Joe Mayo

C# 3.0

With the .NET Framework 3.5

UNLEASHED

Second Edition

 800 East 96th Street, Indianapolis, Indiana 46240 USA

C# 3.0 Unleashed
With the .NET Framework 3.5

Copyright © 2008 by Pearson Education, Inc.

ISBN-13: 978-0-672-32981-4
ISBN-10:   0-672-32981-6

Library of Congress Cataloging-in-Publication Data
Mayo, Joseph.
    C# 3.0 unleashed : with the .NET Framework 3.5 / Joe Mayo. — 1st ed.
       p. cm.
    ISBN 978-0-672-32981-4
  1. C# (Computer program language) 2. Microsoft .NET Framework. I. Title.
    QA76.73.C154M38 2008
    006.7'882—dc22

                              2008026117

Printed in the United States of America
First Printing June 2008

Trademarks

Warning and Disclaimer

Bulk Sales

Sams Publishing offers excellent discounts on this book when ordered in quantity for bulk purchases or special sales. For more information, please contact

U.S. Corporate and Government Sales

1-800-382-3419

corpsales@pearsontechgroup.com

For sales outside of the U.S., please contact

International Sales

international@pearson.com

Editor-in-Chief
Karen Gettman

Executive Editor
Neil Rowe

Acquisitions Editor
Brook Farling

Development Editor
Mark Renfrow

Managing Editor
Kristy Hart

Project Editor
Andrew Beaster

Copy Editor
Keith Cline

Indexer
Brad Herriman

Proofreader
San Dee Phillips

Technical Editors
Tony Gravagno
Todd Meister
J. Boyd Nolan

Publishing Coordinator
Cindy Teeters

Cover Designer
Gary Adair

Composition
Jake McFarland

The Safari® Enabled icon on the cover of your favorite technology book means the book is available through Safari Bookshelf. When you buy this book, you get free access to the online edition for 45 days. Safari Bookshelf is an electronic reference library that lets you easily search thousands of technical books, find code samples, download chapters, and access technical information whenever and wherever you need it.

To gain 45-day Safari Enabled access to this book:

▶ Go to http://www.samspublishing.com/safarienabled

▶ Complete the brief registration form

▶ Enter the coupon code **VDD7-6QGD-AVQZ-VFEX-CZ76**

If you have difficulty registering on Safari Bookshelf or accessing the online edition, please e-mail customer-service@safaribooksonline.com.

Contents at a Glance

Table of Contents

About the Author

Joe Mayo has more than 21 years of software engineering experience and has worked with C# and .NET since July 2000. He regularly contributes to the community through his website, C# Station, which has been running since July 2000. He enjoys giving presentations on .NET, and you can occasionally find him online in a forum or newsgroup, doing what he loves to do—talking about .NET. For his community service over the years, he has been a recipient of multiple Microsoft Most Valuable Professional (MVP) awards. These days, Joe makes a living through the company he founded, Mayo Software Consulting, Inc., delivering value to customers through custom .NET software development services.

Dedication

To my beautiful wife, Maytinee

*You are the vision, the light
guiding my way*

*Your strength and support
enable perseverance*

*Mother of our children and best friend
I love and thank you dearly*

—Joe Mayo

Acknowledgments

Although my name appears on the cover of this book, work of such magnitude could never have occurred without the valuable contributions of many people. To the people at Sams Publishing, Microsoft, and friends and family, I am eternally grateful.

For *C# 3.0 Unleashed* (this version):

- ▶ I' d like to thank Neil Rowe, executive editor, for giving me the opportunity to write the current version of *C# 3.0 Unleashed* and getting it started. Thanks to Brook Farling, acquisitions editor, for leading the bulk of the process and all his help. Andrew Beaster did a great job coordinating author reviews, and Mark Renfrow helped keep my book organized and provided valuable tips along the way. Thanks also to Keith Cline for copyediting that polished the words very nicely.

- ▶ I was pleased to have worked with excellent tech editors for *C# 3.0 Unleashed*. Thanks to Tony Gravagno, Todd Meister, and J. Boyd Nolan for identifying glitches, valuable suggestions, and technical prowess.

- ▶ Thanks to the people at Microsoft who have worked on C#, the .NET Framework, and Visual Studio. Rafael Munoz, my MVP lead, was pivotal in helping me to contact the right people for information.

- ▶ Here's also a shout-out to the user groups on the Front Range who have allowed me to give presentations on .NET subjects and provided me with live feedback: the Boulder Visual Studio .NET User Group, the Colorado Springs .NET User Group, the

Denver Visual Studio .NET User Group, and the Fort Collins .NET SIG. Thanks to everyone for your questions, comments, and willingness to challenge.

For *C# Unleashed* (first version):

▶ For the first version of *C# Unleashed*, I want to thank Shelley Kronzek, executive editor, for finding me and offering this wonderful opportunity. Her leadership is inspiring. Susan Hobbs, development editor, was totally awesome, keeping me on focus and organized. Maryann Steinhart, copyeditor, made my writing look great. Other people at Sams Publishing I'd like to recognize include Katie Robinson, Leah Kirkpatrick, Elizabeth Finney, Pamalee Nelson, and Laurie McGuire. Thanks also to all the editors, indexers, printers, production, and other people at Sams who have contributed to this book.

▶ Special thanks for the first version of *C# Unleashed* goes to Kevin Burton and Bill Craun, technical editors. Their technical expertise and advice was absolutely top-notch. They provided detailed pointers, and their perspectives made a significant difference. Thanks to Keith Olsen, Charles Tonklinson, Cedric, and Christoph Wille for reviewing my early work.

▶ Thanks to all the people at Microsoft who set up author seminars and training. They are transforming the way we do computing and leading the industry in a move of historic proportions—an initiative deserving of much praise. Special thanks to Eric Gunnerson for taking time out of his extremely busy schedule to review chapters of the first version.

Thanks to family members:

▶ Maytinee Mayo, Joseph A. Mayo Jr., Jennifer A. Mayo, Kamonchon Ahantric, Lacee and June Mayo, Bob Mayo, Margina Mayo, Richard Mayo, Gary Mayo, Mike Mayo, Tony Gravagno, Tim and Kirby Hoffman, Richard and Barbara Bickerstaff, Bobbie Jo Burns, David Burns, Mistie Lea Bickerstaff, Cecil Sr. and Margaret Sloan, Cecil Jr. and Jean Sloan, Lou and Rose Weiner, Mary and Ron Monette, Jack Freeman, Sr., and Bill Freeman

Thanks to friends and professional associates:

▶ Evelyn Black, Harry G. Hall, Arthur E. Richardson, Carl S. Markussen, Ruby Mitchell, Judson Meyer, Hoover McCoy, Bill Morris, Gary Meyer, Tim Leuers, Angela Dees-Prebula, Bob Jangraw, Jean-Paul Massart, Jeff and Stephanie Manners, Eddie Alicea, Gary and Gloria Lefebvre, Bob Turbyfill, and Dick Van Bennekom, Barry Patterson, Otis Solomon, and Brian Allen

We Want to Hear from You!

As the reader of this book, *you* are our most important critic and commentator. We value your opinion and want to know what we're doing right, what we could do better, what areas you'd like to see us publish in, and any other words of wisdom you're willing to pass our way.

You can email or write me directly to let me know what you did or didn't like about this book—as well as what we can do to make our books stronger.

Please note that I cannot help you with technical problems related to the topic of this book, and that due to the high volume of mail I receive, I might not be able to reply to every message.

When you write, please be sure to include this book's title and author, as well as your name and phone or email address. I will carefully review your comments and share them with the author and editors who worked on the book.

E-mail: feedback@samspublishing.com

Mail: Neil Rowe

Executive Editor
Sams Publishing
800 East 96th Street
Indianapolis, IN 46240 USA

Reader Services

Visit our website and register this book at www.informit.com/title/9780672329814 for convenient access to any updates, downloads, or errata that might be available for this book.

Introduction

Welcome to *C# 3.0 Unleashed*, a programmer's guide and reference to the C# (pronounced "C sharp") programming language. C# is primarily an object-oriented programming language, created at Microsoft, which emphasizes a component-based approach to software development. In its third version, C# is still evolving, and this book guides you on a journey of learning how that evolution helps you accomplish more in your software engineering endeavors.

C# is one of several languages of the .NET (pronounced "dot net") platform, which includes a runtime engine called the Common Language Runtime (CLR) and a huge class library. The runtime is a virtual machine that manages code and provides several other services. The class library includes literally thousands of reusable objects and supports several user interface technologies for both desktop and Web Application development.

C# is evolving as a programming language. It began life as an object-oriented, component-based language but now is growing into areas that were once considered the domain of functional programming languages. Throughout this book, you'll see examples of objects and components being used as building blocks for applications. You'll also see many examples that include Language Integrated Query (LINQ), which is a declarative way to query data sources, whether the data source is in the form of objects, relational, XML, or any other format.

Just as C# (and the .NET platform) has evolved, so has this book. *C# Unleashed* began as a language-centric learning guide and reference for applying the C# programming language. The audience was varied because C# was new and developers from all types of backgrounds were programming with it. All the applications compiled on the command line, and all you needed was the .NET Framework SDK and an editor to do everything.

At its essence, the same concepts driving the first version of this book made it into this version. For example, you don't need to already know .NET before getting started. If you've programmed with any programming language, *C# 3.0 Unleashed* should be an easy on-ramp for you. This book contains a few command-line examples, especially in the beginning, because I believe that using the command line is a skill that is still necessary and useful. However, I quickly move to the Visual Studio 2008 (VS2008) Integrated Development Environment (IDE) for the largest share of the rest of the book. You aren't required to use VS2008, however; I show you right away how to build your applications without it, and Appendix A, "Compiling Programs," is a guide to command-line options with examples (just like the first version of *C# Unleashed*). However, VS2008 is an incredible tool for increasing productivity, and I provide tips throughout this book for cranking out algorithms with code-focused RAD.

In addition to coverage of VS2008, I've included several new chapters for the newest technologies, such as Windows Presentation Foundation (WPF), Windows Communication Foundation (WCF), and AJAX. If you like the cutting edge, there are chapters on the ADO.NET Entity Framework and ADO.NET Data Services. Speaking of data, I've added an entire part of this book with multiple chapters on working with data.

Since July 2000, when I cracked open the first public pre-beta release of .NET, I've been hooked, with C# as my language of choice. I've made a good living and found my C# skills in demand, even in a difficult economy. Most of all, I've gained an enormous amount of experience in both teaching, as a formal course instructor, and as a developer, delivering value to customers with an awesome toolset. I hope that all the gotchas, tips, and doses of reality that I've encountered and shared in this book will help you learn and thrive as I have.

Why This Book Is for You

If you've developed software in any other computer programming language, you will be able to understand the contents of this book with no trouble. You already know how to make logical decisions and construct iterative code. You also understand variables and basic number systems such as hexadecimal. Novices may want to start with something at the introductory level, such as *Sams Teach Yourself C# in 21 Days*. Honestly, ambitious beginners could do well with this book if they're motivated.

This is a book written for any programmer who wants to learn C# and .NET. It's basic enough for you to see every aspect of C# that's possible, yet it's sufficiently advanced to provide insight into the modern enterprise-level tasks you deal with every day.

Organization and Goals

C# 3.0 Unleashed is divided into eight parts. To promote learning from the beginning, it starts with the simpler material and those items strictly related to the C# language itself. Later, the book moves into other C#-related areas, showing how to use data, user interface technologies, web services, and other useful .NET technologies.

Part 1 is the beginning, covering basic C# language syntax and other essentials. Chapter 1 starts you off by discussing the .NET platform. This is an important chapter because you need to know the environment that you are building applications for. It permeates everything else you do as a C# developer and should be a place you return to on occasion to remind yourself of the essential ingredients of being a successful C# developer. In Chapter 2, you learn how to build a simple C# application using both the command line and VS2008. It is just the beginning of much VS2008 coverage to come. Chapter 3 is another essential milestone for success in developing .NET applications with C#, learning the type system. Chapters 4 and 5 show you how to work with strings and arrays, respectively. By the time you reach Chapter 7, you'll have enough skills necessary to write a simple application and encounter bugs. So, I hope you find my tips on using the VS2008 debugger helpful before moving on to more complexity with object-oriented programming in Part 2.

Part 2 covers object and component programming in C#. In the first version of *C# Unleashed*, I dedicated an entire chapter to basic object-oriented programming concepts. What changed in *C# 3.0 Unleashed* is that I weaved some of those concepts into other chapters. This way, developers who already know object-oriented programming don't have to skip over an entire chapter, but those who don't aren't completely left out. Mostly, I concentrate on how C# implements object-oriented programming, explaining those nuances that are of interest to existing object-oriented programmers and necessary for any C# developer.

Part 3 teaches you some of the more advanced features of C#. With an understanding of objects from Part 2, you learn about object lifetime—when objects are first instantiated and when they are cleaned up from memory. An entire body of knowledge builds upon earlier chapters, leading to where you need to be to understand .NET memory management, the Garbage Collector, what it means for you as a C# developer, and mostly, what you can do to ensure that your objects and the resources they work with are properly managed.

Part 4 gives you five chapters of data. Feedback from the first version of this book indicated that you wanted more. So, now you can learn about LINQ to Objects, LINQ to SQL, ADO.NET, LINQ to DataSet, XML, LINQ to XML, ADO.NET Entity Framework, LINQ to Entities, ADO.NET Data Services, and LINQ to Data Services. Really, five chapters aren't the end of the story, and there is good reason why I moved data earlier in the book: I use LINQ throughout the rest of the book. In addition to learning how to use all of these data access technologies, you'll see many examples in the whole book.

Part 5 demonstrates how to use various desktop user interface technologies. You have choices, console applications, which were beefed up in .NET 2.0, Windows Forms, and WPF. By the way, if you are interested in Silverlight, you'll want to read the WPF chapter first because both technologies use XAML, the same layout, and the same control set. Not only does it help me bring more information to you on these new technologies, but it also should be comforting that what you learn with one technology is useful with another, expanding your skill set as a .NET developer.

Part 6 teaches you how to build web user interfaces. ASP.NET is the primary web UI technology for .NET today, and I provide a fair amount of coverage to help you get up-to-speed with it. You'll want to pay attention to the discussion of the difference between desktop and web applications because it affects how you develop ASP.NET applications. In recent years, Asynchronous JavaScript and XML (AJAX) has become a hot topic. I show you how to use ASP.NET AJAX, which ships with VS2008, to make your ASP.NET pages more responsive to the user. The newest web UI technology is Silverlight, which enables you to build interactive websites that were once only possible with desktop UI technologies. A couple of the new capabilities of Silverlight are easier ways to play audio and video on the web and animation; these new capabilities allow you to build web experiences similar to Adobe Flash.

Part 7 brings you in touch with various communications technologies. In a connected world, these chapters teach you how to use essential tools. You learn how to use TCP/IP, HTTP, and FTP, and send email using .NET Framework libraries. The remoting chapter is still there, as is the web services chapter. However, an additional chapter covers the new WCF web services.

Part 8 covers topics in architecture and design. Many programmers learn C# and all the topics discussed previously and then find their own way to build applications with what they've learned. If they find an effective way to build applications, then that is positive. However, it's common for people to want to know what the best way is for putting together all of these objects, components, and services to build a usable application. I don't have all the answers because architecture and design is a big topic, and there are as many opinions about it as there are questions. However, I've taken a quick foray into the subject, showing you some of the techniques that have worked for me. You learn how C# and .NET support common design patterns and make it easy for you to use these patterns. I show you how to build an n-layered application and describe a couple more ways that you can take what I've presented and use it in your own way. I also show you how to use a couple .NET tools, including the Class Designer, and introduce you to Windows Workflow (WF), which has a graphical design surface for building applications graphically.

Part 9 is a grab bag of technologies that could be important to your development, depending on what you want to do. For example, multithreading is something that most programmers will do on occasion. However, multithreading is a skill that most programmers will need as multiprocessing and multicore CPUs become more common, meaning that I added more multiprocessing/multithreaded information in this version of the book. Depending on where you are in the world, localization and globalization could be very important, so I explain the essentials of resources and satellite assemblies for localization purposes. There is still a lot of legacy code that people need to communicate with, depending on the needs of the project you are working on. To help out, the chapter on Interop covers P/Invoke for interoperating with Win32 DLLs and COM Interop for working with COM. There's also some information on working with COM+. For those of you who like a solution out of the box, I explain how to use the .NET trace facilities for instrumenting and logging. There's also a section on how to use existing performance counters and how to instrument your own code with a custom performance counter for diagnostics through the Windows Performance Monitor.

Part 10 helps you with your ultimate goal: deploying code. This is a series of quick chapters to help you build setup programs and deploy desktop or web applications. Before that, I give you some more information about assemblies and what they are made of. The Security chapter will help you learn how the .NET Code Access Security (CAS) system works. Along the way, I throw in several tips to ensure that your deployment endeavors go more smoothly than if you would have had to do it alone.

That's what this book is all about. I wish you luck in learning C# and hope that you find *C# 3.0 Unleashed* a helpful learning tool and useful reference.

PART 1

Learning C# Basics

CHAPTER 1

Introducing the .NET Platform

As a C# developer, it's important to understand the environment you are building applications on: Microsoft .NET (pronounced "Dot Net"). After all, your design and development decisions will often be influenced by code-compilation practicalities, the results of compilation, and the behavior of applications in the runtime environment. The foundation of all .NET development begins here, and throughout this book I occasionally refer back to this chapter when explaining concepts that affect the practical implementation of C#.

By learning about the .NET environment, you can gain an understanding of what .NET is and what it means to you. You learn about the parts of .NET, including the Common Language Runtime (CLR), the .NET Framework Class Library, and how .NET supports multiple languages. Along the way, you see how the parts of .NET tie together, their relationships, and what they do for you. First, however, you need to know what .NET is, which is explained in the next section.

What Is .NET?

Microsoft .NET, which I refer to as just .NET, is a platform for developing "managed" software. The word *managed* is key here—a concept setting the .NET platform apart from many other development environments. I'll explain what the word *managed* means and why it is an integral capability of the .NET platform.

When referring to other development environments, as in the preceding paragraph, I'm focusing on the traditional practice of compiling to an executable file that contains machine code and how that file is loaded and executed by the operating system. Figure 1.1 shows what I mean about the traditional compilation-to-execution process.

FIGURE 1.1   Traditional compilation.

In the traditional compilation process, the executable file is binary and can be executed by the operating system immediately. However, in the managed environment of .NET, the file produced by the compiler (the C# compiler in our case) is not an executable binary. Instead, it is an assembly, shown in Figure 1.2, which contains metadata and intermediate language code.

FIGURE 1.2   Managed compilation.

As mentioned in the preceding paragraph, an assembly contains intermediate language and metadata rather than binary code. This intermediate language is called Microsoft Intermediate Language (MSIL), which is commonly referred to as IL. IL is a high-level, component-based assembly language. In later sections of this chapter, you learn how IL supports a common type system and multiple languages in the same platform.

.NET STANDARDIZATION

.NET has been standardized by both the European Computer Manufacturers Association (ECMA) and the Open Standards Institute (OSI). The standard is referred to as the Common Language Infrastructure (CLI). Similarly, the standardized term for IL is Common Intermediate Language (CIL).

In addition to .NET, there are other implementations of CIL—the two most well known by Microsoft and Novell. Microsoft's implementation is an open source offering for the purposes of research and education called the Shared Source Common Language Infrastructure (SSCLI). The Novell offering is called Mono, which is also open source.

Beyond occasional mention, this book focuses mainly on the Microsoft .NET implementation of the CLI standard.

The other part of an assembly is metadata, which is extra information about the code being used in the assembly. Figure 1.3 shows the contents of an assembly.

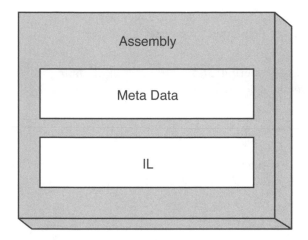

FIGURE 1.3   Assembly contents.

Figure 1.3 is a simplified version of an assembly, showing only those parts pertaining to the current discussion. Assemblies have other features that illustrate the difference between an assembly and an executable file. Specifically, the role of an assembly is to be a unit of deployment, execution, identity, and security in the managed environment. In Part X, Chapters 43 and 44 explain more about the role of the assembly in deployment, identity, and security. The fact that an assembly contains metadata and IL, instead of only binary code, has a significant advantage, allowing execution in a managed environment. The next section explains how the CLR uses the features of an assembly to manage code during execution.

The Common Language Runtime (CLR)

As introduced in the preceding section, C# applications are compiled to IL, which is executed by the CLR. This section highlights several features of the CLR. You'll also see how the CLR manages your application during execution.

Why Is the CLR Important?

In many traditional execution environments of the past, programmers needed to perform a lot of the low-level work (plumbing) that applications needed to support. For example, you had to build custom security systems, implement error handling, and manage memory.

The degree to which these services were supported on different language platforms varied considerably. Visual Basic (VB) programmers had built-in memory management and an error-handling system, but they didn't always have easy access to all the features of COM+, which opened up more sophisticated security and transaction processing. C++ programmers have full access to COM+ and exception handling, but memory management is a totally manual process. In a later section, you learn about how .NET supports multiple languages, but knowing just a little about a couple of popular languages and a couple of the many challenges they must overcome can help you to understand why the CLR is such a benefit for a C# developer.

The CLR solves many problems of the past by offering a feature-rich set of plumbing services that all languages can use. The features described in the next section further highlight the value of the CLR.

CLR Features

This section describes, more specifically, what the CLR does for you. Table 1.1 summarizes CLR features with descriptions and chapter references (if applicable) in this book where you can find more detailed information.

TABLE 1.1   CLR Features

Feature	Description
.NET Framework Class Library support	Contains built-in types and libraries to manage assemblies, memory, security, threading, and other runtime system support
Debugging	Facilities for making it easier to debug code. (Chapter 7)
Exception management	Allows you to write code to create and handle exceptions. (Chapter 11)
Execution management	Manages the execution of code
Garbage collection	Automatic memory management and garbage collection (Chapter 15)
Interop	Backward-compatibility with COM and Win32 code. (Chapter 41)
Just-In-Time (JIT) compilation	An efficiency feature for ensuring that the CLR only compiles code just before it executes
Security	Traditional role-based security support, in addition to Code Access Security (CAS) (Chapter 44)
Thread management	Allows you to run multiple threads of execution (Chapter 39)
Type loading	Finds and loads assemblies and types
Type safety	Ensures references match compatible types, which is very useful for reliable and secure code (Chapter 4)

In addition to the descriptions provided in Table 1.1, the following sections expand upon a few of the CLR features. These features are included in the CLR execution process.

The CLR Execution Process

Beyond just executing code, parts of the execution process directly affect your application design and how a program behaves at runtime. Many of these subjects are handled throughout this book, but this section highlights specific additional items you should know about.

From the time you or another process selects a .NET application for execution, the CLR executes a special process to run your application, shown in Figure 1.4.

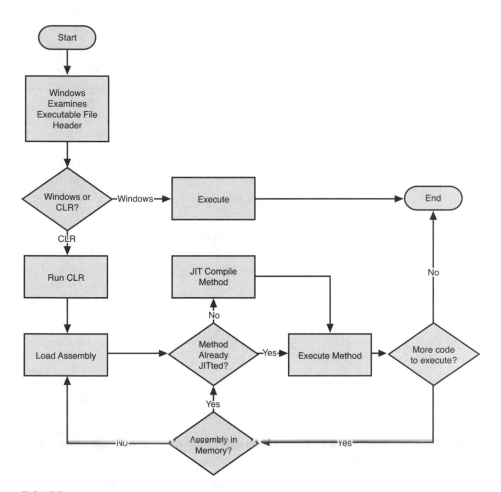

FIGURE 1.4   The CLR execution process (summarized).

As illustrated in Figure 1.4, Windows (the OS) will be running at Start; the CLR won't begin execution until Windows starts it. When an application executes, OS inspects the file to see whether it has a special header to indicate that it is a .NET application. If not, Windows continues to run the application.

If an application is for .NET, Windows starts up the CLR and passes the application to the CLR for execution. The CLR loads the executable assembly, finds the entry point, and begins its execution process.

The executable assembly could reference other assemblies, such as dynamic link libraries (DLLs), so the CLR will load those. However, this is on an as-needed basis. An assembly won't be loaded until the CLR needs access to the assembly's code. It's possible that the code in some assemblies won't be executed, so there isn't a need to use resources unless absolutely necessary.

As mentioned previously, the C# compiler produces IL as part of an assembly's output. To execute the code, the CLR must translate the IL to binary code that the operating system understands. This is the responsibility of the JIT compiler.

As its name implies, the JIT compiler only compiles code before the first time that it executes. After the IL is compiled to machine code by the JIT compiler, the CLR holds the compiled code in a working set. The next time that the code must execute, the CLR checks its working set and runs the code directly if it is already compiled. It is possible that the working set could be paged out of memory during program execution, for various reasons that are necessary for efficient operation of the CLR on the particular machine it is running on. If more memory is available than the size of the working set, the CLR can hold on to the code. Additionally, in the case of Web applications where scalability is an issue, the working set can be swapped out due to periodic recycling or heavier load on the server, resulting in additional load time for subsequent requests.

The JIT compiler operates at the method level. If you aren't familiar with the term *method*, it is essentially the same as a function or procedure in other languages. Therefore, when the CLR begins execution, the JIT compiler compiles the entry point (the Main method in C#). Each subsequent method is JIT compiled just before execution. If a method being JIT compiled contains calls to methods in another assembly, the CLR loads that assembly (if not already loaded).

This process of checking the working set, JIT compilation, assembly loading, and execution continues until the program ends.

The meaning to you in the CLR execution process is in the form of application design and understanding performance characteristics. In the case of assembly loading, you have some control over when certain code is loaded. For example, if you have code that is seldom used or necessary only in specialized cases, you could separate it into its own DLL, which will keep the CLR from loading it when not in use. Similarly, separating seldomly executed logic into a separate method ensures the code doesn't JIT until it's called.

Another detail you might be concerned with is application performance. As described earlier, code is loaded and JIT compiled. Another DLL adds load time, which may or may not make a difference to you, but it is certainly something to be aware of. By the way, after code has been JIT compiled, it executes as fast as any other binary code in memory.

One of the CLR features listed in Table 1.1 is .NET Framework Class Library (FCL) support. The next section goes beyond FCL support for the CLR and gives an overview of what else the FCL includes.

The .NET Framework Class Library (FCL)

.NET has an extensive library, offering literally thousands of reusable types. Organized into namespaces, the FCL contains code supporting all the .NET technologies, such as Windows Forms, Windows Presentation Foundation, ASP.NET, ADO.NET, Windows

Workflow, and Windows Communication Foundation. In addition, the FCL has numerous cross-language technologies, including file I/O, networking, text management, and diagnostics. As mentioned earlier, the FCL has CLR support in the areas of built-in types, exception handling, security, and threading. Table 1.2 shows some common FCL libraries.

WHAT IS A TYPE?

Types are used to define the meaning of variables in your code. They could be built-in types such as int, double, or string. You can also have custom types such as Customer, Employee, or BankAccount. Each type has optional data/behavior associated with it.

Much of this book is dedicated to explaining the use of types, whether built-in, custom, or those belonging to the .NET FCL. Chapter 4, "Understanding Reference Types and Value Types," includes a more in-depth discussion on how C# supports the .NET type system.

TABLE 1.2   Common .NET Framework Class Library Namespaces

System	System.Runtime
System.Collections	System.Security
System.Configuration	System.ServiceModel
System.Data	System.Text
System.Diagnostics	System.Threading
System.Drawing	System.Web
System.IO	System.Windows
System.Linq	System.Workflow.*
System.Net	System.Xml

The namespaces in Table 1.2 are a sampling from the many available in the .NET Framework. They're representative of the types they contain. For example, you can find Windows Presentation Foundation (WPF) libraries in the System.Windows namespace, Windows Communication Foundation (WCF) is in the System.ServiceModel namespace, and Language Integrated Query (LINQ) types can be found in the System.Linq namespace.

Another aspect of Table 1.2 is that I included only two levels in the namespace hierarchy, System.*. In fact, there are multiple namespace levels, depending on which technology you view. For example, if you want to write code using the Windows Workflow (WF) runtime, you look in the System.Workflow.Runtime namespace. Generally, you can find the more common types at the higher namespace levels.

One of the benefits you should remember about the FCL is the amount of code reuse it offers. As you read through this book, you'll see many examples of how the FCL forms the basis for code you can write. For example, you learn how to create your own exception object in Chapter 13, "Naming and Organizing Types with Namespaces," which requires that you use the Exception types from the FCL. Even if you encounter situations that don't require your use of FCL code, you can still use it. An example of when you would want to reuse FCL code is in Chapter 17, "Parameterizing Type with Generics and Writing Iterators," where you learn how to use existing generic collection classes. The FCL was built and intended for reuse, and you can often be much more productive by using FCL types rather than building your own from scratch.

Another important feature of the FCL is language neutrality. Just like the CLR, it doesn't matter which .NET language you program in—the FCL is reusable by all .NET programming languages, which are discussed in the next section.

C# and Other .NET Languages

.NET supports multiple programming languages, which are assisted by both the CLR and the FCL. Literally dozens of languages target the .NET CLR as a platform. Table 1.3 lists some of these languages.

TABLE 1.3   Languages Targeting the .NET CLR

A#	Fortran	Phalanger (PHP)
APL	IronPython	Python
C++	IronRuby	RPG
C#	J#	Silverfrost FTN95
COBOL	Jscript	Scheme
Component Pascal	LSharp	SmallScript
Delphi	Mercury	Smalltalk
Delta Forth	Mondrian	TMT Pascal
Eiffel.NET	Oberon	VB.NET
F#	Perl	Zonnon

Table 1.3 is not a comprehensive list because there are new languages being created for .NET on a regular basis. An assumption one could make from this growing list is that .NET is a successful multilanguage platform.

As you learned earlier in this chapter, the C# compiler emits IL. However, the C# compiler is not alone—all compilers for languages in Table 1.2 emit IL, too. By having a CLR that consumes IL, anyone can build a compiler that emits IL and join the .NET family of languages.

In the next section, you learn how the CLR supports multiple languages via a Common Type System (CTS), the relationship of the languages via a Common Language Specification (CLS), and how languages are supported via the FCL.

The Common Type System (CTS)

To support multiple programming languages on a single CLR and have the ability to reuse the FCL, the types of each programming language must be compatible. This binary compatibility between language types is called the Common Type System (CTS).

The built-in types are represented as types in the FCL. This means that a C# int is the same as a VB.NET Integer type and their .NET type is System.Int32, which is a 32-bit integer named Int32 in the System namespace of the FCL. You'll learn more about C# types, type classification, and how C# types map to the CTS in Chapter 4.

The Common Language Specification (CLS)

Although the CLR understands all types in the CTS, each language targeting the CLR will not implement all types. Languages must often be true to their origins and will not lose their features or add new features that aren't compatible with how they are used.

However, one of the benefits of having a CLR with a CTS that understands IL, and an FCL that supports all languages, is the ability to write code in one language that is consumable by other languages. Imagine you are a third-party component vendor and your language of choice is C#. It would be desirable that programmers in any .NET language (for example, IronRuby or Delphi) would be able to purchase and use your components.

For programming languages to communicate effectively, targeting IL is not enough. There must be a common set of standards to which every .NET language must adhere. This common set of language features is called the Common Language Specification (CLS).

Most .NET compilers can produce both CLS-compliant and non-CLS-compliant code, and it is up to the developer to choose which language features to use. For example, C# supports unsigned types, which are non CLS compliant. For CLS compliance, you can still use unsigned types within your code so long as you don't expose them in the public interface of your code, where code written in other languages can see.

Summary

.NET is composed of a CLR and the .NET FCL, and supports multiple languages. The CLR offers several features that free you from the low-level plumbing work required in other environments. The FCL is a large library of code that supports additional technologies such as Windows Presentation Foundation, Windows Communication Foundation, Windows Workflow, ASP.NET, and many more. The FCL also contains much code that you can reuse in your own applications. Through its support of IL, a CTS, and a CLS, many languages target the .NET platform. Therefore, you can write a reusable library with C# code that can be consumed by code written in other programming languages.

Remember that understanding the .NET platform, which includes CLR, FCL, and multiple-language support, has implications in the way you design and write your code. Throughout this book, you'll encounter many instances where the concepts in this chapter lay the foundation of the tasks you need to accomplish. You might want to refer back to this chapter for an occasional refresher.

This chapter has been purposefully as short as possible to cover only the platform issues most essential to building C# applications. If you're like me, you'll be eager to jump into some code. The next chapter does that by introducing you to essential syntax of the C# programming language.

CHAPTER 2

Getting Started with C# and Visual Studio 2008

When using integrated development environments (IDEs) such as Visual Studio 2008 (VS2008), you don't have to think too much about how a program starts because a shell is automatically in place after running a new project wizard. Nonetheless, it's important to start out the learning process by seeing a minimal program and the important elements of starting a new program.

The first program you see in this chapter is a minimal console application. I've chosen a console application for its simplicity. You won't have extra code for the graphical user interface (GUI) technology obfuscating the core elements of the code, and thus you can concentrate on only those parts that are significant for getting started.

After learning how to code, compile, and execute an application via the command line, you learn how to do the same thing with VS2008. You'll already be familiar with the code, but now the discussion will be in the context of how VS2008 manages projects and several options available to you in the GUI environment.

Before finishing the chapter, you receive a primer on C# types and learn various ways to declare variables. Then you learn a couple more console I/O commands to help you learn how to interact with the user.

Now it's time to see a bare-bones C# program.

Writing a Simple C# Program

In C#, the smallest program you can have consists of a type with an entry point method. Listing 2.1 shows a simple C#

program, named FirstProgram, with only essential elements necessary to compile and run. You can type this into a text editor, such as Notepad, save it as FirstProgram.cs, compile, and run. Here's the command-line instruction to compile this program:

```
C:\>csc FirstProgram.cs
```

COMMAND-LINE TIPS

If you've never used the command-line (aka Command Prompt) or are rusty at it, there are a few gotchas that you might need help with. First, the path to the C# compiler, csc.exe, isn't included in the normal windows command-line. Therefore, you should add C:\WINDOWS\Microsoft.NET\Framework\v2.0.50727 (for .NET v2.0) or C:\WINDOWS\Microsoft.NET\Framework\v3.5 (for .NET v3.5) to your path environment variable. Additionally, the .NET Framework SDK has a command-line that you can find by selecting Start, All Programs, Microsoft .NET Framework SDK <version>, or you can use the VS2008 command-line at Start, All Programs, Microsoft Visual Studio 2008, Visual Studio Tools. The .NET and VS2008 command-line already has the path to the C# compiler in their environments.

Remember that your filename must have a *.cs file extension. By default, Windows explorer hides well-known file extensions, which results in you creating a file named FirstProgram.cs.txt if you're using Notepad. Because of the *.txt extension, csc.exe won't ever find FirstProgram.cs.

I personally prefer using Visual Studio, which I'll show you how to use, starting in this chapter, but you don't have to, and knowing a couple of the problems you might have on the command-line can be helpful.

C# source code files have the .cs file extension. Here's the command-line instruction to run this program:

```
C:\>FirstProgram
```

We're using the command-line compiler first because I want to keep the discussion simple. In the next example, which has more in-depth discussion about the IDE, you learn how to create a new VS2008 project, rather than only the code as we have here. Here's the output:

```
First C# Unleashed program.
```

LISTING 2.1   A Simple C# Program

```
class FirstProgram
{
    static void Main()
    {
        System.Console.WriteLine("First C# Unleashed program.");
```

LISTING 2.1   Continued

```
    }
}
```

Structurally, the code from Listing 2.1 has two major parts whose contents are enclosed in curly braces: a class named FirstProgram and a method named Main.

Curly braces are boundaries that mark the beginning and ending of blocks. Notice that the Main method is physically located inside of the FirstProgram class and that there is a statement inside of the Main method. This is a pattern that you must follow: Classes contain methods, and methods contain statements. Other programming languages, such as C++, can define method prototypes in one location and method implementations in another. However, in C#, the entire definition of a method, including all of its statements, is defined with the method, inside of its containing class.

MATCHING CURLY BRACES

If you aren't accustomed to using curly braces to define blocks of code, one of the most common mistakes you'll make in the beginning is in creating mismatches between beginning and ending braces. To help alleviate the initial frustration, you should get into the habit of typing the beginning and ending curly braces before adding any code between them.

VS2008 helps keep track of curly braces, too. When selecting one curly brace, both the beginning and ending curly braces are selected. In VS2008, you can also use a short-cut key, Ctrl+}, to easily navigate between them.

In later sections of this chapter and throughout the book, the meaning of a class and all of its capabilities and features will gradually emerge into a clear picture. For now, I describe the class in its simplest terms as a container that is required for holding methods. In the case of Listing 2.1, there is one method, named Main, that is contained inside the FirstProgram class. Because a method can't exist on its own, you need to define a class to contain it.

Main is an identifier that defines the entry point of a C# program. Most of the time, your identifiers can be anything you want. In this case, however, Main is telling the C# compiler that this is the first method to begin the program with. Without Main, the C# compiler will emit an error message similar to the following:

```
'FirstProgram.exe' does not contain a static 'Main' method suitable for an entry
point.
```

C# is case-sensitive. Therefore, if you accidentally type lowercase main rather than Main, you'll receive this error message because the two identifiers are different.

C# IS CASE SENSITIVE

Programmers coming from languages that are not case-sensitive are often tripped up by the fact that C# is case-sensitive. Remember that any two identifiers that differ by case represent two different artifacts.

The Main method in Listing 2.1 doesn't accept any parameters, which would have been defined between the parentheses on the right side of the Main identifier, Main(). In a later section, you'll see how to pass information to a program during startup via a Main method parameter.

The void identifier is a C# keyword, meaning that the Main method does not return a value. Later, you learn how Main methods can return an int (integer) when the program terminates.

The static identifier is another C# keyword, meaning that the Main method belongs to the FirstProgram type, rather than a FirstProgram instance. In C#, you can have classes with instance/type members. Instance means that you can create multiple unique copies of a class, and any operations on a single instance affects only that one instance. For example, if you have a Customer class, you want a unique instance of the class in memory for each customer with which your program works. In the case of types or static members, you have only one copy of the class associated with the type. Figure 2.1 illustrates the difference between instance and type member access.

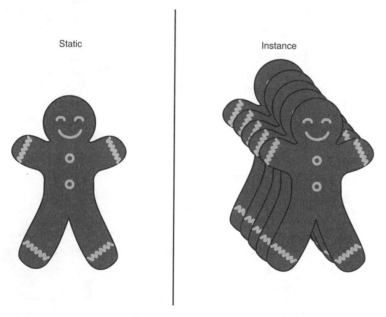

Static

Instance

FIGURE 2.1   Types are like cookie cutters. They create multiple cookies, each a separate instance of the cutter's shape. Static types are a single, shared copy of the cookie.

Static members prove useful if you don't have a need for unique copies of the type, and allow you to simply execute methods based on the type without the overhead of creating an instance. Static types and their members are a single copy of the type, shared with all code in a program. In the case of the Main method, the program is just starting, and no instance has been created. Therefore, it makes sense to associate the Main method with the FirstProgram type by giving it a static modifier. Later, you'll see how to create unique instances and call their members, as well as call static members of a type.

The statement inside of the Main method prints the output to the command line. Recall from Chapter 1, "Introducing the .NET Platform" (in the section "The .NET Framework Class Library (FCL)"), that all FCL code is organized by namespace. System is a top-level namespace. Inside of the System namespace is a class named Console. Notice that FirstProgram is also a class, but in this case FirstProgram is a custom class. Console is a class that is defined as part of the FCL. Console contains a method named WriteLine. Notice that the namespace, class, and method name are written with dotted notation, the member access operator. The WriteLine method contains a single parameter in its parameter list (between the two parentheses). This parameter is a string, enclosed in double quotation marks at beginning and end with text. The WriteLine causes the contained text to be sent to command-line output along with a carriage return and linefeed.

Notice that the statement is terminated with a semicolon as is required of all statements. Adding semicolons to the end of blocks (curly braces) is optional.

You now have a working minimal C# program that you compiled and ran on the command line. Next, you'll see how to do something similar using VS2008.

Creating a Visual Studio 2008 (VS2008) Project

There are many editors and a few nice IDEs for building .NET applications with C#. The IDE I prefer and use the most is Visual Studio 2008 (VS2008), which is also popular among the .NET developer community. Other IDEs are available, including the open source community supported #develop. This book uses VS2008. I give you tips and shortcuts throughout the book to help you become more productive using VS2008. The features described in this book appear in the VS2008 Professional, and some features might not be available in lower-level products, such as Visual C# Express. This section shows you how to start a new project and create another simple program in C#.

Running the New Project Wizard

VS2008 offers a number of project types, including Windows Presentation Foundation, Windows Workflow, Windows Communications Foundation, and ASP.NET. Each of these technology types has its own chapter later in this book. For now, this chapter needs to be simple to help you concentrate on getting started. Therefore, you first learn how to create a new console application.

To create a console application, select File, New, Project (Ctrl+Shift+N) to open the New Project window. Select the Visual C# branch of the Project Types tree and select Console

Application in Templates. Name the program SimpleVS2008Program, and you should have the results shown in Figure 2.2.

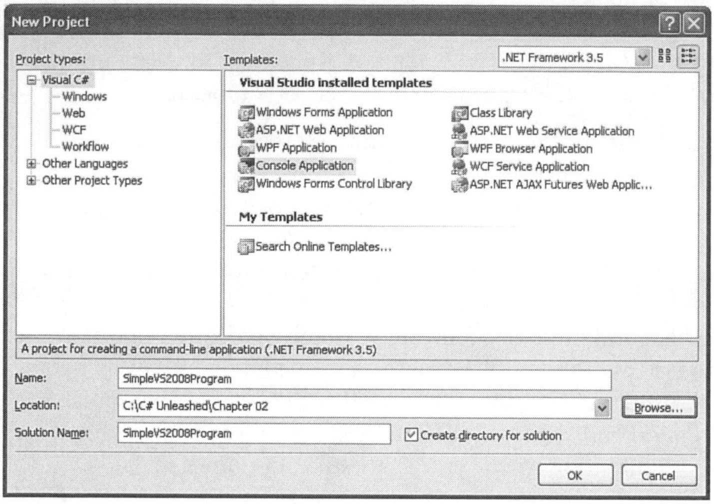

FIGURE 2.2   New Project window.

Notice the drop-down list at the upper right of the New Projects window with .NET Framework 3.5 selected. This is a new feature of VS2008 that enables you to target different versions of .NET. The other options are for .NET Framework 2.0 and .NET Framework 3.0. .NET Framework 1.1 is not supported. There is also no support in VS2008 for letting you know that you are using C# syntax from a higher-level version than the targeted framework, so you must remember this yourself, which may or may not matter depending on who you share your source code with and what IDE they're using. .NET Framework targeting is a useful feature that enables you to build your application and deploy it to a machine that supports only an earlier version of the .NET Framework.

The Location field identifies where your project will be created. The default that appears the first time you run the program is <your MyDocuments folder>\Visual Studio 2008\Projects (<your Documents folder>\Visual Studio 2008\Projects on Vista). You can also change it to a folder, such as C:\Projects, which makes it easy for all those on a team to have their code physically located in the same place. In Figure 2.2, you can see that I found this particular situation better for a folder related to this book, C:\C# Unleashed\Chapter 02.

If you have Create Directory for Solution checked, VS2008 creates a folder under the Location for the solution and also creates another folder under the Solution folder for the project. Otherwise, VS2008 creates a folder only under the Location for the project.

As you type in the Name field for the project, VS2008 completes the Solution field with the identical information. The relationship between solutions and projects is that you work with only one solution at a time. That one solution can have many projects. The relationship can be seen as a single-level hierarchy with the solution at the top and multiple projects, all at the same level, under the solution. Figure 2.3 shows the folder structure created after clicking the OK button.

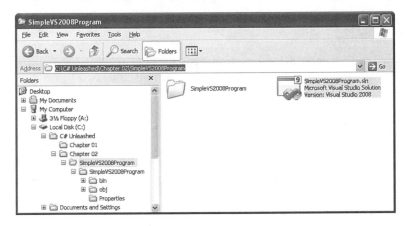

FIGURE 2.3   The Solution folder.

The address bar in Figure 2.3 shows that VS2008 creates a new Solution folder underneath the Location, as expected, because Create Directory for Solution was checked in the New Project window (Figure 2.2). The solution is represented by a file named after the solution name in the New Project window, having the name SimpleVS2008Program.sln. When VS2008 installs, it associates the *.sln extension with itself, meaning that if you double-click a *.sln file, it will open the solution in VS2008. VS2008 created a new project folder, too, shown in Figure 2.4.

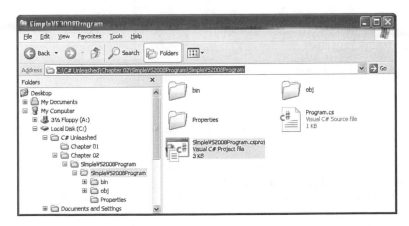

FIGURE 2.4   The Project folder.

Because the Name (of the project) and Solution Name fields were the same in the New Project window (Figure 2.2), VS2008 created an identically named folder,

SimpleVS2008Program, underneath the Solution folder at C:\C# Unleashed\Chapter 02\SimpleVS2008Program. It contains a project file, similarly named SimpleVS2008Program.csproj. VS2008 also created a file association for *.csproj, which will open VS2008 with the containing solution whenever a *.csproj file is double-clicked.

Other folders that VS2008 creates support building the project. For example, the bin\debug folder under the project will hold compiled output from the project.

It's important to know where files and folders are located (by default) in case you want to copy, move, or share files for any reason. However, most work is typically done in the IDE, so the next section explains how to work with files in VS2008.

Understanding Solutions and Projects

When you create a new project, as done in the previous section, VS2008 populates the Solution Explorer window, shown in Figure 2.5, with the solution, project, and project files. Creating a new project this way also opens a starting page with some skeleton code.

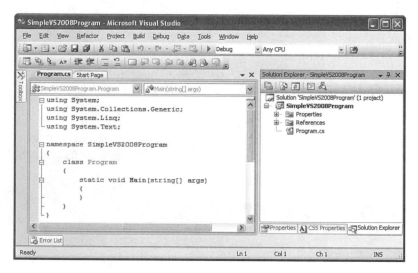

FIGURE 2.5   New project in VS2008.

The Solution Explorer window, on the right side of Figure 2.5, is arranged in the Solution/Project hierarchy the same as the physical file structure.

The Properties folder, under the project, contains metadata for the assembly output of this project. The References folder contains information about assemblies that hold code that is used by this project. Later in this chapter, you learn more about the contents of the Properties and References folders.

The Program.cs file under the project is open in the editor. You can see the tab in the editor with the same name. Hovering over the tab with the cursor, you can see the physical file path of the file. The next section tells you more about this file and other files like it.

Coding in VS2008

The code in Program.cs will compile and run as is, but it doesn't do much. We're going to add code to make the program do something. Before doing so, however, you might want to make sure you have VS2008 open on your computer.

A couple cool features of VS2008, IntelliSense and snippets, help you to be more productive by needing to type less code. I quickly show you how to use IntelliSense and snippets so that you can start being as productive as possible right away with the following steps.

1. Place your cursor, by a single click, immediately after the closing curly brace of the Main method. This highlights the beginning and closing braces.

2. Press Ctrl+Enter. This inserts a new line between the curly braces, moves the cursor to that line, and indents the cursor. Think about the number of keystrokes this saved you.

3. Type **c**. This opens the IntelliSense window to the first command that starts with *c*.

4. Type **w**. This traverses the IntelliSense list and brings you straight to the entry for cw. You can use IntelliSense to rip out code quicker than typing an entire keyword, which saves even more keystrokes. Also, observe that there is a torn-paper icon associated with cw, meaning that this is a snippet.

5. Press Tab. This selects the snippet.

6. Press Tab again. This executes the snippet, giving you a form to fill out. With each snippet, you must always press Tab twice. The first completes the snippet selection, and the second either gives you a form to fill out for changeable items or just places the cursor where you need to type. In this case, the second tab placed the cursor where you need to type.

7. Type "**Simple VS2008 Program**", including the quotes.

What you've done during this procedure was to use IntelliSense and snippets. These are productivity features that will save you a lot of time and put less physical strain on your hands and wrists. Throughout this book, I show you productivity features just like this to make your work easier. Your code should look like Listing 2.2.

LISTING 2.2   A C# Program in VS2008

```
using System;
using System.Collections.Generic;
using System.Linq;
using System.Text;

namespace SimpleVS2008Program
{
    class Program
    {
        static void Main(string[] args)
        {
```

LISTING 2.2   Continued

```
            Console.WriteLine("Simple VS2008 Program");
        }
    }
}
```

There are a few differences between Listing 2.1 and Listing 2.2 to observe: using directives, namespace declaration, and `Console.WriteLine`. The first item to notice is the using directives. If you recall from Chapter 1, the FCL is organized into namespaces. A using directive specifies a namespace. You can write code in your application without needing to fully qualify type names if namespaces are identified with the using directive. In our example, this translates to the fact that there is a using statement for the System namespace. Notice that Listing 2.1 has a statement in the Main method written as `System.Console.WriteLine`, but the similar line in Listing 2.2 is `Console.WriteLine`, without the System namespace qualification. By adding using directives at the top of your file, you can use any of the types in those namespaces without having to qualify the type name with the namespace, just like the Console class that no longer needed to be qualified with System. Adding using directives lets you write less code and is a common coding practice.

The statement `namespace SimpleVS2008Program` puts the Program class into the SimpleVS2008Program namespace. If there were other code that wanted to use the Program class, it would either need to add a `using SimpleVS2008Program` directive to the top of its file or fully qualify the Program class as `SimpleVS2008Program.Program`. You'll learn all the details about Namespaces in Chapter 13, "Naming and Organizing Types with Namespaces." Until then, I add using directives as needed to keep the code as simple as possible.

The class file, Program.cs, isn't the only file that comes with skeleton code. There is a whole library of project items you can use that are but a few clicks away. To use them, right-click the project folder in Solution Explorer, select Add, New Item, and observe the Add New Item window, shown in Figure 2.6.

The Add New Item window (Figure 2.6) allows you to create several different types of files for your project. Each file type includes skeleton code to help you get started creating a specific type of item. Going down the list, you can tell that there are several file types and they are categorized according to options on the left.

After creating, organizing, and coding your solutions and projects, you can use VS2008 to see whether they work. The next section shows you how to build and run your programs.

Building and Running Applications

There are several options for building (compiling) and running your project, each option available from either the Build or Debug menus. Your project must be open in VS2008 for build and run options to be available. Table 2.1 lists the options available from the Build Menu.

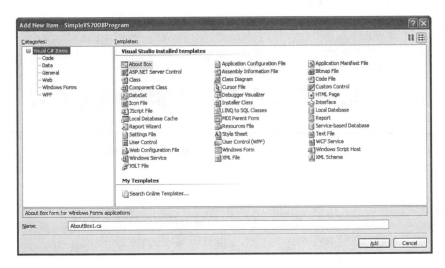

FIGURE 2.6   Add New Item window.

TABLE 2.1   VS2008 Build Menu Options

Menu Option	What It Does for You
Build Solution	Builds any projects that are out-of-date.
Rebuild Solution	Forces build of all projects, regardless of whether they are current.
Clean Solution	Removes all output files from bin\<Project Type> folders. Makes a smaller size for moving files—the output can be re-created any time.
Build <Project Name>	Builds the project if it is out-of-date.
Rebuild <Project Name>	Forces build of project, regardless of whether it is current.
Clean <Project Name>	Removes output files from bin\<Project Type> folder. Makes a smaller size for moving files—the output can be re-created any time.

The difference between Build and Rebuild options is that a Rebuild will force a build, even if the projects are up-to-date. When building, VS2008 already knows the dependencies between projects and will ensure that a referenced project will build before the referring project. A referenced project is typically a reusable class library, DLL. The Build menu is context-sensitive, so whatever file you have open in the editor will determine the project that appears as <Project Name> in the Build menu.

On the Debug menu, there are two options to run a program, Start Debugging (F5) and Start Without Debugging (Ctrl+F5). The differences between these two options are that Start Debugging stops on breakpoints during execution and the console window will close when the Main method completes. However, the Start Without Debugging option will not stop on breakpoints and will stop and leave the console window open when the Main method completes. You can learn more about breakpoints and debugging code in Chapter 7, "Debugging Applications with Visual Studio 2008."

A PROJECT IS REQUIRED FOR COMPILATION

You can open any file you want in the editor and observe syntax highlighting, IntelliSense, and other editor features. However, a common gotcha for beginning VS2008 users is that you can't compile that file. Anything that is compiled must be a part of a project, and that project must be currently open in VS2008.

Press F5 (Start Debugging) to run the program, which will save any unsaved files, build the project, and run the code. If you have compiler errors, they will show up in an error window. You can double-click the line item, which will take you to the offending line. Because I don't know what errors could have happened, the best I can tell you is to look at the code in Listing 2.2 and ensure every single character matches, including semicolons, quotes, and capitalization.

If the code runs without VS2008 showing you errors, it will run and end quickly with you either seeing a short flicker or not seeing the window at all, depending on the speed of your computer. You can press Ctrl+F5 (Start Without Debugging), which will pause the console.

Instead of pressing Ctrl+F5, here's another trick that allows you to press F5 and still see your console output, described here:

1. In the Main method, as the last line of the Main method before the closing curly brace, add a new line.

2. Press C and observe that IntelliSense appears. Initially, IntelliSense will start on the first item starting with the character C. However, after you've used IntelliSense a while, it will be smart enough to go straight to the item you most commonly use, which is often Console. If IntelliSense doesn't select Console, type an **o** and then an **n** and you will see it.

3. Type a period (dot operator). IntelliSense will automatically type the rest of Console, the dot, and show you members of the Console class that you can select. Observe that the dot finished the word. Often, people press Enter or Tab and then the dot, which is an extra keystroke. Remember, you're saving keystrokes, and all you need to do is type the next character that comes after the keyword, whether it is a dot, left parenthesis, semicolon, or other logical character that follows.

4. Type **ReadK**. ReadKey is selected. Again, after you've typed the ReadKey a few times, it will be the first item selected.

5. Type (. This will complete ReadKey.

6. Type); to complete the statement.

7. Press F5. Observe that the program runs and stops when complete. You can press any key to end the program. Here's what the completed line should look like:

```
Console.ReadKey();
```

Another way to end a running program is to select Debug, Stop Running (Shift+F5).

Start Debugging and Stop Running have a green-arrow and blue-square toolbar buttons, respectively. You can right-click the toolbar (or select View, Toolbars, Debug) and modify options, just as with Microsoft Office applications.

The procedure used to run code in this section used default compiler options. However, you can customize these options, as is done in the next section.

Setting Compiler Options

As promised earlier, I'll show you what is available from the Properties folder under the SimpleVS2008Program project. When you want to set compiler options, double-click the Properties folder for the project you want to control. There isn't a way to set compiler options at the solution level, and you'll have to configure compiler options for each individual project. The first set of compiler options are on the Properties Application tab, shown in Figure 2.7.

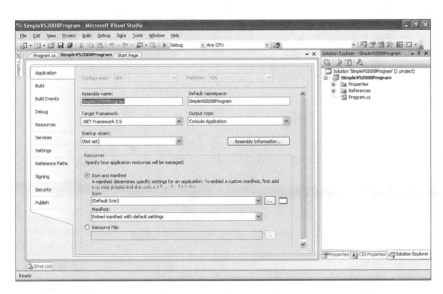

FIGURE 2.7   Application compiler options.

The Assembly name defines the output filename, without the extension, for this project. Recall from Chapter 1 that an assembly name is part of the identity of an assembly. The culture, strong name key, and version number, which are the other parts of an assembly's identity, are covered in Chapter 44, "Securing Code." Every time you add a new file to a project, the generated skeleton uses the namespace defined in the Default Namespace field, leading to the namespace that was defined in Listing 2.2. We discussed the target framework in the previous section, and this is where you can change it after the project is created. The output type of the application created in this section was a console application. You also have the choice of creating a Windows application, as discussed in Chapter 25, "Writing Windows Forms Applications," or a class library, which is a DLL.

This was an essential detour, introducing you to building applications with VS2008. Now it's time to get back to the code, which needs to be documented, as described in the next section.

Commenting Code

Part of writing good code is ensuring it is properly documented. To help you out, there are three types of commenting syntax in C#:multiline, single line, and XML.

Multiline Comments

Multiline comments have one or more lines of narrative within a set of comment delimiters. These comment delimiters are the begin comment /* and end comment */ markers. Anything between these two markers is considered a comment. The compiler ignores comments when reading the source code. Here's an example:

```
/*
 * File Name: Program.cs
 * Author: Joe Mayo
 */
```

The VS2008 editor makes it easy to add multiline comments. First, type **/*** and press Enter; VS2008 will color (green by default) all code that follows and add a ***<space>** on the next line. As soon as you add the */, VS2008 will ensure that only the comment is colored and that the rest of the syntax coloring will go back to normal.

In addition to multiple lines, you can also comment single lines.

Single-Line Comments

Single-line comments allow narrative on only one line at a time. They begin with the double forward slash marker, //. The single-line comment can begin in any column of a given line. It ends at a new line or carriage return. Here's an example:

```
// make the console screen pause
Console.ReadKey();
```

You also get good single-line commenting support with VS2008 via keystroke combinations. You can select any part of multiple lines and use the following key strokes:

▶ Ctrl+K+C adds single-line comments to every highlighted line.

▶ Ctrl+K+U uncomments every highlighted line.

These commenting techniques prove useful any time you want to comment out a block of incomplete code to get a good compile or any other time you want to leave a block of code in place temporarily.

The multiline and single-line comments are great for helping yourself or other programmers understand your code. In addition, C# has a powerful XML documentation commenting feature that is good for both reading code and providing external documentation.

XML Documentation Comments

In addition to providing code commenting, an XML documentation comment supports tools that extract comments into an external XML document. This XML can be consumed by tools or run through XSLT style sheets to produce readable documentation. This is what Microsoft uses to document the .NET FCL APIs that you see in the VS2008 help files.

XML documentation comments start with a triple slash, ///, on each line. They have a begin and end tag that can contain whatever relevant text you choose to add. Comments are enclosed in XML tags. Here's an example of an XML documentation comment:

```
/// <summary>
/// first method executed in application
/// </summary>
/// <param name="args">command-line options</param>
static void Main(string[] args)
{
    // other code
}
```

The .NET C# compiler has an option that reads the XML documentation comments and generates XML documentation from them. XML documentation is extracted to a separate XML file that can then be processed by a tool for creating human-readable documentation.

Here's an example of a command line you can use to get the C# compiler to create an XML documentation file from XML documentation comments in a C# source code file:

```
csc /doc:ProgramComments.xml Program.cs
```

The /doc switch specifies the output file, and the Program.cs file identifies which source code file to extract XML documentation comments from. You can also generate XML files from XML documentation comments in VS2008. If you open project properties (double-click the Properties folder in Solution Explorer) and click the Build tab, you'll see something similar to Figure 2.8.

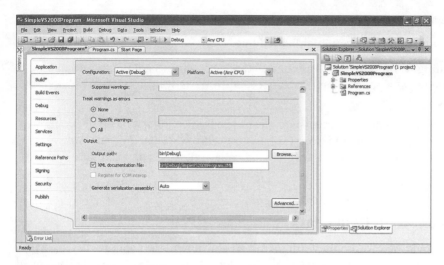

FIGURE 2.8   VS2008 XML documentation comments settings.

In the Output section of Figure 2.8, I checked XML documentation file. VS2008 automatically populated it with the assembly name and an .xml suffix. Because VS2008 generates the documentation file every time you compile the project, you might want to disable this option until you want to generate the XML documentation file. You can also press F6 to compile and generate docs, without running.

Here's some sample output:

```
<doc>
    <assembly>
        <name>Program</name>
    </assembly>
    <members>
        <member name="M:SimpleVS2008Program.Program.Main(System.String[])">
            <summary>
            first method executed in application
            </summary>
            <param name="args">command-line options</param>
        </member>
    </members>
</doc>
```

The preceding code shows only the summary and param elements from the Main method. However, there are many other predefined elements you can add, as shown in Table 2.2.

TABLE 2.2   XML Documentation Tags

`<c>`	`<code>`	`<example>`	`<exception>`	`<list>`
`<param>`	`<paramref>`	`<permission>`	`<remarks>`	`<returns>`
`<see>`	`<seealso>`	`<summary>`	`<value>`	

Although the predefined XML tags suggest their purpose, you can use them any way you want. You aren't limited by this predefined set either—you can add any other XML tags you want. With Intellisense, adding tags is quick and easy.

In addition to commenting, you want to ensure you use good identifiers for the object types and variables in your program. The next section describes what you need to know about C# identifiers.

Identifiers and Keywords

Identifiers and keywords are important because you need to know how to name your variables, custom types, methods, and so on. Identifiers are names of the types and variables in your program. Keywords are reserved words in the C# language. The difference between identifiers and keywords is that keywords are reserved for C# language syntax and can't be used for naming your variables, types, and so on.

Identifiers

Identifiers are names used to identify code elements. The class name `Program` in Listing 2.1 is an example of an identifier. Identifiers are made up of Unicode characters.

WHAT IS UNICODE?

The Unicode standard identifies a 16-bit character set that is large enough to represent any language throughout the world. This differs from ASCII, which is another popular encoding format that preceded Unicode. ASCII is a 7-bit format that can't support as many languages as Unicode. Any Unicode character can be specified with a Unicode escape sequence, `\u` or `\U`, followed by four hex digits. For example, the Unicode escape sequence `"\u0043\u0023"` represents the characters `"C#"`. Visit http://www.unicode.org for more details.

Identifiers can have nearly any name, but a few restrictions apply. Here are some rules to follow when creating identifiers:

▶ Use nonformatting Unicode characters in any part of an identifier.

▶ Identifiers can begin with an allowed Unicode character or an underline.

▶ Begin an identifier with an @ symbol. This allows use of keywords as identifiers.

Here are a few examples of legal C# identifiers:

```
currentBid
_token
@override
\u0043sharp
```

Here are a few examples of invalid identifiers:

```
2threefour      // error – 1st letter is a number
decimal         // error – reserved word
\u0027format // error – Unicode formatting character
```

The first line is invalid because its first character is a number, which is not allowed. The first character of an identifier must be either a letter or an underscore. The second identifier is invalid because it is a keyword. C# keywords are reserved and cannot be used as identifiers. The third line is invalid because the first character is a Unicode formatting character (\u0027 = x1E = Escape). Unicode formatting characters are not allowed in any part of an identifier.

In the next section, you'll see which keywords belong to C#.

Keywords

Keywords are words reserved by the system and have special predefined meanings when writing C# programs. The class keyword, for instance, is used to define a C# class. Another example is the void keyword, which means a method does not return a value. These are words that are part of the language itself. Usage of keywords in any context other than what they are defined for in the C# language is likely to make code unreadable. This is the primary reason why keywords are reserved. They are meant to be used only for constructs that are part of the language. You can see examples of keywords in Listing 2.2: class on line 8, and static and void on line 10. Valid keywords are listed in Table 2.3.

TABLE 2.3   Complete List of C# Keywords

abstract	as	base	bool	Break
Byte	case	catch	char	Checked
Class	const	continue	decimal	Default
delegate	do	double	else	Enum
Event	explicit	extern	false	Finally
Fixed	float	for	foreach	Goto
If	implicit	in	int	interface
internal	is	lock	long	namespace
New	null	object	operator	Out
override	params	private	protected	Public
readonly	ref	return	sbyte	sealed
Short	sizeof	stackalloc	static	String
Struct	switch	this	throw	True

TABLE 2.3   Continued

Try	typeof	uint	ulong	unchecked
Unsafe	ushort	using	virtual	volatile
Void	while			

In the previous section, you learned that keywords, listed in Table 2.3, can't be used as identifiers. However, there is an exception to the rule—you can prefix keywords with the @ character and use it as an identifier. For example, you can do this:

```
int @class = 5;
int @Main = 3;
int @namespace = @class + @Main;
```

The preceding code compiles and runs, but one could say that I took a lot more creative license than should be allowed. It is also a matter of opinion as to whether the preceding code is appropriate. Another similarly subjective topic is style, discussed in the next section.

Convention and Style

This section introduces you to a couple characteristics of C# code layout and common conventions in style. You have the freedom to use the conventions and style you want, but many people will want to be consistent with common conventions.

Whitespace characters (that is, newline, tab, form feed, and Ctrl-Z) separate language elements such as identifiers and keywords. A program may have any amount of whitespace between language elements. It is common practice in C# to use whitespace and indentation to facilitate easier reading of code. VS2008 tries to help by formatting according to settings that you can change by selecting Tools, Options.

When Microsoft created C#, they published a set of design guidelines that you can find in the .NET help files. One of the conventions is how identifiers are structured, using either Pascal casing or camel casing. In Pascal casing the first letter of each word in a name is capitalized, such as `HelloWorld`, `DotProduct`, and `AmortizationSchedule`. This is normally used in all instances except for parameters (passed to methods), private fields (class member variables), and local variables (method variables). Parameters, private fields, and local variables use camel casing. With camel casing, the first letter of the first word is lowercase, and subsequent words are capitalized, as in `bookTitle`, `employeeName`, and `totalCompensation`.

The next section builds upon what you learned about identifiers and conventions, showing how to declare variables.

Variables and Types

Any program will have variables that hold values, and each variable has a meaning, which is its type. This section describes proper C# syntax for declaring variables and then describes many of the predefined types that you can declare variables to be.

Variables

Variables are programming elements that can change during program execution. They're used as storage to hold information at any stage of computation. As a program executes, certain variables change to support the goals of an algorithm. The syntax of a variable definition uses the following pattern:

```
Type Identifier [= Initializer];
```

In this example `Type` is a placeholder, representing one of the types listed in the next section or a user-defined type. Every variable must have a `Type` part in its declaration. Similarly, every variable declaration must have an identifier. Declarations may optionally include an initializer to set the value of a variable when it is created. The type of the value used to initialize a variable must be compatible with the type that the variable is declared as.

Here's an example of a variable declaration without initialization:

```
char middleInitial;
```

You can subsequently assign a value to `middleInitial` like this:

```
middleInitial = 'B';
```

Alternatively, you can declare and initialize on the same line:

```
char middleInitial = 'B';
```

A `char` is a predefined C# type representing a single character. However, sometimes you need to use custom types. In both Chapter 4, "Understanding Reference Types and Value Types," and Chapter 8, "Designing Objects," you learn the details of how to create custom types. For now, and to illustrate variable declaration for custom types, let's assume that a custom class named `Customer` has already been defined. Therefore, if you want to create a variable to hold instances of customer objects, you can do this:

```
Customer cust;
```

The preceding example simply declared `cust`, which will refer to an object of type `Customer`. However, the `cust` variable here just holds the C# value `null` because it doesn't refer to an object yet. Here's what you need to do to get `cust` to refer to an object:

```
cust = new Customer();
```

The new keyword creates a new instance of the `Customer` class in memory and sets `cust` to a value that references that new object. Similar to the previous example for `char` `middleInitial`, you can declare and instantiate a custom class on the same line:

```
Customer cust = new Customer();
```

Alternatively, you can also declare the variable like this:

```
var cust = new Customer();
```

This way, you don't have to specify the type for both the variable and the type of the instance assigned to the variable.

The next section describes the C# simple types with more examples of how to declare variables of each type.

The Simple Types

The simple types consist of Boolean and numeric types. The numeric types are further subdivided into integral types and floating-point types.

The bool Type

There's only a single bool type: bool. A bool can have a boolean value of either `true` or `false`. The values `true` and `false` are also the only literal values you can use for a `bool`. Here's an example of a bool declaration:

```
bool isProfitable = true;
```

> **NOTE**
>
> The bool type will not accept integer values such as 0, 1, or −1. The keywords `true` and `false` are built in to the C# language and are the only allowable values.

The Integral Types

The integral types are further subdivided into eight types plus a character type: sbyte, byte, short, ushort, int, uint, long, ulong, and char. All the integral types except char have signed and unsigned forms. All integral type literals can be expressed in hexadecimal notation by prefixing `0x` to a series of hexadecimal numbers `0` to `F`. The exception is the char.

A `char` holds a single Unicode character. Examples of char variable declarations include the following:

```
char middleInitial;                    // uninitialized
char yesNo = 'Y';
char studentGrade = '\u005A';          // Unicode 'Z'
char studentGrade = '\x0041';          // Unicode 'A'
```

Notice that char literal values, assigned to char variables, are surrounded with single quotes, as opposed to double quotes for string types that I'll discuss later. As discussed in a previous section, Unicode escape character notation requires four hexadecimal digits, prefixed by \u or \U. The digits are left-padded with zeros to make the digit part four-characters wide. A char may also be specified in hexadecimal notation by prefixing \x to between one to four hexadecimal digits, so \x0041 can be written as \x41.

C# has special escape sequences representing characters. They're used for alert, special formatting, and building strings to avoid ambiguity. The following list shows the valid C# escape sequences:

```
\'      Single Quote
\"      Double Quote
\\      Backslash
\0      Null
\a      Bell
\b      Backspace
\f      Form Feed
\n      Newline (linefeed)
\r      Carriage Return
\t      Horizontal Tab
\v      Vertical Tab
```

Here's a common implementation of character literals where you need to escape double-quotes within strings:

```
string thanks = "Hey \"Tony\".\r\nThanks for the great example!";
```

Because the string literal must be defined with double quotes, you need to tell C#, by using \", that it shouldn't interpret the other quotes as the end of the string. Also, if you are writing the string somewhere that expects a carriage return and linefeed sequence, then \r\n is helpful.

A byte is an unsigned type that can hold 8 bits of data. Its range is from 0 to 255. An sbyte is a signed byte with a range of –128 to 127. This is how you declare byte variables:

```
byte age = 25;
sbyte normalizedTolerance = -1;
```

The short type is signed and holds 16 bits. It can hold a range from –32768 to 32767. The unsigned short, ushort, holds a range of 0 to 65535. Here are a couple examples:

```
ushort numberOfJellyBeans = 62873;
short temperatureFarenheit = -36;
```

The integer type is signed and has a size of 32 bits. The signed type, int, has a range of –2147483648 to 2147483647. The uint is unsigned and has a range of 0 to 4294967295. Unsigned integers may optionally have a u or U suffix. Examples follow:

```
uint nationalPopulation = 4139276850;     // also 4139276850u or 4139276850U
int tradeDeficit = -2058293762;
```

A long type is signed and holds 64 bits with a range of –9223372036854775808 to 9223372036854775807. A ulong is unsigned with a range of 0 to 18446744073709551615. Unsigned long literals may have suffixes with the combination of uppercase or lowercase characters UL. Their declarations can be expressed like this:

```
ulong lightSecondsFromEarth = 72038289347236792;
                    // also 72038289347236792ul
                    //   or 72038289347236792UL
                    //   or 72038289347236792uL
                    //   or 72038289347236792Lu
                    //   or 72038289347236792LU
                    //   or 72038289347236792lU
long negativeVariance = -1636409717646593274;
                    // also -1636409717646593274l
                    //   or -1636409717646593274L
```

Each of the types presented to this point have a unique size and range. Table 2.4 provides a summary and quick reference of the size and range of each integral type.

TABLE 2.4   The Integral Types

Type (Keyword)	Size	Range (in Bits)
char	16	0 to 65535
sbyte	8	–128 to 127
byte	8	0 to 255
short	16	–32768 to 32767
ushort	16	0 to 65535
int	32	–2147483648 to 2147483647
uint	32	0 to 4294967295
long	64	–9223372036854775808 to 9223372036854775807
ulong	64	0 to 18446744073709551615

An interesting point to observe is that most of the unsigned types have a u prefix, except for the byte. Because the typical usage of a byte is in an unsigned context, it is just byte and the signed version is sbyte.

The Floating-Point Types

C# provides two floating-point types—float and double—and a new type called decimal. The floating-point types conform to IEEE 754 specifications. You can order the IEEE 754 standard at http://standards.ieee.org/ or visit Wikipedia at http://en.wikipedia.org/wiki/IEEE_floating-point_standard for more details.

Floating-point literals can be specified with exponential notation. This allows specification of large numbers with the least amount of space necessary to write them. The tradeoff between exponential and normal notation is size versus precision. The general form of exponential syntax is

```
N.Ne±P
```

where N is some decimal digit, e can be uppercase or lowercase, and P is the number of decimal places. The ± indicates either a +, −, or neither, which is the same as +. This is standard scientific notation.

The float type can hold a range of around 1.5×10^{-45} to 3.4×10^{38}. It has a 7-digit precision. To designate a floating-point literal as a float, add an F or f suffix. A float literal can be written with or without exponential notation, as follows:

```
float profits     = 36592.73f;    // also 36592.73F
float atomicWeight = 1.54e-15f;
float warpSpeed    = 3.21E3f;
```

A double has a range of about 5.0×10^{-324} to 1.7×10^{308} and a precision of 15 to 16 digits. Double literals may have the suffix D or d. It, too, may have literals expressed with or without exponential notation:

```
double vectorMagnitude   = 8.2e127;
double accumulatedVolume = 7982365.83658341;
                    // also 7982365.83658341D
                    //   or 7982365.83658341d
```

Notice in the examples in the previous code that the numbers don't have a suffix, indicating that the default type for a numeric literal is double. This is a common gotcha that causes a compile error if you try to assign a numeric literal without a suffix to a float or decimal type, which is discussed next.

The decimal type has 28 or 29 digits of precision and can range from 1.0×10^{-28} to about 7.9×10^{28}. Decimal literals are specified with an M or m suffix.

The tradeoff between decimal and double is precision versus range. The decimal is the best choice when precision is required, but choose a double for the greatest range. The decimal type is well suited for financial calculations, as shown in the following example:

```
decimal annualSales = 998735829487698765893483317.95m;
```

The previous example is quite a large number, but Table 2.5 provides a quick lookup of the floating-point types.

TABLE 2.5   The Floating Point Types

Type (Keyword)	Size (bits)	Precision	Range
Float	32	7 digits	1.5×10^{-45} to 3.4×10^{38}
Double	64	15–16 digits	5.0×10^{-324} to 1.7×10^{308}
decimal	128	28–29 decimal places	1.0×10^{-28} to 7.9×10^{28}

A final word on literal suffixes: There are common suffixes for each literal type. Suffixes ensure that the literal is the intended type. This is good for documentation. However, the primary benefit is ensuring that your expressions are evaluated correctly; that is, the compiler will interpret float and decimal literals without suffixes as a double when evaluating an expression. To avoid the associated errors, use an appropriate literal suffix.

The string Type

The string type is made up of a string of Unicode characters. You can create a string literal with any valid set of characters between two double quotes, including character escape sequences.

```
string thankYou = "Grazie!\a"; // Grazie! <ding>
string hello   = "Sa-waht dee\tkrahp!";
                         // Sa-waht dee<tab>krahp!
string kewl = "Das ist\nzehr\ngut!"; // Das ist
                                     // zehr
                                     // gut!
```

You can also create what is called a verbatim string literal. It's made by prefixing a string with an @. The difference between verbatim string literals and normal string literals is that the character escape sequences are not processed but are interpreted as is. Because the double quote escape sequence won't work in a verbatim string literal, you can include two quotes side by side to include one double quote in a string. Verbatim string literals can span multiple lines, if needed. The following examples show various forms of the verbatim string literals:

```
string whoSaid = @"He said, ""She said.""";
                // He said, "She said."
string beerPlease = @"Een \'Duvel\', alstublieft!";
                 // Een \'Duvel\', alstublieft!
string authorList = @"
    select *
    from Authors
    where FirstName = 'Joe';";
```

One of the most common implementations of the verbatim string literal is for file paths, shown here:

```
string logFileName = @"c:\Projects\MyGreatApp\error.log";
```

Notice the single backslash in the file path. The alternative without the verbatim string literal notation is this:

```
string logFileName = @"c:\\Projects\\MyGreatApp\\error.log";
```

Now, you see double backslash characters because, as you learned in the previous section on the char type, a backslash is the escape character. So, you must escape the escape character. The verbatim string literal can make the code easier to read.

Definite Assignment

Definite assignment is a rule simply stating every local variable (inside a method) must have a value before it's read. The process of assigning a value to a variable for the first time is known as initialization. After the initialization process has taken place, a variable is considered initialized. If the initialization process has not yet taken place, a variable is considered to be uninitialized. Initialization ensures that variables have valid values when expressions are evaluated. Uninitialized variables are unassigned variables. If a program attempts to read from an unassigned variable, the compiler generates an error.

Default initialization rules depend on where a variable is declared in a program. Fields, for example, which are class members, fall under default initialization rules.

Local variables are uninitialized. Local variables are those variables declared within a method or other language element defined by a block. Blocks are language elements that denote the beginning and end of a C# language construct. In the case of methods, blocks denote the beginning and end of a method. Methods are C# language constructs allowing programmers to organize their code into groups. If a variable is declared within a method, it is considered to be a local variable.

This is different from fields, which are declared as class members. Class members can be nearly any C# type or language element. Variables and methods are class members. Class variables are initialized to default values if a program's code does not explicitly initialize them. Table 2.6 lists each type's default values.

TABLE 2.6   Default Values of C# Types

Type (Keyword)	Default Value
bool	False
char	\u0000
sbyte	0
byte	0
short	0
ushort	0
int	0
uint	0
long	0

TABLE 2.6   Continued

Type (Keyword)	Default Value
ulong	0
float	0.0f
double	0.0d
decimal	0.0m

Interacting with Programs

Console applications can interact with the user via either the console screen or via the command line. The following sections explain both techniques.

Console Screen Communications

The `Console` class, used in multiple examples in this chapter, has additional methods that enable you to interact with a user. The following example shows a new `Console` class method, `ReadLine()`, for getting input from a user:

```
Console.Write("What is your name? ");
string name = Console.ReadLine();
Console.WriteLine("Hi, {0}", name);
Console.ReadLine();
```

The `Console.ReadLine()` statement causes the console to pause for the user to type some series of characters and press the Enter key. The `ReadLine()` method returns all the characters entered on the command line. Here's the output:

```
What is your name? Joe
Hi, Joe
```

Prompting the user is one way to get user input. You can also extract command-line information when a program is started, which is discussed in the next section.

Command-Line Communications

Many applications have command-line interfaces, regardless of whether they are console or graphical. This facilitates scripting and other administrative tasks. The command-line for the C# compiler itself is an example of a useful implementation of command-line argument handling. Here's an example of accepting command-line arguments:

```
static void Main(string[] args)
{
    Console.WriteLine('Your option is: {0}', args[0]);

    Console.ReadKey();
}
```

The `Main()` method here has a parameter—an array type named args that can hold a list of string types, `string[]`. The system populates args from the entries added in the command line. Chapter 6, "Using Arrays and Enums," contains more details on arrays, but you can rely on the behavior of a C# array to be similar to other languages.

The `Console.WriteLine()` statement accepts an argument of `args[0]`. C# arrays are zero based, and you index into them with square brackets. Therefore, `args[0]` holds the first element of the args array. Subsequent arguments would be in `args[1]`, `args[2]`, ..., `args[n]`. This program replaces the `{0}` parameter with the value of `args[0]` when it prints to the console. Here's an example of how to use this program on the command line and its output:

```
CommandLineInput.exe /doc:myoutput.xml
Your option is: /doc:myoutput.xml
```

As you can see in the preceding example, the assembly name is `CommandLineInput`, and it is not included in the list of options passed to the args parameter in the `Main` method. I arbitrarily used the text `/doc:myoutput.xml` as the command-line option, and that is what was passed to the `Main` method's args parameter.

If you're coding in VS2008, starting up a command line just to test command-line parameters can be more cumbersome than necessary. The next section shows you how to set command-line options with VS2008.

Command-Line Options with VS2008

If you try to run a program that expects command-line arguments, but there are no command-line options, you'll see an error with an `IndexOutOfRangeException` message. This happens because the program is trying to read the `Main` method's args array, but args is empty. If you are doing this in VS2008, you'll probably see something similar to Figure 2.9.

If you encounter an error similar to the one in Figure 2.9, you can stop the application from running by clicking the blue-square Stop Debugging (Shift+F5) button on the toolbar.

To fix this problem, double-click the Properties folder for the project in Solution Explorer. Then select the Debug tab. You'll see a screen similar to Figure 2.10.

Under Start Options in Figure 2.10, I added an entry into the Command line options box. You can add a space separated list of options here that you would normally use via the real command line. Now, you won't see the error from Figure 2.10, and the program will run normally.

Now you've seen how to pass command-line arguments to a program. The next section shows you how to send results from your program back to the command line.

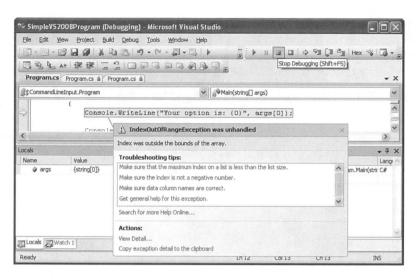

FIGURE 2.9   VS2008 error when reading empty **Main** method **args** parameter.

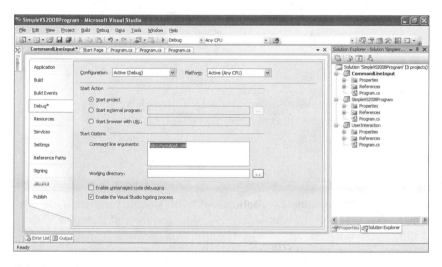

FIGURE 2.10   Setting command-line options in VS2008.

Returning Values from Your Program

In addition to processing command-line arguments, you can send information back to the command line. Typically, this is for relaying the success status via a set of error codes. Here's an example of returning an error code to the command line:

```
static int Main()
{
    return 7;
}
```

Two features of the preceding code enable you to return values to the command line: a return type and `return` statement. In previous examples, the `Main` method has a return type of void, meaning that it doesn't return anything; but this example has a return type of int. `Main` can return only either int or void.

The `return` statement, sends the value 7 back to the command line. The value returned is whatever you define it to be. Typically, the value 0 means success, and any other value is an application-defined error.

You would return values from your program for the same reason that you process command-line arguments: to allow administrative execution via scripting or other tool such as the Windows Scheduler. Here's a batch file you can run, after compiling the preceding example to ReturnIntFromMain.exe, to see how this could be scripted:

```
@echo off
ReturnIntFromMain.exe
echo Result is "%errorlevel%"
pause
```

If you save this to a file, named something like ReturnValView.bat (don't forget the *.bat extension), into the same folder as ReturnIntFromMain.exe and run it (double-click the file), you will see the following output:

```
Result is "7"
Press any key to continue . . .
```

This output demonstrates how a system administrator might use the program in a script and extract the value to see whether the program ran successfully.

Summary

This chapter showed how to build simple C# applications with console programs. In addition to the basic syntax of a C# program, you learned how to declare and initialize variables. You learned how to use both the command line and VS2008 for creating, editing, compiling, and running programs.

You can return to this chapter as a reference for the simple C# types, such as bool, int, and decimal. The next chapter continues where this leaves off by showing you how to write code by creating more sophisticated statements.

CHAPTER 3

Writing C# Expressions and Statements

In Chapter 1, "Introducing the .NET Platform," you learned the basic structure of a C# program, how to compile the application, and some useful information on syntax. This chapter builds upon that to show you how to write algorithms with proper C# expressions and statements.

A large part of this chapter covers the details of C# operators and statements. Along the way, you'll see several tips and gotchas for features that might be different from other languages. We start with operators first.

C# Operators

C# has four types of operators: unary, binary, ternary, and a few others that don't fit into a category. Unary operators affect a single expression. Binary operators require two expressions to produce a result. The ternary operator has three expressions. You'll see the details of other operators, too. Unary operators are first.

Unary Operators

As previously stated, unary operators affect a single expression. In many instances, the unary operators enable operations with simpler syntax than a comparable binary operation. The unary operators include + (plus), - (minus), ++ (increment), − (decrement), ! (logical negation), and ~ (bitwise complement).

The Plus Operator
The plus operator (+) returns the same value of the type it is applied to. Here are a couple examples:

```
int negative = -1;
int positive = 1;
int result;

result = +negative;    // result = -1
result = +positive;    // result = 1
```

The Minus Operator

The minus operator (-) allows negation of a variable's value. In integer and decimal types, the result is the number subtracted from 0. For floating-point types, the operator inverts the sign of the number. When a value is NaN (not a number), the result is still a NaN. Here are some examples:

```
int     negInt = -1;
decimal posDec =  1;
float   negFlt = -1.1f;
double nanDbl = Double.NaN;
int     resInt;
decimal resDec;
float   resFlt;
double  resDbl;

resInt = -negInt;  // resInt = 1
resDec = -posDec;  // resDec = -1
resFlt = -negFlt;  // resFlt = 1.1
resDbl = -nanDbl;  // resDbl = NAN
```

The Increment Operator

The increment operator (++) allows incrementing the value of a variable by 1. The timing of the effect of this operator depends upon which side of the expression it's on.

Here's a post-increment example:

```
int count;
int index = 6;

count = index++;   // count = 6, index = 7
```

In this example, the ++ operator comes after the expression index. That's why it's called a post-increment operator. The assignment takes place and then index is incremented. Because the assignment occurs first, the value of index is placed into count, making it equal 6. Then index is incremented to become 7.

Here's an example of a pre-increment operator:

```
int count;
int index = 6;
count = ++index;   // count = 7, index = 7
```

This time the ++ operator comes before the expression `index`. This is why it's called the pre-increment operator. The `index` variable is incremented before the assignment occurs. Because `index` is incremented first, its value becomes 7. Next, the assignment occurs to make the value of count equal 7.

The Decrement Operator

The decrement operator (--) allows decrementing the value of a variable. The timing of the effect of this operator again depends upon which side of the expression it is on. Here's a post-decrement example:

```
int count;
int index = 6;

count = index--;  // count = 6, index = 5
```

In this example, the -- operator comes after the expression `index`, and that's why it's called a post-decrement operator. The assignment takes place, and then `index` is decremented. Because the assignment occurs first, the value of `index` is placed into count, making it equal 6. Then, `index` is decremented to become 5.

Here's an example of a pre-decrement operator:

```
int count;
int index = 6;

count = --index;      // count = 5, index = 5
```

This time, the -- operator comes before the expression `index`, which is why it's called the pre-decrement operator. `Index` is decremented before the assignment occurs. Because `index` is decremented first, its value becomes 5, and then the assignment occurs to make the value of count equal 5.

The common use of increment and decrement operators is with `int` variables, but you can use them on all simple types other than `bool` and `string`. For `char`, the value moves to the next character.

The Logical Complement Operator

A logical complement operator (!) inverts the result of a Boolean expression. The Boolean expression evaluating to `true` will be `false`. Likewise, the Boolean expression evaluating to `false` will be `true`. Here are a couple examples:

```
bool bexpr   = true;
bool bresult = !bexpr;   // bresult = false
bresult      = !bresult; // bresult = true
```

The Bitwise Complement Operator

A bitwise complement operator (~) inverts the binary representation of an expression. All 1 bits are turned to 0. Likewise, all 0 bits are turned to 1. Here's an example:

```
byte bitComp = 15;                 // bitComp =  15 = 00001111b
byte byteResult = (byte) ~bitComp; // bresult = 240 = 11110000b
```

One thing you might have noticed in the preceding example was the cast operator (byte) on the second line. This will force a conversion from type int to type byte. Since mathematical operations on byte and short types result in an int, the cast is necessary to convert the type to a byte for assignment. I'll discuss cast operators in more detail later.

Binary Operators

Binary operators work with two operands. For example, a common binary expression would be a + b—the addition operator (+) surrounded by two operands. The binary operators are further subdivided into arithmetic, relational, logical, and assignment operators.

Arithmetic Operators

Arithmetic expressions are composed of two expressions with an arithmetic operator between them. This includes all the typical mathematical operators as expected in algebra.

The Multiplication Operator

The multiplication operator (*) evaluates two expressions and returns their product. Here's an example:

```
int expr1 = 3;
int expr2 = 7;
int product;

product = expr1 * expr2;  // product = 21
```

The Division Operator

The division operator (/), as its name indicates, performs mathematical division. It takes a dividend expression and divides it by a divisor expression to produce a quotient. Here's an example:

```
int dividend = 45;
int divisor = 5;
int quotient;

quotient = dividend / divisor;  // quotient = 9
```

Notice the use of integers in this expression. Had the result been a fractional number, it would have been truncated to produce the integer result.

The Modulus Operator

The modulus operator (%) returns the remainder of a division operation between a dividend and divisor. A common use of this operator is to create equations that produce a remainder that falls within a specified range. Here's an example:

```
int dividend = 33;
int divisor = 10;
int remainder;

remainder = dividend % divisor;   // remainder = 3
```

As long as the divisor stays at 10, the remainder will always be set between 0 and 9.

The Addition Operator

The addition operator (+) performs standard mathematical addition by adding one number to another. Here's an example:

```
int one = 1;
int two;

two = one + one;   // two = 2
```

The Subtraction Operator

The subtraction operator (–) performs standard mathematical subtraction by subtracting the value of one expression from another. Here's an example:

```
decimal debt    = 537.50m;
decimal payment = 250.00m;
decimal balance;

balance = debt - payment;  // balance = 287.5
```

The Left Shift Operator

To shift the bits of a number to the left, use the left shift operator (<<). Here's an example.

```
uint intMax = 4294967295; // 11111111111111111111111111111111b
uint byteMask;
byteMask   = intMax << 8; // 11111111111111111111111100000000b
```

The effect of this operation is that all bits move to the left the specified number of times. High-order bits are lost. Lower-order bits are 0 filled. This operator can be used with the int, uint, long, and ulong types.

The Right Shift Operator

The right shift operator (>>) shifts the bits of a number to the right. Here are some examples:

```
uint intMax = 4294967295; // 11111111111111111111111111111111b
uint shortMask;
shortMask = intMax >> 16; // 00000000000000001111111111111111b

int intMax = -1;          // 11111111111111111111111111111111b
int shortMask;
shortMask = intMax >> 16; // 10000000000000001111111111111111b
```

Given a number to operate on and number of digits, all bits shift to the right by the number of digits specified. You can use the right shift operator on int, uint, long, and ulong types. The uint, ulong, positive int, and positive long types shift 0s from the left. The negative int and negative long types keep a 1 in the sign bit position and fill the next position to the right with a 0.

Relational Operators

You can use relational operators to compare two expressions. The primary difference between relational operators and arithmetic operators is that relational operators return a bool type rather than a number. Another difference is that arithmetic operators are applicable to certain C# types, whereas relational operators can be used on every possible C# type, whether built in or not.

The Equal Operator

To see whether two expressions are the same, use the equal operator (==). The equal operator works the same for integral, floating-point, decimal, and enum types. I'll discuss enum types later. It just compares the two expressions and returns a bool result. Here's an example:

```
bool bresult;
decimal debit  = 1500.00m;
decimal credit = 1395.50m;

bresult = debit == credit;  // bresult = false
```

When comparing floating-point types, +0.0 and –0.0 are considered equal. If either floating-point number is NaN (not a number), equal returns false.

The Not Equal Operator

The not equal operator (!=) is the opposite of the equal operator for all types, with a slight variation for floating-point types only:

```
bool bresult;
decimal debit  = 1500.00m;
decimal credit = 1395.50m;
```

```
bresult = debit != credit;     // bresult = true
bresult = !(debit == credit); // bresult = true
```

If one of the floating-point numbers is NaN (not a number), not equal returns true.

The Less Than Operator

Use the less than operator (<) to find out whether one value is smaller than another. Here's an example:

```
short redBeads   = 2;
short whiteBeads = 23;
bool bresult;

bresult = redBeads < whiteBeads; // bresult=true, work harder
```

The expression on the left is being evaluated, and the expression on the right is the basis of comparison. When the expression on the left is a lower value than the expression on the right, the result is true. Otherwise, the result is false.

The Greater Than Operator

You can use the greater than operator (>) to learn whether a certain value is larger than another. Here's an example:

```
short redBeads   = 13;
short whiteBeads = 12;
bool bresult;

bresult = redBeads > whiteBeads; // bresult=true, good job!
```

The preceding example compares the expression on the left to the expression on the right. When the expression on the left is a higher value than the expression on the right, the result is true. Otherwise, the result is false.

The Less Than or Equal Operator

The less than or equal operator (<=) is for learning whether a number is either lower than or equal to another number. Here's an example of the less than or equal operator:

```
float limit     = 4.0f;
float currValue = 3.86724f;
bool bresult;

bresult = currValue <= limit; // bresult = true
```

Above, the expression on the left is compared to the expression on the right. When the expression on the left is either the same value as or less than the one on the right, less than or equal returns true.

The Greater Than or Equal Operator

As its name implies, the greater than or equal operator (>=) checks a value to see whether it's greater than or equal to another. Here's an example:

```
double rightAngle = 90.0d;
double myAngle    = 96.0d;
bool isObtuse;

isObtuse = myAngle >= rightAngle; // Yes, myAngle is obtuse
```

As shown here, when the expression to the left of the operator is the same as or more than the expression on the right, the result is true. The greater than or equal operator is the opposite of the less than operator.

Logical Operators

Logical operators perform Boolean logic on two expressions. There are three types of logical operators in C#: bitwise, Boolean, and conditional.

The bitwise logical operators perform Boolean logic on corresponding bits of two integral expressions. Valid integral types are the signed and unsigned int and long types. C# promotes byte to int, which is why the example in the prevous section worked. The bitwise logical operators return a compatible integral result with each bit conforming to the Boolean evaluation.

Boolean logical operators perform Boolean logic upon two Boolean expressions. The expression on the left is evaluated, and then the expression on the right is evaluated. Finally, the two expressions are evaluated together in the context of the Boolean logical operator between them. They return a bool result corresponding to the type of operator used.

The conditional logical operators operate much the same way as the Boolean logical operators with one exception: When the first expression is evaluated and found to satisfy the results of the entire expression, the second expression is not evaluated. This is efficient because it doesn't make sense to continue evaluating an expression when the result is already known.

The Bitwise AND Operator

The bitwise AND operator (&) compares corresponding bits of two integrals and returns a result with corresponding bits set to 1 when both integrals have 1 bits. When either or both integrals have a 0 bit, the corresponding result bit is 0. Here's an example:

```
byte oddMask  = 1;  // 00000001b
byte someByte = 85; // 01010101b
bool isEven;

isEven = (oddMask & someByte) == 0; //(oddMask & someByte) = 0
```

The Bitwise Inclusive OR Operator

The bitwise inclusive OR operator (¦) compares corresponding bits of two integrals and returns a result with corresponding bits set to 1 if either of the integrals have 1 bits in that position. When both integrals have a 0 in corresponding positions, the result is 0 in that position. Here's an example:

```
byte option1 = 1; // 00000001b
byte option2 = 2; // 00000010b
byte totalOptions;

totalOptions = (byte) (option1 ¦ option2); // 00000011b
```

The Bitwise Exclusive OR Operator

The bitwise exclusive OR operator (^) compares corresponding bits of two integrals and returns a result with corresponding bits set to 1 if only one of the integrals has a 1 bit and the other integral has a 0 bit in that position. When both integral bits are 1 or both are 0, the result's corresponding bit is 0. Here's an example:

```
byte invertMask = 255; // 11111111b
byte someByte   = 240; // 11110000b
byte inverse;

inverse = (byte)(someByte ^ invertMask); //inverse=00001111b
```

The Boolean AND Operator

The Boolean AND operator (&) evaluates two Boolean expressions and returns `true` when both expressions evaluate to `true`. Otherwise, the result is `false`. The result of each expression evaluated must return a bool. Here's an example:

```
bool inStock = false;
decimal price = 18.95m;
bool buy;

buy = inStock & (price < 20.00m); // buy = false
```

The Boolean Inclusive OR Operator

The Boolean inclusive OR operator (¦) evaluates the results of two Boolean expressions and returns `true` if either of the expressions returns `true`. When both expressions are `false`, the result of the Boolean inclusive OR evaluation is `false`. Both expressions evaluated must return a bool type value. Here's an example:

```
int mileage = 2305;
int months = 4;
bool changeOil;

changeOil = mileage > 3000 ¦ months > 3; // changeOil = true
```

The Boolean Exclusive OR Operator

The Boolean exclusive OR operator (^) evaluates the results of two Boolean expressions and returns true if only one of the expressions returns true. When both expressions are true or both expressions are false, the result of the Boolean exclusive OR expression is false. In other words, the expressions must be different. Here's an example:

```
bool availFlag = false;
bool toggle    = true;
bool available;

available = availFlag ^ toggle; // available = true
```

The Conditional AND Operator

The conditional AND operator (&&) is similar to the Boolean AND operator (&) in that it evaluates two expressions and returns true when both expressions are true. When the first expression evaluates to false, there is no way the entire expression can be true. Therefore, the conditional AND operator returns false and does not evaluate the second expression. However, when the first expression is true, the conditional AND operator goes ahead and evaluates the second expression. Here's an example:

```
bool inStock  = false;
decimal price = 18.95m;
bool buy;

buy = inStock && (price < 20.00m); // buy = false
```

Notice that price < 20 will never be evaluated.

The Conditional OR Operator

The conditional OR operator (¦¦) is similar to the Boolean inclusive OR operator (¦) in that it evaluates two expressions and returns true when either expression is true. When the first expression evaluates to true, the entire expression must be true. Therefore, the conditional OR operator returns true without evaluating the second expression. When the first expression is false, the conditional OR operator goes ahead and evaluates the second expression. Here's an example:

```
int mileage = 4305;
int months = 4;
bool changeOil;

changeOil = mileage > 3000 ¦¦ months > 3; // changeOil = true
```

Notice that because `mileage > 3000` is true, `months > 3` will never be evaluated.

Side Effects

Watch out for side effects with conditional Boolean operations. Side effects occur when your program depends on the expression on the right of the conditional logical operator being evaluated. If the expression on the right is not evaluated, this could cause a hard to find bug. The conditional logical operators are also called short-circuit operators. Take a look at this example:

```
decimal totalSpending = 3692.48m;
decimal avgSpending;

bool onBudget = totalSpending > 4000.00m
    && totalSpending < CalcAvg();
```

Notice that the second half of the expression was not evaluated. If `CalcAvg()` was supposed to change the value of a class field for later processing, there would be an error.

> **WARNING ON CONDITIONAL OPERATOR SIDE EFFECTS**
>
> When using conditional AND and conditional OR operators, make sure a program does not depend upon evaluation of the rightmost side of the expression, because it might not be evaluated. Such side effects are common sources of hard-to-find bugs.

Assignment Operators

This chapter has already demonstrated plenty of examples of the simple assignment operator in action. This section builds on that by explaining how the compound operators work. Basically, a compound operator is a combination of the assignment operator and an arithmetic operator, bitwise logical operator, or Boolean logical operator. Here's an example:

```
int total = 7;
total += 3; // total = 10
```

This is the same as saying `total = total + 3`. Table 3.1 shows a list of the available compound assignment operators.

TABLE 3.1   Compound Assignment Operators

Operator	Function
*=	Multiplication
/=	Division
%=	Remainder
+=	Addition

Operator	Function
-=	Subtraction
<<=	Left Shift
>>=	Right Shift
&=	AND
^=	Exclusive OR
¦=	Inclusive OR

The Ternary Operator

The ternary operator contains three expressions, thus the name *ternary*. The first expression must be a Boolean expression. When the first expression evaluates to true, the value of the second expression is returned. When the first expression evaluates to false, the value of the third expression is returned. This is a concise and short method of making a decision and returning a choice based on the result of the decision. The ternary operator is often called the conditional operator. Here's an example:

```
long democratVotes   = 1753829380624;
long republicanVotes = 1753829380713;

string headline = democratVotes != republicanVotes ?
                "We Finally Have a Winner!" : recount();
```

Other Operators

C# has some operators that can't be categorized as easily as the other types. These include the is, as, sizeof(), typeof(), checked(), and unchecked() operators. You'll learn more about the delegate operator in Chapter 12, "Event-Based Programming with Delegates and Events," which is used for creating what are called anonymous methods. The following sections explain each of these operators.

The is Operator

The is operator checks a variable to see whether it is of a given type. If so, it returns true. Otherwise, it returns false. Here's an example:

```
int i = 0;
bool isTest = i is int; // isTest = true
```

This example generates a compiler warning that i will always be an int. However, if you were performing this operation in a method that was testing a parameter passed to it, then the C# compiler wouldn't know this. I'll discuss methods and parameters later.

The as Operator

The as operator attempts to perform a conversion on a reference type. Here's an example:

```
object obj = new Customer();
string cust = obj as string;

Console.WriteLine("cust {0} a string.",
    cust == null ? "is not" : "is"); // cust is not a string.
```

Notice the object type in the preceding example. In C#, all objects can be assigned to the object type. You'll learn more about objects in Chapter 4, "Understanding Reference Types and Value Types."

The preceding example tries to convert the Customer type object, cust, into a string, but the types are clearly incompatible. C# won't compile assignments of incompatible types. If the conversion were successful, which can't be in this example, the string variable, cust, would hold a reference to a string object. When the conversion from an as operator fails, it assigns null to the receiving reference. That's the case in this example where cust is null because obj is really a Customer, not a string.

The sizeof Operator

The sizeof operator returns the number of bytes that a type can hold. Here's an example:

```
unsafe
{
    int intSize = sizeof(int); // intSize = 4
}
```

Notice the unsafe keyword in the preceding code. This defines a block of code that can be used for low-level operations that can't be verified by the Common Language Runtime (CLR). The sizeof operator is used only with unsafe code blocks. You can learn more about unsafe code in Chapter 41, "Performing Interop (P/Invoke and COM) and Writing Unsafe Code."

CONFIGURING UNSAFE CODE

To get unsafe code blocks to work in VS2008, double-click the Properties folder for the project in Solution Explorer, click the Build tab, and check the Allow Unsafe Code check box.

The typeof Operator

The typeof operator returns a Type object, which holds information about a type. The following example extracts details of the int type:

```
Type myType = typeof(int);
Console.WriteLine(
    "The int type: {0}", myType ); // The int type: System.Int32
```

The typeof operator is useful for giving the code information about a given type. In Chapter 16, "Declaring Attributes and Examining Code with Reflection," you can learn how to use Type objects, which are returned by the typeof operator, to perform reflection and work with code dynamically.

The checked Operator

The checked operator detects overflow conditions in certain operations. The following example causes a system error by attempting to assign a value to a short variable that it can't hold:

```
short val1 = 20000, val2 = 20000;
short myShort = checked((short)(val1 + val2)); // error
```

The unchecked Operator

If it is necessary to ignore an overflow error and accept the results regardless of overflow conditions, use the unchecked operator as in this example:

```
short val1 = 20000, val2 = 20000;
short myShort =
    unchecked((short)(val1 + val2)); // error ignored
```

SETTING CHECKED/UNCHECKED

Overflow checking is unchecked by default.

You can use the /checked[+¦-] command-line option when the majority of program code should be checked (/checked+) or unchecked (/checked-).

In VS2008, select the project in Solution Explorer, Properties, Build tab, scroll down to Advanced, and set Check for Arithmetic Overflow/Underflow as you need.

Statements

Statements in C# are single entities that cause a change in the program's current state. A statement ends with a semicolon (;), which will generate a compiler error if forgotten. Statements may span multiple lines, which could help make your code more readable, as the following example shows:

```
decimal closingCosts = loanOrigination
        + appraisal
        + titleSearch
        + insuranceAdvance
        + taxAdvance
        + points
        + realtorCommission
        + whateverElseTheyCanRipYouOffFor;
```

Had the statement been placed on one line, it would have either continued off the right side of the page or wrapped around in an inconvenient location. This way, each item is visible, lined up nicely, and easier to understand. Don't forget your semicolons.

Blocks and Scope

Setting off code in blocks clearly delimits the beginning and ending of a unit of work and establishes scope. Begin a block of code with a left-side brace ({) and end it with a right-side brace (}). Blocks are required to specify the boundaries of many language elements such as classes, interfaces, structures, properties, indexers, events, and methods.

Blocks also specify scope. Here's an example of blocks associated with a method or nested:

```
static void Main(string[] args)
{
    bool myBool = true;

    {
        int myInt = 5;
        myBool = false;
    }

    myInt = 6;

    // code can be here too
}
```

As you know by now, the beginning and ending of a `Main` method, or any other method, is defined by a block. However, the preceding example creates an unnamed block inside of the `Main` method. This is essentially creating a unique scope for `myInt`. Because `myInt` is defined inside of the block, the code following the block that tries to set `myInt` to 6 will cause a compiler error. Outer scopes can't see types defined at inner scopes.

From the perspective of visibility from inner scopes, all variables defined at an outer scope are visible. In the preceding example, `myBool` is defined at the `Main` method scope and is visible to code in the unnamed block.

Similarly, class fields are visible to all methods in a class, but local variables (defined in methods) aren't visible to other methods.

Labels

Labels are program elements that simply identify a location in a program. Their only practical use is to support the `goto` statement. The `goto` statement allows program control to jump to the place where a label is defined. A label is any valid identifier followed by a colon (not a semicolon). Here are two examples:

```
loop:       // a label named "loop"
jumphere:   // a label named "jumphere"
```

You'll see how the goto statement works later in this chapter. Although goto statement usage often leads to bad code and you should avoid them, they are a part of the language. So, I show you how they work.

Operator Precedence and Associativity

When evaluating C# expressions, there are certain rules to ensure the outcome of the evaluation. These rules are governed by precedence and associativity and preserve the semantics of all C# expressions. Precedence refers to the order in which operations should be evaluated. Subexpressions with higher operator precedence are evaluated first.

There are two types of associativity: left and right. Operators with left associativity are evaluated from left to right. When an operator has right associativity, its expression is evaluated from right to left. For example, the assignment operator is right-associative. Therefore, the expression to its right is evaluated before the assignment operation is invoked. Table 3.2 shows the C# operators, their precedence, and associativity.

TABLE 3.2   Operator Precedence and Associativity

Operators	Associativity
x.y f(x) a[x] x++ x- - new	
typeof default checked	
unchecked delegate	Left
+(unary) –(unary) ~ ++x - -x (T)x	Left
* / %	Left
+(arithmetic) –(arithmetic)	Left
<< >>	Left
< > <= >= is as	Left
== !=	Left
&	Left
^	Left
|	Left
&&	Left
||	Left
?:	Right
= *= /= %= += -= <<= >>= &= ^= |=	Right

Certain operators have precedence over others to guarantee the certainty and integrity of computations. One effective rule of thumb when using most operators is to remember their algebraic precedence. Here's an example:

```
int result;
result = 5 + 3 * 9;   // result = 32
```

This computes 3 * 9 = 27 + 5 = 32. To alter the order of operations, use parentheses, which have a higher precedence:

```
result = (5 + 3) * 9;   // result = 72
```

This time, 5 and 3 were added to get 8 and then that was multiplied by 9 to get 72. See Table 3.2 for a listing of operator precedence and associativity. Operators in top rows have precedence over operators in lower rows. Operators on the left in each row have higher precedence over operators to the right in the same row.

Selection and Looping Statements

When coding, you need to make logical decisions, iteratively execute a sequence of instructions, and modify the normal flow of control. Even though selection and looping statements are common to most languages, this section shows you how to do all of that and points out special C# features.

if Statements

if statements allow evaluation of an expression and, depending on the truth of the evaluation, the capability to branch to a specified sequence of logic. C# provides three forms of if statements: simple if, if-then-else, and if-else if-else.

Simple if

A simple if statement takes the following form:

```
if (Boolean expression)
[{]
    true condition statement(s)
[}]
```

The Boolean expression must evaluate to either true or false. When the Boolean expression is true, the program performs the following true condition statements. Here's an example:

```
if (args.Length == 0)
{
  Console.WriteLine("Invalid # of command line args");
}
```

If the preceding code were in a Main method, this would be one way to validate that the user entered a command-line option.

if-then-else

The simple if statement guarantees you can only perform certain actions on a true condition. It's either done or it's not. To handle both the true and false conditions, use the if-else statement. It has the following form:

```
if (Boolean expression)
[{]
    true condition statement(s)
[}]
else
[{]
    false condition statement(s)
[}]
```

Here's an example:

```
if (args.Length == 0)
{
  Console.WriteLine("Invalid # of command line args");
}
else
{
  Console.WriteLine("You entered: {0}?", args[0]);
}
```

The preceding statement behaves the same as the simple if, except when the Boolean expression evaluates to false, the else block is executed.

if-else else-if

Sometimes it's necessary to evaluate multiple conditions to determine what actions to take. In this case, use the if-else else-if statement. Here's its general form:

```
if (Boolean expression)
[{]
    true condition statement(s)
[}]

else if (Boolean expression)


    .

    .

    .


else if (Boolean expression)

else
```

In a sequential order, each statement, beginning with if and continuing through each else if, is evaluated until one of its Boolean expressions evaluates to true. The dots indicate possible multiple else if blocks. There can be any number of else if blocks.

When one of the Boolean expressions evaluates to true, the true condition statements for that if or else if are executed, and then flow of control transfers to the first statement following the entire if-else if-else structure.

When none of the Boolean expressions evaluates to `true`, the `false` condition statements of the last `else` section are executed. Here's an example:

```
if (args.Length == 0)
{
  Console.WriteLine("Invalid # of command line args");
}
else if (args.Length == 1)
{
  Console.WriteLine("You entered: {0}?", args[0]);
}
else
{
  Console.WriteLine("Too many arguments!\a");
}
```

You can include any valid statement inside an `if`, `else if`, or `else` statement block.

In VS2008, you can use the if snippet by typing **if**, and pressing tab, tab, adding the condition and pressing enter, which will add a block and move the cursor into that block.

switch Statements

When there are many conditions to evaluate, the `if-else if-else` statement can become complex and verbose. Sometimes, a much cleaner solution is the `switch` statement. The `switch` statement allows testing any integral value or string against multiple values. When the test produces a match, all statements associated with that match are executed. Here's the basic form of a `switch` statement:

```
switch(integral, enum, or string expression)
{
    case <literal-1>:
        statement(s)
        break;
        .
        .
        .
    case <literal-n>:
        statement(s)
        break;
    [default:
        statement(s)]
}
```

The integral, enum, or string expression is compared against each `case` statement's literal value. You'll learn more about enum types in Chapter 6, "Using Arrays and Enums." Add as many `case` statements as necessary. When there's a match, those statements following the matching `case` are executed. Here's an example:

```
switch (choice)
{
  case "A":
    Console.WriteLine("Add Site");
    break;
  case "S":
    Console.WriteLine("Sort List");
    break;
  case "R":
    Console.WriteLine("Show Report");
    break;
  case "Q":
    Console.WriteLine("GoodBye");
    break;
  default:
    Console.WriteLine("Huh??");
    break;
}
```

The break or other statement that forces an exit from the case block is required. Later in this section, you learn about continue, goto, and return statements, which are also acceptable.

One case can't drop through to another case after executing its statements. There are a few less-common exceptions to this rule. One exception is grouping case statements together, as this example shows:

```
switch (choice)
{
  case "a":
  case "A":
    Console.WriteLine("Add Site");
    break;
  case "s":
  case "S":
    Console.WriteLine("Sort List");
    break;
  case "r":
  case "R":
    Console.WriteLine("Show Report");
    break;
  case "q":
  case "Q":
    Console.WriteLine("GoodBye");
    break;
```

```
  default:
    Console.WriteLine("Huh??");
    break;
}
```

The preceding example shows an exception to the restriction against case fall-through. The case for each capital and small letter are grouped together with one immediately following the other. The top case will fall through to the next case when there are no statements between the two cases. Here's an example of using a goto statement:

```
switch (choice)
{
  case "A":
    Console.WriteLine("Add Site");
    break;
  case "S":
    Console.WriteLine("Sort List");
    break;
  case "R":
    Console.WriteLine("Show Report");
    break;
  case "V":
    Console.WriteLine("View Sorted Report");
    // Sort First
    goto case "R";
  case "Q":
    Console.WriteLine("GoodBye");
    break;
  default:
    Console.WriteLine("Huh??");
    break;
}
```

The preceding example shows the second exception to the restriction against case fall-through. It uses a goto statement to execute another case. It doesn't matter whether the goto case is the next in line or somewhere else in the switch statement. Program control will still transfer to the case specified in the goto statement. When none of the cases match, control transfers to the default case.

The default case in a switch statement is optional. When there is no default case, program control transfers to the next statement following the ending curly brace of the switch statement.

C# Loops

In C#, there are four types of loops: the while loop, the do loop, the for loop, and the foreach loop. Each has its own benefits for certain tasks.

while Loops

To continually execute a group of statements when a condition is `true`, you can use the while loop. The general form of the `while` loop is as follows:

```
while (Boolean expression)
[{]
    true condition statement(s)
[}]
```

When the Boolean expression evaluates to `true`, the `true` condition statements are executed. The following example shows how a `while` loop can be used:

```
string doAgain = "Y";
int count = 0;
string[] siteName = new string[10];

while (doAgain == "Y")
{
  Console.Write("Please Enter Site Name: ");
  siteName[count++] = Console.ReadLine();

  Console.Write("Add Another?: ");
  doAgain = Console.ReadLine();
}
```

A sneaky bug to watch out for with all loops is the empty-statement bug. The following code is for illustrative purposes only, so don't try it:

```
string doAgain = "Y";

while (doAgain == "Y"); // loop forever
{
  // this is never executed
}
```

Because curly braces are optional, the semicolon after the Boolean expression represents the true condition statement. Thus, every time the Boolean expression evaluates to `true`, the empty statement is executed, and the Boolean statement is evaluated again—*ad infinitum*.

The reason the curly braces don't cause a bug is because they represent a block, which is legal syntax in C#.

> **WARNING**
>
> A single semicolon is interpreted as a statement. A common mistake is to put a semi-colon after a loop statement, which causes subsequent loop statements to execute only one time. These are hard-to-find errors.

do Loops

while loops evaluate an expression before executing the statements in a block. However, it might be necessary to execute the statements at least one time. This is what the do loop allows. Here's its general form:

```
do {
    Statement(s)
} while (Boolean expression);
```

The statements execute, and then the Boolean expression is evaluated. If the Boolean expression evaluates to true, the statements are executed again. Otherwise, control passes to the statement following the entire do loop. The following is an example of a do loop in action:

```
do
{
  Console.WriteLine("");
  Console.WriteLine("A - Add Site");
  Console.WriteLine("S - Sort List");
  Console.WriteLine("R - Show Report\n");

  Console.WriteLine("Q - Quit\n");

  Console.Write("Please Choose (A/S/R/Q): ");

  choice = Console.ReadLine();

  switch (choice)
  {
    case "a":
    case "A":
      Console.WriteLine("Add Site");
      break;
    case "s":
    case "S":
      Console.WriteLine("Sort List");
      break;
    case "r":
    case "R":
      Console.WriteLine("Show Report");
      break;
    case "q":
    case "Q":
      Console.WriteLine("GoodBye");
      break;
```

```
    default:
      Console.WriteLine("Huh??");
      break;
  }

} while ((choice = choice.ToUpper()) != "Q");
```

This code snippet prints a menu and then asks the user for input. For this purpose, it is logical to use a do loop, because the menu has to print at least one time. If this were to be done with another type of loop, some artificial condition would have needed to be set just to get the first iteration.

Calling ToUpper will uppercase the string to avoid needing to check for multiple casing scenarios that the user could type in. I'll discuss ToUpper and other string methods in a later chapter.

for Loops

for loops are handy when the number of times to execute a group of statements is known. Here's the general syntax:

```
for (initializer; Boolean expression; modifier)
[{]
    statement(s)
[}]
```

The initializer is executed one time only, when the for loop begins. After the initializer executes, the Boolean expression is evaluated. The Boolean expression must evaluate to true for the statement(s) to be executed. After the statement(s) have executed, the modifier executes, and then the Boolean expression is evaluated again. The statement(s) continue to be executed until the Boolean expression evaluates to false, after which control transfers to the statement following the for loop. The following example illustrates how to implement a for loop:

```
int n = siteName.Length-2;
int j, k;
string save;

for (k=n-1; k >= 0; k—)
{
  j = k + 1;
  save = siteName[k];
  siteName[n+1] = save;

  while ( string.Compare(save, siteName[j]) > 0 )
  {
    siteName[j-1] = siteName[j];
```

```
    j++;
  }
  siteName[j-1] = save;
}
```

The insertion sort in this code shows how a for loop is used in a realistic scenario. Often, for loops begin at 0 and are incremented until a predetermined number of iterations have passed. This particular example starts at the end of the array and moves backward, decrementing each step. When k reaches 0, the loop ends.

When programming in C#, there is a full set of libraries from which to choose premade functions. The Boolean condition of the while loop shows the string.Compare() method. In this particular instance, the program checks to see whether save is greater than siteName[j]. If so, the Boolean result is true. The siteName variable is an array of string objects.

foreach Loops
The foreach loop is excellent for iterating through collections. Here's its syntax:

```
foreach (type identifier in collection)
[{]
    statement(s)
[}]
```

The type can be any C# or user-defined type. The identifier is the variable name you want to use. The collection could be any C# collection object or array.

Upon entering the foreach loop, the identifier variable is set with an item from collection. Then the statement(s) are executed and control transfers back to get another item from the collection. When all items in the collection have been extracted, control transfers to the statement following the foreach loop.

You can learn more about collections in Chapter 17, "Parameterizing Type with Generics and Writing Iterators."

Here's an example that iterates through the siteName array, printing each entry to the console:

```
foreach(string site in siteName)
{
  Console.WriteLine("\t{0}", site);
}
```

Had this been done with another loop, the program would have taken more effort. Then there's always the possibility of corrupting a counter. The foreach loop is a clean and simple way to iterate through an array.

`goto` Statements

The goto statement allows unconditional branching to another program section. The form of the goto statement is as follows:

```
goto label;
```

The destination is marked by a `label`. Legal destinations include the current level of the goto statement or outside of the current loop. The following code shows how a goto statement could be used:

```
do {
  // some processing
  while (/* some Boolean condition */)
  {
    // some processing
    for (int i=0; i < someValue; i++)
    {
      if (/* some Boolean condition */)
      {
        goto quickExit;
      }
    }
  }
} while (/* some Boolean condition */);

quickExit:
```

This example displays a potential scenario where the code is deeply nested in processing. If a certain condition causes the end of processing to occur in the middle of that loop, the program has to make several less-than-graceful checks to get out. The example shows how using a goto might be helpful in making a clean exit from a tricky situation. It might even make the code easier to read, instead of trying to design a clumsy workaround. Again, the decision to use a goto is based on the requirements a project needs to meet.

A goto may never jump into a loop. Here's an example that should help you visualize just how illogical such an attempt might be:

```
// won't compile
while (/* some Boolean condition */)
{
  // some processing
  innerLoop:
  // more processing
}

goto innerLoop;
```

It's normally desirable to have some type of initialization and control while executing a loop. This scenario could easily violate the integrity of any loop, which is why it is not allowed.

GO TO **STATEMENT CONSIDERED HARMFUL**

Much has been said about the value of the goto statement in computer programming. Arguments range from recommending that it be eliminated to using it as an essential tool to get out of a hard spot. Although many people have been able to program without the goto for years, there's always the possibility that someone may still find it necessary. Just be careful with its use and make sure programs are maintainable.

The title of this note echoes the sentiments of the late Edsgar W. Dijkstra and his essay of the same subject, which you can order from the ACM at http://portal.acm.org/citation.cfm?id=1241518&coll=ACM&dl=ACM&CFID=40705154 &CFTOKEN=94932948. Another in-depth discussion can be found at Wikipedia at http://en.wikipedia.org/wiki/Goto.

Another allowed use of goto in C# programs is to move from one case to another in a switch statement, which I covered in the previous section of this chapter on switch statements. See the sidebar "goto Statement Considered Harmful."

break Statements

The switch statement, mentioned previously, showed one way to use the break statement. It allowed program control to jump out of the switch statement. Similarly, the break statement allows jumping out of any decision or loop. Its destination is always the first statement following the most containing decision or loop.

This example shows two ways to break out of a loop:

```
string doAgain = "Y";


while (doAgain == "Y")
{
  Console.Write("Please Enter Site Name: ");
  siteName[count++] = Console.ReadLine();

  Console.Write("Add Another?: ");
  doAgain = Console.ReadLine();

  if (count >= 5)
  {
    break;
  }
}
```

Normally, a user types **Y** to continue or types anything else to leave. However, an array is a specified size and it wouldn't be nice to attempt to overflow its bounds, because this would cause an error. The if statement is present to guard against this happening. When the number of entries in the array exceeds its max capacity, the program breaks out of the loop with the break statement.

The break statement goes only to the next level below its enclosing loop.

continue Statements

continue statements are used in loops. They allow a program to jump immediately to the Boolean expression of the loop. Here's a program snippet that shows how to use a continue statement to discontinue processing during a given iteration:

```
foreach(string site in siteName)
{
  if (response.ToUpper() == "Y" &&
    site != null &&
    site.IndexOf(filter) == -1)
  {
    continue;
  }

  Console.WriteLine("\t{0}", site);
}
```

This example checks the current array entry against a predefined filter. The IndexOf() method, a predefined string function, returns a –1 if the value of filter does not exist in the site string. When the value is –1, the continue statement is invoked. This sends program control back to the top of the foreach loop for another iteration.

VALUE OF THE CONTINUE **STATEMENT**

In practice, I rarely use continue. Every time it looks like a viable option, a more maintainable solution, such as an if statement, often makes more sense.

return Statements

return statements allow jumping out of a method or, in the case of the Main() method, the program. The following example shows how the return statement is used in the Main() method:

```
public static int Main(string[] args)
{
  // other program statements

  return 0;
}
```

The Main() method has a return type of int, as specified by the int declaration in front of the word Main. If the return value were void, there would be two choices: Don't use the return statement, or just use the statement return; with no value. Because the example returns an int, the return statement must return an integer value. Therefore, when this program runs without problems and ends, it returns a value of 0 to the command line.

All methods have return types and have the same return statement options as shown previously. The difference is that the value is returned to the statement making the method call.

Summary

You now have the information necessary to use operators, build expressions, and implement selection or looping statements. Most of the features are common to other programming languages, but there are nuances that you've learned about that make C# unique.

In Chapter 2, "Getting Started with C# and Visual Studio 2008," you learned about C# simple types, and this chapter built on this by showing how to use C# operators with various types. The next chapter takes you even further by exploring the .NET type system with reference and value types.

CHAPTER 4

Understanding Reference Types and Value Types

Deep in the course of coding, you're often immersed in logic, solving the problem at hand. Simple actions, such as assignment and instantiation, are tasks you perform regularly, without much thought. However, when writing C# programs, or using any language that targets the Common Language Runtime (CLR), you might want to take a second look. What appears to be simple can sometimes result in hard-to-find bugs. This chapter goes into greater depth on CLR types and shows you a few things about coding in C# that often catch developers off guard. More specifically, you learn about the differences between reference types and value types.

The .NET type system, which C# is built upon, is divided into reference types and value types. You'll work with each of these types all the time, and it's important to know the differences between them. This chapter shows you the differences via memory allocation and assignment behaviors. This understanding should translate into helping you make smart design decisions that improve application performance and reduce errors.

A Quick Introduction to Reference Types and Value Types

There is much to be said about reference types and value types, but this section gives a quick introduction to the essentials. You learn a little about their behaviors and what they look like in code.

As its name suggests, a reference type has a value that is a reference to an object in memory. However, a value type has a value that contains the object itself.

Up until now, you've been creating custom reference types, which is defined with the class keyword shown here:

```
class Customer
{
    public string Name;
}
```

The Customer class is a reference type because it uses the class keyword in its definition. Value types are similar in syntax but use the struct keyword instead, as shown here:

```
struct Money
{
    public decimal Amount;
}
```

The struct keyword classifies the Money type as a value type.

In both of these examples, I used the public modifier on the Name and Amount fields. This allows code using the Customer and Money types to access the Name and Amount fields, respectively. You can learn more about the different access modifiers in Chapter 9, "Implementing Object-Oriented Principles."

Later sections of this chapter go into even greater depth on the differences between these types, but at least you now know the bare minimum to move forward. The next section starts your journey into understanding the differences between reference types and value types and how these differences affect you.

The Unified Type System

Before looking at the specific behaviors of reference types and value types, you should understand the relationship between them and how the C# type system, the Unified Type System, works. The details described here help you understand the coding practices and performance issues that you learn later in the chapter.

How the Unified Type System Works

Essentially, the Unified Type System ensures that all C# types derive from a common ancestor, System.Object. The C# object type is an alias for System.Object, and further discussion will use a C# perspective and refer to System.Object as object. Figure 4.1 illustrates this relationship.

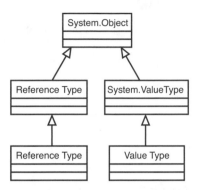

FIGURE 4.1   In the Unified Type System, all objects derive from the object type.

WHAT IS INHERITANCE

Inheritance is an object-oriented principle that promotes reuse and helps build hierarchical frameworks of objects. In the context of this chapter, you learn that all types derive from object. This gives you the ability to assign a derived object to a variable of type object. Also, whatever belongs to object is also a member of a derived class.

In Chapter 8, "Designing Objects," and Chapter 9, "Implementing Object-Oriented Principles," you can learn a lot more about C# syntax supporting inheritance and how to use it. Throughout the rest of the book, too, you'll see many examples of how to use inheritance.

In Figure 4.1, the arrows are Unified Modeling Language (UML) generalization symbols, showing how one type, a box, derives from the type being pointed to. The direction of inheritance shows that all types derive either directly or indirectly from object.

Reference types can either derive directly from System.Object or from another reference type. However, the relationship between value type objects and object is indirect. All value types implicitly derive from the System.ValueType class, a reference type object, which inherits object. For simplicity, further discussion omits the fact of either explicit or implicit inheritance relationships.

At this point, you might be scratching your head and wondering why you should care (a natural reaction). The big deal is that your coding experience with treating types in a generic manner is simplified (the good news), but you must also be aware of performance penalties that are possible when treating types in a generic manner. In Chapter 17, "Parameterizing Type with Generics and Writing Iterators," you can learn about the best way to manage generic code, but the next two sections explain the implications of the Unified Type System and how it affects you.

Using `object` for Generic Programming

Because both reference types and value types inherit object, you can assign any type to a variable of type object as shown here:

```
decimal amount = 3.50m;
object obj1 = amount;
Customer cust = new Customer();
object obj2 = cust;
```

The amount variable is a decimal, a value type, and the cust variable is a Customer class, a reference type.

Any assignment to object is an implicit conversion, which is always safe. However, doing an assignment from type object to a derived type may or may not be safe. C# forces you to state your intention with a cast operator, as shown here:

```
Customer cust2 = (Customer)obj2;
```

The cast operator is necessary because the C# compiler can't tell whether obj2 is actually a Customer type. Chapter 10, "Coding Methods and Custom Operators," goes into greater depth on conversions, but the basic idea is that C# is type-safe and has features that ensure safe assignments of one object to another.

A more concrete example of when you might see a situation where a variable can be assigned to another variable of type object is with standard collection classes. The first version of the .NET Framework Class Library (FCL) included a library of collection classes, one of them being ArrayList. These collections offered many conveniences that you don't have in C# arrays or would have to create yourself.

One of the features of these collections, including ArrayList, was that they could work generically with any type. The Unified Type System makes this possible because the collections operate on the object type, meaning that you can use them with any .NET type. Here's an example that uses an ArrayList collection:

```
ArrayList customers = new ArrayList();
Customer cust1 = new Customer();
cust1.Name = "John Smith";
Customer cust2 = new Customer();
cust2.Name = "Jane Doe";
customers.Add(cust1);
customers.Add(cust2);
foreach (Customer cust in customers)
{
        Console.WriteLine("Customer Name: {0}", cust.Name);
}
```

The preceding example creates a new instance of an ArrayList class, named customers. It creates a couple Customer objects, sets their Name fields, and then adds them to the customers `ArrayList`. Notice that the `foreach` loop works seamlessly with collections as well as it does with arrays.

Again, because the `ArrayList` operates on type object, it is convenient to use with any type, whether it is a reference type or value type. The preceding example showed you how to assign a reference type, the `Customer` class, to an `ArrayList`, which is convenient. However, there is a hidden cost when assigning value types to object type variables, such as the elements of an `ArrayList`. The next section explains this phenomenon, which is known as boxing and unboxing.

Performance Implications of Boxing and Unboxing

Boxing occurs when you assign a value type variable to a variable of type object. Unboxing occurs when you assign a variable of type object to a variable with the same type as the true type of the object. The following code is a minimal example that causes boxing and unboxing to occur:

```
decimal amountIn = 3.50m;
object obj = amountIn; // box
decimal amountOut = (decimal)obj; // unbox
```

Figures 4.2 to 4.4 illustrate what is happening in the preceding algorithm. Figure 4.2 shows the first line.

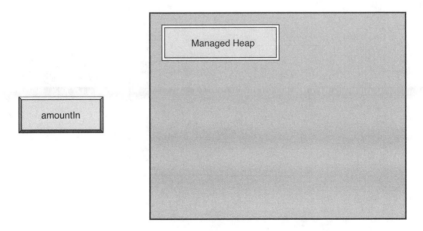

FIGURE 4.2   A value type variable before boxing.

Before boxing, as in the declaration of `amountIn`, the variable is just a value type that contains the data directly. However, as soon as you assign that value type variable to an object, as in Figure 4.3, the value is boxed.

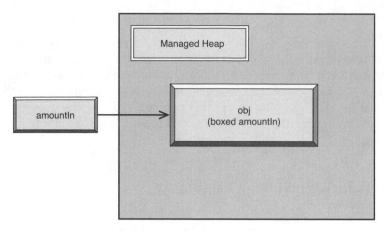

FIGURE 4.3   A boxed value.

As shown in Figure 4.3, boxing causes a new object to be allocated on the heap and a copy of the original value to be put into the boxed object. Now, you have two copies of the original variable: one in amountIn and another in the boxed decimal, obj, on the heap. You can pull that value out of the boxed decimal, as shown in Figure 4.4.

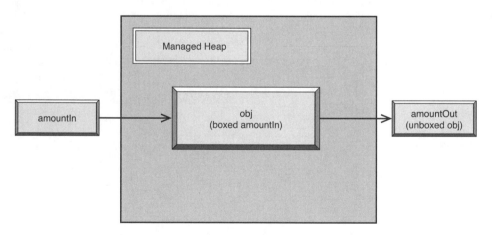

FIGURE 4.4   Unboxing a value.

In Figure 4.4, the boxed value in obj is copied into the decimal variable, amountOut. Now, you have three copies of the original value that was assigned to amountIn.

Writing code as shown here is pointless because the specific example doesn't do anything useful. However, the point of this boxing and unboxing exercise is so that you can see the mechanics of what is happening and understand the overhead associated with it. On the other hand, you could write a lot of code similar to the ArrayList example in the previous section; that is, unless you understood the information in this section. Here's an example, similar to the `ArrayList` code in the previous section, that uses value type variables:

```
ArrayList prices = new ArrayList();


decimal amount1 = 7.50m;
decimal amount2 = 1.95m;


prices.Add(amount1);
prices.Add(amount2);


foreach (decimal amount in prices)
{
        Console.WriteLine("Amount: {0}", amount);
}
```

Because of the Unified Type System, this code is as convenient as the code written for the `Customer` class, but beware. If the `prices ArrayList` held 10, 20, or 100 decimal type variables, you probably wouldn't care. However, what if it contains 10,000 or 100,000? In that case, you should be concerned because this could have a serious impact on the performance of your application.

Generally, any time you assign a value type to any object variable, whether a collection or a method parameter, take a second look to see whether there is potential for performance problems. In development, you might not notice any performance problem; after deployment to production, however, you could get slammed by a slow application with a hard-to-find bug.

From the perspective of collections, you have two choices: arrays or generics. You can learn more about arrays in Chapter 6, "Using Arrays and Enums." If you are programming in C# 1.0, your only choices will be arrays or collections, and you'll have to design with tradeoffs between convenience and performance, or type safety and no type safety. If you're using C# 2.0 or later, you can have the best of both worlds, performance and type safety, by using generics, which you can learn more about in Chapter 17.

Now that you know the performance characteristics of boxing and unboxing, let's dig a little deeper. The next sections tell you more about what reference types and value types are, their differences, and what you need to know.

Reference Type and Value Type Memory Allocation

Reference type and value type objects are allocated differently in memory. This can affect your code in the area of method call parameters and is the basis for understanding assignment behavior in the next section. This section takes a quick look at memory allocation and the differences between reference types and value types.

Reference Type Memory Allocation

Reference type objects are always allocated on the heap. The following code is a typical reference type object declaration and instantiation:

```
Customer cust = new Customer();
```

In earlier chapters, I explained that this was how you declare and instantiate a reference type, but there is much more to the preceding line. By declaring cust as type Customer, the variable cust is strongly typed, meaning that only compatible objects can be assigned to it. Figure 4.5 shows the declaration of cust, from the left side of the statement.

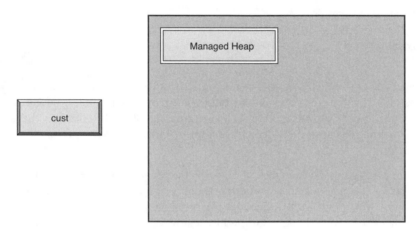

FIGURE 4.5   Reference type declaration.

In Figure 4.5, the cust box is in your code, representing the declaration of cust as Customer. On the right side of the preceding code, the new Customer() is what creates the new instance of a Customer object. The assignment puts a reference into cust that refers to the new Customer object on the heap, as shown in Figure 4.6.

Figure 4.6 shows how the cust variable holds a reference to the new instance of a Customer object on the heap. The heap is a portion of memory that the CLR uses to allocate objects. This is what you should remember: A reference type variable will either hold a reference to an object on the heap or it will be set to the C# value null.

Next, you learn about value type memory allocation and how it is different from reference type memory allocation.

Value Type Memory Allocation

The answer to where value type variables are allocated is "It depends." The two places that a value type variable can be allocated is either the stack or along with a reference type on the heap. See the sidebar "What Is the Stack?" if you're curious about what the stack is.

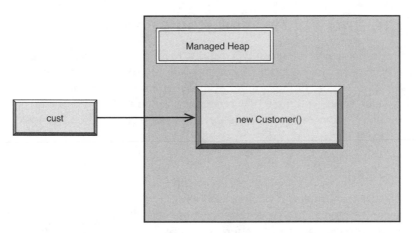

FIGURE 4.6   Reference type object allocated on the heap.

WHAT IS THE STACK?

The CLR has a stack for keeping track of the path from the entry point to the currently executing method in an application. Just like any other stack, the CLR stack works on a last-in, first-out fashion. When your program runs, Main (the entry point) is pushed onto the stack. Any method that Main calls is then pushed onto the top of the stack. Method parameter arguments and local variables are pushed onto the stack, too. When a method completes, it is popped off the top of the stack, and control returns to the next method in the stack, which was the caller of the method just popped.

Value type variables passed as arguments to methods, as well as local variables defined inside a method, are pushed onto the stack with the method. However, if the value type variable is a field of a reference type object, it will be stored on the heap along with the reference type object.

Regardless of memory allocation, a value type variable will always hold the object that is assigned to it. An uninitialized value type field will have a value that defaults to some form of zero (bool defaults to false), as described in Chapter 2.

C# 2.0 and later versions have a feature known as nullable types, which also allow value types to contain the value null. A later section of this chapter explains how to use nullable types.

Now you know where reference type and value type variables are allocated in memory, but more important, you understand the type of data they can hold and why. This opens the door to understanding the assignment differences between reference types and value types, which is discussed next.

Reference Type and Value Type Assignment

Based on what you know so far about reference types and value types—their relationship through the Unified Type System and memory allocation—the step to understanding assignment behavior is easier. This section examines assignment among reference types and assignment among value types. You'll see how reference type and value type assignment differs and what happens when assigned values are subsequently modified. We look at reference type assignment first.

Reference Type Assignment

To understand reference type assignment, it's helpful to look at previous sections of this chapter, focusing on reference type features. Because the value of a reference type resides on the heap, the reference type variable holds a reference (to the object on the heap). Keeping this in mind, here's an example of reference type assignment:

```
Customer cust5 = new Customer();
cust5.Name = "John Smith";
Customer cust6 = new Customer();
cust6.Name = "Jane Doe";

Console.WriteLine("Before Reference Assignment:");
Console.WriteLine("cust5: {0}", cust5.Name);
Console.WriteLine("cust6: {0}", cust6.Name);

cust5 = cust6;

Console.WriteLine("After Reference Assignment:");
Console.WriteLine("cust5: {0}", cust5.Name);
Console.WriteLine("cust6: {0}", cust6.Name);
```

In the preceding example, you can see there are two variables, cust5 and cust6, of type Customer that are declared and initialized. Between sets of Console.WriteLine statements, there is an assignment of cust6 to cust5. The Console.WriteLine statements show the effect of the assignment, and here's what they show when the program runs:

```
Before Reference Assignment:
cust5: John Smith
cust6: Jane Doe
After Reference Assignment:
cust5: Jane Doe
cust6: Jane Doe
```

You can see from the preceding output that the value of the Name property in cust5 and cust6 is different. There are no surprises here because that is what the code explicitly did when declaring and instantiating the variables. What could be misleading is the result, after assignment, where both `cust5.Name` and `cust6.Name` produce the same results. The following statement and results show why the preceding results could be misleading:

```
cust6.Name = "John Smith";
```

```
Console.WriteLine("After modifying the contents of a Reference type object:");
Console.WriteLine("cust5: {0}", cust5.Name);
Console.WriteLine("cust6: {0}", cust6.Name);
```

And here's the output:

```
After modifying the contents of a Reference type object:
cust5: John Smith
cust6: John Smith
```

In the preceding code, the only assignment was to change the `Name` field of `cust6` to `"John Smith"`, but look at the results. The `Name` fields of both `cust5` and `cust6` are set to the same value. What's tricky is that the code in this last example didn't use the `cust5` variable at all.

Now, let's see what happened. To start off, look at Figure 4.7, which shows what the memory layout is right after `cust5` and `cust6` were declared and initialized.

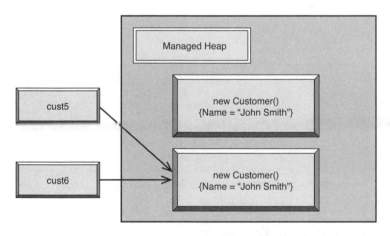

FIGURE 4.7   Two reference type variables declared and initialized separately.

Because `cust5` and `cust6` are reference type variables, they hold a reference (address) of an object on the heap. Figure 4.7 represents the reference as an arrow coming from the variables `cust5` and `cust6` to `Customer` objects. These `Customer` objects were allocated during runtime when the `new Customer` expression ran. Each object contains a different value in its Name field. Next, you see the effects of assigning the cust6 variable to cust5, shown in Figure 4.8.

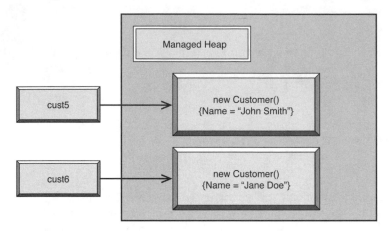

FIGURE 4.8   Assigning one reference type variable to another.

The assignment of cust6 to cust5 didn't copy the object; it actually copied the contents of the cust6 variable, which was the reference to the object. So, as shown in Figure 4.8, both cust5 and cust6 now refer to the same object. Figure 4.9 shows what happens after modifying the Name field of cust6.

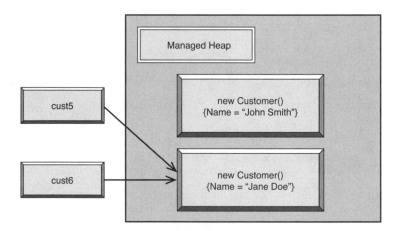

FIGURE 4.9   Affects of modifying the contents of an object that has multiple references to it.

Figure 4.9 shows that changing the Name field of cust6 actually modified the object referred to by cust6. This is important because both cust5 and cust6 refer to the same object, and any modification to that object will be seen through both the cust5 and cust6 reference. That's why the output, after we modified cust6, showed that the Name field of cust5 and cust6 were the same.

Looking at reference type assignment in a more general perspective, you can assume that modifications to the contents of an object are visible through any reference to the same object.

Assignment behavior isn't the same for reference types and value types. The next section shows how value type assignment works and how reference type and value type assignment differs.

Value Type Assignment

Value type assignment is a whole lot simpler than reference type assignment. Because a value type variable holds the entire object, rather than only a reference to the object, no special actions can be occurring behind the scenes to affect that value. Here's an example of a value type assignment, using the Money struct that was created earlier in the chapter:

```
Money cash1;
Money cash2;

cash1.Amount = 50.00m;
cash2.Amount = 75.00m;

Console.WriteLine("Before Value Assignment:");
Console.WriteLine("cash1.Amount: {0}", cash1.Amount);
Console.WriteLine("cash2.Amount: {0}", cash2.Amount);

cash1 = cash2;

Console.WriteLine("After Value Assignment:");
Console.WriteLine("cash1.Amount: {0}", cash1.Amount);
Console.WriteLine("cash2.Amount: {0}", cash2.Amount);
```

The pattern used for value type assignment is similar to that used for the reference type assignment in the previous paragraph. This is intentional so that you can see the differences. In the preceding code, the results after assigning cash2 to cash1 is that the Amount field of both cash1 and cash2 is the same, as shown in the following output:

```
Before Value Assignment:
cash1.Amount: 50.00
cash2.Amount: 75.00
After Value Assignment:
cash1.Amount: 75.00
cash2.Amount: 75.00
```

No surprises here, except perhaps if you expect the same behavior as what you saw in the reference type section, but that isn't the case because value type assignment is not the same as reference type assignment. The next example demonstrates how value types are separate entities that hold their own values:

```
cash2.Amount = 50.00m;
```

```
Console.WriteLine("After modifying contents of Value type object:");
Console.WriteLine("cash1.Amount: {0}", cash1.Amount);
Console.WriteLine("cash2.Amount: {0}", cash2.Amount);
```

After we set the Amount field of cash2 to 50.00m, the output, shown next, demonstrates that there was no affect on cash1, which was set to 75.00 during the previous example:

```
After modifying contents of Value type object:
cash1.Amount: 75.00
cash2.Amount: 50.00
```

When you perform value type assignment, the only object affected is the one being assigned.

Now, you can see that this is different from reference type assignment. Value type assignment affects only the object held by the variable being assigned to, but reference type assignment will affect an object in the heap that could be referred to by multiple variables.

Therefore, while writing code, be aware of the type of the variable being assigned to ensure that subsequent modifications produce the results you expect.

In the next section, you learn a few more of the differences between reference types and value types.

More Differences Between Reference Types and Value Types

In addition to memory allocation, variable contents, and assignment behavior, there are other differences between reference types and value types. These differences can be categorized as inheritance, construction, finalization, and size recommendations. These issues are covered thoroughly in later chapters, so I just give you a quick overview here of what they mean and let you know where in this book you can get more in-depth information.

Inheritance Differences Between Reference Types and Value Types

Reference types support implementation and interface inheritance. They can derive from another reference type or have a reference type derive from them. However, value types can't derive from other value types. Chapter 9 goes into detail about how implementation inheritance works in C#, but here's a quick example:

```
class Customer
```

```
{
    public string Name;
}

class PotentialCustomer : Customer
{
    public string SalesPerson;
}

class RegularCustomer : Customer
{
    public DateTime LastPurchase;
}
```

In the preceding example, Customer is the base class. PotentialCustomer and RegularCustomer derive from Customer, that is, they are types of Customer, as indicated by the : (colon) on the right side of the class identifier.

SINGLE-IMPLEMENTATION INHERITANCE

Reference types support single-implementation inheritance, meaning that they can derive only from a single class. However, both reference types and value types support multiple-interface inheritance where they can implement many interfaces.

Construction and Finalization Differences Between Reference Types and Value Types

Construction is the process that occurs during the instantiation process to help ensure an object has the information you want it to have when it starts up. Chapter 15, "Managing Object Lifetime," discusses this in detail, but for reference, you should know that you can't create a default constructor for a value type. Chapter 3, "Writing C# Expressions and Statements," contains the default values of built-in types, which are some form of zero. Value types are automatically initialized when declared, which is why the cash1 and cash2 variables in the previous section didn't need to be instantiated with new Money().

Finalization is a process that occurs when the CLR is performing garbage collection, cleaning up objects from memory. Value type objects don't have a finalizer, but reference types do. A finalizer is a special class member that could be called by the CLR garbage collector during cleanup. Value types are either garbage collected with their containing type or when the method they are associated with ends. Therefore, value types don't need a finalizer. Because garbage collection is a process that operates on heap objects, it is possible for a reference type to have a finalizer. Chapter 15 goes into the garbage collection process in detail, giving you the information you need to make effective design decisions on implementing finalizers, and other techniques for managing object lifetime effectively.

Object Size Considerations for Reference Types and Value Types

Because of the way an object is allocated differently for reference types and value types, you might need to consider the impact of the size of the object on resources and performance. Reference type objects can generally be whatever size you need because the variable just holds a reference, which is 32 bits on a 32-bit CLR and 64 bits on a 64-bit CLR. However, value type size might need more thought.

If a value type is a field inside of a class or at some level of containment that puts it into a class, its size shouldn't be much concern. However, think about scenarios where you might need to pass a value type to a method. In the case of a reference type argument, it is simply the reference being passed, but for a value type argument, the entire object is passed.

With local variables and parameters that are value types, the CLR pushes the entire object onto the stack when calling the associated method. Now, instead of the 4 or 8 bytes that would have been pushed with a reference type, you have potentially much more information to push, which represents overhead. A recommended rule of thumb for value type size is 16 bytes. I've benchmarked this by calling methods that have value type parameters of differing sizes and verified that performance does tend to deteriorate faster as the size of the value type increases above 16 bytes. That said, you should also look at how many times you'll call the method before the performance implications matter to you; that is, consider whether the method is called frequently or in a loop.

REFERENCE TYPE OR VALUE TYPE: WHICH TO CHOOSE?

As a rule of thumb, I typically create new types as classes, reference types. The exception is when I have a type that should behave more like a value type. For example, a ComplexNumber would probably be better as a struct value type, because of its memory allocation, assignment behavior, and other capabilities such as math operations that are similar to built-in value types such as int and double.

Among the many tips you get from this chapter for working with both reference types and value types, you also have a lot of facts related to tradeoffs. Look at the differences to see what matters the most in your situation and choose the tradeoffs that are best for you.

The next section looks at specific .NET types, building on what you learned so far in this chapter.

C# and .NET Framework Types

In Chapter 1, "Introducing the .NET Platform," you learned about the CTS and in Chapter 3, you learned how to use the C# built-in types. This section melds these two features together and builds upon them so that you can see how C# types support the CTS. We also look at a couple .NET Framework types (specifically, DateTime and Guid) that are important but don't have C# keyword aliases.

C# Aliases and the CTS

C# types are specified with keywords that alias .NET CLR types. Table 4.1 shows all the .NET types and which C# keywords alias them.

TABLE 4.1   .NET Types with Matching C# Aliases

.NET Type	C# Alias
System.Boolean	Bool
System.Byte	Byte
System.Char	Char
System.DateTime	No alias
System.DBNull	No alias
System.Decimal	decimal
System.Double	double
System.Guid	No alias
System.Int16	short
System.Int32	Int
System.Int64	Long
System.IntPtr	No alias
System.Object	object
System.SByte	sbyte
System.Single	Float
System.String	string
System.TimeSpan	No alias
System.TimeZone	No alias
System.UInt16	ushort
System.UInt32	Uint
System.UInt64	ulong
System.UIntPtr	No alias

Some of the types in Table 4.1 are marked as "No alias" because C# doesn't have a keyword that aliases that type, but the type is still important. For example, DBNull is a value that comes from a database field that is set to NULL but is not equal to the C# null value. The following sections show you how to work with the System.Guid and System.DateTime types, which don't have C# aliases either.

Using System.Guid

A globally unique identifier (GUID) is a 128-bit string of characters used whenever there is a need for a unique way to identify something. You can see GUIDs used throughout the Microsoft operating system. Just look at the registry; all of those long strings of characters are GUIDs. Another place GUIDs are used is as unique columns in SQL Server for when you need unique IDs across separate databases. Generally, any time you need a unique value, you can reliably use a GUID.

GUIDs are Microsoft's implementation of universally unique identifiers (UUID), an Open Software Foundation (OSF) standard. You can find more information about UUIDs at Wikipedia, http://en.wikipedia.org/wiki/Universally_Unique_Identifier.

.NET implements the GUID as the System.Guid (Guid) struct. You can use the Guid type to generate new GUIDs or work with an existing Guid value. Here's an example of how you don't want to create a new GUID:

```
Guid uniqueVal1 = new Guid();
Console.WriteLine("uniqueVal1: {0}", uniqueVal1.ToString());
```

The problem here is that Guid is a value type and it is immutable (can't be modified). If you recall from a previous section, value types have a default (no parameter) constructor that you can't override, and the default value is some form of zero. Therefore, the following output from the preceding code makes sense:

```
uniqueVal1: 00000000-0000-0000-0000-000000000000
```

Because Guid is immutable, you can't change this value. Fortunately, if you have a Guid value already defined, you are still able to work with it because Guid has several overloads for specifying an existing GUID. Here's the Guid constructor overload that takes a string:

```
uniqueVal1 = new Guid("89e9f11b-00ee-47dc-be15-01f70eeac3f9");
Console.WriteLine("uniqueVal1: {0}", uniqueVal1.ToString());
```

The preceding code results in the following output:

```
uniqueVal1: 89e9f11b-00ee-47dc-be15-01f70eeac3f9
```

You'll often want to generate your own GUIDs from scratch, and the instance, uniqueVal1, doesn't have methods to accomplish this. In this case, you'll want to use the NewGuid method of Guid to generate a new GUID, like this:

```
uniqueVal1 = Guid.NewGuid();
Console.WriteLine("uniqueVal1: {0}", uniqueVal1.ToString());
```

As you might already expect, the output is a unique ID, as follows:

```
uniqueVal1: cabfe0ba-fa72-4c5c-969f-e76821949ff1
```

In fact, every time you run the preceding code, the output will differ. This is because, for all practical purposes, the GUID will be unique across space and time. Speaking of time, the next section covers another important .NET value type that isn't aliased by a C# keyword, System.DateTime.

Working with `System.DateTime`

Many programs need to work with dates and times. Fortunately, .NET has the `System.DateTime` (`DateTime`) type to help out. You can use `DateTime` to hold `DateTime` values, extract portions such as the day of a `DateTime`, and perform arithmetic calculations. You can also parse strings into `DateTime` instances and emit `DateTime` instances as a string in the format of your choice.

Creating New DateTime Objects

The default value of `DateTime` is Jan 1, 0001 at 12:00 midnight. Here's how to create the default `DateTime`:

```csharp
DateTime date = new DateTime();
Console.WriteLine("date: {0}", date);
```

And the output is as follows:

```
date: 1/1/0001 12:00:00 AM
```

You can initialize the `DateTime` through the constructor, which has several overloads. Here's an example of how to use one of the more detailed overloads:

```csharp
date = new DateTime(2008, 7, 4, 21, 35, 15, 777);
Console.WriteLine("date: {0}", date);
```

Here's the output:

```
date: 7/4/2008 9:35:15 PM
```

Quite often, you'll just need the current date and time, like this:

```csharp
date = DateTime.Now;
Console.WriteLine('date: {0}', date);
```

Which produces the following output:

```
date: 11/4/2007 8:42:39 PM
```

This section worked with the entire `DateTime`, but sometimes you only want to have access to parts of a `DateTime`. The next section shows you how to extract different parts of a `DateTime`.

Extracting Parts of a DateTime

You can access any part of a `DateTime` instance, including parts of the date, day of the week, or day of the year. Here's an example:

```csharp
Console.WriteLine(
    "{0} day {1} of the month is day {2} of the year",
    date.DayOfWeek, date.Day, date.DayOfYear);
```

And here's the output

```
Friday day 4 of the month is day 186 of the year
```

You can also extract other parts of the date (for example, month and hour). If you're using VS2008, you can see all of them in IntelliSense.

Next, you learn how to manipulate `DateTime` objects.

DateTime Math and TimeSpan

You often need to manipulate `DateTime` objects. However, because they are immutable, you need to create a new instance with a modified value. Here's an example:

```
Console.WriteLine("date before AddDays(1): {0}", date);
date.AddDays(1);
Console.WriteLine("date after AddDays(1): {0}", date);
```

The preceding code calls the `AddDays` method, trying to add a day, but the original value, date, doesn't change, as shown by the following output:

```
date before AddDays(1): 11/4/2007 8:48:26 PM
date after AddDays(1): 11/4/2007 8:48:26 PM
```

This just proves that `DateTime` is immutable and hopefully saves you from making this common mistake yourself. Here's how you can change the date variable:

```
Console.WriteLine("date before AddDays(1): {0}", date);
date = date.AddDays(1);
Console.WriteLine("date after AddDays(1): {0}", date);
```

If you look at the documentation for `AddDays` and other methods of `DateTime` that manipulate dates, you see that they return a `DateTime`. Just reassign the return value to the original variable, as in the preceding example, and it will work fine. Here's the output:

```
date before AddDays(1): 11/4/2007 8:52:08 PM
date after AddDays(1): 11/5/2007 8:52:08 PM
```

The preceding date shows that date was truly modified because the day was incremented by one as intended.

You can also use the `DateTime` type for quick-and-dirty performance benchmarks. Here's some code that does `DateTime` math and produces a `TimeSpan` object to tell how long an algorithm took. Here's an example of how you might go about this:

```
int testIterations = int.MaxValue/4;
DateTime start = DateTime.Now;
```

```
for (int i = 0; i < testIterations; i++)
{
    Money cash;
    cash.Amount = decimal.MaxValue;
}

DateTime finish = DateTime.Now;
TimeSpan elapsedTime = finish - start;

Console.WriteLine("Elapsed Time: {0}", elapsedTime);
```

The for loop is code that you might change to hold whatever algorithm you need to benchmark. The example gets the current time before and after the for loop. Notice how the mathematical operation, subtracting start from finish, produced a TimeSpan. A TimeSpan is used to represent an amount of time, as opposed to an exact time as held by DateTime. Any time you perform a mathematical operation on DateTime types, the return value is a TimeSpan. Here's the output:

```
Elapsed Time: 00:00:16.2834144
```

Here's an exercise that you might find fun. Create a few methods that take value type parameters of varying sizes. For example, you could create multiple versions of Money and add more decimal fields to make them bigger. Then use the benchmark preceding code to call each method a specified number of times and compare the TimeSpan results of each. Do the same with a reference type. This exercise will let you know at what point the size of the value type affects performance.

Converting Between DateTime and string Types

If the user inputs a date and/or time, it will often reach the code in the form of a string. Alternatively, sometimes a DateTime needs to be formatted and presented in the form of a string. This section shows you how to read string types into a DateTime and how to format the output of a DateTime.

The DateTime type has a Parse method you can use to get the value of a string. Here's how you can use it:

```
Console.Write("Please enter a date (mm/dd/yyyy): ");
string dateStr = Console.ReadLine();

date = DateTime.Parse(dateStr);

Console.WriteLine("You entered '{0}'", date);
```

The user's input, retrieved by the call to Console.ReadLine, came back in the form of a string, dateStr. The call to DateTime.Parse converted the string to a DateTime, which can now be manipulated with DateTime members as described in previous sections.

You could see an exception message after typing in the date on the command line. This would be because the date was not typed in the correct format. In Chapter 11, "Error and Exception Handling," you'll learn how to handle errors like this, and Chapter 10 shows you how to use the TryParse method, which is effective for handling user input. Here's the output:

```
Please enter a date (mm/dd/yyyy): 11/04/2007
You entered '11/4/2007 12:00:00 AM'
```

Notice from the output that the response to the Please enter a date (mm/dd/yyyy) prompt was 11/04/2007. However, the response included the time, which you may or may not want. In case you don't want the time to show or you want the output to appear differently, you have the option to specify the output format. Here's what you could do to remove the time from the preceding output:

```
Console.WriteLine("Date Only: {0:d}", date);
```

The preceding example used the format specifier in the placeholder of Console.WriteLine's format string parameter. You could have also used the DateTime ToString method like this:

```
Console.WriteLine("Date Only: {0}", date.ToString("d"));
```

A lowercase d means to print a short date time. Here's what it looks like:

```
Date Only: 11/4/2007
```

In addition to the d, there are several other predefined format specifiers, shown in Table 4.2.

TABLE 4.2   Standard **DateTime** Format Strings

Format String	Output for date = new DateTime(2008, 7, 4, 21, 35, 15, 777);
D	7/4/2008
D	Friday, July 04, 2008
T	9:35 PM
T	9:35:15 PM
F	Friday, July 04, 2008 9:35 PM
F	Friday, July 04, 2008 9:35:15 PM
G	7/4/2008 9:35 PM
G	7/4/2008 9:35:15 PM
M ¦ M	July 04
r ¦ R	Fri, 04 Jul 2008 21:35:15 GMT
S	2008-07-04T21:35:15
U	2008-07-04 21:35:15Z
U	Saturday, July 05, 2008 3:35:15 AM
Y ¦ Y	July, 2008

Table 4.2 shows a predefined set of strings for formatting dates, but you aren't limited by this list. You can also customize `DateTime` strings. Here's an example that ensures two characters for each part of the date:

```
Console.WriteLine("MM/dd/yy: {0:MM/dd/yy}", date);
```

Based on the input used for Table 4.2, the output would be this:

```
MM/dd/yy: 07/04/08
```

The number of possible custom format strings is much more than is practical for listing here, but you can find the entire list by opening the .NET Framework Documentation Help file and searching for "formatting strings, custom date and time format strings" in the index. Rather than list all the possible format strings, Table 4.3 lists a few that could be useful; it also includes the ones used in the preceding example.

TABLE 4.3   Common Custom **DateTime** Format Strings

Format String	Purpose
D	Day (1–31)
Dd	Two-digit day (01–31)
Ddd	Abbreviated name of day (for example, Fri)
dddd	Full name of day (for example, Friday)
M	Month (1–12)
MM	Two-digit month (01–12)
MMM	Abbreviated name of month (for example, Jul)
MMMM	Full month name (for example, July)
Yy	Two-digit year
yyyy	Four-digit year
H	Hour (1–12)
Hh	Two-digit hour (01–12)
H	24-hour clock (0–23)
HH	Two-digit 24-hour clock (00–23)
M	Minutes (0–59)
Mm	Two-digit minutes (00–59)
S	Seconds (0–59)
Ss	Two-digit seconds (00–59)

As with `DateTime`, most of the other built-in types are value types whose value is always defined. The next section discusses nullable types and helps you deal with those situations where the value you have to work with is not defined, but is `null`.

Nullable Types

As you've learned previously, the default value for reference types is null, and the default value for value types is some form of zero. Sometimes, you receive values from external sources, such as XML files or databases that don't have a value—they could be nil or null, respectively. For reference types, this is no problem. However, for value types, you have to find your own solution for working with null values.

This problem, not being able to assign null to value types, was alleviated in C# 2.0 with the introduction of a feature called nullable types. It essentially allows you to declare nullable value types to which, as the name suggests, you can assign the value null.

Think about how useful this is. SQL Server has column types that map to the C# built-in types. For example, SQL Server money and datetime column types map to C# decimal and DateTime types. In SQL Server, these values can be null. However, that is particularly problematic when dealing with an application that interfaces with multiple databases. You could be working with FoxPro, SQL Server, and another database, and they all return a different default DateTime value, which makes a mapping between DBNull and the default DateTime value impractical. This is just one element of complexity you have to deal with for null database values, and there are many more. By having nullable types, we can more quickly write easier-to-maintain code.

An entire part of this book, Chapters 19 to 23, provides extensive coverage of working with data in .NET, and this material is applicable in the context of those chapters. However, the examples here assume that there is code that has extracted data from a data source that contains null values. The following example assumes there is a value from a database for the creation date of a record:

```
DateTime? createDate = null;
```

The most noticeable part of the preceding statement is the question mark suffix, ?, on the DateTime type. The proper terminology for this is that the type of createDate is a nullable DateTime. It is explicitly set to the value null, which is not possible in non-nullable value type objects.

There are a couple ways to check a nullable type to see whether it has the value null. Here's an example:

```
bool isNull;


isNull = createDate == null;
isNull = createDate.HasValue;
```

Using the C# equals operator, you can learn whether createDate is set to null. Calling HasValue will return true if createDate is not null. The C# not equals operator, !=, is equivalent in behavior to HasValue.

A common task with nullable types is to see whether they are `null` and take an action. In this case, you can use the C# null coalescing operator, `??`, as a shortcut. Here's an example to show you the alternatives:

```
if (createDate == null)
{
    createDate = DateTime.Now;
}
```

Or

```
createDate = createDate ?? DateTime.Now;
```

As you can see, the `??` operator is quicker to code for such a simple task. Here's another example:

```
DateTime? defaultDate = null;
createDate = createDate ?? defaultDate ?? DateTime.Now;
```

In the preceding code, if `createDate` is `null`, `defaultDate` is evaluated. If `defaultDate` is not `null`, `defaultDate` is assigned to `createDate`. Otherwise, the next expression, `DateTime.Now`, is evaluated. If none of the expressions are non-`null`, the last expression in the chain of `??` operators is returned, even if it's `null`, too.

Summary

Your takeaway from this chapter should be the significant differences between reference types and value types. Because they have different memory allocation and assignment behavior, you must be aware of which you're using in your programs. Much of the material in the rest of this book relies on your understanding of this information and refers back to this chapter for clarification.

A related subject is the C# built-in types and how they relate to .NET types. Some .NET types don't have a C# keyword equivalent, such as `Guid` and `DateTime`. Whereas you might use `Guid` just occasionally, you will probably use `DateTime` a lot, and this chapter showed you much of the common usage you'll need.

This chapter discussed nullable types, which are very applicable for working with value type data. In later Chapters, 19 through 23 to be specific, you'll see extensive discussion of C# and .NET data capabilities, which demonstrates effective implementation of Nullable types.

Up until now, we've mostly discussed the built-in value types. However, there is one built-in reference type, string, that is pervasive for most programs. The next chapter goes into depth about the string type and how to use it.

CHAPTER 5

Manipulating Strings

Strings are ubiquitous in programming, so much so that the .NET Framework Class Library (FCL) has extensive support for strings. Besides the string type with numerous methods, there is a special class called StringBuilder for manipulating strings efficiently. In this chapter, you'll read about the string and StringBuilder types.

A related feature, regular expressions, has FCL APIs that offer even greater flexibility for working with strings. In this chapter, you'll learn how to build a regular expression and use it for pattern matching on blocks of text. Let's look at the C# string type first.

The C# String Type

Among the C# built-in types, string is the only reference type. This suprises people sometimes because of the fact that it is a built-in type and has behavior similar to value types. If you are a little fuzzy on the differences between reference types and value types, you might want to refer to Chapter 4, "Understanding Reference Types and Value Types," for a quick refresher. The features of a string type that makes it behave like a value type are immutability and being sealed.

The string type is immutable, meaning that a string can't be modified once created. All methods that appear to modify a string really don't; they create a new string object on the heap and return a reference to the new string object.

The string type is also sealed, meaning that it can't be derived from.

Being immutable and sealed makes the string type more efficient and secure. The efficiency comes from the way the Common Language Runtime (CLR) manages strings in memory with an intern pool and limits the overhead of changing string content. From a security perspective, sealing a string keeps derived classes from manipulating string content. Sealing also supports CLR memory efficiencies and eliminates the overhead of virtual type member management.

Now, let's check out what you can do with string types. The following sections describe members of the string class. Remember that members called on the string type (for example, string.Format) are static methods, and those called on a string instance are instance methods.

YOU CAN FIND OVERLOADS WITH INTELLISENSE

Many string methods have overloads, allowing you to use the method with different types or numbers of parameters. A quick way to see the overloads is to take advantage of IntelliSense in the editor.

For example, if you type **str**, type **.** (dot) to fill in the string, type **C**, and type **(** (left parenthesis) to fill in the Compare, you'll see IntelliSense pop up. On the left side of the IntelliSense pop-up, you'll find up and down arrows labeled 1 to 8. You can press the up and down arrows on the keyboard to traverse the available overloads.

Formatting Strings

The first string method we cover is Format, which allows you to customize the appearance of a string. If you recall the Write and WriteLine method introduction in Chapter 1, "Introducing the .NET Platform," you already have a good idea of how Format works because the parameter list is the same. The only difference is that Console methods emit output to the OS console, whereas Format returns a new string. Here's an example of how to implement the Format method:

```
string formatString = "{0,15}";

strResult = string.Format(formatString, str2);

Console.WriteLine("string.Format({0}, {1}) = \n",
  formatString, str2, strResult);
```

This example shows the Format method accepting two string parameters. The first parameter, formatString, is a format item that will be applied to the second parameter. Here's the output:

```
string.Format({0,15}, string 2) = [string 2]
```

You might want to take a closer look at how this output occurred by noticing that the formatString variable itself was used as input to the first index, {0}, which is part of

`Console.WriteLine`'s format string parameter. Used with `Format`, the `formatString` variable becomes a format item; otherwise, it is a normal string.

As you can see, the result is a 15-character string, between brackets, with the text right aligned and padded to the left with spaces. The comma between the 0 and 15 in `{0,15}` separates the index from alignment (specifies both alignment and character width).

If you don't want the result to be right-aligned, make the alignment negative so that it reads as `{0,-15}`, which will look like this:

```
string.Format({0,-15}, string 2) = [string 2]
```

In addition to alignment, you can control the output format of the parameter matching an index with a format string. The following example applies a numeric parameter, `10`, to two different format items, currency and hex:

```
strResult = string.Format(
        "Currency: {0:C}, Hex: '{0,2:X}'", 10);
Console.WriteLine(strResult);
```

Format strings follow the index with a colon separator. The format item, `{0:C}`, results in currency output. The hex format item is both setting the size of the output and doing a hex conversion. Notice that there is only a single parameter this time, `10`, but two format items, both set to index `0`, which you might want to do sometime. Here's the output:

```
Currency: $10.00, Hex: ' A'
```

You can see that currency used a U.S. dollar sign and a period to separate dollars from cents. If your machine were set to another locale, the output would have matched your currency symbol and other punctuation. Table 5.1 shows several other standard numeric format strings.

TABLE 5.1   Standard Numeric Format Strings

Standard Numeric Format String	Meaning
C or c	Currency
D or d	Decimal
E or e	Exponential
F or f	Fixed point
G or g	General
N or n	Number
P or p	Percent
R or r	Round trip (guarantees conversion from floating point to string and back again)
X or x	Hexadecimal

The standard numeric format strings are useful because they are quick to use for common scenarios. Sometimes, however, you need more control over the output, building your own custom format strings. Table 5.2 has a list of custom numeric format strings.

TABLE 5.2   Custom Numeric Format Strings

Custom Numeric Format Character	Meaning
0	Zero placeholder
#	Digit placeholder
.	Decimal point
,	Thousands separator
%	Percent placeholder
E/e +/- 0 (for instance, e+0)	Scientific notation
\	Escape character
"XYZ" or 'XYZ'	Literal string
;	Section separator
Other	Literals as they appear

Using Table 5.2, we can re-create the currency format like this:

```
strResult = string.Format(
    "Custom Currency: {0:$#,###.00}", 123456);
Console.WriteLine(strResult);
```

Here's the output:

```
Custom Currency: $123,456.00
```

Of course, that is a single currency value, but sometimes you have to vary financial output depending on whether the input is positive, negative, or zero. Instead of using if statements or some other logic, you can take advantage of the section separator like this:

```
strResult = string.Format(
    "Conditional Currency: {0:$#,###.00;($#,###.00);$0.00}",
    -123456);
Console.WriteLine(strResult);
```

Which produces the following output:

```
Conditional Currency: ($123,456.00)
```

One of the three format strings, $#,###.00;($#,###.00);$0.00, separated by semicolons will be selected, depending on the value of the variable assigned to the format item index.

The first format string matches a positive number, the second format string matches a negative number, and the third format string matches zero.

Comparing Strings

When comparing strings, it's often easier to use comparison operators, such as ==, <, or >. However, the Compare and CompareOrdinal methods are available to retrieve a single int value for the results of the comparison. Some types in the FCL actually require an int value specifying less than, equal, or greater than, so having this available to call is convenient. The following paragraphs discuss the Compare and CompareOrdinal methods. To keep from repeating code, you can assume the values being used are as follows:

```
int intResult;
string strResult;
string str1 = "string 1";
string str2 = "string 2";
```

The Compare method accepts two string parameters and returns the following int results:

- str1 < str2 = negative
- str1 == str2 = zero
- str1 > str2 = positive

An empty string, "", is always greater than null. Here's an example of how to implement the Compare method:

```
intResult = String.Compare(str1, str2);


Console.WriteLine("String.Compare({0}, {1}) = {2}\n",
  str1, str2, intResult);
```

The variable, intResult, is −1.

The CompareOrdinal method compares two strings, independent of localization. It produces the following integer results:

- str1 < str2 = negative
- str1 == str2 = zero
- str1 > str2 = positive

An empty string, "", is always greater than null. Here's an example of how to implement the CompareOrdinal() method:

```
intResult = String.CompareOrdinal(str2, str1);


Console.WriteLine("String.CompareOrdinal({0}, {1}) = {2}\n",
  str2, str1, intResult);
```

Notice how I switched the order of strings from `Compare` to `CompareOrdinal`. The `intResult` from the call to `CompareOrdinal` is 1.

The `CompareTo` method compares the value of the `this` instance with a parameter string. It produces the following integer results:

- `this < string = negative`
- `this == string = zero`
- `this > string = positive`
- `string is null = 1`

An empty string, `""`, is always greater than `null`. If both `this` and `string` are `null`, they are equal (zero result). Here's an example of how to implement the `CompareTo` method:

```
intResult = str1.CompareTo(str2);


Console.WriteLine("{0}.CompareTo({1}) = {2}\n",
   str1, str2, intResult);
```

The result, `intResult`, is –1.

Checking for String Equality

`Compare` methods, as you learned about earlier, are good for sorting algorithms because they help figure out which value comes before another. However, sometimes you just need to know whether two strings are equal (for example, in a search algorithm).

A quick and common way to check for string equality is to use the `==` operator. Here's an example:

```
bool boolResult = str1 == str2;
Console.WriteLine("boolResult: {0}", boolResult);
```

Because `str1` and `str2` have different values, the result is that `bResult` is `false`. You can also use the `!=` operator to see whether two strings are not equal to each other.

You can also check equality via either an instance or static `Equals` method. Here's an example of how to implement the static `Equals` method:

```
boolResult = String.Equals(str1, str2);


Console.WriteLine("String.Equals({0}, {1}) = {2}\n",
   str1, str2, boolResult);
```

The static `Equals` method accepts the two string parameters. The result is a `bool` that will evaluate to `false` because `str1` and `str2` are not the same value.

The instance `Equals` method also determines whether two strings are equal, returning a bool value of `true` when they are equal and a bool value of `false` when they're not. Here's an example:

```
boolResult = str1.Equals(str2);
```

```
Console.WriteLine("{0}.Equals({1}) = {2}\n",
  str1, str2, boolResult);
```

In this example, the `Equals` method accepts one string parameter. Because `str1` has a different value than `str2`, the return value is `false`.

Concatenating Strings

C# has a concatenation operator, +, that makes is easy to concatenate strings. Here's how you can use it:

```
strResult = str1 + ", " + str2;
```

The `strResult` variable will equal "string 1, string 2" after the preceding statement executes. This is equivalent to calling the `Concat` method, but with shorter syntax.

As you've seen previously, most of the `Console.WriteLine` statements have used place-holders to define where a parameter should go. You can also use the concatenation operator instead, like this:

```
Console.WriteLine(strResult);
Console.WriteLine("{0}, {1}", str1, str2);
Console.WriteLine(str1 + ", " + str2);
```

The preceding three statements produce the same output:

```
string 1, string 2
string 1, string 2
string 1, string 2
```

The first string uses the results of the previous statement, the second uses the format string technique you've seen in all earlier examples, and the third uses concatenation to produce a single parameter for the `Console.WriteLine` call. You have several choices, and all are valid.

Yet another concatenation method is the `Concat` method, which creates a new string from one or more input strings or objects. Here's an example of how to implement the `Concat` method using two strings:

```
strResult = String.Concat(str1, str2);


Console.WriteLine("String.Concat({0}, {1}) = {2}\n",
  str1, str2, strResult);
```

The example shows the `Concat` method accepting two string parameters. The result is a single string with the second string concatenated to the first. The `strResult` in this example is "string 1string 2".

Copying Strings

The `Copy` method returns a copy of a string. Here's an example of how to implement the `Copy` method:

```
strResult = String.Copy(str1);


Console.WriteLine("String.Copy({0}) = {1}\n",
  str1, strResult);
```

The `Copy` method makes a copy of `str1`. The result is a copy of `str1` placed in `stringResult`. This is not the same as assignment, shown here:

```
strResult = str1;
```

After executing the preceding line, both `strResult` and `str1` hold identical references to the same string in memory. However, `Copy` created a new instance of the string. Remember that string is a reference type. (Chapter 4 has more info if you need a refresher.)

If you don't want to copy an entire string, perhaps just a subset, you can use the `CopyTo` method, which copies a specified number of characters from one string to an array of characters. Here's an example of how to implement the `CopyTo` method:

```
char[] charArr = new char[str1.Length];


str1.CopyTo(0, charArr, 0, str1.Length);

Console.WriteLine(
  "{0}.CopyTo(0, charArr, 0, str1.Length) = ",
  str1);
```

```
foreach(char character in charArr)
{
  Console.Write("{0} ", character);
}
Console.WriteLine("\n");
```

And here's the output:

```
string 1.CopyTo(0, charArr, 0, str1.Length) =
s t r i n g   1
```

This example shows the CopyTo method filling a character array. It copies each character from str1 into charArr, beginning at position 0 and continuing for the length of str1. The foreach loop iterates through each element of charArr, printing the results.

The Clone method returns a copy of a string. Here's an example of how to implement the Clone method:

```
strResult = (string)str1.Clone();
```

```
Console.WriteLine("(string){0}.Clone() = {1}\n",
  str1, strResult);
```

The Clone method returns a reference to the same instance it is invoked upon, the same as the = (assignment) operator. Because the Clone method returns an object reference, the return value must be cast to a string before assignment to stringResult.

Inspecting String Content

Sometimes you need to search for a string to see whether it begins, ends, or contains a substring anywhere in between. For these tasks, you can use the StartsWith, EndsWith, and Contains string methods.

The StartsWith method determines whether a string prefix matches a specified string. Here's an example of how to implement the StartsWith method:

```
boolResult = str1.StartsWith("Str");
```

```
Console.WriteLine("str1.StartsWith(\"Str\"): {0}",
  boolResult);
```

In this case, the StartsWith method checks to see whether str1 begins with the "Str". The result is false because str1 begins with "str", where the first character is lowercase.

The EndsWith method determines whether a string suffix matches a specified string. Here's an example of how to implement the EndsWith method:

```
boolResult = str1.EndsWith("2");
```

```
Console.WriteLine("{0}.EndsWith(\"2\") = {1}\n",
  str1, boolResult);
```

In this case, the EndsWith method checks to see whether str1 ends with the number 2. The result is false because str1 ends with the number 1.

If you don't have the constraint of a substring being at the beginning or end of a string, you can use the Contains method. Here's an example:

```
boolResult = str1.Contains("ring");
Console.WriteLine("str1.Contains(\"ring\"): {0}", boolResult);
```

The results of the call to Contains are true because the value of str1 does contain "ring".

Extracting String Information

Beyond just checking to see whether a string contains a value, you can find out information about where the string is located by using the IndexOf and LastIndexOf methods. You can use these results in the CopyTo method, shown earlier, or for explicitly extracting the contents of a substring with the SubString method.

The IndexOf method returns the position of a string. IndexOf returns –1 if the string isn't found. Here's an example of how to implement the IndexOf method:

```
intResult = str1.IndexOf('1');
```

```
Console.WriteLine("str1.IndexOf('1'): {0}", intResult);
```

The return value of this operation is 7 because that's the zero-based position within str1 where the character '1' occurs.

The LastIndexOf method returns the position of the last occurrence of a string or characters within a string. Here's an example of how to implement the LastIndexOf method:

```
string filePath = @"c:\Windows\Microsoft.NET\Framework\v3.5.x.x\csc.exe";
```

```
intResult = filePath.LastIndexOf(@"\");
```

```
Console.WriteLine("filePath.LastIndexOf(@\"\\\"): {0}", intResult);
```

The preceding example shows how to use the LastIndexOf method to find the position of the last occurrence of a backslash character, \. Here's the output:

```
filePath.LastIndexOf( 43
```

This example was another opportunity to show you the verbatim string literal symbol, shown in \Windows\Microsoft.NET\Framework\v3.5.x.x\csc.exe". This allows you to avoid writing a double backslash, \\. Similarly, the call to `LastIndexOf` used @"\" for its parameter, which is much more readable than the equivalent string, "filePath.LastIndexOf(@\"\\\"): {0}", used in the call to `Console.WriteLine`. Notice how without the @ (verbatim string literal symbol) all special characters, such as quote and backslash, were escaped, resulting in a less-readable expression.

You can use the `IndexOf` and `LastIndexOf` methods to extract substrings from a string using the `SubString` method. The `SubString` method retrieves a substring at a specified location of a string. Here's an example of how to implement the `SubString` method:

```
strResult = str1.Substring(str1.IndexOf("ring"), 4);
Console.WriteLine("str1.Substring(str1.IndexOf(\"ring\"), 4) : {0}", strResult);
```

Here's the output:

```
str1.Substring(str1.IndexOf("ring"), 4) : ring
```

The first parameter was the position in `str1` to begin, which was returned by the call to `IndexOf`. The second parameter was the length of the substring.

Padding and Trimming String Output

When displaying strings, you'll often want to control the spacing or characters surrounding each side of the string. For example, you might want to apply spacing or zero padding on one side or the other of a string to get it to line up properly, perhaps in a column, in the output. Other times, you'll receive strings with spaces or some other character on the beginning, end, or both sides of a string (things you would rather not see). This section introduces you to padding methods for adding characters and trimming methods for removing characters.

The `PadLeft` method right-aligns the characters of a string and pads the left with spaces (by default) or a specified character. Here's an example of how to implement the `PadLeft` method:

```
strResult = str1.PadLeft(15);

Console.WriteLine("str1.PadLeft(15): ", strResult);
```

In this example, the `PadLeft` method creates a 15-character string with the original string right-aligned and filled to the left with space characters, as shown here:

```
str1.PadLeft(15): [string 1]
```

Opposite to the `PadLeft` method, the `PadRight` method left aligns the characters of a string and pads on the right with spaces (by default) or a specified character. Here's an example of how to implement the `PadRight` method:

```
strResult = str1.PadRight(15, '*');

Console.WriteLine("str1.PadRight(15, '*'): ", strResult);
```

The example shows the `PadRight` method creating a 15-character string with the original string left-aligned and filled to the right with * characters, as shown here:

```
str1.PadRight(15, '*'): [string 1*******]
```

That was how to add characters, with padding. The next couple of methods show you how to remove unwanted characters.

The `Trim` method removes whitespace or a specified set of characters from the beginning and ending of a string. Here's an example of how to implement the `Trim` method:

```
string trimString = "  nonwhitespace  ";


strResult = trimString.Trim();

Console.WriteLine("trimString.Trim(): ",
  strResult);
```

The example shows the `Trim` method being used to remove all the whitespace from the beginning and end of `trimString`, as shown here:

```
trimString.Trim(): [nonwhitespace]
```

If you are concerned about trimming only one side of the string, you can use either `TrimEnd` or `TrimStart`.

The `TrimEnd` method removes a specified set of characters from the end of a string. Here's an example of how to implement the `TrimEnd` method:

```
strResult = trimString.TrimEnd(new char[] {' '});


Console.WriteLine("trimString.TrimEnd(): ",
  strResult);
```

In this example, the `TrimEnd` method removes all the whitespace from the end of `trimString`. The result is "nonwhitespace", with no spaces on the right side.

The `TrimStart` method removes whitespace or a specified number of characters from the beginning of a string. Here's an example of how to implement the `TrimStart` method:

```
strResult = trimString.TrimStart(new char[] {' '});


Console.WriteLine("trimString.TrimStart(): ",
  strResult);
```

Here, the `TrimStart()` method removes all the whitespace from the beginning of `trimString`. The result is "nonwhitespace", with no spaces on the left side.

Modifying String Content

A few string methods return a modified version of a string. You can insert, remove, or replace the content of a string by using the Insert, Remove, and Replace methods, respectively. Other modification methods include ToLower and ToUpper, which convert all string characters to lowercase and uppercase, respectively.

The Insert method returns a string where a specified string is placed in a specified position of an original string. All characters at and to the right of the insertion point are pushed right to make room for the inserted string. Here's an example of how to implement the Insert method:

```
strResult = str2.Insert(6, "1");

Console.WriteLine("str2.Insert(6, \"1\"): {0}",
  strResult);
```

This example places a 1 into str2, producing "string1 2".

MODIFYING STRINGS

Strictly speaking, you never really modify a string. A string is immutable, meaning that it can't change. What really happens when calling a method such as Insert, Remove, or Replace is that the CLR creates a new string object and returns a reference to that new string object. The original string never changed.

This is a common mistake by people just getting started with C# programming, so remember this any time you look at a string after one of these operations, thinking that it should be changed. Instead, assign the results of the operation to a new string variable. Assigning the result of the string manipulation to the same variable will work, too; it just assigns the new string object reference to the same variable.

The Remove method deletes a specified number of characters from a position in a string. Here's an example of how to implement the Remove method:

```
strResult = str2.Remove(3, 3);

Console.WriteLine("str2.Remove(3, 3): {0}",
  strResult);
```

This example shows the Remove method deleting the fourth, fifth, and sixth characters from str2. The first parameter is the zero-based starting position to begin deleting, and the second parameter is the number of characters to delete. The result is "str 2", where the "ing" was removed from the original string.

The Replace method replaces all occurrences of a character or string with a new character or string, respectively. Here's an example of how to implement the Replace method:

```
strResult = str2.Replace('2', '5');
```

```
Console.WriteLine("str2.Replace('2', '5'): {0}",
   strResult);
```

In this example, the `Replace` method accepts two character parameters. The first parameter is the char to be replaced, and the second parameter is the char that will replace the first.

The `ToLower` method returns a copy of a string converted to lowercase characters. Here's an example of how to implement the `ToLower` method:

```
string ucString = "UpperCaseString";
```

```
strResult = ucString.ToLower();
```

```
Console.WriteLine("ucString.ToLower(): {0}",
   strResult);
```

The result of this example converts `"UpperCaseString"` to `"uppercasestring"`.

The `ToUpper` method returns a copy of a string converted to uppercase characters. Here's an example of how to implement the `ToUpper` method:

```
strResult = str1.ToUpper();
```

```
Console.WriteLine("str1.ToUpper(): {0}",
   strResult);
```

In this example, the result converts `"string 1"` to `"STRING 1"`.

Splitting and Joining Strings

Occasionally, you'll need to work with strings that come in a specialized format such as comma-separated value (CSV) or tab delimited. This is common when writing to a format that can be read by spreadsheet applications such as Excel. The `Split` and `Join` methods can prove helpful in such cases.

The `Split` method extracts individual strings separated by a specified set of characters and places each of those strings into a string array. Here's an example of how to implement the `Split` method:

```
string csvString = "one,two,three";
```

```
string[] stringArray = csvString.Split(new char[] { ',' });
```

```
foreach (string strItem in stringArray)
```

```
{
    Console.WriteLine("Item: {0}", strItem);
}
```

The example shows the Split method extracting strings that are separated by commas. The individual strings "one", "two", and "three" are placed into a different index of stringArray.

The new char[] { ',' } used as a parameter to the Split method creates an array of one element, and that one element contains a comma. The character array can contain other separator characters, and the Split method will extract a new entry for its resulting array any time it encounters any of the characters in the array.

The Join method concatenates strings with a specified separator between them. Since the Join method is static, you'll need to call it on the string type. Here's an example of how to implement the Join method:

```
string[] strArr = new string[] { str1, str2 };


strResult = string.Join(",", strArr);

Console.WriteLine(
    "string.Join(\",\", [str1 and str2]) = {0}\n",
    strResult);
```

This example shows how to create a CSV list of strings with the Join method. The first parameter of the Join method specifies the separator character, a comma in this case. The second parameter is an array of strings that will be separated, resulting in a string where each member of the array is separated by the separation character.

Working with String Characters

As you know, strings are made of characters. You'll often need to know information such as number of characters, which character is at a certain position, or perhaps to extract the characters into an array. To accomplish these tasks, you can use the Length property, indexer, and ToCharArray methods, respectively, on a string.

The Length property returns the number of characters in a string. Here's an example of how to implement the Length property:

```
intResult = str1.Length;


Console.WriteLine("str1.Length: {0}",
    intResult);
```

The example shows the Length property being used to get the number of characters in str1. The result is 8.

The string indexer returns a character within the string at a specified location. An indexer is just a set of brackets, commonly used in arrays, to access an element of an object. Here's an example of how to implement the string indexer:

```
char charResult = str1[3];
```

```
Console.WriteLine("str1[3]: {0}",
   charResult);
```

In this example, the indexer extracts the third character from a zero-based count on str1. The result is the character i.

To help you see the usefulness of both the Length property and string indexer, the following example combines them both into a more common usage pattern:

```
for (int i = 0; i < str1.Length; i++)
{
    Console.WriteLine("str1: {1}", i, str1[i]);
}
```

This produces the following output:

```
str1[0]: s
str1[1]: t
str1[2]: r
str1[3]: i
str1[4]: n
str1[5]: g
str1[6]:
str1[7]: 1
```

That was an example of accessing the string array directly. Because strings are immutable, however, you can't change their contents. But if you were working with a character array, you could modify the characters.

The ToCharArray method copies the characters from a string into a character array. Here's an example of how to implement the ToCharArray method:

```
char[] charArray = str1.ToCharArray();
```

```
foreach( char character in charArr )
{
```

```
  Console.WriteLine("char: {0}", character);
}
```

The output of the preceding code is exactly the same as the output from the previous for loop that used a Length property and a string indexer.

Affecting CLR String Handling via the Intern Pool

The Intern method returns a reference to a string in a place called the intern pool. See the note titled "The Intern Pool" if you are curious about what this is. The Intern method will accept a parameter with a string that was programmatically constructed and return a reference to the identical string from the intern pool. Here's an example of how to implement the Intern method:

```
string objStr1   = string.Concat("string ", "1");
string internedStr1 = string.Intern(objStr1);

Console.WriteLine(
  "(object)objStr1 == (object)str1 is {0}\n",
  ((object)objStr1 == (object)str1));

Console.WriteLine(
  "(object)internedStr1 == (object)str1 is {0}\n",
  ((object)internedStr1 == (object)str1));
```

The example shows the effects of using the Intern method on a programmatically constructed string. The Concat method constructs a string on-the-fly, objStr1, that is identical in value to str1. However, objStr1 is a new object on the heap and not yet a member of the intern string pool.

The Intern method added an entry into the intern pool, identical to str1, and returned a reference to the new string in the intern pool. (Values are the same but references are still different.) The first WriteLine method will return the value false because objStr1 refers to the heap object but str1 refers to a literal string that was added to the intern pool. The second WriteLine method returns true because internedStr1 received a reference to the intern pool, which is the same as str1. (References are the same.)

In the example, converting a string type to an object type via the cast operator, (object), caused the equality to be evaluated via the object type, which performs reference equality. This wouldn't have worked with string equality because, as you learned earlier in this chapter, string equality performs value equality. In Chapter 8, "Designing Objects," I show you a better way to check for reference equality when examining members of the object class.

THE INTERN POOL

The intern pool is a system table that eliminates duplication by allowing multiple references to the same constant string when the strings are identical. This saves system memory. The intern-related methods of the string class enable a program to determine whether a string is interned and to place it in the intern pool to take advantage of the associate memory optimizations.

The `IsInterned` method returns a reference to an interned string if it is a member of the intern pool. Otherwise, it returns `null`. Here's an example of how to implement the `IsInterned` method:

```
strResult = string.IsInterned(internedStr1);
```

```
Console.WriteLine("string.IsInterned({0}) = {1}\n",
    internedStr1, strResult);
```

The example shows the `IsInterned` method determining whether a string is in the intern pool. Assuming that the `internedStr1` string parameter has been interned, the `IsInterned` method will return a reference to that string in the intern pool.

In normal .NET development, it is not usual to work with the intern pool via `Intern` and `IsInterned` methods. If you do need to optimize your application to close detail, these methods could prove useful. Any time you try to interact with methods that affect the normal operation of the CLR, you might want to consider using benchmarking and profiling tools to ensure your efforts don't accidentally have an opposite effect or cause other problems.

The **StringBuilder** Class

For direct manipulation of a string, you can use the `StringBuilder` class. It's the best solution when a lot of work needs to be done to change the content of a string. It's more efficient for manipulation operations because, unlike a string object, it doesn't incur the overhead involved in creating a new object on every method call. The `StringBuilder` class is a member of the `System.Text` namespace.

TIP

With `StringBuilder` overhead occurs when instantiating the `StringBuilder` object, but with the string type, overhead occurs on every modification of a string because it creates a new string object in memory. A rule of thumb to know when to use a `StringBuilder` rather than a string is to start using `StringBuilder` after four manipulations of a string.

Many StringBuilder methods are the same as those of string. Rather than be repetitive, I'll show you those methods unique to a StringBuilder. After reading the previous section on the string type, you won't find it difficult to figure out how to use similar methods.

The Append Method

The Append method adds a string object to the end of a StringBuilder. Here's an example of how to implement the Append method:

```
StringBuilder myStringBuilder;
myStringBuilder = new StringBuilder("Original");

myStringBuilder.Append("Appended");

Console.WriteLine(
  "myStringBuilder.Append(\"Appended\"): {0}",
  myStringBuilder);
```

This example shows how to append one string to another with the Append method. The result is "OriginalAppended". The result is similar to the string Concat method.

The AppendFormat Method

The AppendFormat method uses a format string to modify the actual appended string. Here's an example of how to implement the AppendFormat method:

```
myStringBuilder = new StringBuilder("Original");

myStringBuilder.AppendFormat("{0,9}", "Appended");

Console.WriteLine(
    "myStringBuilder.AppendFormat(\"{0,9}\",\"Appended\"): {0}",
    myStringBuilder);
```

This example uses the AppendFormat method to format the "Appended" string, which is 8 characters, to a width of 9 characters and then append it to myStringBuilder. The result is "Original Appended", with a space between words because "Appended" was formatted to 9 characters.

The EnsureCapacity Method

The EnsureCapacity method guarantees that a StringBuilder will have a specified minimal size. Here's an example of how to implement the EnsureCapacity method:

```
int capacity;
myStringBuilder = new StringBuilder();
```

```
capacity = myStringBuilder.EnsureCapacity(129);

Console.WriteLine(
  "myStringBuilder.EnsureCapacity(129): {0}",
  capacity);
```

The example shows the EnsureCapacity method guaranteeing that myStringBuilder will have at least a 129-character capacity.

The ToString() Method

When using a StringBuilder, you need the string that it contains. You can't assign a StringBuilder to a string because they are different types. Instead, you must use the ToString method.

The ToString() method converts a StringBuilder to a string. Here's an example of how to implement the ToString method:

```
myStringBuilder = new StringBuilder("my string");


strResult = myStringBuilder.ToString();

Console.WriteLine(
  "myStringBuilder.ToString(): {0}",
  strResult);
```

The earlier examples that used StringBuilder in Console.WriteLine statements worked because Console.WriteLine implicitly calls ToString on parameters for you. However, if you are extracting the string as the preceding example shows, the call to ToString is required.

Regular Expressions

Using the string type for searching strings via methods such as Contains or IndexOf is good for simple tasks, but sometimes you need sophisticated pattern-matching abilities that string type methods don't give you. For example, you could use the following logic to see whether a simple five-digit U.S. ZIP Code is valid (contains digits):

```
string zip = "1234C";
bool isGoodZip = true;


foreach (char ch in zip)
{
```

```
    if (!char.IsDigit(ch))
    {
        isGoodZip = false;
        break;
    }
}
```

This isn't too bad, as far as complexity goes. However, what if you need to validate whether the U.S. ZIP Code is a nine-digit ZIP Code that has a dash and four extra characters appended? It would take a little more logic, adding to the complexity of the preceding algorithm.

Let's muddy the waters even more and assume that you needed to check for both Canadian, German, and U.S. ZIP Codes. What if you need to validate something even more sophisticated like an email address? The list goes on, but the point is that there is an elegant solution to working with pattern of greater complexity: regular expressions.

Regular expressions provide the ability to manipulate and search text efficiently. The System.Text.RegularExpressions namespace contains a set of classes that enable regular expression operations in C# programs. The next section shows you a better way to perform the U.S. ZIP Code pattern match that was coded previously.

Basic Regular Expression Operations

To perform a simple pattern match with regular expressions, you need a pattern string (the regular expression), a search string, and the RegEx class. To use RegEx, you'll need to either fully qualify it or add a using declaration for the System.Text.RegularExpressions namespace. The following example shows a simple way to match the U.S. ZIP Codes:

```
string searchString = "1234C";
string regExString = @"\d\d\d\d\d";

Regex rex = new Regex(regExString);
bool isMatch = rex.IsMatch(searchString);
```

The Regex class instantiates with the regular expression, which is the pattern string you want to check with. A single instance of \d means match a number, and the entire string means match five numbers in a row. The IsMatch method of Regex takes a parameter that is a string to be checked. Because the fifth digit of searchString is not a digit (it's the character C), isMatch is false.

Now, here's how easy it is to check the nine-digit U.S. ZIP Code. Change the regular expression and search string as follows:

```
string searchString = "12345-6789";
string regExString = @"\d\d\d\d\d-\d\d\d\d";
```

This time `isMatch` will be `true`. If you compare this to the example at the beginning of this section that used the `foreach` loop, you might begin to see how powerful regular expressions are.

Notice how convenient the verbatim string literal syntax is for working with regular expressions. Instead of typing `\\d` for every character, you only need to type `\d`, making the string shorter and more readable.

More Regular Expressions

Digits are only one of many parts of a regular expression. Table 5.3 shows many more.

TABLE 5.3   Common Regular Expression Character Classes

Character Class	Meaning (What It Matches)
.	Any character. Everything matches.
[abcd]	Any of the characters between the brackets.
	For `"[aeiou]"`, `"me"` matches, but `"by"` doesn't.
[^abcd]	Any of the characters that are not between the brackets.
	For `"[^aeiou]"`, `"by"` matches, but `"me"` doesn't.
[a-z]	Any of the characters in the range between the hyphen.
	For `"[5-9]"`, `"7"` matches, but `"3"` doesn't.
\w	Any word character. Same as `[a-zA-Z_0-9]`.
	The string `"_a1"` matches, but `"\r\n"` doesn't.
\W	Any nonword character. Same as `[^a-zA-Z_0-9]`.
	The string `"\r\n"` matches, but `"_a1"` doesn't.
\s	Any whitespace character. Same as `[\f\n\r\t\v]`.
	The string `"\r\n"` matches, but `"_a1"` doesn't.
\S	Any nonwhitespace character. Same as `[^\f\n\r\t\v]`.
	The string `"_a1"` matches, but `"\r\n"` doesn't.
\d	Any decimal digit.
	The string `"1"` matches, but `"a"` doesn't.
\D	Any nondigit.
	The string `"a\n"` matches, but `"3a"` doesn't.

In addition to the character classes from Table 5.3, you can quantify parts of a regular expression. For example, you could have written the nine-digit U.S. ZIP Code regular expression as follows:

```
string regExString = @"\d{5}-\d{4}";
```

This saved a few characters, which might not be much in this example but could be significant in larger strings. Table 5.4 lists a few more common quantifiers.

TABLE 5.4   Common Regular Expression Quantifiers

Quantifier	Meaning (What It Matches)
*	Zero or more matches.
	For `"\d*"`, `""`, `"123"`, `"1234"`, ... matches.
+	One or more matches.
	For `"\d+"`, `"123"`, `"1234"`, ... matches, but not `""`.
?	Zero or one matches.
	For `"\d?"`, `""` and `"1"` matches.
{n}	n matches.
{n,}	n or more matches.
{n,m}	At least n, but not more than m matches.

There are many more regular expression symbols available, and you can find the entire list of them in the .NET Framework SDK documentation. I hope this helps you get started with regular expressions and whets your appetite to explore their effectiveness for solving pattern-matching problems you may encounter.

Application for Practicing Regular Expressions

This section gives you an application to help you practice using regular expressions. It will read a filename, passed in on the command line, open the file, and search the file for a regular expression, also supplied via the user on the command line. Listing 5.1 shows the code for a program similar to grep (Global Regular Expression Print) expressions:

LISTING 5.1   Regular Expressions Application

```
using System;
using System.Text.RegularExpressions;
using System.IO;

class lrep
{
  static int Main(string[] args)
  {
    if (args.Length < 2)
    {
      Console.WriteLine("Wrong number of args!");
      return 1;
    }
```

LISTING 5.1   Continued

```csharp
    Regex re = new Regex(args[0]);

    StreamReader sr = new StreamReader(args[1]);

    string nextLine = sr.ReadLine();

    while (nextLine != null)
    {
      Match myMatch = re.Match(nextLine);

      if (myMatch.Success)
      {
        Console.WriteLine("{0}: {1}", args[1], nextLine);
      }

      nextLine = sr.ReadLine();
    }
    sr.Close();

    return 0;
  }
}
```

> **NOTE**
>
> Global Regular Expression Print (grep), written by Doug McIlroy, is a popular UNIX (AT&T) utility. It enables you to perform a command-line search for regular expressions within the text of one or more files.

The Listing 5.1 program is called lrep, which stands for Limited Regular Expression Print. It might be limited in features, but because of the built-in regular expression classes, it's powerful. Here's an example of how to use it:

```
>lrep str ..\..\Program.cs
```

Assuming you are using VS2008, you would want to cd to the \bin\Debug folder under the project, where the executable file is built. The first parameter, lrep, is the command name of the program. The second parameter, str, is the regular expression. It happens to be a normal string without anything special but can also do something more sophisticated using classes and symbols from Table 5.3, Table 5.4, or others found in the .NET Framework SDK documentation. The third parameter, Program.cs, is the filename to search for the regular expression. In this case, we just used the source code file from Listing 5.1. Here's the output:

```
..\..\Program.cs:       static int Main(string[] args)
..\..\Program.cs:           string nextLine = sr.ReadLine();
```

Each line of output contains the name of the file that was searched. Following that is the text of the line where the regular expression matched. The next example shows how the regular expression is set in the program:

```
Regex re = new Regex(args[0]);
```

This should be familiar because we instantiated `Regex` in earlier examples. The following shows another way to use a regular expression object:

```
Match myMatch = re.Match(nextLine);
```

Earlier examples used the `IsMatch` method, which simply returned a `bool`, but the `Match` method actually collects the string that matches.

The `StreamReader` class might be new to you. I'm using it to read the contents of the specified file. This program opens a file, specified in the command-line arguments, and reads each line to see whether there is a match. By using the `Success` property of `myMatch`, the program can figure out that a match was made and then write the matching lines to the console. Remember to close the `StreamReader` because opening it in this application grabs an OS file lock, preventing reuse of the program.

Summary

There is a plethora of options available in the way of string manipulation with the system libraries. The string type provides basic string handling but has many methods available for returning new strings with various modifications.

For sophisticated string manipulation, use the `StringBuilder` class. It allows modification of the string in the same object without the overhead of creating a new object with each operation.

Strings need to be formatted for many processing activities. There are simple number formatting options as well as picture formatting.

A welcome feature of the FCL is regular expressions. Regular expressions allow easier and more powerful pattern matching than either the string or `StringBuilder`.

CHAPTER 6
Arrays and Enums

Arrays are a common tool in many programming languages, holding lists of objects together in a single collection. The first part of this chapter shows you how to use arrays in C#. You'll learn how to use single-dimension arrays, multidimension arrays, and something called a jagged array. Building upon what you learned about the relationship between the .NET Framework Class Library (FCL) and C# in Chapter 1, "Introducing the .NET Platform," you'll see how the `System.Array` class offers basic functionality for all array types.

Following the thought about how `System.Array` supports C# arrays, the FCL has another type, `System.Enum`, which supports the C# language feature known as enums. If you aren't familiar with enums from other languages, often called enumerations, they are a way to code with meaningful constants, rather than literal values, making your code easier to read and more maintainable. You'll see how to create enum types and then learn how to use the `Enum` class to manipulate an enum.

We'll start with arrays first.

Arrays

An array is a type that holds a list of objects. If you've used arrays in other languages, you might see a few differences in C# arrays, but there aren't any huge surprises. You've already seen a few examples of array usage in previous chapters, typically when implementing a loop that needs to access a group of objects one after the other, like this:

```
char[] bookName = "C# Unleashed".ToCharArray();


for (int i = 0; i < bookName.Length; i++)
{
    Console.WriteLine(bookName[i]);
}
```

You might be a little familiar with how similar this code is to examples from the previous chapter when discussing strings. Above, bookName is an array of type char that is initialized to hold the characters of the string "C# Unleashed". The for loop uses the array indexer, [ ], to extract each element, resulting in a vertical printout of each character.

The following sections go into greater depth, showing you how to use single-dimension, multidimension, and jagged arrays.

Single-Dimension Arrays

Single-dimension arrays let you store and manipulate a list of objects. Every element is of the same (or derived if applicable) type. Here's the basic syntax:

```
Type[] Array-Identifier [initializer] ;
```

Type is any built-in or custom .NET type. The Array-Identifier is any valid identifier (variable name). The optional initializer allocates memory for the array.

ARRAYS ARE FIXED SIZE

After a C# array has been initialized, it can't change its size. You can use a collection class for greater flexibility, as discussed in Chapter 17, "Parameterizing Type with Generics and Writing Iterators."

Here are some examples of single-dimensional array declarations:

```
// uninitialized declaration
MyClass[] myArray;
byte[] inputBuffer = new byte[2048];


// creates an array of 3 strings
string[] countStrings = { "eins", "zwei", "drei" };
```

Arrays can be declared with no initialization. Remember, an array must be initialized before it's used. It may be initialized with an integer type value inside the brackets of the initializer, as the following example shows:

```
// creates an array of 3 strings
string[] countStrings
        = new string[3] { "eins", "zwei", "drei" };
```

Another way to initialize an array is by leaving the space in the brackets of the initializer blank and then following the initializer brackets with an initializer list in braces. The array initializer list is a comma-separated list of values of the array type. The size of the array becomes the number of elements in the initializer list. If an integer value is added to the initializer brackets and there is an initializer list in the same array initializer, make sure the integer value in the initializer brackets is greater than or equal to number of elements in the initializer list. Take a look at this code sample:

```
// error
string[] countStrings
        = new string[3] { "eins", "zwei", "drei", "vier" };
```

The initializer in this code fails with an error because the allocated size of the countStrings array is only 3, but the number of strings in the list is four. The number of strings in the list can't exceed the allocated size.

It's common to use loops to access each element of an array. Here's an example using a for loop:

```
for (int i = 0; i < countStrings.Length; i++)
{
    Console.WriteLine(countStrings[i]);
}
```

Notice how the loop condition uses the array's Length property. In this case, Length is 3. The condition will be where i is less than countStrings.Length because arrays have zero-based indexes. Here's an example of accessing array indexes:

```
string first = countStrings[0];
string last = countStrings[2];
string error = countStrings[3]; // error
```

The top line accesses the first element of the countStrings array—remember that arrays are zero-based. Therefore, each subsequent index is one less than the position in the array. Because the array has three elements, the second preceding statement uses index 2 to access the last element. A nice feature of arrays is that the Common Language Runtime (CLR) will do bounds checking for you, ensuring code doesn't accidentally read places in memory other than the elements of the array. The last line shows how this works because index 3 is trying to access the fourth element, which doesn't exist. This results in a runtime error.

In addition to accessing array elements, you can set them using the array indexer, like this:

```
countStrings[1] = "two";
countStrings[5] = "six"; // error
```

Now the second element of countStrings references the "two" string. Again, access to a nonexistent array element causes a runtime error, as shown by the attempt to assign the string "six" to the sixth (index 5) of the countStrings array.

You can use any of the C# loops to iterate through arrays. Another loop that is commonly used is foreach, shown here:

```
foreach (var count in countStrings)
{
    Console.WriteLine(count);
}
```

Notice how I used var rather than a type. C# knows what the type (string) of countStrings is and will ensure count is strongly typed. Remember that you can't modify count, because foreach loops don't allow you to modify the array objects.

ARRAYS ARE REFERENCE TYPES

An array is a reference type object. Therefore, assigning one array to another just makes the variable assigned to contain an identical reference to the same object in memory. This is consistent with what you learned about reference type objects in Chapter 4, "Understanding Reference Types and Value Types."

Multidimension Arrays

A multidimension array differs from a single-dimension array in that it contains two or more dimensions. Here are a couple examples of how to declare and initialize a multidimension array:

```
long [ , ] determinant = new long[4, 4];
int [ , , ] stateSpace = new int[2, 5, 4];
```

The number of dimensions is one more than the number of commas between brackets of the type declaration. In the preceding example, determinant is a two-dimension array, and stateSpace is a three-dimension array. You initialize multidimension arrays with the syntax new type[dimension sizes], where dimension sizes is a comma-separated list with the size of each dimension.

You also have shortcut syntax for any time you need to hard code a multidimension array. Here's an example:

```
bool [,] exclusiveOr = new bool[2, 2] { {false, true}, {true, false} };
bool[,] exclusiveOr2 = new bool[,] { { false, true }, { true, false } };
```

The initializer list has nested curly braces that go as deep as the number of dimensions of the array. The second preceding statement shows how the integer values in the initializer brackets are optional when including an initializer list. This syntax is convenient for demos, but most of the time, you'll be populating array elements dynamically.

When iterating through a multidimension array, you won't be able to use a foreach loop because you can't get a reference to a single dimension. However, a for loop will work fine, like this:

```
int dimOneSize = 2;
int dimTwoSize = 2;

for (int i = 0; i < dimOneSize; i++)
{
    for (int j = 0; j < dimTwoSize; j++)
    {
        Console.WriteLine(
            "exclusiveOr: {2}",
            i, j, exclusiveOr[i, j]);
    }
}
```

In the preceding example, I used variables set to the size of each dimension as a meaningful way to iterate, instead of hard coding a number. This was necessary because each dimension of a multidimension array doesn't have a Length property. In a later section of this chapter, on the System.Array type, I show you an even better way to automatically obtain dimension size without hard coding the value. Here's the output:

```
exclusiveOr[0, 0]: False
exclusiveOr[0, 1]: True
exclusiveOr[1, 0]: True
exclusiveOr[1, 1]: False
```

The preceding output reflects the Boolean exclusiveOr logic that the array was built to support. Assignment and reading on multidimension arrays are similar to single-dimension arrays, except you specify the element of each dimension. Here's an example:

```
exclusiveOr[0, 1] = true;
bool bResult = exclusiveOr[1, 1];
```

The assignment and read operations on the preceding array were legal because the indexes were within the bounds of the array. Like single-dimension arrays, if any index is beyond the bounds of the array, you'll receive a runtime error.

Another array type, with characteristics of both single-dimension and multidimension arrays, is the jagged array.

Jagged Arrays

Jagged arrays are like multidimension arrays in that you can have multiple dimensions. They differ in that a jagged array will use only the specific amount of memory allocated to it, whereas a multidimension array uses a uniform amount of memory for every dimension. The jagged array has characteristics of a single dimension array in that it is an array of arrays. Here is an example:

```
decimal[][] monthlyVariations = new decimal[12][];
```

The preceding statement is the first part of creating a jagged array. Notice the double set of brackets, [][], meaning that this is a two-dimension jagged array. You can add additional dimensions by increasing the number of bracket sets. As you might expect, the type decimal means that monthlyVariations is a two-dimension jagged array of decimal.

Next, look at the instantiation, new decimal[12][], where only the size of the first dimension is specified. At this point in time, we know that the size of the first dimension is 12. This is an important point—with jagged arrays, you define one dimension at a time. That's because the size of each element of each dimension can vary.

Imagine that monthlyVariations is an array designed to handle some type of financial calculation, and the size of each element of the second dimension will depend on the month it represents. The next set of statements show how to instantiate each element of the second dimension:

```
int jan = 0;
int feb = 1;
int dec = 11;

monthlyVariations[jan] = new decimal[31];
monthlyVariations[feb] = new decimal[28];
.
.
.
monthlyVariations[dec] = new decimal[31];
```

Using meaningful int variables for the months, this shows how monthlyVariations has a different number of entries for each month. Here, you can see the similarity between jagged arrays and single-dimension arrays, where jagged arrays are actually arrays of arrays.

If this had been a multidimension array, you would be required to define the second dimension with 31 elements. However, every month in the year doesn't have 31 days, and that would waste memory space. In this example, it isn't much, but for large financial and scientific applications the savings is often significant.

A similarity between multidimension arrays and jagged arrays is that you have convenient syntax to address each dimension of the array. Of course, the jagged array indexing syntax uses sets of brackets, rather than the comma-separated list between brackets of the multi-dimension array. Here's an example of how to assign and read from jagged arrays:

```
decimal daily = monthlyVariations[jan][15];
monthlyVariations[dec][13] = 1.59m;
```

The first statement shows how to read an element by specifying the index of each dimension, each within its own bracket set, []. You can also assign a value to an element with similar indexing syntax, as shown in the second statement.

Jagged arrays are a little more flexible when it comes to iterating through them with loops. Here's an example of using a `for` loop:

```
for (int i = 0; i < monthlyVariations.Length; i++)
{
    for (int j = 0; j < monthlyVariations[i].Length; j++)
    {
        Console.WriteLine(monthlyVariations[i][j]);
    }
}
```

Notice that with jagged arrays we can take advantage of the array-of-arrays features to access the `Length` property of each dimension. You can also iterate through jagged arrays with `foreach` loops:

```
foreach (var month in monthlyVariations)
{
    foreach (var day in month)
    {
        Console.WriteLine(day);
    }
}
```

Using the `foreach` loop, you can iterate through the array returned by the current jagged array element.

The `System.Array` Class

All arrays implicitly inherit the `System.Array` class. This is convenient because `System.Array` has several useful features, such as searching and sorting. This section outlines members of the `System.Array` class that are self-explanatory and shows you how to use members that require more explanation.

Array Bounds

In the previous section on multidimension arrays, I promised to show you a better way to dynamically ascertain the size of each dimension. The `System.Array` class has two methods for getting the size of dimensions: `GetLowerBound` and `GetUpperBound`. Here's how to use them:

```
for (int i = exclusiveOr.GetLowerBound(0);
        i <= exclusiveOr.GetUpperBound(0); i++)
```

```
{
    for (int j = exclusiveOr.GetLowerBound(1);
            j <= exclusiveOr.GetUpperBound(1); j++)
    {
        Console.WriteLine(
            "exclusiveOr: {2}",
            i, j, exclusiveOr[i, j]);
    }
}
```

The GetLowerBound and GetUpperBound methods have a single parameter, specifying the dimension to search—0 is the first dimension, and 1 is the second dimension. Unlike earlier examples that used the size of the array and set the condition so that the index variable was less than the size, these conditions are for less than or equal. That's because GetLowerBound and GetUpperBound return the index at the beginning and ending of an array, which are 0 and 1.

Notice how I initialize i and j with calls to GetLowerBound. Because arrays default to being zero-based, you might wonder why I didn't just initialize i and j to 0. The answer lies in the fact that zero-based arrays are the default but could possibly have lower bounds based on another number. For example, if you were doing COM Interop to extract a range of cells from an Excel spreadsheet, you would receive a two-dimension array that is one-based. This would produce a one-off error when trying to access the elements of the array. If you know this ahead of time, you can still explicitly initialize i and j to 1.

However, there might be a time when you don't know what the lower bound of an array is. If you were writing a scientific application that requires array calculations with different lower bounds, you could do this:

```
Array kelvinTemperature = Array.CreateInstance(
    typeof(double),
    new int[] { 201 },
    new int[] { -100 });
```

This creates an array of type double from a lower bound of –100 to an upper bound of 100. The second parameter is the size, which can have multiple values for each dimension. The third parameter is an array of lower bounds for each dimension.

Searching and Sorting

Arrays support searching and sorting, and there are a couple things you need to know about how these methods work. Here's an example of using the BinarySearch method:

```
int[] numbers = { 2, 9, 7, 3, 5 };
int position = Array.BinarySearch(numbers, 3);
```

Notice that the contents of the numbers array are out of order. The binary search algorithm being used looks at the middle number in the array, determines whether what it's searching for is higher or lower, and then repeats the search on either the higher or lower half of the array, continuing until the number of items is reduced to one with no matches or it finds the value. In this case, 3 won't be found because it is in the upper half of the array, but the `BinarySearch` method sees a 7 and looks in the lower half of the array. `BinarySearch` returns a negative number if it doesn't find what it's looking for. As you can see, `BinarySearch` expects an array to be sorted, and here's how you do that:

```
Array.Sort(numbers);
position = Array.BinarySearch(numbers, 3);
```

After the preceding code sorts the array and calls `BinarySearch`, `position` will be 1, which is correct because 2 is at index 0, and 3 would be the next number in order.

A couple more search-related `Array` methods are `IndexOf` and `LastIndexOf` for getting the index of the first occurrence and last occurrence of the specified number, respectively. Here's an example:

```
int idxOf = Array.IndexOf(numbers, 9);
int lIdxOf = Array.LastIndexOf(numbers, 5);
```

In the preceding code, `idxOf` is 4 and `lIdxOf` is 2. If the values weren't found, the result would be one less than the lower bound of the array, which would be –1 for zero-based arrays.

You can also reverse the contents of an array. Here's an example:

```
Array.Reverse(numbers);
```

There are several other members of the `System.Array` class, many of them generic methods. I cover generics in greater detail in Chapter 17. Nevertheless, this should give you a big jump on knowing what is possible with arrays and provide you some powerful tools to work with.

As with class and struct, arrays let you create custom types. In the next section, you learn another way to define custom types as enum types.

Using Enum Types

An enum type is a list of strongly typed constant values. Just like a class or struct is used to create custom reference type and value type objects, an enum allows you to create a custom value type. They are meant to be reused across a program, so you typically declare enum types at the namespace level. You can review Chapter 2, "Getting Started with C# and Visual Studio 2008," for more information about what goes where in a C# program. Chapter 13, "Naming and Organizing Types with Namespaces," goes into detail about namespaces.

Although enum types are value types, they don't have the same members as struct types. Members of an enum are values that are expressed pneumonically, rather than via numbers, making it convenient for understanding the meaning of the value being used. Here's an example:

```
enum Months { Jan, Feb, Mar, Apr, May, Jun, Jul, Aug, Sep, Oct, Nov, Dec }
```

In the preceding example, enum means simply that this is a custom enum type. It's name is Months, which is important because you will express enum members in terms of their type name. Between the curly braces is a list of enum members, which are typically related to the purpose of the enum. In the preceding example, each member of the Months enum represents a month in a year. In its most basic form, here's how you can declare and initialize an enum variable:

```
Months currentMonth = Months.Nov;
```

If you type this with VS2008 IntelliSense, type a space right after typing the assignment operator, =, and you'll see Months selected in the list. Type a dot, ., which shows you the members of the Months enum. Type **N**, which selects Nov, and then type a semicolon, ;, to complete the statement. This is another example of how IntelliSense helps you save keystrokes and increases productivity.

While I'm giving you VS2008 tips, here's another trick, using a snippet, which typically receives oohs and aahs in the classroom. Do the following after declaration of currentMonth:

1. Type **sw** and then press Tab (to complete the switch keyword).
2. Press Tab again, which will give you the switch snippet template. The cursor is highlighting the switch parameter, which is part of the snippet form.
3. Type **cur** and IntelliSense will select the currentMonth variable.
4. Press Enter, which fills out the template form with currentMonth. The form is still green.
5. Press Enter and, poof!, the snippet fills every case of the switch statement with a member of the Months enum, shown here:

```
switch (currentMonth)
{
    case Months.Jan:
        break;
    case Months.Feb:
        break;
    case Months.Mar:
        break;
    case Months.Apr:
        break;
    case Months.May:
        break;
    case Months.Jun:
        break;
```

```
case Months.Jul:
    break;
case Months.Aug:
    break;
case Months.Sep:
    break;
case Months.Oct:
    break;
case Months.Nov:
    break;
case Months.Dec:
    break;
default:
    break;
}
```

Besides showing a cool snippet demo, the preceding code makes another important point. Because you can use enum types in switch statements, you don't have to use other weakly typed literal values. If you've ever been on the receiving end of performing maintenance on a switch statement with int values on each case, it might be easier to appreciate the readability that enums give you.

Although you use enums via their pneumonic values, each member of the enum has an underlying integral value. The default integral type is int, but you can also change it to byte or short if you need to save storage space. Here's an example:

```
enum Month: byte
{
    January,
    February,
    March,
    April,
    May,
    June,
    July,
    August,
    September,
    October,
    November,
    December
};
```

Notice the colon, :, between the enum type name, Month, and the underlying type, byte. Maybe you want to save the value to a file or database, and there are many records with this value. Designating the underlying type as byte helps do this. Remember that if you happen to have more than 128 values, or want underlying values that are more than that, which is the max size of a byte, you must change this to a larger integral type.

By default, the first element of an enum has a value of 0. Subsequent elements have a value one greater than their predecessor. You can manipulate these values like this:

```
enum Weekday { Mon = 1, Tue, Wed, Thu, Fri, Sat = 10, Sun }
```

In the preceding example, Mon has the value 1, Tue is 2, Wed is 3, Thu is 4, and Fri is 5. Then, after Sat is changed to 10, Sun becomes 11.

Another way to use an enum is as a method parameter. Here's an example:

```
static DateTime FindAvailableDate(Months monthToSearch)
{
    // some business logic that finds a day
    return DateTime.Now;
}
```

Notice the parameter type is Months. This restricts the input to the values allowable via an enum. You don't have to use an int or string, both of which could have numerous invalid values. You've strongly typed the input so that it will be valid and your program will be more reliable. You could call the FindAvailableDate method like this:

```
DateTime availableDate = FindAvailableDate(currentMonth);
```

The currentMonth argument is a variable of type Months.

Any time you need to use a constant value, consider whether an enum would be a good solution, especially if the constant is reused in multiple places.

There's more you can do with an enum, such as converting it to/from strings and iterating through the members of an enum. The next section shows you the System.Enum struct, which expands the usefulness of C# enum types.

The System.Enum struct

System.Enum is a convenience struct that allows you to manipulate enum types in several ways; you can convert strings to enums, loop through lists of enum members, and more. The following sections show what you can do with System.Enum.

Converting Between Enum Types, Ints, and Strings

A lot of your input comes from the user in the form of strings. For example, your UI could have a combo box or list of items that you need to extract selected items from. The items come in the form of strings, and you'll want to convert the string to your enum type. Here's an example:

```
Console.Write("Enter 3 character day (i.e. Mon): ");
string dayStr = Console.ReadLine();
Weekday wkDay = (Weekday)Enum.Parse(typeof(Weekday), dayStr);
```

In the preceding code, the input came from the call to ReadLine, which brought the user's input back as a string type. The next statement converts that string to a Weekday enum, but it might not be immediately intelligible to you, so I'll do a breakdown. The cast operator for Weekday, (Weekday), is necessary because the return type of the Parse method is type object. Because the System.Enum class operates on any enum type, it has to return object to be generic, and so the conversion is necessary. The requirement to be generic is also the reason for the typeof(Weekday) argument, which tells Parse that it needs to convert the second parameter, dayStr, to a Weekday enum type.

If you're running this code yourself and type in a value that doesn't match a member of the Weekday enum, you'll receive a runtime error. You can learn more about these types of errors, which are called exceptions, in Chapter 11, "Error and Exception Handling." Ensure you type your input, with case-sensitivity, to be a member of the Weekday enum, shown in the previous section on enum types.

You can also convert enum types to strings, like this:

```
dayStr = Enum.GetName(typeof(Weekday), Weekday.Thu);
```

Again, the first parameter, typeof(Weekday), is necessary because GetName needs to be generic and handle any enum type. Here's an easier way to convert an enum to a string:

```
dayStr = Weekday.Thu.ToString();
```

The call to ToString is easier if you have a variable of the enum type or the enum type constant itself, but that won't work if all you have is an int. In that case, you must call GetName, as follows:

```
dayStr = Enum.GetName(typeof(Weekday), 4);
```

I used the constants Weekday, Thu, and 4 in the preceding examples, but you would typically pass in a variable of each type in actual code. Converting from an enum to an int is as simple as using a cast operator, like this:

```
int satVal = (int)Weekday.Sat;
```

This could prove useful if you have an array or collection with elements based on the values of an enum. The elements would be indexed as int, and this gives you a readable approach. Another example might be working with ASP.NET DropDownList controls where the value is an index and the text is a string.

You can also convert between int and an enum type. The following example shows how to do this with the GetObject method:

```
Weekday Sunday = (Weekday)Enum.ToObject(typeof(Weekday), 11);
```

By now, you understand why the first parameter must be a type and the result must be converted to the enum type. With these conversion methods, you can work with enums and any int or string input, or output.

Iterating Through Enum Type Members

Occasionally, you might need to perform some action for each member of an enum. Next, I show you how to iterate through either the pneumonic members or their string representations.

Here's an example of how you can iterate through the members of an enum:

```
foreach (var day in Enum.GetValues(typeof(Weekday)))
{
    Console.WriteLine(day);
}
```

Calling GetValues returns an array of type Weekday[]. The argument to GetValues specifies the enum type to extract values from. You can also retrieve the members of an enum as an array of strings, like this:

```
foreach (var weekDayStr in Enum.GetNames(typeof(Weekday)))
{
    Console.WriteLine(weekDayStr);
}
```

Calling GetNames returns an array of strings, string[]. Its argument specifies which enum to use.

Other System.Enum Members

A couple other methods of System.Enum enable you to inspect the underlying type of an enum and see whether an enum contains a specific member. Here's how to discover the underlying type of an enum:

```
Type enumType = Enum.GetUnderlyingType(typeof(Month));
Console.WriteLine("Month enum underlying type: " + enumType);
```

The FCL has an object that holds type info, named System.Type, which is what enumType is declared as and is the return type of GetUnderlyingType. I used the Month enum, which was declared in the previous section on enum types, because it's underlying type is a byte. Here's the output:

```
Month enum underlying type: System.Byte
```

Notice that it printed out System.Byte, which the C# byte type aliases. Chapter 4 explains how C# types alias .NET types.

Here's how you can find out whether an enum type contains a certain value:

```
bool hasFriday = Enum.IsDefined(typeof(Weekday), Weekday.Fri);
```

If you're using the enum member, as shown here, the answer is pretty obvious. However, if you do need this method, the following example shows a more realistic scenario:

```
hasFriday = Enum.IsDefined(typeof(Weekday), 5);
```

Assuming you received an int as input, you can figure out whether it is valid with the `IsDefined` method. Another possibility is that your input could be a string, which you would check like this:

```
hasFriday = Enum.IsDefined(typeof(Weekday), "Fri");
```

This shows how much flexibility you have with enum types. The `System.Enum` type is useful for working with enums in several different ways.

Summary

As you can now see, C# arrays are a lot like arrays in other languages. You can create single-dimension and multiple-dimension arrays. You also learned about an array type called a jagged-array, which is more like an array of arrays. You saw how all arrays have many special members because they implicitly derive from `System.Array`.

Another FCL type, `System.Enum` helps work with enum types. You learned how to create enum types and received a few tips on how enums are better than using a number that represents a value. In addition, you saw how the `System.Enum` type helps convert between enum, string, and int types.

6

CHAPTER 7

Debugging Applications with Visual Studio 2008

Visual Studio 2008 (VS2008) has extensive debugging support. You can manage breakpoints, inspect values, step through code, and open several other windows that give you a view into the current state of your application. If you've used visual debuggers before, the VS2008 debugger might have a lot of familiar features that you're accustomed to. If you're used to command-line debuggers or come from a web development environment with little debugging support, you're definitely in for a treat.

Stepping Through Code

The first thing you probably want to do when debugging is to set a breakpoint, where the application will stop, inspect values, and step through the code.

The Debugger Demo Program

We'll look at each of these features while using the following simple program as a demonstration tool:

LISTING 7.1   Debugging Demo Program

```
class Program
{
    static void Main()
    {
        int product = Multiply(3, 4);
    }

    private static int Multiply(int num1, int num2)
```

LISTING 7.1   Continued

```
    {
        return num1 * num2;
    }
}
```

The demo program simply calls a method named `Multiply` from the `Main` method. `Multiply` adds a couple numbers and returns them. This will serve as a tool to show you how to navigate in and out of methods with the VS2008 debugger.

Setting Breakpoints

The first thing you need to do with the code in Listing 7.1 is to set a breakpoint, which is where the debugger will stop program execution. Allowable places for breakpoints include any line in the editor that contains code. Figure 7.1 shows a breakpoint set for the demo program in VS2008.

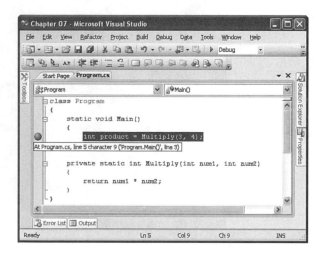

FIGURE 7.1   Setting a breakpoint.

The red dot on the left side of the screen that lies in a vertical area, called the gutter, is the location of the breakpoint. Although you can't see the cursor, you can see the IntelliSense providing details of the breakpoint. The code on that line is highlighted red, too. When the program runs, and it reaches the breakpoint, it will stop there.

In addition, after you set a breakpoint, you can right-click the breakpoint, in the gutter, and set a condition, hit count, filter, or take an action when the breakpoint is hit.

Now, you can begin a debugging session by selecting Debug, Start Debugging (F5) or click the green-arrow Start Debugging button on the debugging toolbar. After your code runs and hits the breakpoint, you're ready to begin inspecting values, which is covered next.

Examining Program State

After your program stops at a breakpoint, you're free to begin inspecting its state. The VS2008 debugger has multiple tools available for you to find out what is happening with your program. There are Watch windows where you can define your own set of variables, a Locals window for seeing everything in scope, and an Autos window for limiting the view to what is current. You'll see each of these and more throughout this chapter.

When your program is stopped at a breakpoint, the line will be highlighted in yellow. (Yellow is the default, but you can always select Tools, Options and change the colors to a scheme you are more comfortable with.) At this point, the line at the breakpoint has not executed. Along the same lines, the variables in the program have the same values that they would have just before this statement executes. Figure 7.2 shows the VS2008 debugger, stopped at a breakpoint, and the Locals window.

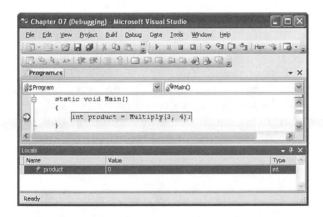

FIGURE 7.2   The VS2008 Locals window.

The Locals window shows all variables currently in scope. In the case of the demo program from Listing 7.1, and shown in Figure 7.2, the only variable in scope is `product`, and it hasn't been set yet. This window can get busy if you have a long algorithm with a lot of variables in scope.

An alternative is to set up one or more Watch windows, found at Debug, Windows, Watch. You can open up to four instances of Watch windows. Figure 7.3 shows a Watch window with a variable that has been added.

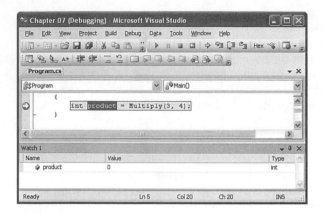

FIGURE 7.3   The VS2008 Watch window.

As you can see from Figure 7.3, the Watch window shows the product variable. Initially, a Watch window is empty, but you can use one of a few different ways to add variables: manual editing, context menu options, or highlight a variable and drag and drop.

Another way to see the value of variables is to hover your cursor over them, which is often a quicker way to inspect their values.

There are other debugging windows, and you can find them on the Debug, Windows menu. Make sure you're stopped on a breakpoint in the debugger because the debug windows are context-sensitive and won't appear when you're not debugging. The next step is to begin navigating through code.

Stepping Through Code

You'll want to follow the logic of your code to see what variables are being set to and the path your code takes, leading you to the reason for the bug. Of course, you could also be stepping through the code because you want to see how it works. In VS2008, you have a few different options to step through your code, and Table 7.1 lists the actions you can take.

TABLE 7.1   Commands to Step Through Code

Action	Description
Step In	Steps into a method at the location of the breakpoint. You can select Debug, Step Into, click the Step Into button on the debug toolbar, or press F11. If the currently highlighted line is not on a method call, the statement on that line is executed and control passes to the next logical place in the program.
Step Out	Steps up and out of a method back to the caller. You can select Debug, Step Out, and click the Step Out button on the debug toolbar, or press Shift+F11. If control is at the top level of a program, Main for console applications, the Step Out button causes the program to resume running as normal.

TABLE 7.1   Continued

Action	Description
Step Over	Steps past a method to the next statement. You can select Debug, Step Over, and click the Step Over button on the debug toolbar, or press F10.
Stop Debugging	Stops a debugging session. You can select Debug, Stop Debugging, and click the Stop Debugging button on the debug toolbar, or press Shift+F5.

Let's use the commands from Table 7.1. As mentioned earlier, the demo program, from Listing 7.1, is stopped at the breakpoint. If you did a Step Into, execution would move into the Multiply method. At that point, the Locals window would show you the values of num1 and num2, which are parameters. Another debugging window that is useful, especially when stepping though code, is the Autos window, shown in Figure 7.4.

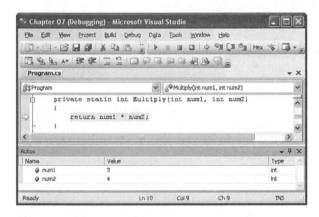

FIGURE 7.4   The VS2008 Autos window.

The Autos window, as shown in Figure 7.4, displays variables for the current and previous lines only. For example, after doing the initial Step Into for the Multiply method, execution stops on the first curly brace. Because there weren't any variables defined on the previous line (parameters don't count), the Autos window was empty. I had to do a Step Over to bring execution to the next line where num1 and num2 are defined so that you could see them in Figure 7.4. You could also do a Step Into, but there isn't a method at the current line, so execution just moves to the next statement.

While stepping through code, you'll often end up in an algorithm that either doesn't offer any information to solve the problem or was accidentally stepped into. The Step Out command is helpful to get back to the next higher level in the stack. It executes all remaining code in the method and then stops at the point where you did a Step Into. After doing a Step Out, the effects of the method still don't appear in the debugger. You must take another step (Step Into or Step Over) for the return value of the method to be assigned (something that could catch you off guard at first). In the case of the demo program, product won't change until you step to the next statement.

There are a couple more debugger commands that aren't really stepping through code, and the next section describes them to you.

Extra Must-Have Debugging Commands

Many times, you know that an entire block of code doesn't have any useful information. For example, you might not have any interest in stepping through a long loop, especially when you know what the results will be.

To make the debugger execute a block of code and stop again afterward, you can set another breakpoint and press F5. However, you have another quick-and-easy option. Find the statement where you want the debugger to stop, right-click, and select Run to Cursor. You'll want to clear any existing breakpoints between the current position and where you want to run to; otherwise, you'll stop at the breakpoint first.

Another debugging feature is Edit and Continue. With the debugger stopped at the first curly brace of the Multiply method, you can add the following lines to the code:

```
int i = 0;
i = 5;
```

Now, step and execute the first line, setting i to 0. So, you can edit your code on-the-fly and continue debugging. You can also go into the Autos, Locals, and Watch windows and alter the value of the variables.

With the debugger stopped, before executing i = 5, move your cursor to the line after that, return num1 * num2, right-click, and select Set Next Statement. The result is that the debugger skipped the lines from the breakpoint to where your cursor was. Run to Cursor executes all the code in between, but Set Next Statement skips over the code.

Finally, here's a useful trick for your toolbox. Notice that there is a yellow arrow in the gutter where the debugger has the program stopped. Click that arrow and drag it back up two lines. You can now step through the same code over again, saving you from restarting your debugging session.

Using the Debugger to Find a Program Error

This section lets you take a look at something a little more realistic and shows a couple more debugger features. Listing 7.2 contains the program that, as you might suspect, has bugs in it. You'll also see compiler warnings, but ignore them for now. Type the program exactly as is, bugs and all. There are two parts of the code listing: Fibonacci and Squares. Both work with sequences of numbers and demonstrate the potential complexity of an algorithm that you could work with. What is important is the techniques being used to solve the problems that I've intentionally added to the code.

LISTING 7.2   A Program with Bugs

```
1: using System;
2:
3: /// <summary>
4: ///  This program prints a couple mathematical sequences.
5: /// </summary>
6: public class MathSequences
```

LISTING 7.2   Continued

```
7: {
8:    public static void Main()
9:    {
10:      string input;
11:      int index;
12:      int number;
13:      int choice;
14:      int count = 0;
15:
16:      do
17:      {
18:        // Print menu.
19:        Console.WriteLine("\nMath Sequences\n");
20:        Console.WriteLine("1 - Fibonacci");
21:        Console.WriteLine("2 - Squares");
22:
23:        Console.WriteLine("3 - Exit\n");
24:
25:        Console.Write("Please Choose (1, 2, or 3): ");
26:
27:        input = Console.ReadLine();
28:        choice = Int32.Parse(input);
29:
30:        // Figure out what user wanted.
31:        switch (choice)
32:        {
33:          // Print Fibonacci Sequence
34:          case 1:
35:            int temp;
36:            int lastnum;
37:            int fibnum;
38:
39:            Console.WriteLine(
40:              "\nFibonacci Sequence\n");
41:
42:            Console.Write("How many numbers? ");
43:            input = Console.ReadLine();
44:            number = Int32.Parse(input);
45:
46:            for (index=0, lastnum=0, fibnum=1;
47:              index < number;
48:              index++);
49:            {
50:              temp = fibnum;
51:              fibnum += lastnum;
```

LISTING 7.2   Continued

```
52:                    lastnum = temp;
53:
54:                    Console.WriteLine("{0}: {1}",
55:                       index+1, fibnum );
56:                 }
57:
58:               break;
59:             // Print Squared numbers sequence
60:             case 2:
61:               // point of int overflow
62:               const int maxSquare = 46352;
63:
64:               Console.WriteLine(
65:                  "Squared Number Sequence");
66:
67:               Console.Write("How many numbers? ");
68:               input = Console.ReadLine();
69:               number = Int32.Parse(input);
70:
71:               for (index=0;
72:                  index < number && index < maxSquare;
73:                  index++)
74:               {
75:                  Console.WriteLine("{0}: {1}",
76:                     index+1, index*index );
77:               }
78:               if (number >= maxSquare)
79:               {
80:                  Console.WriteLine(
81:          "Overflow: Enter a number less than {0}!",
82:                     maxSquare);
83:               }
84:             break;
85:             // Exit Program
86:             case 3:
87:               Console.WriteLine("\nGoodBye\n");
88:               break;
89:             // User entered bad data
90:             default:
91:               Console.WriteLine(
92:                  "No, no , no - That just won't do!");
93:               break;
94:        } // end switch
95:
```

LISTING 7.2   Continued

```
 96:      // Keep going until user wants to quit
 97:      } while (choice != 3);
 98:
 99:      return;
100:   }
101: }
```

Next, run this program and perform the following tasks:

1. At the main menu, select 1 and press Enter for a Fibonacci report. This option is for printing out a sequence of Fibonacci numbers. You'll be asked for a number, so enter **3**.

2. Observe the output. It's the number entered plus one, a colon, and the number 1. However, it really should have printed the number of lines corresponding to the number entered, with the next Fibonacci number on each subsequent line. This is a bug. The program must be fixed to obtain the expected output.

3. Reproduce the problem. This is simple; just select 1 from the menu again and press Enter.

4. During the reproduction step, observe that the problem happens at the time the Fibonacci report is executed.

5. In VS2008, set a breakpoint as close as possible to the place before the problem occurred. The problem occurs when menu option 1 is selected. This is around line 39.

6. To set the breakpoint, click in the gutter on line 39; a red dot appears. This indicates a breakpoint on that line. Now start debugging (F5).

7. You'll see a menu when the console window appears. Select menu option 1 and press Enter to reproduce the problem. The program stops at the breakpoint.

8. Do a Step Over. The highlighted line is now line 41.

9. Now observe the variables to see their values. You can use the Watch window because there are specific items to watch (instead of looking at everything, as the Locals window provides). Do this for the following int variables: number, index, temp, lastnum, and fibnum. You learned earlier in this chapter how to set up a Watch window.

10. Step until the program asks for the number of numbers to generate. Enter the number **5** and press Enter, and step until the program reaches the for loop. Watch the variables in the Watch window with each step.

11. The current line is a for loop, and the index variable is 0. Take another step and observe that number is 5 and index is 0, meaning that the loop condition is true.

12. Take another step. What's this? Instead of moving to line 50, to execute what you expect is the body of the loop, control moves to incrementing i, something that should happen only after executing the body of the loop.

13. If you step through this until i equals 5 and continue stepping, you'll notice that the body of the for loop is executed line by line, and then control moves to the break statement past the body of the for loop.

Take a better look at the line with the `for` loop statement. It appears to look like any other `for` loop. `index`, `lastNum`, and `figNum` were initialized to 0, 0, and 1, respectively. The value of the `index` should be less than 5, the `index` is being incremented, and the statement is terminated with a semicolon. Hmm...a semicolon? `for` loops don't have semicolons.

Remove the semicolon, recompile, and run (or debug, if preferred). Notice that the bug is fixed and that the output prints as expected.

What happened was that the `for` loop interpreted the semicolon as its program statement. Because curly braces are optional, the semicolon was the only statement that belonged to the `for` loop. Therefore, the loop iterated on nothing and then transferred control to the following block. This block printed out the line `"5: 1"` similar to what it should on its first run, executed the `break` statement, and then moved on to show the menu again.

This particular problem will be flagged as a compiler warning. However, when multiple files are being compiled at the same time, a warning can scroll off the screen without being noticed. Also, compiler warnings may be turned off. Therefore, it is good to look at compiler warnings; they'll often help you fix a problem faster than a debugging session.

Attaching to Processes

Sometimes its necessary to begin a debugging session while a program is running. Perhaps there might be a Windows Service process or a custom control acting up. The problem is that you can't debug these by just running the debugger. You need to attach to the process that the code is running in before it's possible to hit a breakpoint.

The next scenario uses the second menu item of the Math Sequences program from Listing 7.2. This part of the program prints a sequence of squared numbers from zero to whatever number the user enters.

Suppose that a user submits a bug with the program that needs to be investigated. He selected menu option number 2, for a square number sequence. His requirements were to obtain the square of 50,000, so that's what he entered at the prompt. The program ran but gave him the wrong number and an error.

To get started, run the program from outside of VS2008. You will find its *.exe file in the project folder in bin/debug. Select menu option number 2 and press Enter. Type **50000** at the prompt and press the Enter key. The program runs and ends with the error message "`Overflow: Enter a number less than 46352!`" Figure 7.5 shows the program output.

As is obvious from the output, some type of error checking is applied; however, it doesn't seem to be working as effectively as it should. The output shows numbers being calculated appropriately and suddenly going negative. Because the program is still running, it is easy to attach to its process and see what's happening inside. To attach to this process, follow these steps:

1. With VS2008 running, select `Debug Processes...` from the `Debug` menu. The `Attach to Process` dialog box, shown in Figure 7.6, appears.

2. Select the Chapter 07.exe process (or the name you used for your project) from the Available Processes list and click the Attach button.

3. VS2008 goes into debug mode and the process is attached for debugging.

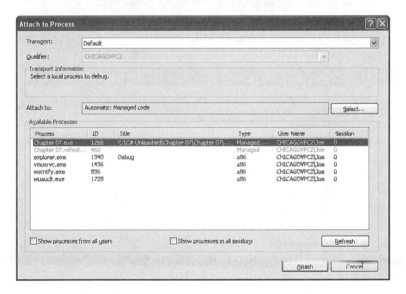

FIGURE 7.5   Listing 7.2 program output.

FIGURE 7.6   Attaching to a process.

Now it's necessary to create a breakpoint in the program to stop execution and examine what's happening. This breakpoint is different from the one used in the Fibonacci example because the number of iterations needed to re-create the problem is much greater. The strategy for this program is to execute a specified number of iterations and then examine what happens when the calculations don't work. This means the program must run for a predefined number of iterations and then stop on a breakpoint. The following steps show how to run a program through a loop for a specified number of iterations:

1. Make sure the file from Listing 7.2 is loaded in the debugger.

2. Scroll down to line 75, where the Console.Writeline statement is.

3. Create a breakpoint by clicking in the gutter of line 75.

4. Right-click the breakpoint, in the gutter, created in the previous step.

5. Select the Hit Count option from the context menu. The Breakpoint Hit Count dialog box appears, as shown in Figure 7.7.

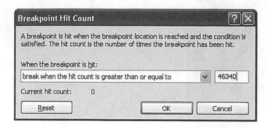

FIGURE 7.7   The Breakpoint Hit Count dialog box.

6. From the When the Breakpoint Is Hit drop-down list, select Break When the Hit Count Is Greater Than or Equal To.

7. In the text field to the right, type the number **46340**.

WHY 46,340?

The number 46,340 is used for the breakpoint because it's the last valid square to be calculated before an overflow condition occurs on the int type.

---

8. Click the Reset Hit Count button to make sure it's set to 0.

9. Click the OK button and observe the + symbol on the break point in the gutter. Now, when the program arrives at line 75 for the 46,340th time, it stops there on the breakpoint.

10. Return to the console window where the program is running and select menu option number 2 and press Enter. Type **50000** at the prompt and press the Enter key. The program will break when the number reaches 46,340.

THE PRODUCTIVITY GAIN

Now is a good time to reflect upon the amount of time this procedure just saved. It would have been time-intensive to have stepped through more than 46,000 individual iterations.

---

11. When the program reaches the breakpoint, add the index variable to the Watch window.

12. Below the index variable in the Watch window, add a new line "index*index". The variable index is 46339, and the "index*index" is 2147302921.

13. Start debugging again. index is 46340, and "index*index" is 2147395600. This is normal.

14. Start debugging again. index is 46341, and "index*index" is –2147479015. This is clearly where the program is going awry. The index variable is never able to reach 46341.

As you can see in Listing 7.2, it's apparent that preventing overflow was a part of this program's design. The for loop on line 72 checks to make sure the program doesn't make a calculation when index reaches the maxSquare variable. In addition, the if statement on line 78 checks to see whether number is greater than or equal to maxSquare. If it is, it prints an error message to the console. The problem is that the program didn't stop before the error occurred.

Take a closer look at maxSquare. It's defined on line 62 as a constant integer with a value of 46352. This is not the correct value. Earlier investigation revealed an overflow condition on an integer occurred at 46342. Therefore, to fix this problem, just change the value of maxSquares to 46341. This will stop the program before it prints out incorrect values.

It's easy to see how this bug happened. Perhaps the developer added the overflow checks after the program was written. He might have seen the overflow occurring in the output at 46342. This is because the line number is printed as index+1. To compound this oversight, a typo was made when creating the maxSquares constant integer initialization by transposing a 4 with a 5 in the tens position. Scenarios such as this are why some bugs are so hard to find. Many times, it's not just a single bug, but a series of mistakes made together.

Summary

An IDE, such as VS2008, can prove useful in finding bugs. In this chapter, two debugging examples demonstrated different techniques for finding bugs. The first was a straightforward explanation about how to set an explicit breakpoint on a line of code. The second debugging example explained how to attach to a process. It also showed how to set a conditional breakpoint.

This completes Part I of C# 3.0 Unleashed. You now know the basic syntax of the C# programming language and have essential knowledge of using VS2008. Part II builds upon what you've learned, covering how to build objects and implement object-oriented programs with C#.

PART 2

Object-Oriented Programming with C#

CHAPTER 8

Designing Objects

In the real world, outside of Second Life and other software endeavors, we handle many kinds of problems every day. Think about how you solve these problems. For example, if you were the one organizing a special event, what would you need? You would select dates and times, entertainment, food, workers, and invitations. You would also coordinate these things with an agenda.

From a software perspective, those items selected are referred to as objects, such as a custom class or struct. You would further refine those objects to hold members, which define attributes and behavior. The attributes and behavior would map to C# language elements. An attribute could be a field or property, and a behavior could be a method or event. This is the world of objects, and by building objects that represent real-world entities, you can build more meaningful systems.

This chapter shows you how to create objects and define their members.

Object Members

Objects should be self-contained with a single purpose in mind. All included members should be compatible and interact effectively to support that purpose. Here's a simple class skeleton:

```
class WebSite
{
    // constructors
```

```
    // destructors

    // fields

    // methods

    // properties

    // indexers

    // events

    // nested objects
}
```

In this example, the `class` keyword tells that this is a class—a custom reference type. The name `WebSite` is the name of the class, and the class members are contained within the braces. This could have been a struct instead, but that would have made it a value type, as explained in Chapter 4, "Understanding Reference Types and Value Types."

THE OVERLOADED TERM: *OBJECT*

The term *object* is used in so many ways that it is no wonder it confuses many people. In computer science, an object is a thing that represents an entity in the domain of the problem you are trying to solve. In .NET terms, the definition of an object is often called a type. In object-oriented programming, an object is an instance of a type. In C#, object is the base type of all other types.

In this chapter, I use the computer science definition of an object for describing how you create objects in C#. You can visit Wikipedia, http://en.wikipedia.org/wiki/Object, for a view of how many meanings there are for the word *object*.

The following sections provide details about each object member. These object members include fields, constructors, destructors, methods, properties, indexers, and events.

Instance and Static Members

Each member of an object can be classified in one of two ways: instance member or static member. When a copy of an object is created, it is considered instantiated. At that point, the object exists as a sole entity, with its own set of attributes and behavior. If a second instance of that object were created, it would normally have a separate set of data from that of the first object instance. In C#, object members belong to the instance, unless modified as static. An example of instance objects is a `Customer` class, where every customer has different information.

If you use the static modifier with an object member, only a single copy of that member can exist at any given time, regardless of how many object instances there are. Static members are useful for controlling access to static fields (object state). We can look at the .NET Framework Class Library (FCL) for good examples of when to use static methods, such as the `System.Math` class, the `System.IO.Path` class, and the `System.IO.Directory` class. Each of these classes has static members that operate on the input and return a value. Because these methods don't depend on any object state, making them static is convenient and avoids the overhead of creating an instance.

Fields

Fields comprise the primary "data" portion of a class. They are the state of an object. They are members of a class as opposed to local variables, which are defined inside of methods and properties.

Fields can be initialized during declaration or afterward, depending on style or the nature of requirements. There are pros and cons each way.

For example, a conservative approach may be to ensure that all fields have default values, which would lead to initialization of fields at declaration or soon thereafter. This is safe, and perhaps it also helps plan design more thoroughly by requiring you to think about the nature of the data up front. Here's an example of a field declaration:

```
string siteName  = "Computer Security Mega-Site";
```

The field declaration and initialization can happen on the same line. However, this isn't an absolute requirement. Fields can be declared on one line and then initialized later, as the following example shows:

```
string url;
```

```
// somewhere in the code
url = "http://www.comp_sec-mega_site.com";
```

If desired, multiple fields can be declared on the same line. They must be separated by commas. This can even include declaration of one or more of the fields, as the following example shows:

```
string siteName, url, description = "Computer Security Information";
```

All three of those fields are strings. The `description` field is initialized with a literal string. The other fields are still uninitialized. They could have been initialized in the same manner as the `description` field.

Constant Fields

When the value of a field is known ahead of time and that value won't change, you can create a constant. A constant field is guaranteed not to change during program execution. It can be read as many times as needed. However, code can't write to them or try to change them in any way.

Constants are efficient. Their values are known at compile time. This enables certain optimizations unavailable to other types of fields. By definition, constants are also static. Here's an example:

```
const string http = "http://";
```

This example shows a constant string declaration, initialized with a literal string. Constants are initialized with literal representations. This was a good selection for a constant because it's something that doesn't change. Think about the way addresses are sometimes entered into web browsers: A user types part of the address, assuming that the Internet protocol will conform to World Wide Web standards. An easy way to accommodate this usage is to have a constant field specifying the HTTP protocol as a default prefix to any web address.

Integral constants could be implemented with the `const` keyword, but it's often much more convenient to implement them as enum types. Using an enum type also promotes a more strongly typed implementation. Chapter 6, "Using Arrays and Enums," discusses enum types in more detail.

readonly Fields

`readonly` fields are similar to constant fields in that they can't be modified after initialization. The biggest difference between the two is when they're initialized: Constants are initialized during compilation, and `readonly` fields are initialized during runtime. There are good reasons for this, including flexibility and providing more functionality for users.

Sometimes the value of a variable is unknown until runtime. The value could depend on several conditions and program logic. `readonly` fields are initialized during object instantiation.

In the following example, `currentDate` is initialized with the date at the time the field is created:

```
readonly DateTime currentDate = DateTime.Now;
```

Because the creation date of an object is something that can't possibly be known at compile time, the `readonly` modifier is the most appropriate way to approach this case.

Methods

Methods are some of the most common object members you'll work with. A C# method is similar to functions, procedures, subroutines, and so on in other programming languages. There's a lot to say about methods in C#, and you can learn more about them in Chapter 10, "Coding Methods and Custom Operators." For now, here's a simple example:

```
void MyMethod()
{
    // statements go here
}
```

The preceding method doesn't return any value, which is why you see the void return type. The name is MyMethod, and you would replace that with a meaningful name of what the method does. This method doesn't accept parameters, but you still have to follow the method name with parentheses. Inside the curly braces, block is the method body.

Properties

A C# property enables you to protect access to the state of your object. You use them like fields, but they operate much like methods. The following sections show you how to declare and use properties. You'll also learn about a new C# 3.0 feature called the auto-implemented property and how to use the VS2008 property snippet.

Declaring Properties

Here's an example of a simple property:

```
private string m_description;


public string Description
{
    get
    {
        return m_description;
    }

    set
    {
        m_description = value;
    }
}
```

The property begins with an access modifier of public, meaning that code outside of this class can see the property. The next item is the property type, string. The name of this property is Description. This property has both a get and a set accessor.

The get and set accessors can have any logic you want to define. A get accessor returns a value, and the set accessor sets a value. Notice the value keyword in the set accessor; it holds whatever value was assigned to the property.

Using Properties

Here's an example to show you how a property can be used:

```
static void Main()
{
    WebSite site = new WebSite();
```

```
        site.Description = "cool site";
        string desc = site.Description;
}
```

Assuming the Description property is defined inside the WebSite class, you would create an instance of WebSite, with its site in the preceding code. Through the site instance, you can access the Description property. Remember the Description property was defined as public, which makes it visible outside the WebSite class, but the m_description field was defined as private, meaning that the preceding code will not see it.

Notice how the "cool site" string is being assigned to site.Description. When this happens, the Description property's set accessor is called. Furthermore, the value inside of the set accessor holds the assigned string, "cool site".

Next, look at how site.Description is being assigned to the desc variable. This causes the Description property's get accessor to be called. The get accessor returns whatever is assigned to m_description, which will be assigned to the desc variable.

This example shows how a property can use a single field as its backing store, where all the property does is get or set on the backing store field, which is a common scenario. In Chapter 9, "Implementing Object-Oriented Principles," you'll learn about the object-oriented principle of encapsulation, which explains why it is important to use properties this way, instead of just accessing a field. Essentially, you want to decouple objects and make maintenance easier, and this helps a lot. The next section shows an easier way for the simple scenario of when you only get and set a single backing store.

Auto-Implemented Properties

The pattern of properties encapsulating a single field is so common that C# 3.0 introduced auto-implemented properties. Here's an example:

```
public int Rating { get; set; }
```

This Rating property encapsulates some value of type int. Because calling code doesn't have access to the backing store anyway, knowing its name doesn't matter. The C# compiler will create an int field behind the scenes for us.

Another benefit of the auto-implemented property is that it eliminates a temptation by programmers to code to the backing store instead of going through the property. For example, in the case of Description, code inside the same class can access the private m_description field. However, what if you later change the implementation of description so that it contains business rules to evaluate what is being assigned. It's possible that other code in the class will not change to operate on the property to take advantage of that business logic, meaning that you have a bug in the code.

The VS2008 Property Snippet

There's another nice snippet in VS2008 that you can use for properties. Here's how to use it:

1. Click inside of the WebSite class. Create a class named **WebSite** if you haven't created it yet.

2. Type **pro**, press Tab, and you'll see prop fill out. There are other property snippets, but we only want to use prop right now.

3. Press Tab again to get the property snippet form. The highlight will be on the property type, which defaults to int.

4. Type **Web**, and then press Tab. You'll see WebSite fill out.

5. Press Tab and you'll see control move to the next place in the form, which is the name of the property.

6. Type **BetaSite** and then press Enter. You'll see the cursor move to the end of the snippet.

This created an automatic property. The propg snippet creates a property with a get accessor, and the propa and propdp snippets create attached properties and dependency properties that are used in Windows Presentation Foundation and Windows Workflow applications, which you'll learn about in Chapter 26, "Creating Windows Presentation Foundation (WPF) Applications," and Chapter 28, "Adding Interactivity to Your Web Apps with ASP.NET AJAX."

Indexers

Indexers let you build objects that can be used like arrays. A useful comparison is to view their implementation as a cross between an array, property, and method.

Indexers behave like arrays in that they use the square-bracket syntax to access their members. The .NET collection classes use indexers to accomplish the same goals. Their elements are accessed by index.

Indexers are implemented like properties because they have get and set accessors, following the same syntax. Given an index, they obtain and return an appropriate value with a get accessor. Similarly, they set the value corresponding to the index with the value passed into the indexer.

Indexers also have a parameter list, just like methods. The parameter list is delimited by brackets. Normally, parameter types are commonly int, so a class can provide array-like operations, but other useful parameter types are string or a custom enum. Here's an example:

```
const int MinLinksSize = 10;
const int MaxLinksSize = 10;
string[] m_links = new string[MaxLinksSize];
```

```csharp
public string this[int i]
{
    get
    {
        if (i >= MinLinksSize && i < MaxLinksSize)
        {
            return m_links[i];
        }
        return null;
    }
    set
    {
        if (i >= MinLinksSize && i < MaxLinksSize)
        {
            m_links[i] = value;
        }
    }
}

// code in another class

static void Main()
{
    WebSite site = new WebSite();

    site[0] = "http://www.mysite.com";
    string link = site[0];
}
```

The indexer in this example accepts an integer argument. The get and set accessors guard against any attempt to retrieve or set out-of-range values.

Using this indexer looks and feels just like an array. At the end of the example, there is an instance of WebSite, the indexer's containing object. Similar to the way a property is used, reading from the indexer calls the get accessor and assigning to the indexer calls the set accessor. The number between brackets is assigned to the i parameter that is used in the accessors; in the preceding example, i is set to 0. The value keyword holds the value being assigned, which is "http://www.mysite.com" in this example.

Reviewing Where Partial Types Fit In

Partial types, introduced in C# 2.0, allow you to divide the definition of a single type into multiple parts. Although the parts can be in the same file, they are typically used to divide an object definition among multiple files. The primary purpose of partial types is tool support in separating machine-generated code from the code you work with. For example, VS2008 ASP.NET and Windows Forms project and item wizards create skeleton classes divided into two files. This reduces the amount of code you have to work with directly because your code is in one file and the machine-generated code is in another.

The syntax identifying a partial type includes a class (or struct) definition with the partial modifier. At compile time, C# identifies all classes defined with the same name that have partial modifiers and compiles them into a single type. The following code shows the syntax of partial types:

```
using System;


partial class Program
{
    static void Main()
    {
        m_someVar = 5;
    }
}


// Located in a different file

using System;

partial class Program
{
    private static int m_someVar;
}
```

The preceding code represents two different files. The second file begins at the second using System statement. Here, I've simply shown the declaration of the partial type where both parts use the partial modifier. Notice that m_someVar is declared in one partial but used in the Main method of the other partial. At runtime, both partials are the same class, but that is not a problem.

This was the basic syntax of a partial type, and you'll be able to see it in action in Chapter 25, "Writing Windows Forms Applications," Chapter 26, and Chapter 27, "Building Web Applications with ASP.NET."

Static Classes

Although normal classes can have both instance and static members, sometimes you want a class to have only static members. In that case, you can create a static class. Here's an example:

```
public static class CustomMathLib
{
    public static double DoAdvancedCalculation(
        double param1, double param2)
    {
        return -1;
    }
}
```

As shown here, just use the `static` modifier. Subsequently, all members of the class must be static.

The `System.Object` Class

As you learned in Chapter 4, all types derive from `System.Object`. Because of this inheritance relationship, all objects also have `System.Object` members. This section discusses what these members are and how you can use them.

Checking an Object's Type

In Chapter 2, "Getting Started with C# and Visual Studio 2008," you learned about the `typeof` operator and saw it used extensively in Chapter 6 when working with the `Enum` class. The thing about `typeof` is that you have to know the type for the parameter, but sometimes you'll get an object and won't necessarily know what type it is. For example, if you have a generic method that accepts a parameter of type object, you might need to check to see whether it is a type you can work with. You'll see this scenario later in Chapter 9 when implementing a custom `Equals` method. To get the type of an object instance, you can call its `GetType` method, like this:

```
Type siteType = site.GetType();
```

In this example, we're calling `GetType` on a `WebSite` instance. Perhaps it's a class that derives from `WebSite` and we need to know which one it is.

Comparing References

Another `System.Object` method is `ReferenceEquals`, which works with reference type objects. It will let you know whether two variables contain references to the same object. Here's an example:

```
WebSite site2 = site;
bool isSameObject = object.ReferenceEquals(site, site2);
```

Because the preceding code assigns `site` to `site2`, their references will be the same, and the call to `ReferenceEquals` will succeed. You could have two different objects with the exact same values, but `ReferenceEquals` will return `false` because the variable references are not the same.

Checking Equality

The purpose of the `Equals` method is to check value equality. For value type objects, the `Equals` method checks every member of the object automatically. However, for reference type objects, `Equals` calls `ReferenceEquals`, which gives you reference equality. Chapter 9 shows you how to add an `Equals` method to your own objects to define value equality. Here are a couple examples of how to use the instance and static `Equals` methods of `System.Object`:

```
WebSite site3 = new WebSite();
WebSite site4 = new WebSite();
site3.Description = "C# Info";
site4.Description = site3.Description;

bool isSiteEqual = site3.Equals(site4);
isSiteEqual = object.Equals(site3, site4);
```

In the preceding example, the `site4.Description` property is set to the `site3.Description` property, giving both objects value equality. That doesn't matter, however, because both calls to `Equals` returns `false` because the variables refer to two different objects. I show you how to fix this in Chapter 9.

Getting Hash Values

A common operation in C# programming is to work with hash tables, which store objects based on an immutable key. These are often called associations, associative arrays, or dictionaries in other languages. To help create these keys, `System.Object` has a `GetHashCode` method, shown here:

```
int hashCode = site3.GetHashCode();
```

Typically, you won't be calling `GetHashCode` like this, unless you're implementing your own hash table. It will be called when you use a `Hashtable` class or a generic `Dictionary` class, which is covered in Chapter 17, "Parameterizing Type with Generics and Writing Iterators." The default implementation of `GetHashCode` in `System.Object` isn't guaranteed to return a unique value, but in Chapter 9 you'll learn how to define your own `GetHashCode` method.

Cloning Objects

`System.Object` also has a method called `MemberwiseClone` for making copies of objects. Here's an example:

```
// member of WebSite
public WebSite GetCopy()
{
    return MemberwiseClone() as WebSite;
}
```

I had to call MemberwiseClone from inside of the WebSite class because it is protected, meaning that only derived classes can access it. You'll learn more about how protected and other access modifiers work in Chapter 9. Here's the code that uses it:

```
WebSite beta = new WebSite();
WebSite site5 = new WebSite();
site5.BetaSite = beta;

WebSite site6 = site5.GetCopy();

bool areSitesEqual = ReferenceEquals(site5, site6);
bool areBetasEqual = ReferenceEquals(site5.BetaSite, site6.BetaSite);

Console.WriteLine(
    "Sites Equal: {0}, Betas Equal: {1}",
    areSitesEqual, areBetasEqual);
```

First, notice how the BetaSite property of WebSite is set to beta. This means that you have a field inside of WebSite with a reference to another WebSite class instance. When calling GetCopy, which calls MemberwiseClone, a new object is assigned to site6, which is a copy of site5.

Here's something that can trick you: MemberwiseClone does just a shallow copy. A shallow copy will only copy objects at the first level of the object graph. Both site5 and site6 are at the first level of their object graph. The beta WebSite instance was at the second level of the site5 object graph. That means that the only thing copied during the call to MemberwiseClone was the reference held through the BetaSite property of site5. So, although site5 and site6 are different objects that really were copied, they both refer to the same object assigned to BetaSite. Here's the output to show this:

```
Sites Equal: False, Betas Equal: True
```

Remember that a MemberwiseClone is a shallow copy. If you want a deep copy, you must implement your own method.

Using Objects as Strings

One thing you might have noticed by now is that you can call ToString on anything. The Console.WriteLine method implicitly calls ToString on whatever is given to it. That's because ToString is a member of System.Object. Here are a couple of examples:

```
string siteStr = site6.ToString();
string fiveStr = 5.ToString();

Console.WriteLine("Site6: {0}, five: {1}", siteStr, fiveStr);
```

We didn't add a `ToString` method to `WebSite`, but can still call it. You can also call `ToString` on a literal value, as the preceding example does with the number 5. Here's the output:

```
Site6: Chapter_08.WebSite, five: 5
```

Output for number 5 isn't too surprising, but look at what happened with `site6`. `Chapter_08` is the namespace of the program I'm using, and `WebSite` is the class name. This is the fully qualified name of the type, which is what `ToString` will give you by default.

DEFAULT TOSTRING **WHEN DEBUGGING**

Occasionally, you might be debugging your program or print out the results of `ToString` and see a fully qualified type name. This often means that you are either looking at or using the wrong object.

For example, in ASP.NET you assign `ListItem` objects, which contain `Text` and `Value` properties, to lists. However, you accidentally call `ToString` on the `ListItem`, rather than its `Text` property, which you intended.

Summary

You now have some familiarity with class members and what can go inside of an object. Properties are useful for encapsulating the state of objects. You can also allow your objects to be used like arrays by implementing indexers.

VS2008 uses partial classes to help make working with ASP.NET and Windows Forms easier by putting parts of a class into different files.

The `System.Object` class, which as you know is the ultimate base class of all C# types, has several members that you can use. You can compare objects for both reference and value equality. In the next chapter, you learn about object-oriented concepts, including polymorphism. You can use polymorphism to override `Equals` and other methods from `System.Object` to make your class more useful.

CHAPTER 9

Designing Object-Oriented Programs

Everything in the world can be described from the perspective of objects. Lawyers have clients, laws, and courts; doctors have patients, illness, and treatments; and software engineers have computers, software, and slices of pizza shoved under the door late at night. All these things can be defined as objects, but each set of objects is specific to its own domain.

After you get used to it, identifying objects from the domain of which to solve a problem is easy. It's even more fun to figure out what to do with those objects after we have them. Often, natural relationships that exist between objects help us define the static structure of our application. An inheritance relationship allows creating a hierarchy of classes, such as a patient (in the doctor domain), where there can be different types of patients, such as a sick patient or a well patient (maybe they just need a physical) that derive from the patient parent. Often, there are compositional relationships, where one object contains another, such as a sick patient who has an illness. Another thing you'll want to do with objects is manage encapsulation. For example, a doctor has patients, but he must protect access to patient information to ensure privacy. Objects also have sophisticated behavior where they communicate among one another. When there is inheritance involved in the communication, you want to make sure the method on the correct object is being called at runtime, meaning that you could use polymorphism.

The following sections drill down on these subjects, which are three of the principles of object-oriented programming: inheritance, encapsulation, and polymorphism. Abstraction, a fourth pillar of object-oriented programming, deals with building objects from a higher-level perspective so that you don't have to be concerned about the lower-level details. In this chapter, you learn about building objects and managing the public members to create new abstractions. However, Chapter 14, "Implementing Abstract Classes and Interfaces," goes into greater depth on the C# language features of abstract classes and interfaces that help you build abstract objects to program with. For now, you learn about how to implement inheritance, encapsulation, and polymorphism with C#, starting with inheritance.

Inheritance

Inheritance is an object-oriented principle relating to how one class, a derived class, can share the characteristics and behavior from another class, a base class. This can be thought of as an "is a" relationship, because the derived class can be identified by both its class type and its base class type. Later in this chapter, I show you how to control whether derived classes can also inherit base class members and use those base class members as if they belonged to the derived class.

The benefits gained by this are the ability to reuse the base class members and to add additional members to the derived class. The derived class then becomes a specialization of the base class (parent). This specialization can continue for as many levels as necessary, each new level derived from the base class above it. In the opposite direction, going up the inheritance hierarchy, there is more generalization at each new base class traversed. Regardless of how many levels between classes, the "is a" relationship holds.

Base Classes

Normal base classes may be instantiated themselves, or inherited. Derived classes inherit each base class member marked with protected or greater access. The derived class is specialized to provide more functionality, in addition to what its base class provides.

A derived class declares that it inherits from a base class by adding a colon, :, and the base class name after the derived class name. Here's an example:

```
public class Contact
{
    public string Name { get; set; }
    public string Email { get; set; }
    public string Address { get; set; }
}


class Customer : Contact
{
    public string Gender { get; set; }
    public decimal Income { get; set; }
}
```

In this example, the `Customer` class derives from the `Contact` class. This means the `Customer` class possesses all the same members as its base class, `Contact`, in addition to its own. In this case, `Customer` has the properties `Name`, `Email`, and `Address`.

Because `Customer` is a specialization of `Contact`, it has its own unique properties: `Gender` and `Income`.

Calling Base Class Members

Derived classes can access the members of their base class if those members have protected or greater access. A later section on the object-oriented principle of encapsulation goes into greater depth on access modifiers. For our discussion, you need to know that a base class member with a `protected` or `public` modifier can be accessed by derived classes. Just use the member name as if that member were a part of the derived class itself. Here's an example:

```
class Contact
{
    public string Address { get; set; }
    public string City { get; set; }
    public string State { get; set; }
    public string Zip { get; set; }

    protected string FullAddress()
    {
        return Address + '\n' + City + ',' + State + ' ' + Zip;
    }
}

class Customer : Contact
{
    public string GenerateReport()
    {
        string fullAddress = FullAddress();
        // do some other stuff...
        return fullAddress;
    }
}
```

In this example, the `GenerateReport` method of the `Customer` class calls the `FullAddress` method in its base class, `Contact`. All classes have full access to their own members without qualification. *Qualification* refers to using a class name with the dot operator to access a class member—`MyObject.SomeMethod`, for instance. You could have also used the base keyword like this:

```
string fullAddress = base.FullAddress();
```

In the preceding example, there is no advantage one way or the other to using the base keyword. However, sometimes a derived class redefines a base class method, making the use of the base keyword necessary to disambiguate the call. The next section discusses redefining, or hiding, base class members.

Hiding Base Class Members

Sometimes derived class members have the same name as a corresponding base class member, meaning that they are redefining the base class method in the derived class. When using an instance of the derived class, you invoke the derived classes specialized behavior and not the behavior of that method in the base class. In this case, the derived member is said to be "hiding" the base class member. When hiding occurs, the derived member is masking the functionality of the base class member. Users of the derived class won't be able to see the hidden member; they'll see only the derived class member. The following code shows how hiding a base class member works. If you're compiling this example now, disregard the compiler warning; it is explained in a couple more paragraphs.

```
class SiteOwner : Contact
{
    public string FullAddress()
    {
        string fullAddress = "";

        // create an address...
        return fullAddress;
    }
}
```

In this example, both SiteOwner and its base class, Contact, have a method named FullAddress. The FullAddress method in the SiteOwner class hides the FullAddress method in the Contact class. This means that when an instance of a SiteOwner class is invoked with a call to the FullAddress method, it is the SiteOwner class FullAddress method that is called, not the FullAddress method of the Contact class.

Versioning

Versioning, in the context of inheritance, is a C# mechanism that allows modification of classes (creating new versions) without accidentally changing the meaning of the code. Hiding a base class member with the methods previously described generates a warning message from the compiler. This is because of the C# versioning policy. It's designed to eliminate a class of problems associated with modifications to base classes.

WATCH THOSE HIDING METHOD WARNINGS

Often, these warning messages scroll off the screen or are overlooked during compilation in an IDE. These overlooked warnings could be early indications of a bug.

In general, warnings are potential bugs or at least indications of code that isn't as clean as it can be. You might want to consider making it a habit of cleaning up all warning messages.

Here's the scenario: A developer creates a class that inherits from a third-party library. For the purposes of this discussion, we assume that the Contact class represents the third-party library. Here's the example:

```
class Contact
{
    // does not include FullAddress() method
}

class WebSite
{
    // members
}

public class SiteOwner : Contact
{
        WebSite mySite = new WebSite();

        public new string FullAddress()
        {
            string fullAddress = mySite.ToString();

            // create an address...
            return fullAddress;
        }
}
```

In this example, the FullAddress method does not exist in the base class, and there is no problem, yet. Later, the creators of the third-party library update their code. Part of this update includes a new member in a base class with the exact same name as the derived class:

```
public class Contact
{
    public string Address = "";
    public string City = "";
    public string State = "";
```

```csharp
    public string Zip = "";

    public  string FullAddress()
    {
        return Address + '\n' + City + ',' + State + ' ' + Zip;
    }
}


class WebSite
{
    // members
}


public class SiteOwner : Contact
{
        WebSite mySite = new WebSite();

        public string FullAddress()
        {
            string fullAddress = mySite.ToString();

            // create an address...
            return fullAddress;
        }
}
```

In this code, the base class method `FullAddress` contains different functionality than the derived class method. In other languages, this scenario would break the code because of implicit polymorphism. (Polymorphism is discussed later in this chapter.) However, this does not break any code in C# because when the `FullAddress` method is called on a variable of type `Contact` that is actually an instance of `SiteOwner`; the `SiteOwner` class' `FullAddress` method won't be called.

As you learn later, polymorphism in C# must be explicitly stated via `virtual` and `override` keywords. Without these keywords, the default behavior is hiding. Again, this explicitness supports the versioning scenario just shown.

This scenario generates the following warning message:

```
'Chapter_09.SiteOwner.FullAddress()' hides inherited member
'Chapter_09.Contact.FullAddress()'. Use the new keyword if hiding was intended.
```

One way to eliminate the warning message is to place a new modifier in front of the derived class method name, as the following example shows:

```csharp
class SiteOwner : Contact
{
        WebSite mySite = new WebSite();
```

```
        public new string FullAddress()
        {
            string fullAddress = mySite.ToString();

            // create an address...
            return fullAddress;
        }
}
```

This has the effect of explicitly letting the compiler know the developer's intent. Placing the new modifier in front of the derived class member states that the developers know there is a base class method with the same name, and they definitely want to hide that member. This prevents breakage of existing code that depends on the implementation of the derived class member. With C#, the compile-time type of a variable determines which nonvirtual method is called. Here's an example:

```
Contact myContact = new Contact();
string address = myContact.FullAddress();

Contact myContactAsSiteOwner = new SiteOwner();
address = myContactAsSiteOwner.FullAddress();

SiteOwner mySiteOwner = new SiteOwner();
address = mySiteOwner.FullAddress();
```

In the preceding code, the compile-time type of myContact and myContactAsSiteOwner is Contact, so calling FullAddress on these instances invokes Contact.FullAddress. The runtime type, defined via the new modifier on myContactAsSiteOwner is SiteOwner, but that doesn't matter. FullAddress is not virtual. The compile-time type of mySiteOwner is SiteOwner, which is the reason why SiteOwner.FullAddress is invoked via the call to mySiteOwner.FullAddress.

You can eliminate any of the problems here by not allowing any class to derive from your class; the next section shows you how.

Sealed Classes

Sealed classes are classes that can't be derived from. To prevent other classes from deriving from a class, make it a sealed class. There are a couple good reasons to create sealed classes, including optimization and security.

Sealing a class avoids the system overhead associated with virtual methods. (The "Polymorphism" section later in this chapter has an in-depth discussion of virtual methods.) This allows the compiler to perform certain optimizations that are otherwise unavailable with normal classes.

Another good reason to seal a class is for security. Inheritance, by its very nature, dictates a certain amount of protected access to the internals of a potential base class. Sealing a class does away with the possibility of corruption by derived classes. A good example of a sealed class is the string class. The following example shows how to create a sealed class:

```
sealed class CustomerStats
{
    public bool Gender { get; set; }
    public decimal Income { get; set; }
    public int NumberOfVisits { get; set; }
}

class CustomerInfo : CustomerStats // error
{
}

class Customer
{
    public CustomerStats Stats { get; set; } // OK
}
```

This example generates a compiler error. Because the CustomerStats class is declared with the sealed modifier, it can't be inherited by the CustomerInfo class. The CustomerStats class was meant to be used as an encapsulated object in another class. This is shown by the declaration of a CustomerStats field in the Customer class.

Encapsulating Object Internals

Encapsulation is the object-oriented principle associated with hiding the internals of an object from the outside world. C# has several mechanisms for supporting encapsulation, including properties, indexers, methods, and access modifiers. In this section, you see how to use the features of C# to achieve encapsulation.

There are several reasons to take advantage of C#'s built-in mechanisms for managing encapsulation:

▶ Good encapsulation reduces coupling. By clearly defining a public interface (what other code sees) and hiding everything else users can write code with less dependency on that object.

▶ Internal implementation of an object can freely change. This reduces the possibility of breaking someone else's code.

▶ An object has a much cleaner interface. Users see only those members that are exposed, which reduces the amount of understanding they need to use the object. It simplifies reuse.

Data Hiding

One of the most useful forms of encapsulation is data hiding. Most of the time, users shouldn't have access to the internal data of an object. Data represents the state of an object, and an object normally has full control of its own state to ensure consistency. Anytime access to data is open, the potential of someone else wreaking havoc with the operation of that object increases.

Sometimes it's logical and necessary to expose object data—especially if it's necessary to expose constants, enumerations, and read-only fields. Perhaps a design goal is to increase the efficiency of data access for a field that's accessed frequently. The decisions made depend on the requirements. However, give serious consideration to proper encapsulation of object state.

Modifiers Supporting Encapsulation

You can manage object encapsulation with appropriate use of C# access modifiers, which specify which code can access class members. They also control the method of access. You apply different sets of access modifiers, depending on whether you are working with objects or object members. You see access modifiers applicable to object members first, followed by which modifiers apply to types.

Public Access

Public access is the least restrictive of all access modifiers. It lets any code have access to class members without restriction. Public access is necessary to publish the interface of a class. It is through these members that communication with a class is accomplished. Great care should be taken to ensure that only those members contributing to effective use of an interface to a class are made public. Here's an example:

```csharp
public string GenerateReport()
{
    string fullAddress = base.FullAddress();
    // do some other stuff...
    return fullAddress;
}
```

This GenerateReport method, with the public modifier, might be a good public method. There's a lot of work that goes into building a report, and that object knows more about it than anyone else. Therefore, creating public methods and other type members that do work for you behind the scenes is a good way to build a public interface on an object.

PAY ATTENTION TO THE INTERFACE THING

You might notice that I keep mentioning this concept of an interface, which is all the members of the object that can be accessed by other code. It is an important concept because interfaces are instrumental to component and object-based systems that promote reuse and maintainability in a system. I want to encourage you to be thinking about interfaces because Chapter 14 shows you how C# formalizes the concept of an interface with language support through abstract classes and a C# type called an ... interface.

Private Access

Private access, the opposite of public, is the most restrictive access modifier. Only members within an object may access another member marked as private. Anyone outside the object can't access this member. They won't even know it's there without source code, reflection tools, or documentation telling them otherwise. Private access is useful because it allows modification of a private member implementation without anyone knowing. Here's an example:

```
private string m_firstName = string.Empty;


public string FirstName
{
    get { return m_firstName; }
    set
    {
        if (!string.IsNullOrEmpty(value))
        {
            m_firstName = value;
        }
    }
}
```

Code outside of the object that contains the preceding code can't see m_firstName because it has a private modifier. Notice that the FirstName property is public, and its set accessor has logic to ensure its backing store, m_firstName, has a valid value. This is a common pattern, where properties encapsulate access to private fields. Another benefit of encapsulating private state with properties is if the implementation of that state changes, you don't break other code. All code can only use the public interface of the class, and as long as you don't change that, you can alter the internals as you need.

Private access is the default for object members that do not have an access modifier.

Protected Access

Protected access is a little less restrictive than private access but more restrictive than public. The only way to use a protected member is via members of the same class or through inheritance. A derived class has full access to protected base class members.

```
class Contact
{
    protected int Age { get; set; }
}

class WebSite
{
    // members
}

class Customer : Contact
{
    public bool IsContentAppropriate(WebSite site)
    {
        return Age > 18;
    }
}
```

Notice that the `Age` property in the `Contact` class has a `protected` modifier. This is plausible because some information shouldn't be available to external code for privacy reasons. However, sometimes there's a balance between full encapsulation and the need for other code to have access to information. In this case, the `Customer` class, which derives from `Contact`, needs access to `Age` in `Contact` so that it can figure out whether a specified `WebSite` is appropriate for the viewer.

Another feature of this particular example is that the protected member is a property and not a field. This gives `Contact` the capability to encapsulate its implementation, yet share access at a level necessary for the job. Had the `Age` information been exposed as a protected field, the coupling between derived classes, such as `Customer`, would constrain `Contact` and make maintenance more difficult.

Internal Access

Internal access restricts visibility to only code within the same assembly. In Chapter 1, "Introducing the .NET Platform," when describing .NET, I briefly described an assembly as a unit of deployment, execution, identity, and security. An assembly is also a unit of containment where you may restrict access via `internal` modifiers.

To use internal access effectively, you create a class library project in VS2008. Any code inside of that class library can access your internal members, but other code that references the assembly can't. Here's an example of internal members:

```
sealed class CustomerStats
{
    internal bool Gender { get; set; }
    internal decimal Income { get; set; }
    internal int NumberOfVisits { get; set; }
}
```

All the properties in this `CustomerStats` class have internal access. This would be valid if there were a group of objects responsible for collecting and manipulating these stats. These hypothetical objects would all have access if they belonged to the same assembly. However, this assembly would be implemented as a DLL so that many other programs can use it. These other programs don't have a need to access the `CustomerStats` members. In fact, you don't want them to touch anything in `CustomerStats` because there are a lot of specialized operations that you don't want other code messing with. Therefore, you have the flexibility to work with multiple objects that do have a need for the data, but it is encapsulated within the assembly to keep outside code from breaking it.

Protected Internal Access

Protected internal is a combination of `protected` and `internal` modifiers. Objects in the same assembly have access because the member is internal. Derived classes inside and outside the assembly have access to protected internal members, too.

```
class Contact
{
    protected internal bool Active { get; set; }
}
```

Perhaps the fact that a `Contact` has `Active` set to `true` or `false` matters only to code in the same assembly or a derived class, such as `Customer`.

As you can see, multiple access modifiers are available, giving you flexibility in how you manage access to members of an object. In addition to object members, you can control access to objects themselves, which is discussed in the next section.

Access Modifiers for Objects

You may also control access to objects, but you have only two options: `public` and `internal`. If objects don't have an access modifier, their access defaults to internal. Therefore, all the class, enum, and struct definitions you've seen so far are internal because their access modifiers were not specified.

VS2008 ITEM TEMPLATE DEFAULTS

Here's a gotcha for you. When in a class library project, you can right-click the project, select Add, New Item, Class. Give it any name you want and click the OK button. The skeleton that VS2008 creates defines a class without an access modifier. Consequently, when you reference the DLL from your program, you get a message telling you that the class doesn't exist. That's because the default is internal. To avoid this, make a mental note to add a `public` modifier to new classes you create in class library projects.

Just like public members, public objects are accessible by any other code. Here's an example:

```
internal sealed class CustomerStats
{
    internal bool Gender { get; set; }
    internal decimal Income { get; set; }
    internal int NumberOfVisits { get; set; }
}

public class Customer : Contact
{
    internal CustomerStats Stats { get; set; }
}
```

In the preceding example, `Customer` is public and `CustomerStats` is internal. Be aware of the accessibility you assign to various objects and the accessibility given to them in other objects because you could receive errors for inconsistent accessibility. For example, if the `Stats` property in `Customer` had a public modifier, rather than `internal`, you would get the following compiler error:

```
Inconsistent accessibility: property type 'Chapter_09.CustomerStats' is less acces-
sible than property 'Chapter_09.Customer.Stats'
```

That would be appropriate because `CustomerStats` is internal. By making it public in `Customer`, you would be trying to give access to an instance of `CustomerStats` to outside code. C# will catch this and let you know that either you need to make `CustomerStats` public, which you probably don't want to do, or make `Stats` internal, which is probably your original intention.

6

Containment and Inheritance

Containment means that one object holds another. This is the "has a" relationship. An object inside another object is a field of its containing object.

When speaking of inheritance, it's useful to think of the "is a" relationship, where a class is a part of the classification hierarchy associated with its parent class.

Inheritance and containment are two different concepts, but one can be used improperly in place of the other. This text has repeatedly spoken of the "natural" inheritance hierarchy that is implemented between objects. Studies have shown inheritance is sometimes used where it doesn't necessarily make sense. For a good discussion, see C++ *Programming Style*, by Tom Cargill (Addison-Wesley, 1992). Inheritance is good when applied naturally and is a good fit for the problem.

An alternative to inheritance is containment. By encapsulating one object within another, a class can control what behavior is used by derived classes. If need be, it can provide access to each member of the contained object through its own methods, which is called delegation. In contrast, all class members in a base class, accessible to a derived class, are also accessible to further derivation.

Another factor to consider is that C# has only single-implementation inheritance. This means it can only inherit functionality from a single base class. Other languages, such as C++, allow one class to derive from multiple other classes, but this isn't allowed in C#. Therefore, if a class already inherits from a base class, containment is the only way to reuse another class.

Although containment helps make it easier to reuse and extend code, you still need inheritance to implement the object-oriented principle of polymorphism, discussed next.

Polymorphism

The object-oriented principle of polymorphism is powerful in building flexible object-oriented systems. Examining the word *polymorphism* reveals clues to its purpose. *Poly* means many, and *morph* means to change to something different. Pulling this definition into where it applies to C# programming, you often need to work with many different objects with a single algorithm. Although they might be different objects, they have commonalities. Therefore, you want to write a single algorithm that operates on each of these different objects in the same way.

The following sections build upon previous examples in this chapter where there is a base class, `Contact`, with derived classes, `Customer` and `SiteOwner`. You see how polymorphism works with those classes.

Examining Problems That Polymorphism Solves

To begin, it's useful to get an appreciation of the problem polymorphism solves. The key factor is the capability to dynamically invoke methods in a class based on their type. Essentially, a program would have a group of objects, examine the type of each one, and execute the appropriate method. Here's an example:

```
public class Contact
{
    public void SendAlert()
    {
        Console.WriteLine("Generic Contact Alert");
    }
}

public class Customer : Contact
{
    public new void SendAlert()
    {
        Console.WriteLine("Alert for Customer");
    }
}

class SiteOwner : Contact
{
    public new void SendAlert()
    {
        Console.WriteLine("Alert for SiteOwner");
    }
}
```

The first thing you should notice about the preceding code is that each class has a
SendAlert method. Customer and SiteOwner derive from Contact. Both Customer and
SiteOwner could have given their SendAlert a unique name, but this isn't necessary
because they can just hide SendAlert in Contact with the new modifier, which clears
compiler warnings, too. A previous section of this chapter covered hiding.

Assuming that our application has built-in support to notify interested parties when something on a website changes, the following method performs that notification:

```
private static void HandleUpdates()
{
    // get contacts
    Contact[] contacts = new Contact[3];
    contacts[0] = new Customer();
    contacts[1] = new SiteOwner();
    contacts[2] = new Contact();

    foreach (var contact in contacts)
    {
        switch (contact.GetType().ToString())
        {
            case "Chapter_09.Customer":
                Customer cust = contact as Customer;
```

```
            cust.SendAlert();
            break;
        case "Chapter_09.SiteOwner":
            SiteOwner owner = contact as SiteOwner;
            owner.SendAlert();
            break;
        case "Chapter_09.Contact":
            contact.SendAlert();
            break;
        default:
            break;
    }
  }
}
```

And here's the output:

```
Alert for Customer
Alert for SiteOwner
Generic Contact Alert
```

If you are trying to compile this code, make sure that the case statements reflect the fully qualified name of your types. The SiteOwner, Customer, and Contact classes in the case statements above are in the Chapter_09 namespace, which might not be the same as yours.

Notice how I build the contacts array, adding Contact, Customer, and SiteOwner instances. This is possible because of the inheritance relation between Contact and its derived classes Customer and SiteOwner. Because Customer and SiteOwner are Contact, they can be assigned to a variable of type Contact—an array element of type Contact in this case.

Because the array is type Contact, the compile-time type of these objects is Contact. However, the runtime type of each object is defined with the new operator. So, contacts has three Contact compile-time elements whose runtime types are Customer, SiteOwner, and Contact. Keeping track of compile-time type and runtime type is important to understanding how polymorphism works. If you breezed by this paragraph, you might want to read it again.

Typically, creating the contacts array would be done in another object that creates each object from a data source or grabs a cached version of the array. However, I put it there so that you can explicitly see the compile-time type and runtime type of each object.

There is a switch statement in the loop that bases its condition on the type of each object it's looking at. Notice the use of the GetType method from System.Object to figure out what the runtime type of the object is. Calling ToString on GetType creates a string of the fully qualified name of each object. You can see what these are by the case statements because I designed each class to be a member of the Chapter_09 namespace.

Again, the compile-time type of each object is `Contact`, but we need to know the runtime type of each object to figure out which method to call. When the program hits a specific case statement, we know the runtime type of the object and can safely convert contact to that type. The reason we need the runtime type is because we have to call the `SendAlert` method on the proper object type. Otherwise, the `SendAlert` in `Contact` will always be called because that is all the compiler knows about the current object.

This is a lot of work and complexity, isn't it? It also opens up a can of worms for maintenance, where the `switch` statement can be modified in all kinds of ways, and duplication of functionality can slip in easily over time. Every new class that needs to provide `SendAlert` functionality must also be added. Knowing this ahead of time is key to putting together an elegant design that avoids such problems in the first place and makes the code easier to work with.

Notice that the whole focus of the `switch` statement was to figure out the runtime type of the object to ensure the right method on the right object gets called. From a general perspective, this is a common scenario. For example, instead of objects for managing website updates, what if you were working with bank accounts, automobile configurations, ordering systems, customer management, or more. The commonality among all these systems would be that there would be a base class with multiple derived classes that specialize that behavior. For example, banks would have an `Account` base class with `SavingsAccount` and `CheckingAccount` derived classes. In each of these cases, the same pattern applies—you want to invoke a method on the runtime type of the object. It would seem that such a common scenario could be resolved by a feature built in to the language so that you don't have to code gargantuan `if-then-else` or `switch` statements—to implement polymorphism.

C# does have support for polymorphism, and the problem previously described can be solved rather elegantly. The next section shows you how.

Solving Problems with Polymorphism

The preceding examples accomplish the task of dynamically invoking object methods. However, there is a more efficient and elegant way to accomplish the same thing—polymorphism. Polymorphism is efficient because C#, rather than explicit coding, is managing this process. It's also more elegant because there is less code, which makes for a simpler implementation.

The following code shows how to modify the classes from the preceding section to implement polymorphism. The process is explicit, and I show you how to modify the base class to enable polymorphism and how to modify derived classes to take advantage of polymorphism. Here's the base class, `Contact`:

```
public class Contact
{
    public virtual void SendAlert()
    {
        Console.WriteLine("Generic Contact Alert");
```

```
    }
}
```

Now, the `SendAlert` method in `Contact` is decorated with the virtual modifier. This says that derived classes can override `SendAlert` to enable polymorphism. As I mentioned earlier, polymorphism in C# is explicit, so just decorating the base class as virtual does not suffice. Here's what you need to do in derived classes to get polymorphism to work:

```
public class Customer : Contact
{
    public override void SendAlert()
    {
        Console.WriteLine("Alert for Customer");
    }
}

class SiteOwner : Contact
{
    public override void SendAlert()
    {
        Console.WriteLine("Alert for SiteOwner");
    }
}
```

The `Customer` and `SiteOwner` classes here use the `override` modifier to explicitly enable polymorphism for the `SendAlert` method. There are a couple other requirements to make this compile: The name and signature of overriding methods in derived classes must match a virtual method in the base class.

HANDLING COMPILER WARNINGS WITH OVERRIDE

In a previous section of this chapter on hiding, using the new modifier was a way to explicitly state that hiding was intentional. The situation was that there is a derived class method with the same name and signature as a base class method. If you recall, the warning message that shows when not using the new modifier states that using the override modifier was another option to resolve the compiler warning message. However, you can't just put an override on a derived class method; you must decorate the base class method with the `virtual` modifier. Another option was to rename the derived class method, but you have to look at your situation and pick the proper resolution strategy: hiding, polymorphism, or just another object method. Whatever your intention, remembering these few simple rules will help you resolve the compiler warning.

Now that the classes are explicitly set with modifiers to support polymorphism, the algorithm that calls these methods can be modified. The following update to the HandleUpdates method shows how elegant an algorithm can be with polymorphism:

```
private static void HandleUpdates()
{
    // get contacts
    Contact[] contacts = new Contact[3];
    contacts[0] = new Customer();
    contacts[1] = new SiteOwner();
    contacts[2] = new Contact();

    foreach (var contact in contacts)
    {
        contact.SendAlert();
    }
}
```

And here's the output:

```
Alert for Customer
Alert for SiteOwner
Generic Contact Alert
```

As you can see in the preceding code, the results are quite dramatic—we've replaced all the code inside of the foreach loop with a single line. The output is exactly the same as the nonpolymorphic implementation from the previous section, but the logic to produce it is much improved. A quick reminder: The array creation is something that must happen and would normally be code inside of another method that you would call to obtain a reference to the array.

The explanation is simple. Remember that we need to know the runtime type of an object to ensure the right method is called. By decorating SendAlert in Contact as virtual and SendAlert in Customer and SiteOwner as override, we accomplish this. C# will ensure that overrides (runtime types) of virtual (compile-time types) methods are called when the method on the compile-time type object is called.

INTELLISENSE FOR OVERRIDES

In VS2008, you have IntelliSense support for implementing overrides. If you're in a derived class and type **public override** and then type a space, IntelliSense will appear. Just type enough characters to select the method you want to override, press Enter, and VS2008 will build the method skeleton for you.

IntelliSense is also smart enough to omit the overrides that you've already implemented from the list.

You're only responsibility now is to ensure you put the right logic associated with each derived class, `Customer` or `SiteOwner`, in its own `SendAlert` method.

Polymorphic Properties

In addition to methods, C# permits polymorphism with property accessors. The same rules applied to methods also apply to properties. Here's an example:

```
public class Contact
{
    public virtual string Email { get; set; }
}

public class Customer : Contact
{
        public override string Email
        {
            get
            {
                // perform specialized logic
                return base.Email;
            }
            set
            {
                // perform specialized logic
                base.Email = value;
            }
        }
}
```

In this example, the `Contact` class declares the `Email` property with a virtual modifier. The `Customer` class overrides the `Email` property.

Polymorphic Indexers

C# permits polymorphism with indexer accessors. The same rules applied to methods and properties also apply to indexers. Here's an example:

```
public class SiteList
{
    protected string[] sites = new string[5];

    public virtual string this[int index]
    {
```

```
        get
        {
            return sites[index];
        }
        set
        {
            sites[index] = value;
        }
    }
}

public class FinancialSiteList : SiteList
{
        public override string this[int index]
        {
            get
            {
                if (index > sites.Length)
                    return (string)null;

                return base[index];
            }
            set
            {
                base[index] = value;
            }
        }
}
```

In this example, the SiteList class declares its indexer as virtual. The FinancialSiteList indexer overrides the indexer of its base class, SiteList. The FinancialSiteList indexer accessors call the SiteList indexer accessors by using the base keyword with the index value.

Overriding System.Object Class Members

In Chapter 8, "Designing Objects," you learned about the members of System.Object and what they meant. This section builds on the capabilities of System.Object, showing how to override specific members. In addition to the previous section, this will give you more practical examples of how polymorphism can benefit you. The following sections show how to override Equals, GetHashCode, and ToString, which are already declared with virtual modifiers in System.Object. All of these examples assume that you are adding the methods to a Customer class that has a public Name property.

Overriding Equals

By default, the Equals method in System.Object performs reference equality for reference types and does a full comparison of every field of the object. If you need to consider two separate reference types with the same key as equal, the default is inadequate. For value types, you might need an equality check that is not so thorough. The following example shows how to override Equals on the WebSite class:

```csharp
public override bool Equals(object obj)
{
    Customer cust = obj as Customer;

    if (cust == null) return false;

    return cust.Name == Name;
}
```

The Equals override here is for the Customer class, which is a reference type. If you recall, the as operator will return null if the conversion won't work; that means obj isn't the right type, and the objects can't possibly be equal. Furthermore, if obj is null in the first place, there is no way the objects can be equal. Checking cust against null catches both of these conditions and returns false right away, saving processing time. This example simply returns the equality comparison for the Name property, but you are free to determine which fields of your objects define equality. Just a tip: Comparing a single ID is much quicker than looking at multiple values.

You can't use the as operator on value type objects, so an Equals implementation would have to be different. The following example shows how to implement Equals for a value type:

```csharp
public struct ComplexNumber
{
    public double RealPart { get; set; }
    public double ImaginaryPart { get; set; }

    public override bool Equals(object obj)
    {
        if (obj == null) return false;

        if (this.GetType() != obj.GetType()) return false;

        ComplexNumber cplxNum = (ComplexNumber)obj;

        return
            this.RealPart == cplxNum.RealPart &&
            this.ImaginaryPart == cplxNum.ImaginaryPart;
    }
}
```

This implementation ensures that the input value isn't `null` but is the same type before doing a comparison. Then the conditional AND ensures both the real and imaginary parts of the number are the same. In this particular example, there might not be much gained in meaning or performance for a `ComplexNumber` type, and perhaps you could find a better implementation. However, the point is that you should think about whether implementing `Equals` on a value type makes sense and then do a benchmark to ensure your implementation is faster than the default.

Whenever you implement the `Equals` method, you receive a compiler warning that you should also implement `GetHashCode`. The next section shows you how to implement `GetHashCode`.

Overriding `GetHashCode`

Using objects in collections, such as dictionaries, is so common that `System.Object` includes a special method, `GetHashCode`, for obtaining a unique ID for the object. The problem with the default implementation of `GetHashCode` is that you aren't guaranteed to get a unique ID. This can slow down your program because duplicates in hash tables and dictionaries cause collisions that increase overhead. How to write good hash functions that make the distribution of hash codes more even over a collection is beyond the scope of this book, but there are many sources of information that cover this topic, and I'm sure you can find decent sources of information on the Internet. However, you do need to know how to override the `GetHashCode`, which is shown here:

```
public override int GetHashCode()
{
    return Name.GetHashCode();
}
```

This `GetHashCode` example belongs to the `Customer` class. You can take a value that represents the object adequately to create your hash value. You must always be able to generate the same hash code for the same object because the object put into the collection must also be found using `GetHashCode`. Because string types implement their own `GetHashCode`, I simply delegated (another object-oriented term for letting another object do the work).

Speaking of strings, a common `System.Object` override is the `ToString` method, discussed next.

Overriding `ToString`

The default implementation of `ToString` in `System.Object` returns the fully qualified name of the type. This isn't useful because calling `GetType.ToString` already does that. It is more useful if `ToString` returns a meaningful representation about an object instance.

If you recall, methods such as `Console.WriteLine` call `ToString` on an object. Also, the VS2008 debugger will call `ToString` when showing the value of a variable in a debugger window, such as Autos, Locals, or Watch. Here's an example of how you can implement a ToString override:

```
public override string ToString()
{
    return Name;
}
```

This ToString override was implemented for the Customer class. It is quite possible that "John Doe" would be a more meaningful result than "Chapter_09.Customer".

Summary

C# supports object-oriented programming, and you have special support for inheritance, encapsulation, and polymorphism. Abstraction is covered in Chapter 14. You learned how to create a base class and the syntax for creating derived classes. You can also access members of the base class and perform hiding so that your derived class methods will be called rather than the base class method.

You saw how to use C# accessors to help manage object encapsulation. Remember that in addition to methods, properties are a great way to help encapsulate the internal state of your objects.

Polymorphism is a sophisticated, but elegant object-oriented principle with support in C#. You can create virtual methods and override them in derived classes. This chapter added to what you learned about System.Object, showing how to override Equals, GetHashCode, and ToString.

CHAPTER 10

Coding Methods and Custom Operators

When cooking a meal, you need to follow a recipe. Whether the recipe is in your head, out of a cookbook, or retrieved from a computer recipe database, a series of steps transforms raw food into fine cuisine. (Some of the things I've cooked in the past have not been referred to as fine cuisine, but that was the original idea.) What happens in each step of a recipe is unique to the cook. For example, your stove might be electric or gas and have a digital panel or dial. Such details don't matter in the recipe, which only specifies the steps needed.

Similar to a recipe, a software developer has a set of objects with members that each performs some work when called. These members can be methods, custom operator overloads, or custom conversion operators. Most of the time, you'll be working with methods, but custom operators and conversions are tools that are available if you should have the need. Methods are like functions or procedures in other languages, custom operators allow you to overload the C# built-in operators such as + and ==, and custom conversions enable you to convert between your custom types and other types. These object members hide the details of how the operation is performed, just like recipes don't specify the details of your kitchen and how you follow a step. This chapter covers methods, operator overloads, and conversion operators; you can learn more about other object members in other chapters. For example, Chapter 8, "Designing Objects," introduced fields, indexers, and properties, and you learn about events in Chapter 12, "Event-Based Programming with Delegates and Events."

Methods

Methods embody a significant portion of an object's behavior. They're the primary mechanism whereby messages may be passed between objects. Each method within an object should be designed with a single purpose in mind. Furthermore, the purpose of the method should contribute to the role of the object and interact cohesively with other object members to support object goals.

This section reviews method signatures, local variables, and parameters.

Defining Methods

Methods have signatures that distinguish them from other class members. The contents of a method perform a single operation and can optionally return a value. Here's the basic format of a method:

```
[modifiers] ReturnType MethodName([parameter list])
{
    [statements]
}
```

Modifiers are optional and can be any number of keywords used throughout this book. For example, Chapter 9, "Implementing Object-Oriented Principles," introduced access modifiers, the `new` modifier, and modifiers supporting polymorphism.

The `ReturnType` value can be a reference type, value type, or `void` (doesn't return a value). The `MethodName` is any valid C# identifier. A method can specify zero or more parameters to be used as input/output parameters. A later section of this chapter discusses method parameters in depth. Following the method parameter is the method body. Here's a method example:

```
private const string m_http = "http://";


public bool IsValidUrl(string url)
{
    if (!(url.StartsWith(m_http)))
    {
        return false;
    }
    else
    {
        return true;
    }
}
```

The purpose of the `IsValidUrl` method is to check the input string, `url`, to ensure it begins with the `const` `http` string, `"http://"`. If so, the return value is `true`, otherwise false. The return value must be the same type as the method's return type. Also, the method must return a value, unless the return type is void. The following example shows how this method could be called:

```
WebSite site = new WebSite();
bool isValid = site.IsValidUrl("http://www.informit.com");
```

To call the IsValidUrl method, create an instance of its containing class, WebSite, and call the method through that instance. The argument is a literal string, but in a real application this would probably be a variable holding a value from a database or, more likely, user input. Notice how the code retrieves the return value through an assignment statement to a local variable.

Local Variables

Methods may declare their own local variables. This is useful when working data is needed only for the purpose of that method. Allocated on the stack, these local variables normally go away after the method has executed. For reference type local variables, the reference itself is allocated on the stack, but the actual object is allocated on the heap and is marked for deletion by the garbage collector when the method ends, provided the reference wasn't returned or made available to the caller. Chapter 4, "Understanding Reference Types and Value Types," explains in greater depth how reference type and value type variables are allocated, and you can learn more about the garbage collector in Chapter 15, "Managing Object Lifetime."

So what happens when you use a local variable with the same identifier as a field, which is declared at the object level? Simple, you prefix the field name with the this operator. Using the name without the this operator addresses the local variable (with the same name as the field). Here's an example:

```
private const string m_http = "http://";


private string fullUrl;

public string EnsureValidUrl(string url)
{
    string fullUrl;

    if (!(url.StartsWith(m_http)))
    {
        fullUrl = m_http + url;
        this.fullUrl = fullUrl;

        return fullUrl;
    }

    return url;
}
```

The preceding example has both a field and local variable with the same name, fullUrl. To distinguish between the two, the this operator identifies the field. Without the this operator, the local variable is accessed.

The preceding example also mixes coding conventions. Notice the m_ prefix for m_http. This is a common way to code field names, as there is just an underscore, such as in _http. Whereas the underscore prefix is popular among VB.NET (and occasionally other languages, including C#) developers, some people avoid it because in languages such as C and C++, double underscores have meaning for special language-specific symbols that you shouldn't use as variable names. Because of the distracting similarity, many people avoid the underscore syntax. Whichever way you prefer, being consistent in usage is good, and you should not mix naming guidelines like the preceding example does.

Method Parameters

In C#, you have four types of method parameters: value, ref, out, and params. Their usage is not always immediately obvious because the effects of modifying a parameter are a combination of the argument type and parameter type. This section goes into greater depth to expose the nuances of different ways to define parameters and pass arguments.

Because the argument type has such an important impact on the results of a method, you might want to review Chapter 4 if you are fuzzy about the differences between value type and reference type variables.

Value Parameters

The default parameter type is value.

Value parameters provide a local copy of themselves to the method. This means that the method may read and write to them as much as needed, but the original copy from the caller is not changed. An argument passed into a method must be the same type as the specified parameter or must be implicitly convertible to that type. Value parameters must be definitely assigned before being passed as an argument. Here's an example:

```
public string Url { get; set; }


public bool UpdateSite(WebSite site)
{
    if (!(site.Url.StartsWith(m_http)))
    {
        site.Url = m_http + site.Url;
        return true;
    }
    else
    {
        return false;
    }
}
```

Here's how you call the preceding method:

```
WebSite site2 = new WebSite();
site2.Url = "www.informit.com";

bool changed = site.UpdateSite(site2);

Console.WriteLine("Changed? {0}, URL: {1}", changed, site2.Url);
```

And here's the output:

```
Changed? True, URL: http://www.informit.com
```

The site2 variable is a WebSite, which is a class (reference type). Notice how the UpdateSite method modifies the URL property of the site parameter. Next, look at the output from the calling code. The change to the URL parameter of site2 that occurred inside of the UpdateSite method is visible to the calling code.

Because the argument, site2, was a reference type variable, the type passed as the value parameter was a reference. The UpdateSite method couldn't modify the reference, but it did modify the contents of the object being referred to, which is why the change can be seen in the calling code.

Alternatively, the effect of passing a value type argument as a value parameter means that any changes to the object are not seen by the calling code. To see how this works, modify WebSite to be a struct rather than a class. Although the UpdateSite method changes the value, it was only a copy that was passed, which is consistent with the behavior of value type variables. Consequently, the calling code doesn't see the change because it has the original copy of the WebSite, not the method's copy.

If you want calling code to see changes to a value type variable, the parameter type should be ref, which is discussed next.

Ref Parameters

Ref parameters can be thought of as in/out parameters. Modifying a ref parameter within the body of a method also changes the original variable passed in as an argument. Ref parameters definitely must be assigned before passing them to a method.

Ref parameters are mostly applicable when a method needs to change a value type so that calling code will receive that change. Here's the value type for following demos:

```
public struct Location
{
    public double Lat { get; set; }
    public double Lon { get; set; }
}
```

To understand the preceding code, suppose, for example, a WebSite object is tracking someone with a mobile device with attached GPS capability. Of course, the delay in satellite communications causes a less-than immediate tracking experience, so the site needs to use an intelligent algorithm for predicting what the true movement is until an accurate update arrives. Here's a sophisticated artificial intelligence algorithm that does the prediction and reports whether the input was a good value and the translation was accurate:

```
public bool PredictLocation(ref Location loc)
{
    bool success = true;

    loc.Lat += 5;
    loc.Lon += 3;

    return success;
}
```

Okay, so the algorithm isn't as sophisticated as advertised. People are building amazing software on the web every day, so maybe a little imagination will help.

What's important about the PredictLocation method is the ref keyword preceding the parameter. Also, the parameter type is Location, which is a value type. This effectively ensures that a reference to location is passed, rather than a copy. More specifically, the PredictLocation method has a reference to the exact same Location type variable passed in by the calling code. Here's what the calling code looks like:

```
var loc = new Location();
loc.Lat = 2;
loc.Lon = 4;

bool success = site.PredictLocation(ref loc);

Console.WriteLine("Lat: {0}, Lon: {1}", loc.Lat, loc.Lon);
```

Similar to how the ref parameter in PredictLocation was defined, you must also use the ref keyword on the argument that is passed in. The C# compiler will emit an error if it isn't there, so you can't forget it. Here's the output:

```
Lat: 7, Lon: 7
```

This proves that the lon variable that was passed to PredictLocation is actually changed.

One possible question about this scenario is, "Why not just return the new value instead of modifying?" In most cases, returning the new value is exactly what you would do and arguably the preferred solution. However, notice how the PredictLocation is implemented by returning a bool. Sometimes you might want to provide a method like this as a way to avoid an error. Again, after you learn about exception handling in Chapter 11, "Error and Exception Handling," you'll see how this is also a questionable practice. Overall, just be aware that using ref parameters cause side effects that could affect the reliability of your code.

What if you pass a reference type as a ref parameter? There is typically no need to create a ref parameter for a reference type variable. The only possible reason is if you want to make the reference refer to a different object. This is possible because what is passed is a reference to a reference. Otherwise, ref parameters for reference type objects are unnecessary and could potentially be a bug waiting to happen if another object is assigned to the ref parameter when that isn't your intention. Imagine how hard of a bug that would be to figure out.

As mentioned at the beginning of this section, ref enables you to pass a value in and out of the method. Optionally, there are cases when you only need to get one or more values from a method, which is discussed next.

Out Parameters

Besides using return statements, another way to return information from a method is via out parameters. You would typically use an out parameter if the return value was already being used for another purpose.

In this section, you see two different examples: one where you implement your own method having an out parameter and another showing a common implementation of out parameters for conversion from string to another type. First, here's how you would implement your own method with an out parameter:

```
public static bool TryParse(string latLonInStr, out Location latLon)
{
    latLon = new Location();
    double lat, lon;
    string[] latLons = latLonInStr.Split(',');

    if (double.TryParse(latLons[0], out lat) &&
        double.TryParse(latLons[1], out lon))
    {
        latLon.Lat = lat;
        latLon.Lon = lon;
        return true;
    }

    return false;
}
```

The parameter, latLon, is decorated with the out keyword, designating it as an out parameter. Out parameters don't need to be definitely assigned before calling the method, but they must be definitely assigned before the method returns, which is why the TryParse method above instantiates latLon in the first line of the method block. You don't have to instantiate on the first line like this—just make sure you assign the out parameter a value before returning from the method. Even if a variable is definitely assigned before a method call, it is considered unassigned once inside the method call. Therefore, any attempt to access the out parameter within the method prior to its initialization is a compile-time error.

Nearly all logic in the preceding method has been covered in previous chapters, so it should make sense—it just converts the string passed via the `latLonInStr` parameter to a `Location` object, which is the second parameter. The `if` statement contains a couple calls to `double.TryParse` to perform conversions on the individual `lat` and `lon` values, and I discuss that after discussing the code that calls the `Location.TryParse` method, shown here:

```
success = Location.TryParse("5.3,7.2", out loc);
Console.WriteLine("Lat: {0}, Lon: {1}", loc.Lat, loc.Lon);
```

This code calls `Location.TryParse` with an input string and receives multiple values back. The `success` return value tells whether the conversion succeeded, and the `out loc` parameter returns the converted values. Here's the output:

```
Lat: 5.3, Lon: 7.2
```

The output verifies that `Location.TryParse` converted the string properly. Normally, you would get this string from either user input or maybe an external text-based data source.

Because it is so common to get data in the form of a string from user input or text-based data sources, the .NET built-in types have `Parse` and `TryParse` methods for converting from the string representation of a value to the type you need. `Parse` will throw an exception, as covered in Chapter 11, and `TryParse` will let you know whether the string input was valid via a bool return value. This design is helpful for avoiding the overhead of exception handling, which is a common scenario with user input that you can't control. Because the return value is being used, the out parameter returns the converted value if the conversion is successful. Otherwise, it returns the default value of whatever was passed in. We covered default values in both Chapter 2, "Getting Started with C# and Visual Studio 2008," and Chapter 4. The following code is a snippet from the preceding example to show how `TryParse` works:

```
if (double.TryParse(latLons[0], out lat) &&
    double.TryParse(latLons[1], out lon))
{
    latLon.Lat = lat;
    latLon.Lon = lon;
    return true;
}
```

In the preceding code, `latLons[0]` and `latLons[1]` hold string representations of `lat` and `lon`, respectively. The goal is to convert them from string to double types. So, the code calls `double.TryParse` for each value. In this case, the code needed a double, but all the built-in value types have `Parse` and `TryParse` methods when you need conversion from string to those types. Here, the `&&` helps to short circuit evaluation in case the string passed in could be recognized as garbage right away. If both calls to `TryParse` return true, the string has valid values, and this method sets the out parameter, `latLon`, and returns `true`. By the way, there are probably permutations of bad input values that you would want to check for in the algorithm, but in the interest of brevity, the code is simplified to drill down on the practical application of out parameters.

The fourth and final parameter type is called params, which is covered next.

Params Parameters

You might not know it yet, but you've already seen methods that used params parameters plenty of times in this book. Think about how `Console.WriteLine` has been used. You give it a format string and then a variable number of parameters after that. This is nice because it makes `Console.WriteLine` easier to use and more flexible than if you would have been forced to use some other technique, like explicitly passing an array of objects. `Console.WriteLine` has the capability to accept multiple parameters through the use of method overloads and the params parameter. A later section of this chapter discusses method overloads, but now you'll learn about how params parameters work and see how you can implement your own methods that accept a variable number of parameters.

The purpose of a params parameter is to allow you to create methods that will accept a variable number of arguments. As you learned previously, `Console.WriteLine` is a ubiquitous example of the value of params parameters. In this chapter, you saw another method with a params parameter, `string.Split`. When I first introduced `string.Split` in Chapter 5, "Manipulating Strings," you saw how it can accept a `char[]`, but in the previous section of this chapter, you saw the following line of code:

```
string[] latLons = latLonInStr.Split(',');
```

What this demonstrates is that an argument for a params parameter can be either an array or a variable number of parameters. The preceding example was only a single parameter but could have also been a comma-separated list of parameters, the same as with `Console.WriteLine`.

You can also write methods that take a variable number of parameters by using a params parameter. The following example shows a method designed to build a file path from a set of file segments. The file segments are represented via the params parameter:

```
public static string CombinePath(params string[] segments)
{
    var segTmp = new string[segments.Length + 1];

    for (int i = 0; i < segments.Length; i++)
    {
        segTmp[i] = segments[i].Trim().Trim('\\');
    }

    return string.Join("\\", segTmp);
}
```

The params parameter, modified with the params keyword in the preceding code, is actually an array of strings. Often, you see it implemented as an array of object to make it more generic. The Console.WriteLine params parameter overload takes an array of type string and calls ToString on each, which it can because ToString is a virtual method of System.Object. The algorithm builds a valid path from a series of segments, ensuring there is only a single backslash between segments. Here's how calling code uses the method:

```
// params parameters
string fullPath = CombinePath(
    Environment.GetFolderPath(Environment.SpecialFolder.ProgramFiles),
    "Microsoft.NET\\", "\\\\\SDK\\", "v3.5");


Console.WriteLine(fullPath);
```

Environment is a class from the Framework Class Library (FCL) for working with the OS environment. Here, it is using the SpecialFolder enum to get a string path to the c:\Program Files folder. This is a handy way to get paths to many of the OS system folders. The other parameters are simply path segments that should be combined to build the path. You'll occasionally need to extract different parts of a path to dynamically account for where customers desire to place files on their system or to facilitate setup programs that give the user a choice of where they want a program installed. Here's the output:

```
C:\Program Files\Microsoft.NET\SDK\v3.5\
```

Notice that I hacked up the path segments, in the calling code, with varying backslashes, \, to represent situations where input data is often inconsistent. As the CombinePath method iterated through the list of segments, provided via the params parameter, it cleaned up these inconsistencies to provide the preceding clean path.

Overloading Methods

Overloading enables you to define multiple versions of a method with the same method name. Think about the Console.WriteLine method and how you can call it different ways with different arguments. You can call it with any built-in type or with a format string and a list of parameters of any type. This is a convenience given to you through the C# feature of overloading.

OVERLOAD AND OVERRIDE, WHAT'S THE DIFFERENCE?

The terms *overload* and *override* may sound similar, but they are two different concepts. Chapter 9 discusses overrides and how polymorphism works where a base class has a virtual method that can be overridden by a derived class method—so override is for implementing polymorphism. On the other hand, overload is for redefining a single method multiple times so that you can use the same method name, but vary the number and types of parameters.

Objects often have multiple methods that effectively do the same thing, but they can be called with different parameters. In languages without overloading, this results in methods with unique names and parameter lists that effectively do the same thing. Just like `Console.Writeline`, you just want to print output to the console, regardless of what parameters are passed. Without overloading, the alternative for `Console.WriteLine` might be `Console.WriteLineChar`, `Console.WriteLineString`, `Console.WriteLineDecimal`, and so on, or some other naming convention that isn't as comfortable as overloads. The capability to overload simplifies this so much more.

Here's an example of the `ValidateUrl` method. Both method perform the same task, but their parameter types differ:

```
public bool IsValidUrl(string url)
{
    if (!(url.StartsWith(m_http)))
    {
        return false;
    }
    else
    {
        return true;
    }
}

public bool IsValidUrl(Uri url)
{
    if (!(url.Scheme.StartsWith(m_http)))
    {
        return false;
    }
    else
    {
        return true;
    }
}
```

Notice that the name and return type of both methods are exactly the same, which is required for overloads. The only difference is the parameter type. This allows you to call whichever method is more convenient. The following example shows how to call this method with either parameter type:

```
isValid = site.IsValidUrl("http://www.informit.com");


Uri url = new Uri("http://www.informit.com");
isValid = site.IsValidUrl(url);
```

10

The first line calls IsValidUrl with a string argument, and the third line, after instantiating a Uri, passes that URI argument to the IsValidUrl method. C# automatically figures out which version of IsValidUrl to call, based on the parameter type.

You can also overload by the number of parameters. What if calling IsValidUrl and assuming the scheme is HTTP is too limiting? Here's an overload that gives the caller more flexibility by adding another parameter for the scheme to compare:

```
public bool IsValidUrl(Uri url, string scheme)
{
    if (url.Scheme == scheme)
    {
        return true;
    }

    return false;
}
```

Now there are three overloads of IsValidUrl, all differentiated by either the type or number of parameters. You would call the preceding IsValidUrl overload like this:

```
isValid = site.IsValidUrl(url, "https");
```

Again, the C# compiler will figure out that the overload of IsValidUrl to be called will be the one that takes a URI as the first parameter and a string as the second parameter.

The order of arguments must match parameters, too. For example, you couldn't call IsValidUrl with a string as the first parameter and a URI as the second. You would have to create another overload for that, but then you would have to evaluate whether doing so is practical.

SIMULATING OPTIONAL PARAMETERS

C# doesn't have optional parameters. However, you can simulate optional parameters by creating additional overloads. For example, the code in this section shows an overload of IsValidUrl with Uri and string parameters and another overload of IsValidUrl with only a Uri parameter. Because both versions of IsValidUrl are available, the caller has the choice of adding a second string parameter. Although the implementation is technically an overload, it appears that string scheme is an optional parameter.

In addition to overloading methods, you can overload operators such as + and ==. The next section shows how.

Overloading Operators

C# has a feature, called operator overloading, allowing you to use operators, such as +, *, and ==, with your own custom objects. Think about situations where you want to create your own custom type that acts like a built-in type. Perhaps you need a custom complex type, matrix, or vector. The commonality of these types is that it would be convenient to perform mathematical operations on them. Another example of practical operator overloading is when overriding the System.Object.Equals method. You would naturally want consistency in your object by allowing calling code to use the == and != operator, which you would define to have the same meaning as Equals, or opposite as applicable for !=. This section shows a couple examples of how and when to use operator overloading.

Mathematical Operator Overloads for Custom Types

The first example you'll see is a Vector object, which acts like a built-in value type. This is meant to be a mathematical-like vector and has no similarity to Java vector types. This Vector lacks a rigorous implementation but should give you a general idea of how you could go about accomplishing the same thing. Because Vector will be used like a built-in value type, it is defined as a struct. It also has overloaded operators to support mathematical calculations. Here's the Vector struct:

```
struct Vector
{
    private const int m_size = 4;
    private double[] m_vect;

    private void InitVector()
    {
        if (m_vect == null)
            m_vect = new double[m_size];
    }

    public double this[int index]
    {
        get
        {
            InitVector();
            return m_vect[index];
        }
        set
        {
            InitVector();
            if (index < m_size)
                m_vect[index] = value;
        }
```

10

```
    }

    public override string ToString()
    {
        return string.Format(
            "X: {0}, Y: {1}, Z: {2}, Magnitude: {3}",
            m_vect[0], m_vect[1], m_vect[2], m_vect[3]);
    }
}
```

The preceding Vector struct has a backing store that is a four-element array of doubles. It also has an indexer that calls InitVector to make sure the backing store is properly initialized before use. One of the things you might want to do with a Vector is add two of them together. That would be a good reason to overload the addition operator, which is what the following code does:

```
public static Vector operator +(Vector vect1, Vector vect2)
{
    Vector vectSum = new Vector();

    for (int i = 0; i < m_size; i++)
    {
        vectSum[i] = vect1[i] + vect2[i];
    }

    return vectSum;
}
```

The preceding operator overload is a member of the Vector struct. Just like all operator overloads, it is static. The result of applying the operator is Vector, which is like a method return type. The operator being overloaded is identified by the operator keyword, followed by the operator (operator + in this case). Operator overloads have either one or two parameters. A single parameter means it is a unary operator overload, and two parameters mean it is a binary operator. In the preceding addition operator overload, the first parameter holds the argument from the left side of the operator, and the second parameter holds the argument on the right side of the operator. The algorithm simply adds matching indexes of each input Vector and assigns them to the matching index of the result Vector and then returns the result Vector, which is the result of the expression using this operator. Here's code that uses the Vector and its + operator overload:

```
        Vector vect1 = new Vector();
        Vector vect2 = new Vector();

        vect1[0] = vect2[0] = 3;
        vect1[1] = vect2[1] = 5;
        vect1[2] = vect2[2] = 7;
        vect1[3] = vect2[3] = 9;
```

```
Vector vectResult = vect1 + vect2;

Console.WriteLine(vectResult);
```

After instantiating and initializing Vectors, the preceding code adds vect1 and vect2, which calls the operator + overload of the Vector struct. Here's the output:

X: 6, Y: 10, Z: 14, Magnitude: 18

Notice that Console.WriteLine doesn't have any formatting information to indicate the output should appear. To make this happen, I added the following override of System.Object.ToString in Vector:

```
public override string ToString()
{
    return string.Format(
        "X: {0}, Y: {1}, Z: {2}, Magnitude: {3}",
        m_vect[0], m_vect[1], m_vect[2], m_vect[3]);
}
```

What's useful to know about this is that it reinforces the method overload discussion from the previous section. Console.WriteLine clearly doesn't have an overload for Vector because Vector is a custom class, but it does have an overload for an object type parameter. Because Console.WriteLine calls ToString on its parameters, the preceding ToString override in Vector is called, resulting in the formatted output you saw earlier.

Getting back on the subject of operator overloads, another scenario for implementing operator overloads is when overriding System.Object.Equals. The next section shows what logical operators apply for that situation.

Logical Operator Overloads on Custom Types

When overloading operators and adding logical methods to an object, pay particular attention to symmetry and consistency. The example I show here involves overloading the == and != operators. The problem is that calling == on two objects doesn't call object.Equals, which means your object will be inconsistent if someone were to use == or !=, expecting proper value equality. By default, == and != perform reference equality on a custom object. Here's a WebSite class that implements the Equals operator:

```
class WebSite
{
    public string Url { get; set; }
    public override bool Equals(object obj)
    {
        if (obj == null) return false;
        if (obj.GetType() != typeof(WebSite)) return false;
```

10

```
            return Url == Url;
    }
}
```

Chapter 9 shows how to use polymorphism and override object.Equals. Here's code that calls and also uses the == operator:

```
        WebSite site3 = new WebSite();
        WebSite site4 = new WebSite();

        site3.Url = site4.Url = "http://www.informit.com";

        bool equalUrls1 = site3.Equals(site4);
        bool equalUrls2 = site3 == site4;

        Console.WriteLine(
            "site3.Equals(site4): {0}\nsite3 == site4: {1}",
            equalUrls1, equalUrls2);
```

If you set a breakpoint on the Equals method, it will hit on the call to site3.Equals(site4), but not on site3 == site4. Here are the results:

```
site3.Equals(site4): True
site3 == site4: False
```

The preceding result shows that Equals is implementing value equality, but the == operator gives only reference equality, which is false because site3 and site4 refer to separate objects. Because this is logically inconsistent, the WebSite class needs the following operator overloads:

```
        public static bool operator ==(WebSite leftSite, WebSite rightSite)
        {
            return leftSite.Equals(rightSite);
        }

        public static bool operator !=(WebSite leftSite, WebSite rightSite)
        {
            return !leftSite.Equals(rightSite);
        }
```

The implementation of these operators is similar to the + operator overload in the previous section. The result is bool, the first parameter is on the left of the operator, and the second parameter is on the right of the operator. The operator itself is defined by operator == and operator !=. Notice how each operator simply delegates to Equals, resulting in a consistent implementation.

Additional Operator Overload Tips

Not all operators can be overloaded. Also, there are restrictions placed on when certain operators can be overloaded, such as requiring == and != to be defined together. This section discusses additional facts associated with operator overloading.

Overloaded unary operators require an argument of the same type of class or struct they are defined in. The following unary operators can be overloaded:

```
+

-

!

~

++

--

true

false
```

PREFIX AND POSTFIX OPERATOR OVERLOADING

The prefix and postfix (++) and (--) operators can't be overloaded separately. If you overload one, you must overload the other.

When overloading binary operators, one parameter must be of the class or struct in which they are defined. The other parameter can be any type. Here's the list of binary operators that can be overloaded:

```
+

-

*

/

%

&

|

^

<<>>==

!=

><>=

<=
```

10

The following list shows operators that are not overloadable:

```
.
f()
[]
=
&&
¦¦
?:
??
new
sizeof
typeof
as
is
checked
unchecked
->
```

CONDITIONAL OPERATOR OVERLOADING

The conditional logical operators can't be overloaded, but they are evaluated using &
and ¦, which can be overloaded.

Compound operators can't be explicitly overloaded. However, when a binary operator is
overloaded, its corresponding compound operator assumes the same overloaded behavior.
For example, when binary + is overloaded, += is also overloaded.

Such rules maintain the consistency of overloading behavior. In that spirit are other rules
governing operator overloading. Any time the == operator is overloaded, the != operator
must also be overloaded and vice versa. The same holds true for the > and < operators and
for the >= and <= operators.

Conversions and Conversion Operator Overloads

C# is strongly typed and protects you from accidental assignment of one incompatibly
typed variable to another. However, sometimes you want to force a conversion. In addition, there aren't any implicit conversions between custom types and other types, with
the single exception that all types can be converted to the object type. This section

discusses the types of conversions you can make, existing conversions between built-in types, and then shows you how to create conversion operator overloads for custom types.

Implicit Versus Explicit Conversions

C# conversions can be classified as either implicit or explicit. Implicit conversions occur automatically, without special method calls or cast operators. For example, converting an int to a long can occur as a normal assignment operation as follows:

```
int  myInt  = 5;
long myLong = myInt;
```

This conversion occurs without a problem because of two simple principles. First, the long is a 64-bit value and the int is a 32-bit value. The int can fit into the long with no problem. Second, no errors will occur. The semantics of an int value don't change when it's put into a long variable. It still represents the same thing—a whole number.

On the other hand, an explicit conversion is required when the same principles don't lead to a positive result. To be more specific, larger types moving to smaller types or anything that can possibly generate an error require an explicit conversion.

For instance, going in the opposite direction of the previous example, long to int would require an explicit conversion because it's possible for a long value to be larger than what can be represented by an int type. This forces the programmer to make a deliberate decision that could cause corruption of data. Here's an example of converting the long type to the int type:

```
long myLong = 5;
int  myInt  = (int)myLong;
```

The other reason to use an explicit conversion is to cover the possibility of an error or exception being thrown. Looking at a scenario with the simple types, imagine what would happen if one was to attempt putting a negative number into an unsigned type. Sure, the unsigned type may be large enough to accept the value, but the results are likely to be undesirable. It causes an error because the value loses its semantics on conversion. This is why an explicit conversion is required, to force a potentially erroneous conversion to occur. Here's an example of converting a signed value to an unsigned type:

```
int  mySigned = -1;
uint myUnsigned = (uint)mySigned;   // myUnsigned = 4294967295
```

Implicit conversion occurs in expressions, too. During evaluation of expressions of two or more variables, some values are automatically converted to a larger type, and the result is of that larger type. Table 10.1 shows the types that convert automatically in expressions.

10

TABLE 10.1   Automatic Expression Conversions

To	From
Int	sbyte, byte, short, ushort
double	float

A little more freedom to perform implicit conversions is available with constant expressions. For instance, implicit conversion is allowed when assigning an int type to either an sbyte, byte, short, ushort, uint, or ulong. Where, in this case, the constant int type is the source and the other types are the target, implicit conversion is allowed when the value of the source type is within the allowable range of the target type. In addition, a constant long may be converted to type ulong when the constant long is positive.

There are essentially two choices when dealing with the results of automatic promotion conversions. The first is to make sure the value returned by the expression is placed into a field of the type that the expression result is promoted to. Here's an example where an expression using ushort types will be promoted to type int:

```
ushort myShort1 = 3, myShort2 = 5;
int result = myShort1 + myShort2;
```

HANDLING AUTOMATIC PROMOTIONS

Explicit conversion enables the results of an arithmetic expression to be the same type as the expression members. Just use a cast operator to force the conversion of the arithmetic result to the smaller type.

Remember, arithmetic expressions where the integral type is smaller than int produce a result of type int. Similarly, arithmetic expressions where the types are float produce a result of type double.

In the preceding example, a compiler error would have been generated if an attempt were made to place the result of the arithmetic operation into a ushort type field. An alternative is to perform an explicit conversion back to the original types in the expression. Here's an example:

```
ushort myShort1 = 3, myShort2 = 5;
ushort result = (ushort)(myShort1 + myShort2);
```

In the preceding example, the expression myShort1 + myShort2 produces a result of type int. Surrounding the expression in parentheses ensures the addition occurs first. Then the cast operator, (ushort), is applied to the results of the parenthesized expression. Had we omitted the parenthesis, the cast operator would have only applied to myShort1, and the result type would have still been promoted to int. This ensures the entire expression is converted via the cast operator and returned.

Conversions that are normally performed implicitly can also be performed explicitly. Performing an explicit conversion where an implicit conversion is possible does not change the results of the conversion that would have resulted from an implicit conversion alone. It's just allowed.

Various results can be obtained from the explicit conversion of a double to a float type. A double type is rounded when converted to a float. If the double is smaller than what can fit into a float, the resulting value is zero. When the double is larger, the result is positive or negative infinity. An explicit conversion of a double to a float where the value of the double is NaN (Not a Number) results in a float that is also NaN. The following example shows these effects:

```
float myFloat;


double posInfinity =
          9999999999999999999999999999999999999999.0;
myFloat = (float)posInfinity;   // myFloat = Infinity

double negInfinity =
          -9999999999999999999999999999999999999999.0;
myFloat = (float)negInfinity;   // myFloat = -Infinity

double zeroDouble =
          0.00000000000000000000000000000000000000001;
myFloat = (float)zeroDouble;   // myFloat = 0

double myDouble = Double.NaN;
myFloat = (float)myDouble;     // myFloat = NaN
```

This example shows various conditions that result from explicit assignment of double type values to float type variables. The first couple of examples show how positive and negative infinity are produced when the double value is too large to fit into a float type variable. The next example shows how values that are too small result in zero when explicitly converted from a double to a float. The last example shows how an explicit conversion from double, with a value of NaN, to float causes a float value to become NaN.

Conversion of a float or double to a decimal type results in a rounded value up to the twenty-eighth decimal place. Values that are too small result in zero. If the value is too large for the decimal to represent, infinity, or NaN, an OverflowException is thrown. Converting the other way, from decimal to double or float, can result in loss of precision but still won't throw an exception. The following example shows a few results of when float and double types are explicitly converted to the decimal type:

```
decimal myDecimal;


double posInfinity =
          9999999999999999999999999999999999999999.0;
```

10

```
double negInfinity =
            -9999999999999999999999999999999999999999.0;
double tooLarge = 9999999999999999999999999999999.0;
double doubleNaN = Double.NaN;
double zeroDouble =
            0.000000000000000000000000000000000000000000000001;

//myDecimal = (decimal)posInfinity; // OverflowException
//myDecimal = (decimal)negInfinity; // OverflowException
//myDecimal = (decimal)tooLarge;    // OverflowException

myDecimal = (decimal)zeroDouble; // myDecimal = 0
```

The positive and negative `infinity` examples cause an `OverflowException` when an attempt is made to move the value of the double type into the decimal type variable.

Custom Value Type Conversion Operators

Conversions with simple types are easy. It's just a matter of putting a cast operator in front of the variable being converted from. For complex types, the expression syntax is the same. However, there's a lot of work going on behind the scenes to make sure complex type conversions happen properly. This section shows how to implement conversions on structs, complex value types.

A conversion definition can be either implicit or explicit. What is important is that one of the types being converted must be the same type as the enclosing class or struct. The following is the signature for defining a conversion operator:

```
public static convType operator toType(fromType typeName)
{
    // conversion code
}
```

The `public` and `static` modifiers are mandatory and must be included as shown. The `convType` can be either the keyword `implicit` or `explicit`. The `operator` keyword is mandatory. There are two types involved in a conversion, `toType` and `fromType`. One of these is the type of the enclosing class or struct. The other is the type being converted either to or from. The `fromType` is the source type, and the `toType` is the destination or target type. The `typeName` is a user-defined identifier.

Listing 10.1 shows how to define implicit and explicit conversion operators for a struct.

LISTING 10.1   Implicit and Explicit Struct Conversions
_____

```
public struct Currency
{
    private double amount;
```

LISTING 10.1   Continued

```csharp
    public Currency(double amount)
    {
        this.amount = amount;
    }

    public static implicit operator Currency(double dbl)
    {
        return new Currency(dbl);
    }

    public static explicit operator float(Currency curr)
    {
        return (float)curr.Amount;
    }

    public override string ToString()
    {
        return String.Format("{0:C}", amount);
    }

    public static Currency operator+(Currency c1, Currency c2)
    {
        Currency cur = new Currency();
        cur.Amount = c1.Amount + c2.Amount;
        return cur;
    }

    public double Amount
    {
        get
        {
            return amount;
        }
        set
        {
            amount = value;
        }
    }
}
```

Below is another custom type, named Currency. It contains both explicit and implicit conversion operators, along with other members to make it a little more useful.

Before moving on to the conversion operators, I'll give you a quick introduction to the Currency constructor. Chapter 15 discusses constructors in depth, but I have to cheat here a little because the example isn't complete without it. Here's the constructor:

```
public Currency(double amount)
{
    this.amount = amount;
}
```

This is the method that is called when a `Currency` object is instantiated, `new Currency(50.00d)`. Its purpose is to initialize the object. Now, back to conversion operators.

The implicit conversion operator converts double to `Currency`:

```
public static implicit operator Currency(double dbl)
{
    return new Currency(dbl);
}
```

Notice that the conversion operator here is static, which is required, just like operator overloads. The `implicit` keyword is what makes this an implicit conversion, meaning that you don't have to use a cast operator for assignment. The `operator` keyword is required. Following the `operator` keyword is the type being converted to, which is `Currency` in this case. The parameter is the type being converted from.

Before showing how this is called, let's do a quick review of the `explicit` conversion operator, which converts `Currency` to double:

```
public static explicit operator float(Currency curr)
{
    return (float)curr.Amount;
}
```

The syntax for the `explicit` conversion operator here is similar to the `implicit` operator except that it uses the keyword `explicit` in its signature, meaning that a cast operator is required for assignment. Also, the conversion is to float and from `Currency`. Making this an explicit conversion was the right thing to do because the value managed by the `Currency` object is type double and converting that to float could result in loss of data or precision.

Here's a block of code that uses both the preceding implicit and explicit conversions:

```
Currency myCurrency;
double   myDouble;
float    myFloat;

myCurrency = 9.3f;
Console.WriteLine("myCurrency: {0}", myCurrency);

myFloat = (float)myCurrency;
Console.WriteLine("myFloat: {0}", myFloat);
```

```
        myDouble = (double)myCurrency;
        Console.WriteLine("myDouble: {0}", myDouble);
```

And here's the output:

```
myCurrency: $9.30
myFloat: 9.3
myDouble: 9.30000019073486
```

The preceding code performs three conversions. The first conversion implicitly converts a float value, 9.3f, to Currency. Although there is no conversion for float to Currency defined in the Currency struct, this is still possible because the float is implicitly converted to double according to built-in implicit conversion of primitive types. After the float is converted to double, the double is implicitly converted to Currency via the Currency struct's implicit double to Currency conversion operator.

The second conversion shows how to copy a Currency value to a float. The cast to float first invokes the explicit conversion of Currency to double and then an explicit conversion from double to float occurs.

The third example invokes the explicit conversion of the Currency struct directly to convert Currency to double.

Another area of conversion for value types that you need to know about is enums. There's only one allowable implicit enum conversion—to convert the integer value zero (0) to an enum. All other enum conversions are explicit. Here's an example:

```
enum CurrencyType
{
    Dollar, Euro, Franc, Lire, Yen
};

...

CurrencyType myCurrType = 0;   // myCurrType = Dollar
```

In the preceding example, the zero (0) is implicitly converted to the CurrencyType enum. One thing to note with this example is that if CurrencyType.Dollar would have been defined as 1, where Dollar = 1, the assignment preceding statement would have resulted in an error because the 0 would be considered an illegal value.

Custom Reference Type Conversion Operators

Reference type conversions are performed the same as value type conversions. However, one difference between reference types and value types is that reference types can also have conversions between basc and derived types.

10

Conversions from a derived class to a base class are implicit. This comes from the fact that the derived class has an "is a" relationship with the base class. Anything that can be done with a derived class can also be done with its base class.

When converting from a base class to a derived class, an explicit conversion is required. Listing 10.2 shows how class conversion works.

LISTING 10.2   Implicit and Explicit Class Conversions

```
using System;

class BaseClass
{
    int baseField;

    public BaseClass(int bf)
    {
        baseField = bf;
    }
}

class DerivedClass : BaseClass
{
    int derivedField;

    public DerivedClass(int df, int bf) : base(bf)
    {
        derivedField = df;
    }
}

class ClassConversions
{
    static void Main(string[] args)
    {
        BaseClass    bc = new BaseClass(1);
        DerivedClass dc = new DerivedClass(2, 3);

        bc = dc;
        //dc = bc;   // compile time error
        dc = (DerivedClass)bc;
    }
}
```

The Main method of Listing 10.2 performs conversions between a base class instance and a derived class instance. The first statement, converting the derived class instance, dc, to the base class instance, bc, works fine. Derived class-to-base class conversions are always implicit.

The next line is commented out because it generates a compile-time error. There is no implicit conversion from a base class instance to a derived class instance.

The last line uses an explicit conversion to assign the base class instance to the derived class instance. This illustrates why base class to derived class conversions must be explicit. In this case, the base class does not have a derivedField field. During the explicit conversion, the derived class instance receives an object with a baseField field only, which leaves the derived class in a potentially inconsistent state.

Partial Methods

Just as you can divide types into separate files, you can now divide methods between files via a feature known as partial methods. Unlike partial types, there are at most two parts of a partial method: a defining part and an implementing part. The example in this section shows a modified Currency struct that implements partial methods. Here's the Currency partial with the defining partial method:

```
public partial struct Currency
{
    private double amount;

    public double Amount
    {
        get
        {
            return amount;
        }
        set
        {
            amount = value;
            AmountChanged(amount);
        }
    }

    partial void AmountChanged(double amount);
}
```

Partial methods are defined inside of partial types and have the partial modifier. The AmountChanged partial method is defined with a return type of void, which is required. You can define partial methods with multiple parameters of any parameter type, except for out parameter types. Notice that AmountChanged doesn't have an implementation and is defined with a semicolon, ;, suffix, meaning that it is a defining partial.

The Amount property's set accessor calls AmountChanged with the new amount. This doesn't call the preceding partial method, which doesn't have an implementation. Instead, it calls a partial method in a separate partial type, shown here:

```
public partial struct Currency
{
    partial void AmountChanged(double amount)
    {
        Console.WriteLine("Amount is " + amount);
    }
}
```

The preceding code belongs to a partial type in another file. This partial AmountChanged method has an implementation, indicating that it is the implementing partial. It is the code called when the Amount property's set accessor calls AmountChanged.

Here are a few more notes about partial methods:

▶ Partial methods must be members of partial types.

▶ There are only two parts of a partial method: a defining partial and an implementing partial.

▶ A defining partial can be defined without an implementing partial. If there is no implementing partial, C# omits it and calling code from the generated Intermediate Language (IL).

▶ An implementing partial can exist only if there is a defining partial. Otherwise, you'll get a compiler error.

PARTIAL METHOD INTELLISENSE

Partial method implementation parts are easy to code in VS2008. Assuming the defining part exists in another partial type, type **partial** and a space to display the list of partial methods in IntelliSense. Type enough characters to select the partial to implement and press Enter. IntelliSense will construct a method skeleton for you.

Extension Methods

C# 3.0 introduces a new feature that allows you to attach methods to object types, called extension methods. Extension methods are a huge part of Language Integrated Query (LINQ), which is introduced in Chapter 19, "Accessing Data with LINQ." Nevertheless, they are handy outside of LINQ for extending libraries that aren't accessible. The example in this section shows how to write an extension method for the string class, which is sealed and immutable.

As you know, the string class is sealed, effectively eliminating any opportunity to extend it via inheritance. However, now you can use extension methods to add new methods that can be invoked via string instances. The example here is a rewrite of the CombinePath method that you saw in the previous section of this chapter on params parameters, except it is now an extension method:

```
public static class StringExtensions
{
    public static string CombinePath(
        this string path,
        params string[] segments)
    {
        var segTmp = new string[segments.Length + 1];
        segTmp[0] = path.Trim().Trim('\\');

        for (int i = 0; i < segments.Length; i++)
        {
            segTmp[i + 1] = segments[i].Trim().Trim('\\');
        }

        return string.Join("\\", segTmp);
    }
}
```

Two features of the preceding code make CombinePath an extension method: a static class and using this as the first parameter. Extension methods must belong to a static class. In addition, the first parameter of the extension methods must have a this modifier, as in this string path. The type of the first parameter establishes which object type the extension method extends, which is string in for the CombinePath method. The path parameter holds the value of the instance used to call the method. The next example shows that this object would be the progFiles variable.

To use an extension method, you can call it on an instance of the extended type. Here's code that calls CombinePath:

```
string progFiles = Environment.GetFolderPath(
    Environment.SpecialFolder.ProgramFiles);

string fullPath = progFiles.CombinePath(
    "Microsoft.NET\\", "\\\\\SDK\\", "v3.5");

Console.WriteLine(fullPath);
```

The progFiles variable is an instance of type string that refers to the Windows Program Files folder, which is C:\Program Files on the machine this example was run on. Notice that CombinePath is called on the progFiles instance. If you have the extension method namespace declared in a using declaration, the extension methods will display via

IntelliSense for their extended types. For example, if you type **progFiles** (followed by a dot, with no space between), you'll see the CombinePath method in the IntelliSense list. Here's the output:

```
C:\Program Files\Microsoft.NET\SDK\v3.5
```

The contents of the extension method eliminated extraneous backslash characters and added a backslash character when there wasn't one. This provides more functionality than the System.IO.Path.Combine method, which would throw an exception for extra backslash characters. In addition, System.IO.Path.Combine accepts only two path segments, but this method uses a params parameter to handle multiple path segments. So, you're probably wondering why I didn't just extend System.IO.Path. I didn't because System.IO.Path is static, and you can't define extension methods for static classes.

Summary

As you can see, there is a lot to know about C# methods. Besides just calling a method and getting a return value, four parameter types (value, ref, out, and params) affect how an argument can be treated within the method and how it affects the calling code after the method executes.

Related to methods are operator overloads. You saw how to implement overloads for a mathematical operator. Another example showed how to implement a logical operator.

Another operator type is a conversion operator. In addition to learning how to implement both implicit and explicit conversion operators, you saw many rules and tips on how to perform conversions between types.

A couple new features of C# 3.0 are partial methods and extension methods. You saw how partial methods allow you to extend code of partial types. In the discussion about extension methods, you saw how to define methods on types, such as string, that you wouldn't be able to extend by other means.

CHAPTER 11

Error and Exception Handling

IN THIS CHAPTER

▶ Why Exception Handling?

▶ Exception Handler Syntax: The Basic try/catch Block

▶ Ensuring Resource Cleanup with finally Blocks

▶ Handling Exceptions

▶ Designing Your Own Exceptions

▶ checked and unchecked Statements

Every programmer wants to create robust applications without bugs and crashes. The idea and the reality of error-free code can often be quite far apart, especially with constant pressure to build software faster and systems that are increasingly larger and more complex than their predecessors. This chapter addresses these concerns that you, as a C# programmer, must be aware of and address to build the most reliable applications possible.

The subjects of error handling and exception handling are closely related, with subtle differences. There are schools of thought about the intricate differences between the two, where an exception is not necessarily an error. In most practical contexts, however, an exception is raised because of an error condition in your code. I'll not split hairs here because what you need to know is how to properly handle error conditions, and the proper way of doing so in C# is by handling exceptions.

In discussing exception handling, this chapter includes the try/catch block for handling exceptions, the throw clause for throwing your own exceptions, and the finally block, which is essential for proper resource cleanup. We also take a look at predefined exception classes and show how to create your own custom exceptions. Finally, you'll also see how checked and unchecked statements work for managing mathematical overflow errors.

Why Exception Handling?

To get an appreciation for C# exception handling, consider the error-handling methods used in programming languages with no built-in exception-handling mechanism. For example, look at the following C programming language error-handling routine:

```
int someMethod();
...
int result;
result = someMethod();
if (result != 0) {
    // do some error handling
}
```

In this example, there's a prototype of someMethod, showing that it returns an int. Under the prototype is code that would normally be part of a routine. The result variable captures the return value from someMethod. Then the program checks the return to see whether it's nonzero. If so, there must have been an error, and it is handled right there.

This is the way C does error handling and is also the standard way of programming the Win32 API. COM programming has a similar protocol where calling code must check an HRESULT return value to see whether the method call succeeded. The problem with this approach is that every method call must have its own error handler. This problem surfaces in algorithms with several method calls. It clutters the code and makes it more difficult to develop as well as maintain. Another problem occurs when programmers fail or forget to check return values from method calls. This means that an error has occurred but no one knows about it, leading to difficult runtime bugs to fix. C# has exception handling mechanisms that avoid the difficulties with this approach.

Moving away from the old style of error handling, you'll want to use exception handling in C#. The next section begins the journey of learning how to handle exceptions, introducing basic syntax.

Exception Handler Syntax: The Basic try/catch Block

The try/catch block is the primary mechanism of C# exception handling. This permits separation of error handling from the normal flow of an algorithm. Essentially, the algorithm is more understandable because its actions relate primarily toward the goal of a method, rather than with the complex mixture of error handling. Here's the basic syntax of the try/catch block:

```
try
{
    // some algorithm
```

```
}
catch (Exception e)
{
    // exception handling code
}
```

The try portion of the try/catch block holding statements could potentially result in an exception being raised. If an exception is raised, it could be handled in the catch portion of the try/catch block. The catch block is where exceptions are handled. The catch blocks have a filter that defines what type of exception they can handle. A later section of this chapter discusses exception objects, how to handle more than one, and how to choose which exception object type to use.

Listing 11.1 has code that executes within a try block. It will cause an error, the error condition will cause an exception to be raised, and the catch block will handle that exception.

LISTING 11.1   A Simple Exception: Exceptions.cs

```
using System;

public class Exceptions
{
    public static int Main(string[] args)
    {
        byte[] myStream = new byte[3];

        try
        {
            for (byte b=0; b < 10; b++)
            {
                Console.WriteLine("Byte {0}: {1}", b+1, b);
                myStream[b] = b;
            }
        }
        catch (Exception e)
        {
            Console.WriteLine("{0}", e.Message);
        }

        return 0;
    }
}
```

And here's the output:

```
Byte 1: 0
Byte 2: 1
Byte 3: 2
Byte 4: 3
Index was outside the bounds of the array.
```

This example shows a try/catch block in action. Before the try block the program declares a three-element array of bytes named myStream. Within the try block, there is a for loop, set to add 10 bytes to the myStream array. It prints out the byte number and then the value. Then it assigns the byte value to the myStream array.

This works well until the fourth iteration of the for loop. Because the myStream array can hold only 3 bytes, trying to add a fourth is an error. This generates an exception, causing program control to jump into the catch block.

Ensuring Resource Cleanup with `finally` Blocks

When your program raises an exception, the Common Language Runtime (CLR) will unwind the call stack, looking for a handler—a catch block. This occurs immediately, skipping any code that follows the last statement where the exception was raised. This makes sense because the program could be in an unstable state, and you don't want to continue executing code. So, the exception behavior is desirable, but you have a tradeoff where there could have been critical code that must run before the CLR moves control back up the call stack. For example, if the code opens a file, database connection, or network connection requiring signoff, it is imperative that you close these resources. Otherwise, you end up with a resource leak that affects your application, the system resources you have open, and any other applications that require access to those resources. This impacts performance/scalability and can quickly bring a busy system to its knees. In these situations, you need to guarantee that these resources are closed (or disposed) regardless of whether an exception occurs.

This is the purpose of the finally block. You can use the finally block to perform any necessary cleanup chores. The finally block is guaranteed to be executed when leaving a try block, whether the code in the try block executes successfully or an exception is raised.

Listing 11.2 shows how to implement a finally block. It opens a file and ensures that the finally block closes the file.

LISTING 11.2   The **finally** Block: Exceptions2.cs

```
using System;
using System.IO;

public class Exceptions2
{
```

LISTING 11.2   Continued

```csharp
public static int Main(string[] args)
{
    byte[] myStream = new byte[3];
    StreamWriter sw = new StreamWriter("exceptions.txt");

    try
    {
        for (byte b=0; b < 10; b++)
        {
            sw.WriteLine("Byte {0}: {1}", b+1, b);
            myStream[b] = b;
        }
    }
    catch (Exception e)
    {
        Console.WriteLine("{0}", e.Message);
    }
    finally
    {
        sw.WriteLine("Close");
        sw.Close();
    }

    return 0;
}
}
```

In this example, the exception occurred, printing the exception message to the console. Then control transferred to the finally block, which closed the file. If this code had not been in the finally block—that is, after the closing curly brace of the finally block—it would not have been executed after the exception was generated.

The finally block is executed regardless of whether there is an exception. To check this, change the condition in the for loop in the try block to "i < 3" and run the program again. The finally block still executes. This is evident by the word "Close" being written as the last line of the exceptions.txt file.

Handling Exceptions

Although setting up try/catch/finally blocks and catching the generic exception is better than not catching errors at all, there are various methods of handling errors to make code more robust. This section shows how to handle errors in a few of different ways, including handling multiple exception types, handling and passing on exceptions, and recovering from exceptions.

Handling Different Exception Types

Previous examples in this chapter demonstrated how to catch the generic exception, `System.Exception`, but that was for demonstration purposes and isn't appropriate for most situations. In most cases, you'll catch an exception derived from `System.Exception` that is more specific for your needs. You'll even define multiple `catch` blocks for the exception types you want to handle.

This works by placing additional `catch` blocks below the `try` block. Your `catch` blocks should be ordered by specificity of the exception they handle. Failure to do so results in a compiler error. Listing 11.3 has a program with multiple `catch` blocks.

LISTING 11.3   Multiple **catch** Blocks: Exceptions3.cs

```
using System;
using System.IO;

public class Exceptions3
{
    public static int Main(string[] args)
    {
        int mySize = 3;
        byte[] myStream = new byte[mySize];
        int iterations = 5;

        StreamWriter sw = new StreamWriter("exceptions.txt");

        try
        {
            for (byte b=0; b < iterations; b++)
            {
                sw.WriteLine("Byte {0}: {1}", b+1, b);
                myStream[b] = b;
            }
        }
        catch (IndexOutOfRangeException iore)
        {
            Console.WriteLine(
                "Index Out of Range Exception: {0}",
                iore.Message);
        }
        catch (Exception e)
        {
            Console.WriteLine("Exception: {0}", e.Message);
        }
        finally
        {
```

LISTING 11.3   Continued

```
            sw.WriteLine("Close");
            sw.Close();
        }

        return 0;
    }
}
```

The example shows two catch blocks. The catch block with the IndexOutOfRangeException handler is more specific than the catch block with the Exception handler. Therefore, when this program executes, an exception is generated that invokes the catch block for the IndexOutOfRangeException. Had the error been another type of exception, the catch block for the Exception handler would have been executed.

Handling and Passing Exceptions

One method of handling exceptions is to pass the exception to the calling program. This is done using a throw statement. The throw statement raises a new exception, and the CLR unwinds the stack looking for an exception handler, try/catch, in the call chain with a catch block that either matches the thrown exception, or the thrown exception is derived from the catch block exception type. Listing 11.4 shows how to use the throw clause to pass an exception to the calling program. It has code that calls a method. That method explicitly throws an exception, which causes the CLR stack to unwind, looking for a catch block.

LISTING 11.4   Passing Exceptions: Exceptions4.cs

```
using System;
using System.IO;

public class Exceptions4
{
    public static int Main(string[] args)
    {
        Exceptions4 myExceptionMaker = new Exceptions4();

        try
        {
            myExceptionMaker.GenerateException();
        }
        catch (Exception e)
        {
            Console.WriteLine("\nNow processing Main() Exception:");
            while (e != null)
            {
```

LISTING 11.4   Continued

```
                Console.WriteLine("\tInner: {0}", e.Message);
                e = e.InnerException;
            }
        }
        finally
        {
            Console.WriteLine("Finally from Main()");
        }

        return 0;
    }

    void GenerateException()
    {
        int mySize = 3;
        byte[] myStream = new byte[mySize];
        int iterations = 5;
        StreamWriter sw = new StreamWriter("exceptions.txt");

        try
        {
            for (byte b=0; b < iterations; b++)
            {
                sw.WriteLine("Byte {0}: {1}", b+1, b);
                myStream[b] = b;
            }
        }
        catch (IndexOutOfRangeException iore)
        {
            Console.WriteLine(
"\nIndex Out of Range Exception from GenerateException: {0}",
iore.Message);

            throw new Exception(
"Thrown from GenerateException.",
iore);
        }
        catch (Exception e)
        {
            Console.WriteLine(
"\nException from GenerateException: {0}", e.Message);
        }
        finally
        {
            Console.WriteLine("Finally from GenerateException.");
```

LISTING 11.4 Continued

```
        sw.WriteLine("Close");
        sw.Close();
    }
  }
}
```

Here's the code's output:

```
Index Out of Range Exception from GenerateException: An exception of type System
.IndexOutOfRangeException was thrown.
Finally from GenerateException.

Now processing Main() Exception:
        Inner: Thrown from GenerateException.
        Inner: An exception of type System.IndexOutOfRangeException was thrown.
Finally from Main()
```

The Main method instantiates an Exceptions4 object and, within a try block, calls its GenerateException method. In the GenerateException method, within a try block, there is a for loop that causes an IndexOutOfRangeException.

This causes the catch block that handles the IndexOutOfRangeException to be executed. Notice the multiple catch blocks.

UNDERSTANDING CLR STACK UNWINDING

The best way to understand how the CLR unwinds the stack is to see it happening. You can do this by setting a breakpoint on the throw statement in Listing 11.4 and then step through the code. This will make the explanation I provided clearer and illuminate what is happening when an exception is raised.

Within the catch block that handles the IndexOutOfRangeException, there is a throw clause, which throws a new exception. The first argument of this new exception is a unique message that will be the Message property. The second argument is the exception object that causes this catch block to be executed.

This second argument becomes the InnerException of the new exception. InnerExceptions are useful for creating exception chains that show what exceptions have been generated in a program. If an exception is purposely thrown for multiple layers, each time adding the original exception as the InnerException, it could have a long exception chain.

When the exception is thrown, it propagates to the calling program, which is the Main method. Because the GenerateException method was called inside a try/catch block, the thrown exception is caught within Main. This causes control to pass to the catch block in Main. Within that catch block, the Message property of each exception in the exception chain is printed to the console. This is made possible by calling the `InnerException` property of each exception to obtain the next exception in the chain.

The output of this program shows some interesting facts about the sequence of events in exception handling. The first line is from the `Console.WriteLine` method of the `catch` block that handles the `IndexOutOfRangeException` in the `GenerateException` method. Notice that the `finally` block of the `GenerateException` method executes before the `catch` block in the `Main` method. Next, the `catch` block in the `Main` method executes, printing the `Message` property from each exception in the exception chain. The last line shows the `finally` block of the `Main` method executing.

Recovering from Exceptions

Any time the CLR unwinds the stack and doesn't find a handler, the program will crash because of the unhandled exception. This is generally an undesirable occurrence, and often a better solution is to degrade gracefully or recover, if possible. This section shows one way to recover from an exception. Listing 11.5 shows how to recover from an exception, perform corrective measures, and keep on processing.

LISTING 11.5   Recovering from Exceptions: ExceptionTester.cs

```csharp
using System;
using System.IO;

public class ExceptionTester
{
    public static int Main(string[] args)
    {
        ExceptionTester myExceptionMaker =
            new ExceptionTester();

        try
        {
            myExceptionMaker.GenerateException();
        }
        catch (Exception e)
        {
            Console.WriteLine(
                "\nNow processing Main() Exception:");
            while (e != null)
            {
                Console.WriteLine("\tInner: {0}", e.Message);
                e = e.InnerException;
            }
        }
        finally
```

LISTING 11.5   Continued

```
        {
            Console.WriteLine("Finally from Main()");
        }

        return 0;
    }


    void GenerateException()
    {
        int mySize = 3;
        byte[] myStream = new byte[mySize];
        int iterations = 5;

        do
        {
            StreamWriter sw =
                new StreamWriter("exceptions.txt");

            try
            {
                for (byte b=0; b < iterations; b++)
                {
                    sw.WriteLine("Byte {0}: {1}", b+1, b);
                    myStream[b] = b;
                }
                break;
            }
            catch (IndexOutOfRangeException iore)
            {
                Console.WriteLine(
"\nIndex Out of Range Exception from GenerateException: {0}",
iore.Message);
                iterations--;
            }
            catch (Exception e)
            {
                Console.WriteLine(
"\nException from GenerateException: {0}", e.Message);
            }
            finally
            {
                Console.WriteLine(
                    "Finally from GenerateException.");
                sw.WriteLine("Close");
```

LISTING 11.5   Continued

```
            sw.Close();
        }
      } while (true);
    }
}
```

Here's the code's output:

```
Index Out of Range Exception from GenerateException:
➥ Index was outside the bound
s of the array.
Finally from GenerateException.

Index Out of Range Exception from GenerateException:
➥ Index was outside the bound
s of the array.
Finally from GenerateException.
Finally from GenerateException.
Finally from Main()
Press any key to continue . . .
```

Within the try block of the GenerateException method in Listing 11.5, a for loop executes until an exception is raised. This exception is generated because the iterations field is set to 5, but the myStream array size is set to 3.

Within the catch block that handles the IndexOutOfRangeException, the iterations field is decremented. This is an error-correction technique because the program knows that the iterations field controls the number of items placed into the myStream array.

This is what happens after the first exception. The iterations field is decremented from 5 to 4 and continues in a degraded state. The program continues because of the do loop enclosing the try/catch/finally block. The while condition is set to true, causing it to loop until some condition causes the program to break out of the loop.

This causes the logic in the try block to execute again, raise another exception, and decrement the iterations field from 4 to 3. The loop keeps the program from crashing again, and the try block is executed once more, but this time the program is no longer in a degraded state.

The program is in a stable state because the iterations field is set to the size of the array. This causes the for loop to execute successfully. Once this happens, control passes to the break statement following the for loop, which allows program control to pass out of the do loop. The program has fully recovered and can now complete as normal.

The output shows results of the sequence of events just described. The first two lines show the exception generated and the finally block being executed as the result of the iterations field set at 5. The next two lines show the same exception generation and finally block from the iterations field set at 4. After the iterations field is set to 3, the fifth line is created by the finally block of the GenerateException method. Control then passes to the finally block of the Main method, as evidenced by the last output line.

Designing Your Own Exceptions

A program is not limited to the predefined C# exceptions. Its possible to create unique exceptions, tailored to a specific application. This section shows how to design your own exception.

Listing 11.6 shows how to create a new exception and how to use it.

LISTING 11.6   Designing an Exception: NewException.cs

```
using System;
using System.IO;

public class TooManyItemsException : ApplicationException
{
    public TooManyItemsException() : base(@"

**TooManyItemsException**  You added too many items
to this container.  Try specifying a smaller number
or increasing the container size.

")
    {
    }
}

public class ExceptionTester
{
    public static int Main(string[] args)
    {
        ExceptionTester myExceptionMaker = new ExceptionTester();

        try
        {
            myExceptionMaker.GenerateException(5);
        }
        catch (Exception e)
        {
            Console.WriteLine("\nMessage: {0}", e.Message);
        }
        finally
```

LISTING 11.6   Continued

```
        {
            Console.WriteLine("Finally from Main()");
        }

        return 0;
    }

    void GenerateException(int iterations)
    {
        int mySize = 3;
        byte[] myStream = new byte[mySize];
        StreamWriter sw = new StreamWriter("exceptions.txt");

        try
        {
            if (iterations > myStream.Length)
            {
                throw new TooManyItemsException();
            }

            for (byte b=0; b < iterations; b++)
            {
                sw.WriteLine("Byte {0}: {1}", b+1, b);
                myStream[b] = b;
            }
        }
        finally
        {
            Console.WriteLine("Finally from GenerateException.");
            sw.WriteLine("Close");
            sw.Close();
        }
    }
}
```

Here's the code's output:

```
Finally from GenerateException.

Message:

**TooManyItemsException**  You added too many items
to this container.  Try specifying a smaller number
or increasing the container size.

Finally from Main()
```

The first class, TooManyItemsException, is the new exception class. It derives from ApplicationException. During initialization of TooManyItemsException, it would have been nice to set the Message property of Exception. However, that isn't possible because its Message property is read-only. Therefore, the TooManyItemsException class uses base class initialization by calling the base class constructor that accepts a string. This effectively updates the Message property with the desired string. This is how a new exception class can be constructed.

This class is used in the GenerateException method of the ExceptionTester class. The GenerateException method tests the value of the iterations argument that was passed in during invocation in the Main method. If that value is larger than the myStream array's length, the TooManyItemsException is thrown.

Notice that the GenerateException method doesn't have a catch block after its try block. This is permissible and purely a matter of style. In this case, the program uses a try/finally block where the finally block guarantees closing the file resource regardless of whether the exception is thrown.

The Main method catches the exception and prints its Message property. The output is as may be expected. When TooManyItemsException is thrown, the finally block of the GenerateException method executes. The exception prints in the catch block of the Main method. Last, the finally block of the Main method executes.

Now that you know the syntax and a couple strategies for exception handling, the next section introduces one area that might require some exception-handling code: checked and unchecked statements.

checked and unchecked Statements

C# has built-in expressions for checking the overflow context of arithmetic operations and conversions. These are checked and unchecked statements. checked statements watch expressions for evidence of overflow. When overflow occurs, the system raises an exception. Listing 11.7 shows how the checked statement causes an OverflowException to be generated.

LISTING 11.7   **checked** Statements: checked.cs

```
using System;

public class ExceptionTester
{
    public static int Main(string[] args)
    {
        int prior = 250000000;
        int after = 150000000;
        int total;
```

LISTING 11.7   Continued

```
        try
        {
            checked
            {
                total = prior * after;
            }
        }
        catch (OverflowException oe)
        {
            Console.WriteLine("\nOverflow Message: {0}",
                                oe.Message);
        }
        catch (Exception e)
        {
            Console.WriteLine("\nMessage: {0}", e.Message);
        }
        finally
        {
            Console.WriteLine("Finally from Main()");
        }

        return 0;
    }
}
```

In the try block of the Main method, there is a checked statement around an arithmetic equation that causes an overflow. When the overflow occurs, this generates an exception, causing program control to branch to the catch block that handles an OverflowException.

Expressions can also be enclosed in unchecked statements. This allows the overflow to proceed, undetected. There are likely to be occasions when this type of behavior is desired.

Listing 11.8 shows how to use the unchecked statement to prevent overflow exceptions.

LISTING 11.8   **unchecked** Statements: unchecked.cs

```
using System;

public class ExceptionTester
{
    public static int Main(string[] args)
    {

        try
```

LISTING 11.8   Continued

```
        {
            unchecked
            {
                int absShortMask = (int)0xFFFF0000;
            }
        }
        catch (OverflowException oe)
        {
            Console.WriteLine("\nOverflow Message: {0}", oe.Message);
        }
        catch (Exception e)
        {
            Console.WriteLine("\nMessage: {0}", e.Message);
        }
        finally
        {
            Console.WriteLine("\nFinally from Main()");
        }

        return 0;
    }
}
```

In the `try` block of the `Main()` method, there is an unchecked statement containing an arithmetic operation that causes an overflow condition. Because it is unchecked, no exceptions are generated, and the program proceeds as normal.

In the preceding example, it was useful to assign the bit pattern to the absShortMask variable. Subsequent possible operations could have been to get the absolute value of a short expression, implicitly cast to an integer, by using a bitwise exclusive or operation.

A program is always running in a checked or an unchecked state. During runtime, the checking context for nonconstant expressions is determined by the environment in which your program is running. The default for the C# compiler in the Microsoft .NET Framework SDK is unchecked. Constant expressions are always in a checked context. Here's an example:

```
Total = 25000000 * 15000000;    // compiler error
```

To turn checked and unchecked on or off for an entire program, C# has a checked/ unchecked compiler switch. Here's an example of turning on the checked context:

```
csc /checked+ myprogram.cs
```

To compile code in an unchecked context, you use a hyphen (-) with the checked switch:

```
csc /checked- myprogram.cs
```

To set checked/unchecked mode in VS2008, you can right-click on the project in Solution Explorer, select properties, select the Build tab, scroll down the page, and click on the Advanced button, and then set Check for arithmetic overflow/underflow.

Summary

This chapter presented C# exceptions and exception handling. The first section introduced `try`/`catch` blocks. It showed how to use `try`/`catch` blocks to wrap up code where a possible exception may occur and to handle the exception when it occurs.

A section on the `finally` block explained how to make sure certain operations are always carried out, regardless of whether an exception occurs. The example showed how to release a system resource when an exception occurs.

Sometimes the predefined exceptions won't meet a program's requirements. This chapter showed how to create a new exception that met the unique requirements of a sample program. It also showed how to determine which predefined exception to inherit and how to throw an exception.

Finally, this chapter covered the `checked` and `unchecked` statements. It showed how to control overflow exception checking for arithmetic operations and conversions. It also explained a situation where generating an overflow condition may be desirable and how to achieve that goal without generating an exception.

CHAPTER 12

Event-Based Programming with Delegates and Events

There are many magazines on the market, covering any topic popular enough to sell. The people who create the magazines are called publishers. They advertise and figure out how to let you know that their magazine exists. If you're interested, you can buy the magazine from a store. Whenever people like a magazine, they also subscribe to it so that they can get the latest issue, usually monthly, whenever it's available. This is a typical publish/subscribe model.

A lot of software uses the publish/subscribe model, too. You have an application that publishes items and other code, observers, that subscribes to those items. Whenever the publisher wants to let the observers know that a new item is available, it goes through its list of observers, those that have subscribed, and notifies them of a new item. This publish/subscribe model is what powers the event-based programming paradigm.

The event-based programming paradigm has been with us for years, especially for GUI programmers. You click a button on a form and then program the code that reacts to that button click. Of course, events aren't limited to GUI programming. You have many situations where one piece of code is interested in an event in another piece of code, which is much more efficient than polling.

This chapter shows how to use the C# features of delegates and events to perform event-based programming. In other languages and platforms, event handling is relatively simple because you just code a method that is magically hooked up to a GUI event. In C#, however, all the plumbing that make the magic happen is now brought to the surface for you to deal with. You must explicitly hook up and remove event handlers. Having to deal with event-based plumbing is certainly different, but more powerful, and now delivers control that you never had before. Whereas it's like pulling teeth to get a magazine publisher to cancel your subscription, it is relatively simple to unsubscribe from an event in C#. This event plumbing code is embodied in a C# language feature called delegates.

Related to delegates are events, a first-class object member that directly supports event-based programming. When you understand how delegates work, bridging the gap to events is a quick step.

Exposing Delegates

A C# delegate is a type-safe method reference. With delegates, a program can dynamically call different methods at runtime. The primary purpose of delegates is to establish an infrastructure to support events. This section shows how to create and use delegates and builds a bridge to your understanding of events.

Defining Delegates

A delegate is a reference type object that defines the signature and return type of a method. Delegate instances are used to refer to methods. Any method that a delegate instance refers to must conform to the signature of the delegate. After a method has been assigned to a delegate, it is called when the delegate is invoked.

Here's how a delegate signature is defined. The specification shows the syntax of creating a delegate:

```
[modifiers] delegate <return type> <delegate name>([parameter list]);
```

Modifiers and parameters are optional. The keyword, `delegate`, states that this is a custom delegate type declaration, just like you would declare custom class or struct types. Of course, the delegate has a type name, which is `delegate name`, so you can declare variables or create instances of the delegate type. The `delegate` keyword and `delegate name` are the only similarities between delegate and class or struct declarations. The rest of the delegate declaration defines the signature of a method that the delegate can refer to. More specifically, the delegate declaration has a return type and parameter list, and any method that a delegate instance of this type refers to must have an identical return type and parameter list.

The following example shows how to declare a delegate:

```
public delegate decimal Calculation(decimal val1, decimal val2);
```

It has `public` accessibility, returns a `decimal`, and accepts two `decimal` parameters. Its type name is `Calculation`. Because a delegate is a type, you declare it at the namespace level, just like class and struct types. If you declare it inside of a class or struct, it will not do any good because it's typical usage is to enable one object to notify another of changes and, both objects need access to the delegate type declaration. You'll see how this works in a little bit, but first you need to see more mechanics to understand what the parts are. Here's how to declare a variable of the delegate type in your code:

```
public Calculation MyCalc;
```

The `MyCalc` variable is a field inside of a class. Delegate variables can also be local variables if you have a reason for doing so—for example, to limit the lifetime within the scope of a method. It's type is `Calculation`, meaning that it can refer to and call methods conforming to the signature defined by the `Calculation` delegate type. The next section describes how to define a method that `myCalc` can refer to.

> ### FOR C++ PROGRAMMERS
>
> Delegates are similar to function pointers in C++, except that they are type safe, object oriented, and secure. C# allows delegates to refer to both instance and static methods.

Creating Delegate Method Handlers

To use a delegate, there must be a delegate method handler. This is a method that adheres to the delegate signature, which includes return type and parameters. The handler method implements some functionality to be executed when the delegate referring to it is invoked. The parameter list must be the same as the delegate type, and it must return the same type. Here's an example that conforms to the signature and return type requirements of a delegate:

```
public decimal Add(decimal add1, decimal add2)
{
    return add1 + add2;
}
```

This example accepts two decimal parameters, operates on them, and returns a decimal value. It conforms to the `Calculation` delegate type signature and is ready to be used as a delegate method handler.

Hooking Up Delegates and Handlers

For a delegate method handler to be invoked, it must be assigned to a delegate object variable. The following example assigns the `Add` method to the `MyCalc` delegate by creating a new instance of the `DelegateExample` delegate type and including the `Add` method handler in the parameter list:

```
DelegateExample del = new DelegateExample();
del.MyCalc = new Calculation(del.Add);
```

The preceding code makes `MyCalc` refer to the `Add` method. The `DelegateExample` class is the containing object for the `Add` method. It also contains the `MyCalc` field, of delegate type `Calculation`. Calling `new Calculation` creates a new instance of the `Calculation` delegate type, assigning the reference to that instance to the `MyCalc` field. Notice the parameter to `new Calculation`—it defines which method that `MyCalc` will refer to.

This is why the `Add` method must conform to the signature of the `Calculation` delegate type. It allows the type-safe assignment of a method to a variable of the delegate type.

Invoking Methods Through Delegates

A delegate method handler is invoked by making a method call on the delegate itself. Another way to look at this is that when invoked, the delegate calls the method it refers to. The next example shows a delegate being called as if it were a method:

```
decimal result = del.MyCalc(5.35m, 9.71m); // result = 15.06m
```

What's happening behind the scenes is that the `Add` method is being called with the `MyCalc` delegate's arguments.

The ability to refer to and invoke a method is powerful because now you can pass the method reference (delegate instance) to other parts of a program that can invoke your method. For example, a Windows Forms button is generic, by necessity, and you have to tell it what to do when clicked. So, you can take a delegate that refers to your method and give it to the button to call when clicked.

This example shows only a single method being referred to. However, another feature of delegates is that they can hold multiple method reference at the same time. They are called multicast delegates, discussed next.

Multicasting with Delegates

A multicast delegate is a single delegate made up of two or more other delegates. It's created by adding one delegate to another with the combine, `+=`, operator. Similarly, individual delegates may be removed from a multicast delegate by using the remove (`-=`) operator.

MULTICAST DELEGATE RETURN TYPES

Double-check method return types to make sure they are `void` before assigning them to a multicast delegate.

Multicast delegates can't have any `out` parameters in their parameter lists. When the multicast delegate is invoked, each individual delegate that has been added is invoked in the order in which it was added. Listing 12.1 shows how to implement multicast delegates.

LISTING 12.1   Creating a Socket Server: MultiCast.cs

```csharp
using System;

public delegate void Calculation(decimal val1,
                                 decimal val2,
                                 ref decimal result);

public class MultiCastDelegateExample
{
    Calculation MyCalc1;
    Calculation MyCalc2;

    public void Add(decimal add1, decimal add2, ref decimal result)
    {
        result = add1 + add2;
        Console.WriteLine("add({0}, {1}) = {2}",
                          add1, add2, result);
        return;
    }

    public void Sub(decimal sub1, decimal sub2, ref decimal result)
    {
        result = sub1 - sub2;
        Console.WriteLine("sub({0}, {1}) = {2}",
                          sub1, sub2, result);
        return;
    }

    public decimal Add(decimal[] addList)
    {
        decimal total = 0;

        foreach( decimal number in addList )
        {
            total += number;
        }

        return total;
    }

    public static int Main(string[] args)
    {
        decimal result = 0.0m;
        MultiCastDelegateExample del = new MultiCastDelegateExample();
```

LISTING 12.1   Continued

```
        del.MyCalc2 = new Calculation(del.Sub);

        del.MyCalc1(5.35m, 9.71m, ref result);
        del.MyCalc2(8.39m, 1.75m, ref result);

        Console.WriteLine();

        Calculation MultiCalc = del.MyCalc1;
        MultiCalc += del.MyCalc2;

        MultiCalc(7.43m, 5.19m, ref result);

        Console.WriteLine();
        Console.WriteLine("MultiCalc(7.43m, 5.19m) = {0}",
                            result);

        Console.ReadKey();
        return 0;
    }
}
```

And here's the output:

```
add(5.35, 9.71) = 15.06
sub(8.39, 1.75) = 6.64

add(7.43, 5.19) = 12.62
sub(7.43, 5.19) = 2.24


MultiCalc(7.43m, 5.19m) = 2.24
```

In Listing 12.1, the delegate to be used is the Calculation delegate. Within the DelegateExample class, a couple Calculation delegate fields are used to create a multicast delegate. In addition, a couple of methods, Add and Sub, conform to the Calculation delegate signature and return type. They are used as delegate method handlers.

After initializing the result field and creating a new instance of the DelegateExample class in the Main method, the two Calculation delegate fields, MyCalc1 and MyCalc2, are instantiated. MyCalc1 holds the Add delegate method handler, and MyCalc2 holds the Sub delegate method handler. These two delegates are invoked, resulting in the first two lines of output.

Next, the multicast Calculation delegate, MultiCalc is created. This occurs by first making MultiCalc equal MyCalc1. Then MyCalc2 is added with the compound addition operator. This also could have been written as follows:

```
Calculation MultiCalc = del.MyCalc1 + del.MyCalc2;
```

The third and fourth lines of the output show invocation of the multicast delegate MultiCalc. Each delegate is invoked in the order it was added. They both operate with the same input values. Remember the ref decimal result parameter? This was to avoid the limitation of not having an out parameter. The last line of output shows what this parameter is after the multicast delegate is invoked. It is the value of the last delegate in the multicast delegate to be invoked. It normally doesn't make sense to return values from individual handlers of a multicast delegate, because each method's output can't be used anyway. However, the ref parameter is available if you can find a practical reason for needing the output of the last delegate of a multicast delegate.

Checking Delegate Equality

Sometimes an application may have a need to evaluate the equality of single or multicast delegates. A possible application for this in single delegates might be to make sure that a certain method is only invoked one time. Such an ambiguous situation could evolve as a result of multiple delegates being dynamically instantiated at different times or places in a program.

Another potential application of equality checking on delegates could arise with multicast delegates. The individual delegates of a multicast delegate are placed and invoked in a specific sequence. If an application has to rely on the sequence of individual delegates in a multicast delegate being different, the equality or inequality operator is handy.

If two delegates reference the same method or one delegate references the other, the equal operator returns true. When two delegates contain separate functions, the equal operator evaluates to false, as shown in the following example:

```
bool equal = del.MyCalc1 == del.MyCalc2; // equal is false
```

Assume del.MyCalc1 and del.MyCalc2 are from the example in the previous section on multicast delegates. Each delegate has different delegate method handlers. Therefore, this equation assigns the Boolean value false to the equal field. If the not equal (!=) operator had been used instead, it would have returned true.

For two multicast delegates to be considered equal, they must have the same number of delegates. In addition, delegates in corresponding positions of each multicast delegate must be equal. For example, assume MyCalc1 and MyCalc2 are multicast delegates. If the sequence of delegates added to MyCalc1 is Add + Sub + Add, the same sequence, Add + Sub + Add, must also be added to MyCalc2. However, if instead the sequence of Add + Add + Add were added to MyCalc2, MyCalc1 and MyCalc2 would not be equal because the second delegate in each sequence is not equal. Similar to single delegates, the not equal (!=) operator is opposite of equal.

This section described the basic syntax of delegates, but as C# matured, new features were added. The next section describes these new features before moving on to where delegates are used the most, to support events.

Implementing Delegate Inference

The C# language designers recognized that delegates are a little harder to work with than they need to be. One area of improvement they added in C# 2.0 was an easier way to assign method handlers to delegate instances, using delegate inference. If you recall from previous discussions, we needed to hook up the Add method with a Calculation delegate variable like this:

```
del.MyCalc = new Calculation(del.Add);
```

Here's how that can be simplified with delegate inference:

```
del.MyCalc = del.Add;
```

Because C# already knows that MyCalc is a Calculation delegate type, you don't need to instantiate the delegate yourself. The C# compiler will figure this out and do the instantiation for you in Intermediate Language (IL).

Another C# 2.0 feature that makes it easier to work with delegates is anonymous methods, discussed next.

Assigning Anonymous Methods

When you think about all the moving parts of getting delegates to work—delegate type definition, delegate instance, handler method, and code to hook up the handler with the delegate variable—it's a lot of work. If the handler method is reusable beyond the delegate, this model is useful. However, a lot of the time a handler method exists only for the purpose of executing when the delegate is invoked and isn't used anywhere else. Therefore, we shouldn't need a named method in a lot of cases. This is where anonymous methods help. They don't have a name, thus the term anonymous, and are attached directly to a delegate variable. Here's an example that replaces the Add method shown earlier:

```
MultiCastDelegateExample del = new MultiCastDelegateExample();


del.MyCalc = delegate(decimal add1, decimal add2)
{
    return add1 + add2;
};
```

Notice the delegate keyword in the preceding example, which signifies that this is an anonymous method. It has a parameter list, just like the Add method did, and the body of the method is enclosed in curly braces. The preceding code would be placed inside of a method, meaning that you have a method definition inside of a method.

If you don't have parameters, you can optionally use a set of empty parentheses or no parentheses at all. In addition, even if the delegate variable the anonymous method is assigned to has parameters, you don't need to specify the parameters in the anonymous method at all. Here's an example:

```
MultiCastDelegateExample del = new MultiCastDelegateExample();
```

```
del.MyCalc = delegate { return 0; };
```

The preceding example doesn't make much sense in the context of trying to perform a calculation on two input parameters. However, it's good to know if you ever find yourself in a situation where it might prove useful. It's more common for delegates with no parameters.

In addition to operating on parameters, anonymous methods can use local variables and fields. Any local variable or field used by an anonymous method is said to be captured. Here's an example:

```
        static decimal capturedVar1 = 3.19m;


        static void Main()
        {
            var capturedVar2 = 9.71m;

            MultiCastDelegateExample del = new MultiCastDelegateExample();

            del.MyCalc = delegate { return capturedVar1 + capturedVar2; };

            decimal result = del.MyCalc(5.35m, 9.71m);
        }
```

The anonymous method here uses capturedVar1, a field, and capturedVar2, a local variable. Notice also that the call to del.MyCalc(5.35m, 9.71m) doesn't use the parameters supplied, which doesn't make much sense, but is allowed—possibly a hidden gotcha.

CAPTURING AND OBJECT LIFETIME

Whenever an anonymous method captures a local variable or field, it holds a reference to it. This could be tricky because you already know that local variables normally go out of scope when a method ends. Of less impact might be a field, but holding a field reference is of concern, too. The danger in this assumption lies in the fact that the anonymous method doesn't let go of the variable reference until it is either removed from its delegate or the delegate it is assigned to has no more references.

As will be discussed in Chapter 15, "Managing Object Lifetime," the Common Language Runtime (CLR) garbage collector won't clean up an object until it no longer has references. Therefore, you need to be aware of any special behavior associated with a captured object to ensure you don't encounter subtle bugs.

LAMBDA EXPRESSIONS AND DELEGATES

C# 3.0 introduced a new language feature called lambda expressions. Although lambda expressions are assigned to delegates, just like anonymous methods, they also have special features that support Language Integrated Query (LINQ) and more. Chapter 18, "Using Lambdas and Expression Trees," provides extensive coverage of lambda expressions, and you can learn more about LINQ beginning in Chapter 19, "Accessing Data with LINQ."

You need to understand the syntax of delegates to understand how they work, which is what this and previous sections help you with. Although there are several cases where you use raw delegates to get the job done, the majority of all delegate work will be with supporting events, which you'll learn about in the next section.

Coding Events

An event is a delegate with special features in the areas of type membership, limitations on invocation, and assignment. By having events as first-class type members, along with fields, methods, and properties, C# becomes a more component-oriented language. This means that other objects can listen for changes in your object and receive notifications via event invocations.

Events offer additional protections that you don't have with raw delegates, one being that the event can be invoked only inside of its containing type. Another protection is preventing direct assignment to the event. Because of these protections, events are preferred over delegates for holding delegate instances and invoking delegates.

The following section shows you how to use events and explains these protections in depth. Different parts of the same application appear in Listing 12.2 through Listing 12.7.

Defining Event Handlers

Events are commonly used in GUIs for things such as button clicks and menu selections. In those cases, the event is already defined, and all that needs to be done is to register with the event. However, events can be defined and used anywhere for GUI or non-GUI purposes. Here are the elements that make up an event:

```
[modifiers] event type name;
```

This line shows optional modifiers, the same as methods, followed by the keyword, event. Next is the type. Because all events are based on delegates, the type must be a delegate type. Following the type is the name of the event. Listing 12.2 shows how to declare an event.

LISTING 12.2   Event Declaration: MenuItem.cs

```
using System;

public delegate void MenuHandler();

public class MenuItem
{
    public event MenuHandler MenuSelection;

    string text;

    public MenuItem(string text)
    {
        this.text = text;
    }

    public void Fire()
    {
        MenuSelection();
    }

    public string Text
    {
        get
        {
            return text;
        }
        set
        {
            text = value;
        }
    }
}
```

The MenuItem class defines an event named MenuSelection. The delegate type of this event is MenuHandler. The MenuHandler delegate is defined just before the MenuItem class declaration.

The next section uses the MenuHandler delegate to hook a method up with the MenuSelection event.

Registering for Events

Programs that want to be notified of when an event occurs register their interest with the event provider. In the preceding section, the MenuItem class was an event provider. Its event is public, and it can also be considered an event publisher. Programs that register can be considered subscribers. This is often referred to as the publisher/subscriber pattern. Listing 12.3 shows how to wire up subscribers to publishers. It uses delegates to connect methods to events.

LISTING 12.3   Event Method Handlers: DelegatesAndEvents.cs

```
using System;

public class DelegatesAndEvents
{
    public static int Main(string[] args)
    {
        // create main menu
        Menu myMenu = new Menu("Financial Sites");

        // create data object
        SiteManager sm = new SiteManager();

        // create menu items
        MenuItem addMenu = new MenuItem("Add");
        MenuItem delMenu = new MenuItem("Delete");
        MenuItem modMenu = new MenuItem("Modify");
        MenuItem seeMenu = new MenuItem("View");

        // add events
        addMenu.MenuSelection += new MenuHandler(sm.AddSite);
        delMenu.MenuSelection += new MenuHandler(sm.DeleteSite);
        modMenu.MenuSelection += new MenuHandler(sm.ModifySite);
        seeMenu.MenuSelection += new MenuHandler(sm.ViewSites);

        // populate menu with menu items
        myMenu.Add(addMenu);
        myMenu.Add(delMenu);
        myMenu.Add(modMenu);
        myMenu.Add(seeMenu);

    // invoke menu for user input
        myMenu.Run();

        return 0;
    }
}
```

Listing 12.3 contains four components: `DelegatesAndEvents`, `Menu`, `MenuItem`, and `SiteManager`. The `DelegatesAndEvents` class is the main component. It sets up the other three components—a `Menu` component, `myMenu`, which takes care of user interface and user interaction; a `SiteManager` component, `sm`, that performs all the data manipulation for the program; and the `MenuItem` components, which represent choices that could be made with a program.

After each object has been created, the program begins connecting them. Because the `SiteManager` class contains the data manipulation, its methods are associated with `MenuItem` objects by assigning the `SiteManager` method to a new `MenuHandler` delegate. In the same call, the `MenuHandler` delegate is assigned to the `MenuSelection` of its corresponding `MenuItem`. For example, the first event registration takes the `AddSites` method from the `sm` object, assigns it to a new `MenuHandler` delegate, and then adds that delegate to the `addMenu` `MenuItem`.

Attaching to an event is performed through the event combine operator (+=). Similarly, the remove event operator (-=) is used to detach a subscriber from an event. Detachment prevents any subsequent notifications from the publisher object.

Each of these `MenuItem`s is then added to the `myMenu` `Menu` object. Now the program has a `Menu` object with `MenuItem`s, and each `MenuItem` has an associated method from `SiteManager`. To get the `Menu` to show on the screen and begin user interaction, the `Run` method of the `myMenu` object is invoked. This ends the `DelegatesAndEvents` class role because when the `Run` method of the `Menu` class completes, it returns to the `Main` method, and the program ends immediately.

So far, you've seen how to create events as type members and how to add methods to them via delegates. The next section shows the methods themselves.

Implementing Events

The methods to implement an event must conform to the signature and return type of the event's delegate type. This way they can be assigned to the delegate before being added to the event. Listing 12.4 shows a class with event method implementations.

LISTING 12.4   Event Method Handlers: SiteManager.cs

```
using System;

public class SiteManager
{
    SiteList sites = new SiteList();

    public SiteManager()
    {
        this.sites = new SiteList();
```

LISTING 12.4   Continued

```
            this.sites[this.sites.NextIndex]
                = new WebSite("Joe",
                              "http://www.mysite.com",
                              "Great Site!");
            this.sites[this.sites.NextIndex]
                = new WebSite("Don",
                              "http://www.dondotnet.com",
                              "okay.");
            this.sites[this.sites.NextIndex]
                = new WebSite("Bob",
                              "www.bob.com",
                              "No http://");
        }


        public void AddSite()
        {
            string siteName;
            string url;
            string description;

            Console.Write("Please Enter Site Name: ");
            siteName = Console.ReadLine();

            Console.Write("Please Enter URL: ");
            url = Console.ReadLine();

            Console.Write("Please Enter Description: ");
            description = Console.ReadLine();

            sites[sites.NextIndex] = new WebSite(siteName,
                                                 url,
                                                 description);
        }


        public void DeleteSite()
        {
            string choice;

            do
            {
                Console.WriteLine("\nDeletion Menu\n");
                DisplayShortList();

                Console.Write("\nPlease select an item to delete:  ");
                choice = Console.ReadLine();
```

LISTING 12.4   Continued

```
                if (choice == "Q" |¦ choice == "q")
                    break;

                if (Int32.Parse(choice) <= sites.NextIndex)
                    sites.Remove(Int32.Parse(choice)-1);

        } while (true);
    }

    public void ModifySite()
    {
        Console.WriteLine("Modifying Sites.");
    }

    public void ViewSites()
    {
        Console.WriteLine("");

        for (int i=0; i < sites.NextIndex; i++)
        {
            Console.WriteLine("Site: {0}", sites[i].ToString());
        }

        Console.WriteLine("");
    }

    private void DisplayShortList()
    {
        for (int i-0; i < sites.NextIndex; i++)
        {
            Console.WriteLine("{0} - {1}", i+1, sites[i].ToString());
        }

        Console.WriteLine("Q - Quit (Back To Main Menu)");
    }
}
```

These methods conform to the signature and return type of the MenuHandler delegate. They don't have parameters and return void, just as the MenuHandler delegate.

Firing Events

When events are invoked, they are also said to be fired. Events are fired from within the class that defines them. Outside of their class, they can be used only on the left side of a combine or remove operation. Listing 12.5 shows how to invoke, or fire, an event.

LISTING 12.5   Firing Events: Menu.cs

```csharp
using System;
using System.Collections.Generic;

public class Menu
{
    List<MenuItem> menuItems = new List<MenuItem>();
    string title;

    public Menu(string title)
    {
        this.title = title;
    }

    public void Add(MenuItem menu)
    {
        menuItems.Add(menu);
    }

    public void Run()
    {
        string choice;

        do
        {
            Console.WriteLine("{0}\n", title);

            foreach(MenuItem menu in menuItems)
            {
                Console.WriteLine("{0} - {1}", menuItems.IndexOf(menu), menu.Text);
            }

            Console.WriteLine("Q - Quit");
            Console.Write("\nPlease Choose:   ");
            choice = Console.ReadLine();

            if (choice.ToUpper() != "Q")
            {
                menuItems[int.Parse(choice)].Fire();
            }

        } while (choice != "Q");
    }
}
```

This example has an array of `MenuItem` objects, a constructor that initializes its title string, an `Add` method, and a `Run` method. The `Add` method adds a new `MenuItem` object to the `menuItems` list. The `Run` method has a do loop that displays a menu, accepts user input, and fires the event corresponding to a user's selection.

The first task of the do loop in the `Run` method is to print the menu title and then each menu item to the console. Each menu item is printed in a `foreach` loop that takes the `Text` property of each `MenuItem` object in the `menuItems` List. Each menu item is associated with its numeric position in the list.

Then the program waits for input from the user. When a menu item is selected, the program uses the input number to index into the `menuItems` list by using the `Parse` method of the int type. The `menuItems` list returns a reference to the `MenuItem` object matching what the user selected.

By using the dot operator, the `Fire` method of the new `MenuItem` object is invoked. This is the same `Fire` method that was shown in the "Defining Event Handlers" section earlier in this chapter. Here it is again for reference:

```
public void Fire()
{
    MenuSelection();
}
```

This example shows how to invoke an event. It must be a member of the class where the event is defined, because events can't be invoked directly. The `Fire` method calls the `MenuSelection` event as if it were another method. Recall that a method was assigned to this event in the `Main` method of the `DelegatesAndEvents` class. It is that method, assigned in the `Main` method, which is invoked.

This section demonstrated one of the protections that events have over delegates. The `MenuSelection` event invocation had to be inside of the same class that `MenuSelection` is defined in. If code from outside the class wants to cause the method to fire, it can call a method like `Fire`. The benefits of this in the area of encapsulation are huge. What if you need to perform some business logic at the time the method fires? By encapsulating this, you can do so as is required.

To see the benefit of this even clearer, think about what would happen if you create a public field of some delegate type. Objects outside of yours could invoke the delegate any time they want. If, in the future, you needed to ensure some type of record keeping or internal logic, changes would be difficult because external code is already relying on that delegate to be there and has no responsibility to do anything else to ensure the internal logic of your class. In the case where all the code belongs to you, it could potentially be a lot of work to change, causing that classic rippling effect throughout your code base that the lack of proper encapsulation is so famous for. In the case of your code being a reusable library for projects beyond your own, the battle will have been lost. That's why the fact that events force encapsulation protects you and is good for your code.

Modifying Event Add/Remove Methods

Adding and removing callback methods to and from events, respectively, is configurable. This technique is most appropriate when you have a large number of events, but only a few are hooked up at a time. This is accomplished by including add and remove accessors with an event declaration. Listing 12.6 is a modification of the `MenuItem` class from a previous example in this chapter.

LISTING 12.6   Event Accessors: MenuItem.cs

```
using System;

public delegate void MenuHandler(object sender, EventArgs e);

public class MenuItem
{
    int    numberOfEvents;
    string text;

    private MenuHandler mh = null;

    public event MenuHandler MenuSelection
    {
        add
        {
            mh += value;
            numberOfEvents++;
        }
        remove
        {
            mh -= value;
            numberOfEvents—;
        }
    }

    public MenuItem(string text)
    {
        this.text = text;
        numberOfEvents = 0;
    }

    public void Fire()
    {
        OnMenuSelection();
    }
```

LISTING 12.6   Continued

```
    protected void OnMenuSelection()
    {
        if (mh != null)
        {
            mh(this, null);
        }
    }

    public string Text
    {
        get
        {
            return text;
        }
        set
        {
            text = value;
        }
    }

    public int NumberOfEvents
    {
        get
        {
            return numberOfEvents;
        }
    }
}
```

The MenuSelection event of Listing 12.6 is different from events in previous listings. It has two accessors, add and remove. The add accessor adds the method, indicated by the value keyword, to the event, and then increments the numberOfEvents field. The remove accessor removes the method, indicated by the value keyword, from the event, and then decrements the numberOfEvents field. This modification could be useful if it were necessary to know how many subscribers there were to an event. To support this, the read-only property NumberOfEvents was added to the class.

Events can be treated much like indexers and properties in using the abstract, overrides, static, and virtual modifiers. Using the overrides modifier, the accessors of an event in a derived class may specialize the implementation of abstract and virtual base class events.

The SiteManager class in Listing 12.4 depends on the WebSite and SiteList classes in Listing 12.7. Therefore, Listing 12.7 is presented for completeness.

LISTING 12.7   The Rest of the Program: WebSites.cs

```csharp
using System;
using System.Collections;

/// <summary>
///     Describes a single website.
/// </summary>
public class WebSite
{
    const string http = "http://";
    public static readonly string currentDate
        = new DateTime().ToString();

    string siteName;
    string url;
    string description;

    public WebSite()
        : this("No Site", "no.url", "No Description") {}

    public WebSite(string newSite)
        : this(newSite, "no.url", "No Description") {}

    public WebSite(string newSite, string newURL)
        : this(newSite, newURL, "No Description") {}

    public WebSite(string newSite,
                   string newURL,
                   string newDesc)
    {
        SiteName    = newSite;
        URL         = newURL;
        Description = newDesc;
    }

    public override string ToString()
    {
        return siteName    +
               ", "        +
               url         +
               ", "        +
               description;
    }

    public override bool Equals(object evalString)
```

LISTING 12.7   Continued

```csharp
{
    return this.ToString() == evalString.ToString();
}

public override int GetHashCode()
{
    return this.ToString().GetHashCode();
}

protected string ValidateUrl(string url)
{
    if (!(url.StartsWith(http)))
    {
        return http + url;
    }
    return url;
}

public string SiteName
{
    get
    {
        return siteName;
    }
    set
    {
        siteName = value;
    }
}

public string URL
{
    get
    {
        return url;
    }
    set
    {
        url = ValidateUrl(value);
    }
}

public string Description
{
    get
```

LISTING 12.7   Continued

```
        {
            return description;
        }
        set
        {
            description = value;
        }
    }


    ~WebSite() {}
}

/// <summary>
///     This object holds a collection of sites.
/// </summary>
public class SiteList
{
    protected SortedList<int, WebSite> sites;

    public SiteList()
    {
        sites = new SortedList<int, WebSite>();
    }

    public int NextIndex
    {
        get
        {
            return sites.Count;
        }
    }

    public WebSite this[int index]
    {
        get
        {
            if (index > sites.Count)
                return (WebSite)null;

            return (WebSite) sites.GetByIndex(index);
        }
        set
```

LISTING 12.7   Continued

```
        {
            if ( index < 10 )
                sites[index] = value;
        }
    }

    public void Remove(int element)
    {
        sites.RemoveAt(element);
    }
}
```

Whereas Listing 12.7 doesn't add any new material to this chapter, it does manage the underlying information for the program and make it more realistic. In addition, you can study the code to reinforce many of the skills you learned in earlier chapters. Listing 12.8 shows how to compile the listings in this chapter so that they may be run as a program.

LISTING 12.8   Compilation Instructions for Chapter 12 listings

```
csc WebSites.cs SiteManager.cs Menu.cs
➥ MenuItem.cs DelegatesAndEvents.cs
```

Summary

This chapter covered delegates and events. It explained how delegates provide the infrastructure for events. One section showed how to define a delegate. It showed how to define delegate method handlers and how to connect them to a delegate. This led to the purpose of delegates and a demonstration of how to invoke methods through delegates. The multicast delegate section showed how to invoke multiple delegates at the same time through a single delegate invocation. Delegates can be compared with the equal (==) and not equal (!=) operators.

You also saw how delegate inferencing works, making the task of hooking up handlers a lot easier. Anonymous methods reduce code by hooking them up directly to either delegates or events.

The section covering events showed how to define event handlers using delegates. Then there was a section on how subscribers can register for events. Once registered, the subscriber is notified when those events are invoked. Another section showed how to invoke or fire events. Finally, there was an example of how to customize events by implementing their add and remove accessors.

CHAPTER 13

Naming and Organizing Types with Namespaces

In a room full of people, perhaps a party or a user group meeting, you might want to get someone's attention. So you say, "Hey, Joe!" but notice that three people turn around to respond at the same time. Then you say, "Sorry, I meant Mayo," and you still have two people responding. Then you say, "Joe Mayo," and finally you are talking to the right person.

Effectively, you had to use the right name and be specific to communicate with the person you wanted to in a crowded room. The same principle holds true when writing C# programs. In a program of so many objects and third-party libraries with their own objects, it is easy to find yourself in a situation where you want to use one object type, but there is ambiguity because of multiple objects with the same type name. This is a common problem that is solved by namespaces in C#.

Throughout this book, namespaces have been used consistently. In the using System; statement at the beginning of each program, the word *System* was a reference to the System namespace. This chapter explains why it was necessary to reference the System namespace in the simplest of programs.

The purpose of namespaces is to help organize code and reduce conflicts between names. The concepts are generally simple, but this chapter points out some strange situations that can occur with namespaces. There's also a section that deals with scope and visibility. C#'s scope and visibility rules are generally similar to other languages, but a few differences need to be identified.

Why Namespaces?

Namespaces are language elements that help organize code and reduce conflicts between various identifiers in a program. By helping organize code, namespaces help programmers manage their projects more efficiently. Reducing conflict is perhaps the greatest strength of namespace. This allows reusable components from different companies to be used in the same program without the worry of ambiguity caused by multiple instances of the same identifier.

C# NAMESPACES AND JAVA PACKAGES

Namespaces are similar to Java packages with a single, significant difference. There are no built-in language rules forcing C# namespaces to conform to the directory placement of the files. C# namespaces are logical rather than physical.

Organizing Code

Namespaces provide a logical organization for programs to exist. C# namespaces provide a hierarchical framework upon which to organize code. Starting with a top-level namespace, subnamespaces are created to further categorize code, based upon its purpose.

A CLR VIEW OF NAMESPACES

The Common Language Runtime (CLR) does not recognize that namespaces exist. For instance, it does not know that Console is a member of the System namespace. It thinks that System.Console is the name of the class and always requires a fully qualified name.

An example of using namespaces for organization is the Framework Class Library (FCL). It begins at the System namespace, which has nested namespaces. There are several classes at the System namespace level, such as Console, DateTime, and Exception. Consider the System.Console.WriteLine method. System refers to the FCL namespace by the same name. Console is a class under the System namespace. WriteLine is a method of the Console class within the System namespace.

There are also nested namespaces within the System namespace, such as the System.Collections, System.Data, and System.Security namespaces. This is along the lines of the hierarchical nature of namespaces. Using nested namespaces is good for categorizing code.

NAMESPACES AND INHERITANCE

The hierarchical organization of code into namespaces is a logical function only. It differs from object-oriented inheritance in that there are no language rules defining the hierarchical relationship. Namespaces can be used to organize code in any way the programmer desires.

Avoiding Conflict

Another service provided by namespaces is the capability to avoid naming conflicts between identifiers. Class and method names often collide when using multiple libraries. This risk increases as programs get larger and include more third-party tools. For example, consider the following program that uses two types of `Console` class from different namespaces:

```
System.Console.WriteLine("Hello from System.");
SomeThirdPartyLibrary.Console.WriteLine("Hello from SomeThirdPartyLibrary.");
```

Notice that the preceding code has two calls to the `WriteLine` method of a `Console` class. The difference is that each `Console` class belongs to unique namespaces, `System` and `SomeThirdPartyLibrary`. By fully qualifying each call, you can ensure the intended code is used.

Generally, you need to fully qualify a type only when a conflict occurs, as shown in the preceding code. As you can see, the code can become a little more difficult to read because of all the extra syntax. Most of the time, you'll want to add `using` directives to the top of a file, as has been done in previous chapters. The next section covers namespace directives in greater depth.

Namespace Directives

Namespace directives are C# language elements that allow a program to identify namespaces used in a program. They allow namespace members to be used without specifying a fully qualified name. When using the entire namespace hierarchy to make a method call, a program uses a method's fully qualified name. If every statement in every method used fully qualified names, a program would be wordy, redundant, and perhaps more difficult to read. C# has two namespace directives: `using` and `alias`.

The using Directive

The `using` directive permits specification of a method call without the mandatory use of a fully qualified name. Here's an example of the `using` directive:

```
using System;

class Program
{
    static void Main(string[] args)
    {
        Console.WriteLine("Hello from System.");
    }
}
```

The first line in the example has the using directive. It states that the programs in this file can use any types within the System namespace without a fully qualified name. In other words, statements don't need the System prefix. This is evident in the Main method where the Console.WriteLine method is invoked. Console is not a namespace. It is the name of a class that holds the static method, WriteLine.

The benefits in clarity and of not needing to type in fully qualified names are apparent with the using directive approach. In cases where there is a possible conflict, the fully qualified name can be used where necessary. The next section discusses another way of avoiding conflict, with the alias directive.

The alias Directive

The alias directive allows a program to have another name for a namespace or type. This is commonly used to provide a shorthand notation to long namespace names. Besides aliasing namespaces, aliases can also be assigned to types within a namespace. Aliases conform to the rules for any other C# identifier. The following example shows how difficult program readability can get when every member is fully qualified.

THE FCL AS A GOOD EXAMPLE OF NAMESPACE USAGE

Check out the .NET Framework Reference in the .NET Framework SDK for a good picture of how the .NET Framework is laid out. It provides some familiarity with what is where.

```
public class AliasExample
{
    public static int Main()
    {
        System.Security.Permissions.FileIOPermissionAccess
            fileAccess = new
        System.Security.Permissions.FileIOPermissionAccess();

        fileAccess =
    System.Security.Permissions.FileIOPermissionAccess.NoAccess;

        System.Console.WriteLine(
            "Level of File IO Access: {0}", fileAccess);

        return 0;
    }
}
```

How many programmers do you think would like to maintain several thousand lines of that? If you like it, you can have it. I'm going to use the language constructs available to make life easier for myself and others. There's absolutely no doubt about what is being executed, but I think we can use C# aliases to make this a bit more palatable. The following example shows how to implement a program with aliases:

```
using System;
using aFilePerm
    = System.Security.Permissions.FileIOPermissionAccess;

public class NewAliasExample
{
    public static int Main()
    {
        aFilePerm fileAccess = new aFilePerm();

        fileAccess = aFilePerm.NoAccess;

        Console.WriteLine(
            "Level of File IO Access: {0}", fileAccess);

        return 0;
    }
}
```

The second line shows how to declare an alias. The alias, aFilePerm, becomes an alias for the enum named System.Security.Permissions.FileIOPermissionAccess. This shows that aliases aren't limited to only namespaces.

Within the program, the alias aFilePerm is used everywhere the fully qualified name would have been. With a combination of the using directive and alias, this program has become much easier to read. The fact that the alias has a meaningful name also facilitates more self-documenting code.

NAMESPACE VERSUS ASSEMBLY REFERENCE

A common problem for programmers who first learn C# is to distinguish between the meaning of a namespace and an assembly reference. As explained earlier in this chapter, a namespace is a logical concept for organizing code and disambiguating type identifiers. Use a namespace to specifically identify the type that is being used, either by fully qualifying the identifier or adding a using or alias directive to the top of your code file.

This differs from assembly references in that an assembly is a physical entity that holds code and other resources in your file system. You add assembly references to your project via either a /r:<assemblyname> option on the command-line or right-click on the project in the VS2008 Solution Explorer and select Add Reference. By adding a reference, you are telling C# to look at that assembly to find types that you want to use in your code. Otherwise, C# wouldn't know how to find those types. When you add a using directive to the top of a file, C# will assume that a reference exists.

Now, here is the real kicker that confuses people a lot–errors for both a missing namespace or a missing reference emit the exact same error message: The type or namespace name '<your type name here>' could not be found. (Are you missing a using directive or an assembly reference?) To fix this problem, look at the type to see if you should either add a using directive or fully qualify the name. Clicking on the identifier in VS2008 will invoke IntelliSense and show you an underline that you can hover over and select the shortcut to add this automatically. Often, you've already done this, and the real problem is that you don't have an assembly reference to the assembly containing the code for that type. You can figure out what that assembly should be by looking at the documentation for the type. In the .NET Framework Class Library Documentation, look for the About page for the type, which displays both the namespace and assembly name for the type.

Creating Namespaces

Creating a namespace is easy. Just use the keyword namespace followed by the name. The contents of a namespace are enclosed in curly braces. The following example shows how to create a namespace and add a class to it:

```
namespace Sams
{
    using System;
    using aFilePerm =
        System.Security.Permissions.FileIOPermissionAccess;

    public class FilePerm
    {
        aFilePerm fileAccess = new aFilePerm();

        public FilePerm()
        {
            fileAccess = aFilePerm.NoAccess;
        }

        public aFilePerm FileAccess
        {
            get
            {
                return fileAccess;
            }
            set
            {
                fileAccess = value;
            }
        }
    }
}
```

The first line shows that this code is in the Sams namespace. The next example shows how to access this class from another class:

```
using System;
using aFilePerm = System.Security.Permissions.FileIOPermissionAccess;

public class AliasExample
{
    public static int Main(string[] args)
    {
        Sams.FilePerm myFilePerm = new Sams.FilePerm();

        aFilePerm fileAccess = myFilePerm.FileAccess;

        Console.WriteLine("Level of File IO Access: {0}",
                          fileAccess);

        return 0;
    }
}
```

This example shows how to access a class in another namespace. Within the Main method, there is a field named myFilePerm of type FilePerm within the Sams namespace. This is declared with the fully qualified name of Sams.FilePerm.

The Sams namespace helps avoid conflicts with other classes that may be named FilePerm, but the namespace name is kind of short. Because the name is short and relatively common, its entirely possible for a name conflict to occur—for instance, there might be another namespace named Sams in a third-party library. In fact, if there were another book within the company using this namespace name, there would definitely be a conflict. Also, just using the name Sams is too generic. It would help to organize this book's code with something more specific.

Nested namespaces help meet both goals of organization and avoiding conflict. A nested namespace makes the category of code more specific and makes more sense. Also, deepening the hierarchy reduces the chance of conflicts. Here's a revised namespace:

```
namespace Sams
{
    namespace Unleashed
    {
        // namespace members
    }
}
```

This shows more specialization in namespaces. However, what if there were a *Visual C# Unleashed*, *ASP.NET Unleashed*, or *.NET Unleashed* that used the Sams.Unleashed namespace? It might be a good idea to go a bit further. Here's another revision.

```
namespace Sams.Unleashed.csharp.Chapter13
{
    // namespace members
}
```

With this new namespace, it's highly unlikely that there will ever be a namespace conflict between code in this namespace and any third-party library. It's nested all the way to four levels to provide a safe degree of uniqueness. It's possible to specialize it even further, but there is such a thing as too far.

Notice that this example used a dot operator between namespace names, whereas the previous example actually reproduced the namespace syntax of the Unleashed namespace within the Sams namespace. The first example could have been written just as well like this:

```
namespace Sams.Unleashed
{
    // namespace members...
}
```

Either method is acceptable, and they both produce the same results. It depends on how a program is written as to which method should be used. The dot operator is quick and short and adapts well to the four-level namespace. On the other hand, if there were two nested namespaces declared in the same file, it might be more convenient to use the more explicit notation. The following example is one way to specify that certain namespace members belong in specific nested namespaces:

```
namespace Sams
{
    namespace Unleashed
    {
        // namespace members...
    }
    namespace TwentyOneDays
    {
        // namespace members...
    }
}
```

Some would find this more expressive. Regardless of how namespaces are declared, they are always accessed with the same type of fully qualified name. Here's a snippet of how that four-level nested namespace would be accessed:

```
Sams.Unleashed.csharp.Chapter13.FilePerm myFilePerm
    = new Sams.Unleashed.csharp.Chapter13.FilePerm();
```

Namespaces are not bound to a single file or directory structure. They're logical, not physical. They can be divided among multiple files. The following examples show how the same namespace can be used in different files. Notice that they're not only in two different files, but they're also in two different directory names and at two different levels.

This code shows the contents of the file located at C:\examples\chapter13.cs:

```
namespace Sams.Unleashed.csharp.Chapter13
{
    // namespace members
}
```

This code shows the contents of the file located at C:\testcode\csharp\alias.cs:

```
namespace Sams.Unleashed.csharp.Chapter13
{
    // namespace members
}
```

Although similar code is normally located in the same place, this shows the logical nature of namespaces.

WHEN TO THINK ABOUT NAMESPACES

Plan out namespaces ahead of time. Good organization avoids problems later. With a good hierarchy in place, new code can be easily developed to fit in logically with no problem.

Namespace Members

Namespaces are at the top of the food chain of the C# language element hierarchy. Although namespaces may contain other namespaces, nothing else can contain a namespace. Here's a list of all the C# language elements that go into namespaces:

▶ Classes

▶ Delegates

▶ Enums

▶ Interfaces

▶ Structs

▶ Namespaces

▶ using directives

▶ alias directives

13

Scope and Visibility

When discussing scope, this section refers to the parts of a program where an identifier refers to a specific declaration. Visibility refers to whether an identifier can be seen by other program elements. This section discusses how these concepts are implemented in C#.

Besides required blocks, it's possible to place blocks within code, independent of supporting other language constructs. This could prove useful if there is an iterative or recursive routine with local variables that isn't necessary for subsequent iterations or recursive calls. By isolating these variables and the data working on them within a block, a local scope can be established where those data items exist only within the scope of that block and aren't carried longer than necessary. This could help conserve system memory.

Visibility of a program's elements exists within their declaring block and within subordinate blocks. Within class, interface, and structure blocks, data may be declared anywhere and still be visible anywhere throughout the block. However, on methods, properties, and indexers, data must be declared before it is referenced. Otherwise, that data won't be visible.

Subordinate program elements may redeclare the visible program elements outside their local scope. Doing so effectively hides the enclosing block's corresponding program element. To access those corresponding program elements within the local scope of a block, use the this operator.

Within methods and property, indexer, and event accessors, program elements may be redeclared. However, redeclaration within an unnamed block or flow-control statement causes an error. Here's an example of both proper and improper redeclaration:

```
using System;
using aFilePerm
    = System.Security.Permissions.FileIOPermissionAccess;

public class NewAliasExample
{
    aFilePerm fileAccess;

    public NewAliasExample()
    {
        fileAccess = aFilePerm.AllAccess;
    }

    public static int Main()
    {
        NewAliasExamplemyAlias = new NewAliasExample();

        myAlias.printFilePerm();
```

```
        return 0;
    }

    public void PrintFilePerm()
    {
        string fileAccess = this.fileAccess.ToString();

        // error - can't redeclare within method
        //if (this.fileAccess != aFilePerm.NoAccess)
        //{
        //    int fileAccess = (int)this.fileAccess;
        //}

        // error - can't redeclare within method
        //{
        //    int fileAccess = (int) this.fileAccess;
        //}

        Console.WriteLine("Level of File IO Access: {0}", fileAccess);
    }
}
```

This code shows legal and illegal examples of class member redeclaration. At the class level, there is a member named fileAccess with a type defined by the aFilePerm alias. Within the scope of the PrintFilePerm method, the visibility of the class member named fileAccess of alias type aFilePerm is effectively hidden by the declaration of the local string field also named fileAccess.

Any unqualified reference to fileAccess within the PrintFilePerm method refers to the local string type fileAccess. In this case, the program needs access to the class-level field fileAccess, so it uses the this keyword.

Two illegal redeclarations are marked out with comments. The first is within an if statement that redeclares the fileAccess name as an int. The second is in an unnamed block that tries to do the same thing. It might work in other languages, but not in C#.

Namespace Alias Qualifiers

On occasion, you'll encounter namespace ambiguity because of an alias that matches a type name. Of course, you could simply change the alias. The problem with changing the alias name is that you'll often have a lot of code that uses that alias, and many files that define the same alias and will want the consistency across your application.

Another alternative is to change the type name you are trying to reference. Many times this isn't an option because the type name comes from a third-party library, and you don't have access to the code. Here's a demo that reproduces this problem by creating an identical alias and type name:

```
using DotNet = System;
```

```
public class DotNet { }
```

Notice that both the alias and type name are named `DotNet`. Typically, the `DotNet` class would be in the third-party library, and the alias would be in your code. The ambiguity occurs because C# doesn't know whether to treat `DotNet` as an alias when a `using System` directive is declared or to treat `DotNet` as a type name when the `using System` directive isn't declared. To fix the problem, you can use a namespace alias operator, `::`, like this:

```
class NamespaceAliasQualifiers
{
    global::DotNet dotNet = new global::DotNet();
    DotNet::DateTime date = new DotNet::DateTime();
}
```

In the first statement, `global::` ensures that `DotNet` is declared as the `DotNet` class. The second statement, with `DotNet::`, ensures that `DotNet` is declared as the `DotNet` alias. When using the namespace alias qualifier, `::`, put the namespace or alias on the left side. You can use `global` for those types that aren't declared in any namespace.

THE BENEFITS OF USING NAMESPACES

As you can see, one of the use cases of applying the namespace alias qualifier, `::`, is to disambiguate between aliases and types without a namespace. The problem occurs because the type doesn't have a namespace. You can avoid this by placing your types in namespaces.

In addition, this problem can occur if your namespace isn't unique. Although this second use case would be extremely rare, you can avoid this problem by ensuring your namespaces are unique.

Don't forget either that using namespaces is good for organizing types.

Extern Namespaces Alias

Another namespace problem occurs when an external DLL contains a type with the same name as a type in your code. You can access the type in your code, but there is no easy way to use the exactly named type in the external DLL. To do so, you must use an extern namespace alias, which is an alias that identifies code in the external DLL. To reproduce the problem, create a new class library project (DLL) in the same solution as the DotNet project from the previous example, I'll call it `ExternDotNet`, with the following code:

```
public class DotNet
{
    public string WhoAmI()
    {
        return "I'm ExternDotNet.";
    }
}
```

Using the `DotNet` class from the previous section in your code, in a separate project, add a new `WhoAmI` method like this:

```
public class DotNet
{
    public string WhoAmI()
    {
        return "I'm DotNet in your code.";
    }
}
```

Right-click the References folder in your project, select Add Reference, click the Projects tab, select the ExternDotNet project, and click OK. This adds a reference for the ExternDotNet DLL to your project. Now you have the preceding code in your project and the previous `DotNet` class defined in an external DLL and a reference from your project to the ExternDotNet DLL. If there were other types declared in the ExternDotNet DLL, you would be able to access them, provided there weren't any name conflicts. However, there is still no way for you to access the `DotNet` class in the ExternalDotNet DLL from your code at this point in time. To fix this problem with VS2008, just follow these steps:

1. Open the References folder in your project and select the ExternalDotNet reference.
2. Right-click the ExternalDotNet reference and select Properties. Observe that there is a property named Aliases that has global already defined.
3. Change the Aliases property to `"global,ExternDotNet"`. Notice that there is a comma between entries. You are allowed to add multiple comma-separated entries for additional aliases. Spaces before or after the comma are allowed.
4. Add the line `"extern alias ExternDotNet;"` as the first line of your code. This is the alias you'll use to access the `DotNet` class in the ExternDotNet DLL.

After you've set up the ExternDotNet DLL with an alias, you can access the `DotNet` class in it with the following code:

```
global::DotNet dotNet = new global::DotNet();
ExternDotNet::DotNet dotNetExtern = new ExternDotNet::DotNet();

System.Console.WriteLine(dotNetExtern.WhoAmI());
System.Console.WriteLine(dotNet.WhoAmI());
```

Notice that the preceding code uses the namespace alias qualifier with the `ExternDotNet` alias, defined as the first line of the file, on the left side, to access the `DotNet` class in the ExternDotNet DLL.

You can avoid these situations by the attentive use of namespaces when defining types. See the tip "The Benefits of Using Namespaces" for clarification.

NAMESPACE MANAGEMENT IN VS2008

If you like to keep your namespaces organized, VS2008 has a couple great new features to help. Just right-click anywhere in the code editor, preferably at the top so that you can see. Select Organize Usings and observe that there are three entries: Remove Unused Usings, Sort Usings, and Remove and Sort. They work exactly as their name implies.

Summary

You should now understand the details of using namespaces. Adding namespace directives helps reduce the amount of code you need to type. The section on creating namespaces gave you ideas about how to add your code to your own namespaces. You also learned how to avoid weird naming conflicts by using namespace aliases operators and extern namespace aliases.

In the next chapter, you learn about two object types that go into namespaces: abstract classes and interfaces.

CHAPTER 14

Implementing Abstract Classes and Interfaces

Automated teller machines (ATM) are everywhere. What do you expect when using an ATM? At a high level, an ATM provides services such as dispensing money, checking balances, and making deposits. To perform these operations, you have to use a number pad and read the console. Money appears in a bin when you withdraw, there is a slot to put the money into when depositing, and you can see balances on the screen. This is what we all expect from an ATM. What would happen, however, if you were to walk up to an ATM that has a joystick? A few people might like it, but the rest of us would be confused and go off looking for an ATM that works the way we expect it to.

Essentially, an ATM has an interface, which is common across all ATMs. It's an implicit contract, and the strange ATM with the joystick effectively breaks that contract—so much that it becomes unusable to most people. The same principles of interface apply with software, too. Whether you build an implementation class or struct with public methods, an abstract class, or a C# type called an interface, you are creating interfaces. Other programmers write code against your interface and develop certain levels of expectations, depending on the nature of the interface you've created.

These expectations of an interface are what people often refer to as a contract. If you change the public interface, just like the joystick on the ATM, you break the contract, which essentially breaks code. This is such an important concept that C# has special features, through abstract classes and interface types, to support hard contracts with code. With interfaces, anyone can write code and be guaranteed he can call the members of that interface.

This chapter shows how to create both abstract classes and interfaces. You'll see how both can help create interfaces for other code to use. Another important point is that you'll see how to write code that implements interfaces.

Abstract Classes

Abstract classes are a special type of base classes. In addition to normal class members, there are abstract class members. These abstract class members are methods and properties declared without an implementation. All classes derived directly from abstract classes must implement these abstract methods and properties. You can look at an abstract class as a cross between normal classes and interfaces, in that they can have their own implementation yet define an interface through abstract members that derived classes must implement. C# interface types are covered later in this chapter, but for right now you need to know that interfaces do not contain any implementation, a fact that differentiates them from abstract classes that can have implementation.

Abstract classes can never be instantiated. This would be illogical, because of the members without implementations. So what good is a class that can't be instantiated? Lots! Abstract classes sit toward the top of a class hierarchy. They establish structure and meaning to code. They make frameworks easier to build. This is possible because abstract classes have information and behavior common to all derived classes in a framework. Take a look at the following example:

```
abstract public class Contact
{
    protected string name;

    public Contact()
    {
        // statements...
    }

    public abstract void GenerateReport();

    abstract public string Name
    {
        get;
        set;
    }
}

public class Customer : Contact
{
    string gender;
    decimal income;
```

```csharp
    int numberOfVisits;

    public Customer()
    {
        // statements
    }

    public override void GenerateReport()
    {
        // unique report
    }

    public override string Name
    {
        get
        {
            numberOfVisits++;
            return name;
        }
        set
        {
            name = value;
            numberOfVisits = 0;
        }
    }
}

public class SiteOwner : Contact
{
    int siteHits;
    string mySite;

    public SiteOwner()
    {
        // statements...
    }

    public override void GenerateReport()
    {
        // unique report
    }

    public override string Name
    {
        get
        {
```

```
        siteHits++;
        return name;
    }
    set
    {
        name = value;
        siteHits = 0;
    }
    }
}
```

This example has three classes. The first class, Contact, is now an abstract class. This is shown as the first modifier of its class declaration. Contact has two abstract members, which includes an abstract method named GenerateReport. This method is declared with the abstract modifier in front of the method declaration. It has no implementation (no braces) and is terminated with a semicolon. The Name property is also declared abstract. The accessors of properties are terminated with semicolons.

The abstract base class Contact has two derived classes: Customer and SiteOwner. Both of these derived classes implement the abstract members of the Contact class. The GenerateReport method in each derived class has an override modifier in its declaration. Likewise, the Name declaration contains an override modifier in both Customer and SiteOwner.

The override modifier for the overridden GenerateReport method and Name property is mandatory. C# requires explicit declaration of intent when overriding methods. This feature promotes safe code by avoiding the accidental overriding of base class methods, which is what actually does happen in other languages. Leaving out the override modifier generates an error. Similarly, adding a new modifier also generates an error. Abstract methods are implicitly virtual. They must be overridden and cannot be hidden, which the new modifier or the lack of a modifier would be trying to do.

Notice the name field in the Contact class. It has a protected modifier. Remember, a protected modifier allows derived classes to access base class members. In this case, it enables the overridden Name property to access the name field in the Contact class.

Abstract Class and Interface Differences

Interfaces are specifications defining the type of behaviors a class must implement. They are contracts a class uses to allow other classes to interact with it in a well-defined and anticipated manner. Interfaces define an explicit definition of how classes should interact.

Abstract classes are a unit of abstraction, whereas interfaces define further specification. Abstract class members may contain implementations. The exception is when an abstract class member has an abstract modifier. Derived classes must implement abstract class members with an abstract class modifier, but they don't have to implement any other method declared virtual. On the other hand, classes inheriting an interface must implement every interface member. Interface members have no implementation.

Implementing Interfaces

As stated in the preceding section, a C# interface defines a contract for all custom class and struct objects that implement that interface. This means that you must write code in the class or struct that implements the interface, to provide the implementation for the interface. Instead of just exposing public members, the interface is enforced by the C# compiler, and you must define the members specified in the interface (contract). First, I show you how to define an interface and then follow up with explanations of how to implement interface members. Later, you see how to use the interface.

Defining Interface Types

The definition of an interface is much like a class or struct. However, because an interface doesn't have an implementation, its members are defined differently. The following example shows how to declare an interface and how an interface is structured:

```
[modifiers] interface IName [: Interface [, Interfaces]]
{
      // methods
      // properties
      // indexers
      // events
}
```

The modifiers can be public or internal, just like other type definitions. Next is the keyword interface followed by the interface name, IName, which is simply an identifier. A common convention is to make the first character of an interface name the uppercase letter *I*. After the name is a colon and a comma-separated list of interfaces that this one inherits. The colon/inherited interface list is optional.

Although classes have only single class inheritance, they have multiple interface inheritance. Along the same lines, structs and interfaces have multiple interface inheritance. Later sections of this chapter explain some of the issues involved with multiple interface inheritance.

Following the interface inheritance list is the interface body, which consists of the members enclosed in curly braces. Legal members are methods, properties, indexers, and events. Interface members are assumed to be public and, therefore, have no modifiers. Interface implementations must also be public.

The following sections explain how to define interface members for the following interface, IBroker:

```
public interface IBroker
{
    // interface members
}
```

Remember, interface members don't have implementations. It is the class or struct that
implements the interface. Those implementations, by whatever classes or structs you code,
must have members that match what the specified interface members.

Methods

Interface methods are defined similarly to normal methods. The difference is that they
have no implementation. The following example shows an interface method:

```
string GetRating(string stock, out string provider) ;
```

Everything is the same as a normal method, except that a semicolon is used at the end in
place of the implementation code block.

Properties

At first, it might seem strange that a property could be an interface member, especially
when the normal implementation of a property is associated with a field. Although fields
can't be interface members, this doesn't prevent the use of properties, because the implementation of a property is independent of its specification.

Remember, one of the primary reasons for properties is to encapsulate implementation.
Therefore, the fact that an interface doesn't have fields is not a limiting factor. For this
reason, property specifications may be added to interfaces with no problem, as shown in
the following example:

```
decimal PricePerTrade
{
    get ;
    set ;
}
```

This property example is structured similarly to a regular property. However, the accessors
don't have implementations. Instead, the get and set keywords are closed with a semicolon.

Indexers

Interface indexer specifications appear similar to normal indexers, but their accessor specifications are the same as property accessors, as shown in the following example:

```
decimal this[string StockName]
{
    get ;
    set ;
 }
```

This example shows an indexer accepting a string argument and returning a decimal value. Its get and set accessors are closed with semicolons, similar to how property accessors are defined.

Events

There is no difference in the way interface events and normal events are declared. Here's an example:

```
public delegate void ChangeRegistrar(object sender,
                          object evnt);
...
event ChangeRegistrar PriceChange ;
```

As you can see, the event has the exact same type of signature that goes in a normal class. No surprises.

Implicit Implementation

It is easy to implement a single interface on a class or struct. It just requires declaration of the class or struct with interface inheritance and the implementation of those interface members. There are two views of implicit interface implementation. The first is the easiest: a single class implementing a single interface. The second uses interface polymorphism by implementing the same interface in two separate classes.

Single Class Interface Implementation

As mentioned previously, it is easy for a class to implement a single interface. Implementation of an interface simply follows the rules set in previous sections. The interface in Listing 14.1 represents a plausible set of class members that a stockbroker or financial company may want to expose to a client.

LISTING 14.1   The **IBroker** Interface Definition

```
using System;
using System.Collections;
```

LISTING 14.1   Continued

```
public delegate void ChangeRegistrar(object sender,
                           object evnt);

public interface IBroker
{
    string GetRating(string stock) ;

    decimal PricePerTrade
    {
        get ;
        set ;
    }

    decimal this[string StockName]
    {
        get ;
        set ;
    }

    event ChangeRegistrar PriceChange ;
}
```

The interface name, from Listing 14.1, begins with the conventional I in IBroker. It has four members: the GetRating method, the PricePerTrade property, an indexer, and the PriceChange event. The delegate type of the PriceChange property, ChangeRegistrar, is defined, too. As mentioned earlier, interface members do not have implementations. It is up to a class or struct to implement interface member declarations. Listing 14.2 shows a class that implements the IBroker interface, which is an object that represents a finance company. It has an overridden constructor to ensure that the pricePerTrade field is initialized properly.

LISTING 14.2   An Implementation of the **IBroker** Interface

```
public class FinanceCompany : IBroker
{
    Dictionary<string, decimal> m_stocks
        = new Dictionary<string, decimal>();

    decimal pricePerTrade;

    public FinanceCompany()
        : this(10.50m)
    {
    }
```

LISTING 14.2   Continued

```
    public FinanceCompany(decimal price)
    {
        pricePerTrade = price;
    }

    public string GetRating(string stock)
    {
        return "Buy";
    }

    public decimal PricePerTrade
    {
        get
        {
            return pricePerTrade;
        }
        set
        {
            pricePerTrade = value;
            PriceChange("FinanceBroker", value);
        }
    }

    public decimal this[string StockName]
    {
        get
        {
            return m_stocks[StockName];
        }
        set
        {
            m_stocks.Add(StockName, value);
        }
    }

    public event ChangeRegistrar PriceChange;
}
```

As the listing shows, the private pricePerTrade field is encapsulated by the PricePerTrade property. The get accessor of the PricePerTrade property simply returns the current value of the pricePerTrade field. However, the set accessor provides more functionality. After setting the new value of the pricePerTrade field, it invokes the PriceChange event.

The PriceChange event is based on the ChangeRegistrar delegate, which specifies two object parameters. When the PriceChange event is invoked in the set accessor of the

PricePerTrade property, it receives two arguments. The string argument is implicitly converted to object. The decimal value is boxed and passed as an object. Event declaration and implementation are normally as simple as shown in Listing 14.2. However, the event implementation can be much more sophisticated if there is a need to override its add and remove accessors.

The GetRating method is implemented to always return the same value. In this context, the broker is always bullish, regardless of the real value of a stock.

The indexer implementation uses the Dictionary<string, decimal> collection for maintaining its data. This is a generic collection where the key is type string and the value is type decimal. You'll learn more about generics in Chapter 17, "Parameterizing Type with Generics and Writing Iterators." The indexer's get accessor returns the value of a stock using Stockname as a key. The set accessor creates a new Hashtable entry by using the indexer string parameter as a key and the value passed in as the hash value.

Now there's a class that faithfully follows the contract of the IBroker interface. What's good about this is that any program can now use that class and automatically know that it has specific class members that can be used in a specific way. Listing 14.3 shows a program that uses a class that implements the IBroker interface.

LISTING 14.3   Implementation of Single Interface Inheritance

```
public class InterfaceTester
{
    public static int Main()
    {
        FinanceCompany  finco = new FinanceCompany();
        InterfaceTester iftst = new InterfaceTester();

        finco.PriceChange += new ChangeRegistrar(
                        iftst.PricePerTradeChange);

        finco["ABC"] = 15.39m;
        finco["DEF"] = 37.51m;

        Console.WriteLine("ABC Price is {0}", finco["ABC"]);
        Console.WriteLine("DEF Price is {0}", finco["DEF"]);

        Console.WriteLine("");

        finco.PricePerTrade = 10.55m;

        Console.WriteLine("");

        string recommendation = finco.GetRating("ABC");

        Console.WriteLine(
```

LISTING 14.3   Continued

```
"finco's recommendation for ABC is {0}", recommendation);

        return 0;
    }

    public void PricePerTradeChange(object sender,
                                    object evnt)
    {
        Console.WriteLine(
            "Trading price for {0} changed to {1}.",
            (string) sender, (decimal) evnt);

    }
}
```

And here's the output from Listing 14.3:

```
ABC Price is 15.39
DEF Price is 37.51

Trading price for FinanceBroker changed to 10.55.

finco's recommendation for ABC is Buy
```

Because the FinanceCompany class implements the IBroker interface, the program in Listing 14.3 knows what class members it can implement. The Main method instantiates a FinanceCompany class, finco, and an InterfaceTester class, iftst.

The InterfaceTester class has an event handler method named PricePerTradeChange. In the Main method, the InterfaceTester class makes itself a subscriber to the finco.PriceChange event by assigning the PricePerTradeChange event handler to that event.

Next, two stocks are added to finco. This is done by using a stock name as the indexer and giving it a decimal value. The assignment is verified with a couple Console.WriteLine methods.

The finco object's PricePerTrade property is changed to 10.55m. Within the FinanceCompany class, this invokes the PriceChange event, which calls the PricePerTrade method of the InterfaceTester class. This shows how events are effective tools for obtaining status changes in an object. Finally, the GetRating method of the finco object is invoked. Method calls are the most typical interface members.

The output follows the sequence of events in Main. The first two lines show the stock values from the indexer. The third line is from the PricePerTradeChange event handler in the InterfaceTester class. The last line of output shows the results of requesting a stock rating from the finco object.

Simulating Polymorphic Behavior

Implementing an interface in a single class and using it is relatively easy, as described in the preceding section. However, the real power of interfaces comes from being able to use them in multiple classes. Let's take a look at using interfaces to implement polymorphism in a program.

We will combine the examples from the previous section in a test program. Listing 14.4 shows another implementation of the IBroker interface. It's a bit more complicated than the FinanceCompany class implementation of IBroker because of additional objects and extra class members with more logic.

LISTING 14.4   Another Implementation of the **IBroker** Interface

```
public enum StockRating
{
    Buy = 0, Accumulate, Hold, Sell
}

public struct Stock
{
    private string name;
    private decimal price;
    private StockRating rating;

    public string Name
    {
        get
        {
            return Name;
        }
        set
        {
            name = value;
        }
    }

    public StockRating Rating
    {
        get
        {
            return rating;
        }
        set
        {
            rating = value;
```

LISTING 14.4   Continued

```
        }
    }

    public decimal Price
    {
        get
        {
            return price;
        }
        set
        {
            price = value;
        }
    }
}

public class StockBroker : IBroker
{
    Dictionary<string, Stock> m_stocks = new Dictionary<string, Stock>();
    decimal pricePerTrade;
    string brokerName;

    public StockBroker()
        : this(13.59m, "Anonymous")
    {
    }

    public StockBroker(decimal price)
        : this(price, "Anonymous")
    {
    }

    public StockBroker(decimal price, string brokerName)
    {
        pricePerTrade = price;
        this.brokerName = brokerName;
    }

    public string GetRating(string stock)
    {
        Stock myStock = m_stocks[stock];
        return Enum.GetName(typeof(StockRating),
                    myStock.Rating);
    }
```

LISTING 14.4   Continued

```csharp
    private StockRating AssignRating(Stock newStock)
    {
        Random myRand = new Random();
        int nextRating = myRand.Next(4);
        return (StockRating)Enum.ToObject(
                            typeof(StockRating),
                            nextRating);
    }

    public decimal PricePerTrade
    {
        get
        {
            return pricePerTrade;
        }
        set
        {
            pricePerTrade = value;
            PriceChange(brokerName, value);
        }
    }

    public decimal this[string StockName]
    {
        get
        {
            Stock myStock = m_stocks[StockName];
            return myStock.Price;
        }
        set
        {
            Stock myStock = new Stock();
            myStock.Name = StockName;
            myStock.Price = value;
            myStock.Rating = AssignRating(myStock);

            m_stocks.Add(StockName, myStock);
        }
    }

    public event ChangeRegistrar PriceChange;
}
```

Two object types are participating in the implementation of the StockBroker class: StockRating and Stock. The StockRating enum is used by the StockBroker class to define its rating system for individual stocks. The Stock struct defines a stock. It has three private fields, encapsulated by three corresponding properties. The name field is a string that holds the name of the stock. A stock's value is held in the decimal price field. The rating field holds a company's assessment of the value of a particular stock. Its type is the StockRating enum. The StockBroker class uses these two objects.

The StockBroker class implements the IBroker interface. It has three fields that support this implementation. The m_stocks field is a Dictionary that holds objects of type Stock struct. A StockBroker object manages the amount it charges for trades through the decimal pricePerTrade field. Its name is saved in the brokerName string field. To support its fields, the StockBroker class implements three overloaded constructors.

Stock objects are created in the StockBroker indexer. The set accessor creates a new Stock object. The name is assigned through the Stock object Name property from the StockName indexer string parameter. The price is set with the indexer value by using the Price property of the Stock object. When creating a rating, the AssignRating() method is used to obtain a StockRating enum value and assign that to the Rating property of the Stock object. Via the Dictionary.Add method, the stock is then added to the m_stocks collection.

The private AssignRating method determines what type of rating each stock has by using the Random class. After instantiating the myRand object of type Random, it calls the Next method and assigns the result to the nextRating field. The Next method of the myRand object accepts an int parameter, indicating upper bound of the result. This produces an int in the range of 0 to 4. This is also the corresponding range of values in the StockRating enum. This value is then translated into a valid StockRating enum value using the ToObject method of the Enum class.

To return a string type, the GetRating method must first obtain the correct Stock object from the stocks collection. It does this by using the string parameter stock as an index for the m_stocks collection. After it has the stock, it uses the GetName method of the Enum class to translate the Rating property, which returns a StockRating type, from the Stock object into a string.

The PricePerTrade property is the same as the one for the FinanceCompany class. Its get accessor simply returns the pricePerTrade field. When setting the property, the set accessor assigns the new value to the pricePerTrade field and then invokes the PriceChange event. Any subscribed classes are notified with the value of the brokerName field and the new pricePerTrade field value.

Despite the increased complexity of the StockBroker class implementation over the FinanceCompany class, they are both used in the same way. They provide the same type of services because they implement the IBroker interface. Listing 14.5 shows a program that uses both of these classes, implementing polymorphic behavior to exploit the power of interfaces.

14

LISTING 14.5   Using Two Classes with the Same Interface

```
public class InterfaceTester
{
    public static int Main()
    {
        string recommendation;
        List<IBroker> brokers = new List<IBroker>();

        brokers.Add(new FinanceCompany(7.32m));
        brokers.Add(new StockBroker(11.51m, "Gofer Broke"));

        InterfaceTester iftst = new InterfaceTester();

        foreach(IBroker broker in brokers)
        {
            broker.PriceChange += new ChangeRegistrar(
                               iftst.PricePerTradeChange);

            broker["ABC"] = 15.39m;
            broker["DEF"] = 37.51m;

            Console.WriteLine("");
            Console.WriteLine("ABC Price is {0}", broker["ABC"]);
            Console.WriteLine("DEF Price is {0}", broker["DEF"]);

            Console.WriteLine("");

            broker.PricePerTrade = 10.55m;

            Console.WriteLine("");

            recommendation = broker.GetRating("ABC");

            Console.WriteLine(
            "Broker's recommendation for ABC is {0}",
            recommendation);
        }

        return 0;
    }

    public void PricePerTradeChange(object sender,
                           object evnt)
    {
```

LISTING 14.5   Continued

```
        Console.WriteLine(
            "Trading price for {0} changed to {1}.",
            (string) sender, (decimal) evnt);
    }
}
```

And here's the output:

```
ABC Price is 15.39
DEF Price is 37.51

Trading price for FinanceBroker changed to 10.55.

Broker's recommendation for ABC is Buy

ABC Price is 15.39
DEF Price is 37.51

Trading price for Gofer Broke changed to 10.55.

Broker's recommendation for ABC is Accumulate
```

Listing 14.5 shows how to implement polymorphism with interfaces. It does this by creating an instance of both the FinanceCompany and StockBroker classes and using each through the IBroker interface. The Main method of the IntefaceTester class begins by declaring a List<IBroker> collection named brokers. Because both FinanceCompany and StockBroker are IBroker classes, they can be assigned to brokers. Each of the IBroker-derived classes is created and added to the brokers collection.

The primary implementation of the Main method is enclosed in a foreach loop. Although both the FinanceCompany and StockBroker objects were instantiated and placed into the brokers collection individually, they're extracted as IBroker objects in the foreach loop. Within the foreach loop, only the IBroker interface members are used on each object.

First, the PricePerTradeChange event handler is added to the PriceChange event of each broker. Any time the PricePerTrade property of a broker changes, this event handler is called. It's interesting to note that this demonstrates how a single event handler can be used as a callback for multiple events. Each of these multiple events is a price change for each of the brokers.

Each broker object's stock list is initialized with the same values, and then these values are printed, which shows that the interface works the same for all IBroker objects, regardless of the IBroker-derived object's underlying implementation.

Then, the PricePerTrade property of each broker is updated. This triggers each broker's PriceChange event and invokes the PricePerTradeChange event handler of the InterfaceTester class. After that, the GetRating method is called. This is more demonstration of the power of interfaces. Interface polymorphism works for all IBroker object members.

Because the first four lines of output are from the FinanceCompany class, they are the same as from the previous section. Then fifth and sixth lines show the stock prices. The seventh line is from the PriceChange event invocation, where it called the PricePerTradeChange event handler. It prints out the name of the StockBroker company and the new trading price. The last line shows the recommendation from the StockBroker class. The recommendation is regenerated every time the program is run and, therefore, will most likely change between program executions.

Explicit Implementation

Sometimes it's necessary to explicitly declare which interface a class or struct member implements. One common reason for explicit implementation is when there is multiple interface inheritance and two or more interfaces declare a member with the same name. Another reason to use explicit interface implementation is to hide a specific implementation.

To perform explicit interface implementation, a class implements an interface member by using its fully qualified name. The implementation is not declared with modifiers, because they are implicitly hidden from an object of the implementing class. However, they are implicitly visible to objects of the explicit interface type. The examples in this chapter show how this occurs.

Disambiguation of interfaces occurs when a class inherits two or more interfaces that have members with the same signature. Normally, a class can just implement the interface member, regardless of which interface it is a part of. However, sometimes it might be necessary to specify the interface in a user class. For this reason, explicit implementation is necessary to specify which implementation serves which interface. Listing 14.6 shows the implementation of two interfaces that have some members in common.

LISTING 14.6   A Couple of Interfaces with Identical Members

```
using System;
using System.Collections;

public delegate void ChangeRegistrar(object sender,
                              object evnt);

public interface IBroker
{
    string GetRating(string stock) ;

    decimal PricePerTrade
    {
```

LISTING 14.6   Continued

```
            get ;
            set ;
        }

        decimal this[string StockName]
        {
            get ;
            set ;
        }

        event ChangeRegistrar PriceChange ;
}

public interface IAdvisor
{
        string GetRating(string stock) ;

        decimal HourlyFees
        {
            get ;
            set ;
        }

        decimal this[string StockName]
        {
            get ;
            set ;
        }
}
```

The IBroker interface in this listing is the same as in previous sections. In the IAdvisor interface, the GetRating method and indexer methods are the same as corresponding members in the IBroker interface.

Sometimes it might be necessary to hide the implementation of an interface so that the particular member is private to the implementing class and users won't know about it. Hiding interface implementations can occur regardless of whether there are one or more inherited interfaces.

Hiding interface members with explicit implementation is not like hiding an inherited method. The difference is that a conversion is required to reference the explicit interface member definition. It generally indicates that the interface is not of particular interest to a user of that class or struct. Listing 14.7 demonstrates explicit interface implementation.

LISTING 14.7   Explicit Interface Implementation

```csharp
public class FinancialAdvisor : IBroker, IAdvisor
{
    Dictionary<string, Stock> m_stocks = new Dictionary<string, Stock>();
    decimal pricePerTrade;
    decimal fee;
    string brokerName;

    public FinancialAdvisor()
        : this(13.59m, 11.73m, "Anonymous")
    {
    }

    public FinancialAdvisor(decimal tradePrice,
                     decimal fee,
                     string brokerName)
    {
        pricePerTrade = tradePrice;
        this.fee = fee;
        this.brokerName = brokerName;
    }

    string IBroker.GetRating(string stock)
    {
        Stock myStock = (Stock)m_stocks[stock];
        return Enum.GetName(typeof(StockRating),
                    myStock.Rating);
    }

    string IAdvisor.GetRating(string stock)
    {
        Stock myStock = (Stock)m_stocks[stock];
        return Enum.GetName(typeof(StockRating),
                        (((int)++myStock.Rating) % 5));
    }

    private StockRating AssignRating(Stock newStock)
    {
        Random myRand = new Random();
        int nextRating = myRand.Next(4);
        return (StockRating)Enum.ToObject(
                        typeof(StockRating),
                        nextRating);
    }
```

LISTING 14.7   Continued

```
    decimal IAdvisor.HourlyFees
    {
        get
        {
            return fee;
        }
        set
        {
            fee = value;
        }
    }

    public decimal PricePerTrade
    {
        get
        {
            return pricePerTrade;
        }
        set
        {
            pricePerTrade = value;
            PriceChange(brokerName, value);
        }
    }

    public decimal this[string StockName]
    {
        get
        {
            Stock myStock = (Stock)m_stocks[StockName];
            return myStock.Price;
        }
        set
        {
            Stock myStock = new Stock();
            myStock.Name = StockName;
            myStock.Price = value;
            myStock.Rating = AssignRating(myStock);

            m_stocks.Add(StockName, myStock);
        }
    }

    public event ChangeRegistrar PriceChange;
}
```

14

Listing 14.7 shows how to use explicit interface implementation to disambiguate the implementation of interface methods and the hiding of interface members. The code is similar to the StockBroker class implementation with a few exceptions.

The FinancialAdvisor class inherits both the IBroker and IAdvisor interfaces. Commas separate multiple interface inheritance in class and struct declarations. This class has three explicit interface member implementations.

The GetRating method has two explicit member implementations. The first is the explicit implementation of the IBroker.GetRating method. It obtains the rating from the Stock object returned from the m_stocks collection.

The second explicit implementation is the IAdvisor.GetRating method. It's similar to the IBroker.GetRating method implementation, except that the myStock.Rating object is manipulated before being converted to a string. This manipulation consists of incrementing its value, casting it to an int type, and performing a modulus operation with the value 5 to keep it in the range of legal StockRating values.

The third explicit implementation is the IAdvisor.HourlyFees property. This property is essentially hidden to a using object of type FinancialAdvisor. This is how interface members are hidden.

The first two properties are also hidden to objects of type FinancialAdvisor class. However, they serve to disambiguate the implementation of that member to using classes. Listing 14.8 shows how these two members are used.

LISTING 14.8   Implementation of Explicit Interface Members

```
public class InterfaceTester
{
    public static int Main(string[] args)
    {
        string recommendation;
        FinancialAdvisor   finad = new FinancialAdvisor();
        InterfaceTester    iftst = new InterfaceTester();

        finad.PriceChange += new ChangeRegistrar(
                            iftst.PricePerTradeChange);

        finad["ABC"] = 15.39m;
        finad["DEF"] = 37.51m;

        Console.WriteLine("ABC Price is {0}", finad["ABC"]);
        Console.WriteLine("DEF Price is {0}", finad["DEF"]);

        Console.WriteLine("");

        finad.PricePerTrade = 10.55m;
```

LISTING 14.8   Continued

```
        // HourlyFees property is hidden and won't compile
        //finad.HourlyFees    = 9.00m;

        Console.WriteLine("");

        recommendation = ((IBroker) finad).GetRating("ABC");

        Console.WriteLine(
            "(IBroker)finad's recommendation for ABC is {0}",
            recommendation);

        recommendation = ((IAdvisor)finad).GetRating("ABC");

        Console.WriteLine(
            "(IAdvisor)finad's recommendation for ABC is {0}",
            recommendation);

        return 0;
    }

    public void PricePerTradeChange(object sender,
                        object evnt)
    {
        Console.WriteLine(
            "Trading price for {0} changed to {1}.",
            (string) sender, (decimal) evnt);
    }
}
```

Listing 14.8 shows how to use class members that were explicitly implemented to avoid ambiguity. It also has a commented member that shows how an error would be generated for an explicit implementation of an interface member for the purpose of hiding. The Main method of the InterfaceTester class contains code that tests the FinancialAdvisor class implementation.

The FinancialAdvisor class is instantiated, the PricePerTradeChange event handler is added to the PriceChange event, and the stock values are instantiated as in examples in previous sections. The first difference in this code is the commented section where there is an instruction to load the HourlyFees property of the finad object with a value. If this were uncommented, it would produce a compiler error because the code wouldn't recognize the HourlyFees property of the FinancialAdvisor class because that property is hidden through explicit interface implementation.

The next portion of code uses the GetRating methods of the FinancialAdvisor class. The difference between the two calls is the object type used. Each is cast to a separate interface type. The object with the `IBroker` cast invokes the explicit implementation of `IBroker.GetRating`. Similarly, the `IAdvisor` cast causes invocation of the `IAdvisor.GetRating` explicit member implementation. This is how explicit implementation for disambiguation of interface implementation is used.

SAFER CONVERSIONS

The example in Listing 14.8 made the assumption that the classes implemented the interfaces. In a production environment, it might be more appropriate to use the `is` and `as` operators to avoid the exception that could be raised.

Interface Mapping

Interface mapping is the method used to determine where and if an interface member is implemented. Interface mapping is important because programmers need a way to figure out why they're getting program errors for not implementing an interface. Another scenario might be strange program behavior because of an interface member implemented somewhere other than the class that directly inherits from the interface. The solution is to understand enough about interface mapping to determine whether and where an interface member was implemented.

In all previous cases, mapping was easy to determine: It happened directly in the derived class that implemented that interface. Most interface implementation occurs that way. However, interface mapping allows alternative ways to determine whether an interface has been implemented. Besides the directly derived class of the interface, an implementation could be in the parent class hierarchy of the class derived from the interface. This follows object-oriented principles where a derived class "is" an inherited class. Remember, when declaring inheritance relationships with both a class and interfaces, the class comes first in the list. Using the `IBroker` and `IAdvisor` interfaces from previous sections in this chapter, Listing 14.9 shows an example of how this could occur.

LISTING 14.9   Interface Mapping Example

```
public class StockBroker
{
    Hashtable stocks = new Hashtable();
    decimal pricePerTrade;
    string  brokerName;

    public StockBroker() : this(13.59m, "Anonymous")
    {
    }

    public StockBroker(decimal price)
                    : this(price, "Anonymous")
```

LISTING 14.9   Continued

```
    {
    }

    public StockBroker(decimal price, string brokerName)
    {
        pricePerTrade = price;
        this.brokerName = brokerName;
    }

    public string GetRating(string stock)
    {
        Stock myStock = (Stock) stocks[stock];
        return Enum.GetName(typeof(StockRating),
                    myStock.Rating);
    }

    private StockRating AssignRating(Stock newStock)
    {
        Random myRand = new Random();
        int nextRating = myRand.Next(4);
        return (StockRating) Enum.ToObject(
                            typeof(StockRating),
                            nextRating);
    }

    public decimal PricePerTrade
    {
        get
        {
            return pricePerTrade;
        }
        set
        {
            pricePerTrade = value;
            PriceChange(brokerName, value);
        }
    }

    public decimal this[string StockName]
    {
        get
        {
            Stock myStock = (Stock)stocks[StockName];
            return myStock.Price;
        }
```

LISTING 14.9   Continued

```
        set
        {
            Stock myStock  = new Stock();
            myStock.Name   = StockName;
            myStock.Price  = value;
            myStock.Rating = AssignRating(myStock);

            stocks.Add(StockName, myStock);
        }
    }

    public event ChangeRegistrar PriceChange;
}
```

Listing 14.9 is the same as the StockBroker class in previous sections of this chapter with one significant exception: It doesn't derive from the IBroker interface. If a class were to derive from the StockBroker class in Listing 14.9, it would inherit the entire implementation. The following example shows how the C# interface mapping strategy works to find the implementation of interface members:

```
public class Accountant : StockBroker, IBroker
{
    // no implementation
}
```

The Accountant class has absolutely no implementation. However, it does inherit from the StockBroker class and, therefore, possesses the implementation of the StockBroker class.

The Accountant class also inherits the IBroker interface. It has no implementation of its own, yet the preceding code compiles perfectly without error. This is because with C# interface mapping, the implementation of the StockBroker class is used to map to the implementation requirements of the IBroker interface. Of note is that the interface mapping would have worked even if the StockBroker class inherited the IBroker interface itself.

If the StockBroker class did not implement a given interface member, the Accountant class would then be required to implement that member. Remember, every member of an interface must be implemented.

Interface Inheritance

Interfaces can inherit from each other. This makes it possible to create an abstract hierarchy of interfaces that support some domain. When interfaces inherit from each other, they inherit the contract of the interfaces above them. Also, interfaces can inherit multiply from other interfaces. The following example shows how one interface can inherit from another:

```
public interface IShareTrade
{
    decimal PricePerTrade
    {
        get ;
        set ;
    }

    event ChangeRegistrar PriceChange ;
}

public interface IBroker : IShareTrade
{
    string GetRating(string stock) ;

    decimal this[string StockName]
    {
        get ;
        set ;
    }
}
```

The IBroker interface inherits the PricePerTrade property declaration and the PriceChange event declaration from the IShareTrade interface. All combined, these are the same interface members from the IBroker interface of previous sections. Therefore, any class inheriting the IBroker interface will have the exact same set of interface members to implement, which is also the exact same contract. Listing 14.10 demonstrates that the contract of inherited interfaces is passed with derived interfaces to derived classes and structs for implementation.

LISTING 14.10   Interfaces Inheriting Other Interfaces

```
public class FinanceCompany : IBroker
{
    Dictionary<string, decimal> m_stocks
        = new Dictionary<string, decimal>();

    decimal pricePerTrade;

    public FinanceCompany()
        : this(10.50m)
    {
    }

    public FinanceCompany(decimal price)
    {
```

LISTING 14.10   Continued

```
        pricePerTrade = price;
    }

    public string GetRating(string stock)
    {
        return "Buy";
    }

    public decimal PricePerTrade
    {
        get
        {
            return pricePerTrade;
        }
        set
        {
            pricePerTrade = value;
            PriceChange("FinanceBroker", value);
        }
    }

    public decimal this[string StockName]
    {
        get
        {
            return m_stocks[StockName];
        }
        set
        {
            m_stocks.Add(StockName, value);
        }
    }

    public event ChangeRegistrar PriceChange;
}
```

In this listing, the FinanceCompany class and the InterfaceTester class that uses it are exactly the same as in previous sections of this chapter. If one of the FinanceCompany class members specified in either the IStockTrade or IBroker interfaces were omitted from the FinanceCompany class implementation, a compiler error would be generated. This proves that an implementing class must fulfill the contract of every interface in the interface inheritance hierarchy.

OBJECT VERSUS INTERFACE INHERITANCE

Interface inheritance is not the same as object inheritance in the areas of implementation and multiplicity. Object inheritance means that all derived objects also inherit implementation of base objects. Because interfaces don't have implementations, derived classes have the responsibility to implement interface members.

Object inheritance is limited in that there is only single implementation inheritance. In other words, derived classes can inherit from only one class. However, classes and structs can inherit as many interfaces as you need.

Summary

You now know how to implement an abstract class. You've seen how abstract classes have normal implementation class members and abstract members.

You also learned about interfaces and their members. I continued by showing how both implicitly and explicitly implement interfaces. You also saw how interface mapping works and how to inherit other interfaces.

This finishes the object-oriented programming part of this book. Now it's time to turn to some more advanced features. In the next section, you learn how to properly manage object lifetime, implement reflection, use lambdas, and learn how to use generic types (after I've been teasing you with generic code snippets for so long already).

14

PART 3

Applying Advanced C# Language Features

CHAPTER 15

Managing Object Lifetime

We enter this world with great fanfare, live our lives, and eventually get old and die. Some people have more drama in their lives than others, but that's often a consequence of the environment they are in and how they're raised. One thing is for sure: The beginning and end of life are significant events.

Similar to people, the objects of our applications have a lifetime, which includes a beginning, middle, and end. Objects begin life via instantiation. In C#, that means a constructor invocation. Just like the level of drama in a person's life, the attributes and behavior of an object interacting with user input determines what happens to that object and its affect on other objects in the system. Predicting when a person will leave this world is as accurate as when the Common Language Runtime (CLR) will clean an object from memory—you don't know. Nevertheless, there is a significant process the CLR engages in to ensure the end of that object's lifetime is handled properly.

Throughout this book, we discuss what happens to an object during its lifetime. However, the purpose of this chapter is to drill down on what happens when an object is first created and when that object is no longer being used. To do this, you learn about constructors to ensure an object is instantiated properly. We also devote significant attention to the CLR memory management process, which is essential to understanding how an object is handled at the end of its lifetime.

Let's start at the beginning, learning about constructors.

Object Initialization

You've been implicitly using constructors in all the C# programs written so far. Every object in C# has a constructor, whether default or defined. When you don't define explicit constructors for an object, C# creates a default constructor behind the scenes. This section shows you how constructors work and covers some tricky scenarios that could catch you off guard if you don't have a full understanding of how constructors work. Much of the material focuses on instance constructors, but I also show you how to define static constructors. C# 3.0 introduced a new way to initialize objects, called type initializers. After you learn how constructors work, I show you how type initializers can make object construction even easier.

Instance Constructors

The purpose of instance constructors is to initialize object instance fields. Instance constructors are convenient because they provide a centralized place to instantiate fields. Instance constructors also enable the ability to dynamically alter the initial values of fields, based on arguments passed to the constructor when the instance of a class is created. Constructors are invoked only on instantiation and can't be called by other programs later.

WHERE ARE CONSTRUCTORS DECLARED?

You can define constructors for both class and struct custom types. This chapter uses the term *object*, but you can't declare constructors for custom delegate, enum, or interface types, which wouldn't make sense because of the way they are used.

Declare constructors with the same name as the class of which they are members. You may include zero or more parameters for users to pass initialization information. Constructors don't have return values. The following example declares a constructor for the WebSite class, which accepts three parameters to initialize the class with:

```
public class WebSite
{

    string siteName;
    string url;
    string description;

    public WebSite(string newSite,
                   string newURL,
                   string newDesc)
    {
        siteName    = newSite;
```

```
    url         = newURL;
    description = newDesc;
  }
}
```

Notice that the constructor name is exactly the same as the class name, which is required. It has three parameters that have values that accept caller arguments, passed whenever the class is instantiated. Constructor parameters are just like method parameters.

Constructors do not have a return value. Their purpose is to instantiate an object and that object is returned when instantiating via the new operator. The following statement uses the new operator to create an instance of the WebSite class, effectively calling the previous WebSite constructor:

```
WebSite mySite = new WebSite(
                  "Computer Security Mega-Site",
                  "http://www.comp_sec-mega_site.com",
                  "Computer Security Information");
```

This example instantiates a new object of class type WebSite. The three arguments are passed to the WebSite constructor so that this WebSite instance can be initialized with the requested data.

Sometimes it's a pain in other languages when trying to figure out new names for the same thing. It often makes sense to use a meaningful name and then have a convention specifying which object is being referred to. That's what the this keyword can be used for, as shown in the following example:

```
public class WebSite
{
    string siteName;
    string url;
    string description;

    public WebSite(string siteName,
                   string url,
                   string description)
    {
        this.siteName    = siteName;
        this.url         = url;
        this.description = description;
    }
}
```

In this example, the constructor parameters have the same name as the fields. You can use the this keyword, just like this example, in your own applications to avoid such ambiguity. The this keyword refers to the current instance of a class. In the example, `this.siteName` refers to the class field `siteName`. Within the constructor, `siteName` (without the `this` key word) refers to the parameter `siteName`.

When the constructor in the example executes, it instantiates fields with the values of the parameters. This is normal—objects are customized by specifying unique arguments during their instantiation.

Overloading Constructors

Objects are not limited to a single constructor because you are allowed to overload constructors. A constructor overload works the same as a method overload where each overload differs by number and type of parameter. The goal of constructor overloads should be to make it easier and more intuitive for the caller to instantiate your object. Here's an example that overloads the `WebSite` class constructors:

```
public class WebSite
{
    string siteName;
    string url;
    string description;

    // Constructors
    public WebSite()
        : this("No Site", "no.url", "No Description") {}

    public WebSite(string newSite)
        : this(newSite, "no.url", "No Description") {}

    public WebSite(string newSite, string newURL)
        : this(newSite, newURL, "No Description") {}

    public WebSite(string newSite,
                   string newURL,
                   string newDesc)
    {
        siteName    = newSite;
        url         = newURL;
        description = newDesc;
    }
}
```

This example shows multiple constructors. They're primarily differentiated by the number of parameters they accept. The last constructor with the three parameters is familiar because it's identical to a previous example. The most notable difference between all the other constructors and the one with three parameters is that the other constructors have no implementation.

The first three constructors also have a different declaration. After the constructor name is a colon and the keyword this. The this keyword refers to the current instance of an object. When used with a constructor declaration, the this keyword calls another constructor of the current instance.

The first three constructors have zero, one, and two parameters in their parameter list. The effect is that the last constructor with three parameters is called. Because none of the other constructors have three parameters of their own, they supply all the information they have available and then add a default value to the argument they don't have a value for.

Each of the first three constructors could have its own implementations. However, this is risky, and any time it becomes necessary to modify an object's initialization, all the constructors would have to be modified. This could lead to bugs, not to mention unnecessary work. By using the this keyword in every constructor to call a single constructor that implements the object initialization, a class becomes more robust and easier to maintain.

In class initialization, there is a defined order of initialization, as follows:

1. Class field initializers. This guarantees they can be initialized before one of the constructors tries to access them.

2. Other constructors called with the this operator.

3. Statements within the constructor's block.

Multiple constructors provide a flexible way to instantiate a class, depending on an application's needs. It can also contribute to making a class more reusable.

Default Constructors

If desired, an object can be declared with no constructors at all—this does not mean that the object doesn't have a constructor, because C# implicitly defines a default constructor. This allows an object to be instantiated regardless of whether it has a constructor. Default constructors have no parameters.

If a class declares one or more constructors, a default constructor is not created automatically. Therefore, it's usually a good idea to include a parameterless constructor, just in case someone tries to instantiate a class with no parameters. A parameterless constructor can also come in handy with automated tools.

Private Constructors

Normally, constructors are declared with public access, but sometimes it's necessary to declare a private constructor. A single private constructor can prevent the class from being derived from or instantiated. This is useful if all of a class's members are static because it would be illogical to try to instantiate an object of this class type.

Here's an example of a class where the constructor is private and the methods are static:

```
public class MortgageCalculations
{
    private MortgageCalculations() {}

    public static decimal MonthlyPayment(
        decimal rate,
        decimal price,
         int years)
    {
        // implementation
    }
    public static decimal TotalInterest(
        decimal rate,
        decimal price,
        int years)
    {
        // implementation
    }
    public static void PrintSchedule(
        decimal rate,
        decimal price,
        int years)
    {
        // implementation
    }
}
```

The MorgateCalculation class here also has no state (fields). Its methods are well-known functions that can be used by many different programs. There is no reason to instantiate a class for calling these methods. Therefore, it is useful to prevent instantiation of this class with a private constructor.

Inheritance and Order of Instantiation

When instantiating classes in an inheritance chain, you need a deterministic way to know which classes instantiate first. This section clarifies what you need to know about the order of invocation for constructors and some tricky scenarios you'll want to know about.

This section concentrates on instance fields, but what about static fields? Static fields shouldn't be accessed within instance constructors because that could possibly create redundant code to execute every time a new instance is created or leave a class in an inconsistent state when subsequent static methods, if any, are invoked. A good rule of thumb is to keep static field initialization in static constructors and instance field initialization in instance constructors. The next section covers static constructors.

Static Constructors

You would use a static constructor any time the static fields of an object need to be initialized to something other than their default values. Static constructors are invoked when a class is loaded. Because classes are loaded only once during the lifetime of a program's execution, static constructors are invoked only one time each time your program runs.

Static constructors can access only static fields. There are two reasons for this. First, static classes are loaded before any instance of an object can be created. It stands to reason, therefore, that instance fields may not have been initialized at that point in time. Certainly, the instance constructor, which is invoked when an object is instantiated, hasn't been invoked yet. It may never be invoked. Therefore, there shouldn't be any attempts to access uninstantiated fields. Such behavior would violate definite assignment and cause funny things to happen to the code (or not so funny, depending on one's perspective).

Second, the purpose of instance fields is just as their name implies, for a specific instance. Static fields are applicable to the type, regardless of instance. Therefore, trying to access instance fields in a static constructor would be illogical. Here's an example of a static constructor, which initializes a static field:

```
public class Randomizer
{
    private static int seed;

    static Randomizer()
    {
        DateTime myDateTime = DateTime.Now;
        seed = myDateTime.GetHashCode();
    }
}
```

Static constructors start with the keyword `static`. They do not return a value. The static constructor name is the same as the class name. It always has an empty parameter list. Because it's never instantiated, parameters wouldn't make sense.

Static constructors cannot be called by programs. They're invoked only when a class is loaded and there is no specified sequence of operations for when a static constructor is invoked, but there are a few conditions that can be relied on:

▶ The type is loaded before the first instance is created.

▶ The type is loaded prior to accessing static members.

15

▸ The type is loaded ahead of any derived types.

▸ The type is loaded only one time per program execution.

Object Initializers

A new feature added to C# 3.0 was object initializers. Instead of calling a constructor, you can provide an initialization list containing fields and properties and the values you want to set them to. The following explanation uses the StaffMember and MedicalOffice classes defined here:

```
class StaffMember
{
    public string Name { get; set; }
}
class MedicalOffice
{
    public StaffMember Doctor { get; set; }
    public StaffMember LeadNurse { get; set; }
    public StaffMember AssistantNurse { get; set; }
    public StaffMember Intern1 { get; set; }
    public StaffMember Intern2 { get; set; }
    public StaffMember Intern3 { get; set; }
    public StaffMember Intern4 { get; set; }
}
```

With type initializers, you don't need to worry about constructors. Here's how you can initialize a StaffMember object:

```
var staffMemberNew = new StaffMember { Name = "Joe" };
```

Between the curly braces, identify the field or property, use the assignment operator, and then specify the value. You can also initialize multiple properties by separating them with commas. Here's a more elaborate example that initializes a MedicalOffice with a Doctor and LeadNurse:

```
var medOff = new MedicalOffice
{
    Doctor = new StaffMember()
    {
        Name = "Marcus"
    },
    LeadNurse = new StaffMember
    {
```

```
            Name = "Nancy"
        }
    };
```

In this case, the values assigned to both `Doctor` and `LeadNurse` are declared with a type initializer, too.

Object Finalization

The original purpose of finalizers was to clean up resources when an object is cleaned up by the Garbage Collector (GC). However, because of the way the CLR GC handles objects, there is the distinct possibility of a finalizer not being called. Furthermore, there is no precise time after which your object is destroyed that a finalizer is called, which causes problems in scalability. This section shows you how finalizers work because they are class members, but you should read the next section to understand the problems with finalizers and the proper way to clean up object resources.

The following example shows how to define a finalizer. It adds a finalizer to the `WebSite` class:

```
public class WebSite
{
    string siteName;
    string url;
    string description;

    public WebSite(string newSite,
                   string newURL,
                   string newDesc)
    {
        siteName    = newSite;
        url         = newURL;
        description = newDesc;
    }

    ~WebSite() {}
}
```

The preceding example shows a typical implementation. All finalizers begin with the tilde, ~, symbol. Their names are the same as their enclosing class name. Their parameter lists are empty. They do not return a value—finalizers can't be called by functions, so return values wouldn't make sense.

Using a finalizer to clean up class resources increases the risk of resource depletion, system corruption, or deadlock. The basic rule is this: Don't depend on a finalizer to release critical resources being held by a class. The next section begins a journey to understanding

15

why finalizers are so problematic and how to solve the problem of ensuring correct resource cleanup.

DESTRUCTOR VERSUS FINALIZER

Prior to C# v2.0, finalizers were actually called destructors. This makes sense if you understand that C# is an evolution of the C++ programming language. A C# finalizer has similar syntax to a C++ destructor, so it was natural for the C# designers to call it a destructor. However, the behavior between a C# finalizer and a C++ destructor is significantly different. In C++ the object is freed from memory deterministically (when deleted/freed in code), but C# object cleanup is nondeterministic (when the GC cleans it up). Because of this significant difference in behavior and purpose, the C# designers renamed destructors as finalizers in C# v2.0, which represents what they are more appropriately and reduces confusion by many C++ programmers adopting C#. The material in this chapter is designed to help you understand the important concepts and practices involved in ensuring your objects and the resources they acquire are cleaned up properly.

Automatic Memory Management

If you're one of the developers who have suffered through years of memory leaks, dangling pointers, memory corruption caused by the misapplication of explicit memory management, you might appreciate the memory allocation and garbage collection features of the CLR. It's a benefit often cited for the migration of programmers to the Java platform and more recently hoards of programmers to .NET languages, especially C#. Although automatic memory management has solved countless problems for programmers who came from languages without it, there are tradeoffs (although much less with automatic memory management) that you need to attend to.

It would be nice if all we needed to do was program business logic without worrying about memory management. In most cases this is true, but you still have responsibility for releasing resources such as file streams, database connections, or operating system handles. Yes, the problems have decreased, but it is still necessary to understand the garbage collection process to ensure that a program runs properly and is a good citizen with resources.

We'll look at memory allocation first and then move on to garbage collection.

Memory Allocation

Reference type objects are allocated on the managed heap (heap) when instantiated with the new operator. CLR memory allocation is efficient because objects are created sequentially on the heap. The heap has a special pointer that begins at position 0 on the heap and is incremented for the size of the allocated object. This establishes the beginning point for the next object to be allocated. The process continues until memory is full.

Figure 15.1 is a graphical representation of the heap after four objects—A, B, C, and D—have been allocated on the heap. After each allocation, the Next Object Pointer points to the top of the last allocated object, marking the location of the beginning of the next object to be allocated.

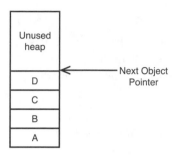

FIGURE 15.1   Memory allocation.

When the heap is full, two things can happen. If all allocated objects are live and in use, an OutOfMemoryException is thrown, and your program must free some objects before allocating any more. The more likely case is that there are unused objects in memory and the GC can kick in and clean up these objects, freeing heap space for the new allocations.

WHEN DOES THE GARBAGE COLLECTOR KICK IN?

Garbage collection is nondeterministic, meaning that there is no way to know for sure when it will run. We can assume that when memory is full, the GC will run, but it is unwise to try to make coding decisions based on assumptions. Microsoft continuously tweaks GC performance for each release of .NET, so any generalization you make today won't necessarily be accurate in the next version. The guidance in this chapter for implementing the dispose pattern is based on the fact that the GC is nondeterministic and is a broadly adopted best practice, recommended by Microsoft, for properly handling release of resources.

Inside the Garbage Collector

In the preceding section, you saw how efficient CLR memory allocation is because it works with a compressed heap. The process that cleans objects from memory and eliminates heap fragmentation is called garbage collection. It is implemented via a CLR service, appropriately called the Garbage Collector (GC).

When an object goes out of scope or all references to it are set to null, that object becomes available for garbage collection. As long as there is an active reference to an object from your program, the GC won't try to clean that object.

Determining which objects are collectable involves a process of creating a graph of live objects and, after all objects have been visited, cleaning up objects that are not in the graph. This graph begins with a set of roots, such as global and static objects. Following each object reference from each root and adding each referenced object creates the graph. The GC algorithm is smart enough to avoid creating circular references in the graph.

The GC then goes to work, clearing the objects that aren't in the graph. The remaining objects are then compacted on the heap, and the pointer to the next available heap memory location is set to the position past the last object in the compacted heap.

Figure 15.2 shows the garbage collection process in three stages:

Beginning—This stage shows the status of objects in memory as the GC constructs the active-object graph. Object A is the root, pointing to objects B and D. Further object visitation discovers that object B contains a reference to object F, which is then added to the graph.

During—Because objects C and E are no longer referenced by any other objects, they're cleaned up. This leaves fragmentation in memory as you can see in the second stage.

After—The last stage shows how heap objects are compacted, eliminating fragmentation, and the Next Object Pointer is reset, ready for the next object to be allocated.

GC Optimization

The GC has several optimizations that increase its execution speed. According to Microsoft, the current execution time for a garbage collection on .NET approximates a typical page fault. Although other optimizations would be interesting to discuss at a theoretical level, the generations optimization is the only one that directly affects you as a programmer. Generations are based on research that has revealed the fact that the older an object is, the more likely it is to stick around.

The GC manages three generations, numbered 0 to 2. All objects begin life at generation 0. Objects that live through a garbage collection are promoted to the next generation, up to level 2. For example, generation 0 objects become generation 1 objects after the first garbage collection occurring after their creation. If generation 1 objects are still alive during the next garbage collection, they're moved to generation 2, which is the highest they can go.

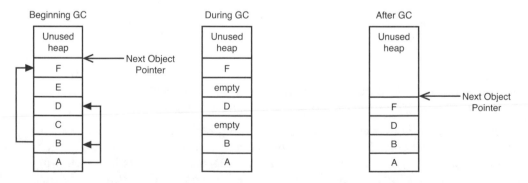

FIGURE 15.2   The garbage collection process.

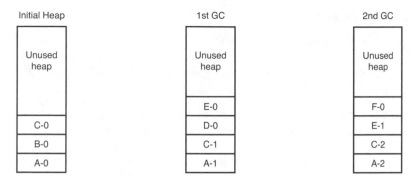

FIGURE 15.3   The generations optimization.

Figure 15.3 shows an example of the three-stage generational optimization:

> **Initial heap**—The first stage shows objects A, B, and C after they have been initialized and their generation set to 0.
>
> **1st GC**—After the first garbage collection, objects A and C are moved up to generation 1. Object B has been removed because it was determined to be unused. Objects D and E were instantiated and set to generation 0, as all newly instantiated objects are.
>
> **2nd GC**—Before the second garbage collection occurs, object D is determined to be unused. Therefore, the second garbage collection moves objects A and C to generation 2, removes object D, and moves object E to generation 1. After the garbage collection, object F is instantiated and becomes a generation 0 object.

If you are a C++ programmer, or other language where you must manage your own memory, the garbage collection process is likely of great concern. There is overhead involved with garbage collection. However, as you can see, there are optimizations in place to improve performance. Memory allocation is faster because of the compressed heap. In addition, because of generations, the GC can perform optimizations, such as collecting only level 0 objects, if that frees up enough memory, resulting in better performance than if all generations were cleaned up.

Now that you understand essentials of the garbage collection process, you're ready to learn how to properly clean up resources with the dispose pattern.

Proper Resource Cleanup

Class instances with finalizers are more expensive to clean up than class instances without finalizers. This is because the GC has to make two passes for objects with finalizers: The first pass executes the finalizer, and the second pass cleans up the object. This means that using finalizers introduces overhead into your application. This section builds on earlier GC knowledge to help clarify exactly what problems finalizers cause and then gives you a practical solution to clean up resources properly.

The Problems with Finalizers

The fact that the GC performs two passes to fully clean up objects with finalizers brings up some immediately obvious prob1lems. First of all, garbage collection on objects with finalizers is expensive. With two passes per object, the amount of time to clean up an object is doubled.

Another set of problems derives from the nondeterministic nature of garbage collection. There is no way to tell when the garbage collection will happen. Some garbage collection methods provide information and allow you to force a garbage collection, but the benefit-to-effort ratio is so small that they would be a waste of time.

Nondeterministic finalization also means that a program has no way to control the release of resources with finalizers alone. There's also no guarantee of the order in which destructors will be called by the GC. Therefore, sequential dependencies between object destructors should be avoided at all cost.

There are also scenarios where the GC might not run at all, such as a program crash. In some cases, such as database connections, the connection will eventually time out, but even that depends on the DBMS you are using. In some cases, such as a custom network connection to a mainframe computer or some other external system, you won't ever get a disconnect if the finalizer isn't called. This has dramatic effects on system availability, reliability, performance, and scalability.

I hope you now have the essential background knowledge of garbage collection, understand how garbage collection affects performance and affects finalizers, and appreciate the serious impact of trying to manage resource cleanup with finalizers alone. Now you're ready to see how to release resources properly.

The Dispose Pattern

The proper alternative to finalizers for releasing resources is use the Dispose pattern. You do this by having your object implement the IDisposable interface.

This is convenient because an object can be checked to see whether it supports the IDisposable interface and, if it does, have its Dispose method called. Listing 15.1 shows how to implement the Dispose pattern.

LISTING 15.1   The Dispose Pattern: DisposePattern.cs

```
class ResourceToDispose : IDisposable
{
    private bool m_disposed = false;

    public void Dispose()
    {
        Dispose(true);
        GC.SuppressFinalize(this);
    }
```

LISTING 15.1   Continued

```
    private void Dispose(bool calledByUser)
    {
        if (!m_disposed)
        {
            if (calledByUser)
            {
                // can clean up other managed objects
            }
            // clean up unmanaged resources

            m_disposed = true;
        }
    }

    ~ResourceToDispose()
    {
        Dispose(false);
    }
}

class DisposePattern
{
    static void Main()
    {
        ResourceToDispose resource = null;

        try
        {
            resource = new ResourceToDispose();

            // use resource
        }
        finally
        {
            if (resource != null)
            {
                resource.Dispose();
            }
        }
    }
}
```

The Dispose pattern is implemented by making a class that needs to release resources implement the IDisposable interface. In Listing 15.1, this class is ResourceToDispose, which implements `IDisposable`. Although the only method of the `IDisposable` interface is `Dispose`, much more goes into proper implementation of the `Dispose` pattern.

First notice that both `Dispose`, with no parameters, and the finalizer call `Dispose`, with the bool parameter. If called with `true`, via `Dispose` without parameters, it means that this object is being called by user code. When called via the finalizer, with `false` as the parameter, this object is being cleaned up via the GC.

After making sure that this object is cleaned up only once, checking `m_disposed`, the `Dispose` (bool) method checks to see whether it was called by either user code or the GC. The difference is significant because you don't ever want the GC thread to try cleaning up other managed objects. You see, it is possible that the GC already cleaned up those objects and you would cause an error, an `ObjectDisposedException`, by trying to access an object that no longer exists. Regardless of whether this object is being called via user code or the GC, you always need to clean up unmanaged resources, such as OS handles and GDI objects.

Notice that the second statement of `Dispose`, with no parameters, calls `SuppressFinalization`. This ensures that the GC won't try to call the finalizer, which wouldn't make sense because we just cleaned up the object. It is also more efficient because it helps avoid a second pass of the GC for finalization.

The `DisposePattern` class instantiates an object of type `DisposableClass`. By performing actions in a `try/finally` block, the program guarantees that the `Dispose` method will always be called, thus releasing resources immediately when they are no longer needed.

The `using` Statement

Hand in hand with the `IDisposable` interface is the `using` statement. The parameter to the `using` statement must be an `IDisposable` object; otherwise, a compile-time error will occur. The following example shows how to implement the `using` statement.

```
using (ResourceToDispose newResource = new ResourceToDispose())
{
    // use resource
} // automatically calls dispose
```

> **NOTE**
>
> The using statement should not be confused with the using declaration, the latter supporting declaration of external namespaces. The using statement supports deterministic resource release through the Dispose pattern.

The preceding code accomplishes the exact same thing as the `try/finally` block in Listing 15.1. In fact, it produces Intermediate Language (IL) code equivalent to the `try/finally` block in Listing 15.1. This is the preferred way to handle `IDisposable` objects, and you would use a `try/finally` only if an object isn't `IDisposable`.

Interacting with the Garbage Collector

For most applications, interacting with the GC will not be necessary. However, some advanced CLR experts might need access to GC APIs.

KNOW WHAT YOU ARE DOING BEFORE USING GC

Microsoft has devoted years of research into optimizing GC performance and has some of the world's best computer scientists working to eke out the next bit of optimization available for each successive version of the CLR. If you attempt to use GC API routines to enhance system performance, you should know for sure that what you are doing is an improvement. Fiddling with these APIs, without the proper knowledge, is likely to slow down performance because you are interfering with the normal operation of the CLR GC.

Controlling Objects

The GC class has several class members for working with the GC; these are shown in Table 15.1. For an example of how to force a garbage collection and observe its effects, see Listing 15.2.

TABLE 15.1 **GC** Class Members

Member Name	Description
MaxGeneration	A property specifying the maximum number of generations the GC supports
Collect	Forces a garbage collection
GetGeneration	Tells what generation an object belongs to
GetTotalMemory	Returns an approximation of allocated memory
KeepAlive	Prevents an object from being finalized
ReRegisterForFinalize	Adds a reference to an object back to the finalization queue
SuppressFinalize	Removes reference to an object from the finalization queue
WaitForPendingFinalizers	Waits for all finalizers for objects referenced in the finalization queue to complete

LISTING 15.2 Interacting with the Garbage Collector: CollectGenerations.cs

```
using System;
using System.Collections;

class CollectGenerations
```

LISTING 15.2   Continued

```
{
    static void Main(string[] args)
    {
        int maxGenerations = GC.MaxGeneration;

        ArrayList heapObjects = new ArrayList();
        string[] IDs = new string[]
            {"A", "B", "C", "D", "E", "F", "G",
             "H", "I", "J", "K", "L", "M", "N"};

        for (int i=0, j=0; i <= maxGenerations; i++, j+=2)
        {
            Console.WriteLine(
                "\nGarbage Collection #{0}: \n", i);

            heapObjects.Add(new AllocatedObject(IDs[j]));
            heapObjects.Add(new AllocatedObject(IDs[j+1]));

            foreach (AllocatedObject obj in heapObjects)
            {
                obj.TellGeneration();
            }

            GC.Collect();
        }
    }
}

class AllocatedObject
{
    string name;

    public AllocatedObject(string name)
    {
        this.name = name;
    }

    public void TellGeneration()
    {
        Console.WriteLine("Object {0} is Generation {1}.",
            name, GC.GetGeneration(this));
    }
}
```

And here's the output:

```
Garbage Collection #0:


Object A is Generation 0.
Object B is Generation 0.

Garbage Collection #1:

Object A is Generation 1.
Object B is Generation 1.
Object C is Generation 0.
Object D is Generation 0.

Garbage Collection #2:

Object A is Generation 2.
Object B is Generation 2.
Object C is Generation 1.
Object D is Generation 1.
Object E is Generation 0.
Object F is Generation 0.
```

The first statement in the Main method of Listing 15.2 uses the GC class to get the maximum number of generations supported by the GC. Then it uses a loop to allocate objects and perform garbage collections. Each of the objects is from the class AllocatedObject, which has a TellGeneration method. On every pass through the for loop, the TellGeneration method is called on each AllocatedObject object. Within the TellGeneration method is a Console.WriteLine method that takes a second parameter telling which generation the object belongs to. The result for the second parameter is produced by a call to the GetGeneration method of the GC class. The parameter to the GetGeneration method specifies the object whose generation will be returned.

Summary

C# gives you features for managing the lifetime of objects in your application. You've learned how to initialize objects properly when instantiated by declaring constructors. You can overload constructors and know how to manage the construction process for inherited objects.

To understand the finalization process and how to properly release resources, you needed to learn about CLR memory allocation and the garbage collection process. This chapter provided this essential knowledge, helping you understand problems with finalizers. And now you have an appreciation for why the Dispose pattern is a best practice and how to release resources properly.

Next, you'll learn about using attributes and reflection.

CHAPTER 16

Declaring Attributes and Examining Code with Reflection

Magicians make everything look too easy on stage. However, a lot of work goes on behind the scenes of a magic show to make the public presentation work well. Similarly, the contents of an assembly are something that most people don't pay attention to, but enjoy the benefits of. Just as the audience doesn't know how all of those scarves can be stuffed into the magician's jacket, abstractions, such as modifiers and parameter types, are attributes that are quietly hidden in the metadata of an assembly so that the programmer can enjoy the benefits without the gory details. Also, the magician uses mirrors to execute a well-timed performance, but the C# programmer can use the feature of reflection to invoke methods on classes where you don't have direct access to the code. For the untrained eye, attributes and reflection seem like magic, but you'll soon learn that they aren't.

Attributes are program elements that decorate code to provide declarative functionality and metadata for a program. Metadata is the information about a program, its internal elements, and any other aspects of the code that may be interesting to developers. Other languages and systems use Interface Definition Language (IDL), interfaces, type libraries, and basic reflection to obtain metadata on programs.

Attributes and reflection have an intimate relationship with assembly metadata. Attributes are a part of that metadata, and reflection understands metadata, allowing you to extract information about attributes and code. By extracting attributes from metadata via reflection, calling code can make assumptions about the code in the assembly. For example, a unit testing program can dynamically extract attributes, at runtime, that identify which classes and methods of an assembly have unit test code. Using reflection, the unit testing tool can do late-bound instantiation, during runtime, of test classes and invoke test methods. This is one example of how attributes and reflection allow building powerful tools that operate on code. You'll see more in this chapter as you learn what attributes are, how to create your own, reading attributes with reflection and using reflection to dynamically discover and run any code in an assembly.

Using Attributes

Using attributes is simple. They are placed on the program element (target) to which they refer and are surrounded by square brackets. Within the square brackets, there are one or more comma-separated attributes. Attribute parameters may be specified as either positional or named. The following sections show how to use attributes and specify their parameters.

Using an Attribute

The simplest attribute to implement is one with no parameters. Listing 16.1 shows an example of the `Flags` attribute, which is used on the `ProblemStatus` enum.

LISTING 16.1   Using a Single Attribute

```
using System;

[Flags]
public enum ProblemStatus
{
    Assigned  = 0x0001,
    NoProblem = 0x0002,
    Open      = 0x0004,
    Resolved  = 0x0008
}

/// <summary>
///     Using a Single Attribute.
/// </summary>
class SingleAttribute
{
    static void Main(string[] args)
    {
        ProblemStatus currentStatus =
            (ProblemStatus.Open | ProblemStatus.Assigned);

        if (((currentStatus & ProblemStatus.NoProblem) != 0) |
            ((currentStatus & ProblemStatus.Resolved)  != 0) )
```

LISTING 16.1   Continued

```
        {
            Console.WriteLine("Problem Closed: {0}",
                currentStatus);
        }
        else
        {
            Console.WriteLine("Problem Still Open: {0}",
                currentStatus);
        }
    }
}
```

And the output is

```
Problem Still Open: Assigned, Open
```

The Flags attribute gives an enum the capability to be treated like a bitfield, using logical operations such as the OR (¦) as done in the Main method in Listing 16.1.

Using Multiple Attributes

Multiple attributes may be specified together. Listing 16.2 demonstrates the proper syntax for using multiple attributes in a single program element.

LISTING 16.2   Using Multiple Attributes

```
[Flags, Serializable]
public enum ProblemStatus
{
    Assigned  = 0x0001,
    NoProblem = 0x0002,
    Open      = 0x0004,
    Resolved  = 0x0008
}
```

Listing 16.2 shows how a comma separates the Flags and Serializable attributes. The Serializable attribute means that a program element can be serialized. Serialization is the process of transforming an object into a form that can be transported out of an AppDomain, typically across a network. In Chapter 32, "Communicating Out of Process with .NET Remoting," you learn how objects can be transported via remoting across a wire in binary serialization format, and in Chapter 33, "Writing Traditional ASMX Web Services," you learn how an object can be sent across a network in XML serialization format. The Flags and Serializable interface could also have been specified as follows:

```
[Flags]
[Serializable]
```

```
public enum ProblemStatus
{
    Assigned  = 0x0001,
    NoProblem = 0x0002,
    Open      = 0x0004,
    Resolved  = 0x0008
}
```

Each attribute of the example is specified in its own square brackets; however, the result is the same, as shown in Listing 16.2. This is just another way to specify the same thing.

Using Attribute Parameters

Attributes have parameters, allowing you to customize their behavior. Because an attribute is actually another object, the parameters act the same as parameters for instance constructors or setting properties and fields.

There are two types of parameters: positional and named. Parameters can include only positional, only named, or a combination of both positional and named. Positional attributes are mandatory and always come before named attributes. The following sections go into more detail about each of these attribute parameter types.

Positional Parameters

Positional parameters correspond to the parameters of an attribute's public constructors. If there's only a single public constructor, the parameters of that constructor must be used. Otherwise, positional parameters for any available public constructor of the attribute may be used. Positional parameters must be specified in total and in the proper order for the attribute constructor being implemented. Listing 16.3 shows an example of using an attribute with positional parameters.

LISTING 16.3   Positional Parameters

```
using System;


/// <summary>
///     Positional Parameter.
/// </summary>
class PositionalParameter
{
    [Obsolete("Use this method at your own risk!")]
    public static void OldMethod()
    {
    }

    static void Main(string[] args)
```

LISTING 16.3   Continued

```
    {
        OldMethod();
    }
}
```

The Obsolete attribute in Listing 16.3 uses a positional parameter, which is a string used to display a message during compilation. By default, this displays a warning when C# compiles the code, but the Obsolete attribute has another positional parameter called IsError. Here's how the second positional parameter is used.

```
[Obsolete("Use this method at your own risk!", true)]
```

The IsError positional parameter generates a compile-time error, displaying the message from the first positional parameter.

Named Parameters

Named parameters correspond to the public fields and properties of an attribute object. It's a compiler error for named parameters to be used for static or read-only fields and properties. Listing 16.4 demonstrates proper use of an attribute with named parameters.

LISTING 16.4   Named Parameters

```
using System;
using System.Runtime.InteropServices;

/// <summary>
///      Named Parameter.
/// </summary>
///
[StructLayout(LayoutKind.Auto, CharSet=CharSet.Unicode)]
class NamedParameter
{
    static void Main(string[] args)
    {
    }
}
```

Listing 16.4 uses StructLayout attribute, showing how to use a named parameter. The StructLayout attribute has its positional parameter, which is required, and then the named parameter. The named parameter has a name label, the equal sign, and then the value of the parameter. The StructLayout attribute is useful for passing classes and structs to unmanaged code where the physical layout of members must be exact.

16

Attribute Targets

Attribute targets specify which program element an attribute is applied to. They're often optional, but can sometimes help make the intent of the attribute more understandable. For example, if there were ambiguity as to whether an attribute applies to a method's return value or the method itself, an attribute target specification would resolve the ambiguity. Listing 16.5 contains an example of how to specify attribute targets.

LISTING 16.5   Attribute Targets

```
using System;


/// <summary>
///     Attribute Targets.
/// </summary>
[assembly:CLSCompliant(false)]
class AttributeTarget
{
    static void Main(string[] args)
    {
    }
}
```

The attribute in Listing 16.5 specifies that the CLSCompliant attribute applies to assembly, rather than to the class it is near. It has the target, assembly, separated from the attribute, CLSCompliant, by a single colon. A CLSCompliant attribute specifies whether the public interface of the targeted program element should conform to the Common Language Specification (CLS). Chapter 1, "Introducing the .NET Platform," discussed the significance of CLS.

Without specifying the target, there would be no way to tell whether this attribute decorates the class it is over or assembly. If the positional parameter were true, the assembly target would have been required before applying the CLSCompliant attribute to any other program element. Table 16.1 shows which targets are available when specifying attribute targets.

TABLE 16.1   Attribute Target Specifiers

Target Name	Applicable To
all	Any element
assembly	Entire assembly
class	A class
constructor	A constructor
delegate	A delegate
enum	An enum

TABLE 16.1 Continued

Target Name	Applicable To
event	An event
field	A field
interface	An interface
method	A method
module	Containing module
param	A parameter
property	A property
return	A return value
struct	A struct

Creating Your Own Attributes

The Framework Class Library (FCL) contains many attributes for various applications—too many to memorize. Because all attributes derive from the FCL Attribute class, you can find them by searching for the Attribute class in the documentation and looking for derived classes. Any time you need an attribute, browse the FCL, which you can learn how to do in Appendix B, "Getting Help with the .NET Framework," to see whether an existing attribute suits your needs. That's what the FCL is there for—reuse.

However, there are times when the predefined system library attributes are not enough for development needs, and it might be desirable to customize your own. Creating a custom attribute is similar to creating a normal class, except that they are decorated with the AttributeUsage attribute and derive from the System.Attribute class. The following sections describe what AttributeUsage is, how to apply it, and how to create a custom attribute with positional and named parameters.

Typically, the reason you would create custom attributes is to support a tool that you've written. For example, CLSCompliant and Obsolete attributes support the C# compiler, Test and TestMethod support the VS2008 unit testing tools, and Browsable and TypeEditor support creation of custom controls for VS2008. The following sections assume that there is a software engineering tool that extracts information about code authors.

The AttributeUsage Attribute

AttributeUsage specifies how a custom attribute can be used in a program. It specifies targets, number of times to use, and inheritance.

Attribute Targets
Some attributes will make sense only on certain program elements. For example, the Flags attribute makes sense only on an enum and would be illogical if applied to anything else such as a class or delegate.

AttributeUsage has a single positional parameter, specifying how its decorated attribute
may be used. Allowable values for this positional parameter may be one of the
AttributeTargets enum members shown in Table 16.2.

TABLE 16.2   **AttributeTarget** Enum Members Applied
with **AttributeUsage**

Target Name	Description
All	Any AttributeTargets member
Assembly	Assemblies
Class	Classes
Constructor	Constructors
Delegate	Delegates
Enum	Enums
Event	Events
Field	Fields
Interface	Interfaces
Method	Methods
Module	Modules
Parameter	Parameters
Property	Properties
ReturnValue	Return values
Struct	Structs

AttributeUsage is used just like any other attribute. It has a positional parameter,
described previously, and two named parameters. Listing 16.6 has the program we'll use in
both this and subsequent sections to describe AttributeUsage and implementation of a
custom attribute. The positional parameter of AttributeUsage in Listing 16.6 is set to
AttributeTargets.All, which means it can be used on any program element.

LISTING 16.6   Custom Attribute Example

```
using System;

/// <summary>
///     Custom Attribute Example.
/// </summary>
[
    Tracker("CR-0001",
            "some fix",
            EngineerId = "Joe",
            ChangeDate = "07/04/2008")
```

LISTING 16.6   Continued

```
]
class SomeProgram
{
    static void Main(string[] args)
    {
        SomeProgram sp = new SomeProgram();
    }
}


[
    AttributeUsage(AttributeTargets.All,
                   AllowMultiple = true,
                   Inherited     = true)
]

class TrackerAttribute : Attribute

{
    public  string   ProblemId;
    public  string   EngineerId;
    private string   fixDescription;
    private DateTime changeDate;

    public string FixDescription
    {
        get
        {
            return fixDescription;
        }
        set
        {
            fixDescription = value;
        }
    }

    public string ChangeDate
    {
        get
        {
            return changeDate.ToString("d");
        }
        set
        {
            changeDate = DateTime.Parse(value);
        }
    }
```

LISTING 16.6   Continued

```csharp
    public TrackerAttribute()
    {
        ProblemId      = "UNASSIGNED";
        EngineerId     = "Unidentified Engineer";
        FixDescription = "No description provided";
        ChangeDate     = "01/01/2009";
    }

    public TrackerAttribute(string problemId, string fixDescription)
    {
        ProblemId      = problemId;
        EngineerId     = "Unidentified Engineer";
        FixDescription = fixDescription;
        ChangeDate     = "01/01/2009";
    }
}
```

In Listing 16.6, the `TrackerAttribute` class has an `AttributeUsage` attribute, showing that this attribute may be used on any type of program element. All attributes inherit the `System.Attribute` class. Parameters of `AttributeUsage` are discussed in following sections.

The `TrackerAttribute` class has two public and two private fields. The private fields are exposed through class properties. The public fields, as expected, are directly exposed to user classes.

FIELD AND PROPERTY REQUIREMENTS

Attribute class fields and properties must be public, and properties must have both get and set accessors.

The `TrackerAttribute` class has a default constructor and a constructor with two parameters. The default constructor initializes all fields and properties to default values. The two-parameter constructor sets the `ProblemId` field and `FixDescription` property, while setting the `EngineerId` field and `ChangeDate` property to default values.

The implementation of the `SomeProgram` class in Listing 16.6 shows how this attribute can be used. It uses the two-parameter constructor implementation and adds the `EngineerId` and `ChangeDate` named parameters.

CUSTOM ATTRIBUTE NAMING CONVENTION

A common naming convention for C# attributes is to add the `Attribute` suffix to the classname. When applying the attribute, you can take a shortcut by leaving off the `Attribute` suffix.

Multiplicity

Controlling the number of times an attribute may be used on a single program element is specified by the AttributeUsage's named parameter, AllowMultiple, which is true in the following example:

```
[
    AttributeUsage(AttributeTargets.All,
                   AllowMultiple = true,
                   Inherited     = true)
]
```

The Tracker attribute in Listing 16.6 may be used multiple times on a program element because AllowMultiple of its AttributeUsage attribute is true. AllowMultiple in other attributes, such as Flags and Serializable, are false because they may be used only one time, which makes sense if you think about how they're used.

Attribute Inheritance

Using the Inherited named parameter of AttributeUsage controls inheritance of attributes. When set to true, the attribute applies to derived classes; false means that the attribute applies only to the immediate object, and derived classes must have their own, if appropriate. The following example shows how the Inherited named parameter is used in AttributeUsage on the Tracker attribute:

```
[
    AttributeUsage(AttributeTargets.All,
                   AllowMultiple = true,
                   Inherited     = true)
]
```

Because Inherited is set to true, the Tracker attribute applies to all derived classes of the class it is applied to.

Using Reflection

Reflection is the capability to inspect the metadata of a program and gather information about its types. Using reflection, it's possible to learn about program assemblies, modules, and all types of internal program elements. You can also use reflection to dynamically build programs and save them as assemblies.

Reflection is particularly useful for design tools, supporting automated building of code based on user selections derived from the metadata of the underlying types being used. Reflection also provides excellent support for late-bound frameworks where runtime determination is required for selecting required libraries or other functionality on-the-fly.

Discovering Program Information

The .NET reflection API is based on a hierarchical model where higher-level items represent composition of one or more lower-level items. Figure 16.1 shows this hierarchy.

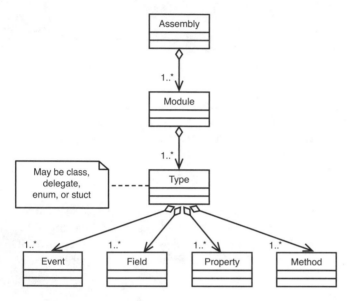

FIGURE 16.1   Reflection API hierarchy.

Assemblies, the basic unit of deployment in .NET, are at the top. Assemblies may be composed of one or more modules. Modules may have one or more types. Types are program elements such as classes, structs, delegates, and enums. Types may contain one or more fields, properties, methods, or events, depending on the type. It might be handy to think about this model as you progress through the sections of this chapter.

Reflection makes it possible to find out all information available about a program. The program elements to be searched include assemblies, modules, types, and type members. Listing 16.7 creates a class that will be reflected upon, and Listing 16.8 demonstrates how to obtain the various reflection objects and inspect their available information.

LISTING 16.7   Class to Reflect Upon: Reflected.cs

```
using System;
using System.Collections;

/// <summary>
///     Reflected Class
/// </summary>
public class Reflected
{
```

LISTING 16.7   Continued

```
public    int        MyField;
protected ArrayList myArray;

public Reflected()
{
    myArray = new ArrayList();
    myArray.Add("Some ArrayList Entry");
}

public float MyProperty
{
    get
    {
        return MyEvent();
    }
}

public object this[int index]
{
    get
    {
        if (index < myArray.Count)
        {
            return myArray[index];
        }
        else
        {
            return null;
        }
    }
    set
    {
        myArray.Add(value);
    }
}

public float MyInstanceMethod()
{
    Console.WriteLine("Invoking Instance MyMethod.");

    return 0.02f;
}

public static float MyStaticMethod()
{
    Console.WriteLine("Invoking Static MyMethod.");
```

LISTING 16.7   Continued

```
        return 0.02f;
    }

    public delegate float MyDelegate();

    public event MyDelegate MyEvent
        = new MyDelegate(MyStaticMethod);

    public enum MyEnum { valOne, valTwo, valThree };
}
```

In the next listing, make sure that the executable filename is Reflecting.exe, otherwise the application won't work as expected. As you'll see, it needs to open the assembly named Reflecting.exe to operate. It is essentially reflecting upon itself.

LISTING 16.8   Performing Reflection: Reflecting.cs

```
using System;
using System.Reflection;

/// <summary>
///     Performing Reflection.
/// </summary>
class Reflecting
{
    static void Main(string[] args)
    {
        Reflecting reflect = new Reflecting();

        Assembly myAssembly
            = Assembly.LoadFrom("Reflecting.exe");

        reflect.GetReflectionInfo(myAssembly);
    }

    void GetReflectionInfo(Assembly myAssembly)
    {
        Type[] typeArr = myAssembly.GetTypes();

        foreach (Type type in typeArr)
        {
            Console.WriteLine("\nType: {0}\n", type.FullName);

            ConstructorInfo[] MyConstructors
```

LISTING 16.8   Continued

```
        = type.GetConstructors();
foreach (ConstructorInfo constructor
        in MyConstructors)
{
    Console.WriteLine("\tConstructor: {0}",
                    constructor.ToString());
}
Console.WriteLine();

FieldInfo[] MyFields = type.GetFields();
foreach (FieldInfo field in MyFields)
{
    Console.WriteLine("\tField: {0}",
                    field.ToString());
}
Console.WriteLine();

MethodInfo[] MyMethods = type.GetMethods();
foreach (MethodInfo method in MyMethods)
{
    Console.WriteLine("\tMethod: {0}",
                    method.ToString());
}
Console.WriteLine();

PropertyInfo[] MyProperties
    = type.GetProperties();

foreach (PropertyInfo property in MyProperties)
{
    Console.WriteLine("\tProperty: {0}",
                    property.ToString());
}
Console.WriteLine();

EventInfo[] MyEvents = type.GetEvents();
foreach (EventInfo anEvent in MyEvents)
{
    Console.WriteLine("\tEvent: {0}",
                    anEvent.ToString());
}
Console.WriteLine();
        }
    }
}
```

16

And the output is as follows:

```
c:\CSharpUnleashed\Chapter 16\Chapter 16>Reflecting.exe

Type: Reflecting

        Constructor: Void .ctor()


        Method: System.Type GetType()
        Method: System.String ToString()
        Method: Boolean Equals(System.Object)
        Method: Int32 GetHashCode()

Type: Reflected

        Constructor: Void .ctor()

        Field: Int32 MyField

        Method: Single get_MyProperty()
        Method: System.Object get_Item(Int32)
        Method: Void set_Item(Int32, System.Object)
        Method: Single MyInstanceMethod()
        Method: Single MyStaticMethod()
        Method: Void add_MyEvent(MyDelegate)
        Method: Void remove_MyEvent(MyDelegate)
        Method: System.Type GetType()
        Method: System.String ToString()
        Method: Boolean Equals(System.Object)
        Method: Int32 GetHashCode()

        Property: Single MyProperty
        Property: System.Object Item [Int32]

        Event: MyDelegate MyEvent


Type: Reflected+MyDelegate

        Constructor: Void .ctor(System.Object, IntPtr)
```

```
        Method: Single Invoke()
        Method: System.IAsyncResult BeginInvoke(System.AsyncCallback, System.Obj
ect)
        Method: Single EndInvoke(System.IAsyncResult)
        Method: Void GetObjectData(System.Runtime.Serialization.SerializationInf
o, System.Runtime.Serialization.StreamingContext)
        Method: Boolean Equals(System.Object)
        Method: System.Delegate[] GetInvocationList()
        Method: Int32 GetHashCode()
        Method: System.Object DynamicInvoke(System.Object[])
        Method: System.Reflection.MethodInfo get_Method()
        Method: System.Object get_Target()
        Method: System.Object Clone()
        Method: System.Type GetType()
        Method: System.String ToString()

        Property: System.Reflection.MethodInfo Method
        Property: System.Object Target

Type: Reflected+MyEnum

        Field: Int32 value__
        Field: MyEnum valOne
        Field: MyEnum valTwo
        Field: MyEnum valThree

        Method: Boolean Equals(System.Object)
        Method: Int32 GetHashCode()
        Method: System.String ToString()
        Method: System.String ToString(System.String, System.IFormatProvider)
        Method: Int32 CompareTo(System.Object)
        Method: System.String ToString(System.IFormatProvider)
        Method: System.TypeCode GetTypeCode()
        Method: System.String ToString(System.String)
        Method: System.Type GetType()
```

Here's how to compile the programs in Listings 16.7 and 16.8:

```
csc Reflecting.cs Reflected.cs
```

The primary purpose of Listing 16.7 is to have a class available with all types of class members to reflect upon. It does nothing more than serves that purpose, and all of its program elements should be familiar by now.

Listing 16.8 is where the interesting bits are. The `Main` method obtains an `Assembly` object by calling the static `LoadFrom` method of the `Assembly` class. The `LoadFrom` method has a string parameter, specifying the name of the executable file, or assembly, to load.

Within the `GetReflectionInfo` method, the `Assembly` object, `myAssembly`, invokes its `GetTypes` method to obtain an array of all types available in the assembly.

YOU CAN SKIP OVER MODULES AS A SHORTCUT TO TYPES

The `Assembly` type has a `GetModule` method that will return an array of modules within an assembly. From each of the modules, it's possible to call `GetTypes` to return an array of types to work with. As a shortcut, Listing 16.8 calls the `GetTypes` method of the `Assembly` type to get all types belonging to all modules within that assembly.

Within the `foreach` loop, each type is extracted and printed. The types are obtained with a `GetX` method, and the result is an `Xinfo` object, where `X` is one of the following type members:

▶ Constructor

▶ Field

▶ Method

▶ Property (including indexer)

▶ Event

Each type member is printed to the console with the `ToString` method, but this isn't the only thing that can be done with each member. Each `XInfo` class includes numerous methods and properties that can be invoked to obtain information. A good source of information on available methods and properties is the .NET Framework SDK documentation.

Reflecting on Attributes

You can extract attributes from an assembly by using the `GetAttribute` and `GetAttribute` methods of the `Attribute` class. They return a single attribute or an array of attributes, respectively. Listing 16.9 demonstrates how to get a single attribute using the `GetAttribute` method. It uses the `Tracker` attribute from earlier in this chapter, which you should include in the same project as the code in Listing 16.9.

LISTING 16.9   Getting Attributes from a Class

```
[
    Tracker("CR-0001",
    "some fix",
    EngineerId = "Joe",
    ChangeDate = "07/04/2008")
```

LISTING 16.9   Continued

```
]
class ReflectingOnAttributes
{
    static void Main(string[] args)
    {
        try
        {
            Type classType     = typeof(ReflectingOnAttributes);
            Type attributeType = typeof(TrackerAttribute);

            TrackerAttribute attrib = (TrackerAttribute)
                Attribute.GetCustomAttribute(classType,
                                             attributeType);

            Console.WriteLine("Problem #:    {0}",
                attrib.ProblemId);
            Console.WriteLine("Engineeer ID: {0}",
                attrib.EngineerId);
            Console.WriteLine("Change Date:  {0}",
                attrib.ChangeDate);
            Console.WriteLine("Description:  {0}",
                attrib.FixDescription);
        }
        catch(Exception e)
        {
            Console.WriteLine(
                "Generic Exception: {0}\nStack Trace:\n{1}",
                e.Message, e.StackTrace);
        }
    }
}
```

The code in Listing 16.9 gets a Type object for the class to be examined and a Type object for the attribute being retrieved. These Type objects are passed to the GetCustomAttribute method to obtain an attribute object, which is an attribute of TrackerAttribute. The public fields and properties of TrackerAttribute are then displayed on the console.

You can use this technique to reflect upon and extract attributes from code in any assembly.

In addition to extracting information from an assembly, you can use reflection to dynamically invoke code at runtime.

Dynamically Activating Code

Dynamic code activation is the capability to make a runtime determination of what code will be executed. This can be useful in any situation where a late-bound framework is required.

Listing 16.10 shows how to perform a late-bound operation by dynamically activating the code in a specified assembly during runtime. The code in Listing 16.10 expects the name of the assembly it is in to be DynamicActivation.exe. You'll get an exception if you name the code anything else. If you do name your project anything else, then change the line with Assembly.LoadFrom() to use your assembly name instead of DynamicActivation.exe.

LISTING 16.10   Dynamically Activating Code: DynamicActivation.cs

```
using System;
using System.Reflection;

/// <summary>
///     Dynamically Activating Code.
/// </summary>
class DynamicActivation
{
    static void Main(string[] args)
    {
        DynamicActivation reflect = new DynamicActivation ();

        Assembly myAssembly
            = Assembly.LoadFrom("DynamicActivation.exe");

        reflect.DynamicallyInvokeMembers(myAssembly);
    }

    void DynamicallyInvokeMembers(Assembly myAssembly)
    {
        Type classType = myAssembly.GetType("Reflected");

        PropertyInfo myProperty
            = classType.GetProperty("MyProperty");

        MethodInfo propGet = myProperty.GetGetMethod();

        object reflectedObject
            = Activator.CreateInstance(classType);

        propGet.Invoke(reflectedObject, null);

        MethodInfo myMethod
            = classType.GetMethod("MyInstanceMethod");

        myMethod.Invoke(reflectedObject, null);
    }
}
```

And here's the output:

```
Invoking Static MyMethod.
Invoking Instance MyMethod.
```

You can compile Listing 16.10 with Listing 16.1 like this:

```
csc DynamicActivation.cs Reflected.cs
```

The Main method of Listing 16.10 gets an Assembly object with the static Assembly.LoadFrom method. The DynamicallyInvokeMembers method uses the Assembly object to get the Type object from the Reflected class. The Type object is then used to obtain the MyProperty property. Next, a MethodInfo object is obtained by calling the GetGetMethod of the PropertyInfo object. The GetGetMethod retrieves a copy of a property's get method, which is, for reflection purposes, treated just like a method.

REFLECTING ON PROPERTY ACCESSORS

Indexer get and set accessors are obtained just like property get and set accessors, with GetGetMethod and GetSetMethod calls.

The Reflected class is instantiated by using the Activator.CreateInstance method. The instantiated object is then used as the first parameter in the Invoke method of the MethodInfo object. This identifies which object to invoke the method on. The Invoke method's second parameter is the parameter list to send to the method, which would be an array of objects if there were parameters. In this case, there are no parameters to send to the method, so the Invoke method's second parameter is set to null.

The next two lines show how to dynamically invoke an instance method. The syntax is the same as just explained for the property get accessor. However, the intermediate step, used in properties, isn't necessary, and the method can be obtained directly with the GetMethod method of the Type object.

If that isn't already the neatest thing you've seen, let's jack up the coolness factor for what you can do with reflection. The next section shows how to dynamically build, execute, and save assemblies at runtime.

Building Runtime Assemblies with `Reflection.Emit`

The Reflection.Emit API provides a means to dynamically create new assemblies. Using customized builders and generating Microsoft Intermediate Language (IL), aka Common Intermediate Language (CIL), code enables programs to create new programs at runtime. These assemblies may be dynamically invoked or saved to file where they may be reloaded and invoked or used by other programs.

16

Dynamic assembly creation can be useful for back ends to compilers or scripting engines on tools such as web browsers. With the `Reflection.Emit` API, any tool can be extended to dynamically support .NET or any other CLI-compliant system. Listing 16.11 shows how to both generate a dynamic assembly and save it as a console program.

Before walking through the code in Listing 16.11, you might want to refer to Figure 16.1, which shows a model of the relationships between reflection API components. The figure may make it clearer as to why each step is necessary.

LISTING 16.11   Dynamic Assembly Generation

```
using System;
using System.Reflection;
using System.Reflection.Emit;

/// <summary>
///     Reflection Emit.
/// </summary>
class Emit
{
    static void Main(string[] args)
    {
        AppDomain myAppDomain = AppDomain.CurrentDomain;

        AssemblyName myAssemblyName = new AssemblyName();
        myAssemblyName.Name = "DynamicAssembly";

        AssemblyBuilder myAssemblyBuilder =
            myAppDomain.DefineDynamicAssembly(
            myAssemblyName,
            AssemblyBuilderAccess.RunAndSave);

        ModuleBuilder myModuleBuilder =
            myAssemblyBuilder.DefineDynamicModule(
            "DynamicModule",
            "emitter.netmodule");

        TypeBuilder myTypeBuilder =
            myModuleBuilder.DefineType(
            "EmitTestClass");

        MethodBuilder myMethodBuilder =
            myTypeBuilder.DefineMethod(
            "Main",
            MethodAttributes.Public|MethodAttributes.Static,
```

LISTING 16.11   Continued

```
            null,
            null);

        ILGenerator myILGenerator
            = myMethodBuilder.GetILGenerator();
        myILGenerator.EmitWriteLine(
            "\n\tI must emit, reflection is pretty cool!\n");
        myILGenerator.Emit(OpCodes.Ret);

        Type myType = myTypeBuilder.CreateType();
        object myObjectInstance
            = Activator.CreateInstance(myType);

        Console.WriteLine("\nDynamic Invocation:");

        MethodInfo myMethod = myType.GetMethod("Main");
        myMethod.Invoke(myObjectInstance, null);

        myAssemblyBuilder.SetEntryPoint(myMethod);
        myAssemblyBuilder.Save("emitter.exe");
    }
}
```

New assemblies must be created in a specific AppDomain. Invocation of members belonging to a Type within an assembly must be done in the current AppDomain. Therefore, when this program begins, it gets a new AppDomain object by calling the CurrentDomain method of the AppDomain class.

To create the entire assembly in Listing 16.11, several steps are required:

1. Create an AssemblyBuilder.
2. Create a ModuleBuilder.
3. Create a TypeBuilder.
4. Create a MethodBuilder.
5. Generate IL.
6. Invoke members or persist assembly.

Each builder is created using a defining method of its parent in the hierarchy. This is another reason why the AppDomain object is required, to get an AssemblyBuilder.

The AssemblyBuilder object is created by calling the DefineDynamicAssembly method of the AppDomain object. The parameters passed to DefineDynamicAssembly are an AssemblyName object and an AssemblyBuilderAccess enum. The AssemblyBuilderAccess enum has four members: ReflectionOnly, Run, RunAndSave, and Save. ReflectionOnly means that the assembly can't execute, Run means the assembly can be invoked only in memory, Save means that the assembly can be persisted (saved) only to file, and RunAndSave means both Run and Save.

With an AssemblyBuilder object, a ModuleBuilder object is created. The parameters of the DefineDynamicModule method are a string with the name for the module and another string with the filename the module will be saved as. The example shows that the module filename will be emitter.netmodule.

AN ASSEMBLY SAVE GOTCHA

The DefineDynamicModule method has four overloads: two are for run-only modules, and the other two are for run and persist modules. To guarantee that a module is included during persistence of an assembly, ensure one of the overloads with the file-name parameter of the DefineDynamicAssembly method is used.

TypeBuilder objects are created with the DefineType method of the ModuleBuilder object. The DefineType method takes a single string parameter with the name of the Type.

The final builder object in Listing 28.6 is the MethodBuilder, which is created using the DefineMethod method of the TypeBuilder object. DefineMethod has four parameters: name, method attributes, return type, and parameter types.

The name parameter is a string with the name of the method. In this case, it's the Main method. Because a Main method must be defined as public and static, the second parameter uses the public and static members of the MethodAttributes enum. The return type is null, which defaults to void, and the parameter types is also null, which means that this method does not accept arguments. When a method accepts arguments, the fourth parameter would be an array with the type definitions of each method parameter.

Next, the code is generated. To accomplish this, invoke the MethodBuilder object's GetILGenerator method. This results in an ILGenerator class that is used to create code.

This is a simple method that writes a line of text to the console and returns. The EmitWriteLine and Emit methods perform this task.

Prior to invoking code, a type instance is created by calling the GetType method of the TypeBuilder object. The resulting Type object is then instantiated with the static Activator.CreateInstance method.

When an object instance is available, the program gets a MethodInfo object and dynamically invokes the method, just like in the last section.

What's really cool about this entire procedure is that you can save the work that was done to a file. With the Assembly object, the SetEntryPoint method is invoked with the MethodInfo parameter for the dynamically generated Main method. Then the file is saved with the Save command, which accepts a single string parameter specifying the assembly filename.

ENSURING AN EXECUTABLE WORKS

One of the goals of Listing 16.11 was to create an executable console application. For a C# program to run standalone, it must have a Main method. Because the program did have a Main method, it would be easy to assume that everything was good to go. However, the SetEntryPoint method of the AssemblyBuilder must still be called or else the program will not run standalone. Remember, the system libraries are cross-language-compatible, and you shouldn't make the assumption that they know C#.

The Save method of the AssemblyBuilder object creates two files. One file is the module named emitter.netmodule. This file can be compiled with other modules to create an executable. The other file is the executable named emitter.exe. This is a standalone program that will execute when invoked from the command line.

Summary

Attributes are a special type of metadata used to decorate program elements with information the programmer chooses. There are several prebuilt attributes, such as the Serializable and CLSCompliant attributes, that you'll use on a regular basis.

When the prebuilt attributes don't meet requirements, it's possible to create custom attributes. Custom attributes are special classes derived from the Attribute class and can be designed to support any metadata requirement imaginable.

The Attribute class has special methods for obtaining attribute metadata from program elements. Single attributes or all attributes associated with a program element may be extracted and read.

Reflection provides the capability to discover information about a program at runtime. Pertinent program items that can be reflected upon include assemblies, modules, types, and other kinds of C# program elements.

Another feature of reflection is the capability to dynamically activate code at runtime. This is especially relevant to situations where late-bound operations are required. With reflection, any type of C# code can be loaded and invoked dynamically.

The Reflection.Emit API provides advanced features for dynamically creating assemblies. This feature could be used in tools such as scripting engines and compilers. After the code has been created, it can be dynamically invoked or saved to file for later use.

Whereas this chapter was very much about runtime operations, the next chapter, on generics, shows you how to gain better compile-time type safety when designing objects.

CHAPTER 17

Parameterizing Types with Generics and Writing Iterators

When we watch television, we're not particularly concerned with the way it works. Of course, maybe someone who is technically inclined will have a natural curiosity, but the average consumer doesn't care. A TV operates the same way regardless of what channel is playing: You can turn it on, change channels, adjust the volume, and turn it back off. What varies, however, is the channel being watched. It could be any type of channel, including news, comedy, drama, and more.

In C# coding terms, we could look at the TV as a generic object. When we tune the TV to a specific channel, we are specifying a type of channel that the TV operates on. What this gives us is a way of reusing code for any object type. This is the concept behind the C# language feature known as generics.

A generic type object is one that has members that can operate on any other type of object. This is similar to a TV as a generic device that operates on multiple channel types. A common implementation of generics in C# is to build different collections, such as dictionaries, lists, stacks, and other data structures. Of course, generics can be used for much more than collections, and you'll see examples of a existing collections, custom collections, and custom generic types in this chapter.

To help you understand why generics are so important, I explain how nongeneric collections work. Then I show you the benefits of greater performance and type safety that generics give you instead. This chapter even includes an entire generic collection so that you can get an in-depth look at how generics can work.

I also show you how to use iterators, a C# feature that enables you to enumerate over a collection of data. I also show you how hard it is to implement the iterator pattern yourself and then show you how easy C# iterators are to implement. I also show you all the different iterator types, give you practical advice on their proper usage, and show you a few pitfalls in nonstandard use of iterators and the need to properly dispose an iterator.

Let's start at the beginning: nongeneric collections.

Nongeneric Collections

Since .NET 1.0, the Framework Class Library (FCL) has offered a set of nongeneric collections in the System.Collections namespace. Nongeneric collections include popular data structures, such as ArrayList and Hashtable. Most people preferred using ArrayList over normal arrays because the ArrayList class had extra features, such as automatic growth and many convenience methods that made working with ArrayList items easier.

Nongeneric collections operated on the System.Object type (or just object in C# terms), which meant that they could hold any type of object, including reference types and value types. You could write classes that derived from them, adding extra functionality necessary for specialized use. Because they operated on type object, they lacked type safety. A common technique for improving the type safety of collections was to write a specialized collection that derived from the CollectionBase class (or DictionaryBase) and write type-safe methods in the derived class.

In most cases, I predict you'll probably want to avoid nongeneric collections and move straight to generic collections, there are still some scenarios in which nongeneric collections are necessary. If you are working with C# 1.x, you must use arrays or nongeneric collections because generics didn't exist until C# 2.0. When exposing parameters or return types from your code and the code is part of a reusable component, you might not use generics. You see, if the component is reusable, it could possibly be used from languages other than C# that don't have generics. The next section explains why you will want to code with generic types.

Understanding the Benefits of Generics

Generic types allow you to parameterize your code and then use that code by filling in a type parameter with whatever object type you want that generic type to work on. A common scenario is when using a generic List, as follows:

```
var letters = new List<string>();


letters.Add("Alpha");
letters.Add("Beta");
letters.Add("Charlie");

foreach (var letter in letters)
```

```
    {
        Console.WriteLine(letter);
    }
```

In the preceding code, `letters` is a generic `List` of `string`. Notice the angle brackets, specifying the string type, new `List<string>()`, for instantiating `letters`. Documentation for `List` shows that it is a parameterized type defined as `List<T>` where `T` is the type parameter. That means you can replace `T` with any type you want, and the `List` will work on that type. In the preceding example, we replaced `T` with `string`, meaning that this is a `List` that works with string types, and the appropriate terminology is `List` of `string`. If the parameter had been defined with `int`, as in `List<int>`, then `letters` would have been a `List` of `int`.

The calls to `Add` will add the new strings to the collection, and then you can iterate through the collection, just as you do for arrays.

This is an example of a using a generic class, but there are other parameterized types, including classes, delegates, interfaces, and structs. You can also parameterize methods.

Generics give you the benefits of better performance with value types, greater type safety, and reduce the number of explicit conversions you need to make. The next section delves into these benefits by explaining the problems that existed in the past, which made generics an essential addition to version 2.0 of the C# programming language.

Problems Solved by Generics

Generics solve three significant problems encountered with nongeneric code that relies on object types (that is, nongeneric collections or code that operates on the object type): lack of type safety, performance degradation with value types, and cluttered code caused by conversions. In this section, I'll concentrate on the first two problems and approach them from the perspective of how generics solve the problems by supplying better type safety and increased performance with value types.

Let's start by examining the most significant problems that generics solve by giving you type safety and better performing code with value types, starting with better type safety.

Generics Give You Type Safety

With nongeneric collections, everything is an object type. In C# 1.x, this was necessary because collections had to handle any type given to them. Because all types, reference and value, implicitly inherit `System.Object`, this helped nongeneric collections achieve a generic-like capability. Unfortunately, there were no controls over what you could add to nongeneric collections. For example, if you instantiate and use an `ArrayList`, you could potentially add anything to it that you want. The code here shows an example:

```
    ArrayList customers = new ArrayList();


    customers.Add(new Customer());
    customers.Add(new Employee());
    customers.Add(15.5f);
```

```
foreach (Customer cust in customers)
{
    Console.WriteLine(cust.ToString());
}
```

In the preceding code, the customers ArrayList should only hold Customer objects. Because of some bug in the program, an Employee object is added to customers. The problem is that this will compile and run. The problem might not be detected until the code is deployed to production, where everything will break. The preceding code is so simple that you will see a runtime InvalidCastException immediately, but that is far from the damage that could be caused if the code tries to access the invalid object later via other logic. Because generics are parameterized with the type of object operated on, they are type safe. You would only be able to assign an object of the appropriate type; anything else causes a compile-time error. The following code shows how generics are type safe:

```
List<Customer> customers = new List<Customer>();


customers.Add(new Customer());
customers.Add(new Customer());
customers.Add(new Employee());

foreach (Customer cust in customers)
{
    Console.WriteLine(cust.ToString());
}
```

The preceding example demonstrates how you can only put Customer object in the customers collection. Because generics are type safe, assigning the Employee instance causes a compiler error.

Notice how the customers collection was declared using List<Customer>. The generic List collection is analogous to the nongeneric ArrayList collection. The <Customer> syntax says that this is a List that operates only on type Customer. You can create a List of any type you want, either built in or custom.

Another convenience of generics is that you no longer need to perform a conversion with either an as operator or cast operator when retrieving an object from the collection. The collection knows what type you are working with and returns that type.

You now know that generics give you type safety, and the significance of type safety is that you can write more robust code. Because the C# compiler checks the type safe syntax of your code, you will see an error when trying to compile the code for generics that isn't type safe.

The fact that nongeneric collections operate on type object leads us to another problem with nongeneric collections and code that works with the object type. When using value types, you encounter a boxing and unboxing penalty. See Chapter 4, "Understanding

Reference Types and Value Types," for an in-depth explanation of boxing and unboxing and the performance implications. The next section explains how generics solve the problem of boxing and unboxing overhead.

Generics Avoid Boxing/Unboxing Performance Penalties

Using value types with nongeneric collections was always a tradeoff. Because the nongeneric collection operated on type `object`, value types were boxed and unboxed every time you, respectively, assigned or retrieved an object. The penalty could be severe. The following example shows what happens when a value type is used with a nongeneric collection:

```
ArrayList myInts = new ArrayList();


myInts.Add(1);
myInts.Add(2);
myInts.Add(3);

foreach (int myInt in myInts)
{
    Console.WriteLine(myInt);
}
```

The preceding code demonstrates assigning a value type to an `ArrayList`. Behind the scenes, the value type is boxed. Reading the value type from the `ArrayList` requires a conversion from the boxed value type to a regular value type variable.

Using generics, you can make assignments in a strongly typed manner. The following code shows how to use generics with Value types:

```
List<int> myInts = new List<int>();


myInts.Add(1);
myInts.Add(2);
myInts.Add(3);

foreach (int myInt in myInts)
{
    Console.WriteLine(myInt);
}
```

As shown here, declaration and use of generics with value types is not different from reference types. In addition, you can just read the value from the collection without needing to use a `cast` operator.

In addition to using a generic type as you've seen here, generic parameters can be used polymorphically. You can also derive classes from generics, as you'll see in the next section.

Generics Are Object-Oriented

This section builds upon the previous section by showing you how generics are object-oriented. You will see how objects assigned to a generic collection can be treated polymorphically and how to write a class that derives from a generic type.

To use generics polymorphically, instantiate the generic type object with a base class parameter. Then code against that generic type instance with instances of objects whose class derives from the base class used as the generic parameter. Listing 17.1 illustrates how this works.

LISTING 17.1   You Can Use Objects Polymorphically with Generics

```
class Shape
{
    public virtual string Name
    {
        get { return "shape"; }
    }
}

// derived type
class Box : Shape
{
    public override string Name
    {
        get { return "box"; }
    }
}

// derived type
class Circle : Shape
{
    public override string Name
    {
        get { return "circle"; }
    }
}

...
    private static void RunShapeList()
    {
        List<Shape> myShapes = new List<Shape>();

        // because Box and Circle are type Shape
        //    they can be added to the collection too
```

LISTING 17.1   Continued

```
        myShapes.Add(new Shape());
        myShapes.Add(new Box());
        myShapes.Add(new Circle());

        // Name is read polymorphically
        foreach (Shape shape in myShapes)
        {
            Console.WriteLine(shape.Name);
        }
    }
...
```

Listing 17.1 has a Shape class and two derived classes, Box and Circle. Notice in the RunShapeList method how the myShapes List is declared with a Shape parameter type. Because Box and Circle are Shape, you can take advantage of their object-oriented inheritance properties to assign them to the myShapes List. You don't loose anything with generics, but you gain substantially in the areas of type safety and performance, as described in previous paragraphs.

Now, here's an example of how you can create a class that derives from a generic type:

```
    public class CustomerList : List<Customer>
    {
        public int DistinctCities
        {
            get
            {
                // compute number of unique cities
                // that customers live in
                return 7;
            }
        }
    }
```

The CustomerList class here derives from List<Customer>. Now you have a type safe way of specializing a collection.

Now that you've been exposed to the basics of generics, the next section presents a few items to consider when making a choice to use an array, nongeneric collection, or generic collection.

Choosing Between Arrays, Nongeneric Collections, and Generic Collections

The preceding section described how generics solve problems associated with nongeneric collections and code that relies on the object type for generic behavior. Consequently, you should see that there is a compelling case for using generics when possible.

Although generics are an excellent choice for working with collections of objects, they aren't the only choice. You still have arrays and nongeneric collections. Here's a list that outlines general situations where you wouldn't want to use generics:

▶ **When exposing a public interface to external libraries**—Nongeneric collections or arrays will both open the API to languages that don't support generics.

▶ **When an API you're calling requests an array or nongeneric collection**—This could be a third-party library or a situation where you have a DLL but not the source code that would enable you to modify the code.

▶ **When you are using version .NET 1.0 and 1.1**—Generics didn't exist until C# 2.0.

Table 17.1 is a decision table that simplifies choosing what type of collection is best for holding your objects.

TABLE 17.1   Collection Types and Possible Choices

Collection Type	When to Consider
Array	Calling a method with an array parameter
	Calling a method that returns an array
	Accessing a type that exposes an array
	Accessing a type property that returns an array
	Implementing utility methods using arrays, such as `string.Join` and `string.Split`
Nongeneric collection	Calling a method with an nongeneric collection parameter
	Calling a method that returns a nongeneric collection
	Accessing a type that exposes a nongeneric collection
	Accessing a type property that returns a nongeneric collection
	Writing a type for reuse with other languages and you need to expose a collection through your type's public interface
Generics	Everywhere, except for the conditions requiring use of other collection types

As always, the choice is yours to use whatever works in your situation, but maybe Table 17.1 could be helpful.

To help you see how generics can be used, the next section demonstrates how to create a collection based on a singly linked list.

Building Generic Types

This section is divided into three parts: "Implementing a Singly Linked List with Generics," "Applying Generics Beyond Collections," and "Defining Type with Generics." In the first part, I show you how to create a custom collection named `GenericSingleLinkedList`, which will serve as a source of ideas for you to implement your own data structures. The second part is a short section designed to help you realize that generics are not just for collections. It gives you a couple tips on opportunities for using generics. The third part is a detailed discussion of using generic constraints. A constraint helps make the generic more specific, by allowing you to make assumptions about the type you are working with. I show you the different constraint types and offer tips on how to get the most out of each one.

Implementing a Singly Linked List with Generics

This section explains how to build a custom generic collection named GenericSingleLinkedList. Because the code to implement this collection has more lines than this chapter, I show you only the relevant parts you need to understand how GenericSingleLinkedList works. The discussion is divided into multiple parts, which logically follow one another. They are all applicable to explaining how GenericSingleLinkedList works. I start off by implementing a generic Node, which shows you how to create the class that will hold each object in the collection. Then I explain the parts of the GenericSingleLinkedList, starting with the constructors. Because GenericSingleLinkedList derives from the IList<T> interface, I show you how GenericSingleLinkedList implements IList<T> members. For future reference, I also have a section titled "Implementing IEnumerable<T> and IEnumerator<T>." Later, when looking at iterators, I refer back to this section so that you can compare the two approaches to see why iterators are an easier solution for creating enumerable types.

HISTORY OF THE GENERICSINGLELINKEDLIST

The code in this section is a singly linked list that I built in the early days of .NET: the beta before .NET 1.0. Generics didn't exist back then, so I had to use System.Object, just as with all the other nongeneric collections. As soon as I got my hands on the .NET 2.0 beta, I did a conversion to generics. Essentially, I changed every object type declaration to a generic parameter, which shows how easy it is to convert your own nongeneric collections to generics.

First, let's look at the Node<T> object, which holds each object contained within the collection.

Implementing a Generic Node

With a single linked list, you need a special object that keeps track of the containing objects and their position in the list, which I'll call a Node. The Node references the object and refers to the next object in the list. Because it is a single linked list, the Node doesn't need to refer to the previous object in the list. The following code shows how to create the generic Node object. The goal of the following code is to build this single linked list with a chain of Node<T> instances that refer to an object and the next node in the list:

```
public class Node<T>
{
```

```
    public T data;
    public Node<T> next;
}
```

This <T> syntax, means that this is an object that accepts a single type parameter. The data field is a reference to the object this node refers to, and the next field refers to the subsequent node in the list. Notice that next is of type Node<T>, which makes it the same type as the current node, which is also Node<T>.

The GenericSingleLinkedList uses Node<T> to initialize the list and is discussed next.

Initializing the Generic Single Linked List

GenericSingleLinkedList needs some initialization code to make sure it is ready for use. For example, it needs to establish where the list starts, create a synchronization object, and have instance and static constructors. The following code shows how GenericSingleLinkedList is initialized:

```
public class GenericSingleLinkedList<T>: IList<T>, IEnumerable
{
    Node<T> head = null;

    private static object syncObj;

    static GenericSingleLinkedList()
    {
        syncObj = new object();
    }

    public GenericSingleLinkedList() {}
}
```

The first part of the preceding code to see is the declaration of GenericSingleLinkedList, where it has the generic parameter <T>. When initialized, this T defines the type that the generic collection operates on. It also defines the type for other generic types, including IList<T> and Node<T>. For example, the type passed to GenericSingleLinkedList determines the type of head, which is type Node<T>. The static constructor initializes the syncObj property so that multithreaded applications can have a common object to put locks on.

After instantiating GenericSingleLinkedList, calling code will begin populating the GenericSingleLinkedList instance and work with its members to manage the collection of objects. Because GenericSingleLinkedList has list semantics, it is natural that GenericSingleLinkedList inherits the IList<T> interface, which defines the members that GenericSingleLinkedList must implement. The next section describes the IList<T> implementation and shows you how an object, referenced by Note<T>, is inserted into or removed from the collection.

Implementing IList<T>

Because GenericSingleLinkedList is a list, it inherits the IList<T> interface. This allows it to be used the same way as any other list. The amount of code for the implementation of this interface is much too voluminous for printing here, but I show some of it in case you're interested in seeing how you would go about implementing this interface yourself. You can also visit www.samspublishing.com to download this and all the other code for this book. Listing 17.2 shows the IList<T> implementation in GenericSingleLinkedList<T>.

LISTING 17.2 **GenericSingleLinkedList<T>** Inherits **IList<T>** and Implements **IList<T>** Members Inherits IList<T> and Implements IList Inherits IList<T> and Implements IList

```csharp
public int IndexOf(T item)
{
    Node<T> curr = head;
    int count = 0;

    while (curr != null && !(curr.data.Equals(item)))
    {
        curr = curr.next;
        count++;
    }

    if (curr != null)
    {
        // return position
        return count;
    }

    return 1;
}

public void Insert(int index, T item)
{
    ...
}

public void RemoveAt(int index)
{
    ...
}

public T this[int index]
```

LISTING 17.2   Continued

```
    {
        get
        {
            ...
        }
        set
        {
            ...
        }
    }
}
```

If you scan the definitions of Inherits IList<T> and Implements IList Inherits IList<T> and Implements IList each `IList<T>` member in Listing 17.2, you'll see a commonality where the object type is represented by the `T` parameter. The exception is `RemoveAt`, which doesn't have a parameter of type `T`, but the implementation does operate on `T`.

The `IndexOf` method initializes by setting the first node at the head of the list. Notice that `curr` is of type `Node<T>`. Inside the `while` loop, the code visits each node until it finds the one it is looking for. If the node is found, `curr` will refer to the node containing the correct object. Otherwise, the algorithm returns a `-1` to indicate that the object wasn't found.

The important thing for you to remember is that algorithm behavior does not change with generics. The only difference is that your code is working on the generic type parameter, rather than the object type.

`GenericSingleLinkedList<T>` also implements `ICollection<T>`, which is implemented in the same manner as `IList<T>` by using the type parameter `T`. If you understand the `IList<T>` implementation, you'll be able to figure out the `ICollection<T>` implementation with no problems. Again, you can get the entire listing from www.samspublishing.com.

UNDERSTANDING GENERICSINGLELINKEDLIST

> It is often instructive to set a debugger breakpoint and step through the example to see everything that is going on.

The `IList<T>` and `ICollection<T>` interfaces represent the meat of how calling code will use `GenericSingleLinkedList` to hold objects. Other interfaces you must understand with collections are `IEnumerable<T>` and `IEnumerator<T>`. These interfaces are key to helping you build enumerable types. You might also be interested in the `IEnumerable<T>` and `IEnumerator<T>` interfaces for a greater appreciation of how iterators, covered later in this chapter, simplify the same task.

Implementing IEnumerable<T> and IEnumerator<T>

In this section, I show you how to implement the `IEnumerable<T>` and `IEnumerator<T>` interfaces. This will help you understand the behavior of types used with a C# foreach loop. In addition, I refer back to this section later, when discussing iterators, so that you can see the difference between the two ways to create enumerable types.

The IEnumerable<T> and IEnumerator<T> interfaces help you build types that can be iterated over—enumerable types. They specify members that are recognized by the C# foreach loop. This is the hard way to create an enumerable type, but it is helpful for you to know so that you understand how iterators work later. Besides, if you ever find yourself debugging someone else's IEnumerable implementation, it could save you a lot of time to know how it works.

Figure 17.1 illustrates what is happening behind the scenes of a foreach loop that calls GetEnumerator.

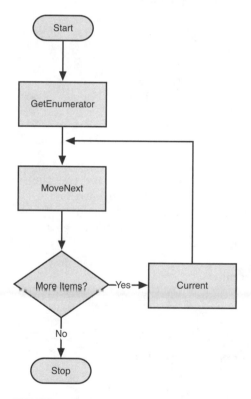

FIGURE 17.1   Flowchart for **IEnumerable<T>** and **IEnumerator<T>** operation.

Here's a quick overview of how Figure 17.1 works:

1. Calling code (that is, foreach) calls GetEnumerator (a member of IEnumerable<T>), which returns an IEnumerator<T>.
2. Calling code then uses IEnumerator<T> to loop through each item of the collection.
3. For each item in the collection, calling code calls the MoveNext method, which tells the IEnumerator<T> to set the position to be the next object that should be read.

4. Calling code then reads the Current property to get the object from the collection.

5. Calling code loops through calling MoveNext and Current until MoveNext returns false, indicating that there are not any more objects in the collection that haven't been read.

In most cases, the calling code that uses an IEnumerable<T>/IEnumerator<T> is inside of a foreach loop, which the C# compiler creates behind the scenes. Every once in a while, you'll see code that uses these interface members explicitly, but not as much as the foreach loop.

First, look at the following implementation of IEnumerable<T>. Any type passed to the foreach loop must implement IEnumerable<T> or its base class, IEnumerable. An IEnumerable<T> type implements the GetEnumerator method, which returns an IEnumerator<T>.

```
public IEnumerator<T> GetEnumerator()
{
    return (IEnumerator<T>)new
        GenericSingleLinkedListEnumerator(head);
}
```

The GetEnumerator method here simply instantiates an IEnumerator<T> and returns it to the calling program.

The next few paragraphs examine the members—MoveNext, Current, and Reset—of the GenericSingleLinkedListEnumerator, which inherits IEnumerator<T>. The MoveNext method and Current property correspond to the MoveNext and Current boxes in Figure 17.1. The Reset method wasn't represented in Figure 17.1 because the foreach statement never calls it. First is the initialization code, shown here:

```
public class GenericSingleLinkedListEnumerator :
    IEnumerator<T>, IEnumerator
{
    Node<T> curr;
    Node<T> head;
    public GenericSingleLinkedListEnumerator(Node<T> head)
    {
        this.head = head;

        curr = new Node<T>();
        curr.next = head;
    }
    ...
```

When reading the preceding code you might wonder why the GenericSingleLinkedListEnumerator class doesn't have a generic type parameter, T. Enumerators are typically implemented as nested classes because their purpose in life is to support their containing type. You don't want them to be explicitly instantiated by other code, so the best implementation is inside their containing type. Because GenericSingleLinkedListEnumerator is a nested type, it can operate on the type parameter of its containing type. Therefore, IEnumerator<T>, which it inherits, uses the same T as the containing type's T, as do all the members of GenericSingleLinkedListEnumerator.

Because nested types can't access the private members of their containing type, the GetEnumerator method needed to pass the first node in the list, head, to the GenericSingleLinkedListEnumerator so that the GenericSingleLinkedListEnumerator instance can save the reference. The GenericSingleLinkedList constructor ensures that the curr reference, of type Node<T>, is initialized properly.

One of the members of the IEnumerator<T> interface is the Reset method. Although the IEnumerable<T> and IEnumerator<T> follow the iterator pattern, common practice is to not reuse an IEnumerator<T>. You don't want to reuse IEnumerator<T>s because their state is undefined after they have been used and doing a reset is complex and fraught with error, especially in more complex data structures. Add multithreading to this scenario and you might be able to imagine the complexity of a Reset on a collection with multiple threads in different states or reading, writing, or traversing the collection. So, if an Enumerator<T> type shouldn't be reused, you probably don't want to implement the Reset method, which implies reuse. The proper implementation of Reset is to throw a NotSupportedException exception to keep callers from trying to reuse your IEnumerator<T>. Here's the implementation of Reset:

```
public void Reset()
{
    throw new NotSupportedException(
        "You can't reuse this IEnumerator<T>!");
}
```

This implementation of Reset properly throws a NotSupportedException exception. This is consistent with the implementation of C# 2.0 iterators, which also throw NotSupportedException. Iterators are covered later in this chapter.

Referring back to the initialization code, the GenericSingleLinkedListEnumerator constructor initialized the first node to reference the head node in its Next property. This is why the foreach loop calls MoveNext before accessing the current item. The first call to MoveNext sets the backing store of the Current property to head. Here's the MoveNext implementation:

```
public bool MoveNext()
{
    if (curr.next != null)
    {
        curr = curr.next;
        return true;
    }

    return false;
}
```

17

When implementing a MoveNext method, you must do two things: set the position of the next node to read, and let callers know whether they can read any more values. For the first task, setting the position of the next node to read, the code makes the curr node refer to the next node in the list. When implementing your own MoveNext, you should do the same thing: Keep track of what the current node is by moving the current node reference to the next node in the collection.

For the second task, letting callers know whether they can keep reading, the code returns true if there is another node in the list. You will know when there are not any more nodes in the list when curr.next is set to null, which means that the algorithm returns false. Therefore, you should expose the same interface from a MoveNext method that you implement: Return true as long as there are nodes to read and return false when all nodes have been read, just like the MoveNext method previously.

When the current item is set, a foreach loop will read the Current property. The following code shows how the Current property is implemented for GenericSingleLinkedListEnumerator:

```
public T Current
{
    get
    {
        return curr.data;
    }
}
```

The Current property above is read-only because calling code should never interfere with enumeration. It all goes back to the principle of encapsulation and the practice of allowing the object to control its own state, which is the safest way to design objects.

Earlier, I mentioned that IEnumerator<T> inherits IEnumerator. Because you must implement all members of all interfaces in the inheritance chain, you must implement IEnumerator.Current, shown here:

```
    ...
    object IEnumerator.Current
    {
        get { throw new NotImplementedException(); }
    }
}
```

If you wonder why you have to implement only IEnumerator.Current and not IEnumerator.MoveNext and IEnumerator.Reset, look at the parameter types and return types of each member. The signatures for MoveNext and Reset are the same for both interfaces. However, IEnumerator<T>.Current operates on type parameter T, but IEnumerator.Current operates on type object. You should follow the example shown in the preceding code: Perform an explicit interface implementation and throw a

`NotImplementedException`. Because `IEnumerator.Current` isn't type safe and causes boxing with value types, you don't want anyone to call it anyway.

The `GenericSingleLinkedList`, although simple, demonstrates how generics can be used to implement data structures. However, it isn't the only way you can take advantage of generics. The next section discusses other applications of generics that you can use in your programs.

This is the end of the `GenericSingleLinkedList` implementation. You can examine the example for ideas on how to create your own generic collection and modify it as needed. Generic collections aren't the only way to apply generics. The next section gives you more ideas on what you can use generics for and provides tips on knowing when you can convert your type to a generic.

Applying Generics Beyond Collections

Collections aren't the only place you would use generics. The .NET Framework uses generics in many types, such as interfaces and delegates. You can even create generic methods.

Here's a tip that will help you recognize when you can adapt your code to use generics: Any time you try to use the object type, consider changing the code to use generics. The reason you want to use object in the first place is because you want the code to operate on any type. Using generics, as I stated earlier, gives you type safety and better performance with value types.

Generic Interfaces

You've already seen generic interfaces in action when implementing the `GenericSingleLinkedList` in the previous section. The `IEnumerable<T>`, `IEnumerator<T>`, and `IList<T>` are all generic interfaces.

An example of using an FCL generic interface that isn't part of a collection is the `IEquatable<T>` interface. Recall from Chapter 4 that the proper way to implement value equality in reference type objects is to override the `Equals` method. The difficulty with the `Equals` override is weak typing, requiring additional code for type checking. Here's how you can accomplish the same task in a strongly typed way by using `IEquatable<T>`:

```
class Person : IEquatable<Person>
{
    public string Name { get; set; }

    public bool Equals(Person cust)
    {
        if (cust == null) return false;
        return cust.Name == this.Name;
    }
}
```

The first thing to notice is that the `Person` class derives from `IEquatable<Person>`. It just means that its implementation of `IEquatable` will be strongly typed. This enables us to add an `Equals` method to `Person` with the parameter specified as `Person`. The following code results in calls to the previous strongly typed `IEquatable<Person>.Equals` method:

```
private static void DemoGenericInterface()
{
    Person cust1 = new Person();
    Person cust2 = new Person();

    cust1.Name = "Joe";
    cust2.Name = "Joe";

    Console.WriteLine(cust1.Equals(cust2));
}
```

This will print true to the console. The magic here occurs when the C# compiler recognizes the strongly typed method and fixes call to `Equals` to call this `IEquatable<Person>.Equals`.

Generic Delegates

Another natural use of generics is with delegates. You can create a single generic delegate that can be reused for many common uses. In the next chapter, you learn about a group of generic delegates named `Func`.

The example in this section shows you how to use an FCL delegate named `EventHandler<T>`. When performing event-based programming where you need to interact with controls on a form or actions, such as key presses or mouse movement, you'll frequently see the nongeneric `EventHandler(object, EventArgs)` delegate being used. In fact, you'll see several variants with a second parameter that is an `EventArgs` derived type. This is where `EventHandler<T>(object, T)` helps. The following code snippets demonstrate how to create a high-precision clock. First is a custom `EventArgs` derived type:

```
public class ClockEventArgs : EventArgs
{
    private DateTime m_time;

    public DateTime Time
    {
        get { return m_time;}
        set { m_time = value;}
    }
}
```

This `ClockEventArgs` derives from `EventArgs`, adhering to a common pattern used throughout the FCL. Here's the high-precision clock:

```
public class Clock
{
    public event EventHandler<ClockEventArgs> Tick;
```

```
public void RaiseTick()
{
    if (Tick != null)
    {
        ClockEventArgs arg = new ClockEventArgs();
        arg.Time = DateTime.Now;

        Tick(this, arg);
    }
}
}
```

Well, maybe you'll need to use your imagination about the high-precision part. Nonetheless, it does demonstrate how to use a generic delegate through the declaration of EventHandler<ClockEventArgs>, which is the delegate type of the Tick event. Next, we need a handler that conforms to the EventHandler<ClockEventArgs> signature, as follows:

```
public class Alarm
{
    public void ListenToTick(object sender, ClockEventArgs e)
    {
        Console.WriteLine("If time then ring.");
    }
}
```

The ListenToTick method has a second parameter of ClockEventArgs, meaning that it matches void EventArgs<T>(object, T), which is defined as EventArgs<ClockEventArgs>(object, ClockEventArgs). The following example shows how to use this code:

```
private static void DemoGenericDelegate()
{
    Clock clock = new Clock();
    Alarm alarm = new Alarm();

    clock.Tick += alarm.ListenToTick;

    clock.RaiseTick();
}
```

The DemoGenericDelegate method here doesn't change anything you already know about how to use delegates. You have a Clock with a Tick event, an Alarm with a ListenToTick handler, and a combine operation that hooks ListenToTick up with Tick. The call to RaiseTick raises the Tick event, which invokes ListenToTick. The important point about the generic delegate is that it can be reused in many scenarios, passing a strongly typed second parameter.

One thing about generics as you've seen them so far is that you can use them with any type for their type parameters. This is great for generic collections or the like where the code is built to handle any type. However, sometimes you might want to make some assumptions about what type is passed. The next section describes how you can make assumptions about the capability of a type parameter using generic constraints.

Defining Type with Generics

The default behavior of generics does not allow you to make any assumptions about how your type will be used. The usage of your type is totally open. In addition, the only type you can work with is the constructed type defined by the code that instantiates the generic type.

Sometimes you do want to make assumptions about type parameters. For example, what if you want to make sure the type parameter implements an interface? If that is all you need, you can choose not to use generics and specify the interface as what your type will operate on. However, you still don't have the ability to make multiple assumptions. For example, what if you want the type to implement multiple interfaces, a base class, and support instantiation? The answer is that you have this ability by decorating your generic parameters with constraints. Table 17.2 shows what generic constraints are available and what they are used for.

TABLE 17.2   Generic Constraints Enable You to Make Assumptions About Type Parameters

Constraint Type	Forces Type Parameter To
Interface	Inherit the interfaces defined by the constraint
Base class	Inherit the base class defined by the constraint
Reference type	Be a reference type object
Value type	Be a value type object
Constructor	Have a default (no parameter) constructor

A constraint can be applied to a generic parameter in a way that allows you to make assumptions about the parameter type. This gives a type-safe way to guarantee, at compile time, that the parameter conforms to the conditions you declare with the constraint. The categories of constraints, discussed in this section and shown in Table 17.2, include interface, base class, reference type, value type, and constructor constraints. The first type of constraint we discuss is interface constraints.

Interface Constraints

An interface constraint allows you to make the assumption that the object passed as a parameter implements specific members. In the following example, the `PrintEnumerableValues` method must implement the `IEnumerable<U>` interface:

```
private void PrintEnumerableValues<T, U>(T myItems)
    where T : IEnumerable<U>
{
    foreach (U item in myItems)
    {
        Console.WriteLine(item);
    }
}
```

This is an example of putting generic parameters on a method. It also shows two generic parameters, separated by commas. The constraint is identified by the where keyword between the method parameters and method body. The where clause states that the type parameter T must implement the IEnumberable<U> interface. The second type parameter, U, is a placeholder for the type inside of the collection that is passed in. Constraints aren't limited to a single interface type. You can add as many as you like in a comma-separated list, like this:

```
where T : IEnumerable<U>, IList<U>, IDisposable, ...
```

Notice that interface constraints define type. Instead of assigning a single type in the parameter list of a method, you can now extend the type you are working with. That is, the parameter is this type, and this type, and this type, which is something you could never do with a nongeneric single typed parameter. Because the compiler can figure out that the parameter implements every constraint type, you don't have to use as or cast operators to explicitly convert the parameter to any of the constraint types. This makes your code easier to read and write.

Base Class Constraints
A base class constraint ensures that a parameter inherits the specified base class. The base class can be arbitrarily high in the inheritance chain. The following code implements a base class constraint:

```
private void PrintStreamValues<T>(T stream)
    where T : Stream
{
    int ByteSize = 1024;
    int count = 0;

    StringBuilder result = new StringBuilder();

    byte[] bytes = new byte[ByteSize];

    do
    {
        count = stream.Read(bytes, 0, ByteSize);

        result.Append(
```

```
            Encoding.Unicode.GetString(bytes).
            Substring(0, count - 1));
    }
    while (count == ByteSize);

        Console.WriteLine(result.ToString());
}
```

Any class that inherits `Stream` can be passed to the `PrintStreamValues` method here. You can only implement a constraint for a single base class, but you can follow the base class constraint with a comma-separated list of interfaces. These are the same rules as for class inheritance, which makes sense because if a class can't inherit more than one base class, then implementing multiple base class constraints for a single type parameter would be illogical. In this example, the value of using a base class constraint is that the method knows it can operate generically on anything that reads and writes to a stream.

Example Interface

For the next few examples, IHoldVal is defined as follows:

```
    private interface IHoldVal
    {
        int Val
        {
            get;
            set;
        }
    }
```

It will be used as an interface constraint, alongside the specific constraint being used, demonstrating also how to implement multiple constraints for a single generic parameter.

Reference Type Constraints

A reference type constraint ensures a parameter is a reference type object. If you have an algorithm that depends on reference type semantics, this is the way to guarantee proper behavior. The following code shows how to implement a reference type constraint:

```
private void CheckForReferenceType<T>(T type)
    where T : class, IHoldVal
{
    type.Val = 5;
}
```

The `class` keyword in the preceding code specifies that parameters of the generic type `T` must be reference types. In addition, you can specify a comma-separated list of interfaces that this type must inherit, as shown with the `IHoldVal` interface.

Value Type Constraints

A value type constraint ensures a parameter is a value type object. If you implement an algorithm that depends on value type semantics, this is the way to guarantee proper behavior. The following code shows how to implement a value type constraint:

```
private void CheckForValueType<T>(T type)
    where T : struct, IHoldVal
{
    type.Val = 5;
}
```

The only difference between this example and the reference type example earlier is that the constraint is using the keyword struct to specify that this is a value type constraint. You will still want to specify an interface constraint if you want to make the assumption that the value type implements certain members.

Constructor Constraints

Sometimes you need to instantiate a type in a method. However, if you don't know what type will be passed, there is no guarantee that the type implements a constructor. The constructor constraint gives you this guarantee. Here's an example of an algorithm that instantiates an object, which is enabled by a constructor constraint:

```
private T CreateNewInstance<T>()
    where T : IHoldVal, new()
{
    T myNewType = new T();
    myNewType.Val = 7;

    // constructor constraint is for
    // default constructors only
    // causes a compile-time error
    //            T anotherNewType = new T(7);

    return myNewType;
}
```

The new() clause is the constructor constraint. It enables the instantiation of T in the first line of the method. Note that you can only call the default constructor, and overloads are not supported, as shown in the commented-out preceding code.

Recall in the previous section that I made the comment that explicitly implementing IEnumerable<T> and IEnumerator<T> is the hard way to make an enumerable collection. C# 2.0 introduced a language feature called iterators that simplifies the process of creating enumerable collections. The next section describes how to use iterators.

Implementing Iterators

Iterators are a C# 2.0 language feature that enables you to work with a sequence of items from a data source. In C# 1.x, you could do this by implementing the IEnumerable and IEnumerator interfaces, which were more complex. C# iterators simplify this task and help make your code easier to maintain. Table 17.3 shows what iterator types are available for you to use in your applications.

TABLE 17.3   C# 2.0 Introduces Iterators with Different Iterator Types

Iterator Type	Capable Of
GetEnumerator	Providing a default iterator for a type
Method	Dynamic runtime control of iterator results
Property	Simple predefined iteration
Indexer	Allowing indexer-like access to collection contents
Operator	Using C# operators to calculate a logical set of results

There are several types of iterators, shown in Table 17.3, which you can create: GetEnumerator, method, property, indexer, and operator iterators. A couple of iterator types, indexer and operator, are ones you probably won't use as often as the others, and I give you some tips to keep you out of trouble if you are tempted to use them. I also show you a different way of looking at iterators, beyond the typical view of returning collection items.

This section is divided into several parts; each part defines a different type of iterator. I explain how each iterator is used. When discussing the first iterator type, GetEnumerator, I also tell you about how C# generates code behind the scenes, which is an implementation of the IEnumerable<T> and IEnumerator<T> interfaces. Let's look at the GetEnumerator iterator first.

The GetEnumerator Iterator

A previous section of this chapter showed how to implement IEnumerable<T> by having the GetEnumerator method return an instance of an IEnumerator<T>. What you are going to see here is much different. I show you the code and then explain it. I chose not to use generics in the following examples so that I could focus specifically on the iterator behavior.

```
public IEnumerator GetEnumerator()
{
    foreach (int i in ints)
    {
        yield return i;
    }
}
```

To understand what is going on, recognize that there is a loop visiting each item in the current collection, and there is also a yield return statement delivering each item to the caller. The purpose of the yield return is to stop on each value and return it to the calling code. Imagine that there is a foreach loop in the calling code using the previous containing type of the GetEnumerator method as the collection it wants to iterate through.

YIELD ISN'T A KEYWORD

The word *yield* is not a C# keyword. Because there are many C# 1.x applications that could be using yield as an identifier (perhaps financial or traffic applications), making it a keyword would have broken much of the existing code. Instead of the lexer, which usually tokenizes keywords, recognizing yield, the parser will recognize clauses of the form yield return <expression> and yield break to ensure the proper code is generated.

You might have noticed that the GetEnumerator method above says that it returns an IEnumerator, but the code doesn't have a return statement that returns an object that is an IEnumerator. It really does return an IEnumerator, but that is generated, behind the scenes, by the C# compiler. Therefore, instead of writing all the complex code to implement an IEnumerator, you can write the previous shorthand code, which performs exactly same task. This is how iterators simplify the task of creating enumerable types.

Iterators are just syntactic sugar over top of the IEnumerable<T> and IEnumerator<T> interfaces. You need to know this because you could encounter code that uses IEnumerable<T> or IEnumerator<T> members, and you might be surprised to see the methods being called and not knowing where the code is. C# generates a full implementation of the IEnumerable<T> and IEnumerator<T> interfaces behind the scenes. The C#-generated code is in the Intermediate Language (IL) produced from the C# compiler, which you won't see unless you inspect the IL. However, to prove that the C# compiler generates a proper implementation of IEnumerable, you can write code that treats your class like an IEnumerable and calls IEnumerator members. Here's an example:

```
IEnumerator enmr = myCollection.GetEnumerator();


while (enmr.MoveNext())
{
    Console.WriteLine(enmr.Current);
}
```

The variable myCollection is a collection instance containing exactly the same code as the previous GetEnumerator method. As you can see, calling GetEnumerator does return an IEnumerator instance. You can call MoveNext and Current in a while loop to visit each instance.

An aspect of the C#-generated IEnumerator code on iterators that you must be aware of is that the Reset method will always be built to throw a NotSupportedException. The reason is that it is not safe to share an IEnumerator, which is the only reason you would want a Reset method. The proper way to work with IEnumerator objects is to use them only one time.

GetEnumerator is limiting in that it allows you to iterate only through a collection one way. C# iterators are more powerful in that they make it easy to build additional iterators that let you enumerate a collection in different ways. For example, what if you have a data structure that is a tree and needs to do pre-order, in-order, and post-order traversals? Explicitly implementing new IEnumerator objects with MoveNext, Current, and Reset would be too much work. The following sections show you how to create different iterators for traversing a collection any way you need.

The next iterator type, method iterator, enables you to pass information to the iterator for custom runtime behavior.

Method Iterators

One of the places you can define iterators is via methods. This is convenient if you want to pass some information that will filter the results of the iteration. The following method iterator accepts a parameter, telling it how many items to return to the caller:

```
public IEnumerable NextN(int itemCount)
{
    int count = 0;

    foreach (int i in ints)
    {
        if (count++ < itemCount)
        {
            yield return i;
        }
        else
        {
            yield break;
        }
    }
}
```

This method iterator returns only the first itemCount number of items from the collection. The preceding code contains a new clause, yield break, which stops returning values. Therefore, calling code, such as the following, will receive only the first two items in the collection:

```
foreach (int i in myCollection.NextN(2))
{
    Console.WriteLine(i);
}
```

Because the NextN method returns IEnumerable, it can be referenced in a foreach loop, as shown here. This code will loop only twice, on the first two items in the collection.

Sometimes you want to have a predefined iterator that always behaves the same way. A simple way to do this is via a property iterator, discussed next.

Property Iterators

When you don't need to dynamically filter iterator results, but want items in a particular order, use a property iterator. The following code defines a property iterator that returns collection results in reverse order:

```
public IEnumerable Reverse
{
    get
    {
        for (int i=ints.Length-1; i >= 0; i—)
        {
            yield return ints[i];
        }
    }
}
```

Notice that the Reverse property iterator here has only a get accessor. C# allows you to define a set accessor, but it doesn't make sense, and you might want to avoid it. The yield return preceding statement shows that you can return an expression. Also, it uses a normal for loop this time, showing that the way you retrieve the values doesn't matter. What matters is that there are yield return statements that make the iterator return results the way you want them. Here's how you could use a property iterator:

```
foreach (int i in myCollection.Reverse)
{
    Console.WriteLine(i);
}
```

The preceding code uses the property iterator as if it were the collection. The interface is simple, and all the caller needs to know is that the collection results are being returned in reverse order.

The next iterator type allows you to build an iterator in an indexer.

Indexer Iterators

Indexer iterators let you use indexer syntax to enumerate a collection. Be careful about how you implement this. Consider how indexers are supposed to be used, to get a specific value from a collection, or, in the case of ADO.NET, to get the value of a column. Maybe you could stretch this concept a bit and get a specific column or property from all the objects in a collection.

The abstraction I've chosen for this example assumes that there is a collection where items are classified into multiple buckets. In this case, the buckets are odd and even numbers. Perhaps you can find a categorization that works for you. Most of the time, it might be better or more intuitive to use a method iterator, unless the solution screams indexer iterator. Here's my implementation of an indexer iterator that classifies the results according to a NumberType enum:

```
public IEnumerable this[NumberType type]
{
    get
    {
        foreach (int i in ints)
        {
            switch (type)
            {
                case NumberType.EVEN:
                    if (i % 2 == 0)
                    {
                        yield return i;
                    }
                    break;
                case NumberType.ODD:
                    if (i % 2 != 0)
                    {
                        yield return i;
                    }
                    break;
                default:
                    throw new ArgumentException("Not Even or Odd!");
            }
        }
    }
}
```

NumberType is defined as:

```
public enum NumberType { EVEN, ODD };
```

The results of this iterator depend on whether the caller asked for even or odd numbers. Also, notice that the indexer contains only a get accessor. You shouldn't implement a set accessor, even if C# allows you to do it, because it doesn't make sense. Here's how you could call this indexer iterator from code:

```
foreach (int i in myCollection[NumberType.ODD])
{
    Console.WriteLine(i);
}
```

The preceding example uses the indexer iterator to extract values from a collection, which is not an iterator type you will often encounter. Again, make sure that your implementation makes sense in the context of how an iterator should be used. Otherwise, you'll confuse users of your collection. Be sure to document it well, too.

Another iterator that could cause confusion is the operator iterator, which I discuss next.

Operator Iterators

An operator iterator allows you to overload an operator with an iterator implementation. The example I use overrides the + operator. The application here is similar to the meaning of the string concatenation operator. In this case, it is being used as an iterator concatenation operator. Here's how it works:

```
public static IEnumerable operator +(
    FakeCollection col1, FakeCollection col2)
{
    foreach (int i in col1)
    {
        yield return i;
    }
    foreach (int i in col2)
    {
        yield return i;
    }
}
```

FakeCollection, referred to in the preceding parameters, is the containing collection type. Notice that the signature of the + operator iterator is the same as a normal operator overload. The difference is that it returns IEnumerable.

The algorithm works by returning each item of the first collection, followed by each item of the second collection. To the caller, it looks like a continuous sequence of data with no interruptions. Here's how this operator iterator could be called:

```
foreach (int i in col1 + col2)
{
    Console.WriteLine(i);
}
```

Although the preceding code has a definite coolness factor that appeals to the geek in me and a love for terse C# syntax, it doesn't strike me as a smart thing to do—even when implemented in the tradition of operators. Also, remember that not all programming languages that target the .NET Common Language Runtime (CLR) support operators, which is an important design factor when building a reusable collection. A method iterator named Concatenate() would probably be more compatible and easier to understand.

Up to this point, you've seen all the iterator types: GetEnumerator, method, property, indexer, and operator. These iterators give you a great deal of flexibility in making your collections enumerable. Be sure to review the purpose of each iterator so that you can choose the one that is right for the needs.

Next I take an alternative view of iterators and what they can do. If you recall, I described an iterator as a feature that returns a sequence of values from a data source. In the next section, I build on that definition by showing you an iterator that reads from a data source that isn't a collection.

Iterators as a Sequence of Values

Looking at an iterator as a mechanism that returns a sequence of data from a data source, you might be able to find new and useful implementations that encapsulate access to the underlying data store and simplify calling code.

The following example is a simplified version of an algorithm that reads data from a file with comma-separated values. It uses an iterator to extract the data and return each item.

```
public IEnumerable YieldCsvDat(string fileName)
{
    using (FileStream   fs = File.OpenRead(fileName))
    using (StreamReader sr = new StreamReader(fs))
    {
        string line = sr.ReadLine();
        string[] items = line.Split(new char[] { ',' });

        foreach (string item in items)
        {
            yield return int.Parse(item);
        }
    }
}
```

The preceding code is a method iterator that accepts the name of a file. It opens the file, reads each line, and splits the results into an array of strings. Then it returns the int value of each of the strings. Again, this shows how you can make the target of a `yield return` statement an expression. The preceding example simplified the results of the data for the user. Here's how this iterator could be called:

```
foreach (int i in myCollection.YieldCsvDat("..\\..\\csvdat.txt"))
{
    Console.WriteLine(i);
}
```

When writing the preceding code, the developer doesn't have to worry about the file format or any of the work required in massaging the data for presentation. The data source could have been anything, including a collection, database, or web service, and the caller doesn't need to know the details.

An important fact about iterators is that they implement the `Dispose` pattern. This means that you can build a collection of objects that need to be disposed and have a reliable way to call their `Dispose` methods. The next section discusses different scenarios that you need to be aware of.

Disposing Iterators

This section identifies potential traps in object disposal that you could fall into if you deviate from the typical use of an iterator. I show you the default behavior, some scenarios that can get you in trouble, and cover the right way to fix any problems.

One of the features of the underlying code that C# generates when compiling iterators is an implementation of the `Dispose` pattern. Under normal conditions, a `foreach` loop, as shown in previous sections, causes the `Dispose` method of the C#-generated code to be called. Chapter 15, "Managing Object Lifetime," has detailed information on CLR garbage collection and why the `Dispose` pattern is important. However, without the `foreach` loop, you are on your own to properly dispose of the iterator. This section presents different scenarios you could encounter when writing your own code that doesn't use `foreach` and how to properly fix problems before they occur. Here's an extreme case of code you should watch out for:

```
IEnumerator myEnumerator = myCollection.DisposeTest.GetEnumerator();


myEnumerator.MoveNext();
Console.WriteLine(myEnumerator.Current);
```

When you run the preceding code, `Dispose` is not called. Therefore, you should explicitly call it yourself, like this:

```
((IDisposable)myEnumerator).Dispose();
```

Preferably, you'll put the call to `Dispose` in the final part of a `try`/`finally` block.

What is also possible is that you might be tempted to put the code in a different type of loop. If you recall, you can't change the contents of a collection inside of a `foreach` loop. If you need to change the contents of a collection in a loop, you must use a different type of loop, similar to the following `while` loop:

```
myEnumerator = myCollection.DisposeTest.GetEnumerator();


while (myEnumerator.MoveNext())
```

```
    {
        Console.WriteLine(myEnumerator.Current);
        break;
    }
```

This example causes `Dispose` to not be called. You will need to call the `Dispose` method, as shown in the previous example. Here's how I recommend that you handle iterator disposal, with a using statement:

```
myEnumerator = myCollection.DisposeTest.GetEnumerator();


using ((IDisposable)myEnumerator)
{
    while (myEnumerator.MoveNext())
    {
        Console.WriteLine(myEnumerator.Current);
        break;
    }
}
```

The `using` statement in the preceding code ensures that `Dispose` gets called on `myEnumerator` after its containing code runs. Don't forget, or you could end up with a resource leak affecting the performance of your application.

Summary

This chapter began by explaining the value of generic collections, including the problems one encounters with nongeneric collections and how generic collections solve those problems. Of course, collections are a heavily used feature and get a lot of attention. However, generics can be used in other scenarios to improve type safety and performance and simplify where code uses type object.

Another advantage of generics is that they can be used for structs, interfaces, and delegates, as well as classes. You can use generics for any situation where you would normally use the object type. You also learned how to make assumptions about generic type parameters through generic constraints.

Another topic, related to collections, is iterators. When first discussing collections, I explicitly showed you an implementation of an enumerable type, in the `GenericSingleLinkedList` collection. I later showed you iterators and how they simplify the task of creating enumerable types.

Generics were used heavily to implement future FCL APIs and support Language Integrated Query (LINQ). You'll learn about LINQ beginning in Chapter 19, "Accessing Data with LINQ," but first you need to understand how lambda expressions work, which is covered in the next chapter.

CHAPTER 18

Using Lambda Expressions and Expression Trees

Serious weather phenomena such as hurricanes, tropical storms, and tsunamis have names. After a pinball dance across islands, they either hit major landfall or fade away at sea. The reason they are important enough to rate a name is because we have to keep track of them, finding out how strong they are and where they're headed. Otherwise, we wouldn't bother giving them a name. Most of the time, there isn't a need to name the weather—the news just says it's going to rain today or maybe a tornado will suddenly drop from the sky, crush a few houses, toss the cat, and quickly fizzle out. Essentially, that bit of weather occurs only one time, so there's no need to give it a name.

Just like the weather, you have methods that you need to name and keep track of so that you can reuse the code and call it again. Other times, you will use code only once or in one place and don't really care whether it has a name. For example, maybe you want to find all the doctors in a hospital who specialize in brain surgery. That's easy; just grab the list of doctors and iterate through it with a loop to filter the ones you want. Another way, introduced in C# 3.0, is to use lambda expressions.

Lambda expressions are C# expressions that don't have a name. You can pass them around in code, just like delegates. In many ways, they are like the anonymous methods you learned about in Chapter 12, "Event-Based Programming with Delegates and Events." What's different about lambdas is that they have minimal syntax and are transferable to and from expression trees. An expression tree is the data representation of an expression, and the lambda is the executable representation of an expression. You'll learn about both in this chapter.

Lambda Expressions

A lambda expression (lambda) is an executable expression that can be transformed into an expression tree. Because of the simplified syntax of lambdas, they are more convenient than anonymous methods, and their capability to transform into an expression tree opens new doors to dynamic coding, expressiveness, and flexibility. In the following sections, we dig into the syntax of a lambda, explain why they were added to C#, and show how you can use them in your code.

Lambda Syntax

Methods have signatures that distinguish them from other class members. The contents of a method perform a single operation and can optionally return a value. Here's the basic format of a method:

```
([parameter list]) =>
```

The optional `parameter list` holds input parameters, passed by value, just like method parameters. The `=>` symbol is often referred to as such that, goes to, or becomes. The return is implied by the results of the expression. Here's an example of a lambda. It doesn't do anything, but is an isolated example so that you can see the syntax a little clearer:

```
lastName => lastName == "Mayo";
```

In the preceding example, the parameter list is a single parameter, `lastName`. In this particular example, the `lastName` parameter's type is a string, which the C# compiler infers from its context. You'll see more complete examples in a little while that help you see exactly how `lastName` can be inferred as a string. The expression, `lastName == "Mayo"`, returns a bool, but you don't need the return statement. Here's a more verbose example that isn't necessary:

```
(string lastName) => { return lastName == "Mayo"; };
```

Because I specified the type, parentheses are required. Parentheses are also required for multiple parameters. In the expression, use of the `return` keyword and curly braces was extraneous. One of the reasons you want to use lambdas is because of the shorter syntax, which is an improvement over anonymous method syntax.

Before going too far with syntactical permutations, I want to show you how elegant a simple lambda can be in your everyday programming.

Using Lambdas

You can use a lambda anywhere you would use an anonymous method. The following example uses the `FindAll` and `ForEach` method of a `List<string>` to filter items in a collection of last names:

```
List<string> lastNames = new List<string> { "Einstein", "Gore", "Mayo" };


 var famousPeople = lastNames.FindAll(lastName => lastName != "Mayo");
famousPeople.ForEach(lastName => Console.WriteLine(lastName));
```

The parameter of FindAll is the Predicate<T> delegate type. Because the lastNames collection contains strings, T becomes a string, and C# can infer that the lastName parameter of the lambda argument passed to FindAll is a string. The lambda simply returns the bool result telling whether the current string being evaluated equals "Mayo". Similarly, the ForEach in the next line takes a parameter of the Action<T> type. Because the lambda matches the Action<T> signature, it works just fine. The lastName parameter for the lambda argument to ForEach is a string for the same reason just described for the FindAll lambda argument. Looking at the preceding example from a more compositional perspective, here's another example that fits into a single statement:

```
lastNames.
    FindAll(lastName => lastName != "Mayo").
    ForEach(lastName => Console.WriteLine(lastName));
```

This code accomplishes the same task as the previous example, except it is a single statement composing multiple method calls that invoke lambda expressions passed as arguments.

By enclosing lambdas in a block, you can accomplish the same thing as anonymous methods. Here's an example:

```
lastNames.ForEach(lastName =>
{
    Console.Write("Name: ");
    if (lastName != "Mayo")
    {
        Console.WriteLine(lastName);
    }
    else
    {
        Console.WriteLine("Who?");
    }
});
```

Okay, I had a little more fun with that than is necessary, but I hope you see how far you can take a lambda if you have the need. Many times, a lambda will be a simple expression.

Delegates and Lambdas

Lambda expressions are special forms of delegates, which also includes anonymous methods. In fact, anywhere you can use a delegate or anonymous method, you can use a lambda. This section shows you how to use a lambda instead of a delegate to write less code that, depending on the situation, could also be more understandable.

You can assign a lambda to a delegate, provided the signatures match. In the previous section, you saw how to use a lambda where Action<T> and Predicate<T> parameter types were expected. Here are a couple examples that demonstrate how to assign a lambda to a delegate variable. Given the following delegates

```
delegate bool NameMatch(string name);
delegate bool TypeMatch<T>(T name);
```

The examples in this section will use the preceding delegates to demonstrate how lambdas can be used in place of delegates.

Here are two delegates, with one of them being generic. You can assign lambdas to each of these delegates like this:

```
NameMatch nameMatch = lastName => lastName == "Mayo";
TypeMatch<string> typeMatch = lastName => lastName == "Mayo";
```

Even though one delegate is generic and the other isn't, both can be used to hold the same lambda. You can use the delegates that hold the preceding lambdas like this:

```
var match1 = GetMatchNormal(lastNames, nameMatch);
var match2 = GetMatch<string>(lastNames, typeMatch);
```

Here we're passing the delegate to the method so that it can invoke the logic defined by the lambda. Here are the methods being called:

```
private static object GetMatchNormal(List<string> lastNames, NameMatch predicate)
{
    List<string> matches = new List<string>();

    foreach (var name in lastNames)
    {
        if (predicate(name))
        {
            matches.Add(name);
        }
    }

    return matches;
}
```

The logic of this method contains syntax you've seen in previous chapters. Notice that the result of the lambda, represented by the NameMatch delegate parameter, predicate, controls whether the item is added to the list. So, it is easy to use a lambda to specify code to execute independent of the algorithm using the lambda. The next method does the same thing as the one above, except it is implemented as a generic method:

```
private static object GetMatch<TMatch>(List<TMatch> lastNames, TypeMatch<TMatch>
predicate)
{
    List<TMatch> matches = new List<TMatch>();

    foreach (var name in lastNames)
    {
        if (predicate(name))
        {
            matches.Add(name);
        }
    }

    return matches;
}
```

The preceding GetMatch<TMatch> method implements the same logic as its nongeneric counterpart, except it could be a little more useful. Instead of operating on strings, you have a generic way of operating on any type and passing in a dynamic block of code to define what a match means for that type.

Although the previous examples show how to use lambdas with custom delegates, you won't normally need to do this. The .Net Framework Class Library (FCL) includes a set of Func<> delegates you can use in the majority of cases. Here are the Func<> delegate overloads:

► Func<TResult>

► Func<T, TResult>

► Func<T1, T2, TResult>

► Func<T1, T2, T3, TResult>

► Func<T1, T2, T3, T4, TResult>

The meaning of the type parameters in the preceding list is that each T is a delegate parameter type and TResult is a return type. Continuing on the example lambda used earlier in this chapter, you can use Func<> as follows:

```
Func<string, bool> matchFunc = lastName => lastName == "Mayo";
bool matched = matchFunc("Beethoven");
```

Here, string is T and bool is TResult in Func<T, TResult>. The result, matched, is false because Mayo is clearly not Beethoven. Okay, maybe that didn't get a chuckle, but the point is that you can use lambdas wherever a Func<> argument is expected.

Recall from Chapter 10, "Coding Methods and Custom Operators," that extension methods allow you to extend other types, including interfaces. Language Integrated Query (LINQ), introduced in Chapter 19, "Accessing Data with LINQ," extends IEnumerable<T> in several areas. Many of those extension methods operate on Func<> parameters. Here's an example of calling an extension method on IEnumerable<T>. It calls the Count method of lastNames, passing the matchFunc Func<> as an argument:

```
int matchCount = lastNames.Count(matchFunc);
```

The call to Count here uses the matchFunc Func<> delegate as a filter to define which items to count. If you recall, the lambda assigned to matchFunc returns true only for values equal to "Mayo".

IEnumerable<T> has many extension methods that take one of the Func<> delegates. Now you have a choice to either pass in a Func<> or a lambda. The difference is that the Func<> can be reused within the scope it is defined in.

Previous examples use a single parameter, which didn't require parentheses. A single parameter is an exceptional circumstance because you must use parentheses for no parameter or more than one parameter. Here's an example of a no-parameter lambda:

```
Func<string> noParamLambda = () => "I'm a no parameter lambda expression";
Console.WriteLine(noParamLambda());
```

If you recall, the return type is implied, so calling Console.WriteLine with the results of noParamLambda simply prints "I'm a no parameter lambda expression". The lambda could have also been a call to another method or other algorithm that used DateTime or Environment settings. Furthermore, perhaps the lambda was used for lazy evaluation, where it was executed only upon a predefined condition.

Here's another example that uses multiple parameters. It's a little more sophisticated, simulating an encryption routine that dynamically allows you to pass in the actual encryption algorithm. It makes it easy for the caller to collect the plain-text encryption key and algorithm all in one spot and allow a third method to run the code:

```
Func<string, int, string> encryptAlgorithm =
    (source, shift) =>
    {
        char[] result = new char[source.Length];

        for (int i = 0; i < source.Length; i++)
        {
            result[i] = (char)(source[i] + shift);
        }

        return new string(result);
    };

string plainText = "HAL";
int privateKey = 1;
```

```
string cryptText = EncryptString(plainText, privateKey, encryptAlgorithm);

Console.WriteLine("Encrypted Secret: " + cryptText);
```

Here, encryptAlgorithm is the Func<>, referring to the lambda with the encryption algorithm. Notice how the lambda itself is defined with multiple parameters, comma separated and surrounded with parentheses. In this case, you need curly braces because of multiple statements and an explicit return statement, to avoid ambiguity about what was being returned. Here's the output:

```
Encrypted Secret: IBM
```

Here's the EncryptString method:

```
private static string EncryptString(string plainText, int privateKey,
    Func<string, int, string> encryptAlgorithm)
{
    return encryptAlgorithm(plainText, privateKey);
}
```

The preceding code simply invokes the Func<> delegate, passing in the other parameters and returning the result. It isn't too sophisticated but could possibly give you ideas about how you can pass lambdas as Func<> delegate arguments and invoke them inside your own algorithms. Perhaps your method would check a condition before invoking encryptAlgorithm.

Because the lambda is assignable to a compatible Func, you could have done away with instantiating the Func and called the EncryptString method like this:

```
cryptText = EncryptString(
    plainText,
    privateKey,
    (source, shift) =>
    {
        char[] result = new char[source.Length];

        for (int i = 0; i < source.Length; i++)
        {
            result[i] = (char)(source[i] + shift);
        }

        return new string(result);
    });
```

In many cases, the lambda won't be this sophisticated, but it does show that you can easily pass the lambda itself directly to a method accepting a Func<>. Here's a simpler example, calling `Count` as we did earlier, but not bothering with the extra step of creating the `Func<>`:

```
matchCount = lastNames.Count(lastName => lastName == "Mayo");
```

This syntax is a little simpler and is a common way to clearly state your intention when using one of the LINQ extension methods. Exactly as earlier, this returns the number of all elements in the `lastNames` array that equal `"Mayo"`.

Another feature of lambdas is that they can be converted between executable code to data via expression trees. The next section shows you how this works.

Expression Trees

As stated earlier, an expression tree is the data representation of a lambda. This opens new ways to parse the code inside of a lambda and translate it into other forms. In fact, expression trees are integral to enabling LINQ to work. In LINQ to SQL, executable code is translated into SQL by passing lambdas to methods with parameters of an expression type. In this section, you'll see how to assign lambdas to expression trees, how to extract information from an expression tree, and how to convert an expression tree to a lambda.

Converting Lambdas to Expression Trees

To convert from a lambda to an expression tree, you need three things: an `Expression` variable, a compatible `Func<>` type for the lambda, and the lambda itself. Here's an example with a lambda from previous examples:

```
Expression<Func<string, bool>> matchExpr = lastName => lastName == "Mayo";
```

The `Expression` type is defined in the `System.Linq.Expression` namespace, and it holds the expression tree, which is data. The type parameter for the `Expression` is a delegate. You'll commonly see `Func<>` as the delegate because that is already a part of the FCL and saves having to create a custom delegate. The delegate type parameter is required and describes how the `Expression` can understand the assigned lambda. With a properly declared `Expression`, you simply assign the lambda as the example above does.

After you have an `Expression`, which is the data representation of the lambda, you can extract its pieces. From the root of the expression tree that the `Expression` variable represents, you can traverse the tree and extract each part of the lambda. Here's an example that uses the preceding `Expression`:

```
Console.WriteLine("Type: " + matchExpr.Type);
Console.WriteLine("Node Type: " + matchExpr.NodeType);

foreach (var parameter in matchExpr.Parameters)
{
```

```
    Console.WriteLine("Parameter: " + parameter);
}

Console.WriteLine("Body: " + matchExpr.Body);
```

Here's the output:

```
Type: System.Func`2[System.String,System.Boolean]
Node Type: Lambda
Parameter: lastName
Body: (lastName = "Mayo")
```

These are the properties of the `Expression` instance. `Type` is the delegate type, `NodeType` is `Lambda`, `Parameters` is a list of lambda parameters, and `Body` is the whole body of the lambda.

You can break the `Body` down even further because it holds the expression tree itself. Here's how:

```
BinaryExpression body = matchExpr.Body as BinaryExpression;
Console.WriteLine(
    "Body Parts:\n\tLeft: {0}\n\tRight: {1}\n\tNode Type: {2}",
    body.Left, body.Right, body.NodeType);
```

Here's the output:

```
Body Parts:
        Left: lastName
        Right: "Mayo"
        Node Type: Equal
```

The `Body` property is type `Expression`, so we have to convert it to `BinaryExpression` to get at its parts. Notice in the `Console.WriteLine` parameter list how it is easy to reference body properties.

Not only can you convert a lambda to an expression tree and read the parts, you can also build an expression tree and convert it to a lambda. The next section shows how.

Converting Expression Trees to Lambdas

In this section, you learn how to dynamically build an expression tree from scratch, compile it, and convert it to a lambda. This capability allows you to dynamically create and run code at runtime, similar to the "reflection emit" features described in Chapter 16, "Declaring Attributes and Examining Code with Reflection." You still can't create assemblies with expression trees, but the automatic code generation for a simple routine is much easier than working at the Intermediate Language (IL) level.

To build an expression tree dynamically, you must create instances of each node and construct the tree from the bottom up. The following snippets write code that re-creates the `matchExpr = lastName => lastName == "Mayo"` lambda. Here's the part that creates the `lastName` and `"Mayo"` nodes:

```
ParameterExpression paramExpr = Expression.Parameter(typeof(string), "lastName");
ConstantExpression constExpr = Expression.Constant("Mayo", typeof(string));
```

The preceding code creates a `ParameterExpression` and a `ConstantExpression`. You'll need to create as many parameters as necessary. The next section pulls everything together in a single statement to create the expression tree:

```
Expression<Func<string, bool>> dynamicExpressionTree =
    Expression.Lambda<Func<string, bool>>(
        Expression.MakeBinary(
            ExpressionType.Equal,
            paramExpr,
            constExpr),
            new List<ParameterExpression> {paramExpr});
```

The static `Lambda` method takes an `Expression` as the body and an `IEnumerable<T>` or `string[]` for a parameter list. In the preceding example, I could have separated the `MakeBinary` call to create a `BinaryExpression` variable as done earlier with `ParameterExpression` and `ConstantExpression` but wanted to show you another way to do the same thing. Finally, call the `Compile` method, of the `Expression` class, to convert the expression tree to a lambda, like this:

```
Func<string, bool> dynamicLambda = dynamicExpressionTree.Compile();


Console.WriteLine("dynamicLambda(\"Mayo\"): " + dynamicLambda("Mayo"));
```

Here's the output:

```
dynamicLambda("Mayo"): True
```

You also have round-trip capability. That is, you can take a lambda, convert it to an expression tree, and then convert the expression tree back into a lambda.

Summary

Lambdas are a more compact form of anonymous method (covered in Chapter 12) that have the additional capability of being convertible to and from an expression tree. Whereas a lambda is an executable entity, an expression tree is a data representation of a lambda. This facilitates building providers for LINQ, which you'll learn about in the next chapter.

PART 4

Learning LINQ and .NET Data Access

CHAPTER 19

Accessing Data with LINQ

Data has become more complex, with an ever-increasing number of systems and libraries for accessing those systems. With the growing tower of Babel in data solutions, including multivalue, object, relational, and XML, to name a few, a developer must learn how to use a multitude of libraries to figure out how to access this data. These data access library choices turn into an explosion of options to evaluate and learn, making what should be simple in this day and age a difficult and often time-consuming task.

Focusing only on what is available in .NET for accessing relational data, we have ADO.NET, which is broken down into multiple providers (ODBC, OleDB, SQL, Oracle, and so on). That's what ships with the .NET Framework, but you also have providers by Oracle and Borland that offer additional options. If you choose not to go the full ADO.NET route, you can use data readers to extract data and populate custom objects. Moving away from ADO.NET, you can also adopt one of the plethora of object-relational data management products available via open source or third party; there are so many to choose from that it would take another paragraph or two to ensure none was left out. In addition, this was just a short description of options available for relational data, without mentioning all the choices you could make for multivalue, object, and XML data sources.

Language Integrated Query (LINQ), as its name implies, is a way to address the data access needs of developers by enabling support directly in the programming language. Data access libraries won't go away, but now we'll have a common way of accessing data, through those libraries. In addition, there has always been a problem bridging the semantic gap between different types of data, whether multivalue, object, relational, or XML—a problem called *impedance mismatch*. For example, if you have relational data in one place and XML data in another, it would be nice to have a similar mechanism to access this data. Furthermore, the chasm between relational, hier-archical, multivalue, and other paradigms with the object-oriented paradigm that a C# developer works in every day can be decreased significantly with LINQ.

Several flavors of LINQ can be used to target different database providers. The chapters following this cover LINQ to ADO.NET, LINQ to Entities, and LINQ to XML. However, before we get there, we cover two popular implementations of LINQ for the C# developer: LINQ to Objects and LINQ to SQL.

LINQ to Objects

Think about how often you need to extract information from a collection of objects—filtering, grouping, and transforming—to obtain the proper output. You probably use `for`, `foreach`, or some other type of loop to iterate through the information, inspecting each object for the condition that matters and manipulating or saving the object. The code is imperative, meaning that each step is explicitly specified, step by step. This is typical and has been a common way of working with objects for many years.

What if it could be easier to accomplish the same task? How would you feel if you could tell the compiler what you want it to do and let it figure out the best way to do it? Such a capability is often referred to as a declarative style of programming. This is what LINQ can do for you.

In this section, you see how to work with objects in a more declarative way. You learn about the SQL-like syntax that is part of C# and how you have syntax highlighting and IntelliSense support with VS2008. Most of all, you see how LINQ can make your task as a C# programmer easier and more productive.

Basic LINQ Syntax

LINQ syntax is SQL-like. It has `from`, `where`, `select`, `join`, `group by`, and `order by` statements. This section introduces the basic syntax, and sections that follow outline more options.

If you just want to select a group of objects, you can use a `from` and `select` statement. The following example selects a group of `StaffMember` objects from a `List` of `StaffMember`. Given this collection

```
List<StaffMember> hospitalStaff = new List<StaffMember>
{
    new StaffMember { Name = "Marcus", Position="Doctor" },
    new StaffMember { Name = "Nancy", Position = "Nurse" },
    new StaffMember { Name = "Chris", Position = "Nurse" }
};
```

You can query it like this:

```
IEnumerable<StaffMember> staffMbrList =
    from staffMbr in hospitalStaff
    select staffMbr;
```

If you're already used to SQL, this example might look familiar. The immediate difference is that the `from` clause comes first. It specifies the target object and the collection being operated on. The `select` clause defines what is being selected, which is the same object queried in this case. The result of this query is assigned to `staffMbrList`. The type of LINQ to Objects queries is always an `IEnumerable` list of objects specified by the `select` clause.

In the preceding query, the result contains the same set of objects from `hospitalStaff`. As you might suspect, querying for the same list isn't of much use. Let's start changing what is returned by modifying the `select` clause. You can extract query results via a loop like this:

```
foreach (var mbr in staffMbrList)
{
    Console.WriteLine(mbr.Name);
}
```

This example uses a `foreach` loop, but you can use the `staffMbrList` any way you want, just like any other collection.

Although usage of query results is the same as any other collection, be aware that the actual query doesn't execute until the `foreach` loop executes. This allows you to define the query in a number of steps without incurring the overhead of reevaluation upon each change, which increases efficiency.

Extracting Projections

In the preceding section, the `select` clause simply specified the exact same object being queried. However, you'll often want to alter the form or shape of the data returned from a query, which is referred to as a projection.

Projections can be in the form of existing objects or anonymous types. This gives you the flexibility to work with the data in any form you need. The following example is a query that forms a projection based on an existing object type, `StaffMbrAbbr`:

```
IEnumerable<StaffMbrAbbr> staffMbrAbbrList =
    from staffMbr in hospitalStaff
    select new StaffMbrAbbr { Name = staffMbr.Name };
```

The `StaffMbrAbbr` class has only a `Name` property, whereas the `StaffMember` class has more. Notice the `select` clause that instantiates a `StaffMbrAbbr` for each record and uses an object initializer to define the new projection, which differs from `StaffMember`.

The previous query assumes that a typed object, `StaffMbrAbbr`, is necessary—perhaps it is a return value from the current method. Sometimes you don't really care what the object type is because you only want to work with the data and you are working with it in the

19

same method that does the query. In this case, you can query with a projection on an anonymous type. Here's an example that returns a projection with the same data as the previous example, for `StaffMbrAbbr`, but uses an anonymous type instead:

```
var staffNameList =
    from staffMbr in hospitalStaff
    select new { Name = staffMbr.Name };
```

Notice two parts of the preceding query: the result and the `select` clause. The `select` clause uses an anonymous type—it doesn't have a type name. Anonymous types were added to C# 3.0 specifically to support flexible projections in LINQ queries. Now, if you have some processing inside of the same method, you don't have to create a special object type that will be used for a single purpose—you can define anonymous types in your query projections. On the other hand, if you do need to return the custom projection to calling code, you must define a custom type, like the `StaffMbrAbbr` in a previous example.

Now that you understand projections with anonymous types, you can better appreciate the value of the `var` keyword (implicitly typed local variables). Thinking logically, if the projection type is anonymous, you don't know its name. However, the return type of a LINQ to Objects query is `IEnumerable<T>`. With no way to specify T, you need a way to assign the return value from the LINQ query to assign to a variable. That's why `var` was added to C# and why you see it being used to hold the results of the projection on an anonymous type.

Remember that `var` is strongly typed. You can't assign its results to a `var` of a different anonymous type.

Filtering Data

You'll need to filter results in queries, which is easy to do with LINQ. Here's an example that gets a list of nurses from the hospital staff:

```
var nurses =
    from staffMbr in hospitalStaff
    where staffMbr.Position == "Nurse"
    select staffMbr.Name;
```

The `where` clause in this example has a simple C# Boolean statement. You can make this more sophisticated with multiple `&&` and `¦¦` conditions, for which the result is always type `bool`.

Ordering Query Results

When you are performing a LINQ query, the default order depends on the type of data source being queried. When you need output to follow a specific order, you can do so in your query, instead of leaving that decision to chance. Here's an example that guarantees that a query result for nurses appears in order:

```
var orderedNurses =
    from staffMbr in hospitalStaff
    where staffMbr.Position == "Nurse"
    orderby staffMbr.Name
    select staffMbr.Name;
```

By default, the preceding `orderby` clause gives you an ascending list. You can use the descending keyword to reverse the order. Here's an example that shows how you can use multiple properties for `orderby` clauses and use `descending`:

```
var orderedStaff =
    from staffMbr in hospitalStaff
    orderby staffMbr.Position descending, staffMbr.Name
    select new { staffMbr.Name, staffMbr.Position };
```

As shown here, you can use a comma-separated list in the `orderby` clause to define the order that properties sort by. To get a reverse sort, follow the property with the `descending` keyword.

Grouping Data

You can also group data on a specified property. Here's an example that groups by `Position`:

```
var groupedStaff =
    from staffMbr in hospitalStaff
    group staffMbr by staffMbr.Position into staffMbrGroup
    select staffMbrGroup.Key;
```

The `group` by statement identifies both the object and property of that object to evaluate. Using the `into` keyword, you can project on a grouping result represented by the `Key` property of the group—the code above projecting on the `Position` property.

Joining Data

When data is divided among objects and you need to combine that data into a single result, you can join it. Here's an example that shows how to join data with a LINQ query:

```
List<Patient> patients = new List<Patient>
{
    new Patient { Doctor = "Marcus", Name = "George" },
    new Patient { Doctor = "Doolittle", Name = "Cat" },
    new Patient { Doctor = "Marcus", Name = "Jane" }
};

var patientsAndDoctors =
    from doctor in hospitalStaff
    join patient in patients on doctor.Name equals patient.Doctor
    select new { Doctor = doctor.Name, Patient = patient.Name };
```

With the `patients` collection previously defined, the query uses a `join` between `patients` and `hospitalStaff`. In the `join` clause, `patient` is the selector on the `patients` collection, and the on keyword leads to the `join` criteria. In this case, the equality is based on whether the patient's doctor matches the doctor's name. On the projection, the anonymous type property is specified to avoid the ambiguity of grabbing the `Name` property for both the `doctor` and `patient`.

Another point you might have noticed is how the syntax is very much like SQL, which could make LINQ easy to adapt to for those who know SQL.

Building Hierarchies with Group Joins

Earlier you learned how to use multiple `from` clauses to perform a `SelectMany` operation that flattened out a hierarchy of objects. You can also perform the opposite operation by performing a `GroupJoin` operation that builds a hierarchy. Here's an example that creates a collection of doctors with a property holding a collection of patients for each doctor:

```
var patientsGroupedByDoctors =
    from doctor in hospitalStaff
    join patient in patients on doctor.Name equals patient.Doctor into
      PatientGroup
    select new { Doctor = doctor.Name, Patients = PatientGroup };

foreach (var doc in patientsGroupedByDoctors)
{
    foreach (var patient in doc.Patients)
    {
        Console.WriteLine("Patient: {0}", patient.Name);
    }
}
```

The first difference between the `join` operation in the previous section and this one is the `into` clause on the end of the `join` clause. The `into` clause grouped patients for each doctor into `PatientGroup`. To build the hierarchy, the `select` clause assigns `PatientGroup` to the `Patients` property of the anonymous type.

As expected, you can access objects in a hierarchy with nested loops. I chose `foreach` in this case to extract all the patients for each doctor.

Querying Relational Data with LINQ to SQL

LINQ to Objects is a good way to query objects that are already in memory, but it is only a single implementation of LINQ. One of the other LINQ implementations that ship with .NET 3.5 is LINQ to SQL. You can use LINQ to SQL to query data from a SQL Server database. If you need to query a database other than SQL Server, you must use a LINQ implementation specific to that database (if available) or use LINQ to Entities, which you learn about in Chapter 22, "Creating Data Abstractions with the ADO.NET Entity Framework."

The following sections show you how to use LINQ to SQL, which enables you to make LINQ queries in code, manipulate data, call stored procedures, and customize queries with additional business logic.

First, you need a `DataContext` to handle your LINQ to SQL data access, which is described in the next section.

Defining a `DataContext`

Before making any queries, you need to set up a `DataContext`, which defines entities you can query. These entities map to relational tables, and the translation between your C# LINQ query and the SQL sent to the database is automatically taken care of by LINQ.

Based on the same hospital paradigm as in the previous section, the examples used here create HospitalStaff and Patients tables in a database named Hospital. Listing 19.1 contains the schema for these tables. You should create the database before running this script.

LISTING 19.1   Hospital Database Schema

```
/****** Object:   Table [dbo].[HospitalStaff]Script Date: 12/29/2007 21:42:42 ******/
SET ANSI_NULLS ON
GO
SET QUOTED_IDENTIFIER ON
GO
IF NOT EXISTS (
SELECT * FROM sys.objects
WHERE object_id = OBJECT_ID(N'[HospitalStaff]')
AND type in (N'U'))
BEGIN
CREATE TABLE [HospitalStaff](
    [HospitalStaffID] [int] IDENTITY(1,1) NOT NULL,
    [Name] [varchar](50)
      COLLATE SQL_Latin1_General_CP1_CI_AS NOT NULL,
    [Position] [varchar](50)
      COLLATE SQL_Latin1_General_CP1_CI_AS NOT NULL,
 CONSTRAINT [PK_HospitalStaff] PRIMARY KEY CLUSTERED
(
    [HospitalStaffID] ASC
)WITH (PAD_INDEX  = OFF, STATISTICS_NORECOMPUTE  = OFF,
IGNORE_DUP_KEY = OFF, ALLOW_ROW_LOCKS  = ON,
ALLOW_PAGE_LOCKS  = ON)
)
END
GO
SET IDENTITY_INSERT [HospitalStaff] ON
INSERT [HospitalStaff] ([HospitalStaffID], [Name], [Position])
VALUES (1, N'Marcus', N'Doctor')
```

19

LISTING 19.1   Continued

```sql
INSERT [HospitalStaff] ([HospitalStaffID], [Name], [Position])
VALUES (2, N'Nancy', N'Nurse')
INSERT [HospitalStaff] ([HospitalStaffID], [Name], [Position])
VALUES (3, N'Chris', N'Nurse')
INSERT [HospitalStaff] ([HospitalStaffID], [Name], [Position])
VALUES (4, N'Doolittle', N'Doctor')
SET IDENTITY_INSERT [HospitalStaff] OFF
/****** Object:  Table [dbo].[Patient]Script Date: 12/29/2007 21:42:42 ******/
SET ANSI_NULLS ON
GO
SET QUOTED_IDENTIFIER ON
GO
IF NOT EXISTS (SELECT * FROM sys.objects
WHERE object_id = OBJECT_ID(N'[Patient]') AND type in (N'U'))
BEGIN
CREATE TABLE [Patient](
    [PatientID] [int] IDENTITY(1,1) NOT NULL,
    [Name] [varchar](50)
      COLLATE SQL_Latin1_General_CP1_CI_AS NOT NULL,
    [DoctorID] [int] NOT NULL,
 CONSTRAINT [PK_Patient] PRIMARY KEY CLUSTERED
(
    [PatientID] ASC
)WITH (PAD_INDEX  = OFF, STATISTICS_NORECOMPUTE  = OFF,
IGNORE_DUP_KEY = OFF, ALLOW_ROW_LOCKS  = ON,
ALLOW_PAGE_LOCKS  = ON)
)
END
GO
SET IDENTITY_INSERT [Patient] ON
INSERT [Patient] ([PatientID], [Name], [DoctorID])
VALUES (1, N'George', 1)
INSERT [Patient] ([PatientID], [Name], [DoctorID])
VALUES (2, N'Cat', 4)
INSERT [Patient] ([PatientID], [Name], [DoctorID])
VALUES (3, N'Jane', 1)
SET IDENTITY_INSERT [Patient] OFF
/****** Object:  ForeignKey [FK_Patient_HospitalStaff]Script Date: 12/29/2007
21:42:42 ******/
IF NOT EXISTS (SELECT * FROM sys.foreign_keys
WHERE object_id = OBJECT_ID(N'[FK_Patient_HospitalStaff]')
AND parent_object_id = OBJECT_ID(N'[Patient]'))
ALTER TABLE [Patient]  WITH CHECK ADD  CONSTRAINT
[FK_Patient_HospitalStaff] FOREIGN KEY([DoctorID])
REFERENCES [HospitalStaff] ([HospitalStaffID])
GO
```

LISTING 19.1   Continued

```
ALTER TABLE [Patient] CHECK CONSTRAINT
[FK_Patient_HospitalStaff]
GO
```

To create a `DataContext` in VS2008, create a new project and complete these steps:

1. Right-click the project and select Add, New Item. You see the Add New Item dialog box.

2. Select Data in the Categories tree, select LINQ to SQL Classes in the Templates list, name the file **Hospital.dbml**, and click the Add button. This creates the Hospital.dbml file in your project that exposes the Object Relational designer surface shown in Figure 19.1.

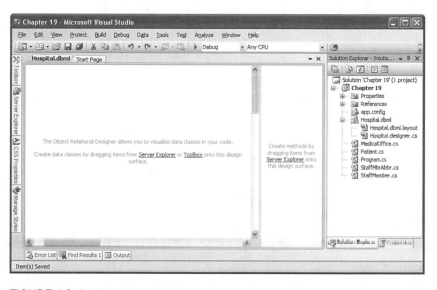

FIGURE 19.1   Object Relational design surface.

3. The designer in Figure 19.1 has two sections: object surface and stored procedure surface. To use these, select View, Server Explorer to open the Server Explorer, ensure the database connection to the database you created earlier is open by right-clicking Data Connections in Server Explorer, select Add Connection, and fill out the Add Connection window for the database you created. If you created the database in VS2008, it should already be in the list. Select the HospitalStaff and Patient tables, and drag and drop them onto the left side of the designer. Figure 19.2 shows the two tables.

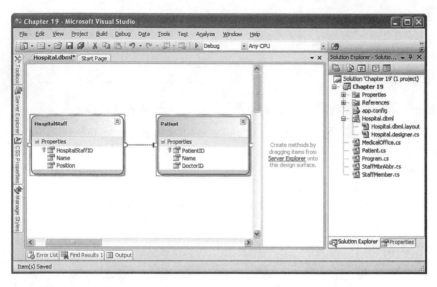

FIGURE 19.2   LINQ to SQL data entities.

The tables in Figure 19.2 are now referred to as entities. Because SQL Server defined the relationship between the two tables, they appear as an association between entities. You can click each entity or association and view the Properties window for their settings, in which you can change various settings. We take a closer look at the Properties window in later sections of this chapter.

With your DataContext created, you can now perform database queries.

Querying Through the `DataContext`

Now you have two data entities that you can program against, as shown in Figure 19.2. They were added to a DataContext-derived class named HospitalDataContext, which was created in step 2 earlier when you were adding the Hospital.dbml item to your project.

Taking what you know about LINQ from previous sections, you just need to create an instance of HospitalDataContext and query against it. Here's how:

```
var hospitalCtx = new HospitalDataContext();


var docs =
    from doctor in hospitalCtx.HospitalStaffs
    where doctor.Position == "Doctor"
    select doctor;
```

Notice that I created an instance of HospitalDataContext, an autogenerated class that was created when adding the Hospital.dbml item to the project. When adding the HospitalStaff and Patients entities, VS2008 also added classes for HospitalStaffs and Patients—plural named container classes to hold HospitalStaff and Patient entities.

Instead of declaring a collection in the `from` clause, as was done for LINQ to Objects, you use the `HospitalDataContext` reference, `hospitalCtx`, to specify the entity collection to query, `HospitalStaffs`.

Modifying `DataContext` Objects

The `DataContext` keeps track of all changes you make to its objects, so you can persist them to the database. This section shows how to do add, update, and delete operations and then persist the changes.

Adding Objects

To add a new object with the `DataContext`, you just need to perform an insert into the `DataContext`-generated collection. Here's an example that adds a new doctor to the `HospitalStaffs` collection:

```
hospitalCtx.HospitalStaffs.InsertOnSubmit(
    new HospitalStaff { Name = "John", Position = "Doctor" });
```

The `InsertOnSubmit` statement adds a new object to the `HospitalStaffs` object, which corresponds to a database table. While this example prepares for the insert, the actual insertion doesn't occur until submitting the changes. You learn how to submit changes in a couple more sections.

Updating Objects

To update an existing object, you need to get a reference to that object and then change its properties. Here's an example that changes one of the doctor's names:

```
IQueryable<HospitalStaff> doctorsToUpdate =
    from doctor in hospitalCtx.HospitalStaffs
    where doctor.Name == "Marcus"
    select doctor;

doctorsToUpdate.First().Name = "Marcus MD";
```

This example uses a LINQ query to find the object to change. Actually, it is a collection of objects. In this case, the collection is a different type, `IQueryable<T>`. LINQ to SQL returns `IQueryable<T>` objects from queries as opposed to the LINQ to Objects queries that return `IEnumerable<T>`. Notice the call to `First` on the `doctorsToUpdate` collection. `First` is a LINQ operator that will return the first object in the collection. With a reference to the object, you simply modify the object contents.

Deleting Objects

Just like an update, you need to get a reference to an object before deleting it. Like an add operation, you must call a method to explicitly delete it. Here's an example that deletes a doctor from the `HospitalStaffs` collection:

```
IQueryable<HospitalStaff> doctorsToDelete =
    from doctor in hospitalCtx.HospitalStaffs
```

19

```
    where doctor.Name == "Doolittle"
    select doctor;
```

```
hospitalCtx.HospitalStaffs.DeleteOnSubmit(doctorsToDelete.First());
```

Make sure you add an entry to the Doctors table in the DB where the Name column contains Doolittle.

The call to `DeleteOnSubmit` removes the object from the collection. Notice that we used the `First` operator again to get a reference to the first object in the collection returned by the query.

Persisting Changes to the Database

None of the previous operations on the collection have persisted changes to the database. You must call `SubmitChanges` on the `DataContext` to make this happen, as follows:

```
        hospitalCtx.SubmitChanges();
```

Now when you do a query, all the changes appear.

UPDATING DATA AFTER RUNNING SAMPLES

After you run the samples in this chapter for modifying the database, your data will change, as expected. Before running the code a second time, make the following changes: change `Marcus MD` to **Marcus**, delete a `John`, and add a `Phil` with a `Position` value of `Doctor`. This will prevent an exception on the next program run.

Calling Stored Procedures

A lot of people have an invested interest in stored procedures. If you fall into this camp, LINQ to SQL has an excellent option for you to call those stored procedures in your source code.

To get started, create the following stored procedure in the Hospital database that you created earlier in the chapter:

```
CREATE PROCEDURE GetDoctors
AS
select Name
from HospitalStaff
where Position = 'Doctor'
```

You need to add the stored procedure to the `DataContext`, which uses the same process as adding tables. Open Hospital.dbml, which you created previously in this chapter. Then open Server Explorer, locate the `GetDoctors` stored procedure, and drag and drop it into the rightmost panel of Hospital.dbml. This adds your stored procedure to `HospitalDataContext`.

Using the stored procedure is as simple as calling the new method in `HospitalDataContext`. Here's how:

```
var doctors = hospitalCtx.GetDoctors();
```

Just use the `HospitalDataContext`, `hospitalCtx`, to call `GetDoctors`. The LINQ to SQL designer names the method the same as your stored procedure. If your stored procedure name contains spaces, LINQ to SQL will replace those spaces with underlines.

You can also use SQL functions in LINQ to SQL, which is discussed in the next section.

Using SQL Functions

In addition to stored procedures, you can use SQL Server functions in your LINQ to SQL queries. To see how this works, add the following function to the Hospital database:

```
CREATE FUNCTION dbo.Doctors()
RETURNS TABLE
AS
RETURN
select * from hospitalstaff
where Position = 'Doctor'
```

As shown in the preceding SQL function, the result is a table that you can query. Drag and drop this function from the Server Explorer to the Hospital.dbml LINQ to SQL designer, and it will appear as a method, named `Doctors()`, above the `GetDoctors()` stored procedure from the preceding section. You can use the `Doctor` function like this:

```
var docNames =
    from docName in hospitalCtx.Doctors()
    select docName.Name;
```

The `Doctors` function is used, just like a table (or an object that returns the contents of a table), in the preceding query.

This was a short detour to show you how to reuse your existing functions in LINQ to SQL. The next section returns to the subject of stored procedures and how you can achieve further integration of them with LINQ to SQL.

Modifying a Database with Stored Procedures

The previous examples for modifying the database used the LINQ to SQL runtime as a default option to dynamically create queries and pass them to the database for execution. However, if you already have stored procedures for performing database modification, you can still use them. This section shows you how to use the LINQ to SQL designer to use stored procedures, instead of LINQ to SQL runtime queries.

19

Inserting via Stored Procedures

Add the following stored procedure to your database to insert a new record:

```
CREATE PROCEDURE dbo.InsertStaff
(
        @Name varchar(50),
        @Position varchar(50)
)
AS

        insert into HospitalStaff
        (Name, Position)
        values (@Name, @Position)
```

To associate the InsertStaff stored procedure above with LINQ to SQL, open Hospital.dbml and drag and drop the stored procedure from Server Explorer to the methods pane of the design surface. Then select the HospitalStaff entity in the designer, open the Properties window, select the Insert property, and click the property value button. The Configure Behavior window will display, as shown in Figure 19.3.

FIGURE 19.3   Configure behavior for insert.

Insert, update, and delete operations are configured to use the LINQ to SQL runtime by default, and the Use Runtime option, shown in Figure 19.3, is chosen. To change this, select Customize, InsertStaff, as shown in Figure 19.3. The Configure Behavior window selects parameters for you, but you can select each parameter and change them if you need to. Notice how the Name parameter is selected, showing the drop-down list where you can change the parameter.

Updating via Stored Procedures

Add the following stored procedure to your database to update an existing record:

```
CREATE PROCEDURE dbo.UpdateStaff
(
        @HospitalStaffID int,
        @Name varchar(50),
        @Position varchar(50)
)
AS
update HospitalStaff
set Name = @Name,
    Position = @Position
where HospitalStaffID = @HospitalStaffID
```

Similar to the steps for adding an insert stored procedure, you should add the UpdateStaff stored procedure to the LINQ to SQL designer, select HospitalStaff, and change the Update property through the Configuration Manager to the UpdateStaff method, as shown in Figure 19.4.

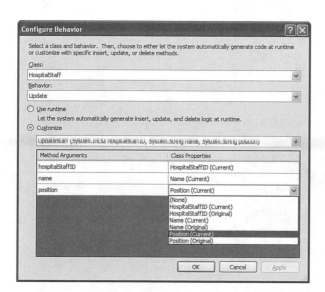

FIGURE 19.4   Configure behavior for update.

When updating records, LINQ to SQL keeps track of the original record, before changes, and the current record, after changes. Notice in Figure 19.4 that LINQ to SQL chooses the current record by default, but you can change it to the original if you want. Suppose, for example, you are reusing existing stored procedures that you can't change and you want to make sure the Position parameter is never changed; you can choose Position (original).

Deleting via Stored Procedures

Add the following stored procedure to your database to delete an existing record:

```
CREATE PROCEDURE dbo.DeleteStaff
(
        @HospitalStaffID int
)
AS
delete from HospitalStaff
where HospitalStaffID = @HospitalStaffID
```

Similar to the steps for adding an insert or update stored procedure, you should add the DeleteStaff stored procedure to the LINQ to SQL designer, select HospitalStaff, and change the Delete property through the Configuration Manager to the DeleteStaff method, as shown in Figure 19.5.

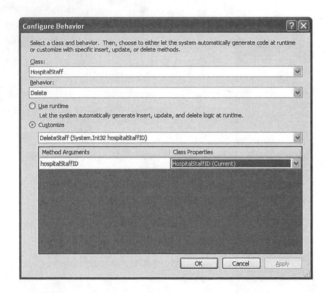

FIGURE 19.5   Configure behavior for delete.

Similar to insert and update, you select Customize and choose the DeleteStaff method, as shown in Figure 19.5. Like update, you have a choice of selecting current or original object values.

You've now seen how to extend the capabilities of LINQ to SQL by using custom stored procedures. Another way to extend LINQ to SQL is via partial methods, discussed next.

Extending Data Handling Logic with Partial Methods

In Chapter 10, "Coding Methods and Custom Operators," I discussed partial methods and promised to discuss a practical implementation of them in this chapter. LINQ to SQL generates partial methods for insert, update, and delete operations for every entity added to the designer. Furthermore, LINQ to SQL generates changing and changed partial methods for every property of each entity. This section shows you how to extend handling logic for all the automatically generated partial methods that LINQ to SQL creates.

Customizing Insert, Update, and Delete with Partial Methods

LINQ to SQL automatically generates partial methods whenever you add a new entity (table) to the LINQ to SQL designer. You can extend the logic of your system by providing an implementation for any of these partial methods. Because the LINQ to SQL code is automatically generated, you don't want to touch that code, which is in the Hospital.designer.cs file for the examples in this chapter. Add a new partial class with a partial method, as shown here, in a separate file of your project:

```
public partial class HospitalDataContext
{
    partial void DeleteHospitalStaff(HospitalStaff staffMember)
    {
        staffMember.Patients.ToList().ForEach(
            patient => DeletePatientCustom(patient.PatientID));

        DeleteStaff(staffMember.HospitalStaffID);
    }
}
```

The code above won't run until after you create the DeletePatientCustom stored procedure, defined here, and add it to the methods pane of your *.dbml design surface.

Notice that both the HospitalDataContext class and DeleteHospitalStaff method are partial. Making the HospitalDataContext class partial allows you to avoid changing LINQ to SQL automatically generated code, and whenever the automatically generated code changes, your partial in a separate file doesn't change.

Whenever you declare a partial method for any of the partial methods that were automatically generated, LINQ to SQL calls your method instead of generating runtime queries. This means that you will be responsible for all operations.

In previous sections, the code deleted HospitalStaff records and didn't encounter errors. That was because the record deleted didn't have Patients. If you recall, the Patient table has a foreign key to the HospitalStaff table, which would generate an error if you tried to delete a HospitalStaff record that had patients. Another fact to consider is that LINQ to SQL does not perform cascading deletes. Therefore, the DeleteHospitalStaff method above maintains the integrity of the database by deleting Patients belonging to a

HospitalStaff member and then deleting the HospitalStaff member. The call to DeletePatientCustom is the following stored procedure:

```
CREATE PROCEDURE dbo.DeletePatientCustom
(
        @PatientID int
)
AS
delete from Patient
where PatientID = @PatientID
```

You would add the DeletePatientCustom stored procedure to the LINQ to SQL designer, just as you did with the stored procedures described earlier in this chapter.

Implementation of insert and update via partial methods follows a similar pattern.

PARTIAL METHODS, STORED PROCEDURES, AND RUNTIME QUERIES ARE MUTUALLY EXCLUSIVE

The default implementation of LINQ to SQL operations is to generate SQL queries at runtime and submit them to the database. In this case, partial methods and stored procedures (not specified) don't run. However, if you change to specifying insert, update, or delete stored procedures, LINQ to SQL won't generate either runtime queries or call partial methods. In fact, LINQ to SQL will remove the partial method reference any time you assign a stored procedure to an insert, update, or delete property for an entity. The same is true for implementing partial methods in that runtime queries aren't generated and stored procedures aren't called.

One aspect of implementing partial methods is that you can't use LINQ operators to affect the change. Furthermore, if you try to call a LINQ to SQL modification method such as InsertOnSubmit or DeleteOnSubmit, LINQ to SQL will throw an exception. That said, you can still call stored procedures in your partial methods.

In addition to customizing insert, update, and delete with partial methods, you can customize property changes via custom methods, as discussed next.

Customizing Property Changes with Partial Methods

To customize and add business logic for property changes, you must create a partial class for the entity holding the property and add a partial method to that partial class for handling the desired change operation. The following example shows how to detect a property change for the Position property of the HospitalStaff entity:

```
public partial class HospitalStaff
{
    partial void OnPositionChanging(string value)
    {
        if (Position != null && Position != value)
```

```
        {
            throw new ArgumentException("Can't change Position.");
        }
    }
}
```

Just add a new class item to your project named `HospitalStaff` and add the `partial` modifier. Notice the `OnPositionChanging` partial method. The string parameter, `value`, is the new value being assigned to the `Position` property. The logic checks to ensure that `Position` doesn't change and throws an exception if it does. You should check for `null`, too, because this method is called when an object is initially populated, meaning that `Position` isn't assigned yet. The following code forces the condition where an exception would occur in the `OnPositionChanging` partial method:

```
IQueryable<HospitalStaff> doctorsToUpdate =
    from doctor in hospitalCtx.HospitalStaffs
    where doctor.Name == "Marcus"
    select doctor;

doctorsToUpdate.First().Position = "Doctor";

hospitalCtx.SubmitChanges();
```

Ensure there is a record in the Doctors table with the Name column set to Marcus and the Position column set to Doctor. Otherwise, you'll receive an exception.

The business logic implemented via `OnPropertyChanging` ensures that the position doesn't change for an existing staff member.

You can also implement the partial method for the `OnPropertyChanged` event. Every property, `Xxx`, has `OnXxxChanging` and `OnXxxChanged` events, where `OnXxxChanging` occurs before the change and `OnXxxChanged` occurs after the change.

Standard Query Operators

Most of the operations used so far query operators that were built in to the C# language syntax. However, many query operators don't have C# syntax aliases. For example, previous examples used the `First` operator to obtain a reference to the first object returned from the query. The following sections provide a quick overview of available query operators—some with C# aliases and others without. These are all part of the .NET Framework documentation, but I cover them briefly for reference and provide a simple example in each category so that you can see how they are used.

Sorting Operators

Sorting operations affect the ordering of the results. Table 19.1 contains sorting operators.

19

TABLE 19.1   Sorting Operators

Operator	C# Alias	Description
OrderBy	order by	Sets sort order
OrderByDescending	order by - descending	Sorts in descending order
ThenBy	order by -, order by	Subsequent sorts
ThenByDescending	order by -, order by - descending	Subsequent sorts in descending order
Reverse	N/A	Reverses results

You've already seen order by and descending operators used with C# syntax earlier in this chapter. The following example shows how to use the Reverse operator:

```
var staffRev =
    (from staff in hospitalStaff
    select staff).Reverse();
```

For hospitalStaff, the members were added with names of Marcus, Nancy, and Chris. By executing the preceding query, you get back Chris, Nancy, and Marcus, in that order. Notice how I enclosed the query in parentheses. In VS2008, you can type the dot operator after the closing parenthesis and get IntelliSense for all of the operators.

Set Operators

Set operators are for set-based operations. Table 19.2 contains set operators.

TABLE 19.2   Set Operators

Operator	C# Alias	Description
Distinct	N/A	Returns unique values
Except	N/A	Like a SQL left join returns results from one set that aren't in another
Intersect	N/A	Returns common elements from each set
Union	N/A	Returns all objects from both sets

The example I'll use from Table 19.2 is for the Distinct operator, which could be a little confusing for some scenarios. Here's an example of Distinct operator usage:

```
hospitalStaff.Add(
    new StaffMember
    {
        Name = "Chris",
        Position= "Nurse"
    }
);
```

```
hospitalStaff.ForEach(
    staff => Console.WriteLine(
        "Name: {0}, Position: {1}",
        staff.Name, staff.Position));

    var distinctStaff =
        (
            from staff in hospitalStaff
            select staff
        )
        .Distinct();

    foreach (var staff in distinctStaff)
    {
        Console.WriteLine(
            "Name: {0}, Position: {1}",
            staff.Name, staff.Position);
    }
```

The preceding code adds a new member to `hospitalStaff`, queries with the `Distinct` operator, and prints the results. The first print shows that a second copy of `Name: Chris, Position: Nurse` was added to the list. It might surprise you to know that the second loop printed exactly the same thing.

The confusion could come from the fact that you are operating on custom reference type objects—instances of the `StaffMember` class. As you may recall from Chapter 8, "Designing Objects," reference type objects default to reference equality. Built-in types already have their equality defined, but you need to define equality for your custom types if you are going to use them in a scenario such as this. The two `StaffMember` instances of `Chris` refer to different instances, and reference equality isn't sufficient.

To solve this problem, you need to use the `Distinct` operator overload that accepts an `IEqualityComparer<T>`. Here's the correct implementation for using the `Distinct` operator on collections of custom types:

```
var distinctStaff =
    (
        from staff in hospitalStaff
        select staff
    )
    .Distinct(new StaffMember());
```

This time, `Distinct` uses an overload that accepts a parameter of type `IEqualityComparer<StaffMember>`. I could have created a special object to implement this interface, but there is already a `StaffMember` class, and it seems to make more sense to implement it there. Here's the change to `StaffMember`, making it an

19

IEqualityComparer<StaffMember>:

```
class StaffMember : IEqualityComparer<StaffMember>
{
    public StaffMember() { }

    public StaffMember(string name)
    {
        Name = name;
    }

    public string Name { get; set; }
    public string Position { get; set; }

    #region IEqualityComparer<StaffMember> Members

    public bool Equals(StaffMember x, StaffMember y)
    {
        return
            x.Name == y.Name &&
            x.Position == y.Position;
    }

    public int GetHashCode(StaffMember obj)
    {
        return obj.Name.GetHashCode() ^ obj.Position.GetHashCode();
    }

    #endregion
}
```

Here you can see Equals and GetHashCode members, required by the contract of IEqualityComparer<StaffMember>. This was a quick implementation, for demo purposes, and you may want to refer to Chapter 8 for more background on proper implementation of equality. Now, Distinct will produce the expected results, where only one object with the name Chris will appear in the results.

Filtering Operators

Filtering operators return a subset of a collection. Table 19.3 describes the filtering operators.

TABLE 19.3   Filtering Operators

Operator	C# Alias	Description
OfType	N/A	Objects of the specified type
Where	Where	Objects meeting specified predicate

The C# where clause aliases the Where operator, but there isn't an alias for the OfType operator. You could give where a predicate, such as where staff.GetType == typeof(TempStaffMember). TempStaffMember is a class that derives from StaffMember. However, you can use the OfType operator directly, like this:

```
hospitalStaff.Add(
    new TempStaffMember
    {
        Name = "Pat",
        Position = "Visiting Intern"
    }
);

var ofTypeStaff =
    (
        from staff in hospitalStaff
        select staff
    )
    .OfType<TempStaffMember>();

    foreach (var ofTypeMbr in ofTypeStaff)
    {
        Console.WriteLine("Name: {0}", ofTypeMbr.Name);
    }
```

TempStaffMember is defined as follows:

```
class TempStaffMember : StaffMember {}
```

After adding a new TempStaffMember to the hospitalStaff collection, which previously held only StaffMember objects, the example uses the OfType operator. All the query operators are generic methods, but you haven't seen me use that syntax yet because the type is inferred. That's different in this case because we need to explicitly specify the return type, requiring that you specify the type parameter when using the OfType operator. The result is the name Pat, which is the only TempStaffMember in the collection.

Quantifier Operators

Quantifier operators return all objects matching the conditions specified by the operator. Table 19.4 describes the quantifier operators.

TABLE 19.4   Quantifier Operators

Operator	C# Alias	Description
All	N/A	All objects meet the condition.
Any	N/A	Any of the objects meet the condition.
Contains	N/A	The specified object is a member.

Using the `Any` operator from Table 19.4, here's how you can check to see whether there are any veterinarians among the hospital staff:

```
bool anyVeterinarians =
    (
        from staff in hospitalStaff
        select staff
    )
    .Any(staff => staff.Position == "Veterinarian");

Console.WriteLine("Any Veterinarians: {0}", anyVeterinarians);
```

Of course, there aren't any veterinarians because I didn't add any to the list.

Projection Operators

Projection operators alter the shape of query results. If a projection operator alters the shape, a projection, the results may contain more or fewer fields or perform some manipulation of an existing field for the result set. Table 19.5 describes the quantifier operators.

TABLE 19.5   Projection Operators.

Operator	C# Alias	Description
Select	select	Defines the fields/properties to return
SelectMany	from y in z	Flattens a multilevel hierachy to access results
	from x in y	

Here's another version of using the `SelectMany`, which uses the `SelectMany` operator rather than nested `from` clauses:

```
var manyPatients =
    hospitalCtx.HospitalStaffs.SelectMany(
        staff => staff.Patients);

foreach (var patient in manyPatients)
{
    Console.WriteLine("Patient Name: {0}", patient.Name);
}
```

What's different about this example is that it uses the `HospitalDataContext`, `hospitalCtx` directly instead of using query syntax in parentheses. It is often simpler to do it this way, especially when the query doesn't do anything more than extract results.

Partitioning Operators

You can use partitioning operators to specify which group of records you want from a collection. Table 19.6 describes the quantifier operators.

TABLE 19.6   Partitioning Operators

Operator	C# Alias	Description
Skip	N/A	Skips over a specified number of records
SkipWhile	N/A	Skips over records while the specified condition is true
Take	N/A	Takes the specified number of records
TakeWhile	N/A	Takes records while the specified condition is true

A common scenario for the partitioning operators is to facilitate paging. In many cases, the number of records in a record set is too large to hold in memory, so you want to bring in only the minimum number necessary. Here's an example of paging using `Skip` and `Take`:

```
int startRecord = 0;
int recordsPerPage = 3;

var page = hospitalStaff
    .Skip(startRecord)
    .Take(recordsPerPage);

foreach (var staff in page)
{
    Console.WriteLine("Staff Member: {0}", staff.Name);
}
```

In the preceding example, the `Skip` operator doesn't skip over any records, because it needs to get the first page, specified as a `startRecord` with a value of 0. If you need the second page, `startRecord` is set to 3. The page size is 3, represented by `recordsPerPage`, which is passed to the `Take` operator. This returns the first three records in the collection.

Join Operators

Join operators enable you to combine sets of data. Table 19.7 describes the quantifier operators.

TABLE 19.7   Join Operators

Operator	C# Alias	Description
Join	join - in - on - equals -	Returns set of records where keys in two sets are equal
GroupJoin	join - in - on - equals - into -	Builds a hierarchy of objects based on child record set keys that match a parent key

19

Earlier sections on `Join` and `GroupJoin` demonstrated the C# alias syntax for these operators. Here's an example of a `GroupJoin` so that you can see the operator syntax:

```
var groupJoinStaff =
    hospitalCtx.HospitalStaffs.GroupJoin(
        hospitalCtx.Patients,
        staff => staff,
        patient => patient.HospitalStaff,
        (staff, patientList) =>
            new
            {
                StaffMemberName = staff.Name,
                Patients = patientList
            });

foreach (var staff in groupJoinStaff)
{
    Console.WriteLine("Doctor: {0}: ", staff.StaffMemberName);

    foreach (var patient in staff.Patients)
    {
        Console.WriteLine("    Patient: {0}", patient.Name);
    }
}
```

This example uses the LINQ to SQL `HospitalDataContext`, `hospitalCtx`, from previous sections. `HospitalStaffs` and `Patients` are the parent and child record sets, respectively. The lambda `staff => staff` denotes the parent key, and `patient => patient.HospitalStaff` denotes the child key. The final lambda performs the projection where the parent record contains the name of the staff member and the child records are represented by a collection assigned to the `Patients` property of the anonymous type. A nested `foreach` loop demonstrates how to traverse the hierarchy.

Grouping Operators

A grouping operator allows you to create groups of data. Table 19.8 describes the grouping operators.

TABLE 19.8   Grouping Operators

Operator	C# Alias	Description
GroupBy	group - by -	Returns set of records where keys in two sets are equal
ToLookup	N/A	Creates an `ILookup` dictionary of lists with specified key

You've seen the C# alias for `GroupBy` in previous sections. Here's an example of `ToLookup`:

```
var lookup =
    hospitalStaff.ToLookup(staff => staff.Position);

foreach (var lkUp in lookup)
{
    Console.WriteLine("Key: {0}", lkUp.Key);

    foreach (var staff in lkUp)
    {
        Console.WriteLine("    Name: {0}", staff.Name);
    }
}
```

The `ILookup`, lookup, has a key and a list of `StaffMember` objects. The key is created by the lambda argument of the `ToLookup` operator.

Generation Operators

The generating operators allow you to form a new sequence of values from a collection. Table 19.9 describes the generation operators.

TABLE 19.9   Generation Operators

Operator	C# Alias	Description
DefaultIfEmpty	N/A	Returns the default value for the collection type if collection is empty (that is, reference types are null and value types are some form of zero, as specified in Chapter 4, "Understanding Reference Types and Value Types")
Empty	N/A	Returns an empty IEnumerable collection
Range	N/A	Returns a sequence of numbers from a starting number for a specified count
Repeat	N/A	Returns a number of objects repeated for a specified count

Operators such as `Range` and `Repeat` can prove useful for generating test data. Here's how to use `Repeat`:

```
var repeatedPatients =
    Enumerable.Repeat<PatientObject>(
        new PatientObject
        {
            Name = "John",
```

```
        Doctor = "Marcus"
    },
    20
);
```

This produces a collection of 20 `PatientObject` objects whose doctor is `Marcus`. Here's the definition for PatientObject:

```
class PatientObject
{
    public string Doctor { get; set; }
    public string Name { get; set; }
}
```

PatientObject is used to demonstrate the use of a custom object.

Equality Operators

There is only one equality operator, which tells you whether two collections are equal. Table 19.10 describes the equality operator.

TABLE 19.10   Equality Operator

Operator	C# Alias	Description
SequenceEqual	N/A	Returns true if two collections are equal

Here's an example of how to use the `SequenceEqual` operator:

```
var staffMemberCopy = new List<StaffMember>
{
    new StaffMember { Name = "Marcus", Position="Doctor" },
    new StaffMember { Name = "Nancy", Position = "Nurse" },
    new StaffMember { Name = "Chris", Position = "Nurse" }
};

bool areEqual =
    hospitalStaff.SequenceEqual(staffMemberCopy);
```

This example creates a `List` of `StaffMember` that doesn't have the same members as `hospitalStaff`. Therefore, the call to `SequenceEqual` returns `false`. The parameter to

SequenceEqual, like the Distinct operator shown previously, requires type
IEqualityComparer<T>.

Element Operators

If you need to return just one record from a collection, you can use an element operator.
Table 19.11 describes the element operators.

TABLE 19.11   Element Operators

Operator	C# Alias	Description
ElementAt	N/A	Returns the element at a specified position
ElementAtOrDefault	N/A	Same as ElementAt, but returns the default value of type if not found
First	N/A	Returns the first element in results
FirstOrDefault	N/A	Same as First, but returns the default value of type if not found
Last	N/A	Returns the last element in results
LastOrDefault	N/A	Same as Last, but returns the default value of type if not found
Single	N/A	Returns only element in results
SingleOrDefault	N/A	Same as Single, but returns the default value of type if not found

Each element operator has a version that returns a default value. The difference is that if
you invoke an element operator that isn't a default version and the collection doesn't
have that value, you'll get an InvalidOperationException exception. By using the
default, you'll get a default value (as described in Chapter 4) any time the results don't
return a value.

In an earlier section of this chapter, the code used the First operator to get the first item
in the results. Another common scenario is performing queries that have only one result.
Here's an example that uses SingleOrDefault to get a specified doctor:

```
var doctorHyde =
    hospitalStaff.SingleOrDefault(
        staff =>
            staff.Name == "Hyde" &&
            staff.Position == "Doctor");
```

In this case, there isn't a record in the hospitalStaff collection meeting the criteria specified by the lambda. Perhaps the name was "Jekyll" at the time.

Conversion Operators

A conversion operator allows you to transform results from one type or collection to another. Table 19.12 describes the conversion operators.

TABLE 19.12   Conversion Operators

Operator	C# Alias	Description
AsEnumerable	N/A	Converts to IEnumerable<T>
AsQueryable	N/A	Converts to IQueryable<T>
Cast	from type - in -	Converts weakly typed collection (for example, ArrayList) to IEnumerable<T>
OfType	N/A	Filters collection based on type
ToArray	N/A	Converts to an array
ToDictionary	N/A	Converts to a dictionary
ToList	N/A	Converts to a list
ToLookup	N/A	Converts to a lookup

You've already seen OfType in the filtering operators and ToLookup in the grouping operators. Because List<T> has many methods that are useful, you'll often want to convert your IEnumerable<T> results, as in the following example:

```
hospitalStaff.ToList().ForEach(
    staff => Console.WriteLine(
        "List Name: {0}", staff.Name));
```

This code performs the conversion to a List<HospitalStaff> (type is inferred) and takes advantage of the ForEach method, passing it a lambda—a technique you might find convenient.

Concatenation Operator

There is one concatenation operator, and it allows you to concatenate one collection to another. Table 19.13 describes the concatenation operator.

TABLE 19.13   Concatenation Operator

Operator	C# Alias	Description
Concat	N/A	Concatenates one collection to another to form a single collection

Here's how you can use the Concat operator:

```
var concatStaff = hospitalStaff.Concat(staffMemberCopy);
```

This implementation of the `Concat` operator appends the `staffMemberCopy` collection to the end of the `hospitalStaff` collection.

Aggregate Operators

An aggregate operator will perform a computation on a group of values and provide a single result. Table 19.14 describes the aggregate operators.

TABLE 19.14 Aggregate Operators

Operator	C# Alias	Description
Aggregate	N/A	Creates a custom aggregation
Average	N/A	Returns an average
Count	N/A	Returns the number of items in a collection of size `int.Max` or less
LongCount	N/A	Returns the number of items in a large collection up to size `long.MAX`
Max	N/A	Returns the max item
Min	N/A	Returns the min item
Sum	N/A	Returns the sum of all items

Here's an example of how to use the `Count` operator—a commonly used operator:

```
int numberOfStaff =
    (
        from doc in hospitalStaff
        where doc.Position == "Doctor"
        select doc
    )
    .Count();
```

Now, `numberOfStaff` holds the number of doctors in the `hospitalStaf` collection.

Summary

LINQ offers a powerful way of querying objects and data in your application. You've learned how LINQ has a SQL-like syntax and makes it easy to select, filter, order, group, and join data. You can query both objects, via LINQ to Objects, and relational data, via LINQ to SQL.

For LINQ to SQL, you need to create a `DataContext`, and the VS2008 tools make this easy to do. You can also perform add, update, and delete operations, but the changes don't persist to the database until you explicitly make it happen.

You saw how you can use stored procedures with LINQ to SQL. You also learned how to customize queries by implementing either stored procedures or partial methods to replace runtime-generated insert, update, and delete queries.

For both LINQ to Objects and LINQ to SQL, you have a plethora of operators to help you work with data in many different ways. In many cases, the C# query syntax aliases operators. However, you can chain collections, queries, and other operators to create complex queries, as was demonstrated with the paging example.

In this chapter, you learned about two dialects of LINQ: LINQ to Objects and LINQ to SQL, but there are more. The next chapter teaches you how to use ADO.NET and then shows you how to use LINQ to DataSet.

CHAPTER 20

Managing Data with ADO.NET

For the past several years, ADO.NET has been one of the primary technologies for connecting to a database with C#. It offers a high level of abstraction, allowing a more object-oriented approach to working with data than was possible with earlier data access technologies. With ADO.NET, a program can view, insert, update, and delete database records. It supports both a connected and disconnected model.

To add ADO.NET to your toolbox, it's helpful to understand the architecture, which describes the participating object types and their relationships. You learn about connected and disconnected strategies you can take. Continuing with our LINQ discussion, you also learn how to implement LINQ to DataSet.

First, let's take a look at ADO.NET architecture.

ADO.NET Architecture

A high-level perspective of the ADO.NET API can help you understand how the pieces fit together and make it easier to figure out which objects you need to use. Here, you learn about ADO.NET components, connected and disconnected modes, and providers.

ADO.NET Components

The architecture in Figure 20.1 maps loosely to specific ADO.NET providers (specific implementations of ADO.NET) but helps focus on purpose. We delve into the details later.

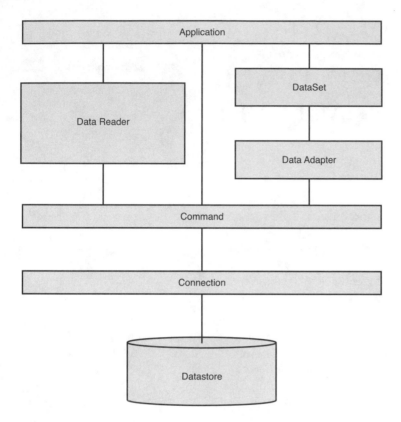

FIGURE 20.1   High-Level ADO.NET architecture.

Looking at Figure 20.1, you see various components reaching from Application down to Datastore. The Application is your program. It could be a web, desktop, or distributed application—any program that requires access to data.

A Data Reader is a fast-forward streaming object for reading data. It is the fastest way to read information from a database. To write to a database, you need to use a Command object for insert, update, and delete operations.

The DataSet is an in-memory snapshot of selected data. It uses a Data Adapter to read and write data to and from the database. The Data Adapter has four Command object properties for select, insert, update, and delete operations.

As you can see from Figure 20.1, all ADO.NET objects use one or more Command objects, and you can use a Command object directly from your application, too. The Command object holds the query that will be sent to a data source.

For every query, you need a Connection object, which knows about the database. A Command doesn't know where it will be executed, which is why it holds a reference to a Connection object. As you learn in this chapter, it is important to keep track of when a

Connection object is opened and closed. The Datasource is an external resource that you are responsible for and properly closing connections is essential to good application performance and scalability.

The Datastore is any system that holds data you are interested in. It is easy to think of the Datastore as a relational database, but it could actually be many things, such as XML or OleDb. For example, you could have an Excel spreadsheet, which has an OleDb interface. You can identify the Datastore with a specific provider, which I tell you about in a following section.

Connected and Disconnected Modes

ADO.NET supports both connected and disconnected modes. You need to look at your application requirements to determine which is best for your situation, but I show you which parts of the ADO.NET architecture fit each mode and a little about what each mode does.

The connected mode of operation means that you must write code that explicitly opens and closes a Connection object. The ADO.NET objects involved in connected mode operations include the Data Reader and Command. You use the Data Reader to select data and the Command to insert, update, and delete.

DATABASE CONNECTION PERFORMANCE AND SCALABILITY

Databases such as SQL Server have a connection pool, meaning that a specified number of connection objects (at the database level) already exist. Because of the connection pool, creating new connections is efficient. Also, the number of these connection objects is limited, and you can check your database documentation for what the connection pool (or similar mechanism) limits are. Because connections are limited, but pooled, it makes a lot of sense to open and close connections on an as-needed basis, instead of keeping a connection open for a long time. Connection pooling gives you the bonofitc of minimizing overhead when creating a connection while still achieving greater scalability by closing connections as soon as your operation is complete, which keeps you from running out of database connection objects.

Disconnected mode means that you can work with data in memory when you don't have an open connection. The DataSet and Data Adapter objects enable disconnected mode operations. Data Adapters are instrumental for disconnected mode by managing the connection. When retrieving data from the database, the Data Adapter opens a connection, fills the specified DataSet, and then automatically closes the connection as soon as the data is read. After you've made changes to the data, you use the Data Adapter again to open the connection, persist changes (whether they are add, update, or delete), and automatically close the connection.

Developers are often concerned about the practicality of the disconnected mode because there is a time between filling a DataSet and updating its data (persisting to the database) where the actual data in the database could have changed. Remember, that although

20

ADO.NET makes it easy to manage data in a disconnected mode, it isn't the recommended solution for all problems. You'll have to make a design decision, based on your application requirements, as to whether working with disconnected mode is more of a benefit than connected mode. If you need data persisted to the database immediately, use connected mode. However, if you have isolated data that no one else will change or the data rarely changes, maybe your analysis will reveal that disconnected mode has a benefit in your situation.

I briefly touched upon providers previously, but the next section explains them in depth.

Data Providers

I mentioned earlier that the components in Figure 20.1 are general. That's because the physical object that you use depend on the provider you use. A provider is a set of ADO.NET objects that work for a specific data source or technology. Specific data sources could be SQL Server or Oracle, and technologies could be ODBC or OleDb (standard data interface technologies that Windows programmers have used for years).

The .NET Framework Class Library (FCL) ships with four providers you can use immediately: SQL, Oracle, ODBC, and OleDb. The SQL provider works for version 7.0 and later of SQL Server. You need to use the ODBC provider for SQL Server 6.5. There is an Oracle provider for accessing Oracle databases. The ODBC provider works with any ODBC data source, which will give you access to a lot of legacy database systems. Microsoft invested a lot into OleDb, making it the ubiquitous standard on Windows for accessing nearly any data source. You can use it with Microsoft Access, Excel, and many other applications that were built in the pre-.NET era.

In addition to the providers that ship with .NET, there are many third-party providers. Oracle has its own provider. Borland has a provider that targets Interbase and has an open API for adapting to many other providers, including SQL Server, Oracle, and IBM DB2. Bluefinity offers MV.NET for IBM Universe, Pick, and other multivalue variants. There are also providers for open source databases such as MySQL, PostgresSQL, and more.

Each provider has its own namespace and uses a convention of a common prefix for provider objects. For example, the SQL Server provider is in the `System.Data.SqlClient` namespace, and objects have a `Sql` prefix, as in `SqlConnection`. Table 20.1 shows .NET FCL provider namespaces and prefixes.

TABLE 20.1   .NET FCL ADO.NET Providers, Namespaces, and Prefixes

Provider	Namespace	Prefix
SQL Server	`System.Data.SqlClient`	`Sql`, as in `SqlConnection` `SqlCommand` `SqlDataReader` `SqlDataAdapter`

TABLE 20.1   Continued

Provider	Namespace	Prefix
Oracle	`System.Data.Oracle`	Oracle, as in `OracleConnection` `OracleCommand` `OracleDataReader` `OracleDataAdapter`
OleDb	`System.Data.OleDb` Note: Remember to add a project reference to the System.Data.OracleClient.dll assembly.	OleDb, as in `OleDbConnection` `OleDbCommand` `OleDbDataReader` `OleDbDataAdapter`
ODBC	`System.Data.Odbc`	Odbc, as in `OdbcConnection` `OdbcCommand` `OdbcDataReader` `OdbcDataAdapter`

Other third-party providers follow the same conventions as the built-in .NET FCL ADO.NET data providers. For example, Borland's data provider prefix is `Bcl`.

WHICH ADO.NET DATA PROVIDER SHOULD I USE?

Generally, you'll want to use the provider that is most specific to the technology you are using. For example, the SQL and Oracle providers perform better because they are built specifically to use the database-specific features and communication protocols. If that isn't available, try to use the OleDb provider that performs better and offers more features than ODBC. Of course, the OleDb provider doesn't perform as well as the platform-specific providers because it uses a COM Interop layer that adds more overhead to communications. The ODBC provider offers more reach for when no other provider will work.

The following sections work from the bottom up, according to Figure 20.1, showing you how to use `Connection` objects first. For brevity, I've chosen to use the SQL provider, which is popular. In concept, most other providers work similarly. Another benefit of using the SQL provider is that you can download SQL Express for free from Microsoft's website, allowing you to practice with the code in this chapter without needing to purchase an expensive DBMS. Other options to avoid purchasing a DBMS to practice with are open source DBMS systems such as MySQL; you can also get developer database editions from other vendors.

Making Connections

Before a program can do anything with a database, your code must make a connection. A connection is the action that establishes a session with a database. A session is the sequence of actions to view, insert, update, delete, and perform other management commands with a database. When a program is connected, a session begins. Likewise, when a program is disconnected, a session ends.

A `SqlConnection` object must be instantiated and opened to establish a database session. `SqlConnection` objects have attributes that define various aspects of the session being initiated, and these attributes depend on the requirements of the underlying database. For example, a name and location are required to indicate which database a program needs to work with. Other common attributes are the username and password to support database security. The following example instantiates a `SqlConnection` object, which establishes a session with a SQL Server database:

```
var conn = new SqlConnection(
➥"Data Source=CHICAGO;
➥Initial Catalog=Hospital;
➥Integrated Security=True");
```

To compile this code ensure that it appears on one line only and include a using directive for the System.Data.SqlClient namespace.

This `SqlConnection` instantiates with a connection string. The connection string is unique to the specific provider you are using, and you can consult the documentation for your database to see what valid connection strings are. In the preceding connection string, `Data Source` is the name of the database server, which is `CHICAGO` on my computer. `Initial Catalog` is the name of the database, which is Hospital. We're going to use the same Hospital database that we created in Chapter 19, "Accessing Data with LINQ." `Integrated Security` means that the provider will connect with the Windows credentials that the current program is running with. Because this is a simple console program, the credentials will be my identity. If you were running an ASP.NET application via Internet Information Services (IIS), the identity would be the machine ASPNET user for IIS5.x and the machine NETWORKSERVICE account for IIS6 and above. The point to remember about user identity is that your database system security must be configured to allow whomever you log in as.

DATABASE LOGIN SECURITY FOR ADO.NET

If you're doing ASP.NET, you don't want to configure the ASPNET or NETWORK SERVICE machine users because multiple applications on the same server will have access to each other's database. A common practice for configuring security for logging in to a database is to create a user for your specific application and then setting the connection string in your ADO.NET code for that user. The connection string parameters for a SQL provider are `User ID=login ID` and `Password=password`, and they look like this:

```
var conn = new SqlConnection(
➥"Data Source=CHICAGO;
➥Initial Catalog=Hospital; User ID=UserID;
➥Password=Password");
```

To compile the code above ensure that it appears on one line only and include a using directive for the System.Data.SqlClient namespace.

Because this is all about making sure that your applications are as secure as possible, here is a list of things *not* to do:

1. Don't literally create a user with the name UserID and a password of Password just like in this book. Your password should be secure.

2. Don't use the database administrator credentials, say for SQL Server, or use a blank password. I can't tell you how many times I've seen connection strings with this, and it is the wrong thing to do. If you don't believe me, do a search with your favorite search engine for the term "SQL Slammer."

3. Don't post your connection string in a public forum where everyone can read it. You can delete the connection string and replace it with "connection string goes here." This is another huge security mistake that I see people make with connection strings, and you'll see the same thing over and over if you watch the newsgroups.

Viewing Data

An efficient way to view database information is through a SqlDataReader, which is used to obtain a forward-only, read-only data stream from a database. A SqlDataReader may not be written to or modified and is an efficient means of obtaining data when the only action required is to view information. To create a SqlDataReader, you need to instantiate a SqlConnection, a SqlCommand that uses the connection and specifies the query, and then use the SqlCommand to get the SqlDataReader. Also, make sure you open and close the SqlConnection appropriately. Here's an example:

```
var conn = new SqlConnection(
➥"Data Source=CHICAGO;
➥Initial Catalog=Hospital;
➥Integrated Security=True");

var cmd = new SqlCommand("select * from Patient", conn);

conn.Open();

SqlDataReader rdr = cmd.ExecuteReader();

while (rdr.Read())
{
    Console.WriteLine("Name: {0}", rdr["Name"]);
}

rdr.Close();
conn.Close();
```

To compile the code above ensure that it appears on one line only and include a using directive for the System.Data.SqlClient namespace.

The example shows how to create an `SqlCommand`, `cmd`, to create a `SqlDataReader`, `rdr`. You can instantiate `cmd` with the `select` statement to execute and the connection that specifies which database to communicate with.

Notice the call to `rdr.Read` as the `while` loop condition. Every time the loop invokes `Read`, it loads the next record into the reader. The contents of the `while` loop get the value by indexing into the column via a string with the column name. Remember to always close both the connection and the reader.

As a matter of fact, the preceding code was not the best example of how you should build an ADO.NET algorithm. It was explicit to show how to instantiate the objects and served for learning how they fit together, but it wasn't safe. For example, if there were an exception anywhere in the code, which is common, the calls to `Close` on the connection and reader would never execute. Furthermore, the `Command` object wasn't closed properly either. These are all important resource issues that affect the performance and scalability of your application. Here's a better way to code this algorithm:

```
string connStr =
➥"Data Source=CHICAGO;
➥Initial Catalog=Hospital;
➥Integrated Security=True";

string queryStr = "select * from Patient";

using (var conn = new SqlConnection(connStr))
using (var cmd = new SqlCommand(queryStr, conn))
{
    conn.Open();

    using (SqlDataReader rdr = cmd.ExecuteReader())
    {
        while (rdr.Read())
        {
            Console.WriteLine("Name: {0}", rdr["Name"]);
        }
    }
}
```

To compile the code above ensure that it appears on one line only and include a using directive for the System.Data.SqlClient namespace.

The point to make about the preceding code is the `using` statements. They ensure that `Dispose` is called, meaning that critical resources get released in a timely manner.

We can improve the performance of the preceding code even more. Notice the call to the `rdr` indexer with the column name, which is a string. Internally, the reader maps that name to an ordinal position in the results and then retrieves the column value. Therefore, something like this would be faster:

```
Console.WriteLine("Name: {0}", rdr[1]);
```

Although better performing, the problem with that code is that you don't know for sure that `Name` will be in the second position (0 is first). For example, if the query changes, you'll have a subtle bug to deal with. Second, the return value is type object, which forces a conversion and boxing and unboxing penalties for value type objects. Here's an example that is more verbose, but fixes these two problems:

```
using (var conn = new SqlConnection(connStr))
using (var cmd = new SqlCommand(queryStr, conn))
{
    conn.Open();

    using (SqlDataReader rdr = cmd.ExecuteReader())
    {
        int namePos = rdr.GetOrdinal("Name");

        while (rdr.Read())
        {
            Console.WriteLine("Name: {0}", rdr.GetString(namePos));
        }
    }
}
```

The first thing the preceding code does is figure out the ordinal position of columns. In this case, there is only `Name`, but you would make a call to `GetOrdinal` for each column you want to extract. Then you can use a strongly typed reader method to get the column, using the ordinal position. Because it is using the ordinal position, there isn't overhead for translation, and you also avoid conversion and boxing and unboxing overhead.

In addition to `GetString`, `SqlDataReader` has several strongly typed accessor methods. You can see each one in Table 20.2

TABLE 20.2 **SqlDataReader** Typed Methods and Return Types

Method	Return Type
GetBoolean	Bool
GetByte	Byte
GetBytes	Array of bytes
GetChars	Array of chars
GetDateTime	DateTime object
GetDecimal	Decimal
GetDouble	Double

20

TABLE 20.2   Continued

Method	Return Type
GetFloat	Float
GetGuid	GUID object
GetInt16	Short
GetInt32	Int
GetInt64	Long
GetString	String
GetTimeSpan	TimeSpan object

In addition to reading data, you can also manipulate data with insert, update, and delete operations, discussed next.

Manipulating Data

Data-manipulation commands (insert, update, and delete) are executed by calling the ExecuteNonQuery method of the Command object. The following sections show how to perform insert, update, and delete commands.

Inserting Data

The following example combines some of the code you've seen already with some new code to execute an insert operation:

```
string insertStr = "insert into Patient
➥(Name, DoctorID) values (@Name, @DoctorID)";


using (var conn = new SqlConnection(connStr))
using (var cmd = new SqlCommand(insertStr, conn))
{
    cmd.Parameters.AddWithValue("@Name", "Joe");
    cmd.Parameters.AddWithValue("@DoctorID", 1);

    conn.Open();

    cmd.ExecuteNonQuery();
}
```

The first thing to notice is the way the insert command is specified in the string, insertStr. The actual parameters are specified with @ symbols. With the OleDb provider, these are replaced with question mark symbols, ?, and parameters must be added in order.

Within the code, you can see that the @Name and @DoctorID parameters are added to the command via the AddWithValue method. I hard-coded the arguments, "Joe" and 1, but these would often come from a variable set by some type of user input.

The ExecuteNonQuery method executes the command. You can use the ExecuteNonQuery with any type of database command, including updates, which is next. ExecuteNonQuery also returns the number of rows affected by the query.

Updating Data

You can update existing records similar to the way inserts work. The following example shows how to perform an update:

```
string updateStr = "update Patient
➥set Name = @Name,
➥DoctorID = @DoctorID
➥where PatientID = @PatientID";


using (var conn = new SqlConnection(connStr))
using (var cmd = new SqlCommand(updateStr, conn))
{
    cmd.Parameters.AddWithValue("@PatientID", 6);
    cmd.Parameters.AddWithValue("@Name", "JoeM");
    cmd.Parameters.AddWithValue("@DoctorID", 1);

    conn.Open();

    cmd.ExecuteNonQuery();
}
```

The string, updateStr, contains parameters, and the code adds values to those parameters and then calls ExecuteNonQuery. Deletes, shown next, work similarly.

Deleting Data

Similar to the techniques for inserting and updating data, you can delete data, too. The following example shows how:

```
string deleteStr = "delete from Patient where PatientID = @PatientID";


using (var conn = new SqlConnection(connStr))
using (var cmd = new SqlCommand(deleteStr, conn))
{
    cmd.Parameters.AddWithValue("@PatientID", 6);

    conn.Open();

    cmd.ExecuteNonQuery();
}
```

This time the only parameter is the `PatientID`. You add that parameter in the code and call `ExecuteNonQuery`, just as with insert and update operations.

PARAMETER VALUES SHOULD BE VARIABLES

The examples in this section hard-coded parameter values, such as `PatientID` and `DoctorID`. This was to simplify the example without needing to add a bunch of extraneous code. You should look at the IDs in your database and use those. Or better yet, write a program with a `Main` method that takes these values from the user and passes them to methods for each of these examples. You can use a `SqlDataReader` to get the ID of a record, too.

All the code you've seen so far uses a query string in code, but you can also use stored procedures, which you'll learn about next.

Calling Stored Procedures

If you already have stored procedures or want to use them, you can do so with ADO.NET. You just make a couple adjustments to your `Command` object and it will work fine. Here's an example:

```
using (var conn = new SqlConnection(connStr))
using (var cmd = new SqlCommand("InsertPatient", conn))
{
    cmd.CommandType = CommandType.StoredProcedure;

    cmd.Parameters.AddWithValue("@Name", "Joe");
    cmd.Parameters.AddWithValue("@DoctorID", 1);

    conn.Open();

    cmd.ExecuteNonQuery();
}
```

To compile this code, add a using directive for the System.Data.SqlClient namespace. Also, add a stored procedure, named InsertPatient, to your database to insert the record.

The difference between the insert preceding code and the previous one is that the `SqlCommand` is instantiated with the name of the stored procedure and not the query to execute. Also, you must explicitly set the `SqlCommand` object's `CommandType` property to the `StoredProcedure` value of the `CommandType` enum. Parameter passing and all other code is exactly the same as previous examples. You use the same pattern for updates and deletes, too.

Working with Disconnected Data

All examples in this chapter so far have made a connection to a database, performed whatever operations were pertinent, and disconnected. This is different with disconnected data, which also connects and disconnects. The difference is that the data is stored in a DataSet object that you can work with after the connection is closed.

Reading Data into a `DataSet`

A DataSet is an in-memory database. In the context of the DataSet, the term *disconnected* means that a connection is made to establish a session with the database, the required data is read into a DataSet, and then the session is closed by disconnecting from the database. At the point the session is closed by disconnecting from the database, the DataSet becomes a disconnected database:

```
var dsConn = new SqlConnection(connStr);


var dsPatients = new DataSet();

var daPatients =
    new SqlDataAdapter("select * from Patient", dsConn);

daPatients.Fill(dsPatients, "Patients");

foreach (DataRow row in dsPatients.Tables["Patients"].Rows)
{
    Console.WriteLine("Patient Name: {0}", row["Name"]);
}
```

The two objects to pay attention to in the preceding listing are the DataSet and SqlDataAdapter. The DataSet is a simple instantiation, but the SqlDataAdapter is instantiated with both a command string and a reference to a SqlConnection. In other literature, you'll also see where the code passes an instance of a SqlConnection to the SqlDataAdapter. Call the Fill method on the SqlDataAdapter to execute the selection and populate the DataSet with the query results.

In the preceding example, the select query returned the entire Patient table, but you can also use a much more sophisticated query that limits the chosen columns or performs a multitable join. Regardless, the result is a new DataTable added to the Tables collection inside of the DataSet. The second parameter to the Fill method gave the DataSet table a name. (The default name is Table.)

The foreach loop demonstrates how to access the newly created DataTable, using the table name specified as the second parameter to the Fill method for indexing into the

Table collection. A DataTable has a Rows collection that you can iterate through. As shown by the Console.WriteLine statement inside of the foreach loop, you can also index into the table using a column name, which was inferred by the results of the SQL query.

One last point you should know about working with DataSets is that the SqlDataAdapter manages the connection for you. In previous examples, showing connected operations, the code is required to explicitly open and close the connection. However, when invoking the Fill method, the SqlDataAdapter automatically opens the connection, reads in the data, and closes the connection for you.

When instantiated, the SqlDataAdapter assigns a SqlCommand object to one of its properties named SelectCommand, using the select string. If it receives a SqlCommand object directly, it just assigns that to its SelectCommand property. If you are thinking that having a SelectCommand property implies that there are also InsertCommand, UpdateCommand, and DeleteCommand properties, you are correct. The next section shows you how to populate these properties and push modifications to a DataSet back to the database.

Saving DataSet Modifications to the Database

Whenever you modify the data of a DataSet, it will keep track of changes. Then you can save those changes back to the database. You have the ability to insert, update, and delete data, as covered in the following sections.

Inserting Data into a DataSet

An insert command needs a SqlCommand object and parameters. Here's an example that adds a record to the DataSet created in the previous section:

```
var insertCommand = new SqlCommand(
    "insert into Patient (Name, DoctorID)
➥values (@Name, @DoctorID)",
    dsConn);

insertCommand.Parameters.AddRange(
    new SqlParameter[] {
        new SqlParameter()
            {
                ParameterName = "@Name",
                SourceColumn = "Name"
            },
            new SqlParameter()
            {
                ParameterName = "@DoctorID",
                SourceColumn = "DoctorID",
                SqlDbType = SqlDbType.Int
            }
        }
    );

daPatients.InsertCommand = insertCommand;
```

The preceding code does three things: instantiates a `SqlCommand` with the `insert` statement, populates `insert` statement parameters, and assigns the `SqlCommand` to the `InsertCommand` property of the `SqlDataAdapter`. The `SqlParameter` objects require the name of the parameter (with the @ prefix) and the name of the column that maps to the parameter. The column was defined by the `select` statement that originally populated the `DataTable`. The data type defaults to string (`SqlDbType.VarChar`), so you need to be explicit for any other type, as is the case with the `@DoctorID` parameter.

Here's how to insert a new row:

```
DataTable tblPatient = dsPatients.Tables["Patients"];


DataRow newRow = tblPatient.NewRow();

newRow["Name"] = "Jane";
newRow["DoctorID"] = 1;


tblPatient.Rows.Add(newRow);
```

This is a little tricky because you have to call `NewRow` on the table you want to get a row for. It ensures you have a row with the right schema. Calling `NewRow` returns only a new instance of a `DataRow`, so remember that you still need to add the row to the table after adding data to each column.

Updating DataSet Data

The process of updating an existing record is similar to inserting, with a few differences unique to updating a record. Here's an example that modifies the contents of the first record:

```
var dcConn = new SqlConnection(connStr);


var dsPatients = new DataSet();

var daPatients =
    new SqlDataAdapter("select * from Patient", dsConn);

var updateCommand = new SqlCommand(
    "update Patient
➥set Name = @Name,
➥DoctorID = @DoctorID
➥where PatientID = @PatientID",
    dsConn);


updateCommand.Parameters.AddRange(
    new SqlParameter[] {
```

20

```
            new SqlParameter()
            {
                ParameterName = "@Name",
                SourceColumn = "Name"
            },
            new SqlParameter()
            {
                ParameterName = "@DoctorID",
                SourceColumn = "DoctorID",
                SqlDbType = SqlDbType.Int
            },
            new SqlParameter()
            {
                ParameterName = "@PatientID",
                SourceColumn = "PatientID",
                SqlDbType = SqlDbType.Int
            }
        }
);

daPatients.UpdateCommand = updateCommand;
```

This code shows how an update is set up by instantiating the SqlCommand, assigning parameters, and assigning the SqlCommand to the UpdateCommand property of the SqlDataAdapter. This is the part that is similar to insert statement preparation, except for the purpose of the command.

Here's how you can update the data:

```
DataTable tblPatient = dsPatients.Tables["Patients"];


tblPatient.Rows[0]["Name"] += "X";
```

The preceding statement indexes into the Rows collection, getting the first record. Then it indexes into the Columns collection of the row, appending an "X" to the end of the current value of the Name column.

Deleting DataSet Data

Following the same pattern as insert and update, you can delete DataSet items with a SqlCommand object. Here's an example:

```
var deleteCommand = new SqlCommand(
    "delete from Patient where PatientID = @PatientID",
    dsConn);

deleteCommand.Parameters.Add(
    new SqlParameter()
```

```
        {
            ParameterName = "@PatientID",
            SourceColumn = "PatientID",
            SqlDbType = SqlDbType.Int
        }
);


daPatients.DeleteCommand = deleteCommand;
```

As this code shows, you instantiate a `SqlCommand` object with a query, set its parameter, and add it to the `DeleteCommand` property of the `SqlDataAdapter`. Instead of calling `AddRange`, the code calls only `Add` because there is only a single parameter.

The ParameterName property of SqlParameter maps to the SourceColumn property of SqlParameter. Whenever, a record is deleted from the Patient table, the DataSet will replace the delete query parameter @PatientID, which is the same as the SqlParameter ParameterName property that was set to @PatientID with the value of the PatientID column, which is the same as the SqlParameter SourceColumn property, PatientID. Here's code that shows how to delete a record:

```
DataTable tblPatient = dsPatients.Tables["Patients"];


foreach (DataRow row in tblPatient.Rows)
{
    if (row["Name"] as string == "Joe")
    {
        row.Delete();
        break;
    }
}
```

To delete a record, you need a reference to its `DataRow` object. The `foreach` loop facilitates finding the desired record, calls `Delete` on the identified `DataRow`, and breaks out of the loop.

Now that you know how to insert, update, and delete `DataSet` data, it's time to see how to push these changes down to the database.

Pushing Modifications to the Database

If you recall, when populating a `DataSet`, you call `Fill` on the `SqlDataAdapter`. Going the other way, you can persist `DataSet` changes in the database by calling `Update` on the `SqlDataUpdater`. Here's how:

```
daPatients.Update(dsPatients, "Patients");
```

That's it. Just like `Fill`, call `Update`, passing in the `DataSet` reference as the first parameter and the name of the `DataSet` table to use.

LINQ to DataSet

There are projects out there with a heavy investment in DataSets for managing data. If your project is one of those, you aren't left out when it comes to LINQ. In fact, Microsoft ships a LINQ provider called LINQ to DataSet with .NET.

In addition to a need to support DataSet developers, another motivation for LINQ to DataSet comes from the fact that a DataSet is not as easy as it should be to query. LINQ to DataSet offers sophisticated query capability to make you more productive to working with DataSets.

A couple of the fundamental skills required to code LINQ to DataSet is transforming DataTables into IEnumerable<T> types and accessing fields in a strongly typed manner. These are covered in the next couple of sections.

DataTables as Data Sources

With LINQ to DataSet, the basic unit to query is the DataTable, which you can access through the DataSets Tables collection. You can use AsEnumerable, as follows, to query the data:

```
DataTable tblPatient = dsPatients.Tables["Patients"];


var patientsEnumerable =
    from patient in tblPatients.AsEnumerable()
    select patient;

foreach (var patient in patientsEnumerable)
{
    Console.WriteLine("Enumerable Patient: {0}", patient["Name"]);
}
```

Notice how the from clause calls AsEnumerable on the DataTable, tblPatients, to produce an IEnumerable<T> to query. In the case of DataTables, AsEnumerable produces an IEnumerable<DataRow>. Because the collection type is DataRow, you can use the DataRow indexer, as shown in the foreach loop, to access specific columns.

The next section demonstrates a better way to access DataRow columns.

Strongly Typed Field Access

The example in the previous section called patient["Name"] to get the Name field from each DataRow. The compile-time type of the result is object, even though the runtime type is string. LINQ to DataSet helps give you strongly typed access to fields with templates. Here's an example of how to filter a query using strongly typed field access:

```
DataTable tblPatient = dsPatients.Tables["Patients"];

var patientsFields =
    from patient in tblPatients.AsEnumerable()
    where patient.Field<string>("Name").StartsWith("George")
    select patient;

foreach (var patient in patientsFields)
{
    Console.WriteLine(
        "Strongly Typed Patient Field: {0}",
        patient.Field<string>("Name"));
}
```

The preceding code uses the `Field<T>` operator to select the `Name` field and specify that it is a string. Because it is strongly typed, you can type the dot operator and get VS2008 IntelliSense to access string methods, like the preceding `StartsWith` method.

There's also a difference between the `foreach` loop in the previous section and this one where the field is also accessed in a strongly typed manner.

Summary

This chapter covered many of the main aspects of ADO.NET. It explained ADO.NET architecture and what managed providers are.

You saw how to read and manipulate database data by performing insert, update, and delete operations on a database. Another section showed how to perform the same types of operations with stored procedures.

You also learned how to work with disconnected data. The `DataSet` object is a means of holding partial or full databases supporting disconnected, webcentric scenarios.

Finally, you learned how to use LINQ to DataSet, which is a LINQ provider for querying `DataTable` objects. Of course, LINQ to DataSet isn't the last LINQ provider you learn about in this book. The next chapter shows you how to work with the .NET XML APIs and follows up with a discussion of LINQ to XML.

CHAPTER 21

Manipulating XML Data

If you've ever traveled to another country, one of the gotchas that you don't always think about is how to use your electronic gear. You see, electrical outlets are different shapes, and power is delivered at different voltages, depending the country. You'll either need an adapter for that electric razor, iPod recharger, or laptop—or not be able to use them at all. Okay, I'm busted—yes, I use my laptop on vacation. Nonetheless, wouldn't it be nice if all the countries could just get together and figure out a standardized way of providing electrical power, hold hands, and sing *Cumbaya*? Not in this lifetime! Well, common power outlets and world peace might be a long way off to never, but at least for us programmers there is a lot of standardization going on in a technology called Extensible Markup Language (XML).

Because XML is an international standard, computer systems can communicate effectively, applications can read and parse information with a common API, and humans can read documents in the form of XML. You don't need to buy a third-party adapter to accomplish what you need because most platforms today have built-in tools to work with XML APIs. Unlike electrical power, XML is an open standard that can work everywhere, regardless of your hardware platform, operating system, programming language, or where you live.

XML permeates nearly every part of the .NET. It is the essential data transport format for web services, the format for configuration files, and the source of data from external systems. The .NET APIs make it easy to use XML as a standardized method of passing information between programs, file saving and reading, data validation, and many other useful tasks. This chapter explains how to use C# and the

XML class libraries to interact with XML data. You'll also learn how to use LINQ to XML, an easy and intuitive API that takes advantage of the common LINQ query capabilities in C#.

Streaming XML Data

There are a couple different ways to work with XML data in .NET: streaming and Document Object Model (DOM). Each has its pros and cons. Streaming provides fast-forward movement through the XML stream, and DOM offers in-memory flexibility for working with a whole document. This section covers the writing and reading streaming APIs, and the section after covers DOM.

A LITTLE RUSTY ON XML?

This chapter assumes that you already know XML. If you are a little rusty and need a refresher, here's a nice free site that can help:

http://www.w3schools.com/

Writing XML

Writing XML documentation is greatly simplified with the System.XML class library. The particular class used in this section is the XMLTextWriter class. It has numerous convenience methods that make producing XML documents a snap. The .NET Framework documentation lists all the available methods for the XMLTextWriter class. Listing 21.1 shows how to write XML data to a file.

LISTING 21.1   Writing an XML Document with **XmlTextWriter**

```
using (var xr = new XmlTextWriter(FileName, null))
{
    xr.Formatting = Formatting.Indented;
    xr.Indentation = 4;

    xr.WriteStartDocument();
    xr.WriteComment(
        "Holds data for the MoneyTalk program.");

    xr.WriteStartElement("moneyTalk");

    xr.WriteElementString(TalkNode,
        "A penny saved is too small, make it a buck.");
    xr.WriteElementString(TalkNode,
        "Keep your wooden nickel.It'll be worth something someday.");
    xr.WriteElementString(TalkNode,
```

LISTING 21.1   Continued

```
        "It's your dime, but you're better off dialing 10-10-XXX.");

    xr.WriteEndElement();

    xr.Flush();
}
```

The code in Listing 21.1 opens the file stream in a using statement, so the file will auto-matically be closed (disposed). It's important to close the file so that your program doesn't unnecessarily hold file locks that prevent other applications from accessing the file. Opening the file stream is performed at the same time as creation of the XmlTextWriter object:

```
XmlTextWriter xr = new XmlTextWriter(fileName, null);
```

The XmlTextWriter constructor in this example accepts two parameters. The first parame-ter is a string denoting the name of the file to be written to. The second parameter is the text encoding written to the file; passing a null parameter here causes the constructor to use the default encoding, UTF8. Possible encodings could be ASCII, BigEndianUnicode, Unicode, Default, UTF7, UTF8, or UTF32.

The XmlTextWriter class uses the Formatting enum to set its Formatting property, which specifies the way XML data is written:

```
xr.Formatting  = Formatting.Indented;
xr.Indentation = 4;
```

This example sets the Formatting and Indentation properties. The Formatting.Indented enum causes child elements to be indented. The behavior of this indentation is controlled by the Indentation and IndentChar properties. This example sets the Indentation prop-erty to 4. The default is 2. The XmlTextWriter has another property called IndentChar with a default value of a space character. Because we want space characters, the code takes the default and does not set IndentChar.

When the stream is open and set up, the next step is to write the XML data to the file. The XmlTextWriter class has several methods for writing standard XML tags to file. The first is the standard XML 1.0 header tag:

```
xr.WriteStartDocument();
```

Formatted comments are also easy to place into the XML document. Just use the WriteComment method. It takes a single string parameter:

```
xr.WriteComment("Holds data for the MoneyTalk program.");
```

The XmlTextWriter class provides a simple method of creating a hierarchical organiza-tion of tags:

```
xr.WriteStartElement("MoneyTalk");
```

The WriteStartElement method creates a start tag for a new level of organization. This example creates a start tag with the text "moneyTalk". Next, Listing 21.1 writes child elements of the moneyTalk node:

```
xr.WriteElementString(TalkNode,
"A penny saved is too small, make it a buck.");

xr.WriteElementString(TalkNode,
"Keep your wooden nickel. It'll be worth something someday.");

xr.WriteElementString(TalkNode,
"It's your dime, but you're better off dialing 10-10-XXX.");
```

The TalkNode value, which is the first parameter to each WriteElementString method call, is defined as follows:

```
public const string TalkNode = "talk";
```

This is a common technique for making the code more maintainable, because if the node name changes, you need only change the TalkNode constant. The second string parameter is the element value. There's no need for formatting, because the WriteElementString method calls do it automatically.

Just as there was a start element ("moneyTalk"), there is a corresponding end element. For each WriteStartElement method call, there must be a WriteEndElement method call, which the matching end tags to the file:

```
xr.WriteEndElement();
```

When all writing of XML data to the file is complete, you can flush the file to ensure buffered modifications are written to disk.

```
xr.Flush();
```

The end of the using statement block ensures that the file is closed after the call to Flush.

In addition to writing streams of data, you can also use XML streaming APIs to read data, as explained next.

Reading XML

The XML streaming APIs encapsulate the code necessary to parse XML files and obtain data related to specific tags. Listing 21.2 shows how to read and parse pertinent data from the moneyTalk file that was written by the code from Listing 21.1.

LISTING 21.2   Reading an XML Document with **XmlTextReader**

```
List<string> m_talkList = new List<string>();


using (var xr = new XmlTextReader(FileName))
{
    string nodeName;

    while (xr.Read())
    {
        nodeName = xr.Name;

        if (nodeName == TalkNode)
        {
            m_talkList.Add(xr.ReadString());
        }
    }
}
```

The example in Listing 21.2 opens an XmlTextReader object in a using statement. This ensures that the file stream associated with the reader will be closed (disposed) appropriately.

The XmlTextReader constructor accepts a single string parameter that designates the file to open. When the file is open, it can be read using the Read method, which sets the value of the XmlTextReader object to the next available node (XML tag).

```
while (xr.Read())
```

Each node has a name; the name is the text value inside the tag. To obtain this value, use the Name property:

```
nodeName = xr.Name;
if (nodeName == TalkNode)
{
    m_talkList.Add(xr.ReadString());
}
```

When this `while` loop completes, the `List<string>`, `m_talkList`, will contain all the "talk" elements from the document, and you can process the data as you need.

This was how to work with the FCL streaming APIs, but you also need to know how to work with DOM data, which is covered next.

Working with the XML DOM

Sometimes you need the flexibility of working with XML data in memory, via the Document Object Model (DOM). The tradeoff between this and the streaming APIs, discussed previously, is that sometimes an XML document is too large to hold in memory. Therefore, you have a tradeoff to make as to which is more appropriate.

This section shows you an efficient way to search read-only XML documents and how to manipulate XML documents in memory.

Reading XML with `XPathDocument`

To work with XML in memory, you can use an `XPathDocument` and then use an `XPathNavigator` to read each node efficiently. The difference between this technique and the `XmlTextReader`, in addition to what has been previously stated, is that an `XPathNavigator` can move anywhere in the document, whereas an `XmlTextReader` is forward only. Here's an example of how to use an `XPathDocument` with an `XPathNavigator` to traverse the moneyTalk document used in the previous section:

```
var xPathDoc = new XPathDocument(FileName);


XPathNavigator xPathNav = xPathDoc.CreateNavigator();
XPathNodeIterator xPathIter = xPathNav.Select("//talk");

foreach (var node in xPathIter)
{
    Console.WriteLine("Money Talk: {0}", node.ToString());
}
```

To get the listing above to compile, you should add a using directive for the System.Xml.XPath namespace.

The `XPathDocument` constructor overload in the preceding example takes a string with the name of the file to read. `XPathDocument` has multiple overloads where you can pass in a stream or even an `XmlTextReader`, which was discussed previously.

After you have the XML document in memory, you can call the `CreateNavigator` factory method to obtain an `XPathNavigator` instance. `XPathNavigators` allow you to move throughout the document with full freedom.

True to its name, the XPathNavigator supports XPath queries, as you can see in the example that uses the Select method to obtain a reference to all the <talk /> nodes in the document. The Select method instantiates and returns a new object of type XPathIterator. You can then use the XPathIterator instance to iterate through the selected nodes as demonstrated in the foreach loop.

Instead of an XPathDocument, you could have used an XmlDocument for this also, but the XPathDocument is faster for reading. Because the XPathDocument supports only read-only data, you would need to use XmlDocument for modifying a document, which is discussed next.

Manipulating XML with `XmlDocument`

The task of modifying an XML document in memory requires using the XmlDocument and XPathNavigator. Here's how you can load an XmlDocument:

```
var xDoc = new XmlDocument();
xDoc.Load(FileName);
```

The Load method has a few different overloads, including streams and XmlTextReaders. The preceding example uses the name of the file to load. Similar to XPathDocument, you also call CreateNavigator for an instance of an XPathNavigator, as shown here:

```
var xPathNav = xDoc.CreateNavigator();
```

You can use any of the several MoveToXxx methods of the XPathNavigator to move around the document. To operate on the document, you move to the location where you want to perform an operation and then do it. Here's how to insert a new node into the moneytalk.xml document:

```
xPathNav.MoveToFirstChild();
xPathNav.MoveToNext();
xPathNav.AppendChild(
    "<talk>Money isn't e...? Wait a minute - what planet are you from?</talk>");
```

In the preceding code, calling MoveToFirstChild moves the position to the comment node. After calling MoveToNext, the position is at the <moneyTalk /> node. Therefore, the call to AppendChild adds a new child node to the <moneyTalk /> node.

In addition to inserting new nodes, you can modify existing nodes. Here's an example:

```
xPathNav.MoveToFirstChild();
xPathNav.SetValue(xPathNav.Value.Replace("buck", "dollar"));
```

If you recall, the position at the last move was on the <moneyTalk /> node. Calling MoveToFirstChild sets the position to the first <talk /> node. The code uses the Value property to read and the SetValue to replace the contents of the <talk /> node.

The next example shows how to delete a node:

```
xPathNav.MoveToNext();
xPathNav.DeleteSelf();
```

This code moves the position to the second node in the list. Calling `DeleteToSelf` will remove the node, and all its children, at the current position. Of course, there aren't any children in this case, so only the second `<talk />` node is deleted.

After you've modified the document, you can save it back to disk, like this:

```
xDoc.Save(FileName);
```

Similar to the `Load` method, the `Save` method is overloaded to accept parameters of type `Stream` or `XmlTextReader`. This example uses the filename, which is a string.

You'll see a lot of .NET versions 1.x, 2.0, and 3.0 code written using the streaming and DOM APIs from this and the previous sections of this chapter. However, .NET 3.5 shipped with a new XML API called LINQ to XML, discussed next.

Easier Manipulation with LINQ to XML

LINQ to XML opens up the common way of querying data that is used for other LINQ implementations. Because of this commonality and ease of use, LINQ to XML is becoming a preferred way of working with XML in .NET. The following sections shows you how to use LINQ to XML, starting with an overview of LINQ to XML objects, how to create an XML document, and reading and validating existing XML documents.

LINQ to XML Objects

LINQ to XML includes an entire set of objects for representing parts of an XML document. Table 21.1 describes these objects and the parts of an XML document they represent.

The following sections use many of the objects in Table 21.1 to demonstrate essential tasks you'll need to accomplish with LINQ to XML.

Creating XML Documents

One of the great features of LINQ to XML is that it is easy and intuitive to create XML documents. The following example shows how to create the moneyTalk document that was used in previous sections of this chapter:

```
XDocument doc =
    new XDocument(
        new XElement("moneyTalk",
            new XElement("talk",
"A penny saved is too small, make it a buck."),
            new XElement("talk",
"Keep your wooden nickel.It'll be worth something someday.")));
```

TABLE 21.1 LINQ to XML Objects

Object Name	How It's Used
XAttribute	For working with XML attributes.
XCData	For working with CDATA sections.
XComment	For working with XML comments.
XContainer	Contains other nodes.
XDeclaration	Lets you work with version and encoding in the XML document declaration.
XDocument	Holds an entire XML document in memory.
XDocumentType	For working with Document Type Definitions (DTD).
XElement	For working with any type of XML element.
XName	The name of an XElement or XAttribute.
XNamespace	For working with namespaces.
XNode	Holds any type of node in a document—abstract base class that many types in this table derive from.
XNodeDocumentOrderComparer	Compare nodes to find out what order they appear in document.
XNodeEqualityComparer	Compare nodes for value equality.
XObject	Abstract base class for XNode and XAttribute.
XObjectChange	Enum with list of reasons for why an object in a document changed. Possible values are Add, Remove, Name, Value. Can be accessed through the EventArgs-derived parameter, XObjectChangeEventArgs, as the ObjectChange property.
XObjectChangeEventArgs	EventArgs derived property for XML document Changing and Changed events. See XObjectChange for a description of how to figure out what changed.
XProcessingInstruction	For working with XML processing instructions.
XStreamingElement	Streams elements for deferred execution.
XText	For working with text nodes.

To compile this example, you should add a using directive for the System.Xml.Linq namespace.

The first thing you might notice about the preceding code is the hierarchical layout. This helps makes working with LINQ to XML more intuitive because it resembles the structure of the XML document being created. Both XDocument and XElement have constructor overloads that allow you to instantiate your document in this flexible way.

The XDocument represents an entire document, and the XElement is used for nodes within the document. Instead of making each node an element, you could have used attributes instead. Here's an example that shows how to use the XAttribute:

```
XDocument doc =
    new XDocument(
        new XElement("moneyTalk",
            new XElement("talk",
                new XAttribute("quote",
"A penny saved is too small, make it a buck.")),
                new XElement("talk",
                    new XAttribute("quote",
"Keep your wooden nickel.It'll be worth something someday."))));
```

The preceding example passes an XAttribute instance to the XElement instead of a string. You can add a comma-separated list of XAttributes to the XElement constructor for more attributes.

This example didn't qualify names with namespaces, which is something you probably want to do and is discussed next.

Working with Namespaces with LINQ to XML

Working with namespaces with LINQ to XML is easy because the XNamespace object overloads the concatenation operator to work with strings. Here's an example:

```
XNamespace moneyNames =
"http://www.samspublishing.com/CSharp30Unleashed/XML";

XDocument doc =
    new XDocument(
        new XElement(moneyNames + "moneyTalk",
            new XElement(moneyNames + "talk",
"A penny saved is too small, make it a buck."),
            new XElement(moneyNames + "talk",
"Keep your wooden nickel.It'll be worth something someday.")));
doc.Save("moneytalk.xml");
```

The preceding moneyNames variable is declared as an XML namespace with the XNamespace type. As you can see, an implicit conversion occurs between type string and XNamespace. To fully understand how this works, you can visit Chapter 10, "Coding Methods and Custom Operators," and review custom conversion operators. Both when instantiating moneyNames and then adding moneyNames to each element, you can use the namespace like a string. The result is a simpler and more intuitive interface for working with XML namespaces.

In addition to creating XML documents, you'll want to read XML created from other sources, which is discussed next.

Reading XML Documents

In addition to writing, you'll also need to read XML documents from different locations. Here's an example of how to read an XML document using LINQ to XML:

```
var doc = XDocument.Load("moneytalk.xml");
```

If you look for the Load method on an instance, you won't find it. As previously shown, the Load method is static, and you can pass it a string or stream.

After you have the document in memory, you'll want to query/manipulate it. The next section shows you how to query the XML document.

Querying XML Documents

Just like all the other implementations of LINQ, you have a common syntax for querying data sources with LINQ to XML. The data source just happens to be XML in this case. Here's an example that queries the moneyTalk document:

```
var talkElements =
    from talk in doc.Element("moneyTalk").Elements()
    where talk.Value.Contains("dime")
    select talk;

talkElements.ToList().ForEach(
    talkElement => Console.WriteLine(
        "Talk Element: {0}", talkElement.Value));
```

You might need to regenerate the moneyTalks.xml file without the moneyNames namespace in the previous listing to get an XML file that will work in this listing.

This query is similar to any other LINQ query. The main difference is in specifying the elements to query. Calling Element selects the moneyTalk node, and then calling elements on that selects all the talk nodes, which can then be searched.

Notice the ToList operator on talkElements so that I could use the ForEach and a lambda for a quick operation on the results. You can access each element's Value property to read its contents.

Besides just reading and querying, you'll also want to modify the contents of an XML document, which is shown next.

Modifying XML Documents

You can use LINQ to XML to insert, update, and delete nodes from an XML document. Here's an example showing how to perform an insert:

```
doc.Element("moneyTalk").Add(
    new XElement("talk",
        "Keep your wooden nickel.It'll be worth something someday."));
```

As shown here, you can use the `Add` method to insert a new `XElement` into the document. There are other `Add` methods you also can use, such as `AddBeforeSelf` and `AddAfterSelf`.

For deleting elements, you need to obtain a reference to the element(s) and call `Remove`, like this:

```
var talkElements =
    from talk in doc.Element("moneyTalk").Elements()
    where talk.Value.Contains("dime")
    select talk;

talkElements.Single().Remove();
```

You need to ensure that the current version of the XML file you're reading from includes the element containing dime for this example to work.

The preceding example uses LINQ to get a reference to the object to delete. If it is only one object, you can use the `Single` operator to reference it from the collection and then call `Remove`. Just as with `Add`, there are other methods, such as `RemoveAll` and `RemoveNodes`, to help you delete items.

Finally, you can also modify the document. Here's an example that replaces an existing node, calling the `ReplaceWith` method from an `XElement`:

```
talkElements =
    from talk in doc.Element("moneyTalk").Elements()
    where talk.Value.Contains("dollar")
    select talk;

talkElements.Single().ReplaceWith(
    new XElement("talk",
        "A penny saved is too small, make it a buck."));
```

You need to ensure that the current version of the XML file you're reading from includes the element containing dollar for this example to work.

Again, the query locates the node you want to operate on. Then you can get a reference to the one `XElement` returned and call `ReplaceWith`.

Summary

You now have a few different APIs to work with XML in your C# programs: streaming, DOM, and LINQ to XML. The streaming APIs are good for working with XML that is either too large to fit in memory or if you want the most efficient way to work with the document. The DOM APIs allow you to work with XML when it can fit in memory or when you need to move around the document freely.

A recent API added in .NET 3.5 is LINQ to XML. This chapter demonstrated how to use LINQ to XML to create new documents and read existing documents. You also learned how to leverage the common C# LINQ syntax to perform queries on data exposed through the LINQ to XML API.

Another data access API in the .NET Framework is the ADO.NET Entity Framework, which offers a higher-level object-oriented abstraction of a data source. It also has a LINQ implementation called LINQ to Entities. Continuing with our data and LINQ story, the next chapter shows you how to use the ADO.NET Entity Framework and LINQ to Entities.

21

CHAPTER 22

Creating Data Abstractions with the ADO.NET Entity Framework

People tend to enjoy socializing with others who share the same interests. Along these lines, C# developers go to .NET user group meetings to watch presentations and meet other like-minded people. Just visit www.ineta.org, the International .NET Association, to view the multitude of .NET user groups around the world.

What if you don't have a C# user group in your area and have a desire to meet other people with interest in .NET? Some people would find other user groups that at least had programmers, even if the group wasn't particularly about .NET. Other programmers would socialize online in various forums and lists. The problem is that it isn't quite as good as the real thing.

A similar situation exists with data APIs. We program in an object-oriented environment but have been forced to work with data in a relational or other data-specific paradigm that isn't object-oriented. Just like a C# developer who can't find a .NET user group, programmers often have trouble finding a good way to work with data from the object-oriented perspective. In Chapter 19, "Accessing Data with LINQ," we discussed LINQ to SQL, but that still forces you to reason about data from a relational perspective. Many object persistence frameworks (OPFs) are on the market, and there are reasons for using these frameworks and solutions, but this chapter shows you another, attractive, option.

To solve the problems of being able to reason about your data from a true object-oriented perspective and offer the common query capabilities of LINQ, Microsoft has created the ADO.NET Entity Framework. The ADO.NET Entity Framework is based on Dr. Peter Chen's 1976 paper "The Entity-Relationship Model—Toward a Unified View of

Data." You can read more about this at http://en.wikipedia.org/wiki/
Entity_relationship_model.

To learn how to use ADO.NET Entity Framework, you need to understand what an entity
is, the relationships that exist between entities, and how to map entities to data. The
sections of this chapter approach this task via VS2008 designers.

You learn how to create a conceptual view of your data that models the objects you design
your application with. Further, you build upon your existing knowledge of LINQ, from
earlier chapters, to work with data via a provider named LINQ to Entities.

An Overview of Entities

An entity is an object that represents data. It may or may not hold the same data as a
table, but the primary purpose of having an entity is the ability to program against an
object abstraction, rather than being confined to an object that maps one-to-one with a
relational table.

The major benefit of this approach is to enable you to design an object-oriented system
from the perspective of objects. You aren't forced to build objects that mirror the relational structure of your database.

You also have relationships between entities. In this chapter, we use the same Hospital
database as used in Chapter 20, "Managing Data with ADO.NET." The Hospital database
has a relationship between HospitalStaff and Patient tables, where patient records have
foreign keys to HospitalStaff rows who are doctors. In the ADO.NET Entity Framework,
you could create a Nurse class and a Doctor class, and the Doctor class will have a collection of Patients—a conceptual view of the data that represents an object-oriented top-
down design.

> **WHAT YOU NEED TO GET STARTED?**
>
> As I wrote this chapter, the ADO.NET Entity Framework was prerelease software that is
> not a part of the VS2008 release. To run the samples, you need to visit http://msdn.
> microsoft.com or http://www.asp.net and search for "ADO.NET Entity Framework" to
> find the most recent software and download it to your system.

Starting the Entity Data Model in VS2008

To start creating entities and associations, you can use the VS2008 tools for creating an
Entity Data Model (EDM). To do so, right-click your project in Solution Explorer, select
Add, New Item, and select ADO.NET Entity Model, as shown in Figure 22.1.

As shown in Figure 22.1, give the item a name like Hospital.edmx. Clicking the Add
button starts the Entity Data Model Wizard, shown in Figure 22.2, where you have a
choice of how to initialize the model contents.

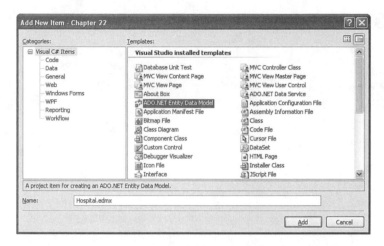

FIGURE 22.1   Adding a New ADO.NET entity model item.

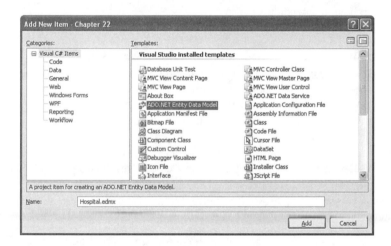

FIGURE 22.2   Choosing model contents.

As shown in Figure 22.2, you have two choices: Generate from Database, or Empty Model. If you create an empty model, you must add entities and map them to database tables manually. We'll look at that when discussing schemas and mapping later in this chapter. Right now, select Generate from Database, which helps introduce basic concepts and click the Next button. Figure 22.3 shows the next wizard screen, letting you choose a database connection.

FIGURE 22.3   Choosing a database connection.

The wizard enumerates all existing database connections from the VS2008 Server Explorer and populates the drop-down list in Figure 22.3. If you already have a connection to the Hospital database that we've used in previous chapters, select it from the list. When an existing connection doesn't appear in the list, you can click the New Connection button to create a new database connection. The wizard also automatically provides a connection string name after selecting the connection. You can change this or take the suggestions. This connection string appears in a new file added to your project called App.config (web.config for Web apps), which compiles to projectname.exe.config, and your program automatically reads the connection string from this file. Clicking the Next button shows the Choose Your Database Objects window, shown in Figure 22.4, in which you can select tables, views, and stored procedures.

The Hospital database doesn't have any views, but it does have a couple tables and several stored procedures—all of which are selected. These tables and stored procedures map to entities and methods that can be called in your C# code. Clicking Finish creates the App.config file that holds the new connection string and the Hospital.edmx file for the new EDM. You can see these files in the Solution Explorer along with the visual design surface for Hospital.edmx in Figure 22.5.

The design surface in Figure 22.5 contains two entities, HospitalStaff and Patient, that map to the same named database tables. There is also an association describing the relationship between the entities that maps to the FK_Patient_HospitalStaff database foreign key constraint. Because this EDM was generated from the database, you have a one-to-one mapping between database objects and EDM objects.

The Mapping Details window shows mapping for the HospitalStaff entity, which is currently the selected entity. Notice how the database column mapping with database types on the left are matched up on the same row with entity attributes with .NET types on the right. This demonstrates the one-to-one mapping.

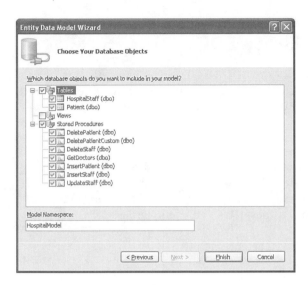

FIGURE 22.4   Choosing database objects.

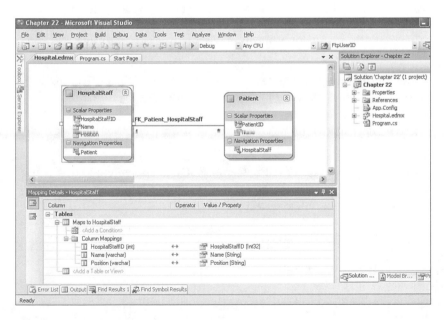

FIGURE 22.5   EDM design surface.

You have now created an EDM. The significance of this is that you can now write code against the HospitalStaff and Patient entities, which simplifies your code. The

ADO.NET Entity Model runtime will take care of ensuring your queries on this EDM work with the database—automatically. The next section shows you how to query the EDM with ADO.NET Entity Framework tools.

Querying Entities with Entity SQL

Entity SQL is a language built specifically for the ADO.NET Entity Framework. It is SQL-like, enabling you to query entities. The following sections show how to select, insert, update, and delete entity objects. First, you need to know how to access entities.

Accessing Entities

When creating the EDM in the previous section, VS2008 created a `HospitalEntities` object that derives from an ADO.NET Entity Framework class named `ObjectContext`, which I refer to as the object context. You need to create an instance of `HospitalEntites` to access the `HospitalStaff` and `Patient` entities. Here's an example:

```
using (var hospital = new HospitalEntities())
{
    // use hospital to access entities
}
```

When instantiating an entity context, such as `HospitalEntities`, you want to implement it with a `using` statement as shown in the preceding code. The object context, `hospital`, maintains a database connection, and you want to make sure it is closed (disposed) properly.

The Data Model Wizard automatically generates code inside of a namespace. For our example, the namespace is `HospitalModel`, and you need to add a `using` declaration for `HospitalModel`.

Selecting Entities

Entity SQL has `select` statements to query entities. Entity SQL is implemented as a string that is passed to an `ObjectQuery<T>` instance, where `T` is the object type returned. Here's an example that retrieves doctors from the `HospitalStaff` entity:

```
using (var hospital = new HospitalEntities())
{
    ObjectQuery<HospitalStaff> hospitalStaffQuery =
        new ObjectQuery<HospitalStaff>(
            "select value Staff from HospitalEntities.HospitalStaff as Staff where
Staff.Position = 'Doctor'",
            hospital);

    foreach (var doc in hospitalStaffQuery)
    {
```

```
        Console.WriteLine("Doctor: {0}", doc.Name);
    }
}
```

You need to add a using directive for the System.Data.Objects namespace for this to compile.

There are two parameters sent to the previous ObjectQuery constructor, query and entity context. This describes what to query and where to get the results.

Within the query string, the select statement gets all columns via Staff, which is an alias for the fully qualified entity HospitalEntites.HospitalStaff. The where clause uses the alias to filter results where the Position property is set to Doctor. The entity and its attributes must exist in the EDM.

WHEN DO QUERIES EXECUTE?

For efficiency purposes, the ADO.NET Entity Framework runtime doesn't execute queries until the code actually accesses the results. In the preceding code, that means the query doesn't execute until the foreach loop executes.

You can also filter attributes in the results. However, the results are of type DbDataRecord, as shown here:

```
ObjectQuery<DbDataRecord> hospitalStaffQuery =
    new ObjectQuery<DbDataRecord>(
        "select Staff.Name, Staff.Position from HospitalEntities.HospitalStaff as
Staff where Staff.Position = 'Doctor'",
        hospital);

foreach (var doc in hospitalStaffQuery)
{
    Console.WriteLine("Doctor: {0}", doc.GetString(0));
}
```

You need to add a using directive for the System.Data.Common namespace for this code to compile.

Notice that the ObjectQuery type parameter is DbDataRecord, instead of HospitalStaff. This is so the select statement can return only the Name and Position properties. Also, the GetString method of the doc instance in the foreach loop indexes by position, rather than by column name. The Name property appears first in the select statement, which is why the GetString parameter is 0. The Position property would have been at index 1. GetString is strongly typed, but you could also use the weakly typed approach of doc[0], which returns an object type.

Creating Custom Entities

Generating an EDM directly from a database does nothing more than duplicate your physical database schema in your application. You will still be writing code from the perspective of your relational model. This bottom-up approach makes it difficult to create a true object-oriented design.

One of the great advantages of the ADO.NET Entity Framework is that it makes it easier (than writing a custom DAL by hand) for you to take a top-down approach to designing an application. The validity of this approach is proven in the multitude of projects that use OPFs and custom data access layers (DALs).

The magic of the ADO.NET Entity Framework approach occurs with a set of XML documents that declaratively defines entities and how they map to the physical database. The next section explains how this works.

Mapping and Schemas

You must create three primary document types to have an EDM: Conceptual Schema Definition Language (CSDL), Mapping Schema Language (MSL), and Storage Schema Definition Language (SSD). They are XML documents, and their contents describe the parts of your EDM and how they fit together. Figure 22.6 illustrates the relationships between these documents.

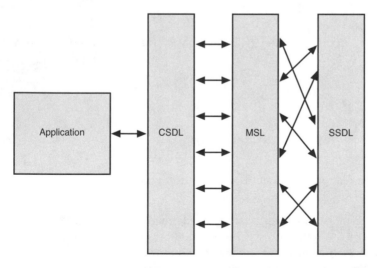

FIGURE 22.6   EDM XML mapping and schema document relationships.

As shown in Figure 22.6, an application communicates directly with the CSDL. It is the CSDL that contains the entities, such as HospitalStaff and Patient, that are objects for code to interact with. The CSDL represents your conceptual model.

Furthest to the right in Figure 22.6 is the SSDL. It contains a representation of the relational tables, foreign keys, constraints, stored procedures, and other database-specific artifacts. The SSDL represents your physical model.

With CSDL and SSDL, there is a representation of two sides of the data environment. There could be a one-to-one mapping between CSDL and SSDL, as in the last section that generated the EDM directly from the database. However, you also have the capability for the CSDL and SSDL to diverge significantly in representation. That is, you won't have an exact one-to-one mapping between entities and database tables.

The MSL gives you the flexibility to have CSDL that doesn't map directly to SSDL. The MSL maps information from various parts of the SSDL to the CSDL, demonstrating that the CSDL and SSDL can vary independently. This gives you much more flexibility to adapt your CSDL to conceptual model changes (entity modifications) or modify SSDL for physical model changes (database changes). You just modify the MSL to map the new changes. This way, changes in one model don't break the other.

Adding a Custom Entity to a Model

Instead of a bottom-up approach, shown in the previous section, you now have the ability to create a top-down design. The benefits of this approach are that it is easier to capture and model customer requirements, you can reason about your design from an object-oriented perspective, and you minimize strange alterations in your model when the database schema changes.

To get started, select your project in Solution Explorer, right-click, select Add, New Item, and create a new ADO.NET entity model named **CustomHospital.edmx**. You see the Entity Data Model Wizard screen as shown in Figure 22.7

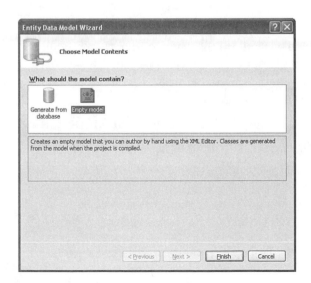

FIGURE 22.7   Creating a custom EDM.

Choose the Empty Model option, as shown in Figure 22.7, and click the Finish button. This will give you a blank design surface. You can now add your own entities from the object-oriented perspective of the code. The following steps describe how to build a custom entity. Warning: The following steps were written for Beta software and its possible that the exact steps could change:

1. Drag an `Entity` control from the toolbox onto the design surface. You see a new entity named `Entity1`, as shown in Figure 22.8.

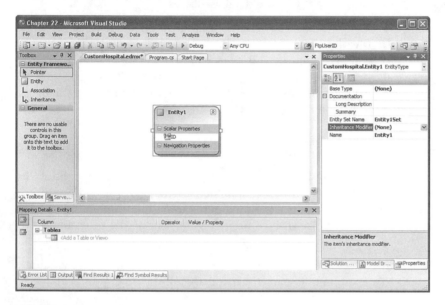

FIGURE 22.8 Adding a new entity.

Entity1, on the design surface, has an `ID` attribute, as all entities should have. The ADO.NET Entity Framework runtime depends on this ID to keep track of modifications. Mapping Details is empty and properties are at defaults, both of which need to be changed.

2. In the Properties window, make the following changes:

   a. Enter Long Description of **Part of HospitalStaff where Position is Doctor**.

   b. Enter Summary of **Doctor Objects**.

   c. Change Entity Set Name to **Doctors**.

   d. Change Name to **Doctor**.

3. Select the `Doctor` entity (just created), right-click, and select Add, Scalar Property, and call the new property **Name**.

4. Select the new `Name` property, open the Properties window, and change the following properties:

    a. Change Type to String.

    b. Change Max Length to 50.

    c. Change Nullable to False.

    d. Change Unicode to False.

When creating new entities, you can repeat the previous step and this one to add as many properties as you need.

5. Add a new entity to the design surface, name it **Patient**, and call its entity set **Patients**. Add a new property named **Name**.

6. Select the new Name property, open the Properties window, and change the following properties:

    a. Change Type to String.

    b. Change Max Length to 50.

    c. Change Nullable to False.

    d. Change Unicode to False.

7. Select the Association control in the toolbox, select Doctor, and then select Patient. This creates an association between Doctors and Patients.

8. With the DoctorPatient association selected, select Association, <Add a Table or View> in the Mapping Details window. Select the Patient table, map ID of Doctor to DoctorID and ID of Patient to PatientID.

9. Right-click the CustomHospital.edmx design surface and select Validate. Select the Hospital database connection in the Entity Data Model Wizard screen and click the Finish button.

10. Open the Model Browser window, select CustomHospital.Target, right-click, and select Update Model from Database. Select all the tables and stored procedures in the list and then click the Finish button.

11. Select the Doctor entity in the EDM designer. In the Mapping Details window, select Tables, <Add a Table or View>, and select HospitalStaff.

12. Select the Condition branch and select Position. You see a condition designer appear where you can specify which records will appear in the Doctor entity. It will say "When Position = ??". Click the cell with ?? and change it to **Doctor** (without quotes).

13. In the Column Mappings section of the Mapping Details window, map HospitalStaffID to ID and leave Position blank.

14. Select the Patient entity in the EDM designer. In the Mapping Details Window, select Tables, <Add a Table or View, and select Patient.

15. In the Column Mappings section of the Mapping Details window, map PatientID to ID and Name to Name.

You now have a custom EDM to program with. Here's code that reads all of the Doctor entities:

```
using (var custHospital = new CustomHospitalEntities())
    {
        ObjectQuery<Doctor> doctorQuery =
            new ObjectQuery<Doctor>(
                "select value Doc from
                ➥CustomHospitalEntities.Doctors as Doc",
                custHospital);

        foreach (var doc in doctorQuery)
        {
            Console.WriteLine("Name: {0}", doc.Name);
        }
    }
```

This is the same type of query you saw in the previous section, except that the ObjectQuery type parameter is Doctor and the select statement accesses the fully qualified name CustomHospitalEntities.Doctors.

Now you can program against the object you design in your domain, and if any changes are necessary for either the entities or the physical database, you can change your mappings. Remember to open the Model Browser and update the model before adjusting mappings.

Coding with LINQ to Entities

If you've read previous chapters on LINQ, everything you've learned about LINQ so far still applies with LINQ to Entities. LINQ to Entities gives you a simple and common API for querying entities produced by the ADO.NET Entity Framework. First, I show you how to query entities and then how to manipulate entity data.

Querying Entities

To perform a LINQ query, all you need to do is get a reference to the entity in the object context. Here's an example the performs a simple select query:

```
using (var custHospital = new CustomHospitalEntities())
{
    var doctors =
        from doc in custHospital.Doctors
        select doc;

    foreach (var doc in doctors)
    {
        Console.WriteLine("Name: {0}", doc.Name);
    }
}
```

Again, you still need the using statement because the connection held by the object context, custHospital, must be closed (disposed). The LINQ query uses the Doctors entity in custHospital to access objects.

All other LINQ queries work the same.

Modifying Entity Data

Some of the tasks you'll want to accomplish include insert, update, and delete on entities. This section shows you how to combine LINQ and auto-generated methods of the object context and entities to modify entity data.

Adding New Entities

The auto-generated object context will offer an AddToXxx convenience method for each entity in the EDM. Here's an example that adds a new Doctor entity:

```
using (var custHospital = new CustomHospitalEntities())
{
    custHospital.AddToDoctors(
        new Doctor
        {
            Name="90210"
        }
    );

    custHospital.SaveChanges();

    foreach (var doc in custHospital.Doctors)
    {
        Console.WriteLine("Name: {0}", doc.Name);
    }
}
```

In the preceding example, AddToDoctors was automatically generated when the Doctor entity was added to the CustomHospitalEntities object context. It is strongly typed, meaning that it will take a new Doctor instance. Also notice how the Doctors entity set in the foreach loop provides default select behavior for all the available entities.

The SaveChanges method of the object context will persist all pending modifications to the database.

Updating Entities

In addition to inserting new entities, you can update existing entities. Here's an example that modifies the doctor named 90210:

```
using (var custHospital = new CustomHospitalEntities())
{
    var doctors =
```

```
        from doc in custHospital.Doctors
        where doc.Name == "90210"
        select doc;

    var doctor = doctors.FirstOrDefault();

    doctor.Name += "-0000";

    custHospital.SaveChanges();

    foreach (var doc in custHospital.Doctors)
    {
        Console.WriteLine("Name: {0}", doc.Name);
    }
}
```

This example uses LINQ to Entities to find the doctor named 90210. After it has a reference to that object, it appends -0000 and then saves the changes. The example used
FirstOrDefault, which is an operator that would have returned null if there weren't any
entities available.

Deleting Entities

Another operation you need to perform is deleting entities. Here's an example that shows
you how to delete the doctor named 90210:

```
using (var custHospital = new CustomHospitalEntities())
{
    var doctors =
        from doc in custHospital.Doctors
        where doc.Name == "90210"
        select doc;

    doctors.ToList().ForEach(
        doc => custHospital.DeleteObject(doc));

    custHospital.SaveChanges();

    foreach (var doc in custHospital.Doctors)
    {
        Console.WriteLine("Name: {0}", doc.Name);
    }
}
```

This example is a little different from how LINQ to SQL deletes objects because entities themselves don't have a `Delete` method. You need to use the `DeleteObject` method of the object context, `custHospital`. Again, `SaveChanges` persists the object context modifications to the database.

Summary

You are now able to use the ADO.NET Entity Framework to access data sources. You saw how to create an EDM and generate entities from a database. Then there was a section explaining how to implement entity SQL queries.

The purpose of showing how to create an EDM from a database was mostly to explain the various parts of the VS2008 designer. It was a bottom-up approach that a lot of developers prefer to avoid. Therefore, I showed you a top-down approach on how to build custom entities that helped you build an object-oriented conceptual model.

You also learned how to use LINQ to Entities, which takes advantage of the common query capabilities of LINQ. Finally, you learned how to manipulate the model to insert, update, and delete entities.

In addition to the ADO.NET Entity Framework, Microsoft is working on another new data access technology called ADO.NET Data Service, which makes it easy to access data over the Internet. You can learn about ADO.NET Data Services, and how it works with the ADO.NET Entity Framework, in the next chapter.

CHAPTER 23

Working with Data in the Cloud with ADO.NET Data Services

It's somewhat timely that my wife and I were discussing the Sunday newspaper today. In light of the Internet, we were wondering why we still maintain the subscription. On the Internet, we can visit our favorite sites and receive near real-time news. Most Internet news portals are quick and easy to navigate, and we can drill down on the subjects we want. The Internet has become very convenient.

Just like the news, data can sometimes be more convenient over the Internet. Many applications use a local database or a common database server on a network, but an increasing amount of data is finding its way to the Internet. We use various protocols and even web services to access data, and as time goes by, working with data over the Internet will become convenient for a growing number of applications.

Microsoft is introducing a new API for accessing information over the Internet called ADO.NET Data Services. What's different about ADO.NET Data Services is that it is easy to access by any application, including ASP.NET AJAX and Silverlight applications, which are covered in Chapters 28, "Adding Interactivity to Your Web Apps with ASP.NET AJAX," and 29, "Crafting Rich Web Applications with Silverlight." This chapter explains how ADO.NET Data Services, which I also refer to as just data services, uses standard Internet protocols to work with data over the Internet.

Adding ADO.NET Data Services to Your Project

VS2008 has ADO.NET Data Services projects that are easy to use. To get started, create a new WCF Service Application. Then right-click your new project, select Add, New Item, and select ADO.NET Data Services. Name the file **HospitalDataService.svx** and click the OK button.

This creates a new project for publishing a Windows Communications Foundation (WCF) web service. We won't cover the details of WCF until Chapter 34, "Creating Web and Services with WCF," but I give you enough information here to get by so that you can understand how to properly set up an ADO.NET Data Services project.

Your next task is to create a data source to be exposed via the new data service. To meet this need, create an ADO.NET Entity Framework Entity Data Model (EDM), just as you did in the preceding chapter. For simplicity, generate your EDM directly from the Hospital database, including the HospitalStaff and Patient tables.

After you have your data source, open the file named HospitalDataService.svc.cs; there will be a class named HospitalDataService that derives from WebDataService<T>. In the skeleton template, there is a TODO comment in the place of T, and you should replace that with the new EDM object context, HospitalEntities, so that it will read as WebDataService<HospitalEntities>. Within the InitializeService method, uncomment the call to config.SetResourceContainerAccessRule and replace the first parameter with "*". Also, change ResourceContainerRights.AllRead in the second parameter to ResourceContainerRights.All so that later examples will be able to perform insert, update, and delete operations. The following example shows how the code in HospitalDataService.svc.cs should look:

```
using HospitalModel;
using Microsoft.Data.Web;

namespace HospitalService
{
    public class HospitalDataService :
        WebDataService<HospitalEntities>
    {
        public static void InitializeService(
            IWebDataServiceConfiguration config)
        {
            config.SetResourceContainerAccessRule(
                "*", ResourceContainerRights.All);
        }
    }
}
```

You now have a web service that can be used to access data exposed via an ADO.NET Entity Framework EDM. Users will access this data with Representational State Transfer

(REST) web service APIs. In case you aren't familiar with REST, it is just a way to write HTTP URLs to access web services. REST has gained much popularity because it uses HTTP and is simpler than XML web services.

Accessing ADO.NET Data Services via HTTP URIs

You can use the ADO.NET Data Services REST API and a browser to perform many types of queries. This section shows you how to do this so that you gain a better understanding of the basic mechanisms of how ADO.NET Data Services work.

Viewing Entity Sets

You can see a list of all entity sets the data service has to offer through a browser. To do so, right-click the data service project and select Set as Startup Project. Then press F5 or click the Run button on the toolbar. Because data services are exposed as XML conforming to the Atom Publishing Protocol (AtomPub): RFC 5023, browsers such as IE7 and Firefox try to interpret results as RSS, but don't show content. You can get around this by right-clicking the page and selecting View Source for IE7 or View Page Source for Firefox. Figure 23-1 shows the AtomPub document in IE7.

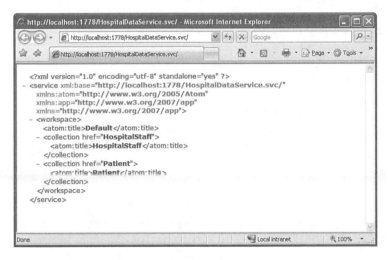

FIGURE 23.1   Querying a data service.

The title elements in Figure 23.1 contain the names of each entity that the data service exposes. These are the same entities that represent tables exposed as entities in the EDM that the data service is based on.

Selecting Entity Items

You can drill down on the entities in Figure 23.1 with specific queries. Type the following address into the browser address bar to list the members of the HospitalStaff entity:

```
http://localhost:1778/HospitalDataService.svc/HospitalStaff
```

Remember to right-click and select View Source to see the results, summarized here:

```
<feed xml:base="http://localhost:1778/HospitalDataService.svc/"
xmlns:ads="http://schemas.microsoft.com/ado/2007/08/dataweb"
xmlns:adsm="http://schemas.microsoft.com/ado/2007/08/dataweb/metadata"
xmlns="http://www.w3.org/2005/Atom">
  <id>http://localhost:1778/HospitalDataService.svc/HospitalStaff</id>
  <updated />
  <title>HospitalStaff</title>
  <link rel="self" href="HospitalStaff" title="HospitalStaff" />
  <entry adsm:type="HospitalModel.HospitalStaff">
    <id>http://localhost:1778/HospitalDataService.svc/HospitalStaff(1)</id>
    <updated />
    <title />
    <author>
      <name />
    </author>
    <link rel="edit" href="HospitalStaff(1)" title="HospitalStaff" />
    <content type="application/xml">
      <ads:HospitalStaffID adsm:type="Int32">1</ads:HospitalStaffID>
      <ads:Name>Marcus</ads:Name>
      <ads:Position>Doctor</ads:Position>
    </content>
    <link rel="related" title="Patient" href="HospitalStaff(1)/Patient"
        type="application/atom+xml;type=feed" />
  </entry>...
  <entry adsm:type="HospitalModel.HospitalStaff">
    <id>http://localhost:1778/HospitalDataService.svc/HospitalStaff(41)</id>
    <updated />
    <title />
    <author>
      <name />
    </author>
    <link rel="edit" href="HospitalStaff(41)" title="HospitalStaff" />
    <content type="application/xml">
      <ads:HospitalStaffID adsm:type="Int32">41</ads:HospitalStaffID>
      <ads:Name>90210-0000</ads:Name>
      <ads:Position>Doctor</ads:Position>
    </content>
    <link rel="related" title="Patient" href="HospitalStaff(41)/Patient"
        type="application/atom+xml;type=feed" />
  </entry></feed>
```

This output shows the first and last entry elements in the results. You can select specific items from the list if you know their index. The following URL will return the first element in the list:

```
http://localhost:1778/HospitalDataService.svc/HospitalStaff(1)
```

Notice the (1) appended to HospitalStaff; the parentheses are used to select an item based on the primary key of the entity, which is HospitalStaffID. Here are the results:

```
- <entry xml:base="http://localhost:1778/HospitalDataService.svc/"
xmlns:ads="http://schemas.microsoft.com/ado/2007/08/dataweb"
xmlns:adsm="http://schemas.microsoft.com/ado/2007/08/dataweb/metadata"
adsm:type="HospitalModel.HospitalStaff" xmlns="http://www.w3.org/2005/Atom">
 <id>http://localhost:1778/HospitalDataService.svc/HospitalStaff(1)</id>
 <updated />
 <title />
- <author>
 <name />
 </author>
 <link rel="edit" href="HospitalStaff(1)" title="HospitalStaff" />
- <content type="application/xml">
 <ads:HospitalStaffID adsm:type="Int32">1</ads:HospitalStaffID>
 <ads:Name>Marcus</ads:Name>
 <ads:Position>Doctor</ads:Position>
 </content>
 <link rel="related" title="Patient" href="HospitalStaff(1)/Patient"
       type="application/atom+xml;type=feed" />
 </entry>
```

Looking at the HospitalStaffID, you can see that the entry element for 1 was returned, matching what was requested in the URL. The next section discusses more sophisticated queries.

Filtering Entity Results

You can filter results, based on any entity properties. For example, if you want all the doctors from HospitalStaff, you could use the following URL:

```
http://localhost:1778/HospitalDataService.svc/HospitalStaff?$filter=Position eq
'Doctor'
```

As shown, filters are implemented by appending the query with ?$filter= and adding criteria. Here are the results:

```
<feed xml:base="http://localhost:1778/HospitalDataService.svc/"
xmlns:ads="http://schemas.microsoft.com/ado/2007/08/dataweb"
xmlns:adsm="http://schemas.microsoft.com/ado/2007/08/dataweb/metadata"
xmlns="http://www.w3.org/2005/Atom">
  <id>http://localhost:1778/HospitalDataService.svc/HospitalStaff</id>
```

```
<updated />
<title>HospitalStaff</title>
<link rel="self" href="HospitalStaff" title="HospitalStaff" />
<entry adsm:type="HospitalModel.HospitalStaff">
  <id>http://localhost:1778/HospitalDataService.svc/HospitalStaff(1)</id>
  <updated />
  <title />
  <author>
    <name />
  </author>
  <link rel="edit" href="HospitalStaff(1)" title="HospitalStaff" />
  <content type="application/xml">
    <ads:HospitalStaffID adsm:type="Int32">1</ads:HospitalStaffID>
    <ads:Name>Marcus</ads:Name>
    <ads:Position>Doctor</ads:Position>
  </content>
  <link rel="related" title="Patient" href="HospitalStaff(1)/Patient"
        type="application/atom+xml;type=feed" />
</entry>...
<entry adsm:type="HospitalModel.HospitalStaff">
  <id>http://localhost:1778/HospitalDataService.svc/HospitalStaff(41)</id>
  <updated />
  <title />
  <author>
    <name />
  </author>
  <link rel="edit" href="HospitalStaff(41)" title="HospitalStaff" />
  <content type="application/xml">
    <ads:HospitalStaffID adsm:type="Int32">41</ads:HospitalStaffID>
    <ads:Name>90210-0000</ads:Name>
    <ads:Position>Doctor</ads:Position>
  </content>
  <link rel="related" title="Patient" href="HospitalStaff(41)/Patient"
        type="application/atom+xml;type=feed" />
</entry></feed>
```

The preceding output is a listing of all entity elements that match the criteria in the URL, `Position eq 'Doctor'`, where the `Position` property is equal to the string `'Doctor'`. Table 23.1 shows some additional queries that perform different filtering tasks you'll want to use.

TABLE 23.1   Data Services Filter Queries

$filter=	Returns entity objects matching filter value.
Position eq 'Doctor'	Position property is equal to 'Doctor'.
Position ne 'Doctor'	Position property is *not equal* to 'Doctor'.

TABLE 23.1   Continued

`HospitalStaffID lt 4`	Value of the `HospitalStaffID` is less than 4.
`HospitalStaffID le 4`	Value of the `HospitalStaffID` is less than or equal to 4.
`HospitalStaffID gt 4`	Value of the `HospitalStaffID` is greater than 4.
`HospitalStaffID ge 4`	Value of the `HospitalStaffID` is greater than or equal to 4.
`HospitalStaff lt 4 and Position eq 'Nurse'`	Value is less than 4 *and* equal to `'Nurse'`.
`HospitalStaff gt 4 or Position eq 'Nurse'`	Value is either greater than 4 or `Position` is equal to `'Nurse'`.
`not (Position eq Doctor)`	Expression result within parentheses is not true.

As you can see from Table 23.1, you have several combinations of relational operators to apply toward filtering results. You can use parentheses anywhere in your filter to affect the ordering of an expression.

Sorting Entities

You can also sort results with the $orderby operator. Here's an example that sorts doctors by their name:

```
http://localhost:1778/HospitalDataService.svc/HospitalStaff?$filter=Position eq
'Doctor'&$orderby=Name
```

The results from the preceding query will be appear in ascending order. Notice how the query contains a filter and the $orderby is separated with an &.

It's amazing how intuitive the API is in some parts. For example, the first time I tried a descending sort, it looked something like this:

```
http://localhost:1778/HospitalDataService.svc/HospitalStaff?$filter=Position eq
'Doctor'&$orderby=Name desc
```

All I did was add desc, and it worked the first time!

Traversing Entity Associations

The HospitalStaff entity has a one-to-many association with the Patients entity. Another task you'll want to accomplish is retrieving a list of patients for a specified doctor. Here's how you do it:

```
http://localhost:1778/HospitalDataService.svc/HospitalStaff(1)/Patient
```

The HospitalStaff object with key, HospitalStaffID, equal to 1 has several patients, which are retrieved by the preceding query. Here is a summary of the results:

```
<feed xml:base="http://localhost:1778/HospitalDataService.svc/"
```

```
xmlns:ads="http://schemas.microsoft.com/ado/2007/08/dataweb"
xmlns:adsm="http://schemas.microsoft.com/ado/2007/08/dataweb/metadata"
xmlns="http://www.w3.org/2005/Atom">
  <id>http://localhost:1778/HospitalDataService.svc/HospitalStaff(1)/Patient</id>
  <updated />
  <title>Patient</title>
  <link rel="self" href="Patient" title="Patient" />
  <entry adsm:type="HospitalModel.Patient">
    <id>http://localhost:1778/HospitalDataService.svc/Patient(1)</id>
    <updated />
    <title />
    <author>
      <name />
    </author>
    <link rel="edit" href="Patient(1)" title="Patient" />
    <content type="application/xml">
      <ads:PatientID adsm:type="Int32">1</ads:PatientID>
      <ads:Name>GeorgeXXXXXX</ads:Name>
    </content>
    <link rel="related" title="HospitalStaff" href="Patient(1)/HospitalStaff"
type="application/atom+xml;type=entry" />
  </entry>...
  <entry adsm:type="HospitalModel.Patient">
    <id>http://localhost:1778/HospitalDataService.svc/Patient(85)</id>
    <updated />
    <title />
    <author>
      <name />
    </author>
    <link rel="edit" href="Patient(85)" title="Patient" />
    <content type="application/xml">
      <ads:PatientID adsm:type="Int32">85</ads:PatientID>
      <ads:Name>Jane</ads:Name>
    </content>
    <link rel="related" title="HospitalStaff" href="Patient(85)/HospitalStaff"
type="application/atom+xml;type=entry" />
  </entry></feed>
```

This output shows the AtomPub output of the patients from the specified query.

Typically, you'll use the query syntax shown in this section with AJAX or Silverlight applications, which you can learn more about in Chapters 28 and 29, respectively. The next section shows you how to write server-side code that lets you use data services.

Writing Code with the ADO.NET Data Services Client Library

The REST API, described in the previous section, is convenient for AJAX and Silverlight applications that use JavaScript. However, you might want to access data services via client applications, such as Windows Presentation Foundation (WPF) or server-side code in an ASP.NET web application. Microsoft provides a client-side API for accessing data services for client applications.

This section shows you how to query, add, update, and delete data using the ADO.NET Data Services Client Library, which I'll refer to as the client API. You also learn how to use the LINQ to Data Services flavor of LINQ.

Setting Up Your Client Project

Previous sections of this chapter showed you how to create a WCF project for exposing data services. The examples in this section use a console application, but you can use the client API with C# code in any project type.

Go ahead and create a new console project, which you are probably accustomed to doing by now—Chapter 1, "Introducing the .NET Platform," explains how to do this.

Next, add a reference to `Microsoft.Data.WebClient`. To do so, right-click your new project, select Add Reference, wait a couple seconds for the Add New Reference window to appear, and select `Microsoft.Data.WebClient` from the list on the .NET tab. If you don't see it listed there, select the Browse tab, navigate to \Program Files\Reference Assemblies\Microsoft\Framework\ASP.NET 3.5 Extensions and select the Microsoft.Data.WebClient.dll library.

You're now ready to write code to perform queries.

Querying Entities with `WebDataQuery`

The following code shows how to perform a query, retrieving a list of doctors, using the client API:

```
var webCtx = new WebDataContext(
    new Uri("http://localhost:1778/HospitalDataService.svc"));

var docs = webCtx.CreateQuery<HospitalStaff>("/HospitalStaff");

docs.ToList().ForEach(
    doc => Console.WriteLine('Name: {0}', doc.Name));
```

The `WebDataContext` in the preceding example is like a connection object that abstracts the logic of communicating with the data service. You just need to give it the URL of the data service. Remember to change the port number from 1778 to whatever port that VS2008 is running your data service from, which does change.

The parameter of `CreateQuery` is the same as what is described in the previous section of this chapter. The `WebDataContext` will append this parameter to the URI that addresses the data service. Therefore, the query from the preceding code would be the same as typing the following into your browser address bar:

```
http://localhost:1778/HospitalDataService.svc/HospitalStaff
```

Another gotcha to avoid is that you shouldn't pass a URI to your `WebDataContext` with a trailing /. Because the query parameters are appended, you would end up with the following invalid query:

```
http://localhost:1778/HospitalDataService.svc//HospitalStaff
```

Because of the double slashes between the service name and the query, you'll get an HTTP 403, Bad Request error. This can happen easily if you copy and paste the URI from the browser to the code after typing it into your browser to verify that it is typed correctly.

When calling `CreateQuery` on the `WebDataContext`, `webCtx`, pass in the type you expect to get back. The type you use needs to be named the same as the data service type with public fields or properties that match the names and types of the entity type returned. Here's the class I created:

```csharp
public class HospitalStaff
{
    public int HospitalStaffID { get; set; }
    public string Name { get; set; }
    public string Position { get; set; }
}
```

Typically, your data service will have many more entities, and I'm sure you don't want to manually duplicate type definitions by hand. To help out, Microsoft ships a command-line tool called WebDataGen.exe, which is located at \Program Files\Microsoft ASP.NET 3.5 Extensions. Here's how you would extract the types from HospitalDataService.svc:

```
Webdatagen.exe/mode:ClientClassGeneration/outobjectlayer:HospitalTypes.cs/uri:http:
//localhost:1778/HospitalDataService.svc
```

The mode option, `ClientClassGeneration`, specifies that it should generate classes, `outobjectlayer` is the name of the file to produce, and `url` addresses the data service.

To use the new file, right-click the project, select Add, Existing Item, navigate to the folder where you created the HospitalTypes.cs file, select HospitalTypes.cs, and click the Add button. You'll see HospitalTypes.cs appear as a file in your project.

The HospitalTypes.cs file contains code that matches the EDM created for the HospitalDataService.svc, meaning that the code is in the `HospitalModel` namespace. To see this, compare the HospitalTypes.cs code to the Hospital.Designer.cs code in the

HospitalService project. To use these types, add a using declaration for the `HospitalModel` namespace to your client code.

Adding Entities

You can insert new objects through data services by using the `WebDataContext`. The following example shows how to add a new doctor to `HospitalStaff`:

```
var webCtx = new WebDataContext(
    new Uri("http://localhost:1778/HospitalDataService.svc"));

webCtx.AddObject("HospitalStaff",
    new HospitalStaff
    {
        Name = "No",
        Position = "Doctor"
    });

webCtx.SaveChanges();
```

The first parameter to `AddObject` is a string that must be one of the entities in the data service, and the second parameter is the new object to insert. Calling `SaveChanges` on the `WebDataContext` causes the client API to send updates to the data service.

If you are getting HTTP 403 Forbidden errors, double-check to ensure that the second parameter to `config.SetResourceContainerAccessRule` in the `InitializeService` method of the `HospitalService` class in the HospitalDataService.svc.cs file in the HospitalService project is set to `ResourceContainerRights.All` and not the default value of `ResourceContainerRights.AllRead`.

Updating Entities

To update an entity, query for references to the entities you want to change, modify them, perform the update, and persist the changes back to the data service. The following example shows how this works:

```
var webCtx = new WebDataContext(
    new Uri("http://localhost:1778/HospitalDataService.svc"));

webCtx.MergeOption = MergeOption.AppendOnly;

var docs = webCtx.CreateQuery<HospitalStaff>(
    "/HospitalStaff?$filter=Name eq 'No'&$top=1");

var drNo = docs.ToArray()[0];
drNo.Position = "Nurse";

webCtx.UpdateObject(drNo);
```

```
webCtx.SaveChanges();

docs = webCtx.CreateQuery<HospitalStaff>(
    "/HospitalStaff");

docs.ToList().ForEach(
    doc => Console.WriteLine(
        "Update - Name: {0}, Position: {1}",
            doc.Name, doc.Position));
```

After instantiating webCtx, set its MergeOption to AppendOnly to turn on tracking, which ensures that changes persist to the database. The system raises an exception as soon as the query is executed without this.

> **PRERELEASE SOFTWARE GLITCHES?**
>
> In this chapter, I used docs.ToArray()[0], to get a reference to the first entity from the previous query. It would have been more elegant to use the LINQ First() operator, but there is a bug in the version of ADO.NET Data Services the code was written with. So, docs.ToArray()[0] is just a workaround.

After getting a reference to the entity instance to modify, the code changes the Position property. You want a reference to the object that will be updated because webCtx is keeping track of the fact that it has been modified, which you indicate by calling UpdateObject. To send changes to the data service, call SaveChanges on the WebDataContext instance.

A similar process helps to delete entities.

Deleting Entities

To delete entities, get references to the entities to delete, mark them for deletion, and then persist changes back to the data service. Here's an example of how to delete:

```
var webCtx = new WebDataContext(
    new Uri("http://localhost:1778/HospitalDataService.svc"));

webCtx.MergeOption = MergeOption.AppendOnly;

var docs = webCtx.CreateQuery<HospitalStaff>(
    "/HospitalStaff?$filter=Name eq 'No'");

docs.ToList().ForEach(
    doc => webCtx.DeleteObject(doc));
```

```
webCtx.SaveChanges();

docs = webCtx.CreateQuery<HospitalStaff>(
    "/HospitalStaff");

docs.ToList().ForEach(
    doc => Console.WriteLine(
        "Delete - Name: {0}, Position: {1}",
            doc.Name, doc.Position));
```

This is similar to the previous update example, except the call to `DeleteObject` on each of the entity references is selected. Again, remember to set the `MergeOption` on `WebDataContext` to `MergeOption.AppendOnly`.

Querying Entities with LINQ to Data Services

All the examples in this section called `CreateQuery` with parameters that match the data service URL parameters. Because it uses a string parameter that isn't strongly typed and represents yet another query language to be learned, it might not be the most optimal solution. Instead, you might find it much easier to use LINQ, which is strongly typed and takes advantage of your intellectual investment in query language knowledge. The good news is that Microsoft is releasing LINQ to ADO.NET Data Services so that you will be able to query data services through the ADO.NET Data Services Client Library.

Here's an example of how to use LINQ to Data Services with the `WebDataContext`:

```
var hospital = new WebDataContext(
    new Uri("http://localhost:1778/HospitalDataService.svc"));

var docs =
    from doc in hospital.CreateQuery<HospitalStaff>("/HospitalStaff")
    where doc.Position == "Doctor"
    select new { doc.Name };

docs.ToList().ForEach(
    doc => Console.WriteLine(
        "LINQ - Name: {0}", doc.Name));
```

In this example, you're still using `CreateQuery` to get a reference to the `HospitalStaff` collection. The rest of the LINQ query works the same as you have learned in the last few chapters, except that it is operating on a `WebDataContext`.

Using the WebDataGen.exe-Generated Classes

In a previous section of this chapter, you learned how to use the WebDataGen.exe utility to create local versions of entities exposed through a data service. The file produced, HospitalTypes.cs contained a class called `HospitalEntities` that derives from `WebDataContext`. If you are beginning to get the idea that `HospitalEntities` would be a good source to query, you would be on the right track. As a reminder, here's how the HospitalEntities and other types were generated with the WebDataGen.exe command-line tool:

```
Webdatagen.exe/mode:ClientClassGeneration/outobjectlayer:HospitalTypes.cs/uri:http:
//localhost:1778/HospitalDataService.svc
```

Here's an example that performs LINQ to Data Services queries with HospitalEntities:

```
var hospital = new HospitalEntities(
    new Uri("http://localhost:1778/HospitalDataService.svc"));

var docs =
    from doc in hospital.HospitalStaff
    where doc.Position == "Doctor"
    select new { doc.Name };

docs.ToList().ForEach(
    doc => Console.WriteLine(
        "LINQ with HospitalEntities - Name: {0}", doc.Name));
```

The preceding example instantiates a new HospitalEntities with a URI, just like the WebDataContext. However, unlike the WebDataContext, the LINQ query from clause is much simpler and more strongly typed by just calling hospital.HospitalStaff.

Although all the queries for select, insert, update, and delete in previous sections used a WebDataContext instance, they could have also used a HospitalEntities instance.

Summary

In this chapter, you've learned how ADO.NET Data Services enables you to work with data over the Internet. It uses a REST API, which you saw how to query with URLs in a browser window.

The chapter continued with examples of how to use the ADO.NET Data Services Client Library to make queries from C# code. You also saw how to perform inserts, updates, and deletes.

Finally, you also learned how to use LINQ to Data Services, which works like LINQ to other providers, giving you a common way to query data.

This is the last chapter on working with data in .NET using C#. However, it won't be the last time you'll see these data access technologies or LINQ used because they are an integral part of most .NET development. There will be many examples throughout this book that help remind you how to use what you've learned (and how to apply it).

Next, we start looking at many other .NET technologies for building applications, starting with desktop programs. To keep it simple, the next chapter delves deeper into building console applications, before moving on to Windows Forms and WPF.

PART 5

Building Desktop User Interfaces

CHAPTER 24

Taking Console Applications to the Limit

Y ou've probably heard some form of the saying "everything old is new again." In the 1970s, we had hip-hugger jeans, but today we have low-rider jeans. Even though the jeans back then were skintight and now they're baggy, the concept is the same in that parents are still telling their kids to pull up their pants.

Similarly, in the 1970s, we had text-based consoles for user interfaces. Today, we can have the same thing with console applications. While back then a console was a modern step above a card reader or teletype and consoles today are a step down from modern graphical user interfaces (GUIs), the concept is the same in that there are times when interfacing with a console is something you might want to do. Therefore, we have .NET console applications for those scenarios where text is the preferred means of communication.

With .NET console applications, you have an API for interacting with the user and managing I/O—via text. Think about all the .NET command-line utilities that are available in %windir%\Microsoft.NET\Framework/ in the v2.0.50727, v3.0, and v3.5 subfolders. Some have GUIs, and others work only with command-line arguments and communicate with text via the console. This chapter shows you how to use the features of the Console API, which can be useful when writing utility or command-line applications.

Introducing the PasswordGenerator Console Application

The sample application for this chapter is a password generator, appropriately named PasswordGenerator. With the ever-increasing need for better security in the workforce, this program will help people select a password better than the name of their dog.

We start off with the simplest console application that can be written and build upon this so that you can see the power of the .NET Console API. Listing 24.1 shows the first version of PasswordGenerator.

LISTING 24.1   A Simple Console Application

```
class PasswordGenerator
{
    static void Main()
    {
        System.Console.WriteLine(
            "Your new password:  M3yz*aHc");
    }
}
```

The PasswordGenerator program in Listing 24.1 uses the WriteLine method of the Console class to tell you what your new password was. This section introduces you to more of the Console class API, showing you different ways to display information and how to receive input from the user.

Interacting with the User

The following example makes the task of getting the password more interactive. It asks users for their name and then gives them a new password. You'll also see how to keep the command prompt window from closing when the program is finished executing:

```
Console.Write("User Name: ");


string userName = Console.ReadLine();

Console.WriteLine();
Console.WriteLine(
    "Hi {0}!  Your new password is {1}.",
    userName, "M3yz*aHc");

Console.WriteLine("Press any key to continue...");

Console.ReadKey();
```

Most of the Console API you've seen so far used WriteLine, which prints a newline, \n, after the specified text. The Console.Write, shown here, only prints the text, and the cursor sits on the same line at the end of the text. This was useful in this program because we want to see the user's name appear on the same line.

The Console.ReadLine call will make the program wait for the user to enter text and will return after the user presses the Enter key. The return value from ReadLine is the string holding the characters that the user typed, which is expected to be a name in this case.

The first WriteLine call simply prints a newline to the console for output formatting. The next WriteLine uses a parameterized string to format the rest of the output, which echoes the user's name and that user's new password.

Calling Console.ReadKey is a useful way to get the command prompt window, which shows the command line, to continue showing. It waits for the user to press any keyboard key. Without Console.ReadKey, the program exits and closes the window right away. Any time you see the command prompt window flash open and close right away, you can use the Console.ReadKey to keep this from happening.

There are many members of the Console class, and Table 24.1 describes how each Console method is used.

TABLE 24.1   Console API Methods for Communicating with Users

Console Member	Usage
Write	Emits text to the console and leaves the cursor on the same line. When users type, their input appears on the same line.
ReadLine	Allows reading user input and returns input as a string that can be assigned to a variable.
WriteLine	Emits text to the console and performs a new line so that the cursor is setting at the beginning of the next line. The first parameter is a format string, containing the text to display on the console and, optionally, multiple format placeholders.
ReadKey	Pauses the console, waiting for any key press.

TABLE 24.1   Continued

Console Member	Usage
Read	Reads each character of user input until the user presses the Enter key. One of the primary differences between ReadKey and Read is that Read will read every character, but ReadKey will read each keystroke, which could represent more than one character. The most notable instance is when pressing the Enter key. An Enter key emits two characters: a carriage return (\r) and a line feed (\n). To use Read to recognize the Enter key, you must add logic that recognizes these two characters in sequence. However, ReadKey just recognizes that the user pressed a key and doesn't need any additional logic. Read will return the integer representation of the character entered, but ReadKey is much richer in that it returns an object of type ConsoleKeyInfo that you can inspect for more information about what key or key combination was pressed.

These APIs aren't the final story in user I/O. You can also handle command-line input, which you learn about in the next section.

Handling Command-Line Input

If you are going to write a utility program, you'll often want to give users the ability to pass information via the command line. For power users, this makes the program quick and easy to use, rather than requiring the user to navigate a series of prompts, which is more appropriate for beginners. This section demonstrates how to allow users to run your program efficiently by passing command-line arguments.

In Listing 24.2, instead of prompting and getting input from the user, this program reads command-line arguments for input.

LISTING 24.2   Retrieving User Input from the Command-Line

```
using System;

class ChangePasswordOption
{
    static void Main(string[] args)
    {
        string userName = args[0];
```

LISTING 24.2   Continued

```
        Console.WriteLine(
            "Hi {0}!  Your new password is {1}.",
            userName, "M3yz*aHc");

        Console.WriteLine("Press any key to continue...");
        Console.ReadKey();
    }
}
```

The Main method in Listing 24.2 has an argument named args, whose parameter type is array of string, string[].

When a user runs this program on the command line, they can follow it with as many space-separated arguments they desire. Each of these arguments is passed to the Main method as an element in the args array. For the purpose of this program, the first command-line argument is the only one we care about. If your program needs more arguments, it could read each element of the args array. The first element of the args array, args[0], retrieves the first command-line argument and assigns the string value to the local userName variable, which is also type string.

If you're using VS2008, remember to add command-line args by double-clicking on the project's Properties folder, selecting the Debug tab, and then setting Command line arguments.

The rest of the program works similarly to previous examples.

Now you know how to make your programs more useful by accepting command-line input. In the next section, you can have a little fun playing with the different Console API members for positioning and color.

Adding Color and Positioning to Consoles

If you decide that you need or want to build a console application, there is more available for you in the way of the user interface than just reading and writing text. The Console class also has several methods that enable you to build text-based graphical interfaces. You can set color, position text on the screen, and make sounds.

The version of PasswordGenerator in this section has some fun with the Console API by going a little retro with green screens. Many of the first monitors available for computer operators and programmers had green screens, and this program captures the essence of that time. The program also borrows from a later time in history when American National Standards Institute (ANSI) commands were common for color and text positioning on personal computers.

Figure 24.1 shows the new user interface, using color and positioning.

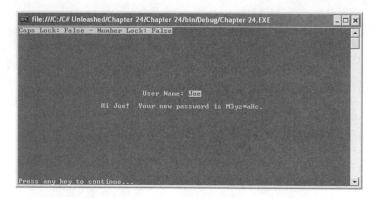

FIGURE 24.1   Adding color and positioning to a console application.

Although it appears as black and white in this book, the screen background is dark green, and the foreground is normal green. Just a warning: This program uses the Console.Beep command to make a few sounds. If you have your speakers turned up, it could startle you.

Just like the PasswordGenerator program you saw earlier in this chapter, enter your name at the prompt and press Enter. Then you'll see your new password. Here's the code that produced the screen for Figure 24.1:

```
Console.BackgroundColor = ConsoleColor.DarkGreen;
Console.ForegroundColor = ConsoleColor.Green;

Console.Clear();

Console.SetCursorPosition(0, 0);

Console.BackgroundColor = ConsoleColor.Green;
Console.ForegroundColor = ConsoleColor.DarkGreen;

Console.Write(
    "Caps Lock: {0} - Number Lock: {1}",
    Console.CapsLock, Console.NumberLock);

Console.BackgroundColor = ConsoleColor.DarkGreen;
Console.ForegroundColor = ConsoleColor.Green;

Console.SetCursorPosition(30, 10);

Console.Write("User Name: ");
```

```
Console.BackgroundColor = ConsoleColor.Green;
Console.ForegroundColor = ConsoleColor.DarkGreen;

string userName = Console.ReadLine();

Console.BackgroundColor = ConsoleColor.DarkGreen;
Console.ForegroundColor = ConsoleColor.Green;

Console.SetCursorPosition(20, 12);

Console.Beep(1000, 100);
Console.Beep(900, 50);
Console.Beep(1100, 200);

Console.Write(
    "Hi {0}!  Your new password is {1}.",
    userName, "M3yz*aHc");

Console.SetCursorPosition(0, Console.WindowHeight - 1);

Console.Write("Press any key to continue...");

Console.ReadKey();
```

Besides meeting the requirements of the application to serve up a new password, the goal of the preceding code is to ensure that colors and positioning are set properly in the right places. Starting from showing the CapsLock and NumLock at the beginning, the program interacts with the user in the center of the screen and then gives a command to press a key at the end of the routine. Table 24.2 provides details for each Console member shown above and how it is used.

TABLE 24.2   Console API Members for Color, Positioning, and Sound

Console Member	Usage
BackgroundColor, ForegroundColor, ConsoleColor	Used to set screen color. You can see how the screen background and foreground are set with ConsoleColor members to set the colors on the screen. These same commands are used throughout the listing to alter colors for specific visual effects.
Clear	Clears all text from the screen. In addition to clearing text from the screen, the code uses the Clear method to paint the screen background with the current background color.

TABLE 24.1   Continued

Console Member	Usage
SetCursorPosition	Sets the location on the screen where the next `Console` member will operate. The screen buffer is organized by columns and rows with `0, 0` being the upper-left corner. Columns increase in number toward the right, and rows increase in number toward the bottom. The call to `SetCursorPosition` puts the cursor in the upper-left corner, in preparation for printing the `CapsLock` and `NumLock` values. Notice in Figure 24.1 that I had turned on the Caps Lock key before running the program. If you are working with passwords, knowing something like this is important.
CapsLock, NumberLock	Allows you to set or get the value of the Caps Lock or Number Lock keys. You can see how the example reads these values and prints them.
Beep	Emits a sound to the computer speakers. The first parameter is `frequency` and the second is `duration`. The set of three `Beep` commands sounds a little like a whistle that blows just before printing out the password. You could probably use the `Beep` command to play a basic tune. In addition, it is sometimes useful to provide an audible alarm when you detect bad input.

Back in the early 1980s, there was an arcade game named Space Invaders that was popular. When Microsoft added the color, positioning, and sound capabilities to the `Console` class in .NET 2.0, they re-created this game as a demonstration of how sophisticated this API was and what you could do with it. To see the full capabilities of the Console API, you can download the Space Invaders program and C# source code from MSDN at http://msdn2. microsoft.com/en-us/netframework/aa569267.aspx. If they move the URL, you can do a search at MSDN, http://msdn.microsoft.com, for "space invaders demo," which brought the link to the top of the list for me. If you are ever feeling nostalgic and have a desire to re-create your own favorite arcade game of the past, now you know how to do it.

Summary

In this chapter, you learned how to perform different tasks with console applications. By using the Console API, you can interact with the user and even to fun things such as color the screen, position text, and play sounds.

Although there is a place for console applications, most of the desktop applications you write will require a more sophisticated GUI. The next chapter shows you how to use Windows Forms as a GUI.

CHAPTER 25

Writing Windows Forms Applications

A few years back, one of the popular TV news shows did a piece on the difference between the way people are treated based on their appearance. They took a couple women where one woman was more attractive than the other and a couple men where one of the men was more attractive than the other and performed some experiments with a hidden camera. They had each pair of people apply for the same jobs, rent the same apartment, and try to get assistance in the same department store. The results for the attractive people was overwhelmingly positive, whereas the other people didn't have as much luck.

If you take the same situation with software where you have a console application and a GUI application, what do you think customer response would be like? Let's even say that the console application has more features, less errors, and performs better than the GUI application. The results would still be that a customer would prefer the GUI application more often than the console application because it is more attractive to look at.

For this reason and the fact that you can make the user experience more positive, most applications being written today use some form of GUI where a customer can use a mouse to interact with buttons, drop-down lists, and many other types of graphical controls. This chapter shows you how to build GUI applications with Windows Forms. You'll see the basic parts of an application, how VS2008 helps you, essential controls, menu handling, and 2D drawing with GDI+.

Windows Forms Fundamentals

The rapid application development (RAD) features of modern IDEs often lull developers into a sense of not truly understanding the fundamentals of what makes the technology work. Too many times, the answers to problems are right under a programmer's nose in the form of language knowledge and object-oriented principles. I'll definitely talk about VS2008 and RAD development in this chapter, but first I want to cover some fundamentals, which I think will help you a lot in the long run.

To get started, create a new Windows Forms application named **WinFormFundamentals**. You can do this in VS2008 by creating a new project and selecting Windows Forms Application, or right-click an existing Solution file and select Windows Forms Application. The results are that you have a new project with references to System.Windows.Forms.dll, which is the library holding the Windows Forms API.

Next, delete Form1.cs, Form1.designer.cs, and Program.cs. You'll use these files in other projects, but for current purposes, we don't want these files getting in the way. Then create a new class file and call it **SimpleForm.cs**. Replace the skeleton code in SimpleForm.cs with the contents of Listing 25.1. The code in Listing 25.1 creates a new window with a button that pops up a message when clicked.

LISTING 25.1   Windows Forms Application Showing Fundamentals

```
using System.Windows.Forms;

class SimpleForm : Form
{
    static void Main()
    {
        Application.Run(
            new SimpleForm());
    }

    public SimpleForm()
    {
        var warnBtn =
            new Button
            {
                Text = "Don't Click Me!",
                Width = 150,
                Height = 50,
                Left = ClientRectangle.Width/2 - 75,
                Top = ClientRectangle.Height/2 - 25
            };

        warnBtn.Click +=
```

LISTING 25.1   Continued

```
            (sender, evtArgs) => MessageBox.Show(
                "I thought I told you not to click!");

        Controls.Add(warnBtn);
    }
}
```

Although Listing 25.1 doesn't have many lines of code, the application it creates is powerful. It is also instructive from the perspective of reinforcing C# language concepts and object-oriented programming.

The first thing to notice is that `SimpleForm` derives from the `Form` class. If you look in the .NET Framework documentation for the `Form` class, you'll see that it has an inheritance chain that extends several classes. Essentially, `SimpleForm` inherits the benefits of all these classes, meaning that it displays a window with title bar, minimize and maximize buttons, context menu, close button, and resizable borders. Actually, there is much more there behind the scenes, but you got it all through the object-oriented principle of inheritance.

Just like console applications, a Windows Forms application begins life through an entry point, `Main`. The `Main` method in Listing 25.1 uses the `Application` class, which is another member of the Windows Forms API. `Application` has several members, including `Exit` to stop execution of a program. Listing 25.1 starts the program by executing the `Run` method on `Application`, passing in an instance of a Form-derived object, which is `SimpleForm`, repeated here for your convenience:

```
Application.Run(new SimpleForm());
```

The `Run` method keeps the program alive, listening for events such as mouse clicks and key presses. When a user chooses to exit the program, the `Run` method returns. As you know, a program ends when the `Main` method ends, effectively meaning that the code in Listing 25.1 stops executing after `Run` returns.

Title bars and close buttons are impressive, but we know that an application has to do something to be useful. You can say that Listing 25.1 is an application with attitude for functionality. Like a kid with attitude, this application has some growing up to do, but you can still push its buttons. Speaking of buttons, here's how the button in Listing 25.1 is defined:

```
var warnBtn =
    new Button
    {
        Text = "Don't Click Me!",
        Width = 150,
        Height = 50,
        Left = ClientRectangle.Width/2 - 75,
        Top = ClientRectangle.Height/2 - 25
    };
```

Using object-initialization syntax, the `Button` control here is initialized with several property settings. `Text` is a standard property across most of the UI controls. Whereas `Width` and `Height` are hard-coded (for this example), the `Left` and `Top` positioning properties are set dynamically. `ClientRectangle` is a property of the containing form that has properties for `Top`, `Left`, `Width`, and `Height` of the area of the form that is left after subtracting title bar, borders, menus and status bars. The `Top` and `Left` positions start at `0` and increase downward and to the right. The initialization on `Left` and `Top` centers the button in the form's client area.

After you've created controls that will appear on the page, you must decide how to add behavior to the controls. With a `Button` control, you are typically interested in providing some type of action that occurs when a user clicks that button. Recall from Chapter 12, "Event-Based Programming with Delegates and Events," that a C# Event is a class member that is used to notify someone of things that happen in an application. In this case, the thing we care about is a button click, and it is convenient that the `Button` class has an event that is named `Click`. You also learned in Chapter 12 what a delegate is and how it facilitates hooking events up to code. In our case, that code is the action we went to take when someone clicks the button, so we need a delegate to hook up the `Click` event on the button to code that we want to run. The next example doesn't use a delegate, but it does use a C# lambda, which can do the same thing:

```
warnBtn.Click +=
    (sender, evtArgs) => MessageBox.Show(
        "I thought I told you not to click!");
```

As you learned in Chapter 18, "Using Lambdas and Expression Trees," a lambda is a method without a name, similar to anonymous methods, but without the extra syntax. The preceding code uses a lambda to hook up code with the `Click` event of the button, using the combine syntax (+=) you learned about in Chapter 12.

The preceding code also shows you how to use a Windows Forms `MessageBox`, the lambda expression, which displays a small window with a single OK button. The `Show` method of a `MessageBox` has several overloads you can use to set an icon, choose buttons, set captions, and set display text, as shown previously.

For all the work done so far, you still won't see the button on the form until you explicitly add it. Here's the code that adds the button to the form:

```
Controls.Add(warnBtn);
```

Container controls, such as `Form`, `Panel`, and `GroupBox`, have a property named `Controls`, which is a collection of all the controls they contain. You can use the `Add` method to add a control, but you can also use many other methods to iterate through controls on the page and perform other actions, such as `Remove`. This is powerful, especially if you need to dynamically build or change the appearance of a form.

There you have it—a basic Windows Forms application. Here's what you should take away from this discussion:

▶ A form is a class, just like any other type you write C# code against.

▶ All controls on the form are also classes, and you use them just like any other type in C#.

▶ Windows Forms is a classic example of the effective implementation and use of delegates and events. You have the Windows Forms API that belongs to the .NET Framework Class Library that exposes events. Then you use the delegates that those events are based on to connect your code to the API to make your program work.

▶ Don't be fooled by the designer in the VS2008 IDE as being a mysteriously opaque container. The IDE generates code; it's all just a bunch of objects, and you use all the C# techniques that you've already learned from previous chapters to make those objects do your will.

Although this section has been instructive from the perspective of learning the object-oriented fundamentals of Windows Forms, most people don't build applications like this in practice. The next section brings you into a comfort zone where there is much support for building Windows Forms applications with VS2008.

VS2008 Support for Windows Forms

This section examines the visual design environment, shows which files are part of a Windows Forms application, and shows you the magic of what code is created as you work with the Visual Designer.

The Visual Design Environment

VS2008 has a helpful visual design environment that helps you build user interfaces with ease. Figure 25.1 shows the Windows Forms design environment.

On the left of Figure 25.1 is the toolbox, which contains controls that you can drag and drop onto the design surface. The design surface is in the middle of the screen. You can see that it is a WYSIWYG environment, where you can resize the form and visually see the results of your work. Although not shown in this example, nonvisual controls appear below the form in the visual designer in an area called the component tray. The two sections to the right in Figure 25.1 are the Solution Explorer and Properties window. You've see the Solution Explorer already when building console applications, and it is a necessary part of every application. The Properties window is context-sensitive. It will change, depending on which window or control that is selected on the design surface. Sometimes one control or window will overlap another and make it hard to select on the design surface. In such cases, you must use the drop-down window at the top of the Properties window to select the control.

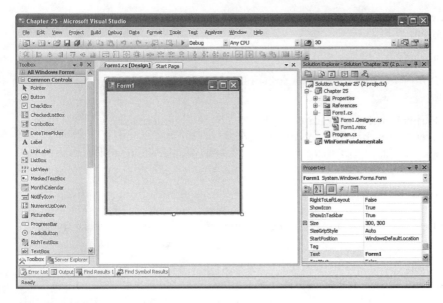

FIGURE 25.1   Windows Forms design environment in VS2008.

Files in a Windows Forms Application

Looking at the Solution Explorer window in Figure 25.1, you can see that there are a few different files that were created by the Windows Application Project Wizard. Table 25.1 lists those files and their purpose.

TABLE 25.1   Initial Windows Forms Application Files

Filename	Purpose
Form1.cs	User code for working with the form. You normally work in this file most of the time. All your event handlers and code that call your business logic are added here.
Form1.Designer.cs	Visual Designer–generated code. You normally don't ever need to open this file. If you need to write your own code to work with the form, it will typically be done through Form1.cs.
Form1.resx	Resource file for bitmaps, strings, icons, and so on. Chapter 40, "Localizing and Globalization," discusses resource files in greater depth.
Program.cs	Contains the Main method.

In addition to these initial files, the References folder is automatically populated with reference to several assemblies, most notably the Windows.Drawing.dll and Windows.Forms.dll assemblies. The next section shows you what's inside these files.

How the Visual Designer Works

This section expands on the points made in the first part of this chapter that showed you basic code that serves as the foundation of Windows Forms and how it relates to the Visual Designer in this section. We'll look at each of the files initially created with a Windows Forms project and the parts they play when working with the Visual Designer.

The Windows Forms Entry Point

If you open the Program.cs file, you'll see a Main method similar to Listing 25.2.

LISTING 25.2   The Windows Forms Program.cs File

```
using System;
using System.Collections.Generic;
using System.Linq;
using System.Windows.Forms;

namespace Chapter_25
{
    static class Program
    {
        /// <summary>
        /// The main entry point for the application.
        /// </summary>
        [STAThread]
        static void Main()
        {
            // other code omitted

            Application.Run(new Form1());
        }
    }
}
```

This is much like you've seen in console applications, whose entry point is also the Main method. It's also similar to Listing 25.1, where you learned that the Application.Run method will start the program and not return until the application closes.

In Chapter 16, "Declaring Attributes and Examining Code with Reflection," you learned about attributes, helping you recognize that [STAThread] on the Main method is also an attribute. This attribute makes your Windows Forms application run in what is called a single threaded apartment (STA). Because the operating system is built with Component Object Model (COM) technology, it also uses the COM thread model. Windows Forms works by calling into the Win32 API, which is STA, but .NET is inherently multithreaded, which is equivalent to a COM multithreaded apartment (MTA). Running multithreaded code in an environment built for single threads only is a prescription for disaster, so decorating your application at the entry point with the [STAThread] attribute makes your C# code run in an STA, and keeps things safe.

User Code

When adding specific behavior to a Windows Forms application, you'll use the Form1.cs class. Listing 25.3 shows what the Windows application project creates for you. You can see this code by right-clicking either the form in the Visual Designer or Form1.cs in Solution Explorer and selecting View Code.

LISTING 25.3   The Windows Forms Form1.cs File

```csharp
using System;
using System.Collections.Generic;
using System.ComponentModel;
using System.Data;
using System.Drawing;
using System.Linq;
using System.Text;
using System.Windows.Forms;

namespace Chapter_25
{
    public partial class Form1 : Form
    {
        public Form1()
        {
            InitializeComponent();
        }
    }
}
```

Listing 25.3 doesn't contain a lot of code, but there are a couple significant observations to make at this point. First, Form1 is a partial class. You learned about partial types in Chapter 8, "Designing Objects," where they received brief coverage. However, now you can see their practical application. This is only one part of the Form1 class definition. This is where you put your code, and the Visual Designer uses another partial, in Form1.Designer.cs, to put its code.

The second observation that you should make is that the Form1 constructor calls a method named InitializeComponent, but you don't see the definition of this method in Listing 25.3. The next section shows you where InitializeComponent is defined and what it does.

Visual Designer–Generated Code

Considering that Form1 is a partial class and its constructor calls an InitializeComponent method that isn't defined in Listing 25.3, you might be curious as to whether there is code defined somewhere else and what it contains. This section unravels the mystery, which is hidden in the Form1.Designer.cs file. Listing 25.4 shows the other Form1 partial class and the definition of the InitializeComponent method.

LISTING 25.4   The Windows Forms Form1.Designer.cs File

```
namespace Chapter_25
{
    partial class Form1
    {
        #region Windows Form Designer generated code

        /// <summary>
        /// Required method for Designer support - do not modify
        /// the contents of this method with the code editor.
        /// </summary>
        private void InitializeComponent()
        {
        }

        #endregion
    }
}
```

As you can see in Listing 25.4, Form1.Designer.cs holds the matching partial to the Form1 partial class defined in Form1.cs. When this code is compiled, C# combines these two files into a single class definition.

The purpose of the InitializeComponent method is so the Visual Designer can automatically generate code that produces the UI you create when dragging and dropping controls onto the design surface and setting properties in the Properties window.

Separating the code into two partial types increases productivity and improves safety. Because the auto-generated code is in Form1.Designer.cs, it won't be in the way when working in Form1.cs, which simplifies your coding experience, helping your productivity. Another benefit of not having auto-generated code in Form1.cs is that you, and other team members, aren't tempted to modify auto-generated code, making the coding experience safer. If someone does go into Form1.Designer.cs, he must do so explicitly, and you'll have a source control record of it (if you're using source control, which is a good idea), making it easier to back out of mistakes being made. Remember, as I just explained why, the comment on the InitializeComponent method in Form1.Designer.cs, shown in Listing 25.4, is there for good reason.

What Happens When Modifying the Visual Designer
Now that you know about the Visual Designer, the files in a Windows Forms application, and the reason for the contents of each file, I want to show you what happens when you

drag and drop a control onto the design surface. This will demonstrate to you how the Form1.cs and Form1.Designer.cs work together while you're building a UI.

To do this, we'll produce the same results as the code in Listing 25.1. The code in this example will be different because VS2005 will take the long way around and explicitly qualify and specify every bit. To get started, complete the following steps:

1. Drag and drop a `Button` control onto the design surface. If you want to delete anything that you accidentally drop on the design surface, select the control and press the Delete key or right-click the control and select Delete.

2. Go to the Properties window and set the following properties. (You can find Height and Width under Size.)

   a. Set Text to **Don't Click Me!**.

   b. Set Height to **50**.

   c. Set Width to **150**.

   d. Set (Name) to **btnWarn**.

3. Open Form1.cs and modify the Form1 constructor as follows:

```
public Form1()
{
    InitializeComponent();

    btnWarn.Left =
        ClientRectangle.Width / 2 -
        btnWarn.Width / 2;
    btnWarn.Top =
        ClientRectangle.Height / 2 -
        btnWarn.Height / 2;

}
```

This code sets the top and left coordinates of where the button, btnWarn, will appear on the form.

At the top of the Properties window, there is a toolbar with a lightning bolt button, which switches the context of the Properties window to a list of available events. If you hover your cursor over this button, the tooltip will say Events. Click the lightning bolt button. Remember that the Properties window is context-sensitive, meaning that you must select the `Button` control.

4. If you haven't selected anything else, you'll notice that the `Click` event is already selected and that its value is empty. In the value column, you have the option of typing in a name (of your choice) for a method that will be called when the `Click` event occurs. Instead of doing that, just double-click the `Click` event, which causes VS2008 to open the Form1.cs source code view with a new method. This method should be named `btnWarn_Click` if you completed step 2.d. above properly. If you don't give your control a name, the generated event handler name will use whatever default name the control was given. Therefore, if you see `Button1_Click` as the name

of your handler, you know you didn't give your button a name first. You can fix this by deleting the generated handler code and delete the contents of the value column of the Click event in the Properties window.

DEFAULT EVENTS

Controls have default events. The default event is highlighted when you open the Events panel in the Properties window. Most noticeably is that when you double-click a control on the design surface, VS2008 automatically creates an event handler for the default event. It works exactly the same as if you had double-clicked the event in the Properties window. For a Button control, the default event is Click. Therefore, you would have received the same results as in step 4 if you would have just double-clicked the Button control. Of course, knowing how to get to the Events panel in the Properties window is essential to being able to work with nondefault events and delete or modify existing events.

---

5. Modify the generated btnWarn_Click method as follows:

```
private void btnWarn_Click(
    object sender, EventArgs e)
{
    MessageBox.Show(
        "I thought I told you not to click!");

}
```

6. Run the program and verify that it behaves exactly like Listing 25.1.

The previous six steps represent a scenario that is typical for how most developers will build UIs with Windows Forms. After adding controls to the design surface, it's usually more convenient to set their properties, especially control names, because everything you do after that can be influenced by the properties. For example, the Click event handler method is named after the button, and the location is set in the Form1 constructor based on the size of properties that have already been set. Listing 25.5 shows all the modifications from the preceding steps.

LISTING 25.5   Form1.cs After Adding and Configuring a Button

```
using System;
using System.Collections.Generic;
using System.ComponentModel;
using System.Data;
using System.Drawing;
using System.Linq;
using System.Text;
using System.Windows.Forms;
```

LISTING 25.5   Continued

```csharp
namespace Chapter_25
{
    public partial class Form1 : Form
    {
        public Form1()
        {
            InitializeComponent();

            btnWarn.Left =
                ClientRectangle.Width / 2 -
                btnWarn.Width / 2;
            btnWarn.Top =
                ClientRectangle.Height / 2 -
                btnWarn.Height / 2;
        }

        private void btnWarn_Click(
            object sender, EventArgs e)
        {
            MessageBox.Show(
                "I thought I told you not to click!");
        }
    }
}
```

Going back to the Form1 constructor in Listing 25.5, notice that constructor modifications follow the call to InitializeComponent. This is intentional because the rest of the code depends on btnWarn being instantiated. For instance, the code would have thrown a NullReferenceException if you tried to access members of btnWarn, such as Height or Width, before calling InitializeComponent. Listing 25.6 shows updates to the code from Form1.Designer.cs so that you can see why the code behaves like this.

LISTING 25.6   Form1.Designer.cs After Adding and Configuring a Button

```csharp
namespace Chapter_25
{
    partial class Form1
    {
        #region Windows Form Designer generated code

        /// <summary>
        /// Required method for Designer support - do not modify
        /// the contents of this method with the code editor.
        /// </summary>
        private void InitializeComponent()
```

LISTING 25.6   Continued

```
    {
        this.btnWarn = new System.Windows.Forms.Button();
        //
        // btnWarn
        //
        this.btnWarn.Name = "btnWarn";
        this.btnWarn.Size = new System.Drawing.Size(150, 50);
        this.btnWarn.Text = "Don\'t Click Me!";
        this.btnWarn.Click += new System.EventHandler(this.btnWarn_Click);
        //
        // Form1
        //
        this.Controls.Add(this.btnWarn);
    }

    #endregion

    private System.Windows.Forms.Button btnWarn;
    }
}
```

When a Button was added to the design surface and configured with an event handler, VS2008 serialized the modifications to the InitializeComponent method in Form1.Designer.cs, shown in Listing 25.6, in the form of code.

Notice that the btnWarn button is declared at the bottom of the Form1 class. VS2008 avoids namespace clashes by fully qualifying all references, which is why the type isn't specified as only Button.

The accessibility of btnWarn is private, but that's okay because Form1 is a partial, meaning that the Form1 partial class in Form1.cs can access it, as was done in the constructor shown in Listing 25.5. This brings up another benefit of the partial type: It allows partial types, of the same type, to share private members without breaking encapsulation.

Within the InitializeComponent method, btnWarn is instantiated and then initialized. Also, notice that the btnWarn_Click handler method is combined with the Click event via an EventHandler delegate—the Click event's delegate type is EventHandler. In the spirit of being explicit, VS2008 uses the current object reference, this, to access type members. Finally, notice how btnWarn is added to the Controls collection.

As you can see, the code is different but accomplishes the same thing. Remember, the InitializeComponent method belongs to VS2008. Instead of altering code in InitializeComponent, you should remove controls by deleting on the Visual Designer (preceding step 1), change properties via the Properties window (preceding step 2), and remove or modify event handlers via the Events panel on the Properties window (preceding step 4).

In this section, you used only a Button control, but there are many more that ship with .NET. The next section discusses the other controls in the toolbox.

Using Windows Forms Controls

A control is a specialized window with specific features and a unique purpose. These are things like buttons, labels, and lists. Table 25.2 introduces each of the standard Windows Forms controls and explains how they're used.

TABLE 25.2   Windows Forms Controls

Control	Description
Button	Control that can be clicked to perform some desired action.
CheckBox	Primarily used for displaying a binary state of an object. Clicking the check box causes it to toggle between a checked or unchecked state.
CheckListBox	List box with a column of check boxes.
ComboBox	A drop-down list of choices that operates similar to the list box. The primary difference is that the combo box is more compact and efficient with screen real estate.
DataGridView	An extremely powerful control that permits a program to bind to a data source.
DateTimePicker	Provides a capability to select a date and time without typing.
DomainUpDown	Permits a user to scroll through a list of data items that can only be shown one at a time.
Form	The main window of an application, a dialog, or a multiple-document interface (MDI) child. It provides all the capabilities for hosting child controls.
GroupBox	Houses a group of other controls, often used to encapsulate a group of radio buttons. It can help organize a form and has a customizable title.
Label	Primarily used to display static text but can also contain images.

TABLE 25.2   Continued

Control	Description
LinkLabel	The same as a label, but it can contain an URL that can be clicked to invoke an Internet connection.
ListBox	Holds selectable lists of data items. When the viewable portion of the list box is filled, a scrollbar appears so that all of its contained items may be selected.
ListView	Provides capabilities for multiple columns, column headers, column resizing, and list sorting. It can also be configured in four different display modes. More sophisticated than a list box.
MessageBox	Provides notifications to users on certain program events. It has a configurable message, title bar, icon, and button.
MonthCalendar	A visual calendar control.
NumericUpDown	The same as a DomainUpDown, with the restriction that its contents are numeric.
Panel	Blank forms with little or no decoration that are used primarily for organization and form layout.
PictureBox	Displays an image.
ProgressBar	Used to display the status of an ongoing operation. It has a graphical indicator, set by a program to show the percentage of task completion.
PropertyGrid	For user interface type applications, to set and display a list of properties associated with a certain component.
RadioButton	Mutually exclusive buttons that permit users to make a choice. Also called option buttons.

25

TABLE 25.2   Continued

Control	Description
RichTextBox	An enhanced text box control that provides more control over its text. It has the capability of creating Rich Text Format (RTF) files.
ScrollBar	Often used to help position the current location in a document that's too large to fit onscreen or in whatever space is available.
Splitter	Permit a user to resize multiple portions of a workspace. When the splitter is moved, one portion of the workspace gets larger, and others become smaller.
StatusBar	Performs multiple functions. Primarily it's a place to notify users of a program's status or other forms of current information.
TabControl	User interfaces that appear like file folder tabs. When selected, they open a specific page where the tab and content match.
TextBox	Allows a user to type text. They can be single line or multiline and have many capabilities for text manipulation such as selection, cut, copy, and paste.
Timer	Nonvisual controls that raise events at specified intervals. They can be used for such things as reminders or auto-save operations.
ToolBar	Permits a user to invoke selected operations in a program; similar in functionality to menus.
ToolTip	Helpful messages that appear when a cursor hovers over a control for a specified amount of time.

TABLE 25.2   Continued

Control	Description
TrackBar	Controls that provide a means to establish settings for a certain purpose. They are often handy in specifying the frequency or speed in which an operation should occur.
TrayIcon	Icons displayed on the icon tray of the window's taskbar. They usually have different pictures to indicate the current state of a program.
TreeView	Displays items in a hierarchical fashion. It has a root node at the top of the tree and can have multiple branches and nodes. Traditionally, it has collapsible branches and is coordinated with another control to display details of selected nodes.

It's evident from Table 25.2 that there is a plentiful supply of graphical components and controls available with Windows Forms. Most of these controls work like the Button control with various levels of sophistication.

MenuStrip, StatusStrip, and ToolStrip Controls

Most applications have a main menu, which is a quick way to access all the functionality of an application. Another popular feature of programs is to offer context-sensitive menus via right-click on parts of the program where they might make sense.

For a quick overview on how to work with menus, perform the following steps on the sample program from the previous section:

1. Drag and drop a MenuStrip control onto the form in the design surface. You'll see the menu appear with a box to visually edit the contents, but don't change it yet.

2. The Menu control has an Action list on its top-right corner. Action lists are a short list of the most commonly used properties and actions from the Properties window. Click the small arrow to open the Action list and select Insert Standard Items. Poof! You now have a full menu with all the standard menu items that you see on many other applications. Notice the Properties window, where the ShortCut property is selected. This has a drop-down designer allowing you to customize shortcut keys for menu items.

3. On the new `MenuStrip`, select File and double-click the Exit menu item.

4. Modify the new handler for the Exit menu item so that it will close the form, effectively ending the application by calling the `Close` method on the form:

```
private void exitToolStripMenuItem_Click(
    object sender, EventArgs e)
{
    Close();

}
```

5. Drag and drop a `ContextMenuStrip` onto the design surface.

6. Any time you need to modify a context menu, you must select it in the component tray. After you do so, it will appear in the Visual Designer. So, select the new `ContextMenuStrip` and add a new menu item by typing **E&xit**. The ampersand, &, means that the character following it, x, should be underlined and used for standard Windows Alt key menu navigation.

7. With the new Exit menu item selected, open the Event panel in the Properties window, select (don't double-click) the value column for the `Click` event, select the drop-down that appears in the value column, and select `exitToolStripMenuItem_Click`. This made the Exit on the context menu call the same handler you just created for the Exit on the main menu. Now, when you right-click the form at runtime, you'll see the context menu that offers an Exit option.

8. Drag and drop a `StatusStrip` control onto the form. You can now use the drop-down on the `StatusStrip` to add items.

9. Select the drop-down on the StatusStrip and notice that you can add a label, progress bar, drop-down, or split button (separates items). Add a Label to the StatusStrip.

10. Add code to set the new status bar label in the `Form1` constructor. The label is the first item, which is why the code sets index 0 of the `statusStrip1`'s `Items` collection:

```
public Form1()
{
    InitializeComponent();

    btnWarn.Left =
        ClientRectangle.Width / 2 -
        btnWarn.Width / 2;
    btnWarn.Top =
        ClientRectangle.Height / 2 -
        btnWarn.Height / 2;

    statusStrip1.Items[0].Text = "Ready...";

}
```

11. Drag and drop a `ToolStrip` control onto the form.

12. Select the new `ToolStrip` control's Action menu and select Insert Standard Items. Poof! You now have a full-featured toolbar. Figure 25.2 shows all the modifications so far.

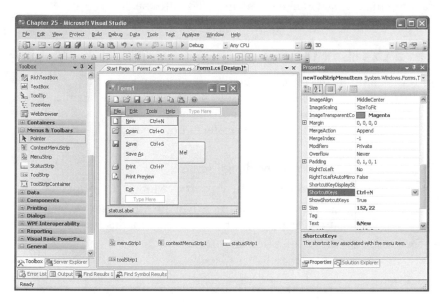

FIGURE 25.2   Form with **MenuStrip**, **ToolStrip**, and **StatusStrip** controls.

The preceding steps added several items to your window that are standard for many Windows Forms applications. Each of the controls has an `Items` collection that you can access from the Properties window and use the Visual Editor to manipulate those items. Steps 4 and 7 show you how to work with event handlers.

Data Grids and Data Binding

Many Windows Forms applications need to display lists of items, whether through `ListBox`, `ComboBox`, or `DataGridView` controls. This section shows you how to perform data binding to make it easier for you to display your data.

Setting Up a Project for Data Binding

In this section, we build upon the Hospital database examples from previous chapters that worked with doctors and patients. This sets up a foundation for further demonstrations in data binding. To set up the project, complete these steps.

1. Create a new Windows Forms application named **HospitalDataDemo**.

2. Select the new form in the design surface and set its `Text` property in the Properties window to **Hospital Data**. You'll see the title bar on the form change to be the same as the text you just updated.

3. Change the name of the form, using the Properties window, to **frmHospitalData**.

4. Right-click the HospitalDataDemo project, select Add, New Item, select LINQ to SQL Classes, name the file **Hospital.dbml**, and click the Add button.

5. Open the Server Explorer, expand the Hospital database, expand the Tables node, and drag and drop the HospitalStaff and Patient tables onto the design surface.

You now have a project with a data access layer (DAL).

Binding Data to a `ListBox` Control

With `ListBox` controls, you can manually open their `Items` property in the Properties window and add entries, which is fine for a static list of items, but not very flexible. Many times, you'll need to fill the `ListBox` dynamically, most likely with values from a database. Before proceeding, change back to the form designer. Here's how you would populate a `ListBox` from a database:

1. Drag and drop a `ListBox` control onto the design surface.

2. Set the name of the `ListBox` control, using the Properties window, to **lbDoctors**.

3. Double-click the title bar of the form (not the `ListBox`). This will create an event handler named `frmHospitalData_Load`, which handles the form's `Load` event. The `Load` event occurs whenever the form displays.

4. Modify the `frmHospitalData_Load` handler as follows:

```
private void frmHospitalData_Load(object sender, EventArgs e)
{
    var docs =
        from doc in new HospitalDataContext().HospitalStaffs
        where doc.Position == "Doctor"
        select doc;

    lbDoctors.DataSource = docs;
    lbDoctors.DisplayMember = "Name";
    lbDoctors.ValueMember = "HospitalStaffID";

}
```

The LINQ to SQL query, covered in Chapter 19, "Accessing Data with LINQ," gets all the doctors from the `HospitalStaffs` entity, which is the HospitalStaff table in the database.

The code uses data binding to assign the results to the `DataSource` property of the `lbDoctors ListBox`. The `DisplayMember` is the field that the user sees (`Name`) and the `ValueMember` is for your code to use to know which item to work with (`HospitalStaffID`) when someone selects it in the list box.

You now have a list box of doctors from the database on a form.

Binding Data to a `DataGridView`

Another popular control is the `DataGridView`. You use the `DataGridView` to show multiple rows of data with multiple columns from each row. The following steps demonstrate how to do data binding with a `DataGridView`:

1. Drag and drop a `DataGridView` control onto the same form where the list box is. You might need to adjust the size of controls and the form itself to get them to display properly.

2. Change the `Name` property, through the Properties window, of the `DataGridView` to **dgvPatients**.

3. Double-click the `lbDoctors` list box. This will create a `SelectedIndexChanged` event handler for the list box. The `SelectedIndexChanged` event occurs when you select an item in the list box.

4. Modify the `SelectedIndexChanged` event handler as follows:

```
private void lbDoctors_SelectedIndexChanged
    (object sender, EventArgs e)
{
    dgvPatients.DataSource =
        from patient in new HospitalDataContext().Patients
        where patient.DoctorID == lbDoctors.SelectedIndex
        select patient;

}
```

Just like the `ListBox` control in the previous section, you set the `DataSource` for a `DataGridView` with query results. This example filters patients based on which doctor was selected. Notice that it does this by looking at the `SelectedIndex` property of the `ListBox`, which holds the `ValueMember` that was created during `ListBox` data binding. As a side note, `DisplayMember` in `ListBox` corresponds to `SelectedValue` when an item is selected.

5. Run the program. Select different doctors and notice that the `DataGridView` updates with patients. You now have a master/detail relationship between doctors and patients, as shown in Figure 25.3.

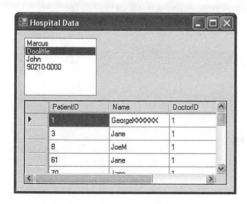

FIGURE 25.3   Master/Detail relationship between doctors and patients.

There are dozens of class members for Windows Forms controls that help you data bind and work with data—enough to fill an entire book. Realizing this, here's what is valuable to retain from this section:

▶ The Windows controls, including `ListBox` and `DataGridView`, are classes with members, just like any other C# class.

▶ You populate the data controls by binding an `IEnumerable` or `IEnumerable<T>` type to their `DataSource` properties. When you think about all the types of collections and LINQ query results that implement these interfaces, you might begin to see the practical use of interfaces and how they help you build flexible, maintainable, and reusable code.

GDI+ Essentials

In addition to the plethora of controls available and the simplicity of creating attractive UIs, you have a powerful 2D drawing capability called GDI+. This section covers the essentials for implementing GDI+ in your applications.

Much of what you do with GDI+ uses brushes and pens. A brush enables you to paint backgrounds with colors and patterns. Pens let you draw lines.

Brush, Pen, and Graphics Objects

Before you can use brushes and pens, you must have a `Graphics` object, which defines the surface you will be drawing on. You'll typically want to get a `Graphics` object in an override of the `Form` class `OnPaint` method. The reason is because there are often many things happening on your screen that your program can't predict, such as one window being covered by another or your program being minimized and maximized or resized. In each case, you must always be prepared to redraw your screen. Windows Forms knows when these events occur and calls `OnPaint` so that you have the opportunity to redraw.

To see how this works, create a new Windows Forms application and add the following `OnPaint` method to your `Form` class:

```
protected override void OnPaint(PaintEventArgs e)
{
    var pen = new Pen(Color.LavenderBlush, 5);
    var brush = new SolidBrush(Color.Goldenrod);

    e.Graphics.FillRectangle(brush, ClientRectangle);
    e.Graphics.DrawRectangle(
        pen,
        ClientRectangle.X + 20,
        ClientRectangle.Y + 20,
        ClientRectangle.Width - 40,
        ClientRectangle.Height - 40);

    base.OnPaint(e);
}
```

The pen in the preceding example is set to the LavenderBlush member of the Color enum and has a width of 5. The Color enum has 141 members, including transparent, and although I chose colors that might make you gag, you can still select the standard Red, Green, and Blue if you like. Alternatively, you can use the SystemColors enum, which will allow your application colors to automatically change whenever a user changes his or her Windows OS color scheme. The Pen class has various constructor overloads, including one that defaults to a width of 1 if you don't specify the second parameter and one that takes a brush as a background.

Speaking of brushes, the brush in the preceding example paints the background with a solid color. Instead of a SolidBrush, you can also use TextureBrush, HatchBrush, LinearGradientBrush, and PathGradientBrush for various effects.

Notice how I accessed the PaintEventArgs parameter, e, to get a reference to the Graphics object. Through the Graphics object, you have an entire set of shape drawing objects. Those that start with FillXxx allow you to fill their background, and those that begin with DrawXxx allow you to draw the shape with a transparent background. In addition to rectangles, you can draw ellipses, arcs, polygons, and more.

Remember to call base.OnPaint. OnPaint is an override, which means that your OnPaint is called rather than the OnPaint in the base class. Important tasks must be performed by base class methods, and you'll find that your application won't always work as you expect if you forget to call the base class methods that you override. For a refresher on why the code behaves this way, review inheritance and polymorphism in Chapter 9, "Implementing Object-Oriented Principles."

Fonts and Drawing Text

In addition to drawing shapes, you'll also want to draw text. To do so, you can use a Font object and then draw the text you want with the DrawString Graphics object. The following example shows how:

```
protected override void OnPaint(PaintEventArgs e)
{
    var pen = new Pen(Color.LavenderBlush, 5);
    var brush = new SolidBrush(Color.Goldenrod);

    e.Graphics.FillRectangle(brush, ClientRectangle);
    e.Graphics.DrawRectangle(
        pen,
        ClientRectangle.X + 20,
        ClientRectangle.Y + 20,
        ClientRectangle.Width - 40,
        ClientRectangle.Height - 40);
```

25

```
var textPos = new PointF(
    ClientRectangle.X + 25,
    ClientRectangle.Y + 25);

(from fontFamily in FontFamily.Families
 select fontFamily)
    .Skip(15)
    .Take(9)
    .ToList()
    .ForEach(
        fontFamily =>
        {
            var currFont = new Font(fontFamily, 15);

            e.Graphics.DrawString(
                fontFamily.Name,
                currFont,
                Brushes.DarkOrchid,
                textPos);

            textPos.Y += currFont.Height;
    });

    base.OnPaint(e);
}
```

If you have a font on your system that causes an error, reset the Skip value to one number past the position of that font.

The preceding example initializes `textPos` as a `PointF` as a starting point for drawing multiple lines of text.

The LINQ to Objects query performs font selection, iteration, and drawing—all in a single statement. The `Families` property of the `FontFamily` class returns a list of every font family on the system, `Skip` passes over the first 15 font families, `Take` gets the next 10 font families, and `ToList` returns a `List<FontFamily>` so that we can use the `ForEach` to iterate through the results.

Using the `FontFamily` passed in on each iteration, the lambda that is passed to the `ForEach` creates a new `Font` object. Remember that `Font` objects are immutable. (You can't change an existing `Font` instance.) Therefore, you must create a new `Font` if you need a `Font` with different parameters, which is why the lambda initializes a new `Font` on each iteration.

`DrawString` is another `Graphics` object, and it draws text, specified as the first parameter, to the screen, which is the name of the font family. The second parameter specifies the font to use when drawing text. You can see that the brush is the third parameter, and the left and top position to start drawing is the fourth parameter. The lambda must adjust the position on each iteration so that the next line is in the proper location.

Figure 25.4 shows the code that OnPaint produces.

FIGURE 25.4   2D graphics example with GDI+.

Additional Windows and Dialogs

Most applications are not so simple that they run in a single window. You'll need additional ways to communicate with the user, which is supported through modal and modeless dialogs. You might want to communicate with the window that pops up, either setting a value or retrieving user input, for which there are right ways and wrong ways to do so. Also, Windows Forms offers a number of common dialog boxes, such as FileOpenDialog and FileSaveDialog, that allow you to create UIs with common interfaces like any other Windows application.

Modal Versus Modeless Dialog Boxes

A modal dialog box will force you to close it before allowing you to work with the main application. Whenever you open or save a file, the dialog box is typically modal. However, a modeless dialog box allows you to move between windows freely, much like the Find dialog box that is common to many applications. To create a modal dialog box, call the ShowDialog method of a Form instance. To create a modeless dialog box, call the Show method of the Form instance.

Follow these steps to set up a program that demonstrates how to create modal and modeless dialog boxes:

1. Create a new Windows Forms application project.
2. Add two Button controls to the form.
3. Set the name of one Button control to **btnModal** and its text to **Modal**.
4. Set the name of the other Button control to **btnModeless** and set its text to **Modeless**.

5. Create a new form by right-clicking the project, selecting Add, New Item, About Box, and naming the new item **About.cs**. This is a form that comes with VS2008 containing information about an application or company that you might want to put in an About box.

6. Create a new form by right-clicking the project, selecting Add, New Item, Windows Form, and naming the new item **Info.cs**. This could be a typical input form that accepts input from a user.

7. Add a `TextBox` control to the Info form and give it the name **txtName**.

8. Add a `Button` control to the Info form and give it the name **btnOK**, set Text to OK, and `DialogResult` to OK.

9. On the main form, double-click `btnModal` and add the following code to its `Click` event handler:

```
private void btnModal_Click(object sender, EventArgs e)
{
    var info = new Info();

    DialogResult result = info.ShowDialog();

    if (result == DialogResult.OK)
    {
        MessageBox.Show("OK");
    }
}
```

Info is the class created in step 6 that inherits `Form`. To make the form appear, call `ShowDialog`. By setting the OK button's `DialogResult` to OK, we are now able to get the result back in the form of a `DialogResult` enum, which has other members for Yes, No, Cancel, and so on.

10. Double-click `btnModeless` and add the following code to its `Click` event handler:

```
private void btnModeless_Click(object sender, EventArgs e)
{
    new About().Show();
}
```

We don't need a reference to the About form because we just want to read it and close it. Using the `Show` method ensures that we close the window before returning to the application—typical modal dialog box behavior.

11. Run the application and verify the modal and modeless behavior of each type of window.

Window Communication

In the previous example, the modeless dialog box, Info, gave the user an opportunity to enter text into the text box before clicking the OK button. You'll often need to extract the information from a dialog box for use in your application, and there is a right way and a wrong way to do it. Unfortunately, I have to show you the wrong way first. If I don't, someone else will, and you'll forever learn a bad habit and not understand why.

The problem you'll encounter is that you want to get the information from a `TextBox` or other control, but it won't appear in your IntelliSense, and you get a compiler error when you try to type it in anyway. You can verify this by going back to the `btnModal_Click` event handler from the previous section, typing info, and then dot (.) and not being able to see `txtName` in the IntelliSense list. The reason is because VS2008 declares controls with private access when you drop them onto the form. This should not be a problem because VS2008 is ensuring you have proper encapsulation of `Form` members. There are a couple kludges people use to get around this: (1) Open Form1.Designer.cs and change the `TextBox` control's access modifier to `public` or (2) select the `TextBox` control, go to the Properties window, and change the `Modifiers` property from `private` to `public`. Go ahead and try it and then make the following changes to the `btnModal_Click` event handler:

```
private void btnModal_Click(object sender, EventArgs e)
{
    var info = new Info();

    DialogResult result = info.ShowDialog();

    if (result == DialogResult.OK)
    {
        string name = info.txtName.Text;

        MessageBox.Show(name);
    }
}
```

Notice how, within the `if` statement, the code can read `txtName` into a variable and display it on the screen.

However, you just broke encapsulation of `Info`. To understand the impact of this, go back to `Info`, delete the `TextBox` control, drag and drop a `ComboBox` control onto the form, name the combo box **cbNames**, open the `Items` property (from the Properties window) and add a few names (Joe, May, and George) separated by newlines. Then compile and notice that you get a compiler error because C# can't find `txtName` from code in the `btnModal_Click` event handler. No duh! I asked you to delete `txtName`!

The point to be made here is not that you broke the code you are working on today. The point is that you need to write code that will withstand change in the future. As in many projects, you will take common code, perhaps like the previous dialog box, and put it in a separate library because it could be useful in other parts of this project or in a later project. That's the huge benefit you get out of component and object-oriented programming. However, by ignoring the object-oriented principle of encapsulation, a change like this can have a rippling effect across not only the code you are working on today, but also projects in the future. If you needed to change the code, you would either have to engage in an expensive and time-consuming rewrite of a lot of other code (which can accidentally

25

break working code) or concoct an unsightly kludge to fix the first kludge. It gets uglier as time goes on, until you just want to rewrite the entire application.

Here's what you can do if you have the vision to anticipate change and build maintainable code. Add a property to the Info form that wraps access to the information you need, which the control holds, like this:

```
public partial class Info : Form
{
    public string UserName
    {
        get { return cbNames.SelectedItem as string; }
        set { cbNames.SelectedItem = value; }
    }

    public Info()
    {
        InitializeComponent();
    }
}
```

The UserName property wraps the SelectedItem property of the ComboBox control, cbNames. This way, calling code doesn't have to know that this is a ComboBox; it only knows that it should call the UserName property. Here's a rewrite of the btnModal_Click event handler that demonstrates this:

```
private void btnModal_Click(object sender, EventArgs e)
{
    var info = new Info();

    info.UserName = "Joe";

    DialogResult result = info.ShowDialog();

    if (result == DialogResult.OK)
    {
        //string name = info.txtName.Text;
        string name = info.UserName;

        MessageBox.Show(name);
    }
}
```

The two changes here are that the new UserName property is set to Joe after Info is instantiated and the if statement reads the value of the UserName property, instead of accessing the control directly.

Now, any time you want to change the Info form, you can make the change and remember to modify the code in the UserName property so that the get and set accessors operate on the new control.

The real kicker is that you modify only the Info form, but never have to touch any of the code that uses the Info form—good encapsulation.

Common Dialogs

There are many common scenarios that you shouldn't have to write new code for, such as opening and saving files or printing. This is why Windows Forms offers several common dialogs for you to reuse. Table 25.3 lists those that are available.

TABLE 25.3   Windows Forms Common Dialogs

Common Dialog Name	Purpose
ColorDialog	Pick colors
FolderBrowserDialog	Create and view directories
FontDialog	Configure and select fonts
OpenFileDialog	Open files
PageSetupDialog	Settings for printable pages
PrintDialog	Print documents
PrintPreviewDialog	Preview before printing
SaveFileDialog	Save files

You already have much information about how to show a dialog. This next example uses the PrintPreviewDialog to give you a better idea about how the common dialogs work. In addition, PrintPreviewDialog has extra features and more sophistication than the other common dialogs.

To prepare for using PrintPreviewDialog, add another Button control to a form, give it a Name of **btnPrint**, and set its Text to **Print**. Double-click the Print button and code the btnPrint_Click event handler like this:

```
private void btnPrint_Click(
    object sender, EventArgs e)
{
    var printDlg = new PrintPreviewDialog
    {
        Document = new PrintDocument()
    };

    printDlg.Document.PrintPage +=
```

```
    (sdr, pea) =>
    {
        var font = new Font(Font.FontFamily, 30);
        var printText = "Print Page Test!";

        SizeF size = pea.Graphics.MeasureString(
            "Print Page Test!", font);

        var location = new PointF
        {
            X = pea.PageBounds.Width / 2
                - size.Width / 2,
            Y = pea.PageBounds.Height / 2
                - size.Height / 2
        };

        pea.Graphics.DrawString(
            printText,
            font,
            Brushes.Black,
            location);

        pea.HasMorePages = false;
    };

    printDlg.ShowDialog();
}
```

You should add a using directive for the System.Drawing.Printing namespace for this to compile.

Much of what you see for `PrintPreviewDialog` works the same as `PrintDialog`. It's just that `PrintPreviewDialog` won't make you waste paper as you try this demo yourself. When instantiating `PrintPreviewDialog`, it has a new `PrintDocument` object, which is used to manage printing of the document itself.

The `PrintDocument`, exposed through the `Document` property of the `PrintPreviewDialog`, has a `PrintPage` event that keeps getting called until you tell it not to call anymore. This supports paging, where each call to the `PrintPage` event handler, which is a lambda in the preceding example, will print one page at a time. When done printing pages, you set the `HasMorePages` of the `PrintEventArgs`, pea, to `false` so that the `PrintPage` event handler won't be called anymore. In the example, the last line of the `PrintPage` event handler sets `HasMorePages` to `false` because it only prints one page.

The first thing to notice in the `PrintPage` event handler above is the call to `MeasureString`, which returns a `SizeF` that we'll use later to get the height and width of the string, based on the `Font` size.

Next, we create a location, which is a `PointF` for specifying the top and left position on the page to start drawing. The `PaintEventArgs`, `pea`, has properties that tell you a lot of information about the printer and page being drawn to. When setting the location, the code uses the `PageBounds` property to figure out where it is allowed to draw. The code ensures that the text will be centered on the page.

Then we access the `Graphics` context and call `DrawString` to write the text out. If you are guessing that you can reuse what you've learned about GDI+ from previous sections, you are correct.

Summary

The fundamental knowledge you should have about working with Windows Forms is that everything is an object, and in this chapter you saw code that showed the basics of a Windows Forms application. You also learned how Windows Forms keeps track of changes and what each file in the application does to support this.

You also learned how to override the `OnPaint` method and use the `Graphics` object to produce 2D drawings with pens, brushes, and other objects.

You learned how to create both modal and modeless dialog boxes. Windows Forms has some common dialog boxes that you can use to interact with the user, and you saw how to use the `PrintPreviewDialog` as a typical example.

Several C# language features, such as delegates, events, interfaces, inheritance, and polymorphism, were reinforced. These are practical examples of how several complex features of C# come together in a powerful way to help you build sophisticated applications.

25

CHAPTER 26

Creating Windows Presentation Foundation (WPF) Applications

The history of sports is filled with superstars that we admire. Think about your favorite football player and how exciting it is when he's at the top of his game. Of course, football players get old. Some of them retire while people can still remember how great they are, and others hold on and fade away slowly.

Desktop user interface (UI) technologies are like football players; they're hot stuff the first time you see them. Just like the football player who's the best in the league, many programmers are convinced that their current UI technology is better than anything that came before it. Of course, there are always exceptions because use cases exist where a console application is the best solution to a problem. Generally, however, we look forward to the future and are excited for promising new football players and new advances in UI.

This chapter is about a new kid on the team, named Windows Presentation Foundation (WPF). Windows Forms, which you learned about in the last chapter, is a great technology, and people will continue to use it for some time. However, WPF offers several compelling and new features that you should take a look at. As a UI developer, you'll be able to work with a dialect of XML called Extensible Application Markup Language (XAML, pronounced Zamel), which enables greater separation of UI and business logic. Code is more declarative, and controls are more composable. WPF is the new superstar.

Just Enough XAML

In WPF, screens are built with a dialect of XML called Extensible Application Markup Language (XAML). This is more declarative than the imperative style used with Windows Forms in Chapter 25, "Writing Windows Forms Applications." By declarative, I mean that a control is specified as an XML element with attributes and subelements to describe what the control will look like. You aren't concerned with how this is done because when you tell WPF what you want, it will figure out how to build the controls (instantiating objects and assigning properties) behind the scenes.

To get started, the following sections show you the parts of a WPF project and describe enough XAML to help you understand what is happening when you are building WPF UIs.

Introducing the WPF Application

Just like other projects in VS2008, you run a Project Wizard to create a WPF application. Select New, Project, WPF Application, name the project, and click the OK button. VS2008 sets up a project that looks like Figure 26.1.

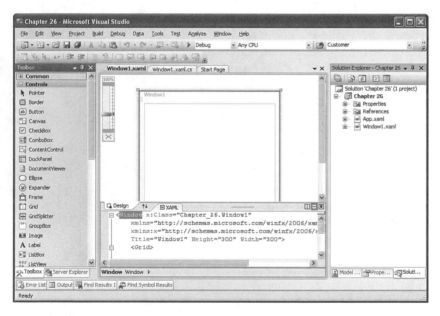

FIGURE 26.1   New WPF application.

Similar to a Windows Forms application, you'll notice, from Figure 26.1, that VS2008 has a toolbox to the left with controls, a Solution Explorer and Properties window to the right, and a designer in the middle.

The WPF designer is different in that it doesn't give the exact WSYWYG appearance that Windows Forms applications have. In addition, the designer is split between a graphical design surface on top and XAML on the bottom. The designer works the same as Windows Forms in that you can drag and drop controls onto it and edit them in the Properties window. However, the XAML is new, and the next section gives you a closer look.

Examining XAML

In Windows Forms, everything translates directly into code. However, WPF translates its user interface to XAML, which gets compiled into code later. More precisely, when working in the UI designer for a WPF project, VS2008 produces XAML, instead of code for all UI elements. VS2008 takes care of all tasks required to translate from XAML to Intermediate Language (IL). Listing 26.1 shows the skeleton XAML produced by the WPF Application Wizard.

LISTING 26.1   Skeleton XAML for a WPF Application

```
<Window x:Class="Chapter_26.Window1"
    xmlns="http://schemas.microsoft.com/winfx/2006/xaml/presentation"
    xmlns:x="http://schemas.microsoft.com/winfx/2006/xaml"
    Title="Window1" Height="300" Width="300">
    <Grid>

    </Grid>
</Window>
```

The XAML in Listing 26.1 defines a window with a title, dimensions, and an empty grid. A later section on layout explains the grid. Because it's XML, you also have namespaces: xmlns and xmlns:x.

Windows are often associated with a code-behind file, which is C#. I'll bet with all this talk of XAML you are wondering where the C# code fits in. WPF uses events, just like Windows Forms, so you need a place for the handlers to go, which is the code-behind. Listing 26.2 shows the code-behind from Window1.xaml.cs.

LISTING 26.2   Code-Behind File

```
using System;
using System.Collections.Generic;
using System.Linq;
using System.Text;
using System.Windows;
using System.Windows.Controls;
using System.Windows.Data;
using System.Windows.Documents;
using System.Windows.Input;
using System.Windows.Media;
using System.Windows.Media.Imaging;
```

26

LISTING 26.2   Continued

```csharp
using System.Windows.Navigation;
using System.Windows.Shapes;

namespace Chapter_26
{
    /// <summary>
    /// Interaction logic for Window1.xaml
    /// </summary>
    public partial class Window1 : Window
    {
        public Window1()
        {
            InitializeComponent();
        }
    }
}
```

Notice that the Window1 class in the code-behind is partial and that its constructor calls InitializeComponent. In Windows Forms, the InititalizeComponent was in a separate file that you could get to. However, WPF generates InitializeComponent from the XAML. You see, WPF will ensure that the XAML creates a partial class named Window1 with an InitializeComponent method, and then C# will combine and compile the partials. That's another benefit of XAML because now teammates that think they know more than the IDE can't accidentally mess up the UI code serialization in InitializeComponent anymore.

Controls in XAML

Many people will use the drag-and-drop capabilities of the WPF designer to build their UIs, but others will want to work directly in XAML. I often find myself using both, and the split window makes it much easier. To try out the designer, drag and drop a Label control onto the window in the designer. If you have the split window open, you'll see the XAML for the Label come into view. In the XAML, change the text inside of the new Label tags from Label to **XAML Spoken Here**. Figure 26.2 shows what this should look like.

You can see the Label control in the XAML code in Figure 26.2 and how the text inside of the Label tag has been changed. There are also attributes on the Label that match properties that you'll see in the Properties window. The Name attribute is the variable name you use in code to access this label if you need to, and VerticalAlignment describes how this control will align within its parent element, which means that this Label will align inside the top border of the grid. I discuss Margin in a later section of this chapter when talking about layout, but in case you're curious now, it means that the top, left, right, and bottom borders are the specified distance from the containing control, which is the Grid.

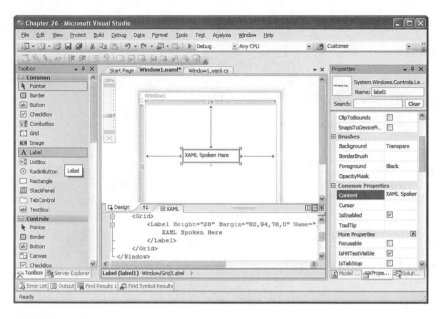

FIGURE 26.2   A **Label** control in the Visual Designer.

Notice that the Content property matches the Label text, but the XAML doesn't show a Content property. The XAML we used was a shortcut for the following:

```
<Label Height="28" Margin="80,94,78,0"
      Name="label1" VerticalAlignment="Top">
   <Label.Content>
       XAML Spoken Here
   </Label.Content>
</Label>
```

If you want to use text only, which is the most typical content, you don't need to wrap the text in the property-specific content element. However, one of the cool things about XAML controls is their composability. Whether it is a label, button, text box, or any other type of control, you can add any type of content to them that you want.

You can put only one item inside of the Content element, but that one element can be a layout control that can hold many controls. The next section discusses the layout controls.

Managing Layout

One of the subjects I breezed over in the previous section was how WPF determined where the Label control should appear on the page, its size, and its relationship to other controls. Whereas Windows Forms applications have absolute positioning and layout support via anchoring and docking, WPF is more sophisticated and has more options. For WPF, you need to know about control alignment and sizing, borders and margins, and layout controls for defining the relationship of containing controls and where they appear.

Control Alignment, Sizing, and the Box Model

With WPF controls, you can control their alignment and size. You can also manage their content, borders, and margins, which is often referred to as the box model.

Default Alignment

The default behavior of a WPF control is to stretch to fill its contents. If you are using a ListBox or Grid, filling the entire area might be the desired appearance, but you might not want this to happen with Button or Label controls. The following Label control demonstrates stretching behavior:

```
<Label Name="label1" Background="AliceBlue">
    XAML Spoken Here
</Label>
```

This Label doesn't have any attributes that specify its size or position, so the default is to stretch (see Figure 26.3).

FIGURE 26.3 Control stretch behavior.

To demonstrate the stretch behavior you see in Figure 26.2, I set the Background of the Label to AliceBlue, which covers the entire client area. I know, you're reading the book and all you can see is shades of gray, but if you run the code you'll see AliceBlue, really.

Explicit Alignment and Size

Stretch may be the default behavior, but you can still explicitly specify size and alignment. The following snippet shows two Label controls at opposite corners of the window:

```
<Label Name="lblTopLeft"
       Height="25" Width="75"
       VerticalAlignment="Top"
       HorizontalAlignment="Left"
       Background="AliceBlue">
    Top/Left
</Label>
<Label Name="lblBotomRight"
       Height="25" Width="75"
       Background="AliceBlue"
       VerticalAlignment="Bottom"
       HorizontalAlignment="Right">
    Bottom/Right
</Label>
```

The `lblTopLeft` Label is in the upper-left corner, and the `lblBottomRight` Label is in the lower-right corner. Both Labels are the same size, 25 x 75.

Canvas Layout

Using the `Canvas` layout, it's possible to explicitly specify where you want controls to appear on a form. The following example centers a `Label` in the client area:

```
<Canvas>
    <Label Name="lblTopLeft"
           Height="25" Width="75"
           Canvas.Left="100"
           Canvas.Top="125">
        Top/Left
    </Label>
</Canvas>
```

Here, you can see that the `Label` resides inside a `Canvas` layout control. It uses `Canvas.Left` and `Canvas.Top` to specify X and Y coordinates in the client area.

One of the problems with `Canvas` layout is that you do have to explicitly specify the location of each element. This is restricting, which is why there are other options, such as the `WrapPanel`, which is discussed next.

WrapPanel Layout

If you're familiar with web development, the `WrapPanel` is a familiar control. A `WrapPanel` lays out controls next to each other from left to right and starts a new row when there isn't any more room on the current row. Here's an example that wraps multiple `Label` controls:

```
<WrapPanel>
    <Label>The</Label>
    <Label>Quick</Label>
```

26

```
    <Label>Brown</Label>
    <Label>Fox</Label>
    <Label>Jumped</Label>
    <Label>Over</Label>
    <Label>The</Label>
    <Label>Lazy</Label>
    <Label>Dog's</Label>
    <Label>Back</Label>
</WrapPanel>
```

In Figure 26.4, the preceding code causes the labels for Dog's and Back to wrap to the next line.

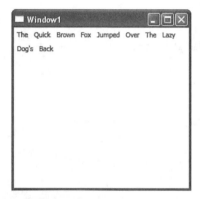

FIGURE 26.4   Using a **WrapPanel** for layout.

StackPanel Layout

A common way to lay out controls is for them to be in-line horizontally or vertically. You can use the StackPanel layout control to accomplish this. Here's an example:

```
<StackPanel Orientation="Horizontal">
    <Label>Label1</Label>
    <Label>Label2</Label>
    <Label>Label3</Label>
</StackPanel>
```

You can add numerous items to the StackPanel, as you saw previously with the Label controls, and it will line them up. Figure 26.5 shows what this looks like.

The example sets the Orientation property to Horizontal, but Orientation will default to Vertical if you omit it.

FIGURE 26.5   Using a **StackPanel** for layout.

UniformGrid Layout

The UniformGrid control divides the size of each cell evenly for all of its controls. The following example shows how this works:

```
<UniformGrid Height="100"
             Name="uniformGrid1"
             Width="200">
    <Label>O</Label>
    <Label>X</Label>
    <Label>O</Label>
    <Label>X</Label>
    <Label>O</Label>
    <Label>X</Label>
    <Label>O</Label>
    <Label>X</Label>
    <Label>O</Label>
</UniformGrid>
```

Because there are nine items, the grid will look like a tic-tac-toe board. If you need more explicit control of grid layout, you should use the Grid layout control.

Grid Layout

Another layout arrangement you'll need is to place items in tabular format with rows and columns, which is the role of the Grid layout. If you noticed, the WPF Application Wizard adds a Window with a Grid as its only content, which you can see in Listing 26.1. That Grid was empty, but you'll often want to create rows and columns. Listing 26.3 shows you how to use a Grid.

26

LISTING 26.3 Using the **Grid** Layout Control

```xml
<Window x:Class="Chapter_26.Window1"
    xmlns="http://schemas.microsoft.com/winfx/2006/xaml/presentation"
    xmlns:x="http://schemas.microsoft.com/winfx/2006/xaml"
    Title="Window1" Height="300" Width="400">
    <Grid ShowGridLines="True">
        <Grid.ColumnDefinitions>
            <ColumnDefinition Width="125" />
            <ColumnDefinition Width="2*" />
            <ColumnDefinition Width="Auto" />
        </Grid.ColumnDefinitions>
        <Grid.RowDefinitions>
            <RowDefinition Height="25" />
            <RowDefinition />
            <RowDefinition />
            <RowDefinition />
            <RowDefinition />
            <RowDefinition />
        </Grid.RowDefinitions>
        <Label Grid.Row="0"
                Grid.Column="0"
                Grid.ColumnSpan="3"
                HorizontalAlignment="Center">
            Grid Facts
        </Label>
        <Label Grid.Row="1" Grid.Column="0">
            Width="125"
        </Label>
        <Label Grid.Row="1" Grid.Column="1">
            Absolute Column Width
        </Label>
        <Label Grid.Row="1" Grid.Column="2">
            Grid.Column
        </Label>
        <Label Grid.Row="2" Grid.Column="0">
            Width="2*"
        </Label>
        <Label Grid.Row="2" Grid.Column="1">
            Proportional Spacing
        </Label>
        <Label Grid.Row="2" Grid.Column="2">
            Grid.Column
        </Label>
        <Label Grid.Row="3" Grid.Column="0">
            Width="Auto"
```

LISTING 26.3 Continued

```xml
        </Label>
        <Label Grid.Row="3" Grid.Column="1">
            Fill Remaining Space
        </Label>
        <Label Grid.Row="3" Grid.Column="2">
            Grid.Column
        </Label>
        <Label Grid.Row="4" Grid.Column="0">
            Height="25"
        </Label>
        <Label Grid.Row="4" Grid.Column="1">
            Absolute Row Height
        </Label>
        <Label Grid.Row="4" Grid.Column="2">
            Grid.Row
        </Label>
        <Label Grid.Row="5" Grid.Column="0">
            Grid.ColumnSpan="3"
        </Label>
        <Label Grid.Row="5" Grid.Column="1">
            Cover 3 Columns
        </Label>
        <Label Grid.Row="5" Grid.Column="2">
            Control Attribute
        </Label>
    </Grid>
</Window>
```

The first two items to notice in Listing 26.3 is Grid.ColumnDefinitions and Grid.RowDefinitions, which define the columns and rows, respectively. Combined with the Label controls, Figure 26.6 shows the resulting window.

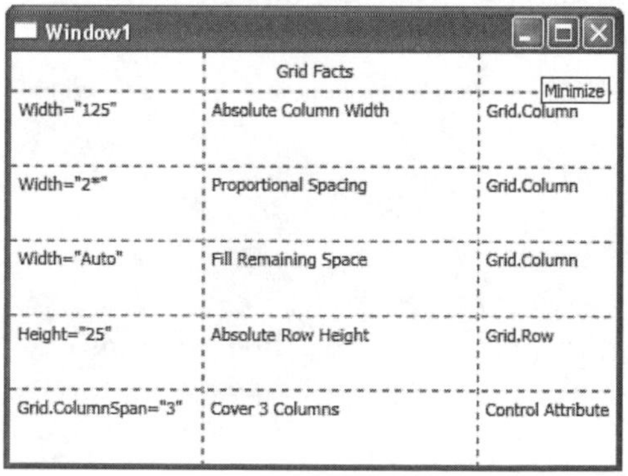

FIGURE 26.6 **Grid** layout demo

Figure 26.6 shows grid lines so that you can see the effects of sizing on rows and columns. Here's the line that makes this happen:

```
<Grid ShowGridLines="True">
```

You can use three settings to control the size of columns: absolute, proportional, and auto fill. Here's how they're used:

```
<Grid.ColumnDefinitions>
    <ColumnDefinition Width="125" />
    <ColumnDefinition Width="2*" />
    <ColumnDefinition Width="Auto" />
</Grid.ColumnDefinitions>
```

Absolute sets an explicit width, and auto fills in the rest of the width of the Grid layout's containing control. Proportional is a little different because it is proportional to the size of the other controls. The second column in the preceding example is two times the current average size of a column. Therefore, if the width of the Grid's container is 400 and there are three columns, the average size of a column is approximately 133. Because the proportional coefficient is 2, the width of the second column is 2 x 133 = 266. You can use absolute, proportional, and auto fill spacing on the Height property of RowDefinition elements, too.

After you've defined columns and rows, you must specify which column and row that controls go into. This example uses all Label controls, but you can put any WPF controls into the grid. Here's the control for the first column of the second row:

```
<Label Grid.Row="1" Grid.Column="0">
    Width="125"
</Label>
```

See how the attributes Grid.Row and Grid.Column reference the row and column to put this control into. You can look at each of these controls and see in Figure 26.3 how they appear.

The first row has a single Label that spans all columns of the Grid, shown here:

```
<Label Grid.Row="0"
       Grid.Column="0"
       Grid.ColumnSpan="3"
       HorizontalAlignment="Center">
    Grid Facts
</Label>
```

Notice the Grid.ColumnSpan, which means that this control covers all three columns in the grid. If you need a control to cover multiple rows, you can use Grid.RowSpan the same way. You can also set horizontal alignment of content with HorizontalAlignment or set vertical alignment with VerticalAlignment.

INDENTATION HELPS

Listing 26.4 is longer than most XAML I've shown you so far. Generally, you'll have long lists of XAML to read, which means that you'll want to make reading as easy as possible. Therefore, you'll want to use proper indentation so that you can see the relationship between elements.

With IntelliSense and auto-formatting in VS2008, it's a lot easier. One useful feature is whenever a block of XAML gets out of whack, you can highlight the block and press Ctrl+K+F to auto-format.

If you don't like the default auto-format, you can change it yourself. Just select Tools, Options, Text Editor, and then select the XAML branch. You'll see a few subbranches that give you many options for how to format XAML.

DockPanel Layout

If you've been using Windows Forms and have grown accustomed to docking layout, WPF keeps you in your comfort zone with the DockPanel. You can use the DockPanel to position controls onto the top, left, bottom, right, and center of the client area. Here's an example:

```
<DockPanel>
    <Label DockPanel.Dock="Top"
           Background="CornflowerBlue">Top</Label>
    <Label DockPanel.Dock="Bottom"
           Background="Fuchsia">Bottom</Label>
    <Label DockPanel.Dock="Left">Left</Label>
    <Label DockPanel.Dock="Right">Right</Label>
    <Label Background="Chartreuse">Center</Label>
</DockPanel>
```

Each control, except Center, in the DockPanel has its DockPanel.Dock set to the side of the client area it occupies. Controls, such as Center, without DockPanel.Dock will fill in the remaining space. Figure 26.7 shows what this looks like.

Background colors show what space is occupied by each control. This isn't too bad in black and white, but after running this program, you might firmly believe that the author should never pick your application's color scheme. Top and Bottom span the width of the client area because they are the first controls entered. Left and Right occupy remaining space. If Right had been placed in the listing before Bottom, it would have extended downward to the bottom of the client area, and Bottom would have stopped at Right's left border.

26

FIGURE 26.7   **DockPanel** layout.

WPF Controls

Just like Windows Forms, WPF has many controls that help you build an attractive and useful UI. This section describes those controls so that you will know what is available. For all controls, you drag and drop them from the Toolbox and then open the Properties window and modify their settings. Optionally, you can type XAML into the XAML Editor, which has nice IntelliSense support. A later section in this chapter describes in general terms how to define event handlers for controls. The following sections list each of the WPF controls in the order that you'll see them in the Toolbox window.

Border

A `Border` allows you to draw a border around a group of controls. Here's an example:

```
<Border Height="100"
        Margin="33,28,45,0"
        VerticalAlignment="Top"
        BorderThickness="1"
        BorderBrush="BurlyWood">
    <StackPanel>
        <Label>Label1</Label>
        <Label>Label2</Label>
    </StackPanel>
</Border>
```

Some commonalities of all controls are that they have `Height`, `Width`, `Margin`, and other related properties for layout. The `Border` control is the same.

In addition, a control can have only a single other control for its content. You might think that this is limiting, but it isn't because that one control can be any of the layout controls. In the preceding example, the one control is a `StackPanel`. Because layout controls can contain as many child controls as needed, there isn't a problem. Actually, it could be considered helpful that WPF forces you to define a layout control, to hold multiple controls, so that you explicitly choose how your controls appear.

A gotcha with borders is that they don't appear automatically. BorderThickness defaults to 0, and BorderBrush, which defines color, defaults to null. You must explicitly set these two values, as done on the preceding Border example, to ensure your border appears.

Button Control

The Button control is a standard button that you click and provide code in an event handler for. A later section in this chapter on event handling demonstrates how to use a Button control.

CheckBox Control

A CheckBox control will normally take one of two states, checked or unchecked. Here's how to use it:

```
<CheckBox IsChecked="True">CheckBox</CheckBox>
```

The IsChecked property tells whether the CheckBox is checked. You can also set the IsThreeState property to true, which means that you can set the IsChecked property to {x:Null} in addition to true and false.

ComboBox Control

A later section of this chapter on DataBinding shows you how to use the ComboBox control. You use a ComboBox control whenever you need to show a list of items where the user can pick only one; you can save screen real estate with its drop-down functionality.

ContentControl Control

Controls that host content derive from the ContentControl class. It is simply a container for other controls. WPF hosts it in the Toolbox window (in case you would like to use it to group other controls). Here's an example:

```
<ContentControl>
    <StackPanel>
        <Label>Label</Label>
    </StackPanel>
</ContentControl>
```

Here the ContentControl contains a StackPanel that can hold multiple other controls. If you gave the ContentControl a Name, you could access it from other code and perhaps do things such as toggle its visibility between true and false or set styles (discussed later in this chapter) that affect all the controls inside of it.

DockPanel Control

As discussed earlier, the `DockPanel` control helps layout by docking controls to the sides of the window.

DocumentViewer Control

Whenever you need the capability to view a document that was produced in the Microsoft XPS file format, you can use the `DocumentViewer` control. To do this, you must add a `DocumentViewer` control to the window and then add code in the `DocumentViewer`'s `Loaded` event to specify the document to read. Here's an example of the `DocumentViewer` control:

```
<DocumentViewer Name="dvAppDesign" />
```

This was placed in the ControlsWindow.xaml file on my system. Be sure to give the `DocumentViewer` a `Name` so that you can access it from code. Here's how to obtain a document:

```
public ControlsWindow()
{
    InitializeComponent();

    dvAppDesign.Loaded +=
        (sender, args) =>
        {
            dvAppDesign.Document =
                new XpsDocument(
"This is an XPS Document.xps", FileAccess.Read)
                .GetFixedDocumentSequence();
        };
}
```

On my system, this code is the constructor for the `ControlsWindow` window in the ControlsWindow.xaml.cs file. Notice the lambda expression for the `Loaded` event. After instantiating a new `XpsDocument`, it calls `GetFixedDocumentSequence` and assigns the results to the `Document` property on the `DocumentViewer` control.

Remember that the document type must be *.xps. Also, you need to add a project reference to the ReachFramework.dll assembly and add a `using` declaration for `System.Windows.Xps.Packaging` before you can use the `XpsDocument` class.

PRODUCING XPS DOCUMENTS

You can use Microsoft Word 2007 to create an XPS document, but the feature isn't installed by default; you need an add-in. To get the add-in, select the Office button in Microsoft Word, hover over Save As, and select the option for getting the PDF or XPS add-in. After you install that add-in, you will be able to use the Save As option again to perform the conversion.

Ellipse Control

In Windows Forms, you need to get a reference to a graphics object and then draw shapes. Windows Forms also requires you to keep the state of your drawing so that you can repeat it at any time because of minimization/maximization or your window being covered by another and needing to repaint. With WPF, you don't need to do this anymore.

The Ellipse control enables you to draw an ellipse shape on the screen without needing to get a reference to a graphics object. Furthermore, the shape stays there, and you don't need to handle the paint event. In addition, an Ellipse control is an object, and you can give it a Name and then manipulate its properties from code. Here's an example:

```
<Ellipse Height="100"
         Name="ellipse1"
         Stroke="Black"
         Width="200" />
```

That's all there is to it. You can select the Ellipse in the designer, go to the Properties window, and modify it as you like.

Expander Control

With the Expander control, you can combine a number of contained controls that can be hidden or revealed when clicking the Expander. Here's an example of how to use the Expander control:

```
<Expander Header="Special Settings">
    <StackPanel>
        <Button>Click Me</Button>
        <CheckBox>Check Me</CheckBox>
    </StackPanel>
</Expander>
```

Just like other controls that can only hold a single control in their Contents, an Expander requires a layout control to hold multiple child controls. The Header property appears by the Expander chevron in the UI.

Frame Control

You can use a Frame control for hosting HTML content. This content is specified via a URL. The Frame control is a simple control, and if you need more power, consider using the Windows Forms WebBrowser control. Here's an example of how to use a Frame control:

```
<Frame Source="http://www.csharp-station.com/" />
```

Notice that the URL is specified via the Source property.

Grid Control

The Grid control was demonstrated in the previous section on layout controls. It allows you to lay out controls via a table-like structure.

GridSplitter Control

It's possible to allow the user to modify the size of a column or row in a grid by using a GridSplitter control. You place it in the column or row that is resizable. Here's an example:

```
<Grid>
    <Grid.ColumnDefinitions>
        <ColumnDefinition />
        <ColumnDefinition />
    </Grid.ColumnDefinitions>
    <Grid.RowDefinitions>
        <RowDefinition />
    </Grid.RowDefinitions>
    <Label Grid.Column="0" Grid.Row="0">
        Left Column
    </Label>
    <GridSplitter
        Grid.Column="0" Width="3" />
    <Label Grid.Column="1" Grid.Row="0">
        Left Column
    </Label>
</Grid>
```

Notice that this GridSplitter control specifies the first column and first row. This allows the first column to be resizable. Remember to give the GridSplitter a Width; otherwise, you won't be able to use it.

GroupBox Control

Another container control is the GroupBox control. What's handy about the GroupBox control is that it takes a header and has a border to visually identify its contents. Here's how you can use it:

```
<GroupBox Header="GroupBox"
          Height="100"
          Name="groupBox1"
          Width="200">
    <StackPanel Height="100"
          Name="stackPanel1"
          Width="200">
        <Label>Label</Label>
        <Button>Button</Button>
```

```
        </StackPanel>
    </GroupBox>
```

The Header shows up in at the top of the GroupBox, and its child controls appear inside.

Image Control

The Image control displays images. Here's an example of how to use it:

```
<Image Stretch="Fill"
        Source="file:///C:/Documents and Settings/All Users/Documents/My
Pictures/Sample Pictures/sunset.jpg" />
```

The Source specifies the URL to use, which is a file in this case. The possible Stretch values are None, Fill, Uniform, and UniformToFill. None makes the picture stay its original size, Fill stretches to fit the rectangle dimensions, Uniform keeps aspect ratio, and UniformToFill keeps aspect ratio even when destination aspect ratio stretches.

Label Control

We've been using the Label control throughout this chapter. It displays text.

ListBox Control

A later section of this chapter on DataBinding shows how to use the ListBox control to display a list of items.

ListView Control

The ListView control is described in the DataBinding section later in this chapter. It's similar to a ListBox but makes it easier to create grids and headers.

MediaElement Control

One of the great new features of WPF is the capability to add media, such as movies, to your application. This is accomplished through the MediaElement control. Here's an example that plays a movie from Microsoft's Channel 9 website where Kevin Moore discusses what's new in WPF 3.5:

```
<MediaElement Source="http://channel9.msdn.com/videos/new_in_wpf3point5.wmv" />
```

Just specify the URL for the Source property and it will play in your application. Yes, it's that easy!

Menu Control

Many applications need menus, and you can use a Menu control for this. You typically populate Menu controls with MenuItem and Separator control, but you can put anything into a menu that you want. Here's an example of a Menu control:

```
<Menu>
    <MenuItem Header="_File">
        <MenuItem Header="_Open" />
        <Separator />
        <MenuItem Header="_Exit" />
    </MenuItem>
</Menu>
```

The `Header` property is the text that appears on the `Menu`. Instead of an ampersand, `&`, as used in Windows Forms, for underlining the Alt+shortcut key, you use an underline character.

PasswordBox Control

Instead of using a `TextBox` control for passwords, you should use the `PasswordBox` control, which ensures that keystrokes are covered with a special character. Here's an example of a `PasswordBox` control:

```
<PasswordBox Height="23" Width="200" PasswordChar="-" />
```

The `PasswordChar` is the character that shows up for every key press. The default is a dot, but you can replace it with the character of your choice, as is done here where the password character is now a dash, `-`.

ProgressBar Control

You've seen `ProgressBar` controls plenty of times, giving you status of some long-running operation. The WPF `ProgressBar` control enables you to put the same functionality into your UI. Here's how:

```
<ProgressBar Height="23"
            Name="pbStatus"
            Width="100" />
```

In code, you would reference `pbStatus` and call `SetValue` or set its `Value` property to specify progress. It has `Minimum` and `Maximum` properties to define its bounds, which default to 0 and 100, respectively.

RadioButton Control

For mutually exclusive selection of items, you can use a `RadioButton` control. Here's an example:

```
<RadioButton
    Name="radioButton1"
    GroupName="CustomGroup"
    IsChecked="True">
    Option 1
</RadioButton>
```

```
<RadioButton
    Name="radioButton2"
    GroupName="CustomGroup">
    Option 2
</RadioButton>
```

This example uses the GroupName property to keep the RadioButton controls in the same group, with the value of your own choosing. Also, you can use the IsChecked property to initially select one of the RadioButton controls.

Rectangle Control

Just like the Ellipse control, you can add a Rectangle control to your window. The following code creates a Rectangle control:

```
<Rectangle Height="100"
           Name="rectangle1"
           Stroke="Black"
           Width="200" />
```

You don't need to have a graphics device reference or handle the paint method because WPF takes care of redrawing the Rectangle.

RichTextBox Control

The RichTextBox control enables you to add an editor to your application with extensive formatting capabilities. Here's an example of how to add the RichTextBox to your application:

```
<RichTextBox Name="richTextBox1" />
```

Generally, you'll write code that accesses the RichTextBox control to access its data. You could even take it to the limits by defining a Menu control and implement code in menu item handlers to operate on the RichTextBox control—effectively creating your own version of Windows WordPad.

ScrollBar Control

Scroll bars are often used for page navigation or setting a value. You can add a scroll bar to your application with the following Scroll Bar control code:

```
<ScrollBar Height="100"
           Name="scrollBar1"
           Width="18" />
```

This adds a vertical scroll bar to your application. Via code, you can interact with the scroll bar and hook up to its events to know when it is moved.

ScrollViewer Control

Instead of manually working with ScrollBar controls for page navigation, the ScrollViewer might be an easier choice. You can add a ScrollViewer to your window and then add content that exceeds the size of the ScrollViewer for navigation. Here's an example:

```xml
<ScrollViewer>
    <StackPanel>
        <DocumentViewer Name="dvAppDesign" />
        <Border Height="100"
            Margin="33,28,45,0"
            VerticalAlignment="Top"
            BorderThickness="1"
            BorderBrush="BurlyWood">
            <StackPanel>
                <Label>Label1</Label>
                <Label>Label2</Label>
            </StackPanel>
        </Border>
        <Button Height="23" Name="button1"
            Width="75">
            Button
        </Button>
...

        <RichTextBox Name="richTextBox1" />
        <ScrollBar Height="100"
                Name="scrollBar1"
                Width="18" />

    </StackPanel>
</ScrollViewer>
```

This ScrollViewer control contains all the examples from this section, which are much longer than the containing window.

Separator Control

Sometimes you need to separate groups of controls in a window and don't need the containment of a GroupBox control. The Separator control enables you to do this with a line between controls. Here's an example:

```xml
<Rectangle Height="100"
        Name="rectangle1"
        Stroke="Black" Width="200" />
<Separator Height="5"
        Name="separator1"
```

```
           Height="5" Width="120" />
<RichTextBox Name="richTextBox1" />
```

This `Separator` puts a line between the `Rectangle` and `RichTextBox` controls. You've
already seen this control being used to separate `Menu` and `Toolbar` items, too.

Slider Control

A nice way to adjust linear settings is via a `Slider` control. Here's an example of how to
use one:

```
<Slider Height="21" Name="slider1" Width="100" />
```

You can specify the `Minimum` and `Maximum` properties to define its range, and there are
various settings for ticks.

StackPanel Control

You've already seen the `StackPanel` control being used in the previous section of this
chapter on layout controls. It's also been used several times in this section to show how to
add multiple child controls to another control's content.

StatusBar Control

Many applications have a status bar at the bottom of the window to provide feedback to
users. You can accomplish the same thing with the `StatusBar` control, as follows:

```
<StatusBar Height="23" Name="statusBar1" />
```

Just like other controls, you can add any other controls to the `StatusBar`.

Tab Control

To separate items into tabs, you can use the `Tab` control. Here's an example:

```
<TabControl Height="100"
            Name="tabControl1"
            Width="200">
    <TabItem Header="Tab 1">
        <Label>Tab 1 Content</Label>
    </TabItem>
    <TabItem Header="Tab 2">
        <Label>Tab 2 Content</Label>
    </TabItem>
</TabControl>
```

The `TabItem` defines content for each tab, and the text on the tab is specified with the
`Header` property. This example uses a single `Label` control as content, but you would
normally use a layout control, such as `StackPanel`, to add multiple controls as tab
content.

TextBlock Control

Optimized for small amounts of data, TextBlock enables you to display formatted text. It can have formatting elements to customize text appearance. Here's an example:

```
<TextBlock>
    <Italic>This</Italic> is <Bold>formatted</Bold> <Underline>text</Underline>.
</TextBlock>
```

The preceding example sprinkles the text with italic, bold, and underlined content. You can use several other elements, such as Hyperlink and LineBreak, for further customization.

TextBox Control

The TextBox control enables you to enter text and capture it programmatically. Here's an example:

```
<TextBox Height="23" Name="textBox1" Width="120" />
```

TextBox controls have a Text property that you can use in code to access their text.

ToolBar Control

You can add ToolBar controls to your applications to expose options that are convenient for users to access. The following example shows a ToolBar control with three buttons:

```
<ToolBar Width="150">
    <Button>Option 1</Button>
    <Button>Option 2</Button>
    <Button>Option 3</Button>
</ToolBar>
```

Although this ToolBar control contains only Button controls, you can add any control type you want, including Menu controls. Notice that I set the width to 150. This causes the buttons to overflow, and any overflowed controls will be accessible via a drop-down list at the end of the toolbar.

ToolBarPanel Control

To explicitly specify which items overflow, you can use a ToolBarPanel. Here's an example:

```
<ToolBar Height="26" Name="toolBar1">
    <ToolBarPanel ToolBar.OverflowMode="Always">
        <Button>Button 1</Button>
        <TextBox Width="50"></TextBox>
    </ToolBarPanel>
    <Button>Button 2</Button>
</ToolBar>
```

Notice that ToolBar.OverflowMode on the ToolBarPanel is set to Always, indicating that its contents will always appear in the overflow menu at the end of the toolbar. Other OverFlowMode options are Always and Never.

ToolBarTray Control

Some ToolBar controls can undock and move around the screen, which is what the ToolBarTray allows you to do. Here's an example:

```
<ToolBarTray>
    <ToolBar>
        <ComboBox>
            <Label>Item 1</Label>
            <Label>Item 2</Label>
            <Label>Item 3</Label>
        </ComboBox>
    </ToolBar>
    <ToolBar>
        <Button>Button 1</Button>
    </ToolBar>
</ToolBarTray>
```

This ToolBarTray has two ToolBar controls. Now, you can rearrange the toolbars. To prevent movement of toolbars, you can set the IsLocked property to true.

TreeView Control

You can use a TreeView control to display a hierarchical list of items. Here's how you can build the TreeView control with a root and multiple branches:

```
<TreeView Height="200" Name="treeView1" Width="120">
    <TreeViewItem Header="Root">
        <TreeViewItem Header="Item 1" />
        <TreeViewItem Header="Item 2" />
    </TreeViewItem>
</TreeView>
```

The content of the TreeView control is made of a hierarchical list of TreeViewItem controls, each with a Header property for the text to display. This example shows only two levels, but you can add as many levels as you need.

UniformGrid Control

A previous section on layout explained how the UniformGrid control allows you to layout controls with the same amount of space.

26

Viewbox Control

The Viewbox control lets you shrink contents so that it is visible in a smaller space. This is useful if you need to provide small thumbnail previews of a document, image, or screen without taking up too much screen real estate. The following example shrinks a label to fit into the space of its containing Viewbox:

```
<Viewbox Height="100" Name="viewbox1" Width="200">
    <StackPanel>
        <Label>This text is wider than the containing control.</Label>
    </StackPanel>
</Viewbox>
```

The Width property of the Viewbox constrains the size of the output. This results in the text being rendered in a smaller font to make it fit in the Viewbox.

WindowsFormsHost Control

Earlier, when discussing the Frame control, I mentioned that the Windows Forms WebBrowser control was more powerful. However, that is a Windows Forms control, and you're working in WPF. Fortunately, there is a way to use the many Windows Forms controls that have been created over the years by using the WindowsFormsHost control. Here's how to use the WindowsFormsHost control to add the Windows Forms WebBrowser control to your application:

```
<Window x:Class="Chapter_26.ControlsWindow"
    xmlns="http://schemas.microsoft.com/winfx/2006/xaml/presentation"
    xmlns:x="http://schemas.microsoft.com/winfx/2006/xaml"
    xmlns:wf="clr-namespace:System.Windows.Forms;assembly=System.Windows.Forms"
    Title="ControlsWindow" Height="300" Width="300">

...

        <my:WindowsFormsHost Height="100"
Name="windowsFormsHost1" Width="200"
xmlns:my="clr-namespace:System.Windows.Forms.Integration;assembly=WindowsFormsInte-
gration">
            <wf:WebBrowser Name="webBrowser"
Url="http://www.informit.com/" />
        </my:WindowsFormsHost>

...

</Window>
```

Before the WindowsFormsHost control will work, the first thing you need to do is add a namespace declaration to the Window, which I did with the wf alias for the clr-namespace

System.Windows.Forms and assembly of System.Windows.Forms.dll. You don't specify the .dll part for the assembly because it is the assembly name, which doesn't include the extension.

When you drag and drop the WindowsFormsHost control onto the designer, it adds the my namespace, which is also required.

The wf:WebBrowser uses the wf namespace to state that this is referenced through the System.Windows.Forms namespace. The Name property provides access via code, just like WPF controls.

The Url property is a property of the WebBrowser control. You can access any of WebBrowser's controls this way. When you run the program, it will display the InformIT website, which is where you can go to get a copy of the source code for this book.

WrapPanel Control

The WrapPanel control was discussed in an earlier section on layout controls. It allows each control to flow one after the other and wrap to the next line when there isn't any more room, much like the default behavior of HTML controls on a web page.

Although it is relatively easy to drag and drop controls onto a Window, you will surely need to add code to manage the logic associated with these controls. The next section discusses event handling and how to hook up code to the many events exposed by WPF controls.

Event Handling

Event handling in WPF works the same way as Windows Forms, but the XAML syntax is new. The following example is in two parts: XAML and code-behind. It detects a ListBox selection and shows the selected item. Here's the XAML first:

```
<ListBox Name="Doctors"
SelectionChanged="Doctors_SelectionChanged">
    <Label>Doolittle</Label>
    <Label>Marcus</Label>
    <Label>Drew</Label>
</ListBox>
```

See the SelectionChanged event on the ListBox? XAML allows you to declaratively hook up event handlers with attribute syntax. On my system, the preceding XAML is in the file named Window1.xaml. Notice also that the Name property is set to Doctors, which is the name of the variable to access this control with.

Whenever an item in the ListBox is selected, the SelectionChanged event invokes the following method:

```
private void Doctors_SelectionChanged(
    object sender, SelectionChangedEventArgs e)
```

```
{
    MessageBox.Show("You selected Dr. " +
        (Doctors.SelectedItem as Label).Content);
}
```

The preceding method resides in the code-behind file at Window1.xaml.cs on my system. The `Doctors` variable corresponds to the `Name` property on the `ListBox` control in the matching XAML file. Because `SelectedItem` is type object, you need to perform a conversion to get to the proper control's contents.

Data Binding

For many user interfaces, you need to display data to lists and other controls. Data binding makes this task easy by automatically updating target controls based on source objects. The following sections explain how data binding works and how you can use it to display data in your applications.

Overview of Data Binding

You need four items to perform data binding: source object, source property, target object, and target property. The source object can be a WPF control or a custom object. You identify a property on the source object that will provide information that binds to a target property in a target object. The target object is typically a UI control. Here's an example that uses data binding to update a `Label` control when the value in a `TextBox` changes:

```
<StackPanel>
    <TextBlock>Please Enter Name:</TextBlock>
    <TextBox x:Name="txtName"></TextBox>
    <TextBlock>You Entered:</TextBlock>
    <Label>
        <Label.Content>
            <Binding ElementName="txtName" Path="Text" />
        </Label.Content>
    </Label>
</StackPanel>
```

As discussed earlier in this chapter, text content is often implied, but in the preceding example, the `Label` needs to explicitly define its content, which is a `Binding` element. `ElementName` defines the source object, and `Path` defines the source property. The `Label` containing the binding is the target object, and the property that the binding is defined for is the target property.

Whenever the `txtName` `TextBox` is modified, WPF automatically updates the `Label`.

This was a simple example of binding, but you also need to bind collections to lists, which is discussed in the next section.

Displaying Lists of Data

A common requirement is to take a collection of data and bind it to an `ItemControl`, which includes `ComboBox` and `ListBox` controls. The following sections explain how to declare a `DataContext`, which defines the data source, and how to bind to various `ItemControls`.

Declaring a DataContext

The `DataContext` defines the object you'll read data from. The two tasks that you need to complete to make this happen are to create a business object to return a collection of objects to bind and then modify XAML markup to expose the collection to controls. Here's the business object definition:

```
using System.Collections.Generic;
using System.Linq;

namespace Chapter_26
{
    public class HospitalManager
    {
        public List<HospitalStaff> GetHospitalStaff()
        {
            return new HospitalDataContext()
                .HospitalStaffs.ToList();
        }
    }
}
```

The `HospitalManager` class is in the `Chapter_26` namespace and contains a single method that returns a `List<HospitalStaff>`. If you need a refresher on how the LINQ to SQL code in the `GetHospitalStaff` method works, you can review Chapter 19, "Accessing Data with LINQ."

The `GetHospitalStaff` method provides the collection that will be bound to controls. To access this method, modify the XAML as follows:

```
<Window x:Class="Chapter_26.Window1"
    xmlns="http://schemas.microsoft.com/winfx/2006/xaml/presentation"
    xmlns:x="http://schemas.microsoft.com/winfx/2006/xaml"
    xmlns:local="clr-namespace:Chapter_26"
    Title="Window1" Height="300" Width="300">
    <Window.Resources>
        <ObjectDataProvider x:Key="hospitalDataSource"
            ObjectType="{x:Type local:HospitalManager}"
            MethodName="GetHospitalStaff">
        </ObjectDataProvider>
    </Window.Resources>
    ...
</Window>
```

26

The first important part of the code above is the local namespace declaration. This demonstrates that you can use clr-namespace to map C# namespaces to XAML namespaces. Now XAML code can access C# types via the local alias.

The Window.Resources element contains various resources you can use in the rest of the XAML. In the current situation, it enables us to define an ObjectDataProvider that the rest of the XAML can access.

The ObjectDataProvider is convenient for using a method in a class to obtain data, which is what this section will be doing. Key is what controls use to identify the ObjectDataProvider as the source object for data binding, ObjectType specifies the type that the ObjectDataSource will instantiate, and MethodName is the method that WPF data binding will call to retrieve data.

Now that we have the DataContext set up, we can use it with controls.

Binding a ComboBox

This section shows you how to use the DataContext, created in the previous section, to bind data to a ComboBox control. ItemControls, such as ComboBox, have properties called ItemSource, which is the target property for data binding. The following code shows you how to bind the DataContext to a ComboBox control:

```
<ComboBox Height="23"
        ItemsSource=
"{Binding Source={StaticResource hospitalDataSource}}"
        DisplayMemberPath="Name">
```

The Binding for ItemSource uses the Key property from the ObjectDataProvider to specify the source object for data binding. Remember that the default implementation of calling ToString on an object is to print out the type name, which means that you must specify DisplayMemberPath to declare the source property for data binding. Name is a property of the HospitalStaff class, which is the type of List<HospitalStaff> returned by the ObjectDataSource method, GetHospitalStaff.

Binding to a ListBox and Using DataTemplate

A single column of bound data isn't adequate for most purposes. You need to display your data in a tabular or other way that makes more sense to the application. Like a ComboBox, the ListBox control binds to ItemSource but is more appropriate for displaying multiple tabular or custom formatted data items at the same time.

You first need to define the DataTemplate and then tell the ListBox control to use it. Here's an example of a DataTemplate:

```
<Window.Resources>
...
    <DataTemplate x:Key="hospitalStaffTemplate">
        <Grid>
```

```
            <Grid.ColumnDefinitions>
                <ColumnDefinition />
                <ColumnDefinition />
            </Grid.ColumnDefinitions>
            <Grid.RowDefinitions>
                <RowDefinition />
            </Grid.RowDefinitions>
            <Label Grid.Row="0"
                Grid.Column="0"
                Content="{Binding Path=Name}" />
            <Label Grid.Row="0"
                Grid.Column="1"
                Content="{Binding Path=Position}" />
        </Grid>
    </DataTemplate>
</Window.Resources>
```

As shown here, you define the template with whatever layout you need to control the appearance of each object bound to the control. This example uses a Grid with two columns.

Next, you need to tell the ListBox control to use the DataTemplate. Here's how:

```
<ListBox ItemsSource=
"{Binding Source={StaticResource hospitalDataSource}}"
        ItemTemplate=
"{Binding Source={StaticResource hospitalStaffTemplate}}"
        HorizontalContentAlignment="Stretch" />
```

The ItemTemplate uses a binding expression to specify that it wants to use the DataTemplate with the Key of hospitalStaffTemplate. The HorizontalContentAlignment ensures controls use all the horizontal width available to them. Figure 26.8 shows what this looks like.

FIGURE 26.8   Using a **DataTemplate** for tabular layout.

Binding to a `ListView`

The `ListView` control is convenient because it's easy to create column headers and put the data in a grid format without a separate `DataTemplate`. Here's how it works:

```
        <ListView  ItemsSource=
"{Binding Source={StaticResource hospitalDataSource}}">
            <ListView.View>
                <GridView>
                    <GridViewColumn
                        Header="Name"
                        DisplayMemberBinding=
                          "{Binding Path=Name}" />
                    <GridViewColumn
                        Header="Position"
                        DisplayMemberBinding=
                          "{Binding Path=Position}" />
                </GridView>
            </ListView.View>
        </ListView>
```

Just like `ListBox`, you have an `ItemSource` to reference the resource that defines where to get the data. The `ListView.View` element defines the headers and bindings via `GridViewColumn` elements.

Using Styles

WPF enables you to set size, color, and fonts for each control, and you can see all that is available via either the Properties window or IntelliSense in XAML. However, adding styles to each individual element can be tedious. Fortunately, WPF allows you to create styles that can apply to multiple controls.

For an individual page, you can set styles in the `Window.Resources` element. Here's an example that sets styles for all `Label` controls on the page:

```
<Window.Resources>
    <Style x:Key="labelStyle"
          TargetType="{x:Type Label}">
        <Setter Property="BorderThickness"
                Value="10" />
        <Setter Property="BorderBrush"
                Value="Black" />
    </Style>
    <ObjectDataProvider x:Key="hospitalDataSource"
        ObjectType="{x:Type local:HospitalManager}"
        MethodName="GetHospitalStaff">
    </ObjectDataProvider>
```

```
        <DataTemplate x:Key="hospitalStaffTemplate">
            <Grid>
                <Grid.ColumnDefinitions>
                    <ColumnDefinition />
                    <ColumnDefinition />
                </Grid.ColumnDefinitions>
                <Grid.RowDefinitions>
                    <RowDefinition />
                </Grid.RowDefinitions>
                <Label Grid.Row="0"
                       Grid.Column="0"
                       Content="{Binding Path=Name}"
                       Style="{StaticResource labelStyle}" />
                <Label Grid.Row="0"
                       Grid.Column="1"
                       Content="{Binding Path=Position}"
                       Style="{StaticResource labelStyle}" />
            </Grid>
        </DataTemplate>
    </Window.Resources>
```

The Style element in the Window.Resources element has a Key that controls refer to for having that style. The TargetType identifies the control type to apply styles to. You can have multiple Style elements for any set of styles you need.

The Style contains Setter elements to define the properties being styled. You can select a control in the Visual Designer and then look at the Properties window to see what is available to style.

Inside of the DataTemplate, Label controls have a Style property that identifies the labelStyle Key for the Style. Figure 26.9 shows the new Style element being applied.

FIGURE 26.9   Using styles.

Setting styles in `Window.Resources` affects only UI elements on the current window. Generally, you'll want styles to apply consistently across an entire application, and setting styles on every window could become tedious. The solution is to put the applicationwide styles in App.xaml, like this:

```
<Application.Resources>
    <Style x:Key="labelStyle"
           TargetType="{x:Type Label}">
        <Setter Property="BorderThickness"
                Value="10" />
        <Setter Property="BorderBrush"
                Value="Black" />
    </Style>
</Application.Resources>
```

In a way, WPF styles are like Cascading Style Sheets (CSS) for web applications. With CSS, styles on a control have precedence over page styles, and page styles have precedence over site styles. In the same way, WPF property settings on controls have precedence over `Window.Resources`, and `Window.Resources` has precedence over `Application.Resources`.

Summary

WPF uses XAML to declaratively define UI elements. It offers many layouts to give you a lot of flexibility in positioning controls.

The WPF controls include many of the same UI controls as in Windows Forms. In addition, you have new controls, such as `MediaElement` (which allows you to add video to your page).

You can perform declarative data binding either between controls or from various data sources. This chapter showed how to bind controls to the results of a LINQ query.

PART 6

Designing Web User Interfaces

CHAPTER 27

Building Web Applications with ASP.NET

I think it's fair to say that before 1991, when Tim Berners Lee created the World Wide Web, few people could have predicted the amazing changes in communications technology and the rise and dominance of the web in our daily lives. Sure, there are people around the world who don't even have a computer today, but the web is still a significant influence in the lives of many others who do have access to it.

The web is so important that learning how to program for it is an essential tool for many software developers. Customer demand for web applications continues to grow and multiply the need for web development technology.

Microsoft's answer to the increasing need for web UI development technology is ASP.NET, ASP.NET AJAX, and Silverlight. Today, you can get by with just knowing ASP.NET, but that is changing quickly or has already changed in many places where there is a demand for interactive websites that use AJAX and JavaScript. JavaScript and Silverlight help you build more interactive applications, which Microsoft refers to as rich Internet applications (RIAs). Before we get into RIA technologies, you need to know how to use ASP.NET, which this chapter is about.

The Web Application Model

Previous chapters discussed desktop applications, such as Console, Windows Forms, and WPF. If you're coming from a web development background, the workings of ASP.NET will be familiar. However, developers who have traditionally written desktop applications will need to make a few adjustments, such as knowing where code is executing, understanding the stateless nature of the web, and working with perceived performance issues.

A High-Level View of an ASP.NET Page Request

When writing for the web, you need to understand where code resides and executes. An ASP.NET application is hosted on a web server, which is where C# executables reside, but it renders HTML to clients via browsers such as Internet Explorer (IE) and Firefox. Figure 27.1 illustrates this.

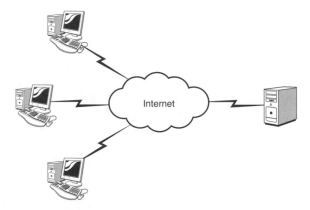

FIGURE 27.1   ASP.NET web model.

As shown in Figure 27.1, on the web you have multiple clients with browsers who make web page requests, often by typing a web address into the browser. The infrastructure of the web translates the request into an address that finds the server where the web page resides. On the server, web server software, such as Internet Information Services (IIS), intercepts the request, recognizes that it is for an ASP.NET web page, and passes the request to ASP.NET for processing. ASP.NET then processes the web page, renders HTML, and returns the rendered HTML (and other JavaScript and objects) to the browser, which understands HTML.

Where Does Your C# Code Reside?

In all of this processing, your assemblies, which were built with C# (or other .NET language), stay on the server. When ASP.NET receives the request, it sends it to your code for processing. The great majority of the time, you don't ever have to emit HTML manually because the object-oriented ASP.NET APIs take care of it for you. The most important point to remember is that your C# code runs on the server, not on the browser.

Where Does Scalability and State Management Come In?

Scalability is a property of software that defines how well it can handle an increased workload. Applications that reach a threshold and then crash or slow to a crawl aren't very scalable. You want a scalable application that performs well at the projected peak capacity for your requirements.

Because a web application exposed to the Internet could have a potentially huge number of requests coming in at any given time, scalability is a concern. Fortunately, web technologies recognize this and have special features for handling it. These special features are what you learn about in this chapter.

For example, in a desktop application, you have only a single user, so it's fine to load hundreds of database records that are unique to you to cache in an in-memory variable to increase performance. However, this same trick in a web application could get you in trouble when there are hundreds of requests for the same web page in a short amount of time. You would be effectively multiplying all those unique sets of records for each person visiting the site, which would kill scalability.

As you can see, there is a scalability/performance tradeoff that you need to balance to make your application more responsive, but let's get back to talking about state management.

Because you can't possibly hold everything in memory for a web application as you can for a desktop application, the web application must have a different state management model. Going back to Figure 27.1, whenever ASP.NET receives a request, it instantiates a new Page object. Again, everything is an object even if it is called a Form, Window, or Page. The Page object processes the request, and then ASP.NET lets go of the Page object's reference. If you paid attention in Chapter 1, "Introducing the .NET Platform," and in Chapter 4, "Understanding Reference Types and Value Types," you'll see where this is leading. Because objects that don't have a reference are eligible for garbage collection, that object will eventually be cleaned up. This is good because now you don't have a bunch of objects hanging around, filling up memory and degrading scalability. Your application is more scalable.

Because the object that processes the request goes away after the request, all fields in that object holding information no longer have that information available because the field isn't there if the object isn't there. In fact, if the same user sends another request to the site, ASP.NET instantiates a brand new Page object to service the request.

This discussion highlights one of the important distinctions between desktop applications and web applications: Desktop applications hold their state in variables, but web applications can't. Therefore, web applications must use a different way to manage state. ASP.NET answers this question with special features such as Application and Session state, which are discussed later in this chapter.

How Do I Comprehend Perceived Performance?

Perceived performance is what the user can see. Desktop UIs (typically) react immediately to changes. You click a button, select a menu item, or perform some other action and the UI changes in real time. On the other hand, nearly every time you do anything with a web page, you have to sit and wait on it to process. Technologies such as AJAX and Silverlight, discussed in upcoming chapters, alleviate the frustration, but the delay is the nature of the beast with web applications.

Whereas the perceived performance of a desktop application is quick, it is generally not so with a web application. It doesn't matter how fast your C# code it. Referring to

Figure 27.1, notice that requests and responses travel over the Internet. The further the distance that a request has to travel, the longer it will take to get a response. Your C# code is running on the server. Therefore, the request must come to the server, via HTTP, with request parameters and all. Then the response is via HTTP with text formatted as HTML and increasingly JavaScript and objects that run in the browser, such as ActiveX or Java applets. The increased bandwidth, the number of bytes to transfer, increases the processing time of the request.

Because of slower perceived performance with web applications, you need to design your pages differently. You can't allow your page to post back to the server every time something changes. This would aggravate your customers or slow down company employees who need the application, which increases cost. Technologies such as ASP.NET AJAX and Silverlight, discussed in later chapters, help improve the user experience many times over, and you'll want to begin using them shortly after you have enough ASP.NET skills to move forward.

Why Should I Use ASP.NET

Because you need to make smart decisions on which technology to use, I want to outline some of the problems that you need to work around with web applications. However, ASP.NET is an awesome technology, with several compelling reasons to use it for your applications.

One big benefit is that you can perform a single deployment, and everyone has access. With desktop applications, the overhead of maintenance and installation can be quite expensive, depending on the size of your company.

With ASP.NET, everyone gets updates right away. As soon as you publish your new features, anyone can use them. Of course, you have controls over who sees what, but those controls are quite easy to implement.

You can expose your application to a wider audience. On the web, anyone can find you. You can expose parts of your application for free and offer premium services for a fee.

Web applications are generally cross-platform. It doesn't matter whether someone is using Linux, Apple, or Windows or what browser they have, you can write an application that works for everyone.

Enough gushing about how great ASP.NET is. Let's go write some code, starting with creating a project in VS2008.

Starting an ASP.NET Project with VS2008

Although you can use any text editor for ASP.NET applications, its much easier with VS2008. Just select File, New, Web Site, and select options as shown in Figure 27.2.

The Location drop-down has three values that specify where you want your project files to reside: File System, HTTP, or FTP. I typically use the File System option because it works better with source control in a team environment. If you choose to use HTTP or FTP, your files will reside on the web server, which could be hazardous, from a versioning and concurrent modification perspective, in a team environment unless you are careful. This chapter assumes the file system scenario.

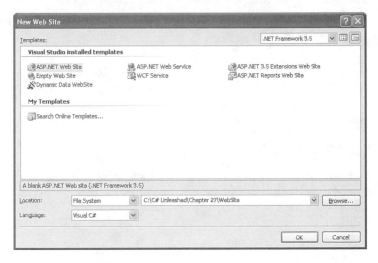

FIGURE 27.2   Creating a new website.

SPECIAL CHARACTERS IN PATHS

If you notice strange behavior in your projects, such as designers not showing controls properly, errors in finding controls, or ASP.NET Configuration returning errors, check the file path for your project. Special characters, such as # and &, tend to confuse VS2008, causing these problems.

After your select File System, modify the file path and click the OK button. You'll see the project files shown in Figure 27.3.

FIGURE 27.3   An ASP.NET website solution.

The website in Figure 27.3 is visible via the C:\...\WebSite\ pathname. App_Data holds local SQL Server Express databases, which we'll create later in this chapter. Default.aspx and Default.aspx.cs are the starting Web form and code-behind files, respectively. This chapter spends an extensive amount of time explaining how to use these to build pages on your site. A web.config file holds a wide array of configuration settings for your application. I explain many parts of what can go into web.config as we go along.

A Lap Around an ASP.NET Page

ASP.NET pages are made up of a web form and an optional code-behind file. To code a page effectively, you need a general understanding of the ASP.NET page life cycle. The following sections show you the essential ingredients and relationships between the ASP.NET web form and code-behind and page life cycle events that you need to know.

What Makes a Web Form?

A web form is HTML that contains markup for page layout, script, and controls. The following code shows the default contents of the Default.aspx web form with a label to demonstrate basic functionality:

```
<%@ Page Language="C#"
    AutoEventWireup="true" CodeFile="Default.aspx.cs"
    Inherits="_Default" Title="Untitled Page" %>

<!DOCTYPE html PUBLIC "-//W3C//DTD XHTML 1.0 Transitional//EN"
"http://www.w3.org/TR/xhtml1/DTD/xhtml1-transitional.dtd">

<html xmlns="http://www.w3.org/1999/xhtml">
<head runat="server">
    <title>Untitled Page</title>
</head>
<body>
    <form id="form1" runat="server">
    <div>
        <asp:Label ID="Label1" runat="server"
                    Text="Label"></asp:Label>
    </div>
    </form>
</body>
</html>
```

The first thing you'll probably notice about the preceding code is the @Page directive at the top. Every web form has an @Page directive. In addition, throughout this chapter, you'll see other types of directives for different types of ASP.NET objects, such as user controls.

The Language attribute specifies the language being used, either C# or VB, and the CodeFile will be a page called a code-behind file, which we'll cover soon in a later section of this chapter. The code-behind file enables you to handle events that occur on the web form.

WHAT IS HTML AND XHTML?

Hypertext Markup Language (HTML) is a standard for communicating content over the web. Extensible HTML (XHTML) is a more recent standard for making HTML more well formed and easier for software to work with. Browsers understand how to interpret HTML and make it viewable in a readable format. You can view the raw HTML for any page through most browsers, which have a View Source option. At its core, HTML is just text where special parts of the text are enclosed or mixed with markup tags, which are special sequences of text. For example, This is bold text will appear as bold text in the browser.

A popular place on the Internet to get a quick start with HTML, XML, and XHTML is http://www.w3schools.com. In addition, you can access the formal standards for HTML and XHTML at http://www.w3c.org.

The rest of the page is laid out with XHTML, with includes special tags for ASP.NET. The DTD for the page defaults to XHTML Transitional, which is one of a set of standards to help people write well-formed content. (See the note "What Is HTML and XHTML?" for more info.)

ASP.NET content renders in a form tag and will work in only one form tag.

What is important to remember when working with ASP.NET tags is that they need the runat="server" attribute, which tells ASP.NET that it must process that tag on the server. A common mistake for people who type in ASP.NET text themselves is to accidentally forget the runat="server", and then their control doesn't render on the client. You see this if you select View Source in your browser and see the raw ASP.NET tag. All ASP.NET content that does have the runat="server" tag will be rendered to HTML, and you won't see the <asp:Xxx> tags in the browser's View Source window.

In the preceding example, you can see an ASP.NET Label control. It has the asp:Label tag name, ID set to Label1, runat set to server, and text that will appear. You could always type your text without using the Label control, but the Label makes it easy to access the content in code because it has an ID, which is the variable name you use to access the Label. Therefore, one of the first things you'll want to do when putting controls on your page is to give them meaningful names to make them easier to use in code.

If you run this page in the browser, by pressing F5, VS2008 will ask you about a file named web.config. You will be told that it doesn't exist and needs to be created to put the application in debugging mode. Answer "Yes" to this because you generally do want a web.config file and will be creating it later anyway.

When the page appears, you'll see the text that was in the Label. Go ahead and select View Source, and you'll notice that the Label control renders to content inside of a span tag.

You've successfully created an ASP.NET page. Now let's make it do something by implementing event handlers in the code-behind file.

27

Code-Behind and the Page Life Cycle

There is much more to an ASP.NET web form than HTML. As you would imagine, you must write code to handle events. However, the web form is more extensive because it has a life cycle, which is referred to as the page life cycle.

Because the web is a stateless environment, ASP.NET must accommodate for that and perform special actions behind the scenes to still allow you to write a meaningful application. Whenever a user selects an option on a page that requires processing, the page does a postback to the server to process that page. The postback needs to read the HTTP request and translate the current state of the page, which was at the browser, to objects when the request reaches the server.

Page Events

ASP.NET gives you many hooks into the processing that occurs, via events, so that you can manage how your application works with the page life cycle. Table 27.1 lists some of the events that you will typically work with on a regular basis.

TABLE 27.1   Typical ASP.NET Page Life Cycle Events

Event	Purpose
Init	Initializes controls on the page
Load	The first time that you can work with page controls
PreRender	Your last opportunity to work with controls before the final page rendering to HTML

In ASP.NET 2.0, Microsoft added several new events that surround the existing events both before and after their processing. For example, there is a `PreInit` event that occurs before `Init`.

Knowing the order of event processing is important because when you make changes during a postback, you want to make sure that the changes you make aren't overwritten or ignored.

Cached and Postback Events

Posting back every time the user changes something on the page would be slow and aggravating, so ASP.NET divides the processing of control events between cached and postback. Cached events occur for items that don't cause an immediate postback—for example, `TextBox` changes or `RadioButton` selections. Controls, such as `Button`, do cause immediate postback because that's the typical behavior that you would expect of them. You can alter the default behavior of controls by changing their `AutoPostBack` properties.

You only have one postback event, which is the control that caused the postback. If the user clicks a button, the button's `Click` event is the postback event.

Cached events always occur before the one postback event. You can have numerous cached events, each representing some action that the user took in the browser. The user could have entered text into a `TextBox` control, selected items in a `ListBox`, and checked a `CheckBox`. When that user clicks a button, or some other action that causes a postback, the browser sends the request to the server for processing. Then, each of the cached events is processed in the order that they appear on the page.

Again, there are many events in a page life cycle, but the following sequence depicts common events so that you can get a general understanding of the order in which they occur:

1. Init
2. Load
3. Cached events
4. Postback events
5. Prerender events

To help you visualize this, Listings 27.1 and 27.2 show a web form and its code-behind, with handlers for multiple page events.

LISTING 27.1   Web Form with Multiple Controls

```
<%@ Page Language="C#"
    AutoEventWireup="true"
    CodeFile="PageEvents.aspx.cs"
    Inherits="PageEvents" %>

<!DOCTYPE html PUBLIC "-//W3C//DTD XHTML 1.0 Transitional//EN"
"http://www.w3.org/TR/xhtml1/DTD/xhtml1-transitional.dtd">

<html xmlns="http://www.w3.org/1999/xhtml">
<head runat="server">
    <title>Untitled Page</title>
</head>
<body>
    <form id="form1" runat="server">
    <div>

        <asp:TextBox ID="TextBox1" runat="server"
            ontextchanged="TextBox1_TextChanged">
        </asp:TextBox>
        <asp:Button ID="Button1" runat="server"
            onclick="Button1_Click" Text="Button" />

    </div>
    </form>
</body>
</html>
```

27

To get the controls onto this page, you can type them into the HTML editor, but it's often easier to drag and drop them from the toolbox. Although drag and drop is quick and efficient for building UIs, IntelliSense in the HTML editor has made typing these in productive, too. Either option beats Notepad for productivity! Listing 27.2 shows the code-behind for the web form in Listing 27.1.

LISTING 27.2   Code-Behind Demonstrating Page Life Cycle

```
using System;

public partial class PageEvents : System.Web.UI.Page
{
    protected void Page_Init(object sender, EventArgs e)
    {
        Response.Write("Page_Init<br />");
    }

    protected void Page_Load(object sender, EventArgs e)
    {
        Response.Write("Page_Load<br />");
    }

    protected void TextBox1_TextChanged(
        object sender, EventArgs e)
    {
        Response.Write(
            "TextBox1_TextChanged to " +
            TextBox1.Text + "<br />");
    }

    protected void Button1_Click(
        object sender, EventArgs e)
    {
        Response.Write("Button1_Click<br />");
    }

    protected void Page_PreRender(
        object sender, EventArgs e)
    {
        Response.Write("Page_PreRender<br />");
    }
}
```

I've listed the event handlers in Listing 27.2 in the order that they will occur. Again, the order of the handlers doesn't affect the order of the events, and you should refer to the previous numbered order of events in this section. When you run this, add text to the `TextBox` and click the button. You'll see the order of events by the order that their `Response.Write` statements execute.

`Response.Write` emits output immediately, as opposed to control output, which renders only during the `Page Render` event.

Controls

ASP.NET controls are typically classified as either server controls or HTML controls. Server controls are ASP.NET controls that either emulate existing HTML tags, such as `TextBox`, or build upon them for a much more sophisticated control, as in the `Calendar` control. However, HTML controls map one-for-one with HTML tags.

Generally, you want to use server controls whenever possible. They are object-oriented, consistent in use, and support events and methods. The HTML controls have attributes and could be processed on the server if you give them an ID and `runat="server"` attributes, but are more limiting. One of the main reasons HTML controls are available is for easier migration from HTML and classic ASP pages. On occasion, some HTML tags don't have server control equivalents, such as a horizontal rule <hr>.

Server Controls

Server controls are graphical user interface items that a user interacts with to run a web application. Although server controls have parallel HTML controls, such as text boxes and buttons, some of the server controls—the ad rotator and calendar, for instance—are much more sophisticated. Table 27.2 lists the ASP.NET server controls.

TABLE 27.2   ASP.NET Server Controls

Name	Description
AdRotator	Displays a sequence of advertisements
Button	Can be clicked for an event
BulletedList	Shows a bullet list of items
Calendar	Displays a monthly calendar
CheckBox	Boolean state check box
CheckBoxList	Multiselection check box group
CompareValidator	Compares the entry against another value
CustomValidator	Used to create custom validators

27

TABLE 27.2   Continued

Name	Description
DetailsView	Shows a single record of data
GridView	Displays database data in multiple columns
DataList	Drop-down list with database data
DropDownList	Single selection drop-down list
FileUpload	Supports uploading files
FormView	Same as DetailsView, but allows templating
HiddenField	Holds data that won't display
HyperLink	Link to other websites
Image	Displays a picture
ImageButton	Button with an image
ImageMap	Lets you create clickable image regions
Label	Static text label
LinkButton	Button that works like a hyperlink
ListBox	Scrollable list of items
ListView	Same as GridView but provides more features
MultiView	Useful for tabbed interfaces
Panel	Contains other controls
RadioButton	Single option button
RadioButtonList	Group of radio buttons
RangeValidator	Ensures entry is between upper and lower bounds
RegularExpressionValidator	Checks entry to see whether it matches a given regular expression
Repeater	Container for each item in a data list
RequiredFieldValidator	Ensures entry exists

TABLE 27.2   Continued

Name	Description
Substitution	Prevents caching its contents
Table	Holds tabular data
TextBox	Free-form text entry
ValidationSummary	Shows a summary of the results of all validations for a page
View	A single tab of a MultiView
Wizard	Lets you build wizards
Xml	Makes it easy to combine XML with XSLT

The controls in Table 27.2 are rendered as their HTML tag equivalents for presentation in a browser.

HTML Controls

HTML controls perform the same functions as their HTML tag equivalents. The primary difference is that HTML controls can be accessed via server code by adding an ID attribute, with an identifier, and a runat="server" attribute. Than you can programmatically access the control via the ID value you provided. Table 27.3 shows the HTML controls.

TABLE 27.3   ASP.NET Server Controls

Name	HTML Equivalent
HtmlAnchor	<a>
HtmlButton	<button>
HtmlForm	<form>
HtmlGenericControl	Tags such as <span>, <div>, <body>, and <font> that don't map to another HTML control
Image	<img>
HtmlInputButton	<input type = button¦submit¦reset>
HtmlInputCheckBox	<input type = checkbox>
HtmlInputFile	<input type = file>
HtmlInputHidden	<input type = hidden>
HtmlInputImage	<input type = image>
HtmlInputRadioButton	<input type = radio>
HtmlInputText	<input type = text¦password>
HtmlSelect	<select>

27

TABLE 27.3   Continued

Name	HTML Equivalent
HtmlTable	`<table>`
HtmlTableCell	`<td>` or `<th>`
HtmlTableRow	`<tr>`
HtmlTextArea	`<textarea>`

HTML controls are specified the same way as their HTML tag equivalents except for an additional attribute.

State Management

As explained earlier, ASP.NET applications must have special features for managing state. To accomplish this, ASP.NET has Application, Cache, Context, Session, and ViewState. Each of these state management techniques operate on type object and have dictionary usage semantics. By handling type object, the state management collections can operate on any type you give them, so watch out for boxing/unboxing penalties, as explained in Chapter 4. The dictionary access means that you need to use these state management collections with key/value pairs. You add items to them with a key and then use that key to pull the item back out.

Global State with Application

On the web, you'll have many people using the same application at the same time. On occasion, there might be a reason to hold information common to all of these application instances. This is where Application state can be used. Here's an example of how to use Application state:

```
Application["SharedKey"] = "Shared Object";
string sharedObject = Application["SharedKey"] as string;
```

This example shows the key/value semantics of using Application state. In practice, you probably won't use Application state a lot because each request to the application runs on a separate thread, which could corrupt the values being held in Application state if they modify the information.

Holding Updatable Information in Cache

ASP.NET Cache state has the same scope as Application state in that all page requests have access to it. The primary difference between Application and Cache state is that what you put in cache can be removed, or evicted, based on memory availability, nonuse, or a specified time. The purpose of Cache is to hold information in memory to avoid the overhead of creating or retrieving that information yourself (for example, keeping a lookup table that is quick to refer to, instead of a costly request across the Internet or other system that is slow). Of course, you'll have to determine whether the effort required to implement cache, memory constraints and resulting performance justify the effort. The following demonstrates a simple use of Cache and then shows you the other features available to you:

```
Cache["TempKey"] = "Cached Object";
string cachedObj = Cache["TempKey"] as string;
```

As you can see, Cache can use dictionary semantics to add and remove items. For the greatest flexibility, you'll want to use one of the many Cache APIs to add and remove items. The following example demonstrates the Add method and several of its options:

```
protected void Page_Load(object sender, EventArgs e)
{
    CacheItemRemovedCallback callback =
        new CacheItemRemovedCallback(
            CacheItemRemovedHandler);

    Cache.Add(
        "TempKey", // key
        "Cached Object", // object to cache
        null, // CacheDependency object
        Cache.NoAbsoluteExpiration, // absolute expiration
        new TimeSpan(0, 0, 60), // sliding expiration
        CacheItemPriority.High, // priority
        callback); // removed callback

    Cache.Remove("TempKey");
}

public void CacheItemRemovedHandler(
    string key, object item, CacheItemRemovedReason reason)
{
}
```

The priority setting enables you to specify how important a particular item is. When ASP.NET begins running out of memory, it could begin evicting items from cache to keep going, and lower-priority items will go first.

There are two options for keeping items in cache: sliding and absolute time. Sliding expiration means that if the cached item isn't accessed for the specified amount of time, it will be evicted. Absolute time will evict an item at the specified time.

Cache dependencies allow the cached item's eviction to be tied to another item, which could be the eviction of another cached item or a file change.

As you may recall from Chapter 12, "Event-Based Programming with Delegates and Events," where I spoke about delegates and explained how the typical usage of delegates is

27

to assign them to events, you won't normally use a delegate variable in your applications. However, now I'm going to show you an example of when you will use a delegate. The `CacheItemCallback` delegate, in the preceding example, enables you to detect when an item is evicted from cache. The callback handler, previously shown, gathers information about why the item was removed from cache and performs whatever actions you need.

Holding State for a Single Request

The other state management features hold on to that state for an extended period of time. Holding too much information in memory affects the scalability of your application, so you'll want to ensure you don't go overboard. One technique that comes in handy on occasion is to hold state in `Context`, which exists only for the life of a single request. Here's an example that uses `Context` state:

```
Context.Items["ContextKey"] = "Context object";
string contextObj = Context.Items["ContextKey"] as string;
```

Notice that we access the `Context` object on the page to save information. Remember that this information will not be available on the next request.

Issuing Cookies

A cookie is information with a max size of 4K that you can ask users to hold in their browsers. Whenever the browser visits your site, it presents all cookies that your site gave to it. Here's an example you could use:

```
// set cookie
HttpCookie responseData = new HttpCookie("CookieKey");
responseData.Value = "some ID";
responseData.Expires = DateTime.Now + new TimeSpan(30, 0, 0, 0);
Response.Cookies.Add(responseData);

// retrieve cookie
HttpCookie requestCookie = Request.Cookies["CookieKey"];
string cookieData = requestCookie.Value;
```

Notice how I set the expiration date, meaning that the cookie is not good after that time. Remember that because the cookie resides on the user's system, you have no control over it—for example, the user could delete cookies. In addition, you must consider the fact that users could have cookies turned off in their browsers, which is a factor you must consider when determining how to implement your application.

Remember to read cookies from `Request` and write cookies to `Response`, as shown previously.

User-Specific Information with `Session` State

A common state feature is `Session`, which holds information for a specific user. When the user visits the page, ASP.NET issues a cookie with a session ID. It then manages `Session` state for that user, based on the user's session ID. Here's an example of how to use `Session` state:

```
Session["SessionKey"] = "per user object";
string userObj = Session["SessionKey"] as string;
```

On the web, there is no way to know exactly when a user leaves a site. You could have login and logout, but there is still no guarantee that you can get a user to click the logout button. Therefore, `Session` state uses a sliding expiration of 20 minutes, as a default.

Understanding Page State in `ViewState`

The mechanism that makes the page life cycle work is heavily supported with `ViewState`. When your page processes, it creates an HTML hidden field called __VIEWSTATE, which you can see via View Source in your browser. This tag holds the serialization of the values of each control on the page. For instance, it could hold the value of a `TextBox` control at the time the page was rendered. When you change the value of controls, these values are sent as form values with the HTTP post to your page. During processing of the page life cycle, ASP.NET compares `ViewState` with form variables to detect events, such as `TextChanged`, that you have subscribed to and raises that event so that your handlers are called during the page life cycle. You can also place items in `ViewState` yourself, like this:

```
ViewState["ViewStateKey"] = "page specic data";
string viewStateObj = ViewState["ViewStateKey"] as string;
```

This makes the state reside in that particular page, which means that it will be available if the page is posted back. All information you add to `ViewState` also affects processing because it increases the size of the information being sent over HTTP. You would use `ViewState` when you care about the information that existed before a single request, it is okay if the user goes to another page and then posts back, and the performance characteristics are acceptable.

Page Reuse with Master Pages and Custom Controls

Most websites need a common interface (for example, a title area, menus, and other information that stays the same from page to page). It's more work than necessary to duplicate this information on each page, especially with ASP.NET, which instead enables you to implement user controls and master pages.

User Controls

A user control is an object that enables you to reuse UI elements. For example, if you have an advertisement, or group of ads, that needs to show up on multiple pages, you can combine the ad content into a user control and then add that user control to whichever pages you want—no duplication of work.

27

To create a new user control, right-click the web project (in Solution Explorer), select Add
New Item, Web User Control, and name it **AdControl.ascx**. Here's what the control
looks like:

```
<%@ Control Language="C#" AutoEventWireup="true"
CodeFile="AdControl.ascx.cs" Inherits="AdControl" %>
```

Two immediate differences between ASP.NET web forms and user controls are the directives and filename extensions. A web form has a @Page directive and a file extension of
*.aspx, but a user control has a @Control directive and a file extension of *.ascx.

Another difference is that all the web forms you've seen have <html />, <head />, and
<body /> tags, but user controls don't have these structural tags. The reason is that the
HTML from a user control is injected as is into the page that contains it.

To see how the user control works, make sure the AdControl.ascx is in design view and
drag and drop two HyperLink controls onto the page and configure their properties, as
shown here:

```
<%@ Control Language="C#"
    AutoEventWireup="true"
    CodeFile="AdControl.ascx.cs"
    Inherits="AdControl" %>
<asp:HyperLink ID="HyperLink1" runat="server"
    NavigateUrl="http://www.informit.com">
    <asp:Image ID="Image1" runat="server"

ImageUrl="http://www.informit.com/display/InformIT/images/header/informit.png" />
</asp:HyperLink>
<br />
<asp:HyperLink ID="HyperLink2" runat="server"
    NavigateUrl="http://www.csharp-station.com">
    <asp:Image ID="Image2" runat="server"
        ImageUrl="http://www.csharp-station.com/Images/cstationlogo.jpg" />
</asp:HyperLink>
```

The preceding code places two HyperLink controls on the page, each with its own image
to create a user control for advertisements. VS2008 lets you drag and drop user controls
from Solution Explorer to the design surface of a web form. The design-time experience
for this isn't so great for file-based websites, so double-check your HTML to ensure it looks
like the following code, which is the WebForm containing the control after it has been
dragged and dropped:

```
<%@ Page Language="C#"
    AutoEventWireup="true"
    CodeFile="Default.aspx.cs"
    Inherits="_Default" %>
<%@ Register
```

```
    Src="~/AdControl.ascx"
    TagName="AdControl"
    TagPrefix="csu" %>

<!DOCTYPE html PUBLIC "-//W3C//DTD XHTML 1.0 Transitional//EN"
"http://www.w3.org/TR/xhtml1/DTD/xhtml1-transitional.dtd">

<html xmlns="http://www.w3.org/1999/xhtml">
<head runat="server">
    <title>Untitled Page</title>
</head>
<body>
    <form id="form1" runat="server">
    <asp:Label ID="Label1" runat="server" Text="Label" />
    <br />
    <csu:AdControl ID="AdControl1" runat="server" />
    </form>
    </body>
</html>
```

This example has another directive, called @Register, which is used to help the page locate the user control. Src is the path to the user control. By the way, the tilde, ~, resolves to the full path of the control for runat="server" controls. The TagPrefix and TagName establish the link between the control in the Src and the control declaration on the page, which is <csu:AdControl ID="AdControl1" runat="server" />.

You could use user controls for a common UI across every page. This would save you from duplicating the UI across every page, but you would still need to add multiple user controls to every page for header, menu, footer, and so on. Fortunately, a more elegant approach exists through the use of master pages, discussed next.

Master Pages

Master pages enable you to build a template for common elements of each page on an entire site. You can have a single master page on a site and then have each web form use that master page for common page items, such as header, footer, and so on.

The first thing I normally do when creating a new website is to delete the Default.aspx that the wizard creates for me, define a master page, and then start creating web forms that use that master page.

To create a master page, right-click the web project, select Add New Item, Master Page, and name it **Hospital.master**. Doing so produces a file with HTML that looks like this:

```
<%@ Master Language="C#"
    AutoEventWireup="true"
    CodeFile="Hospital.master.cs"
    Inherits="Hospital" %>
```

```
<!DOCTYPE html PUBLIC "-//W3C//DTD XHTML 1.0 Transitional//EN"
"http://www.w3.org/TR/xhtml1/DTD/xhtml1-transitional.dtd">

<html xmlns="http://www.w3.org/1999/xhtml">
<head runat="server">
    <title>Untitled Page</title>
    <asp:ContentPlaceHolder id="head" runat="server">
    </asp:ContentPlaceHolder>
</head>
<body>
    <form id="form1" runat="server">
    <div style="border: 1px solid Black">
        <h1>Hospital Management Application</h1>
    </div>
    <div>
        <asp:ContentPlaceHolder
            id="ContentPlaceHolder1" runat="server">

        </asp:ContentPlaceHolder>
    </div>
    <div style="border: 1px solid Black">
        <asp:HyperLink ID="HyperLink1" runat="server">
            Terms of Use
        </asp:HyperLink>
    </div>
    </form>
</body>
</html>
```

The preceding example introduces another directive, @Master, which is for master pages. Properties for @Master are the same as @Page and @Control. This also means that a master page has a code-behind file that you can use for master-page-specific processing.

The ContentPlaceHolder control is where each individual page can add unique content. Notice that the default skeleton code adds two ContentPlaceHolder controls: one for the <head> and another for <body>. I added <div> tags to separate header, content, and footer, but you could use any type of layout you want and place the ContentPlaceHolder wherever you want content to be.

To pull this all together, you need to add a content page, but there's an important step you can't forget. When you right-click the web project, select Add New Item, Web Form, and name it **Doctors.aspx**; don't forget to check the Select Master Page box. When you click the Add button, you see a Select a Master Page window that lets you assign the master page for this content page. After you click the OK button, you see a skeleton web form with nothing in it. The following code adds content to the web form so that you can have a better idea of how to use a content page:

```
<%@ Page Language="C#"
    MasterPageFile="~/Hospital.master"
    AutoEventWireup="true"
    CodeFile="Doctors.aspx.cs"
    Inherits="Doctors"
    Title="Doctors" %>

<asp:Content ID="Content1"
    ContentPlaceHolderID="head" Runat="Server">
    <meta content="hospital info" />
</asp:Content>
<asp:Content ID="Content2"
    ContentPlaceHolderID="ContentPlaceHolder1"
    Runat="Server">
    <hr />
    <asp:BulletedList ID="BulletedList1" runat="server">
        <asp:ListItem Text="Doolittle"></asp:ListItem>
        <asp:ListItem Text="Marcus"></asp:ListItem>
        <asp:ListItem Text="Jekyl"></asp:ListItem>
    </asp:BulletedList>
    <hr />
</asp:Content>
```

First, notice that the @Page directive has a new property called MasterPageFile that identifies this content page's master page. Another important addition to the @Page directive is Title, which is how you can set the title for this page.

Content pages don't have the <html>, <head>, or <body> tags that you saw previously in a web form. Because this content page has a MasterPageFile directive, ASP.NET will render this page with its contents injected into the master page. This is why there are Content controls with ContentPlaceHolderID properties. The ContentPlaceHolderID properties identify the ContentPlaceHolder control in the master page where the Content control's HTML is injected.

If you recall, the ContentPlaceHolder1 was in the <head> of the master page, and the ContentPlaceHolder2 was in the <body>. Figure 27.4 shows how this page renders, with <div> tags for the common master page content at the top and bottom and page content in the middle.

Navigation

So far, you've seen how to use a HyperLink control, but that is a pretty limited version of navigation. What you need is a way to add menus and other sophisticated controls, like breadcrumbs, to make a site more usable. ASP.NET enables you to do this with Menu, TreeView, and SiteMapPath controls. They all work with a common mechanism to lay out a site's logical organization via an XML-formatted web.sitemap file. The following sections show how to set up the various navigation controls, starting with the web.sitemap file.

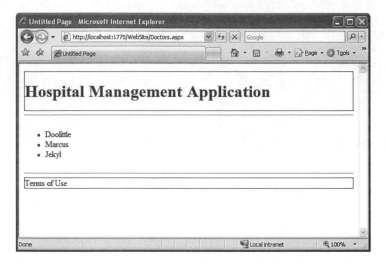

FIGURE 27.4   Using a master page.

Defining Site Layout with Web.sitemap

The web.sitemap file is an XML file that allows you to specify what the logical organization of your site is. To create this file, right-click the web project, select Add New Item, Site Map, don't change the name, and click the Add button. The following example shows a modified web.sitemap file for the Hospital application being built:

```
<siteMap xmlns="http://schemas.microsoft.com/AspNet/SiteMap-File-1.0" >
    <siteMapNode url="~/Default.aspx" title="Home"
                 description="Go Home">
      <siteMapNode url="~/Doctors.aspx" title="Doctors"
                   description="View Doctors">
        <siteMapNode url="~/AddDoctor.aspx" title="Add"
                     description="Add a New Doctor" />
        <siteMapNode url="~/DeleteDoctor.aspx" title ="Delete"
                     description="Remove a Doctor" />
      </siteMapNode>
        <siteMapNode url="~/Patients.aspx" title="Patients"
                     description="View Patients" />
    </siteMapNode>
</siteMap>
```

The content of web.sitemap is a hierarchical list of siteMapNode elements. The url is the page to navigate to when clicked, title appears on the menu, and description is a tooltip that appears when hovering over a menu item. A web.sitemap file is used by multiple navigation controls, including the Menu control.

Navigation with the Menu Control

You can add pop-out menus with the ASP.NET Menu control. You just need to configure its orientation, style, and point it at the web.sitemap file. Start by dragging and dropping a Menu control from the Navigation tab in the toolbox to the designer for the master page, inside the first <div>. After viewing the following configured Menu control, you can see how to build it with step-by-step instructions.

```
<asp:Menu ID="Menu1" runat="server"
    DataSourceID="SiteMapDataSource1"
    Orientation="Horizontal"
    StaticDisplayLevels="2">
</asp:Menu>
<asp:SiteMapDataSource
    ID="SiteMapDataSource1" runat="server" />
```

The following steps describe one of the many configurations you can perform with the Menu control:

1. Set Orientation to Horizontal via the Properties window. As you will see, the default is vertical.

2. Initially, the Menu control displays only the root node with subnodes hierarchically below that. You can flatten out menu by setting its StaticDisplayLevels property, which I usually set to 2.

3. Point the Menu at the web.sitemap. As you may have noticed, web controls have an Action list in the upper-right corner in the Visual Designer. Select the Menu Action list, select New Data Source from the Choose Data Source drop-down, select SiteMap, and then click the OK button. You'll see a SiteMapDataSource control appear on the page. This is a nonvisual control that lets the Menu control know where to get its data.

4. From the Action list, select Auto Format and then select Professional. This gives the Menu a pr-defined style, which you can alter via the Properties window. Later, when I discuss themes, you learn how to skin and style menus and other controls for a consistent look and feel across all controls on a site.

Figure 27.5 shows the Hospital page with the new Menu control. Because it was added to the master page, it will appear on all content pages that use that master page.

The page you see in Figure 27.5 is from a new Default.aspx web form. I deleted the original, created a new one, and added the text "Welcome to the Hospital Application" to the Content control.

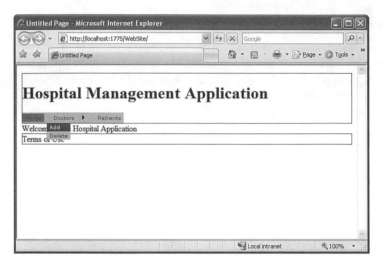

FIGURE 27.5   Implementing a **Menu** control.

Implementing a `TreeView`

`TreeView` implementation is similar to `Menu` implementation in that it can be bound to a web.sitemap file. Because you've already set up a web.sitemap and data source, you only need to drag and drop a `TreeView` control on to the page, select the SiteMapDataSource1 from the Action list and set Auto Format. Here's an example:

```
<%@ Master Language="C#"
    AutoEventWireup="true"
    CodeFile="Hospital.master.cs"
    Inherits="Hospital" %>

<!DOCTYPE html PUBLIC "-//W3C//DTD XHTML 1.0 Transitional//EN"
"http://www.w3.org/TR/xhtml1/DTD/xhtml1-transitional.dtd">

<html xmlns="http://www.w3.org/1999/xhtml">
<head runat="server">
    <title>Untitled Page</title>
    <asp:ContentPlaceHolder id="head" runat="server">
    </asp:ContentPlaceHolder>
</head>
<body>
    <form id="form1" runat="server">
    <div style="border: 1px solid Black">
        <h1>Hospital Management Application</h1>
        <asp:Menu ID="Menu1" runat="server"
            BackColor="#B5C7DE"
```

```
        DataSourceID="SiteMapDataSource1"
        DynamicHorizontalOffset="2"
        Font-Names="Verdana" Font-Size="0.8em"
        ForeColor="#284E98"
        Orientation="Horizontal" StaticDisplayLevels="2"
        StaticSubMenuIndent="10px">
        <StaticSelectedStyle BackColor="#507CD1" />
        <StaticMenuItemStyle HorizontalPadding="5px"
            VerticalPadding="2px" />
        <DynamicHoverStyle BackColor="#284E98"
            ForeColor="White" />
        <DynamicMenuStyle BackColor="#B5C7DE" />
        <DynamicSelectedStyle BackColor="#507CD1" />
        <DynamicMenuItemStyle HorizontalPadding="5px"
            VerticalPadding="2px" />
        <StaticHoverStyle BackColor="#284E98"
            ForeColor="White" />
    </asp:Menu>
    <asp:SiteMapDataSource ID="SiteMapDataSource1"
        runat="server" />
</div>
<div style="width: 150px; float: left;">
    <asp:TreeView ID="TreeView1" runat="server"
        DataSourceID="SiteMapDataSource1"
        ImageSet="Msdn" NodeIndent="10">
        <ParentNodeStyle Font-Bold="False" />
        <HoverNodeStyle BackColor="#CCCCCC"
            BorderColor="#888888" BorderStyle="Solid"
            Font-Underline="True" />
        <SelectedNodeStyle BackColor="White"
            BorderColor="#888888" BorderStyle="Solid"
            BorderWidth="1px" Font-Underline="False"
            HorizontalPadding="3px"
            VerticalPadding="1px" />
        <NodeStyle Font-Names="Verdana" Font-Size="8pt"
            ForeColor="Black"
            HorizontalPadding="5px" NodeSpacing="1px"
            VerticalPadding="2px" />
    </asp:TreeView>
</div>
<div>
    <asp:ContentPlaceHolder
        id="ContentPlaceHolder1" runat="server">

    </asp:ContentPlaceHolder>
</div>
```

27

```
        <div style="border: 1px solid Black; clear: both;">
            <asp:HyperLink ID="HyperLink1" runat="server">
                Terms of Use
            </asp:HyperLink>
        </div>
        </form>
</body>
</html>
```

In the highlighted portion of the preceding code, you can see where I added the TreeView control and how its DataSourceID is set to SiteMapDataSource1, just like the Menu control. The Auto Format I selected was MSDN, which fills out all the styles you see, which you can also change via the Properties window.

Notice that I'm using CSS layout with style attributes. By setting width and floating the TreeView to the left and clearing the footer, I've created master page content that wraps from top to left and around the bottom, leaving page content for the middle-right of the page, which you can see in Figure 27.6.

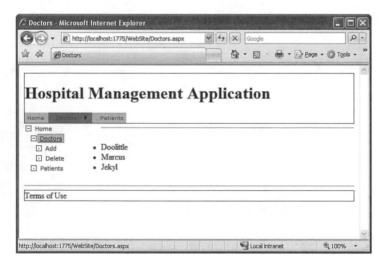

FIGURE 27.6   Implementing a **TreeView** control.

SETTING STYLES

If you're new to CSS, you might want to take a look a the tutorial at http://www.
w3schools.com, which will help you get up to speed. You might also want to get one of
the many books available on the subject.

Until then, you don't need to be a CSS expert to add styles to your page. Just select
the control or <div> that you want to apply styles to, go to the Properties window, and
click the button for the styles property. It pops up a Modify Style dialog box that allows
you to visually build a style.

Adding Breadcrumbs with `SiteMapPath`

A breadcrumb trail is a navigational aid that tells you where you are in a site and provides links to help step back any number of levels toward where you originated. This feature is easy to implement with the `SiteMapPath`. You just drag and drop it on to your page. It will find the web.sitemap file automatically and work. Here's an example:

```
<body>
    <form id="form1" runat="server">
    <asp:SiteMapPath ID="SiteMapPath1" runat="server">
    </asp:SiteMapPath>
    <div style="border: 1px solid Black">
        <h1>Hospital Management Application</h1>
```

The preceding snippet shows that I placed the `SiteMapPath` above the top `<div>` on the master page. This time, I didn't use auto formatting. I also didn't need to specify a `SiteMapDataSource` because it will automatically use web.sitemap, which is another reason why you don't want to rename web.sitemap. Figure 27.7 shows the preceding `SiteMapPath`.

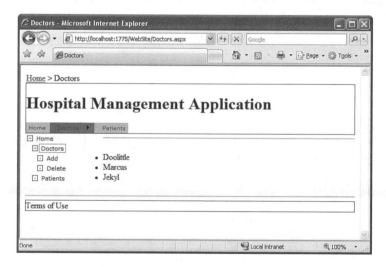

FIGURE 27.7   Implementing a **SiteMapPath** control.

The `SiteMapPath` is in the upper-left corner of Figure 27.7. You can see that I've navigated to the Doctors page, and the `SiteMapPath` shows where we are in the logical hierarchy of the site. You can also click the Home link to go to Default.aspx, as defined in web.sitemap.

Theming a Site

In the preceding section, I teased you with control appearance and styles, promising a better way than putting styles on tags and using Auto Format. The better solution in

ASP.NET is themes. With themes, you can design a set of skins and CSS styles that apply to the entire site.

Setting Up a Theme

To add a theme, right-click the web project, select Add ASP.NET Folder, Theme, and name it **Custom**. You can add multiple themes; they must have different names.

To enable the theme, open web.config (create a web.config if you don't already have one), and add the following <pages> element:

```
<configuration>
        <system.web>
              <pages theme="Custom">
                  </pages>
        </system.web>
```

This code doesn't show a lot of the content—just enough for you to see where the <pages> element is. The applicable content is the theme="Custom", which sets the theme for the entire site.

Within the Custom folder, you can add skins and CSS style sheets, which are discussed in the following sections.

Creating Skins

Skins define the appearance of a control type. For example, if I add a Label skin to a control, it can apply to all labels throughout the site. Alternatively, skins can have a SkinID that controls what the skin type can target directly. The following steps, using a Label control, enable you to quickly create your own skins:

1. Add a Label control to a page and italicize its font and give it a 2-pixel-wide green border, as follows:

   ```
   <asp:Label ID="Label1" runat="server" Text="Label"
       BorderColor="Green"
          BorderWidth="2" Font-Italic="True"></asp:Label>
   ```

2. Right-click the Custom theme folder, select Add New Item, Skin File, name the file **Custom.skin**, and click the Add button.

3. Open Custom.Skin, copy the Label control from step 1, paste the Label control into the Custom.skin file, and delete the ID attribute from the Label in Custom.skin. Custom.skin should look like this:

   ```
   <%—
   Default skin template. The following skins
   are provided as examples only.

   1.Named control skin. The SkinId should be
     uniquely defined because
   ```

```
   duplicate SkinId's per control type are
   not allowed in the same theme.

<asp:GridView runat="server"
   SkinId="gridviewSkin" BackColor="White" >
   <AlternatingRowStyle BackColor="Blue" />
</asp:GridView>
2. Default skin. The SkinId is not defined.
   Only one default
   control skin per control type is allowed
   in the same theme.

<asp:Image runat="server"
    ImageUrl="~/images/image1.jpg" />
—%>
<asp:Label runat="server" Text="Label"
BorderColor="Green" BorderWidth="2"

   Font-Italic="True"></asp:Label>
```

I've included the instructions that you'll see in the skin file, which is descriptive of the type of content you can add.

4. Delete the Label control on the original page and add a brand new one in its place. This time, don't change any of the styles.

5. Run the site, navigate to the page you created and observe that the label has the style defined in the skin. Every Label control you add to the site will have the style defined by the Label skin added to Custom.skin.

6. To implement multiple skins for the same control type, open Custom.skin, copy the Label skin, and paste a copy of it right below the first. Add a SkinID="Green" attribute to the first Label and add a SkinID="Red" attribute to the second (new) Label. Change the BorderColor of the second Label to BorderColor="Red". You now have two custom Label skins.

7. Go back to your skin demo page, select the Label control, select SkinID in the Properties window, and select the Red skin. As you can see, VS2008 reads the Custom.skin file based on the fact that the <pages> element specified the theme and obtains the available skins for this control to populate the list. Here's what the control on your page should look like:

```
<asp:Label SkinID="Red" ID="Label1" runat="server"
Text="Label" BorderColor="Green" BorderWidth="2"

   Font-Italic="True"></asp:Label>
```

Because the SkinID specifies the skin in Custom.skin with a SkinID ="Red", this label will use that skin at runtime.

In addition to skins, you can use CSS style sheets in a theme.

Creating Style Sheets

Skins are easy to use, but you also still have full support for CSS style sheets in your application. Just right-click the Custom theme, select Add New Item, select Style Sheet, name it **Custom.css**, and click the Add button.

This gives you a style sheet and an outline control for easily working with styles. In addition, VS2008 introduced a few more windows that make it easier for you to work with CSS styles on your site: Apply Styles, Manage Styles, and CSS Properties. In the CSS Properties window, you can select an element and alter its CSS properties. Apply Styles lets you attach new style sheets and also modify styles via the window. Manage Styles is for moving styles from inline to different style sheets or changing the order of styles.

Securing a Website

With only a few steps, you can have a website that supports login, roles, registration, and more. To get started, install the ASP.NET databases, which work with either SQL Server or SQL Server Express. VS2008 creates a SQL Express DB for you when you configure the site.

You can configure security through VS2008, via the ASP.NET Configuration tool. The following steps walk you through this process:

1. Select WebSite, ASP.NET Configuration. If you created a website by selecting File, New, Project, ASP.NET Web Application, you'll find ASP.NET Configuration in the Projects menu.

2. Click either the Security link or the Security tab.

3. Click Use the Security Setup Wizard. The wizard, which walks you through seven steps, will open.

4. The first screen is a welcome message. Click Next.

5. ASP.NET enables you to use Windows or ASP.NET security. If you choose From the Internet, a security system is set up via a database for your site, which is ASP.NET security. If you choose From a Local Area Network, you'll be using the same Windows security as the machine hosting the site. If your website is designed to run inside of your company only, Windows security allows you to use preexisting accounts, which decreases administration. However, it is better to use ASP.NET security if your site resides on the Internet and you don't know who will be logging in to your site (and if you may have visitors from non-Windows environments). For our purposes, select From the Internet (so that you can see how to set up ASP.NET security) and then click the Next button.

6. Click Next (because we will be using the built-in SQL Express database). To set up a custom database, run aspnet_regsql.exe, which creates the appropriate tables for you in a SQL Server database. Then you can follow the instructions to configure your provider. Click Next to define roles.

7. Check the Enable Roles for This Web Site check box. ASP.NET will issue a cookie to each user with his or her roles. Click Next.

8. Most sites need an administrator. So, type **Administrator** in New Role Name and click Add Role. You can add as many roles as you want. In ASP.NET, the role system is flat, so you can't assign one role under another. Click Next.

9. You also need to create a user, so fill in the Create User window and click the Create User button. Click Next.

10. Normally, you'll want to force people to log in to your site. Therefore, you should choose Anonymous Users and Deny. You can apply multiple rules, and ASP.NET will read the rules one at a time, stopping on first match. Therefore, order counts. Click Next and then click Finish, which brings you back to the main Security tab.

11. One final task you need to perform is to associate the user you created with the Administrator role. Click Manage users, click Edit Roles for the User, and check the Administrator box.

12. Close the ASP.NET Configuration window. You now have security set up and ready to use.

Now that you've set up security, you can run your site. Notice the error that states "The resource cannot be found." This error occurs because the URL in the address bar of the browser is looking for a nonexistent login.aspx. The rest of the address displays the page that ASP.NET will forward you to after a successful login.

To fix this problem, close the browser and create a new web form named **Login.aspx**. Then drag and drop a Login control onto Login.aspx.

SETTING A START PAGE

For your convenience, VS2008 will launch the current web form in the browser that you were working on. This can be tricky when testing out your Login control because the Login control will redirect you to the page that you originally requested. (Well, if the page that was brought up was Login.aspx, you will log in, but stay on the same page, which makes you think that you haven't logged in, but you really did.)

To fix this confusion, you can set a start page by right-clicking the page you want (for example, Default.aspx) and selecting Set as Start Page from the context menu.

Run your application and observe that it redirected you to Login.aspx. Enter your credentials. You will be redirected to the page that you set as the start page or whatever page you tried to address in your browser.

Now that security is set up and working, notice that there is a SQL Express database under the App_Data folder with tables that have an aspnet_ prefix. Don't modify these tables; they belong to ASP.NET.

In addition to the Login control, you can use the CreateUserWizard, ChangePassword, and other security controls by just dragging and dropping them onto a web form. They all use the security system set up in the same database.

Data Binding

With ASP.NET, you can perform data binding on a number of controls, including `ListView`, `FormView`, `ListBox`, `DropDownList`, and others. Each of these controls has a `DataSource` property that takes an `IEnumerable` collection to bind to.

Several data-binding scenarios and controls are available with ASP.NET. Some are useful for simple applications, and others are better for professional multilayered application development. Many articles on MSDN and across the Internet describe how hobbyists can bind data directly to UI controls; that often leads to code that is difficult to maintain, so I avoid them here. The following sections show techniques that are useful for professional developers.

Setting Up a Business Object

For a maintainable layered application, you can create business objects and let those business objects take care of implementing business rules associated with working on data. To add a business object to your ASP.NET application, follow these steps:

1. Right-click your project, select Add New Item, Class, name the file **HospitalManager.cs**, and click the Add button.

2. You'll immediately see a Warning dialog box that says you need to add an App_Code folder. I did this on purpose so that you would see this dialog box. Click the Yes button. Class files in ASP.NET need to go into the App_Code folder or a separate Class Library project. It's common to add folders under App_Code to organize your classes.

3. Next, add a LINQ to SQL item to your project and name it **Hospital.dbml**. You can get instructions for this from Chapter 19, "Accessing Data with LINQ." Add the HospitalStaff and Patients tables from the Hospital database that was created in Chapter 19. Because the entities aren't created, and won't show up in IntelliSense, until you save the *.dbml file, remember to save the Hospital.dbml file before moving on.

4. Add the following method to the `HospitalManager` class:

```
public IList<HospitalStaff> GetStaff()
{
    using (var hospCtx = new HospitalDataContext())
    {
        return
            (from staff in hospCtx.HospitalStaffs
             select staff)
            .ToList();
    }
}
```

Based on your review of Chapter 19, this should be familiar, in that it will retrieve all records from the HospitalStaff table. Notice that I called `ToList` in the query. This forces LINQ to SQL to materialize the query and return data immediately, which is essential when passing information out of the method. That's because the `using` statement disposes of the `DataContext`, meaning that the calling code can't use it, which is the proper procedure.

Simple Data Binding

In a previous section, I manually entered items for the `BulletedList` control, but you'll often need to dynamically populate data for `BulletedList`, `ListBox`, and `DropDownList` controls from the database.

To get started, drag and drop a `ListBox` control onto a page and press F7 to go to the code-behind file. Add the following code to the `Page_Load` method:

```
if (!IsPostBack)
{
    ListBox1.DataTextField = "Name";
    ListBox1.DataValueField = "HospitalStaffID";
    ListBox1.DataSource =
        new HospitalManager()
        .GetStaff();
    ListBox1.DataBind();
}
```

Setting the `DataTextField` defines what shows in the `ListBox`, and `DataValueField` allows me to store the `ID` so that I can retrieve it later, for another query by `ID`, when the user selects an item. A common gotcha is to forget to define these and then seeing a list of fully qualified names of the type being bound. This is why I covered the object type in Chapter 4, so you would understand the default behavior of `ToString` is to return the fully qualified name of the type. By now, you can guess that the default behavior of the `ListBox` control is to call `ToString` on each object.

I'm using the `HospitalManager` business object to get data. That's where I would put any business rules associated with the query—not in my code-behind.

Always remember to call `DataBind`. Another common gotcha is to forget to call `DataBind` and, as a result, then not seeing data when the page executes.

I checked `IsPostBack` because the bound data is part of `ViewState` and I don't need to rebind on every postback. You might have situations where the currency of the data being bound must be more up-to-date. In those cases, you might want to leave out the `IsPostBack` check and reload on every postback—it depends on your application.

Data Binding with an `ObjectDataSource`

Instead of adding code to your code-behind file, you can declaratively bind a control to a business object with an `ObjectDataSource` control. This is a useful way to code because you can still use your custom business object, rather than binding data directly to your UI.

Any time you bind data directly to your UI, you make code harder to maintain, because adding business logic, later in the application life cycle, will be cumbersome.

The `ObjectDataSource` control allows you to specify data binding in the UI but enables you to bind to your own business object for a cleaner and more maintainable application. The following steps walk you through the process of using an `ObjectDataSource` control:

1. Drag and drop a `ListView` control onto the design surface of a web form.

2. From the `ListView` Action list, select New Data Source in the Choose Data Source area. After a couple seconds, the Data Source Configuration Wizard will appear.

3. You'll see several data sources, most binding directly to the data source. Select Object, which is the `ObjectDataSource` control, and click the Next button.

4. Select `HospitalManager` and click the Next button. If you recall, `HospitalManager` is the business object we created in the preceding section.

5. Select the `GetStaff` method and click the Finish button. The new `ObjectDataSource` will use this method to select records.

After the `ListView` has been bound to the `ObjectDataSource`, you must define templates for layout and data placement in the form of a `LayoutTemplate` and `ItemTemplate`, respectively. Here's how to do so:

```
<asp:ListView ID="ListView1" runat="server"
    DataSourceID="ObjectDataSource1">
    <LayoutTemplate>
        <table>
            <tr>
                <th>ID</th>
                <th>Name</th>
                <th>Position</th>
            </tr>
            <tr id="itemPlaceholder"
                runat="server" />
        </table>
        <asp:DataPager ID="DataPager1"
            runat="server" PageSize="4">
            <Fields>
                <asp:NumericPagerField />
            </Fields>
        </asp:DataPager>
    </LayoutTemplate>
    <ItemTemplate>
        <tr runat="server">
            <td><asp:Label runat="server">
```

```
                    <%# Eval("HospitalStaffID") %>
                </asp:Label></td>
            <td><asp:Label runat="server">
                    <%# Eval("Name") %>
                </asp:Label></td>
            <td><asp:Label runat="server">
                    <%# Eval("Position") %>
                </asp:Label></td>
        </tr>
    </ItemTemplate>
</asp:ListView>
<asp:ObjectDataSource
    ID="ObjectDataSource1" runat="server"
    SelectMethod="GetStaff"
    TypeName="HospitalManager">
</asp:ObjectDataSource>
```

The LayoutTemplate defines the overall layout of all the data. In this example, I've used a table for a traditional tabular layout. The second <tr>, the placeholder, is required, and it must have ID="itemPlaceholder" and runat="server". The placeholder is where each row of data is rendered, which is defined in ItemTemplate.

Before we look at ItemTemplate, one more important part of LayoutTemplate is the DataPager, which defines how the ListView will page through all the records bound to it. Here, I've set the PageSize to 4 so that you will be able to see paging with a smaller set of data. The NumericPagingField causes the DataPager to show page numbers. There is also a NextPreviousPagerField that shows only next and previous links, and yet another TemplatePagerField for full customizability of paging.

The ItemTemplate defines the data and layout for each record that is placed into the location defined by the placeholder in the LayoutTemplate. You can use any controls that you need, and Label controls are typical. Key to making this work are the binding expressions, <%# Eval("") %>, for each column. These define which properties from the data source are bound against each column.

The ListView is more customizable than you see here. For example, you can use <div> and <span> tags for layout rather than tables. Other customizations are supported through additional templates for alternating rows, inserting, updating, and deleting items.

Summary

ASP.NET has myriad features that enable you to build web applications. In this chapter, after explaining the importance of ASP.NET and what it can do for you, I discussed ASP.NET architecture so that you would have a better idea about how everything fits together.

It is important that you understand the page life cycle so that you know the order in which events fire. In addition, understanding the stateless nature of the web should help you appreciate the need for using state management features, such as `Application`, `Session`, and `Cookie` state.

Many HTML and web server controls are available for your reuse. You can also create custom user controls. For a common look and feel across an application, you can implement master pages. Themes and skins help round out page appearance by giving you a way to efficiently affect the look and feel of individual controls and elements across the entire site. Controls, such as `Menu`, `TreeView`, and `SiteMapPath`, combined with a web.sitemap file enable sophisticated navigation that is hard to get with other controls.

Finally, you have extensive support for data binding, whether it is simple or complex. `ObjectDataSource` controls enable you to bind to your own business objects and still enjoy RAD support when building UIs.

A new feature added to ASP.NET 3.5 is ASP.NET AJAX, which enables you to build more responsive and dynamic UIs than with ASP.NET alone. We continue our discussion of this new and exciting addition in the next chapter.

CHAPTER 28

Adding Interactivity to Your Web Apps with ASP.NET AJAX

Can you count the number of times you've clicked a web page and then sat there, tapping your fingers, waiting for a response? I can't, but I know it's been a lot over the years. Because it's the web, we might not ever get rid of the delay altogether, but new technologies, such as AJAX, are making the user experience much better.

The Microsoft version of AJAX is called ASP.NET AJAX. There are many implementations of AJAX that you can use, and there are techniques for implementing AJAX on your own. This chapter focuses on Microsoft's implementation, which I refer to as just AJAX for simplicity. AJAX comes with several controls and a client library to help you build more interactive sites. The AJAX client library is written in JScript (Microsoft's version of JavaScript), which is cross-platform-compatible. This chapter shows you how to use the ASP.NET AJAX controls that ship with VS2008. Because this is a book about the C# programming language, discussing the JavaScript programming language or JavaScript libraries is out of scope. That said, there's a lot you can do with ASP.NET AJAX controls and VS2008.

What Is AJAX?

AJAX is an acronym for Asynchronous JavaScript and XML. JavaScript is a scripting language that is supported by all of the major browsers. With AJAX, an application running in the browser can use JavaScript to send an XML message to the server, the server works on the request and sends an XML response back to the browser client, and the browser uses JavaScrip to process the response. All of this happens asynchronously, meaning that while the page is loaded in the browser, requests are sent and responses are received while the user works on the page. Figure 28.1 illustrates this process.

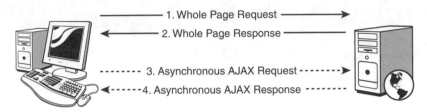

1. Whole Page Request
2. Whole Page Response
3. Asynchronous AJAX Request
4. Asynchronous AJAX Response

FIGURE 28.1   How AJAX works.

The arrows between the client computer and Web server in Figure 28.1 demonstrate communication. The top two arrows, step 1 and 2, show how a normal request for a Web page occurs–the browser makes a request and then the entire page returns. Steps 1 and 2 demonstrate how a typical Web page request works.

AJAX adds to the user experience through asynchronous calls, shown by the dotted arrows, step 3 and 4, in Figure 28.1. While the whole page is loaded into the browser, an asynchronous request, step 3, occurs and then the response, step 4, returns asynchronously.

There's a lot of work that occurs behind the scenes to make the request and response occur in a way that the user experience is satisfying. Additionally, this work is complicated by the fact that different browsers have different objects for making these asynchnonous calls. Most AJAX libraries build an abstraction layer on top of this complexity, so you can just use AJAX without all of the work.

ASP.NET AJAX, which this chapter is about, also has a client library that makes it easy to write AJAX code and frees you from needing to learn the underlying details of browser object models. In addition to client libraries, ASP.NET AJAX ships with controls that help you add asynchronous behavior to your applications. You'll continue the ASP.NET AJAX journey in the next section, where you learn how to set up an ASP.NET AJAX site with VS2008.

Setting Up an ASP.NET AJAX Site

An AJAX site in VS2008 is the same as a normal ASP.NET site, with AJAX controls on it. Select File, New, Project, ASP.NET Web Application, give it a name, and then click the OK button.

Before you can use any of the AJAX controls, you must have a ScriptManager control on the page. There can be only one ScriptManager on the page. Normally, you'll be adding AJAX controls to multiple pages, so it makes sense to add the ScriptManager to a master page, where it will be available to all content pages. Therefore, one of the first tasks you perform when creating a website is to add the `ScriptManager` to your master page. Here's the HTML for the basic `ScriptManager`:

```
<%@ Master Language="C#"
    AutoEventWireup="true"
    CodeBehind="Hospital.master.cs"
    Inherits="Chapter_28.Hospital" %>

<!DOCTYPE html PUBLIC "-//W3C//DTD XHTML 1.0 Transitional//EN"
"http://www.w3.org/TR/xhtml1/DTD/xhtml1-transitional.dtd">

<html xmlns="http://www.w3.org/1999/xhtml" >
<head runat="server">
    <title>Untitled Page</title>
    <asp:ContentPlaceHolder ID="head" runat="server">
    </asp:ContentPlaceHolder>
</head>
<body>
    <form id="form1" runat="server">
    <div>
        <asp:ScriptManager
            ID="ScriptManager1" runat="server">
        </asp:ScriptManager>
        <asp:ContentPlaceHolder
            ID="ContentPlaceHolder1" runat="server">
        </asp:ContentPlaceHolder>
    </div>
    </form>
</body>
</html>
```

By placing the `ScriptManager` on the master page, as shown here, you enable all of the other controls to work. The purpose of the `ScriptManager` is to manage loading the client library, loading JavaScript in your libraries, facilitating web service calls, and managing the AJAX page life cycle. Let's look at the AJAX page life cycle first.

The AJAX Page Life Cycle

Just as you have a life cycle for page events on the server, AJAX has a life cycle for page events on the client. Table 28.1 identifies the primary AJAX page events.

28

TABLE 28.1   AJAX Page Events

Event	Purpose
pageLoad	Called after page is loaded from the Web server
pageUnload	Called when page redirects, posts back, or makes an asynchronous call to the server

These events in Table 28.1 execute on the client side only, and you use JavaScript to access them. Here's an example of how to use both events:

```
<%@ Page Language="C#"
    MasterPageFile="~/Hospital.Master"
    AutoEventWireup="true"
    CodeBehind="Default.aspx.cs"
    Inherits="Chapter_28.Default"
    Title="Untitled Page" %>
<asp:Content ID="Content1"
    ContentPlaceHolderID="head" runat="server">
    <script type="text/javascript">
        function pageLoad(sender, args)
        {
            alert("Page Loaded.");
        }
        function pageUnload(sender, args)
        {
            alert("Page Unload.");
        }
    </script>
</asp:Content>
<asp:Content ID="Content2"
    ContentPlaceHolderID="ContentPlaceHolder1"
    runat="server">
</asp:Content>
```

This is a content page where the JavaScript is added to the ContentPlaceHolder that goes into the <head> of the master page. In JavaScript, objects are functions, and methods are functions, and everything is case-sensitive. ASP.NET AJAX automatically recognizes the pageLoad and pageUnload functions and hooks them up as handlers to their respective events.

The alert function shows a message box with the string parameter shown as its text. When you first run this page, the pageLoad method invokes its alert. If you refresh the page in the browser or close the browser window, you see the alert from the pageUnload event.

COPYING EXAMPLES

If you're coding while following along, remember the structure of an ASP.NET page. For example, the HTML in this example has a @Page directive with a Codebehind attribute set to Default.aspx.cs and an Inherits attribute for Chapter_28.Default. If you create an ASP.NET WebForm named WebForm1.aspx, it will have a code-behind file named WebForm1.aspx.cs and an Inherits attribute set to WebForm1. If you then copy-and-paste all of the HTML in the example into WebForm1.aspx, your code will probably break, especially if you don't have Default.aspx.cs or a type named Chapter_28.Default in your project. This is the way ASP.NET works. If you copy only the code that pertains to the current discussion, you shouldn't encounter any problems getting it to run.

Loading Custom Script Libraries

You could write all the JavaScript you want inside of <script> tags on a page, as shown in the preceding section, but that wouldn't be conducive to reuse. To load your script, you can use the ScriptManager to specify where your script is.

First, create a file to hold your JavaScript by right-clicking the web project, select Add New Item, JScript File, name the file **HelloDemo.js**, and click the OK button. Add the following script to the file and save it:

```
// JScript File


function sayHello()
{
    return "The Doctor is In!";
}
```

Next, set up the ScriptManager to use that file and then call the sayHello function. Put the ScriptManager control in the Master Page so that it will be available to all content pages. Here's an example:

```
<asp:ScriptManager ID="ScriptManager1" runat="server">
    <Scripts>
        <asp:ScriptReference Path="~/HelloDemo.js" />
    </Scripts>
</asp:ScriptManager>
```

The preceding code defines where the HelloDemo.js library can be found and where the ScriptManager will load and cache the script for greater performance. Here's the code that calls sayHello. (You might want to comment-out the previous pageLoad if you're coding while following along.)

```
function pageLoad(sender, args)
{
    //alert("Page Loaded.");
    alert(sayHello());
}
```

This code was in the Default.aspx page, inside of <script> tags like the earlier version. The alert function invokes sayHello and displays the string that it returns.

Looking back at placement of the ScriptManager, it was convenient to place it in the master page. However, now we have a problem: Any script that is loaded is now being loaded for every content page that uses that master page. This is inefficient, especially for scripts that aren't used by every page.

There can be only one ScriptManager to a page, so you can't add that control twice to any page to get the specialized behavior. The alternative of taking ScriptManager off the master page and placing it on each individual content page is not as productive as it should be either. Fortunately, there is a solution to this problem: another control, called ScriptManagerProxy.

You can add a ScriptManagerProxy to content pages, and it will communicate with the ScriptManager for you. To solve the problem of needing the sayHello script on only one page, remove the ScriptReference and its containing <scripts> tags from the ScriptManager, add a ScriptManagerProxy to your content page, and add the ScriptReference to the ScriptManagerProxy, like this:

```
<%@ Page Language="C#"
    MasterPageFile="~/Hospital.Master"
    AutoEventWireup="true"
    CodeBehind="Default.aspx.cs"
    Inherits="Chapter_28.Default"
    Title="Untitled Page" %>
<asp:Content ID="Content1"
    ContentPlaceHolderID="head" runat="server">
    <script type="text/javascript">
        function pageLoad(sender, args)
        {
            //alert("Page Loaded.");
            alert(sayHello());
        }
        function pageUnload(sender, args)
        {
            alert("Page Unload.");
        }
    </script>
```

```
</asp:Content>
<asp:Content ID="Content2"
    ContentPlaceHolderID="ContentPlaceHolder1"
    runat="server">
    <asp:ScriptManagerProxy
        ID="ScriptManagerProxy1" runat="server">
        <Scripts>
            <asp:ScriptReference Path="~/HelloDemo.js" />
        </Scripts>
    </asp:ScriptManagerProxy>
</asp:Content>
```

Remember that `ScriptManager` must appear first on the page. That's why the preceding code puts `ScriptManagerProxy` in the content area that will appear after `ScriptManager`, which is the first control on the master page. Had I placed `ScriptManagerProxy` in the `ContentPlaceHolder` that goes into `<head>`, ASP.NET would have given a runtime error.

ASP.NET AJAX Controls

A few AJAX controls ship with VS2008: `Timer`, `UpdatePanel`, and `UpdateProgress`. Like other web controls, you drag and drop them onto a page and configure them via the Properties window.

The difference between AJAX controls and web controls is that the AJAX controls facilitate asynchronous communication with the server, resulting in a more pleasant user experience. In particular, when updating content, the user doesn't experience a flicker associated with a page reload. In addition, the page stays in place, instead of scrolling back to the top after a postback. The following sections show you how to use these controls to produce pleasant user experiences in your own site.

The `UpdatePanel` Control

The `UpdatePanel` enables partial-page updates, which is one of the most compelling reasons to use AJAX. It is responsible for eliminating the page flicker and scrolling back to the top of the page after postback—experience that people have become accustomed to but are still uncomfortable with all the same.

To enable partial-page updates, drag and drop an `UpdatePanel` onto your page and then add web controls that will cause the page to post back. Here's an example:

```
<asp:Content ID="Content2"
    ContentPlaceHolderID="ContentPlaceHolder1"
    runat="server">
    <br />
    ...
    <br />
```

28

```
<asp:UpdatePanel ID="UpdatePanel1" runat="server">
    <ContentTemplate>
        Name:
        <asp:TextBox ID="txtName" runat="server">
        </asp:TextBox>
        <asp:Button ID="btnHello" runat="server"
            Text="Button"
            onclick="btnHello_Click" />
        <br />
        <br />
        <asp:Label ID="lblResponse" runat="server"
            Text=""></asp:Label>
    </ContentTemplate>
</asp:UpdatePanel>
</asp:Content>
```

If you're coding while following along, remember to add the btnHello_Click event handler in the code-behind file, shown here:

```
protected void btnHello_Click(object sender, EventArgs e)
{
    lblResponse.Text = "Hello " + txtName.Text;
    Thread.Sleep(3000);
}
```

The preceding code contains several <br /> tags to push the UpdatePanel down the page, meaning that you need to scroll down the page in the browser to see the TextBox and Button. What this demonstrates is that when you enter your name in the TextBox and click the button, the entire page does not post back. Instead, the UpdatePanel makes an asynchronous call back to the web form, invokes the Click event for the button, and processes the result. Then, the UpdatePanel takes care of updating the page in place. The page doesn't scroll back to the top or flicker.

This worked because the Button control was inside of the UpdatePanel, but you might need to cause the contents of the UpdatePanel to update from an external event. This is where triggers come in handy. Here's an example that causes the a partial-page update via a Button control that is outside of the UpdatePanel:

```
<asp:UpdatePanel
    ID="UpdatePanel1" runat="server">
    <ContentTemplate>
        Name:
        <asp:TextBox ID="txtName"
            runat="server"></asp:TextBox>
        <br />
        <br />
        <asp:Label ID="lblResponse"
```

```
                runat="server" Text=""></asp:Label>
        </ContentTemplate>
        <Triggers>
            <asp:AsyncPostBackTrigger
                ControlID="btnHello" EventName="Click" />
        </Triggers>
</asp:UpdatePanel>
    <asp:Button ID="btnHello" runat="server" Text="Button"
        onclick="btnHello_Click" />
```

Notice the `Triggers` element, outside of the `ContentTemplate`, but inside the `UpdatePanel`. You can have multiple controls outside the `UpdatePanel` that can cause the partial-page update.

The `UpdateProgress` Control

Sometimes a partial-page postback takes longer than normal. Instead of making the user sit there wondering what is happening, it would be better to give the user some type of status. The `UpdateProgress` control helps in this area by letting the user know that progress is being made. The following example shows how to use the `UpdateProgress` control:

```
<asp:UpdatePanel ID="UpdatePanel1" runat="server">
    <ContentTemplate>
        Name:
        <asp:TextBox ID="txtName"
            runat="server"></asp:TextBox>
        <br />
        <br />
        <asp:Label ID="lblResponse" runat="server"
            Text=""></asp:Label>
    </ContentTemplate>
    <Triggers>
        <asp:AsyncPostBackTrigger
            ControlID="btnHello" EventName="Click" />
    </Triggers>
</asp:UpdatePanel>
<asp:Button ID="btnHello" runat="server" Text="Button"
    onclick="btnHello_Click" />
<asp:UpdateProgress ID="UpdateProgress1" runat="server">
    <ProgressTemplate>
        Forumulating Response...
    </ProgressTemplate>
</asp:UpdateProgress>
```

As shown here, you don't put the `UpdateProgress` inside of the `UpdatePanel`. It will know when the partial-page update occurs and display its message. To see this work, call

28

System.Threading.Thread.`Thread.Sleep(3000)` in your event handler to make the page wait a few seconds.

The Timer Control

In the past, you might have seen a stock ticker or small portion of a screen that updates the latest news. Knowing how web pages work with their natural delay, such feats can be amazing. Now, it is easy for you to accomplish the same thing with the `Timer` control.

You can trigger partial-page updates in periodic increments using the `Timer` control. Just set its frequency and add your server logic to process the partial-page update. Here's an example:

```
<asp:UpdatePanel ID="UpdatePanel2" runat="server">
    <ContentTemplate>
        <asp:Label ID="lblTime" runat="server"
            Text="Label"></asp:Label>
        <asp:Timer ID="Timer1" runat="server"
            Interval="3000" OnTick="Timer1_Tick">
        </asp:Timer>
    </ContentTemplate>
</asp:UpdatePanel>
```

Here's the Timer1_Tick event handler:

```
protected void Timer1_Tick(object sender, EventArgs e)
{
    lblTime.Text = DateTime.Now.ToString();
}
```

The preceding code shows the `Timer` inside of an `UpdatePanel`. This prevents the `Timer` from performing a full-page postback. The `Timer1_Tick` event sets `lblTime` with the current `DateTime`, demonstrating the how the page can be updated asynchronously via time intervals.

Accessing Controls via JavaScript

In JavaScript, it's easy to get a reference to an HTML control by using its ID. However, accessing the ID of a managed control (an ASP.NET control with the runat="server" attribute) isn't as intuitive. The following sections explain the easy way to access both HTML and ASP.NET controls. Then you see an example representing showing you the difficulties you'll encounter when trying to access ASP.NET controls with mangled names.

Simple Control ID Access in JavaScript

It's relatively easy to access HTML elements in JavaScript. Much of the time, ASP.NET controls are easy to access, too. This section explores each of these simple cases. To start off, the following examples show how to acces a HTML control in JavaScript. First, here's a script block that you should put in the head section of the page:

```
<head runat="server">
    <script type="text/javascript">
        function pageLoad()
        {
            var label = document.getElementById("htmlLabel");
            var textBox = document.getElementById("htmlText");

            label.innerHTML = textBox.value;
        }
    </script>
</head>
```

The call to getElementById accepts a parameter that is the id of the HTML element and returns a reference to the HTML element. After you have a reference to an HTML element, you can access its properties. In the preceding example, the value property of the textbox is assigned to the innerHTML property of the label. The following code should be placed in the body element of the same page as the preceding JavaScript

```
<body>
    <form id="form1" runat="server">
        <asp:ScriptManager ID="ScriptManager1" runat="server">
        </asp:ScriptManager>
        <span id="htmlLabel">Label</span>
        <input id="htmlText"
                type="text"
                value="This is HTML Text" />
    </form>
</body>
```

This example contains a ScriptManager control, which is how we get the pageLoad to execute, as explained earlier in this chapter. Notice the span and input HTML elements with htmlLabel and htmlText ids, respectively. These are the HTML elements that were passed to getElementById in the previous script.

With ASP.NET AJAX, you can take a shortcut and use $get instead of getElementById, like this:

```
var label2 = $get("htmlLabel");
var textBox2 = $get("htmlText");

label2.innerHTML = textBox2.value = "Accessed via $get";
```

The previous code would go inside of the pageLoad method, seen earlier. This book doesn't teach JavaScript, but you still might be interested in the fact that the ASP.NET AJAX client library also has several other shortcut methods and an entire object library for String and other objects.

Accessing HTML controls is easy and, sometimes accessing ASP.NET controls is just as easy. Here's script that you can put in pageLoad to access an ASP.NET Label and TextBox control:

```
var label3 = $get("aspDotNetLabel");
var textBox3 = $get("aspDotNetTextBox");

label3.innerHTML = textBox3.value;
```

The aspDotNetLabel and aspDotNetTextBox parameters passed to $get are the id values for an ASP.NET Label and ASP.NET TextBox, respectively, on the page. Notice that I use the same innerHTML and value properties for each control as I did the span and input controls earlier. That's because if you run the page and select View Source from your browser (the way to do it is different for each browser), you'll find the following HTML among all the other HTML on the page:

```
<span id="aspDotNetLabel">Label</span>
<input name="aspDotNetTextBox"
       type="text"
       value="This is text"
       id="aspDotNetTextBox" />
```

ASP.NET renders controls to plain HTML. You can use this technique to figure out how to get to an ASP.NET control from JavaScript code and how to find the ID. Of course, one of the reasons I'm taking you through this tour is to lead you to a solution to when you need to access an ASP.NET control when it isn't as easy. Please read on for the rest of the story.

The following HTML shows what these controls look like on the ASP.NET page, which you will program. It goes into the body section of the ASP.NET page:

```
<form id="form1" runat="server">
    <asp:ScriptManager ID="ScriptManager1"
                       runat="server">
    </asp:ScriptManager>

    <asp:Label ID="aspDotNetLabel"
              runat="server"
              Text="Label"></asp:Label>
    <asp:TextBox ID="aspDotNetTextBox"
                runat="server">
        This is text
    </asp:TextBox>
</form>
```

This HTML is from ASP.NET controls that you can drag and drop onto the page. The Label and TextBox control have the ID properties that the javascript used to gain references the Label and TextBox, which rendered to span and input, respectively.

This section showed you the easy way to access control IDs. However, sometimes ASP.NET control IDs are not as easy to work with, as explained in the next section.

Accessing Mangled ASP.NET Control IDs

Sometimes ASP.NET control names are mangled–that is, they render to HTML in a form that is barely readable. For example, consider the following ASP.NET Wizard control with a Finish button:

```
<asp:Wizard ID="Wizard1" runat="server" ActiveStepIndex="1">
    <WizardSteps>
        <asp:WizardStep ID="WizardStep1"
                        runat="server" Title="Step 1">
        </asp:WizardStep>
        <asp:WizardStep ID="WizardStep2"
                        runat="server" Title="Step 2">
            <asp:CheckBox ID="CheckBox1" runat="server"
                Text="I Agree! Now, let me use the Program!!" />
        </asp:WizardStep>
    </WizardSteps>
    <FinishNavigationTemplate>
        <asp:Button ID="FinishPreviousButton"
            runat="server"
            CausesValidation="False"
            CommandName="MovePrevious" Text="Previous" />
        <asp:Button ID="FinishButton"
            runat="server" CommandName="MoveComplete"
            Text="Finish" />
    </FinishNavigationTemplate>
</asp:Wizard>
```

This Wizard control is the same Wizard control that ships with ASP.NET. You can drag and drop it from the Toolbox on to your page and select Convert to FinishNavigation Template in the Action list. I also dropped a CheckBox control onto Step2 that reflects what most people really think about I Agree check boxes. What we're most interested in is the Button control named FinishButton. It is common to encounter a wizard where you must check the I Agree box before moving on. Additionally, the Finish button (or similarly named button) is normally disabled until you check the box. The problem is that the CheckBox and Button controls are nested deep inside of the Wizard control when ASP.NET renders the page to HTML. Here's the portion of the page, you can see with View Source (different on each browser), to witness how the controls inside the Wizard control render. Here's the CheckBox control:

```
<input id="Wizard1_CheckBox1"
       type="checkbox"
       name="Wizard1$CheckBox1" />
```

As you can see, CheckBox1 now has the mangled name Wizard1_CheckBox1. That is
understandable because you can still read it. What's even harder to read is the Finish
button, shown here:

```
<input type="submit"
       name="Wizard1$FinishNavigationTemplateContainerID$FinishButton"
       value="Finish"
       id="Wizard1_FinishNavigationTemplateContainerID_FinishButton" />
```

The Finish button name is now mangled to Wizard1_FinishNavigationTemplateContainerID_
FinishButton. With this knowledge, you might be tempted to write JavaScript that used
the mangled name IDs. For example, you might put the following code in pageLoad to
start off with a disabled Finish button:

```
var finish = $get("Wizard1_FinishNavigationTemplateContainerID_FinishButton");
finish.disabled = true;
```

Notice the mangled FinishButton name as the $get parameter. Then you could modify the
CheckBox like this:

```
                    <asp:CheckBox ID="CheckBox1" runat="server"
                        Text="I Agree! Now, let me use the Program!!"
                        onClick="IAgreeClicked()" />
```

The addition to the CheckBox above was the onClick event, which calls the following
function, which you would put in the head part of the page (doesn't matter where in
head):

```
        function IAgreeClicked()
        {
            var agree = $get("Wizard1_CheckBox1");
            var finish = $get(
"Wizard1_FinishNavigationTemplateContainerID_FinishButton");

            if (agree.checked)
            {
                finish.disabled = false;
            }
            else
            {
                finish.disabled = true;
            }
        }
```

Again, notice that both the CheckBox and Finish button references are accessed via their mangled names. This runs fine, and you can see that the page starts off with a disabled Finish button and changes when you click the CheckBox.

Now, let me throw a wrench in the engine to show you how easily this can break. Rename the Wizard control ID from Wizard1 to CoolWiz and run the page again. What you should notice is that nothing, script-wise, works. That's because your mangled names have changed, which you can see by looking at View Source in your browser. What you see should look like this portion of the HTML source:

```
<input id="CoolWiz_CheckBox1"
       type="checkbox"
       name="CoolWiz$CheckBox1"
       onclick="IAgreeClicked();" />
<input type="submit"
       name="CoolWiz$FinishNavigationTemplateContainerID$FinishButton"
       value="Finish"
       id="CoolWiz_FinishNavigationTemplateContainerID_FinishButton" />
```

I removed all of the other HTML that surrounds the CheckBox and Button, but you can see that the mangled names are different because of the change of the ASP.NET Wizard control name from Wizard1 to CoolWiz. This wasn't so cool because it broke your code, which could have been much more sophisticated. You might say that you have to just watch out for name changes and adjust accordingly, but the problem is worse than that. Anytime, you change the naming of anything in the document object model (DOM) leading to your control, the mangled name will change. Additionally, the mangled name could change if you rearrange controls on the page.

At this point, you might be a little worried about using AJAX and JavaScript and the maintenance nightmares this situation could cause, but I'll soon relieve your fears. Here's a trick you can use to mangle-proof your ASP.NET control access, which uses an ASP.NET binding expression. Instead of the previous JavaScript, you can use this for CheckBox1:

```
var agree = $get("<%= CheckBox1.ClientID %>");
```

Notice the binding expression, <%= CheckBox1.ClientID %>, used as the argument to $get. The syntax <%= %> runs on the server and means to return the results of the expression it contains. The expression, CheckBox1.ClientID, will return the results of the ClientID property, which is the mangled name of the control. You've already seen the mangled name of CheckBox1. This binding expression allows you to move the control, in a way that makes sense, and the code will still work because ClientID will return the new mangled name.

The story is different for the Finish button. CheckBox1 was easy to access because it was in the editable region of the wizard where all controls can be accessed via their ID in the code behind page. However, the Finish button is nested deep within the guts of the Wizard control. You wouldn't know this by looking at the HTML from View Source, which is a simplification of the real code, but setting the Wizard control to Convert to

FinishNavigation Template caused ASP.NET to render the HTML that way. If you try to use the following code, your page won't compile because it can't find the FinishButton button:

```
var finish = $get('<%= FinishButton.ClientID %>');
```

As mentioned earlier, if you can't get to the control from code-behind, you won't be able to bind to it using a binding expression like this. Fortunately, I have a hack you can use to get around this problem.

Because there isn't a FinishButton exposed on the page, I wrote a public FinishButton property in the code behind file. This FinishButton property will find the Finish button inside of the Wizard control and return it, where the binding expression can call that button's ClientID property. Here's the FinishButton property:

```
public Button FinishButton
{
    get
    {
        var finishButton =
            FindNestedControl(
                CoolWiz, "FinishButton") as Button;

        return finishButton;
    }
}
```

The FinishButton property calls a method named FindNestedControl, which returns an object of type Control. FinishButton will then convert the object to type Button so that the page will have a strongly typed object to work with. Next, I'll show you what the FindNestedControl, a custom method that I wrote, does.

To understand how FindNestedControl works, you need to understand a little more about the internal structure of the Wizard control. The ASP.NET Wizard control is a control made up of controls in a hierarchy. Each control has a controls collection. Taking advantage of this fact, I wrote a recursive method named FindNestedControl to travers this hierarchy and find the control I need. Here's the implementation of FindNestedControl:

```
public Control FindNestedControl(
    Control currCtrl,
    string controlName)
{
    var ctrl = currCtrl.FindControl(controlName);

    if (ctrl != null)
    {
        return ctrl;
    }
```

```
    foreach (Control findCtrl in currCtrl.Controls)
    {
        var resultCtrl =
            FindNestedControl(findCtrl, controlName);

        if (resultCtrl != null)
        {
            return resultCtrl;
        }
    }

    return null;
}
```

The first action that occurs in the FindNestedControl algorithm, is to see if the current control has the control being searched for in its child controls. The call to FindControl only looks one level deep, which is why we need the recursive algorithm in the first place. When the algorithm finds the control, the algorithm starts unwinding back up the call stack until the found control is given to the caller. Otherwise, the algorithm will delve deeper into the hierarchy visiting each child control through the foreach loop. Notice that the algorithm checks to see if the Control has been found inside the foreach loop, which prevents unnecessary lookups if the control is found in the current child control iteration.

Although a recursive C# algorithm doesn't support AJAX directly, you can see that it is possible to access any managed control in a reliable way by leaning on server side behavior through properties. This enables the Javascript on your page to access Managed controls and execute reliably on the client side, taking advantage of ASP.NET AJAX to provide a more positive experience to users.

Now that you know how to access Managed Code with Javascript, you can use that JavaScript to do useful things in the browser, like calling Web Services using ASP.NET AJAX. The next section shows you how to use ASP.NET AJAX to call a Web Service.

Calling Web Services with ASP.NET AJAX

You've seen, in earlier sections of this chapter, how to use the AJAX UpdatePanel control for asynchronous calls back to a WebForm. The UpdatePanel is a quick and easy way to add AJAX functionality to a page, but it isn't the only option. You can also use AJAX to make an asynchronous web service call. The following sections will give you reasons why you might want to use AJAX with Web Services and tradeoffs between web services and the UpdatePanel for implementing AJAX.

28

Reasons and Tradeoffs in Using AJAX with Web Services

A couple reasons to use a Web Service instead of an UpdatePanel is speed and availability of information. One reason why you might choose a web service instead of calling back to the web page is speed. When you use an UpdatePanel, a call goes back to the hosting web page and runs through nearly the entire page lifecycle, which you learned about in Chapter 27, "Building Web Applications with ASP.NET." A web service call doesn't have a page lifecycle. It just calls the operation (implemented as a method with .NET Web Services) on the service, the request is processed, and the Web Service returns the results. Because of this, using web services with AJAX is the preferred way to go when performance trumps all other requirements.

Another reason to use a web service is availability of information. Perhaps the information you need is only available via the web service, but not via the hosting page. Of course, the hosting page could make the web service call for you, but that goes back to the performance issue because you would be taking the long way to solve a problem.

The tradeoff in this case is that the UpdatePanel is easier to use. The recipe is easy: Drop an UpdatePanel on the page, add controls, and you have AJAX. Using a web service, you are responsible for processing the results. You have a choice, use a web service and go back years to manual rendering of data on your page or use an UpdatePanel and take advantage of the power of modern object-oriented controls and components, like ListView, Calendar, and more.

Using AJAX with Web Services

Talking about web services right now puts the book a little bit ahead of itself because I haven't taught you how to build them yet. If you would like an introduction before moving forward, you can review Chapter 33, "Writing Traditional ASMX Web Services." To keep the subject on track, I'll just tell you what you need to do and explain the parts that are necessary to get AJAX to work.

There are a few different steps necessary to get AJAX to work with web services: Create the web service, set up the Script Manager so the page can recognize the web service, and then write the JavaScript code that makes the AJAX call to the web service. The following sections shows you how to perform each step.

1. You can either create a new ASP.NET project or use an existing ASP.NET project to get started.

2. When the project is open, add the following Doctor class to the web project:

```
[DataContract]
public class Doctor
{
    [DataMember]
    public string Name { get; set; }

    [DataMember]
    public string Hospital { get; set; }
}
```

3. Remember to use the DataContract attribute on the class and DataMember on properties. Otherwise, it won't serialize and your web service won't be able to return it to the page.

4. Right-click on the project in Solution Explorer, select Add, New Item, select Web in Categories, select Web Service in Templates, name the service DoctorService.asmx, and click the Add button.

Modify DoctorService.asmx.cs as follows:

```
using System.ComponentModel;
using System.IO;
using System.Runtime.Serialization.Json;
using System.Text;
using System.Web.Services;
using System.Xml.Serialization;

namespace Chapter_28
{
    [WebService(Namespace = "http://tempuri.org/")]
    [WebServiceBinding(
        ConformsTo = WsiProfiles.BasicProfile1_1)]
    [ToolboxItem(false)]
    // To allow this Web Service to be called from script,
    // using ASP.NET AJAX, uncomment the following line.
    [System.Web.Script.Services.ScriptService]
    public class DoctorService : System.Web.Services.WebService
    {
        [WebMethod]
        [XmlInclude(typeof(Doctor))]
        public object GetDoctorViaXml()
        {
            var doc = CreateDoctor();
            return doc;
        }

        [WebMethod]
        [XmlInclude(typeof(Doctor))]
        public object GetDoctorViaJson()
        {
            var doc = CreateDoctor();

            var ser =
                new DataContractJsonSerializer(
                    typeof(Doctor));
            var memStr = new MemoryStream();
```

```
        ser.WriteObject(memStr, doc);
        string jsonStr =
            Encoding.Default.GetString(
                memStr.ToArray());

        return jsonStr;
    }

    private Doctor CreateDoctor()
    {
        return
            new Doctor
            {
                Name = "Marcus",
                Hospital = "Mercy"
            };
    }
  }
 }
```

The ScriptService that decorates the DoctorService class in the preceding code is required for making this work. There are two methods: GetDoctorViaXML for returning results in XML and GetDoctorViaJson for returning results in JavaScript Object Notation (JSON). You'll call these web service methods via JavaScript in a Web page.

Another important attribute is XmlInclude, which ensures that metadata for the Doctor type is included in the response.

The call to GetDoctorViaXml is simple because the object is serialized to XML automatically. For the GetDoctorViaJson, you have to do a bit more work. The method uses DataContractJsonSerializer to serialize the Doctor object into JSON format. The call to WriteObject performs the serialization of the second Doctor type argument, doc, to the first MemoryStream argument, memStr. Then the code makes the MemoryStream convert its contents to a byte, so it can be converted into a JSON string and returned.

5. Add a new web form to your project named DoctorInfo.aspx. This is the web page that will call the web service and display results.

6. Add a ScriptManager control to DoctorInfo.aspx, as the first control inside of the form or Content area, and add a Services section in the HTML as follows:

```
<asp:ScriptManager ID="ScriptManager1" runat="server">
   <Services>
       <asp:ServiceReference Path="DoctorService.asmx" />
   </Services>
  </asp:ScriptManager>
```

Notice the Services section and the ServiceReference control. The Path property of the ServiceReference control holds the name of the web service file that you created in step 3.

7. Add the following HTML below ScriptManager on your page:

```
Via XML: <br />
<asp:Label ID="XmlLabel"
            runat="server"
            Text="Label" />
<br /> <br />
Via JSON: <br />
<asp:Label ID="JsonLabel"
            runat="server"
                Text="Label" />
```

These labels will display the web service results.

8. Add the following JavaScript to the head of the page or the top of the Content control contents:

```
<script type="text/javascript">
    function pageLoad()
    {
        Chapter_28.DoctorService
            .GetDoctorViaXml(completedXmlCall);
        Chapter_28.DoctorService
            .GetDoctorViaJson(completedJsonCall);
    }

    function completedXmlCall(result)
    {
        var doctor = eval(result);

        $get("<%= XmlLabel.ClientID %>").innerHTML =
            doctor.Name + ": " + doctor.Hospital;
    }

    function completedJsonCall(result)
    {
        var doctor = eval( "(" + result + ")" );

        $get("<%= JsonLabel.ClientID %>").innerHTML =
            doctor.Name + ": " + doctor.Hospital;
    }
</script>
```

28

Notice the use of the Namespace in the calls to the DoctorService Web Service in pageLoad. This is the exact same namespace as what you see from step 4. If you forget this, you'll receive a web service not defined error in the browser. The web service calls to GetDoctorViaXml and GetDoctorViaJson take parameters that are the callback routines that execute when the web service response returns to the browser.

After doing an eval on the results, each callback method can use the returned object normally, accessing its properties.

That's what you need to do for using web services with AJAX. There were several required details, each potentially breaking the program if forgotten, so you need to pay close attention to the steps.

Summary

ASP.NET AJAX is a UI technology for enhancing the browsing experience of Web Application users. It enables partial-page updates that avoid the discomfort of full-page reloads.

To use AJAX in VS2008, you need to add a ScriptManager to your page and take advantage of the ScriptManagerProxy for content pages when the ScriptManager is in the master page.

ASP.NET AJAX also offers controls that you can use to enhance the user experience. UpdatePanels are the primary mechanism for enabling partial-page updates. You can use UpdateProgress controls to communicate longer-running processes with users. Finally, you can implement polling updates with the Timer control to keep a page fresh with current information.

When working with AJAX, you often use JavaScript that needs to access controls. You learned how working with ASP.NET controls can be tricky because of mangled naming. You also saw some ways to work around control access problems.

You now know how to use web services with AJAX, too. The examples demonstrated how to return data from a web service as XML or as JSON. Additionally, you know reasons why using AJAX with web services would be desirable and some of the tradeoffs between web services and the ASP.NET AJAX UpdatePanel control.

ASP.NET AJAX isn't the only new technology for enhancing the user experience in web applications. The next chapter covers a new technology named Silverlight, which introduces easier multimedia and interactivity than any of the previous technologies discussed so far.

CHAPTER 29

Crafting Rich Web Applications with Silverlight

Meet the new rock star of .NET user interfaces: Silverlight. In previous chapters, you've seen ASP.NET and ASP.NET AJAX. Silverlight kicks the Web experience up several notches to present what is known as a rich Internet application (RIA).

With Silverlight, you can enjoy many of the benefits of desktop applications by having your UI respond in a timely manner. More than that, you have impressive 2D graphics, and multimedia is much easier, allowing you to effortlessly add audio and video to your site. This chapter gets you started with Silverlight so that you can begin building your own RIAs.

What Makes Silverlight Tick?

Silverlight is a combination of different technologies, working harmoniously together to make it easier to build RIAs. Essentially, you can take parts of what you know about Extensible Application Markup Language (XAML), Windows Presentation Foundation (WPF), ASP.NET, JavaScript, and AJAX combined with a lightweight runtime to create incredible browser experiences that were once only the domain of Flash.

Where Do WPF and XAML Come In?

Microsoft first announced the first beta version of Silverlight, which was called Windows Presentation Foundation/Everywhere, or just WPF/E at Mix '07. Essentially, Silverlight is a subset of WPF, which you already learned about in Chapter 26, "Creating Windows

Presentation Foundation (WPF) Applications." You write the XAML the same way, as long as you stay in the subset of features.

In Silverlight 1.0, the only layout you have is canvas; you can use shapes such as circle, ellipse, and rectangle; you can perform animations; you can use the Media control; and the only language available is Javascript. In Silverlight 2.0, you have the full suite of WPF controls, and you can write code in C# (and other managed languages). Because of the subject of this book, it makes the most sense that the material covers Silverlight v2.0, which allows you to code with the C# programming language.

This chapter doesn't repeat any of the information about XAML basics, layout, or controls. If you aren't already familiar with WPF, you might want to go back and review Chapter 26 before continuing. Although WPF is for desktop UIs, Silverlight uses the same technology that's essential for being able to understand the material in this chapter.

How Does Silverlight Relate to ASP.NET, JavaScript, and AJAX?

Silverlight runs on the Web, meaning that it will run as a control on a web form. In Silverlight 1.0, you are restricted to JavaScript as your only language for handling events and manipulating Silverlight objects. Because ASP.NET AJAX runs with JavaScript, you can use methods in the AJAX client library to interact with Silverlight controls at the same time you are implementing AJAX functionality.

This chapter doesn't repeat any of the information about how to build Web Applications with ASP.NET. If you aren't already familiar with ASP.NET, you might want to go back and review Chapter 27, "Building Web Applications with ASP.NET," before continuing. Although Silverlight doesn't require ASP.NET to run, you can run it on an HTML page. This chapter uses ASP.NET in all of its examples, which you might want to understand so that you can see the relationship between Silverlight and ASP.NET.

GETTING SILVERLIGHT

At some point in the future, Microsoft might add Silverlight as a feature of Visual Studio. As of the first release of VS2008, however, you must visit http://www.silverlight.net to download it. Because Silverlight is a growing technology at this time, read the instructions on the Silverlight site to ensure you get the right version. Here, I let you know which versions you are working with. The rest of this chapter assumes that you've downloaded the appropriate Silverlight SDK to get started.

Starting a Silverlight Project in VS2008

In Silverlight 2.0, you have several options when creating a project. This section guides you through the issues you need to know and explains the parts of a Silverlight project.

Creating a Silverlight Project

To create a Silverlight application in VS2008, select File, New, Project, Silverlight Application, and name the solution and project as you prefer. After clicking the OK button, you see the Add Silverlight Application window, as shown in Figure 29.1.

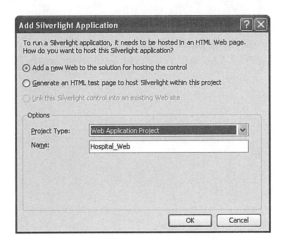

FIGURE 29.1   The Add Silverlight Application window.

If you click Generate an HTML Test Page to Host Silverlight Within This Project, you get an HTML page with skeleton code for running Silverlight. Most of the time, however, you want to use ASP.NET, rather than a plain HTML page.

Clicking Add a New Web to the Solution for Hosting the Control allows you to use ASP.NET. There are two choices: a Web Site or a Web Application. As you can see in Figure 29.1, I've selected the Web Application Project option.

WEB APPLICATION OR WEBSITE?

In Visual Studio 2003 and earlier, ASP.NET developers had only a choice of a Web Application. Problems with this model were being tied to Internet Information Server (IIS) and FrontPage Server Extensions, limited flexibility for Web developers, and a requirement to compile an entire site the first time a page was accessed. In Visual Studio 2005 (VS2005), Microsoft changed this model to website, where the application ran from a Web server inside of the IDE, a project system based on the contents of folders rather than a project, and a single-page assembly. Although the new website model appealed to developers who needed those features, other developers who experienced benefits in the Web Application model were alienated and forced to change the way they worked. So, shortly after the release of VS2005, Microsoft released a plug-in for adding Web Application projects back to the IDE and later made the change more permanent through VS2005 Service Pack 1. VS2008 now supports both web application and website projects, and Silverlight gives you a choice of what type of ASP.NET project you want to build.

29

The contents of both a Web Application and website are the same except for the differences in project types. In the next section, you learn about the files in Silverlight projects.

Understanding the Parts of a Silverlight Project

The Silverlight Wizard created two projects: a Silverlight Web Application and a Silverlight class library. Shown in Figure 29.2, the Silverlight Web Application, Hospital_Web, contains ASP.NET web forms, and the Silverlight class library, Hospital, contains XAML files. This section ties together the relationships between these files and projects to help you learn how a Silverlight application works.

FIGURE 29.2   The Add Silverlight Application window.

Relationship Between Silverlight Application and Silverlight Class Libraries

If you look at the references in Hospital_Web, you won't find a branch for the Hospital class library, which is what you might normally expect for one VS2008 project to reference another. However, there is a good reason for this because Silverlight class libraries reside in a folder named ClientBin, as opposed to where normal class libraries reside in Bin. So, you need a different way to identify references to Silverlight class libraries, which is by creating a Silverlight Link. If you double-click the Properties branch in the Hospital_Web project and then click the Silverlight links, you see the link to the Silverlight class library, as shown in Figure 29.3.

Figure 29.3 shows the Add Silverlight Link window that appears after clicking the Add button. At this point, you don't have to do anything because the default project template already added this link for you. However, if you ever add another library project, you need to know how to add a link to your main application, and this is the way to do it.

The Silverlight Control

The HospitalTestPage.aspx web form contains a Silverlight control that specifies the XAML file to use and its size on the page. Listing 29.1 shows the HTML from HospitalTestPage.aspx.

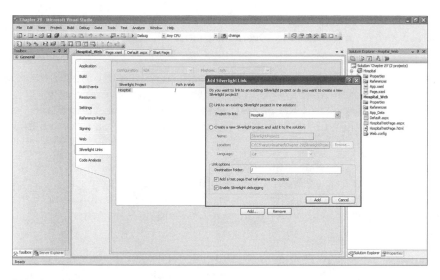

FIGURE 29.3   Adding a Silverlight link to a Silverlight class library.

LISTING 29.1   A Silverlight Control on a Web Form

```
<%@ Page Language="C#" AutoEventWireup="true" %>


<%@ Register Assembly="System.Web.Silverlight" Namespace="System.Web.UI.Sil-
verlightControls"
    TagPrefix="asp" %>

<!DOCTYPE html PUBLIC "-//W3C//DTD XHTML 1.0 Transitional//EN"
"http://www.w3.org/TR/xhtml1/DTD/xhtml1-transitional.dtd">


<html xmlns="http://www.w3.org/1999/xhtml" style="height:100%;">
<head runat="server">
    <title>Test Page For Hospital</title>
</head>
<body style="height:100%;margin:0;">
    <form id="form1" runat="server" style="height:100%;">
        <asp:ScriptManager ID="ScriptManager1" runat="server"></asp:ScriptManager>
        <div  style="height:100%;"> <asp:Silverlight ID="Xaml1" runat="server"
Source="~/ClientBin/Hospital.xap"
Version="2.0" Width="100%" Height="100%" />
        </div>
    </form>
</body>
</html>
```

Listing 29.1 has an @Register directive that maps the System.Web.UI.SilverlightControls namespace to the asp prefix. You can see the Silverlight control itself in a div, inside of the form tags.

The Source property is a little different from what you might have seen in other types of applications, specifying a *.xap file that is located in the ClientBin folder. You won't see the ClientBin folder until after building the project for the first time. Now, you have another folder, in addition to Bin, to pay attention to for deployment because *.xap files reside in ClientBin.

A *.xap file is a compressed Zip file that contains XAML files and other resources. Because Silverlight applications deploy to the Silverlight plug-in that runs in the browser, you want to minimize the amount of network traffic incurred for the page. Compressing the XAML that is sent to the browser helps make your page load and perform better.

Files in the Silverlight Class Library

If you've read Chapter 26 or are already familiar with WPF, the files in the Hospital class library should be familiar. There is an App.xaml and Page.xaml file, which are XAML files that have C# code-behind files. App.xaml specifies that the hospital.xaml in Page.xaml is the start page. The contents of Page.xaml, which is a UserControl, are shown in Listing 29.2.

LISTING 29.2   A Silverlight User Control

```
<UserControl x:Class="Hospital.Page"
    xmlns="http://schemas.microsoft.com/client/2007"
    xmlns:x="http://schemas.microsoft.com/winfx/2006/xaml"
    Width="400" Height="300">
    <Grid x:Name="LayoutRoot" Background="White">

    </Grid>
</UserControl>
```

An immediate difference between Listing 29.2 and a WPF page is that the XAML is a UserControl, rather than a Window. Beyond that, coding is the same. If you add the following TextBlock to the page

```
    <Grid x:Name="LayoutRoot" Background="White">
        <TextBlock Text="Silverlight Control" />
    </Grid>
```

and then run the application, pressing F5, you'll see the web page in Figure 29.4. The Silverlight control is hosted in ASP.NET, so you'll see the familiar message for creating web.config the first time the site runs. Also, notice that ASP.NET creates the ClientBin folder, containing Hospital.xap (or whatever you named your project with the .xap file extension), discussed earlier. If you recall, from the earlier discussion about Silverlight Links, VS2008 copies Silverlight class libraries, *.xap files, to ClientBin, instead of Bin, which is important to know for deployment.

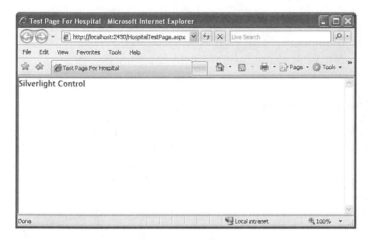

FIGURE 29.4   A simple Silverlight application.

You can see the text, Silverlight Control, in the top left of the browser screen in Figure 29.4.

WHERE DOES SILVERLIGHT RUN?

In Chapter 27, I made an explicit point in explaining how ASP.NET applications run on the server, mostly to help you properly understand how to code a Web Application. That differed from desktop applications that normally run on the machine you are using. Silverlight applications are somewhere in between pure desktop and pure Web Applications from the perspective of where the code runs.

The Silverlight control is hosted on a web server, making it accessible to anyone who can access that web server, which is often across the entire Web. Furthermore, you can host the Silverlight control in ASP.NET web forms, meaning that you can write ASP.NET code that runs on the server on the same web form that hosts your Silverlight control.

Although the Silverlight control is hosted on the Web, it executes in a browser. The customer installs the Silverlight plug-in for one of the many browsers and platforms supported and the Silverlight control, and associated XAML executes on the customer's computer. Overall, this means that you get the responsiveness of a desktop application with the deployment benefits of the Web.

29

Handling Silverlight Events with C#

Silverlight 1.0 introduced the capability to program Silverlight applications with JavaScript, and Silverlight 2.0 adds the capability of programming with managed languages, including, of course, C#.

The model is event-driven, just like WPF, but with a code-behind file, just like ASP.NET. The code is packaged with the *.xap file, allowing it to be loaded and executed in the user's browser. This section builds out a Silverlight control with functionality so that you can see how Silverlight events work, understand the Silverlight object model, and work with Silverlight controls.

Adding a C# Handler for a Silverlight Control Event

Normally, VS2008 allows you to select a control and set its event handlers through the Properties window or to double-click the control to create a default event handler for that control. However, I'm writing this chapter on a beta version of Silverlight 2.0 that requires adding event handlers through XAML. I'm sure you can figure out how to use the visual editor when the product ships for RTM, but the XAML editor is nice, too, delivering the code-focused RAD that Visual C# developers have grown accustomed to over the years.

By selecting the TextBlock control and placing the cursor after the last attribute inside of the TextBlock control, you can type the character **M** and see IntelliSense pop up with other members that can be added to a TextBlock control. Continue typing **MouseEnter** and press the = sign as soon as it appears in the list. VS2008 puts your cursor between two quotes and gives you the option of creating a new event handler. Select New Event Handler and notice that the method name TextBlock_MouseEnter appears. Press F7 to view the code-behind. The following code shows how I coded the handler to modify the Text property of the TextBlock:

```
private void TextBlock_MouseEnter(
    object sender, MouseEventArgs e)
{
    (sender as TextBlock).Text = "Mouse Entered";
}
```

As you can see, the handler uses the familiar pattern of object- and EventArgs-derived type parameters with a void return as in other .NET UI technologies. The only problem with this example was that I was forced to use the sender argument because I haven't given the TextBlock a name yet. Another way to look at it could be that this is a generic way for multiple TextBlock controls to use the same event handler. If that wasn't your intention, however, you should modify the TextBlock control as follows:

```
<TextBlock
    x:Name="SilverlightMessage"
    Text="Silverlight Control"
    MouseEnter="TextBlock_MouseEnter"
    MouseLeave="SilverlightMessage_MouseLeave" />
```

The x:Name property is set to SilverlightMessage. Now, when I create an event handler using IntelliSense, the name of the control is included with the name of the handler, as shown for the MouseLeave event. The handler, SilverlightMessage_MouseLeave, is shown here:

```
private void SilverlightMessage_MouseLeave(
    object sender, MouseEventArgs e)
{
    SilverlightMessage.Text = "Mouse Left";
}
```

Now, it's easy to address the TextBlock control, SilverlightMessage, directly. When running this program, hovering the cursor over the area of the TextBlock control changes the text to Mouse Entered and moving off of the TextBlock control changes the text to Mouse Left.

Working with Data in Silverlight

Recalling that the Silverlight control executes in the browser, you might be wondering how to display data, which resides on the server. Although web services are covered in more detail in Chapters 33, "Writing Traditional ASMX Web Services," and 34, "Creating Web Services with WCF," I'm going to step ahead just a little bit to show you how to pull data over a web service.

To get started, add a LINQ to SQL item to your Hospital_Web Web project. This chapter uses the Hospital database, the same example as in Chapter 22, "Creating Data Abstractions with the ADO.NET Entity Framework."

Next, add a web service to your Web Application: Right-click the project, select Add, New Item, select WCF Service, name it **HospitalService.svc**, and click Add. You'll see a file named IHospitalService, and you should change the DoWork (default skeleton method) to GetHospitalStaff, returning a List<HospitalStaff> like this:

```
[ServiceContract]
public interface IHospitalService
{
    [OperationContract]
    List<HospitalStaff> GetHospitalStaff();
}
```

As explained in Chapter 34, this is the contract for the web service. Next, implement the IHospitalService interface in the HospitalService class as follows. You can right-click the HospitalService.svc file and select View Code to find this file:

```
public class HospitalService : IHospitalService
{
    public List<HospitalStaff> GetHospitalStaff()
```

29

```
        {
            using (var hospCtx = new HospitalDataContext())
            {
                return
                    (from staff in hospCtx.HospitalStaffs
                     select staff)
                    .ToList();
            }
        }
    }
}
```

This is a normal LINQ to SQL call. The difference is that it is being returned from a web service, which means that the object must be able to be passed across the Internet via a process known as serialization.

To enable serialization on LINQ to SQL objects, open the Hospital.dbml file and select a blank area on the designer surface, open the Properties window, and change the Serialization Mode property to Unidirectional. If you forget to do this, you'll have an exception when calling the web service.

To consume this data, you need to add a service reference to the Hospital project, where your XAML control resides. Before doing so, modify the service reference in Web.config. Change it from

```
<endpoint address=""
    binding="wsHttpBinding"
    contract="Hospital_Web.IHospitalService">
```

To

```
<endpoint address=""
    binding="basicHttpBinding"
    contract="Hospital_Web.IHospitalService">
```

Notice that the endpoint binding attribute changed from wsHttpBinding to basicHttpBinding, which is explained in Chapter 34. For a quick explanation, think of the binding as the communications protocol that controls how the communication occurs between your application and the web service.

Then right-click the project, select Add Service Reference, click the Discover button on the Add Service Reference page, select HospitalService.svc, change Namespace to Services, and click the OK button.

Add a Button and DataGrid to Page.xaml, setting their properties as follows:

```
<Grid x:Name="LayoutRoot" Background="White">
    <StackPanel>
```

```
            <TextBlock
                x:Name="SilverlightMessage"
                Text="Silverlight Control"
                MouseEnter="TextBlock_MouseEnter"
                MouseLeave="SilverlightMessage_MouseLeave" />
            <Button x:Name="LoadButton"
                    Content="Load"
                    Click="LoadButton_Click" />
            <my:DataGrid x:Name="HospitalDataGrid"
                        AutoGenerateColumns="True"
                        Width="400" Height="200"/>
        </StackPanel>
    </Grid>
```

The DataGrid has its AutoGenerateColumns set to True, which means we don't need to define a template or columns to perform the binding. The Button has a Click event handler defined, and here's the implementation:

```
        private void LoadButton_Click(object sender, RoutedEventArgs e)
        {
            Services.HospitalServiceClient hospSvc =
                new Services.HospitalServiceClient();

            hospSvc.GetHospitalStaffCompleted +=
                (hospStaffSender, hospStaffEvtArgs) =>
                {
                    HospitalDataGrid.ItemsSource =
                        hospStaffEvtArgs.Result;
                };

            hospSvc.GetHospitalStaffAsync();
        }
```

The HospitalServiceClient is a proxy object that was created when adding the service reference to the project. It takes care of the network communications plumbing associated with calling the web service. That means when you call GetHospitalStaffAsync, the call goes from the browser to the Web Application, and the results are returned, making it look like a local call, but really the web service call happened behind the scenes.

Another point is that the call occurred asynchronously. This is important because communication between the browser and the server takes time, and you don't want to make the browser block, waiting for the reply. The lambda that is hooked up to the GetHospitalStaffCompleted event executes when the web service reply returns to the

29

Silverlight control. Setting `ItemSource` of the `DataGrid`, `HospitalDataGrid`, makes the data appear in the `DataGrid`, as shown in Figure 29.5.

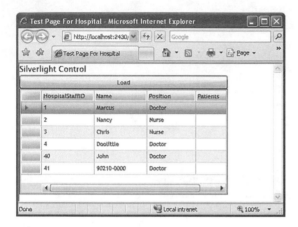

FIGURE 29.5   A Silverlight **DataGrid** populated from a web service.

Playing Media

One of the useful capabilities that Silverlight introduces is an easy way to add media to a website. ASP.NET includes a Silverlight Media control that you can add to a web form, like any other control. Besides pointing the control at a video source, you can interact with and manipulate the Media control through code, which the following sections show you how to do.

Adding the MediaPlayer to a WebForm

The easiest way to play media is via the ASP.NET MediaPlayer control, which is installed with the Silverlight SDK. To get started, create a new Web Application, open Default.aspx in design view, locate the Silverlight controls Toolbox tab, and drag the MediaPlayer control from the Toolbox to the design surface. You'll see a screen similar to Figure 29.6, where the MediaPlayer control resides on the design surface with an open Action List.

As shown in Figure 29.6, you can add a skin, image, or source and set volume, mute, or set to autoplay. Initially, a Web Application doesn't have skins, so you can click the Import Skins link, which will open a folder to the Silverlight SDK where you can select a predefined set of skins. I configured the MediaPlayer to show a video of Scott Guthrie discussing new features of Silverlight that they introduced at Mix '08. Here's the markup:

```
<asp:MediaPlayer ID="MediaPlayer1" runat="server" Height="240px"
    Width="320px" AutoPlay="True" MediaSkinSource="~/Basic.xaml"
    MediaSource="http://mschnlnine.vo.llnwd.net/d1/ch9/0/ScottGuPart2.wmv"/>
```

Since AutoPlay is set to true, the MediaPlayer begins showing the video immediately when the page executes. You can write Javascript to manage this control, but since

Silverlight 2.0 supports C#, I'll show you how to use C# to manage the MediaPlayer in a Silverlight control.

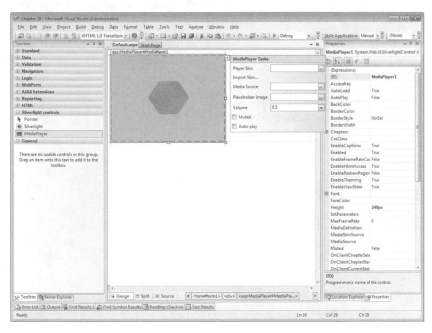

FIGURE 29.6   The Silverlight Media Control,

Manipulating the MediaElement with C#

A counterpart control to the ASP.NET MediaPlayer is the Silverlight MediaElement. The easiest way to demonstrate how to manipulate the MediaElement with C# is to create a new Silverlight application. For this demo, I chose the option to create a new Web Application and named it SilverlightMedia, which created a Web Application named SilverlightMedia_Web and a Silverlight class library for the *.xap file named SilverlightMedia.

When VS2008 creates the project, you'll see a Page.xaml file in the designer, which belongs to the SilverlightMedia project. Add a MediaElement control with a Name of CSharpUnleashed media set like this:

```
<UserControl x:Class="SilverlightMedia.Page"
    xmlns="http://schemas.microsoft.com/client/2007"
    xmlns:x="http://schemas.microsoft.com/winfx/2006/xaml"
    Width="400" Height="300">
    <Grid x:Name="LayoutRoot" Background="White">
        <MediaElement x:Name="CSharpUnleashedMedia">
        </MediaElement>
    </Grid>
</UserControl>
```

29

We need the Name property for the MediaElement to access it from code, but the other properties aren't necessary, because they'll be set as needed in code. The following XAML shows a more filled out control with buttons and text boxes designed to provide a better experience where the user can provide a video address and start and stop the MediaElement:

```
<Grid x:Name="LayoutRoot" Background="White">
    <StackPanel>
        <TextBlock Text="Address:" />
        <TextBox x:Name="AddressText" />
        <MediaElement x:Name="CSharpUnleashedMedia"
                    Height="200"
                    Width="200"/>
        <StackPanel Orientation="Horizontal"
                    HorizontalAlignment="Center">
            <Button x:Name="PlayButton"
                    Content="Play"
                    Click="PlayButton_Click"
                    Margin="5" />
            <Button x:Name="StopButton"
                    Content="Stop"
                    Click="StopButton_Click"
                    Margin="5" />
        </StackPanel>
        <TextBlock x:Name="MessageTextBlock" />
    </StackPanel>
</Grid>
```

All of the XAML should be understandable if you've reviewed Chapter 26 or are already familiar with WPF. It creates a UI that includes an address box, MediaElement, start and stop buttons, and a couple TextBlock controls for communication. What's pertinent about the example for this discussion is the Click event handlers, StartButton_Click and StopButton_Click, for the Button controls. Their implementation in the Page.xaml.cs code-behind file is shown here:

```
private void PlayButton_Click(object sender, RoutedEventArgs e)
{
    if (AddressText.Text != string.Empty)
    {
        CSharpUnleashedMedia.Source =
            new Uri(AddressText.Text);

        CSharpUnleashedMedia.Play();
    }
    else
    {
        MessageTextBlock.Text = "No Address";
```

```
        }
    }

    private void StopButton_Click(object sender, RoutedEventArgs e)
    {
        CSharpUnleashedMedia.Stop();
    }
```

It was important to set the Name properties of the controls, so they can be accessed in the code. The Play ensures that the AddressText control contains a string to make sure it doesn't start the MediaElement with bad data. The MediaElement's Source property is a URI, which is the Internet address of the video to play. I used an address from another site in this example for convenience, but you can also provide an address from your website to show your own videos. In addition to video, you can also provide a URI to an audio source.

Setting the Source and then calling Play, as in the preceding example causes a rewind to the beginning of the media. If you call only play, without setting source, the media will resume where it last left off. There is also a Pause method that will suspend the media at the current position, waiting for a call to Play or Stop. Calling Stop will end playing of the media.

Animating UI Elements

Prior to Silverlight, the primary technology for animated graphics on the Web was Adobe Flash. If you've ever noticed a Flash animation, there are graphical shapes and text moving around the screen in fascinating ways. You can do the same in Silverlight. I'll show you a simple animation that you can do in VS2008, but Microsoft also has a software package named Expression Blend that makes it much easier to create sophisticated graphics and animation with Silverlight.

There are three types of values you can animate in Silverlight: double, color, and point. A double animation could change the length of a line, the width of a shape, or perhaps the opacity of an object—anything with a value of type double. Color animations are self-explanatory, allowing you to change colors. Point animations allow you to change the location of objects, which are specified by Point parameters.

To get started, create a new Silverlight Web Application named Animation, which will produce a Web Application named Animation_Web with a Silverlight class library named Animation. The animation itself is a resource called a Storyboard. The Storyboard identifies the object and property to animate, and the animation type, double, color, or point, defines the parameters of the animation. Here's an example that moves the text, C# Unleashed, from one side of the screen to the other:

```
<UserControl x:Class="Animation.Page"
    xmlns="http://schemas.microsoft.com/client/2007"
    xmlns:x="http://schemas.microsoft.com/winfx/2006/xaml"
    Width="400" Height="300">
```

```
<UserControl.Resources>
    <Storyboard x:Name="CSharpStoryboard" RepeatBehavior="Forever">
        <DoubleAnimation
            Storyboard.TargetName="CSharpUnleashedText"
            Storyboard.TargetProperty="(Canvas.Left)"
            AutoReverse="True"
            From="0"
            By="5"
            To="150"
            Duration="00:00:01" />
    </Storyboard>
</UserControl.Resources>
<Canvas>
    <TextBlock x:Name="CSharpUnleashedText" Text="C# 3.0 Unleashed" />
    <Button x:Name="Play"
            Click="Play_Click"
            Content="Play"
            Canvas.Top="50"/>
    <Button x:Name="Stop"
            Click="Stop_Click"
            Content="Stop"
            Canvas.Top="50"
            Canvas.Left="100" />
</Canvas>
</UserControl>
```

The TextBlock and Button controls in the example are normal XAML for Silverlight controls. What's new is the Storyboard in the UserControl.Resources section. The Name is required on the Storyboard to make it accessible from code and RepeatBehavior, set to Forever, which makes the the animation repeat without stopping. Without RepeatBehavior specified, the animation would run one time. Alternatively, you can set the repeat behavior to a time span or hours:minutes:seconds to determine how long the animation should run, such as in the following example:

```
<Storyboard x:Name="CSharpStoryboard" RepeatBehavior="0:0:4">
```

In the example, the animation will repeat for 4 seconds.

The Storyboard contains the DoubleAnimation element, which performs an animation on a property of type double. The TargetName specifies the control to animate, and TargetProperty specifies the property. In this case, the Left position of the Textblock is being animated so that the text will move position. However, notice that the value is surrounded by parenthesis. The parenthesis are required because the code animates an attached property, which is the property given to it by its parent Canvas control. If you aren't animating an attached property, you could leave the parenthesis out.

AutoReverse means to run the animation in the opposite direction after the animation runs. The animation starts at From, moves the number of units specified with By, and stops at To. This will occur in the time specified by the Duration. The result is that the text C# 3.0 Unleashed will move from the left to the right, by 150 pixels and then back again, continuing forever.

You can control the animation through code, which the code does by specifying Click event handlers for the Start and Stop buttons. Here's the code for those event handlers:

```
private void Play_Click(object sender, RoutedEventArgs e)
{
    CSharpStoryboard.Begin();
}

private void Stop_Click(object sender, RoutedEventArgs e)
{
    CSharpStoryboard.Stop();
}
```

Each handler either calls Begin, to start the animation, or Stop, to end the animation through the CSharpStoryboard instance, which is the identifier for the Storyboard you see in the preceding XAML.

Summary

Silverlight is a new UI technology that gives you the best capabilities of WPF and ASP.NET. In this chapter, you learned how to create a Silverlight project and what the various parts are. Then you saw how to handle C# events and manipulate controls. In addition, you saw how to use a web service to return data that can be displayed in a DataGrid.

You learned a couple ways to play media: either through the ASP.NET MediaPlayer control or via a Silverlight MediaElement control. The benefit of using the Silverlight MediaElement control is that you can use C# to control media events through code.

Silverlight also supports sophisticated animation, just like Flash. You can perform double, color, or point animations by building storyboards. Through C# code-behind, you can also handle animation events to control the animation dynamically.

Upcoming chapters discuss the techniques we briefly covered on web services in this chapter. Before going to web services, the next chapter introduces you to some useful communications technologies that ship with the .NET Framework.

29

PART 7

Communicating with .NET Technologies

CHAPTER 30

Using .NET Network Communications Technologies

The C# language has access to an entire suite of networking libraries. Some of the capabilities range from low-level socket connections to wrappered HTTP classes.

An understanding of TCP/IP would be helpful in understanding the sockets implementation. However, I have tried to explain it in a way that most programmers will understand. The examples demonstrate a client and a server communicating with TCP/IP, using socket library classes.

It would also be advantageous to understand HTTP. The HTTP example implements a client program that requests a web page from an Internet server. It uses special library objects to send a request for a web page and retrieve a response.

Implementing Sockets

A lot of systems on the Internet and inside of companies use TCP/IP sockets to communicate. A socket is just an address and a port that create a communications channel for computing systems to communicate. The .NET Framework Class Library (FCL) makes it easy to work with sockets, as you'll see in the following sections.

The examples in the following sections have two components: a client and a server. The client requests a quote from the server, the server returns a quote (money quotes), and then the client prints the quote to the console after receiving it from the server. When testing the programs yourself, bring up the server first and then start the client in a different process or window.

A Socket Server

The server program uses sockets to deliver information (quotes) to requesting clients. Listing 30.1 demonstrates how to create a server program with sockets.

LISTING 30.1   Creating a Socket Server

```csharp
using System;
using System.Collections.Generic;
using System.Net;
using System.Net.Sockets;
using System.Text;

class MoneyServer
{
    static void Main()
    {
        const int StreamSize = 256;
        const int  Port = 2010;

        var ipAddr = new IPAddress(
            new byte[] { 127, 0, 0, 1 });

        var talk = new List<string>
        {
"A penny saved is too small, make it a buck.",
"Keep your wooden nickel. It'll be worth something someday.",
"It's your dime, but you're better off dialing 10-10-XXX."
        };

        var mSvr = new MoneyServer();
        var AsciiEnc = new ASCIIEncoding();
        var inStream = new byte[StreamSize];
        var outStream = new byte[StreamSize];

        Random rnd = null;
        string reqString = string.Empty;
        int index = 0;

        var tcpl = new TcpListener(ipAddr, Port);

        tcpl.Start();

        Console.WriteLine("Server is Running...");

        do
```

LISTING 30.1   Continued

```csharp
        {
            try
            {
                Socket sock = tcpl.AcceptSocket();

                int count = sock.Receive(
                    inStream, inStream.Length, 0);
                reqString = AsciiEnc.GetString(
                    inStream, 0, count);

                Console.WriteLine(reqString);

                rnd = new Random();
                index = rnd.Next(talk.Count);

                outStream = AsciiEnc.GetBytes(
                    talk[index] as string);

                sock.Send(outStream, outStream.Length, 0);
            }
            catch (SocketException sockEx)
            {
                Console.WriteLine(
                "Generic Exception Message: {0}",
                sockEx.ToString());
            }

        } while (reqString != "bye");

        tcpl.Stop();
    }
}
```

This server program instantiates a List<string>, talk, and initializes it with quote strings during constructor processing. The real action for this program starts in the Main method.

Socket operations are encapsulated in the TCP classes. This program uses the TcpListener class to create a socket connection on the local host. The example accepts a single parameter, indicating the port number. After the TcpListener class is instantiated, it must be started with the Start method. The following snippet shows how to instantiate and share a TcpListener:

```csharp
var tcpl = new TcpListener(ipAddr, Port);
tcpl.Start();
Console.WriteLine("Server is Running...");
```

30

After the TcpListener has been started, it must listen for client connections. This happens by calling its AcceptSocket method, which causes the program to remain idle, in a listening state, until it receives a connection request from a client on port 2010. When a client connects, the AcceptSocket method returns a Socket object. The following code line shows how to accept a client connection and retrieve a Socket object:

```
Socket sock = tcpl.AcceptSocket();
```

After the Socket object is created, it's used to read the input from the client. This program uses the Receive method of the Socket object, which has three parameters. The first parameter is a byte array to store input, the second is the maximum number of bytes to read, and the third is the offset into the byte array to begin filling. The Receive method returns the number of bytes read. This command is shown in the following code lines:

```
int count = sock.Receive(
inStream, inStream.Length, 0);
```

The client sends data in the form of a byte array, which needs to be converted to a string so that the program can deal with it appropriately. This program uses an ASCIIEncoding object to transform a byte array to a string. The GetString method of the ASCIIEncoding class performs this function. Its first parameter identifies the byte array to be converted. The second parameter is the byte array offset to begin at, and the third parameter is the number of bytes to read. This conversion is in the following code lines:

```
reqString = AsciiEnc.GetString(
    inStream, 0, count);
Console.WriteLine(reqString);
```

After receiving the request string from the client and printing it to the console, the program obtains a random string from the talk. To send this string to the client, the server must convert it to a byte array. It does so by invoking the GetBytes method of the ASCIIEncoder object, AsciiEnc. The GetBytes method takes a single string parameter. This task is shown in the following code:

```
rnd = new Random();
index = rnd.Next(talk.Count);

outStream = AsciiEnc.GetBytes(
    talk[index] as string);
```

To actually send the quote back to the client, the program uses the Socket class Send method, which takes three parameters. The first parameter is the byte array to be sent, the second is the number of bytes to send, and the third is the offset in the byte array to begin reading. The Send method is shown in the following code line:

```
sock.Send( outStream, outStream.Length, 0 );
```

The client can keep sending requests for quotes as long as it wants to. When it no longer wants to interact, it sends the string "bye". The server ends operations when it reads this string and then closes the socket connection. The following code lines show the end of the do loop where a stop or go decision is made and the invocation of the Stop method of the TcpListener class when the client breaks the connection:

```
} while (reqString != "bye");


tcpl.Stop();
```

That's all there is to implementing a TCP server. Open a socket, listen for clients, and respond to their requests. The next section shows how to build a client that talks to this server.

A Socket Client

The client program uses sockets to request information from a server. It makes a socket connection, sends a request, and receives a reply. Listing 30.2 shows how a client program is built using sockets. You should create Listing 30.2 as a separate project from Listing 30.1 to enable executing each application separately.

LISTING 30.2   Creating a Socket Client

```
using System;
using System.IO;
using System.Net;
using System.Net.Sockets;
using System.Text;

class MoneyClient
{
    static void Main()
    {
        const int StreamSize = 256;
        const int  Port = 2010;
        const string LocalHost = "localhost";
        var ipEndPt = new IPEndPoint(
            new IPAddress(
                new byte[] { 127, 0, 0, 1 }),
            Port);
        var AsciiEnc = new ASCIIEncoding();
        var inStream = new byte[StreamSize];
        var outStream = new byte[StreamSize];
```

30

LISTING 30.2   Continued

```
        string freeAdvice;
        string choice = "Q";

        do
        {
            try
            {
                Console.WriteLine("\nMoney Line\n");
                Console.WriteLine("1 - Get Advice");
                Console.WriteLine("Q - Quit");
                Console.Write("\nPlease Choose:  ");
                choice = Console.ReadLine();
                Console.WriteLine();

                var myClient = new TcpClient(LocalHost, Port);
                Stream myStream = myClient.GetStream();

                outStream = AsciiEnc.GetBytes(
                    "What is the secret of making money?");

                if (choice == "1")
                {
                    // send request to server
                    myStream.Write(
                        outStream, 0, outStream.Length);

                    // clean garbage chars from byte array
                    for (int i = 0; i < inStream.Length; i++)
                    {
                        inStream[i] = 0;
                    }

                    // retrieve response from server
                    myStream.Read(
                        inStream, 0, inStream.Length);
                    freeAdvice = AsciiEnc.GetString(
                        inStream, 0, inStream.Length);
                    Console.WriteLine("Server Response: {0}",
                                      freeAdvice);
                }
                else
                {
                    // close session with server
                    outStream = AsciiEnc.GetBytes("bye");
                    myStream.Write(
```

LISTING 30.2   Continued

```
                    outStream, 0, outStream.Length);
            }
        }
        catch (InvalidOperationException ioe)
        {
            Console.WriteLine(
                "Invalid Operation Message: {0}",
                ioe.Message);
        }
        catch (Exception e)
        {
            Console.WriteLine(
                "Generic Exception Message: {0}",
                e.Message);
        }
    } while (choice == "1");
    }
}
```

The client application connects to a server, retrieves quotes, and ends a session based on user input. After presenting a menu to the user, the program opens a connection to the server with the TcpClient class. The TcpClient object, myClient, is instantiated with a constructor that accepts two arguments. The first argument indicates the DNS hostname of the server, which is "localhost" because the server is on the same machine. The second argument is the port number, 2010, which is the same port used by the server in Listing 30.1. Here's the statement that creates a TcpClient object and makes a connection:

```
var myClient = new TcpClient(LocalHost, Port);
```

> **TIP**
>
> The listings in this chapter use try/catch blocks for processing exceptions, which is especially important because of the nature of network communications. Most of the time, there is no way to know what will happen on the other end of the network connection. Effective use of exception handling gives programs a way to gracefully degrade in the face of network errors.

The TcpClient class has an alternate constructor that accepts an IPEndPoint object. An IPEndPoint object is constructed with an IPAddress object, which holds a numeric IP address and a port number.

Instead of getting a Socket object as the server did, the TcpClient program obtains a stream. Here's the code line that uses the GetStream method of the TcpClient class to obtain a stream to the server:

```
Stream myStream = myClient.GetStream();
```

30

The client program converts a string to a byte array by using an object of the
ASCIIEncoding class. The following code lines create the request stream that is sent to the
server to obtain a quote and then, assuming the user chose to get a quote, sends the
request to the server with the Write method of the Stream object. The parameters for the
Write method are, in order, the byte array, the offset to begin reading, and the number of
bytes to read:

```
outStream = AsciiEnc.GetBytes(
    "What is the secret of making money?");

if (choice == "1")
{
    // send request to server
     myStream.Write(
        outStream, 0, outStream.Length);
```

Between requests, the program cleans old data out of the byte array used to obtain input.
Otherwise, when a shorter piece of information is retrieved, it would have garbage from
the previous quote hanging off the end of the string. The for loop accomplishes this task:

```
// clean garbage chars from byte array
for (int i=0; i < inStream.Length; i++)
{
    inStream[i] = 0;
}
```

Obtaining the quote from the server requires reading data from the input stream and
converting the bytes to a string. Reading from the server occurs through the Read method
of the Stream object, myStream. Its parameters are, in order, the byte array to read data
into, the offset into the byte array to begin placing data, and the maximum number of
bytes to read. As seen in previous explanations, the GetString method of the
ASCIIEncoding class converts the byte array to a string. The following code lines show
these methods, along with the statement to print the results to the console:

```
// retrieve response from server
myStream.Read(
    inStream, 0, inStream.Length);
freeAdvice = AsciiEnc.GetString(
    inStream, 0, inStream.Length);
Console.WriteLine("Server Response: {0}",
    freeAdvice);
```

When the user wants to quit the program, he selects the Q—or anything other than 1—
option from the menu. This runs the following code lines, which send a message to the
server indicating that the client wants to end its session. The GetBytes method of the
ASCIIEncoding class and the Write method of the Stream class operate as previously
described:

```
// close session with server
outStream = AsciiEnc.GetBytes("bye");
myStream.Write(
    outStream, 0, outStream.Length);
```

This client hooks up to the server in Listing 30.1.

Another important Internet protocol is HTTP, which is covered in the next section.

Working with HTTP

HTTP is what enables communication across the Web. Knowing how to request a web page can be useful for caching or screen scraping, which is a good application of regular expressions that you learned about in Chapter 5, "Manipulating Strings." Listing 30.3 uses the FCL HTTP API to request a web page via HTTP.

LISTING 30.3 Creating an HTTP Client

```
using System;
using System.IO;
using System.Net;
using System.Text;

namespace HttpRequestDemo
{
    class Program
    {
        static void Main()
        {
            const int BufferSize = 2048;

            try
            {
                var AsciiEnc = new ASCIIEncoding();
                var buf = new byte[BufferSize];

                HttpWebRequest httpReq =
                    WebRequest.Create(
                        "http://www.csharp-station.com")
                    as HttpWebRequest;

                HttpWebResponse httpResp =
                    httpReq.GetResponse() as HttpWebResponse;

                Stream httpStream = httpResp.GetResponseStream();
```

LISTING 30.3   Continued

```
            int count = httpStream.Read(buf, 0, buf.Length);

            Console.WriteLine(
                AsciiEnc.GetString(buf, 0, count));
        }
        catch (Exception e)
        {
            Console.WriteLine("Generic Exception: {0}",
                              e.Message);
        }
    }
}
}
```

NOTE

You might want to change your Internet Information Services (IIS) authentication method to Anonymous. Otherwise, you may receive security problems when trying to access a web page on localhost.

The example in Listing 30.3 shows how to obtain a web page by using HTTP classes. The primary classes for making an HTTP request are HttpWebRequest and HttpWebResponse. The statement that instantiates an HttpWebRequest class uses the static Create method of the WebRequest class and returns a WebRequest object. WebRequest is the abstract parent class of HttpWebRequest. Therefore, a cast operation is necessary to convert the return value of the Create method to an HttpWebRequest object. The Create method accepts a string representation of an URL. Here's the statement:

```
HttpWebRequest httpReq =
    WebRequest.Create(
        "http://www.csharp-station.com")
    as HttpWebRequest;
```

After an HttpWebRequest object is created, it can be used to obtain an HttpWebResponse object. This happens by invoking its GetResponse method, which returns a WebResponse object. The WebResponse object is an abstract base class of the HttpWebResponse class, and a cast operation is necessary for conversion. The following statement from Listing 24.3 shows how to use the GetResponse method:

```
HttpWebResponse httpResp =
    httpReq.GetResponse() as HttpWebResponse;
```

The only thing left to do is get the response stream and print it to the console. Use the GetResponseStream method of the HttpWebResponse class to obtain a Stream object. The following code lines get the response stream, convert it, and print it to the console:

```
Stream httpStream = httpResp.GetResponseStream();


int count = httpStream.Read(buf, 0, buf.Length);

Console.WriteLine(
    ASCII.GetString(buf, 0, count));
```

Then, the `Read` method of the `Stream` object fills a byte array. The method's three parameters are the byte array to fill with stream data, the offset into the byte array to begin, and the maximum number of bytes to read. The byte array is converted to a string with the `GetString` method of the `ASCIIEncoding` class. The `GetString` method accepts three parameters—in order: a byte array to read from, the offset into the byte array to begin reading, and the number of bytes to read.

This code performed only one read, which probably won't get all the bytes on a typical web page. Therefore, you want to iterate until `Read` returns a byte count less than the size of the buffer.

Beyond the basic functionality explained in this section, the `HttpWebRequest` and `HttpWebResponse` classes have several methods and properties for using HTTP. This capability includes functionality such as setting and reading headers and cookies.

Performing FTP File Transfers

Another Internet protocol for moving files around is FTP, which is supported by the .NET FCL. The following sections show you how to get and put files with FTP.

Putting Files on an FTP Server

To upload files to an FTP server, you need to create an `FtpRequest` object, get a stream reference to where you want to put the file, and write the file to the stream. Listing 30.4 shows how to do this.

LISTING 30.4   Uploading a File to an FTP Server

```
using System;
using System.IO;
using System.Net;

class FtpPut
{
    static void Main()
    {
        string ftpDest = "ftp://www.myftpsite.com/MyFile.txt";
        string fileSource = "MyFile.txt";
        string userName = "username";
        string password = "password";
```

LISTING 30.4   Continued

```csharp
        FtpWebRequest request =
            WebRequest.Create(ftpDest)
            as FtpWebRequest;
        request.Method =
            WebRequestMethods.Ftp.UploadFile;

        request.Credentials =
            new NetworkCredential(userName, password);

        using (Stream requestStream =
            request.GetRequestStream())
        {
            const int bufferLength = 2048;
            var buffer = new byte[bufferLength];
            int count = 0;
            int readBytes = 0;

            using (FileStream stream =
                File.OpenRead(fileSource))
            {
                do
                {
                    readBytes = stream.Read(
                        buffer, 0, bufferLength);
                    requestStream.Write(
                        buffer, 0, readBytes);
                    count += readBytes;
                }
                while (readBytes != 0);
            }

            request.ContentLength = count;
        }

        using (FtpWebResponse response =
            request.GetResponse()
            as FtpWebResponse)
        {
            Console.WriteLine(
                "Upload File Complete, status {0}",
                response.StatusDescription);
        }
    }
}
```

As demonstrated in Listing 30.4, the first step when uploading an FTP file to a server is to create an FTP request. Here's the code that does this:

```
FtpWebRequest request =
    WebRequest.Create(ftpDest)
    as FtpWebRequest;
request.Method =
    WebRequestMethods.Ftp.UploadFile;
```

Notice that you don't directly instantiate an `FtpWebRequest`, but rather call the `Create` method of the `WebRequest` type. Remember to specify that you want to perform an Upload.

FTP servers require some type of credentials, even if it's anonymous access with a username of "anonymous" and a password that consists of your email address. The following shows how to pass credentials to the FTP site:

```
request.Credentials =
    new NetworkCredential(userName, password);
```

`NetworkCredential` is a common class used to pass credentials with other network communication APIs in the .NET Framework. So, it's a good thing to remember for future reference.

The rest of the code uses the `using` statement to open the request stream. Then, it opens the file stream of the file to send. The file must be translated into a byte array for sending. At the end of the listing, you can see that we open the response stream to read and print the response from the FTP server.

That was how you can put files on an FTP server, but you'll also need to retrieve files from FTP servers, which you learn about in the next section.

Getting Files from an FTP Server

To get a file from an FTP server, you need to create the `FtpWebRequest`, open the stream to the file, read the bytes, open the stream to the file you need to create, and write the bytes to the new file. Listing 30.5 shows how to do this.

LISTING 30.5   Getting Files from an FTP Server

```
using System.IO;
using System.Net;

class FtpGet
{
    static void Main(string[] args)
```

30

LISTING 30.5   Continued

```
    {
        string ftpSource =
            "ftp://www.mysite.com/MyFile.txt";
        string fileName = "MyFile.txt";
        string userName = "username";
        string password = "password";

        FtpWebRequest downloadRequest =
            WebRequest.Create(ftpSource)
            as FtpWebRequest;

        downloadRequest.Credentials =
            new NetworkCredential(userName, password);

        FtpWebResponse downloadResponse =
            downloadRequest.GetResponse()
            as FtpWebResponse;

        using (var responseStream =
                downloadResponse.GetResponseStream())
        {

            if (fileName.Length == 0)
            {
                using (var reader =
                        new StreamReader(responseStream))
                {
                    reader.ReadToEnd();
                }
            }
            else
            {
                using (FileStream fileStream =
                        File.Create(fileName))
                {
                    const int BufferSize = 1024;

                    var buffer = new byte[BufferSize];
                    int bytesRead;
                    while (true)
                    {
                        bytesRead = responseStream.Read(
                            buffer, 0, buffer.Length);
                        if (bytesRead == 0)
                            break;
                        fileStream.Write(
```

LISTING 30.5   Continued

```
                           buffer, 0, bytesRead);
                   }
               }
           }
       }
    }
}
```

Getting an FTP file is different from putting because you need to get the response stream to read from as soon as you instantiate the request stream. Here's the code that does this:

```
FtpWebRequest downloadRequest =
    WebRequest.Create(ftpSource)
    as FtpWebRequest;

downloadRequest.Credentials =
    new NetworkCredential(userName, password);

FtpWebResponse downloadResponse =
    downloadRequest.GetResponse()
    as FtpWebResponse;
```

You need to supply network credentials in the form of a `NetworkCredential` object. You'll use the `FtpWebResponse` object to read the file from the FTP server.

The rest of the code uses `using` statements to open the response stream, read bytes from the FTP server, open a file stream to the new file, and then write those bytes to the new file. Remember that the `using` statements are essential because they close the file streams for you.

Sending SMTP Mail

Almost every single application that I write these days uses some form of email. Because of that, I add a global error handler to applications and add an option to email to a specified address. Another common use is to add a contact form to a web page, rather than stick your email out there to get spammed at. This section shows you how to send a quick email and how to add an attachment to an email.

A Quick Way to Send Email

Here's an email in one statement:

```
new SmtpClient
    {
        Host = "mail.myplace.com"
    }
```

```
.Send(
    "sender@myplace.com",
    "recipient@yourplace.com",
    "test",
    "This is a test.");
```

When using the email types in the .NET Framework Class Library, you should add a using directive for the System.Net.Mail namespace.

The example above sends an email. It's critical that you set the mail server address when instantiating the SmtpClient, which I did with object initialization syntax. The four parameters of the Send method are sender, recipient address list, subject, and body.

Sending Emails with Attachments

To send an attachment, you need three statements: create a MailMessage, add the attachment to the MailMessage, and then send the email. Here's the code to do it:

```
var mailMsg = new MailMessage(
    "sender@myplace.com",
    "recipient@yourplace.com",
    "Attachment Test",
    "Please see attachment");

mailMsg.Attachments.Add(
    new Attachment("MyFile.txt"));

new SmtpClient
    {
        Host = "mail.myplace.com"
    }
    .Send(mailMsg);
```

If you're curious, as I was, whether you can get this into a single statement, give it a shot. You'll quickly find that the To property of the MailMessage is read-only, meaning that you can't set it with object initialization syntax. Also, you can't initialize the attachment collection with collection initialization syntax either.

Note that MailMessage has a lot of other properties, such as CC, Headers, ReplyTo, and more. Therefore, if you need a quick email, you can use the SmtpClient.Send method but use the MailMessage with SmptClient.Send for more sophisticated options.

Summary

This chapter showed how to uses library classes for sockets and HTTP operations. Sockets are easily managed with the TcpClient and TcpListener classes. The examples used these classes to implement both a socket server and a corresponding socket client.

Another section of this chapter showed how to use the HTTP classes to read a web page. Some of the same classes were used for both the HTTP and socket examples. These included encoders and streams that worked with byte arrays.

You also learned to use FTP to put files onto an FTP server and get files from an FTP server. A common task in modern programs is to be able to send email. You saw how to use the `MailMessage` and `SmtpMail` classes to send email.

30

CHAPTER 31

Building Windows Service Applications

Every big event has people working behind the scenes. At a music concert, you don't think about what a fantastic job the people did to set up the stage or the promoters who advertised. You think about the musicians and how they performed because they are what you see in front of you. If you think about it, without all the behind-the-scenes people, the concert wouldn't have been so great.

Similarly, when you use applications such as SQL Server, plug a device into a USB port, or even browse the Internet, you enjoy the benefits of behind-the-scenes software. In particular, this behind-the-scenes software is called a Windows service, which I refer to as just a service, and it runs in the background. SQL Server has services for several of its functions, including the storage engine, scheduling agent, and reporting services. USB ports are supported by the Plug and Play service and Internet web servers (IIS) are supported by the World Wide Web Publishing Service.

There are several situations in which Windows services can be vital parts of your application. Anytime you need software to be running when a computer is running but no one needs to be logged on, you can use a Windows service. If you need to host a remoting object, a web service, or a specialized TCP/IP server, a Windows service can be a good choice. Windows services make a nice host for any type of server application that you build. If you just want a piece of software to execute on a periodic basis on its own, you can use a Windows service. This chapter shows you how easy it is to build a Windows service with VS2008 and C#.

Creating Windows Service Projects in VS2008

Visual Studio has supported Windows service projects since .NET 1.0. You just run the wizard, hook up to service events, and then deploy the service. This first section explains how to create the service with VS2008.

Running the Windows Service Wizard

To create a Windows service project, select File, New, Project, select the Visual C#\Windows branch of the navigation tree, and then select Windows Service.

Examining Windows Service Project Items

The Windows service project contains a couple items that are unique. This section explains what they are and how to get to the code. You can refer to Figure 31.1 to see what files are created on a new Windows service project.

SPACES IN WINDOWS SERVICE PROJECT NAMES

This time, I named the solution Chapter 31, but named the project MoneyServer. Notice that there aren't any spaces in the name of the project, which names the assembly by default. That's because spaces don't work with Windows services. You can do this by creating a blank solution project and then adding a new Windows Service project to the Solution.

FIGURE 31.1   A New Windows service project.

When you first create a Windows service project, it creates a file named Service1.cs, as shown in Figure 31.1, with a special component icon. Another visual on the Windows service is that if you double-click Service1.cs, you'll see a blank design surface in the designer, rather than code. The purpose of this design surface is to allow you to drag and drop components, such as timers, performance counters, and installers that you can configure through the Properties window.

Along with Service1.cs, Figure 31.1 shows a class named Service1.Designer.cs. The purpose of this file is the same as in Windows Forms applications, where Service1.Designer.cs contains a partial class with an `InitializeComponent` method that serializes. In code, the settings for all the components dropped onto the design surface of Service1.cs. Listing 31.1 shows the code inside of Service1.Designer.cs.

LISTING 31.1   Partial Class for a Windows Service

```
namespace MoneyServer
{
    partial class Service1
    {
        /// <summary>
        /// Required designer variable.
        /// </summary>
        private System.ComponentModel.IContainer components = null;

        /// <summary>
        /// Clean up any resources being used.
        /// </summary>
        /// <param name="disposing">true if managed resources
        ➥should be disposed; otherwise, false.</param>
        protected override void Dispose(bool disposing)
        {
            if (disposing && (components != null))
            {
                components.Dispose();
            }
            base.Dispose(disposing);
        }

        #region Component Designer generated code

        /// <summary>
        /// Required method for Designer support - do not modify
        /// the contents of this method with the code editor.
        /// </summary>
        private void InitializeComponent()
        {
            components = new System.ComponentModel.Container();
            this.ServiceName = "Service1";
        }

        #endregion
    }
}
```

Just like with Windows Forms, you shouldn't modify the InitializeComponent method. After several years of experience with building Windows services, I still haven't encountered a reason to "manually" change anything in this file because the Properties window works just fine. In later sections in this chapter, when discussing Windows service settings, I show you Property window settings that you need to know.

The Program.cs file, just like Program.cs in nearly every other executable project in VS2008, contains the application entry point. Listing 31.2 shows the contents of Program.cs and how it starts the Windows service.

LISTING 31.2   The Windows Service Entry Point

```
using System;
using System.Collections.Generic;
using System.Linq;
using System.ServiceProcess;
using System.Text;

namespace MoneyServer
{
    static class Program
    {
        /// <summary>
        /// The main entry point for the application.
        /// </summary>
        static void Main()
        {
            ServiceBase[] ServicesToRun;
            ServicesToRun = new ServiceBase[]
                    {
                            new Service1()
                    };
            ServiceBase.Run(ServicesToRun);
        }
    }
}
```

The Main method, the application entry point, instantiates and executes the Windows service. You generally don't need to change this file, unless you are launching multiple services. Here's an example of how you would do that:

```
ServiceBase.Run(
    new ServiceBase[]
    {
        new Service1(),
        new Service2()
    });
```

Again, I'm having fun refactoring the code into a single statement, but the result is the same. Now, you can instantiate and launch both `Service1` and `Service2`. There's more to it than that because you need to create a `ServiceInstaller` for each service, which I show you how to do in a later section of this chapter, but that's all the changes you need to make to this file.

Coding Windows Services

The guts of a Windows service consist of method overrides that you implement to make your service work. The following sections describe those method overrides and then show how to implement them.

Available Windows Service Method Overrides

The code for a service has several overridden methods, corresponding to the events of a service, such as `Start`, `Pause`, `Continue`, and `Stop`. Table 31.1 explains the purpose of each of these overrides.

TABLE 31.1   Windows Service Event Overrides

Event Method Override	Purpose
OnContinue	Continues execution of a service that was previously in the paused state
OnCustomCommand	Handles commands from a controller
OnPause	Pauses execution of a service that was previously in the started state
OnPowerEvent	Called when power system changes state
OnSessionChange	Occurs when a Terminal Server session change occurs
OnShutdown	Allows you to perform actions before the system shuts down
OnStart	Called when the Windows service first starts
OnStop	Called when the Windows service stops from a started state

As a minimum, you always want to implement `OnStart` and `OnStop`, which are already provided in the shell code that the Windows Service Project Wizard creates for you. To view the code for the Windows service, either select the blank design surface or the Solution Explorer file for Service1.cs, right-click, and select View Code. Listing 31.3 shows what this code looks like initially.

LISTING 31.3   Windows Service Code

```
using System;
using System.Collections.Generic;
using System.ComponentModel;
using System.Data;
using System.Diagnostics;
using System.Linq;
using System.ServiceProcess;
using System.Text;

namespace MoneyServer
{
    public partial class Service1 : ServiceBase
    {
        public Service1()
        {
            InitializeComponent();
        }

        protected override void OnStart(string[] args)
        {
        }

        protected override void OnStop()
        {
        }
    }
}
```

The Service class in Listing 31.3 is a partial class, which matches the partial class in Listing 31.1. To implement this service, you add code to the OnStart, OnStop, and other method overrides from Table 31.1 as needed. The next section describes how a Windows service could be coded.

Implementing Windows Service Method Overrides

You must add code to the method overrides in a Windows service to get your program to work. As mentioned in the preceding section, you need to implement OnStart and OnStop methods as a minimal implementation. The following sections describe how to do this.

Implementing the OnStart Method

The OnStart method can be called when the OS boots and starts services marked as Automatic. It can also be called manually via the Services console that you can find via your OS Administrative Tools panel.

This example implements the MoneyServer logic from the previous sections, except this time the MoneyServer will start up and run as long as the machine is running because it is hosted in a Windows service. Listing 31.4 shows the OnStart implementation for the MoneyServer.

LISTING 31.4   Implementing **OnStart**

```
TcpListener m_tcpl;


protected override void OnStart(string[] args)
{
    const int  Port = 2010;

    var ipAddr = new IPAddress(
        new byte[] { 127, 0, 0, 1 });

    m_tcpl = new TcpListener(ipAddr, Port);
    m_tcpl.Start();

    new Thread(
        () => ListenForQuoteRequests())
        .Start();
}
```

Chapter 30, "Using .NET Network Communications Technologies," explained what the MoneyServer does, and you can refer there for the details. Here, I point out the differences that are necessary to implement this as a Windows service.

The first line of Listing 31.4 is a declaration of a TcpListener, m_tcpl. This was moved from a local variable because you need access to it across multiple methods.

After TcpListener is instantiated, the OnStart method invokes the ListenForQuoteRequests on a thread. You'll learn more about threads in Chapter 39, "Managing Processes and Threads," but I'll give you a quick explanation here. The Thread class must be instantiated with a reference to a method that will execute on the thread, which is ListenForQuoteRequests. The delegate type for this overload of the Thread constructor is ThreadStart, which I chose to implement as a lambda. The thread doesn't begin execution until invoking Start on the Thread instance.

LAUNCHING A THREAD IN ONSTART **AVOIDS TIMEOUTS**

The OnStart method of a Windows service has a total of 60 seconds to complete. After that, Windows will fail your service, which you can verify by looking at the Windows Event Log if it happens to you. To avoid the timeout, you can launch long-running processes on a thread, which enables the OnStart method to finish on time.

For completeness, I've listed the implementation of the MoneyServer in the ListenForQuoteRequests method in Listing 31.5.

LISTING 31.5 **MoneyServer** Implementation

```
        private void ListenForQuoteRequests()
        {
            const int StreamSize = 256;

            Random rnd = null;
            string reqString = string.Empty;
            int index = 0;

            var talk = new List<string>
            {
"A penny saved is too small, make it a buck.",
"Keep your wooden nickel. It'll be worth something someday.",
"It's your dime, but you're better off dialing 10-10-XXX."
            };

            var AsciiEnc = new ASCIIEncoding();
            var inStream = new byte[StreamSize];
            var outStream = new byte[StreamSize];

            while (!m_stopping)
            {
                try
                {
                    Socket sock = m_tcpl.AcceptSocket();

                    int count = sock.Receive(
                        inStream, inStream.Length, 0);
                    reqString = AsciiEnc.GetString(
                        inStream, 0, count);

                    Console.WriteLine(reqString);

                    rnd = new Random();
                    index = rnd.Next(talk.Count);

                    outStream = AsciiEnc.GetBytes(
                        talk[index] as string);

                    sock.Send(outStream, outStream.Length, 0);
                }
                catch (SocketException sockEx)
```

LISTING 31.5   Continued

```
        {
            Console.WriteLine(
            "Generic Exception Message: {0}",
            sockEx.ToString());
        }
    }
}
```

Instead of a do/while loop to listen for when the client sends a "bye" string, as was done in Chapter 30, the implementation in Listing 31.5 uses a while loop that loops until a field named m_stopping is true, which is set when the service stops. The AcceptSocket call makes the loop wait for a new request. Let's see how to stop this service next.

Implementing the OnStop Method

If you recall, I made m_tcpl a field so that we could get to it from other methods. In particular, I use it in the OnStop method to stop the service. Listing 31.6 shows how the OnStop method is implemented.

LISTING 31.6   Implementing **OnStop**

```
protected override void OnStop()
{
    m_stopping = true;
    m_tcpl.Stop();
}
```

Listing 31.6 calls only the Stop method on the TcpListener, m_tcpl. Most important, it sets m_stopping to true, which discontinues the loop in ListenForQuoteRequests in Listing 31.5. Calling Stop on the TcpListener makes the call to AcceptSockets break so that the loop can iterate one more time and m_stopping will be checked. If you have a more extensive server, you might need to call dispose on resources or other actions in the OnStop method.

Remember that OnStop isn't called only when the OS is shutting down. Users could stop the service via the Administrative Tools Services console, meaning that they can start the service back up after that. You'll have to consider all the scenarios for your service when starting and stopping.

Configuring a Windows Service

There are different configuration settings for a Windows service, and you need to know where to find each. The service itself permits specifying logging options, naming, and allowed states (for example, continue and pause). To see the configuration options, open Service1.cs so that you can see its design surface. Then open the Properties window, as shown in Figure 31.2.

FIGURE 31.2   Windows service properties.

AutoLog means that there will be a log entry in the Windows Event Log every time the service changes state. Beyond immediate debugging to know that your service started properly, you might want to just turn this off, instead of filling up the Windows Event Log with information messages that won't have useful meaning in production, but that's your choice.

Several CanXxx properties allow you to turn state on and off. CanStop is true by default because you want to use it most of the time, but it's possible that you don't want users to manually stop your service. It is important to know where these options are because the gotcha is that you'll override OnContinue and OnPause, and they'll never be called because CanContinueAndPause defaults to false.

Installing a Windows Service

You need to add an installer before you can deploy a Windows service. The installer has two parts: a ServiceProcessInstaller and a ServiceInstaller. The ServiceProcessInstaller sets up the Windows process for your Windows service. The ServiceInstaller provides setup for individual services, meaning that you can have multiple services running in the same process.

To add an installer, right-click the design surface for a Windows service and click Add Installer. VS2008 adds a component for a ServiceProcessInstaller and a ServiceInstaller to the design surface of a new file called ProjectInstaller.cs. The following sections describe how to configure the ServiceProcessInstaller and ServiceInstaller components.

Configuring a `ServiceProcessInstaller`

Select the `ServiceProcessInstaller` and open the Properties window to configure it. The most important property to set is `Account`. The available settings are one of the `ServiceAccount` enum's values, described in Table 31.2.

TABLE 31.2   Service Account Types

ServiceAccount Enum Member	Permissions
LocalService	A nonprivilege user on the local computer that presents anonymous credentials to other computers
LocalSystem	Has extensive privileges on the local computer and represents the computer on a network
NetworkService	Possesses several privileges on the local machine and will present credentials to other computers
User	Allows you to specify a user

As you can see, there are options for you to control what you want to allow your Windows service to do. If you want it to have maximum control, you can set it as `LocalSystem`.

The most configurable option is `User`, where you can give the service a machine or domain account. If you don't supply credentials, you'll be prompted when the service starts. This can be cumbersome on servers where a human isn't present for every reboot. If you press F7 or right-click and select View Code on the Project Installer, you can add credentials to the project installer like this:

```
public ProjectInstaller()
{
    InitializeComponent();
    serviceProcessInstaller1.Username = "username";
    serviceProcessInstaller1.Password = "password";
}
```

This is the constructor for the `ProjectInstaller`. You can set the `Username` and `Password` properties of the `ServiceProcessInstaller` here. Remember to set them "after" the call to `InitializeComponent` because `serviceProcessInstaller1` is instantiated inside of `InitializeComponent` and won't exist earlier. Next, you need to configure installers for individual services.

Configuring a `ServiceInstaller`

As mentioned earlier, you need a `ServiceInstaller` for each service in the process. Select the `ServiceInstaller` component and open the Properties window to configure the `ServiceInstaller`. Four important configuration options are `Description`, `DisplayName`, and `StartType`, and `ServiceName`.

The `Description` and `DisplayName` properties are what people see when they are looking at the service in the Administrative Tools Service console. These help give a professional presentation to your service.

`StartType` defaults to `Manual`, meaning that a user must go to the Administrative Tools Service console to manually start the service. Another option is `Disabled`, meaning that a user will have to manually enable the service, via the Services console, by putting it in the `Manual` or `Automatic` mode to start it. If you want the service to start every time the machine starts, switch this to `Automatic`.

If you are building a `ServiceController`, discussed later in this chapter, use the `ServiceName` property from the `ServiceInstaller` to properly identify the service.

The `ServiceInstaller` configuration defines how other programs and people can work with the service. However, before working with a service, you must install it, which is the subject of the next section.

Deploying the Windows Service

The InstallUtil.exe program ships with both the .NET Framework SDK and the .NET Runtime libraries, meaning that you can deploy your service to any machine with .NET installed and run the InstallUtil application to install it.

WHERE IS INSTALLUTIL?

Finding InstallUtil is tricky in .NET 3.0 and 3.5 because both of these .NET versions use the .NET 2.0 Common Language Runtime (CLR). If you open a .NET Framework 2.0 SDK command prompt, Windows SDK CMD shell, or a Visual Studio 2008 command prompt, this location is already in the path. Otherwise, you can find it at %windir%\Microsoft.NET\Framework\v2.0.50727, which is where the .NET 2.0 utilities are located.

The following command installs the `MoneyServer` Windows service:

```
InstallUtil MoneyServer.exe
```

If you open the Administrative Tools Service console, you'll see your Windows service listed. On first install, it won't start automatically, even if you set `StartType` to `Automatic` during `ServiceInstaller` configuration. So, you must start it yourself the first time.

To test that this Windows service works property, you can run the MoneyClient.exe application from Chapter 30, which will run just fine. It's a console application, so you might want to try your hand at converting it to a Windows Forms, Windows Presentation Foundation (WPF), or ASP.NET application with AJAX or Silverlight to see how an application can communicate with a server that you hosted via a Windows service.

The following command uninstalls the MoneyServer Windows service:

```
InstallUtil /u MoneyServer.exe
```

At a minimum, you'll probably want to create a batch file to run these commands for you, but a better solution is to use an installer application. In Chapter 45, "Creating Visual Studio 2008 Setup Projects," I show you how to add a custom installer component to a setup project to specifically perform this task.

UNINSTALL BEFORE REDEPLOYING

During the development cycle, you'll often change code and redeploy it to test. In addition, you'll probably be installing the executable that resides in the bin\debug folder that VS2008 creates for you.

Remember to uninstall your service before doing a build or in VS2008. Many times, you won't have a problem if you forget to do this. Sometimes, however, the build and the installed service can get out of whack, and the service won't uninstall. After going through several cycles of uninstalls, shutting down VS2008, and occasionally a reboot, you can get the old service to break free and uninstall. By making it a habit to uninstall before rebuilding the service, you can avoid a lot of headaches.

Building a Controller to Communicate with a Windows Service

Sometimes you need to control a Windows service from a separate application. The SQL Server taskbar app is a good example, in that it allows you to start and stop SQL Server instances. This section shows you how to build a ServiceController that lets you start and stop the MoneyServer Windows service.

The example we use is a WPF application. So if you are following along, create a new WPF application and add a couple buttons to the window with Content properties set to Start and Stop and with Name properties set to btnStart and btnStop, respectively. Chapter 26, "Creating Windows Presentation Foundation (WPF) Applications," provides instructions on how to create a WPF application (if you need help doing so). I'm naming this application MoneyServerController.

After you have the project in place and buttons created, write handlers for the buttons as shown in Listing 31.7. This is code that starts and stops the MoneyServer.

LISTING 31.7   Implementing a **ServiceController**

```
using System.ServiceProcess;
using System.Windows;

namespace MoneyServerController
{
    /// <summary>
    /// starts and stops Money Quote Server
    /// </summary>
    public partial class Window1 : Window
    {
        private ServiceController m_moneyCtrl;

        public Window1()
        {
            InitializeComponent();

            m_moneyCtrl = new ServiceController
            {
                ServiceName = "Service1"
            };
        }

        private void btnStart_Click(
            object sender, RoutedEventArgs e)
        {
            m_moneyCtrl.Refresh();
            if (m_moneyCtrl.Status ==
                ServiceControllerStatus.Stopped)
            {
                m_moneyCtrl.Start();
            }
        }

        private void btnStop_Click(
            object sender, RoutedEventArgs e)
        {
            m_moneyCtrl.Refresh();
            if (m_moneyCtrl.Status ==
                ServiceControllerStatus.Running)
            {
```

LISTING 31.7   Continued

```
            m_moneyCtrl.Stop();
        }
    }
  }
}
```

As shown in Listing 31.7, you need to add a using declaration for the System.ServiceProcess namespace to use the ServiceController class. In addition, you must add a reference to the System.ServiceProcess.dll assembly.

The constructor for Window1 instantiates ServiceController, m_moneyCtrl. Notice that ServiceName is set to "Service1". To figure out what this name should be, look at the ServiceName property of the ServiceInstaller for the service you want to communicate with. I'll rephrase this to ensure you don't accidentally set this incorrectly—don't use the ServiceName property on the service itself, but use the ServiceName property on the ServiceInstaller instead. You'll probably want to change it to something meaningful.

Notice that handlers btnStart_Click and btnStop_Click check the status of the service before changing its state. It is important that you invoke Refresh on the service to get the latest state. Otherwise, you'll be working with the last state that was set, when m_moneyCtrl was instantiated. Also, you or someone else could change the status of the service via the Administrative Tools Service console; if you do so, your application won't know it.

Summary

You now know how to create a Windows service to host your own server application. Windows services are configurable and have various states, such as start, stop, and others that you write code for via method overrides.

To deploy a Windows service, you need to create installer objects for the whole process and for each service in the application. Then you can use InstallUtil to install the service on the machine it is being deployed to.

On occasion, you might need to communicate with a Windows service. This chapter showed you how to build a controller application that can start and stop a Windows service.

Along the lines of servers and communications, the next chapter explains how to create remoting objects that enable communication between applications.

Remoting

Many of today's enterprise applications employ distributed applications for scalability. Remoting is a new technology supporting this goal, allowing objects to communicate across AppDomains with minimal overhead. The remoting architecture abstracts as much of the underlying communications plumbing associated with distributed computing. It's easy to set up communication between multiple distributed objects and communicate as if the objects were in the same process space.

Remoting can be approached at many different levels. One of the significant differences between remoting and other distributed object technologies is its architectural extensibility. The remoting architecture is very flexible, enabling the capability to extend an application by adding custom components that participate in the communication process.

An integral feature of remoting is lifetime management of remote server components through leases. Client applications communicate with a lease manager to control the lifetime of these components.

Basic Remoting

At its most basic level, remoting is the capability to communicate with components in separate AppDomains. Figure 32.1 shows a simplified view of two objects communicating via remoting: a client component in AppDomain A communicates with a server component in AppDomain B.

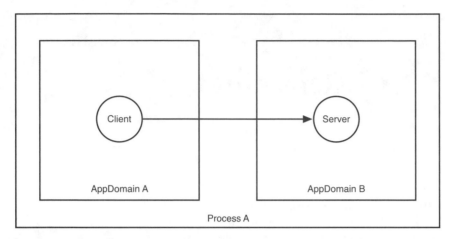

FIGURE 32.1   Basic remoting diagram.

WHAT IS AN APPDOMAIN?

An AppDomain is an execution environment within a process. It separates managed applications during execution. This provides several benefits including reliability and security.

Because remoting supports multitiered as well as distributed architectures, the server component in AppDomain B could easily be extended to a client role, communicating with a server component in another AppDomain. Furthermore, a remote component could be located in another process on either the same or a different machine. When a component is set up, the underlying plumbing required to maintain remote communications is hidden by the remoting architecture.

There are several examples in the following sections that all fit together to help you build a small remoting system. There is a server, which is a DLL that must be hosted by another application, either IIS or a custom host that you build. There is also a client, which is an executable that makes an out-of-process call to communicate with the remoting server. I'll show you how to build the remoting server first, and then the client, and finally, I'll show you a couple ways to host the server. After the server is hosted and the host is running, you can run the client, which will call the server, facilitated by the host.

Remoting Server

A remoting server object is just a class that derives from MarshalByRefObject. Listing 21.1 shows how to implement a remoting server object.

LISTING 32.1   Remoting Server Demo: BasicRemotingServer.cs

```
using System;

namespace BasicServer
{
    /// <summary>
    /// Basic Remoting Server Demo.
    /// </summary>
    public class BasicRemotingServer : MarshalByRefObject
    {
        public string GetServerResponse()
        {
            return
"Greetings from the BasicRemotingServer component!";
        }
    }
}
```

The BasicServer class in Listing 32.1 inherits MarshalByRefObject, which supports the basic functionality for a callable component over the remoting architecture. This class is implemented as a DLL, negating the need for a Main method. The only method in this class is the GetServerResponse method, keeping things simple. This is the remoting server object used in the rest of the examples in this chapter.

Each remoted component requires a configuration file, named web.config, to specify necessary operating parameters. The web.config file for the remote server component in Listing 32.1 is shown in Listing 32.2.

LISTING 32.2   Remote Server Component Configuration File: web.config

```
<configuration>
    <system.runtime.remoting>
        <application>
            <service>

                <wellknown mode="SingleCall"
type="BasicServer.BasicRemotingServer, BasicServer"
objectUri="BasicRemotingServer.soap" />

            </service>
        </application>
    </system.runtime.remoting>
</configuration>
```

The configuration file in Listing 32.2 is located in the same directory in which Listing 32.1 was built. It contains a special section for remoting, marked by a tag named after the remoting namespace, `<system.runtime.remoting>`. Further down the hierarchy is an `<application>` tag, containing a `<service>` tag. The `<service>` section has a `<wellknown>` tag with three attributes that assist in making this remoted object run properly: `mode`, `type`, and `objectUri`.

A `mode` has two possible values: `SingleCall` and `Singleton`. These values identify basic lifetime issues associated with a remote object.

`SingleCall` components are activated and live for the duration of a single call from the remote client. For example, when a remote client calls the `GetServerResponse` method of the `BasicRemotingServer` class (from Listing 32.1), a new `BasicRemotingServer` object is instantiated when the call begins. When the call ends, the server object is destroyed. Furthermore, each client receives a reference to a unique server object whenever it makes a call.

`Singleton` components are the only instance of a given class. They stick around to provide service to every call of every client.

The decision to designate a remote server component depends on the nature of the application. There are a couple tradeoffs to consider. `SingleCall` components are more scalable, supporting an increasing number of clients as hardware constraints allow. A potential drawback to `SingleCall` components is that they lose state between method invocations and don't support shared state between clients. A solution to this is to have a separate component supporting state management to a backing store such as a database or file. `Singleton` components are good for sharing information between clients and their method invocations. This also increases complexity associated with managing the integrity of state between clients. In addition, `Singleton` components are not as scalable as `SingleCall` components. It's also conceivable that a hybrid system of remote `SingleCall` and `Singleton` objects can be established. Just remember that a single class can't have both `SingleCall` and `Singleton` instantiations.

The `type` attribute of the `<wellknown>` tag has a quoted pair of values that identify the remote server object. The first value is the fully qualified name of the class. The second value is the executable filename of the assembly to which the class belongs.

The last attribute of the `<wellknown>` tag is the `objectUri`, which holds the Universal Resource Identifier (URI) of the server component. A URI is a unique identifier for an Internet resource.

WHAT IS A URI?

A URI is a more generic term for objects on the Internet, such as those objects used in remoting. However, a Universal Resource Locator (URL) is more specific to the web and uniquely identifies a web page.

Remoting Client

Writing a remoting client is just a little more involved than writing a remoting server. Basically, writing a client requires finding out the type and location of the remote server object, initializing configuration from a file, and creating an instance of the remote object with the type and location information obtained earlier. Listing 32.3 shows how to write a basic client for a remote server component.

LISTING 32.3   Basic Remoting Client: BasicRemotingClient.cs

```csharp
using System;
using System.Runtime.Remoting;
using BasicServer;

/// <summary>
/// Basic Remoting Client Demo.
/// </summary>
class BasicRemotingClient
{
    static void Main(string[] args)
    {
        Type   type = typeof(BasicRemotingServer);
        String url  =
"http://localhost/BasicServerDemo/BasicRemotingServer.soap";

        RemotingConfiguration.Configure(
            "BasicRemotingClient.exe.config", false);

        BasicRemotingServer brs =
          (BasicRemotingServer)Activator.GetObject(type, url);

        Console.WriteLine(brs.GetServerResponse());
    }
}
```

And here's the output:

```
Greetings from the BasicRemotingServer component!
```

Listing 32.3 uses two additional namespaces: System.Runtime.Remoting and BasicServer. The System.Runtime.Remoting namespace contains all the basic remoting classes. Our remote server component that will be instantiated and called is in the BasicServer namespace.

Within the Main method, the type of the BasicRemotingServer class is obtained with the typeof operator and stored in a Type object. Next, the URL of the BasicRemotingServer component is specified. Notice that it appends the `BasicRemotingServer.soap` URI to the full URL definition. This is the same URI specified in the web.config file (Listing 32.2) for the remote server. Then the client must configure itself in preparation for communication with the remoting system. It does so with the static `Configure` method of the `RemotingConfiguration` class. The string parameter, `"BasicRemotingClient.exe.config"`, of the `Configure` method specifies the configuration file to use. This is similar in purpose to the web.config file but specialized for the needs of the client. Listing 32.4 shows the configuration file for the remoting client.

LISTING 32.4   Client Configuration File: BasicRemotingClient.exe.config

```
<?xml version="1.0" encoding="utf-8" ?>
<configuration>
  <system.runtime.remoting>
    <application>
      <client>
        <wellknown
          type=
"BasicServer.BasicRemotingServer, BasicServer"
          url=
"http://localhost/BasicServerDemo/BasicRemotingServer.soap"
          />
      </client>
    </application>
  </system.runtime.remoting>
</configuration>
```

A client configuration file must be named after the executable of the client with the .config extension. Because the executable name of the program in Listing 32.3 is BasicRemotingClient.exe, the configuration filename must be BasicRemotingClient.exe.config.

If you're using VS2008, you can add a new application configuration file item to your project, which produces a file named App.config. The neat thing about App.config is that VS2008 enables you to modify this file in the IDE, but during compilation, it copies App.config to <AssemblyName>.exe.config in the output folder for you.

VERIFYING ASSEMBLY NAME

Make sure your Assembly name in VS2008 is what you expect; double-click the Properties folder in your project, click the Application tab, and inspect Assembly name. It defaults to what you named the project, but you can change it to what you want.

The first difference between the web.config file and BasicRemotingClient.exe.config is that the `<application>` tag has a `name` attribute defined. This is the name of the client class, `BasicRemotingClient`.

Lower in the hierarchy is the <channels> tag, where a channel is defined. Channels are discussed in more detail later, so this is just a brief explanation. The <channels> section has a <channel> tag with a type attribute that has a string with two values. The first value specifies what type of channel will be used to communicate with the server component. The second parameter identifies the namespace associated with the channel.

After the client has been configured, it may obtain a reference to the remote object. This is accomplished by calling the static GetObject method of the Activator class. The two parameters to the GetObject method are the type and url, respectively, that were obtained earlier. Because the reference is returned as an object type, the return value is cast to BasicRemotingServer. Here's the code obtaining a reference to the remote server component:

```
BasicRemotingServer brs =
    (BasicRemotingServer)Activator.GetObject(type, url);
```

After the remote server component reference is obtained, it can be used just like any other reference. In the following example, the getServerResponse method of the remote server component is invoked, returning a string to the Console.WriteLine method for printing to the console:

```
Console.WriteLine(brs.GetServerResponse());
```

Remoting Setup

There are two ways to get a remoting application up and running: via a web server or a host utility. The first example will use Microsoft Internet Information Services (IIS) as the web server to host the remote server component. Demonstrating the host utility requires code for a new client and server program and the utility.

Web Server Setup

The following steps show how to set up a remote server component via the IIS web server:

1. Before actually starting this procedure, work out a directory structure so that it will be easy to follow along. Given an arbitrary path, <path>, to the source code files, you'll have two directories at the end of this path, BasicServer and BasicClient. Put the BasicServer.cs file from Listing 32.1 and web.config file from Listing 32.2 into the BasicServer directory. Then put the BasicRemotingClient.cs file from Listing 32.3 and the BasicRemotingClient.exe.config file from Listing 32.4 into the BasicClient directory. Next, create a directory named bin under the BasicServer directory. Here's what your directory structure should look like:

```
<path>\BasicServer
    BasicServer.cs
    Web.config
    <path>\BasicServer\bin
```

```
<path>\BasicClient
    BasicClient.cs

        BasicClient.exe.config
```

2. Compile the server component from Listing 32.1 in the BasicServer directory with the following command line:

```
csc /t:library BasicServer.cs
```

This produces the BasicServer.dll file, which should be copied to <path>\BasicServer\bin. This is the location where the web server will be looking. Optionally, copy BasicServer.dll into the bin folder under your VS2008 project.

3. Open Internet Information Services (IIS). The following steps work for Windows XP but are different for other operating systems. For example, WinNT, Win2K, Win2003, Win2008, and Vista are all different. If the actions don't match your OS exactly, consult your documentation to accomplish the same tasks.

4. Expand the server node under which you want to create a virtual directory and right-click Default Web Site. From the menu, select New, Virtual Directory. This opens the Virtual Directory Creation Wizard. Click Next.

5. In the text box for an Alias, type in any meaningful name for the virtual directory, such as **BasicServerDemo**. Click Next.

6. In the text box for the physical path that the virtual directory will refer to, enter the **<path>\BasicServer** directory, where <path> is the actual directory you specified in step 1. I'm personally a big fan of using the Browse button because, more often than not, I'll mistype the path and end up scratching my head later when things don't work. Click Next.

7. There are several access permissions from which to choose. The Read and Run Scripts (such as ASP) options are already checked, and that's fine. Accept the defaults, click Next, and then click Finish on the last screen. IIS will use the web.config file in the BasicServer directory when it loads the server component. The remote server component is now set up. If you're using Visa, remember to right-click on the virtual directory and select Make Application.

8. Use the following command line to compile the remoting client program from Listing 32.3:

```
csc /r:..\BasicServer\BasicServer.dll BasicClient.cs
```

Optionally, you can just build the project with VS2008. Remember to add a reference to the BasicServer project; right-click the References folder in BasicClient, select Add Reference, click the Projects tab, select the BasicServer project, and click the OK button. You'll also need to add a using declaration for the BasicServer namespace.

9. Finally, run the BasicClient.exe program in the BasicClient folder to test the system out. If all goes well, the following output will be printed to the console:

```
Greetings from the BasicRemotingServer component!
```

Host Utility Setup

The host utility setup method uses a program that configures the remote server component so that clients can find it. The process isn't necessarily easier or harder than the web
server setup method—it's just different. As with the web server setup method, an organized approach simplifies things.

Follow a similar directory-naming scheme as described in step 1 of the preceding section.
Replace the BasicServer with HostedServer and the BasicClient with the HostedClient
directory names. To be organized, you may want to create a new directory, at the same
level as HostedServer and HostedClient, named RemotingHost to hold the source and
executable for the host utility.

The server and client components of this example are pretty much the same as the previous
listings in this section. However, for demonstration purposes, it's necessary to have unique
listings to keep track of what's going on. Listing 32.5 shows the remoting server
component.

LISTING 32.5   Hosted Server Demo: HostedServer.cs

```
using System;

namespace Host
{
    /// <summary>
    /// Hosted Server Component Demo.
    /// </summary>
    public class HostedServer : MarshalByRefObject
    {
        public string GetServerResponse()
        {
            return
                "Greetings from the HostedServer component!";
        }
    }
}
```

No surprises in Listing 32.5: The names were changed to protect the innocent, and the
text of the return string from the GetServerResponse method is different. The code in
Listing 32.5 can be compiled with the following command line:

```
csc /t:library HostedServer.cs
```

If using VS2008, you can create a class library project, which will also create the same
DLL when you build. Listing 32.6 shows the client code, which calls the server, and
Listing 32.7 shows its configuration file.

LISTING 32.6   Remoting Client Demo: HostedClient.cs

```csharp
using System;
using System.Runtime.Remoting;
using Host;

namespace HostedClient
{
    /// <summary>
    /// Client for a Hosted Remote Server.
    /// </summary>
    class HostedClient
    {
        static void Main(string[] args)
        {
            Type    type = typeof(HostedServer);
            String url  =
"http://localhost:8000/HostedServer/HostedServer.soap";

            RemotingConfiguration.Configure(
                "HostedClient.exe.config", false);

            HostedServer hostedServer =
                (HostedServer)Activator.GetObject(type, url);

            Console.WriteLine(
                hostedServer.GetServerResponse());
        }
    }
}
```

LISTING 32.7   Remoting Client Configuration File: HostedClient.exe.config

```xml
<configuration>
    <system.runtime.remoting>
        <application name="HostedClient">
            <client url="http://localhost:8000/HostedServer">

                <wellknown
type="Host.HostedServer, HostedServer"
url="http://localhost:8000/HostedServer/HostedServer.soap" />

            </client>
            <channels>
```

LISTING 32.7   Continued

```
                <channel
type="System.Runtime.Remoting.Channels.Http.HttpChannel,System.Runtime.Remoting" />

            </channels>
        </application>
    </system.runtime.remoting>
</configuration>
```

Again, the code in Listing 32.6 doesn't present anything new. The code for listing 32.6 can be compiled with the following command line:

```
csc /r:..\HostedServer\HostedServer.dll HostedClient.cs
```

You could also use VS2008 and build normally.

A host utility enables clients to find a remote server component. Its implementation is straightforward, just configuring the remote server component and pausing for a length of time necessary for the server to be used. Listing 32.8 shows how to implement a host utility.

LISTING 32.8   Host Utility Demo: RemotingHost.cs

```
using System;
using System.Runtime.Remoting;

/// <summary>
/// Summary description for RemoteHost.
/// </summary>
public class RemoteHost
{
    public static void Main()
    {
        RemotingConfiguration.Configure(
            "RemotingHost.exe.config", false);

        Console.WriteLine("Press any key to exit...");
        Console.ReadLine();
    }
}
```

The Main method of the RemoteHost class in Listing 32.8 begins by configuring the remote server component. Then it pauses, prompting the user to press a key to continue. It's necessary for the host utility to remain running while the server is being used. This guarantees that the remoting system will recognize the server and provide a path for clients to find it. Listing 32.9 is the host utility configuration file.

LISTING 32.9   Host Utility Configuration File: RemotingHost.exe.config

```
<configuration>
    <system.runtime.remoting>
        <application name="HostedServer">
            <service>

                <wellknown mode="SingleCall"
                    type="Host.HostedServer, HostedServer"
                    objectUri="HostedServer.soap" />

            </service>
            <channels>

                <channel port="8000"
type="System.Runtime.Remoting.Channels.Http.HttpChannel,System.Runtime.Remoting" />

            </channels>
        </application>
    </system.runtime.remoting>
</configuration>
```

This file has both `<service>` and `<channels>` sections. These are defined pretty much the same as corresponding sections in previous configuration file listings. The difference is that port 8000 is specified in the location data. You will recall that the client configuration file in Listing 32.7 specified the same port. The following example shows how to compile the host utility in Listing 32.8:

```
csc RemotingHost.cs
```

To test this out, copy HostedServer.dll into the same output directory as RemotingHost. Alternatively, you can reference the HostedServer project in VS2008, which will copy the file for you. Run the RemotingHost application and then run the HostedClient application to see the output.

Channels

Channels marshal, format, and transmit messages across AppDomains. Each of a channel's tasks opens new opportunities for extensibility. For example, message contents can be marshaled to conform to the proper data representation using custom sinks. The message itself can be formatted via the built-in Simple Object Access Protocol (SOAP) or binary formatters. In addition, transport protocols, such as HTTP or TCP, which are built in, can be configured with ease. The architecture also supports customizable marshalling, formatting, and transmission components that can be plugged in as needed. Figure 32.2 shows the relationship of the channel to other remoting architecture components. The HTTPChannel, linking the proxy in AppDomain A to the stub in AppDomain B, is a built-in channel component supporting default marshalling, XML/SOAP formatting, and HTTP protocol transmission.

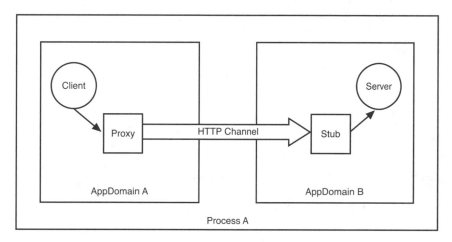

FIGURE 32.2   Remoting channels.

Previous listings in this chapter used configuration files to specify their channels. The following example is an excerpt from one of the configuration files:

```
<channels>

    <channel ref="http" port="8000" />

</channels>
```

The <channels> section in the previous example contains channel information for remoting components. When the configuration file is read by the RemotingConfiguration.Configure method, the specified channel is registered with the remoting system. The <channel> tag has a type attribute, specifying the channel type to be used, as its first value and the applicable namespace as the second parameter. All the previous programs in this chapter used these parameters, meaning that they used an HttpChannel as their remoting channel.

Instead of configuration files, a program may register its channels programmatically. At the most basic level, all that's required is to invoke a single registration command and the channel is registered. Listing 32.12 shows how to register a remoting channel.

LISTING 32.12   Programmatic Remoting Channel Registration: RemotingProxyClient.cs

```csharp
using System;
using System.Runtime.Remoting;
using System.Runtime.Remoting.Channels;
using System.Runtime.Remoting.Channels.Http;
using BasicServer;

/// <summary>
/// Remoting Proxy Client.
/// </summary>
class RemotingProxyClient
{
    static void Main(string[] args)
    {
        ChannelServices.RegisterChannel(new HttpChannel(), false);

        BasicRemotingServer brs = new BasicRemotingServer();

        Console.WriteLine("\nServer Response: {0}",
            brs.GetServerResponse());
    }
}
```

The program in Listing 32.12 registers an `HttpChannel` with the static `ChannelServices.RegisterChannel` method. After that, it instantiates the remote server component, just like any other object, and invokes a remote server component method. Instead of the `HttpChannel` object, the program could have just as easily created a new `TcpChannel` object, which uses the binary formatter and TCP transport protocol. The program in Listing 32.12 can be compiled with the following command line:

```
csc /r:..\BasicServer\BasicServer.dll RemotingProxyClient.cs
```

WHAT'S THE DIFFERENCE BETWEEN HTTP AND TCP CHANNELS?

The `HttpChannel` is good for open standards communication. It uses SOAP to format messages in XML and HTTP for transport. However, XML/SOAP formatted messages are much larger packages than a traditional binary formatted message. The larger messages, which consume more network bandwidth, may be an issue for some projects. If standards are not a concern and your application needs speed, use the `TcpChannel`. It uses a binary formatter, leading to more compressed data, and the TCP transmission protocol, leading to faster transmission speeds.

Lifetime Management

When left alone, a remote server component exists for a default amount of time and then makes itself available for garbage collection. It's often more desirable to explicitly manage the lifetime of remote components. This is why the remoting framework provides a leasing mechanism for finer granularity of control in remote component lifetime management.

Remote leasing operates via a collaborative protocol between one or more client components, a server component, and a lease manager.

Remote server components begin life with a designated amount of time before garbage collection. Client components register with the server component's lease manager for notification of when the server's lifetime is expiring. The lease manager keeps track of server components and notifies clients of when the server will expire. When a server has reached its expiration time, the lease manager notifies the client and waits for a designated amount of time for a reply from the client. If the client wants the server to remain alive, it returns the amount of time the server can live to the lease manager. If the designated reply time from the client to the lease renewal query expires, the lease manager marks the server object for garbage collection.

To participate in remote server component lifetime management, a client must implement the ISponsor interface. This interface has a single method, Renewal, which the lease manager calls when a remote server component needs its lifetime updated. Listing 32.13 shows how to implement a client that uses remote leasing.

LISTING 32.13   Remote Leasing Demo: LeasingDemo.cs

```
using System;
using System.Runtime.Remoting;
using System.Runtime.Remoting.Channels;
using System.Runtime.Remoting.Channels.Http;
using System.Runtime.Remoting.Lifetime;
using BasicServer;

/// <summary>
/// Remoting Object Lifetime Demo.
/// </summary>
class LeasingDemo : ISponsor
{
    ILease lease;

    // implement lease logic
    public void ImplementLease()
    {
        BasicRemotingServer brs = new BasicRemotingServer();
```

32

LISTING 32.13   Continued

```csharp
        lease = (ILease)brs.InitializeLifetimeService();
        lease.Register(this, new TimeSpan(0, 0, 3));

        PrintLeaseInfo();

        Console.WriteLine("\nServer Response: {0}",
            brs.GetServerResponse());
    }

    // ISponsor.Renewal - called to renew lease
    public TimeSpan Renewal(ILease myLease)
    {
        TimeSpan timeSpan = new TimeSpan(0, 0, 3);

        Console.WriteLine("\nLease Renewed.\n");

        PrintLeaseInfo();

        return timeSpan;
    }

    // print lease info
    void PrintLeaseInfo()
    {
        if (lease != null)
        {
            Console.WriteLine("Lease Info\n");
            Console.WriteLine("  CurrentLeaseTime: {0}", lease.CurrentLeaseTime );
            Console.WriteLine("  InitialLeaseTime: {0}", lease.InitialLeaseTime);
            Console.WriteLine("   RenewOnCallTime: {0}", lease.RenewOnCallTime);
            Console.WriteLine("SponsorshipTimeout: {0}", lease.SponsorshipTimeout);
        }
    }

    // entry point
    static void Main(string[] args)
    {
        ChannelServices.RegisterChannel(new HttpChannel(), false);

        LeasingDemo leaseDemo = new LeasingDemo();
        leaseDemo.ImplementLease();
    }
}
```

And here's the output:

```
   CurrentLeaseTime: 00:00:02.9499280
   InitialLeaseTime: 00:05:00
    RenewOnCallTime: 00:02:00
SponsorshipTimeout: 00:02:00


Server Response: Greetings from the BasicRemotingServer component!

Lease Renewed.

Lease Info

   CurrentLeaseTime: -00:00:07.1145440
   InitialLeaseTime: 00:05:00
    RenewOnCallTime: 00:02:00
SponsorshipTimeout: 00:02:00


Lease Renewed.
```

The Main method of the LeasingDemo class in Listing 21.14 registers an HttpChannel, instantiates a LeasingDemo object, and calls the ImplementLease method to run this program.

The leasing demo method initializes a lease manager for the remote server component and receives a lease manager object, which implements the ILease interface. The following line shows how to initialize the lease manager:

```
lease = (ILease)brs.InitializeLifetimeService();
```

With the lease manager object, the client registers itself to receive notifications of the remote server component's lifetime expiration. In addition, the second parameter to the Register method provides the lease manager with the remote server components initial lifetime, using a TimeSpan object, as shown here:

```
lease.Register(this, new TimeSpan(0, 0, 3));
```

All the client needs to do now is invoke methods on the server component and wait for renewal requests from the lease manager. The lease manager calls the client's Renewal() method when the lifetime of the remote server component expires. The client in this example simply creates a new TimeSpan object and returns it to the lease manager to keep the remote server component alive for three more seconds. The TimeSpan constructor overload in the example of Listing 21.14 uses three parameters: hours, minutes, and seconds, respectively.

Summary

In its most basic form, remoting is a mechanism enabling communication across AppDomains between client and server components. Remote server components expose their methods to be consumed by one or more clients. Clients use configuration files to specify remoting parameters that help them use the remoting framework to find and invoke methods on remote server components. Remote server components can be set up via a web server or a specialized host utility.

The remoting framework is extensible, with a flexible channel mechanism with configurable marshalling, formatting, and transport services. These channel services can be replaced with custom components.

Remote server component lifetime can be managed via a leasing mechanism. This leasing mechanism exposes a lease manager, assisting collaboration of lifetime issues between remoting client and server components. The leasing mechanism allows clients to control the lifetime of remote server components.

The next chapter presents another distributed computing technology, web services. Although remoting and web services are two separate technologies, the concepts from this chapter should provide insight into the inner workings of web services.

CHAPTER 33

Writing Traditional ASMX Web Services

A web service is a distributed computing technology that enables the exposure and reuse of logical business entities over the Internet. There are all types of distributed computing technologies, but the emphasis here is on open standards. In particular, these are based on World Wide Web Consortium (W3C) protocols and communications standards.

With open standards, businesses can deploy components on the Web to be consumed by anyone, anywhere. It does not matter what computer is being used, its operating system, or the programming language used to implement the logic. Applicable bits include the communications protocol, data formats, and registry interaction, which are defined by open W3C standards.

Web Service Basics

Creating ASP.NET web services is incredibly easy. ASP.NET web services are web services supported by the ASP.NET infrastructure. This provides an environment where all the underlying plumbing is encapsulated. The net result is reduced complexity and more time for a developer to concentrate on business logic rather than plumbing.

Web Service Technologies

Several open standards technologies play a significant role in making web services a reality. These standards can be categorized by description, discovery, and transmission.

Description

The Web Services Description Language (WSDL) is an XML-based format for describing a web service. It describes what the web service is, its parameters, and how to use it.

Discovery

Universal Description Discovery and Integration (UDDI) directories support discovery. These directories manage WSDL documents and provide a means for clients to find and use web services.

UDDI is interesting for historical purposes. The fact is that it was never widely adopted and practically no one uses it. Instead, most web service implementations use other forms of documentation to publish their web services. For example, Amazon.com has web services that anyone can use; you just visit its site and read its documentation, which includes all the information you need for finding and using its web services.

Transmission

The Simple Object Access Protocol (SOAP) is a communications protocol that enables clients to interact with UDDI directories and web services. It's an open standard protocol that wraps a method call into an envelope for delivery between endpoints. SOAP rides upon other open standard transmission protocols, such as HTTP (very common) or TCP.

As of the SOAP Standard 1.1, the acronym SOAP no longer means Simple Object Access Protocol. Some would say that it isn't as simple as it was first thought to be after some revision. It isn't object-oriented but is message-based instead. Finally, it is more of a message format than a protocol. However, the name SOAP stuck.

A Basic Web Service

With ASP.NET web services, hereafter referred to as web services, the underlying technologies supporting description, discovery, and transmission are hidden with the rest of the system plumbing. To make a web service, you should create two files. The first file is an ASP.NET header, as shown in Listing 33.1. The second is a code-behind file with business logic, as shown in Listing 33.2.

LISTING 33.1   Web Service Header: BasicWebService.asmx

```
<%@ WebService Language="c#" Codebehind="BasicWebService.asmx.cs" Class="BasicWeb-
Service.BasicWebService" %>
```

Similar to an ASP.NET web page header, the web service header in Listing 33.1 communicates with the ASP.NET system to enable compilation and the underlying plumbing that supports the web service. The @WebService directive tells the ASP.NET system that this is a web service, as opposed to the @Page directive, which identifies an ASP.NET web page. The @WebService directive has three attributes: Language, Codebehind, and Class.

The Language attribute specifies the language that this web service will be compiled with. It could have been any .NET-compatible language, but here we're interested only in C#.

The Codebehind attribute identifies the source code file holding the actual code. The current convention is to use *<filename>.asmx.cs*, where *<filename>* can be any name.

The Class attribute indicates the web service class that clients must instantiate. In Listing 33.1, the class is shown as BasicWebService, which is part of the identically named namespace BasicWebService. The contents of the BasicWebService class are shown in Listing 33.2.

LISTING 33.2   Web Service Code: BasicWebService.asmx.cs

```
using System;
using System.Web;
using System.Web.Services;

namespace BasicWebService
{
    /// <summary>
    /// Basic Web Service Demo.
    /// </summary>
    [WebService(Namespace="http://SAMS/C#.Unleashed/WebServices")]
    public class BasicWebService : System.Web.Services.WebService
    {
        [WebMethod]
        public string Greetings(string name)
        {
            return "Hello " + name + "!";
        }
    }
}
```

The BasicWebService class in this listing defines a single method, Greetings, which accepts a string parameter and returns a string. The only noticeable difference from any other class is the inheritance chain and attributes.

A web service class may optionally inherit from the WebService class, which is part of the System.Web.Services namespace. Doing so provides the class with access to ASP.NET objects such as application and session state. In the case of Listing 33.2, the inheritance of the WebService class could have been left out with no implications.

An optional attribute, WebService, decorates the BasicWebService class. Its purpose in Listing 33.2 is to define the XML namespace in which this web service resides. The only requirement is that the namespace be unique, unless it is supposed to be a member of an existing XML namespace. The named parameter, Namespace, sets the BasicWebService web service into the http://SAMS/C#.Unleashed/WebServices namespace.

Exposed methods for web services must be decorated with the WebMethod attribute. In addition, these classes must be public, which makes sense because external components must be able to see and access the method.

BUILDING WEB SERVICES WITH VS2008

The explanation of code in this chapter describes how you can create a web service with nothing more than your favorite editor (or Notepad if you're daring). If you are using VS2008, it will probably be easier to create a new project of type ASP.NET web service application. If you have an ASP.NET web application, you can also add an ASP.NET web service item to it.

You can deploy the source files in Listing 33.1 and Listing 33.2 by copying them to an appropriate web server directory.

Viewing Web Service Info

The ASP.NET infrastructure provides the means to view information and test the operation of a web service. To do so, point your browser to the location of the web service on a web server. Figure 33.1 shows the results of pointing a browser at a web service.

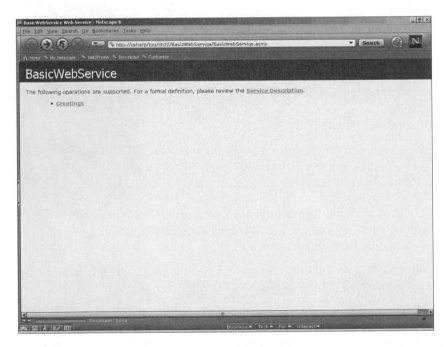

FIGURE 33.1   Locating a web service with a browser.

The screen in Listing 33.1 shows a list of all available operations for a web service. The BasicWebService web service has only a single operation, Greetings. Clicking the greetings hyperlink results in the page, as shown in Figure 33.2.

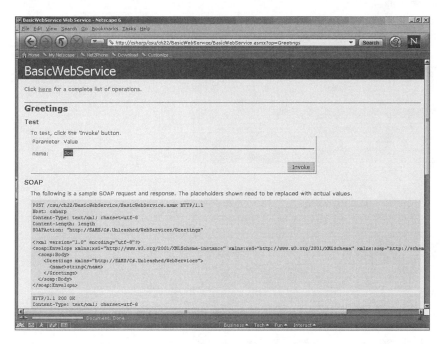

FIGURE 33.2   Testing a web service.

The name parameter with the text box following it is where a string can be entered as a parameter to the Greetings operation. In the example, the string "Joe" is entered as the name parameter. Clicking the Invoke button does what one would expect; it invokes the Greetings method. There's more information on the test page, and I explain that in a little bit.

Figure 33.3 shows the text string returned from invoking the Greetings operation on the BasicWebService web service. However, the actual result is not this simple, because the web browser interpreted the XML before displaying a result. The behavior is browser-specific, so you might see a different result.

The real reply that was returned is shown in Figure 33.4.

The top of the display in Figure 33.4 shows a standard XML header. What is most interesting is the next line with the <string> tag, which has an xmlns attribute. This attribute identifies the XML namespace of which this web service is a part. The namespace is exactly the same namespace specified in the WebService attribute of the BasicWebService class definition in Listing 33.2. The value is the same string reply shown in Figure 33.3, with the difference being that Figure 33.4 shows the full XML reply. Now, looking back at the test screen, Figure 33.5 shows the message format.

Figure 33.5 shows the format of the SOAP request and response for the Greetings operation of the BasicWebService web service. The first code block shows the SOAP request with the first five lines being the HTTP headers. After the XML header is the SOAP envelope, the outer layer of a SOAP message. Within the SOAP envelope is the SOAP body, which in turn holds the Greetings request. The tag of the Greetings request has an xmlns namespace attribute. This is the same namespace specified in the WebService attribute decorating the BasicWebService class in Listing 33.2. When a SOAP request is made for the Greetings operation, the string is entered in the name element when the call is invoked.

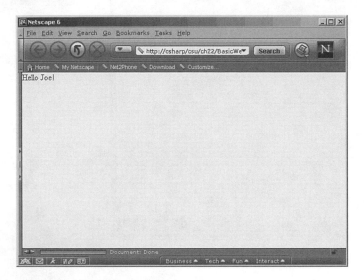

FIGURE 33.3   Web service invocation results: text reply.

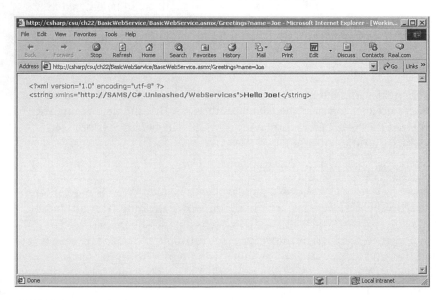

FIGURE 33.4   Web service invocation results: XML reply.

The SOAP response for the Greetings operation is similar to the request with three HTTP response headers, the XML header, and a SOAP envelope with a SOAP body. The difference is that the name of the operation is appended with the word Response,

`GreetingsResponse`, and the result is the name of the operation appended with the word `Result`, `GreetingsResult`. The result will be a string returned from the `Greetings` operation of the `BasicWebService` web service.

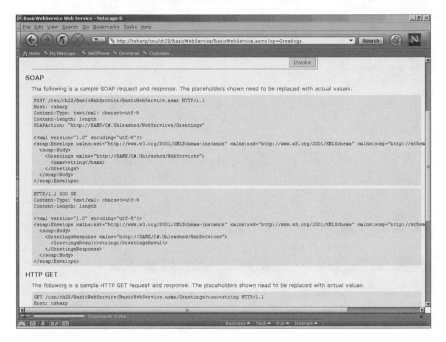

FIGURE 33.5   SOAP message format.

A web service may also be called with HTTP `PUT` and `GET` operations, as shown in Figure 33.6. Examining the HTTP `GET` request command and comparing it to the URL from the browser in Figure 33.4 indicates that the invoke operation from the test page in Figure 33.2 uses an HTTP `GET` operation. Comparing the XML portion of the HTTP `GET` response from Figure 33.6 to the XML output in Figure 33.4 confirms this. An HTTP `POST` message is formatted differently, according to HTTP `POST` protocol, yet returns a response in exactly the same format as the HTTP `GET` response.

Using Web Services

If an application wraps a method call into a SOAP envelope and uses HTTP, it could use the method described in Figure 33.5 to communicate with the `BasicWebService` web service. Alternatively, the client could use one of the HTTP `GET` or `POST` methods from Figure 33.6. It's possible, but that would be a lot of work.

The .NET Framework comes with a utility called `wsdl` that frees a client from creating all this plumbing. This utility takes the URL to a web service and creates a proxy, which is used by the client to call the web service. The following command line creates a proxy to the `BasicWebService` web service with the name `BasicWebService.cs`, shown in Listing 33.3:

```
wsdl http://csharp/csu/ch22/BasicWebService/BasicWebService.asmx?wsdl
```

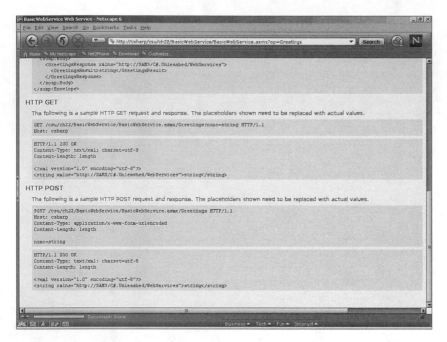

FIGURE 33.6   HTTP message formats.

WARNING

Although experimentation with the code of a proxy can certainly be cool and education-al, be careful. If you later try to use the code and it doesn't work, you might have to regenerate the proxy all over again to get things working.

LISTING 33.3   Autogenerated Web Service Proxy: BasicWebService.cs

```
//------------------------------------------
// <autogenerated>
//     This code was generated by a tool.
//     Runtime Version: 1.0.2914.14
//
//     Changes to this file may cause incorrect behavior and will be lost if
//     the code is regenerated.
// </autogenerated>
//------------------------------------------

//
// This source code was auto-generated by wsdl, Version=1.0.2914.14.
//
using System.Diagnostics;
```

LISTING 33.3   Continued

```
using System.Xml.Serialization;
using System;
using System.Web.Services.Protocols;
using System.Web.Services;


[System.Web.Services.WebServiceBindingAttribute(Name="BasicWebServiceSoap", Name-
space="http://SAMS/C#.Unleashed/WebServices")]
public class BasicWebService : System.Web.Services.Protocols.SoapHttpClientProtocol {

    [System.Diagnostics.DebuggerStepThroughAttribute()]
    public BasicWebService() {
        this.Url = "http://csharp/csu/ch22/BasicWebService/BasicWebService.asmx";
    }

    [System.Diagnostics.DebuggerStepThroughAttribute()]
    [System.Web.Services.Protocols.SoapDocumentMethodAttribute
    ➡("http://SAMS/C#.Unleashed/WebServices/Greetings",
    ➡RequestNamespace="http://SAMS/C#.Unleashed/
    ➡WebServices", ResponseNamespace="http://SAMS/C#.Unleashed/
    ➡WebServices", Use=System.Web.Services.Description.
    ➡SoapBindingUse.Literal, ParameterStyle=System.
    ➡Web.Services.Protocols.SoapParameterStyle.Wrapped)]
    public string Greetings(string name) {
        object[] results = this.Invoke("Greetings", new object[] {
                    name});
        return ((string)(results[0]));
    }

    [System.Diagnostics.DebuggerStepThroughAttribute()]
    public System.IAsyncResult BeginGreetings(string name,
    ➡System.AsyncCallback callback, object asyncState) {
        return this.BeginInvoke("Greetings", new object[] {
                    name}, callback, asyncState);
    }

    [System.Diagnostics.DebuggerStepThroughAttribute()]
    public string EndGreetings(System.IAsyncResult asyncResult) {
        object[] results = this.EndInvoke(asyncResult);
        return ((string)(results[0]));
    }
}
```

The BasicWebService class from the proxy in Listing 33.3 inherits from the
System.Web.Services.Protocols.SoapHttpClientProtocol, indicating that the client
request and response will be wrapped in the SOAP protocol, similar to that shown in

Figure 33.5. Another item of interest is the `Greetings` method, decorated with the `SoapDocumentMethod` attribute. One of the great things about this whole process is that the internals of the proxy class and other underlying plumbing can be ignored. It may be interesting to know but is not necessary to use the web service.

Using a web service requires a client to declare an instance of the proxy class and then call the necessary web service operation, defined in the proxy class. Listing 33.4 shows how to do this.

LISTING 33.4   Using a Web Service: WebServiceClient.cs

```
using System;

namespace WebServiceClient
{
    /// <summary>
    /// Summary description for Class1.
    /// </summary>
    class WebServiceClient
    {
        static void Main(string[] args)
        {
            BasicWebService myWebService =
                new BasicWebService();

            Console.WriteLine(myWebService.Greetings("Joe"));
        }
    }
}
```

And here's the output:

```
Hello Joe!
```

Make sure that the namespace of the Web Service, Reference Name, matches the namespace in your code, WebServiceClient, or else you won't be able to reference it properly. Otherwise, you'll need to fully qualify the type name.

The `Main` method of Listing 33.4 instantiates a new `BasicWebService` object. Then within a `Console.WriteLine` statement, it calls the `Greetings` method with a string parameter. Actually, it's calling these methods on the proxy, which is hiding all the underlying details of communicating with the web service.

It's evident from Listing 33.4 that using a web service is as easy as calling a method in any other class. The secret is the proxy, which uses several classes of the base class library to package the request and response messages into SOAP format messages and transport them via HTTP. The following command line creates the client:

```
csc WebServiceClient.cs BasicWebService.cs
```

CREATING A WEB REFERENCE IN VS2008

In VS2008 you don't need to use the WSDL.exe command-line utility. Just right-click the References folder in the client project, select Add Service Reference, and put the URL of the web service in the address bar (or click the Discover button if the web service is in the same solution). The namespace name you put in the Add Web Reference window is the namespace you can use, with IntelliSense, to add a reference to the web service proxy in your code.

33

Summary

Web services provide a platform-independent means of exposing business logic over the Internet. They are created using several open standards technologies.

Creating ASP.NET web services is easy and abstracts much of the complexity associated with Internet communications. This allows developers to concentrate on business logic rather than underlying plumbing.

Use of a web service involves creating a proxy class that communicates with the web service on behalf of a client. The client application then communicates directly with the proxy to invoke necessary web service operations.

CHAPTER 34

Creating Web Services with WCF

With the Internet, the world is getting smaller, but it can be more complex in some ways. When we're walking down the street in our own country, we can talk to people in our own native language. Of course, there are those people who don't communicate so well regardless of what language they're speaking, but that's another story. All this changes when we leave our own country or travel to another website on the Internet that is in a different language.

Although we can use online translation tools, it's cumbersome, and we can't even wave our hands and point. The same problem exists with computers. If a program is written by the same shop or inside the same company, it isn't so hard to find an easy way to get the computers to communicate or standardize on a protocol. However, when two different companies try to get their computers to talk, the problem becomes much more challenging. Now, multiply that by many network communication interfaces by several cooperating companies.

Many communications protocols available today aim to solve the interoperability problems between computing systems, but none have become a single standard that everyone uses. That is changing with web services. As you might have read in the last chapter on ASMX web services, there are standards, such as XML, SOAP, WSDL, and multiple building blocks of the Web Services Interoperability (WS*) stack.

Microsoft's next generation of web services, part of the Windows Communications Foundation (WCF) brings all these standards together to make it easier to build standards-compliant web services. This chapter introduces you to this technology so that you can begin creating all of your new web services with WCF.

Creating a WCF Application in VS2008

To create a new WCF application in VS2008, select File, New, Project, WCF Service Application, set Name and Location, and click the OK button. Figure 34.1 shows the resulting solution.

FIGURE 34.1   A new WCF solution.

As shown in Figure 34.1, a WCF application is much the same as an ASP.NET application in composition in that it has the same assembly references, a web.config file, and will appear in a browser when you run it, as shown in Figure 34.2.

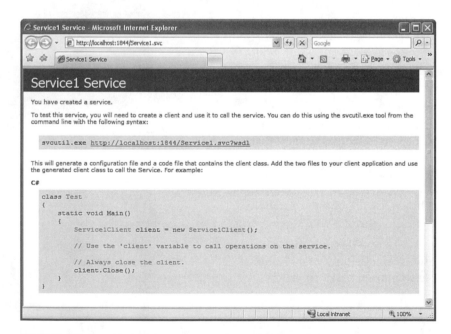

FIGURE 34.2   A WCF web service launched in a browser.

As shown in Figure 34.2, you can run the svcutil.exe utility to generate a proxy, which is a class that a client application can use to call the web service. However, I show you in a later part of this chapter how to create a service reference in VS2008 that will automatically generate the proxy for you.

Figure 34.2 also shows a code snippet that could be used to call the web service from a client. You'll see a similar example later in this chapter.

If you click the http://localhost:1844/Service1.svc?wsdl link in Figure 34.2, the browser will navigate to the Web Service Description Language (WSDL) for this file. In a nutshell, the WSDL is an XML document that describes the types, methods, protocols, formats, and location of this web service. Because WSDL is standardized (you can read the standard at http://www.w3.org/), anyone on any platform (regardless of hardware, OS, or programming language) can write software that reads it and generates a proxy.

WSDL is like an interface; it defines a contract that anyone can write code against without needing to know the low-level details of code that implements to the contract. Speaking of interfaces, the next section describes how interfaces help you write WCF web services.

Creating a Web Service Contract

Just as WSDL is a contract for describing a web service in a platform-independent way, C# interfaces are contracts that describe the WCF web service for the C# coder. The following sections show how to define or work with an existing WCF interface, including attributes that define the web service as a whole and other attributes that define the web service methods.

Creating a WCF Web Service Interface

When creating a WCF web service, the VS2008 wizard adds a skeleton file named IService1.cs. As its name suggests, the IService.cs file contains an interface named IService. The interface is important because it contributes directly to being able to automatically generate the WSDL file used by platform-independent clients desiring to consume the web service that implements the contract. The IService1.cs file also has a skeleton for a custom type, shown in Listing 34.1.

LISTING 34.1   The IService1.cs Skeleton Code

```
using System;
using System.Collections.Generic;
using System.Linq;
using System.Runtime.Serialization;
using System.ServiceModel;
using System.Text;

namespace Chapter_34
{
```

LISTING 34.1   Continued

```
// NOTE: If you change the interface name
// "IService1" here, you must also update
// the reference to "IService1" in Web.config.
[ServiceContract]
public interface IService1
{

    [OperationContract]
    string GetData(int value);

    [OperationContract]
    CompositeType GetDataUsingDataContract(
        CompositeType composite);

    // TODO: Add your service operations here
}


// Use a data contract as illustrated in the
// sample below to add composite types to
// service operations.
[DataContract]
public class CompositeType
{
    bool boolValue = true;
    string stringValue = "Hello ";

    [DataMember]
    public bool BoolValue
    {
        get { return boolValue; }
        set { boolValue = value; }
    }

    [DataMember]
    public string StringValue
    {
        get { return stringValue; }
        set { stringValue = value; }
    }
}
}
```

The focus of this section is the interface IService1, and I discuss the CompositeType class in more detail in a later section of this chapter. The application that I'll build is a WCF web service version of the MoneyTalk application from earlier chapters, which will be called MoneyTalkService.

First, let's give this interface a more meaningful name, perhaps IMoneyTalkService. VS2008 makes this easy because if you rename the file from IService.cs to IMoneyTalkService.cs in Solution Explorer, it will pop up a window that asks whether you want to do the refactoring for types with the same name. Clicking the Yes button will change the interface name from IService1 to IMoneyTalkService. Next, open web.config and change

```
<endpoint address=""
        binding="wsHttpBinding"
        contract="Chapter_34.IService1">
```

to

```
<endpoint address=""
        binding="wsHttpBinding"
        contract="Chapter_34.IMoneyTalkService">
```

I discuss the WCF web service settings in a later section of this chapter, but looking at the fact that you changed the definition of the contract attribute to the new interface name should give you a clue that the interface participates in creating the WSDL contract. Chapter_34 is the namespace that was created when I ran the WCF Application Wizard and named the project as Chapter 34.

Continuing with building the interface, rename GetData to GetQuoteString and delete the parameter. Then rename GetDataUsingDataContract to GetQuote and delete its parameter. You can write web service methods with parameters with no problem, but this application doesn't need them. Delete the Note comments, too, because you've already done the work they require. Listing 34.2 shows what the modified IMoneyTalkService interface looks like:

```
[ServiceContract]
public interface IMoneyTalkService
{

    [OperationContract]
    string GetQuoteString();

    [OperationContract]
    CompositeType GetQuote();
}
```

The preceding interface must be implemented by a web service class, as is the purpose of a C# interface. Along these lines, the class must implement GetQuoteString and GetQuote methods.

The only parts of the code I haven't discussed much yet are the attributes: `ServiceContract` and `OperationContract`. I discuss them in the following sections, before writing an implementation class for the interface. Notice how the attributes have `Contract` suffixes—a meaningful indicator that they participate in defining the web service interface.

Declaring the ServiceContract Attribute

The `ServiceContract` attribute states that your interface is the contract for a web service. Your web service won't work without it. All of its parameters are optional but still useful. The following code enhances the `ServiceContract` attribute from previous listings:

```
[ServiceContract(
    Namespace=
    "http://www.InformIT.com/SamsPublishing/CSharpUnleashed")]
```

This example uses the `Namespace` property, meaning that the WSDL for this web service will have `http://www.InformIT.com/SamsPublishing/CSharpUnleashed` as its `targetNamespace`. If you don't declare the `Namespace` property, the default `targetNamespace` will be `http://tempuri.org/`, which isn't a good idea because you could loose the uniqueness of your web service.

Declaring OperationContract Attributes

To expose a method as a web service operation, you must decorate it with the `OperationContract` attribute. The following example describes how to enhance `OperationContract` attributes that you've already seen with a `Name` property:

```
        [OperationContract(Name="GetQuote")]
        CompositeType GetQuote();

        [OperationContract(Name = "GetQuoteByID")]
        CompositeType GetQuote(int id);
```

The `Name` is necessary in this case because web services don't support method overloads. Considering that web services are a platform-neutral, message-passing mechanism for computing system interoperability, object orientation and other platform-dependent details can't be exposed. However, the `Name` attribute lets you code like you want but still expose the interface you want. Consuming code will use the value of the `Name` property to call the web service and won't be aware of the method name you used. WCF will handle the mapping because it knows about `OperationContract` attribute that you decorated the method with.

Constructing Data Contracts

As explained earlier, web services are message-based, meaning that clients call a web service with a SOAP-formatted XML message and receive a SOAP-formatted XML response message. You won't have problems with the simplest examples that pass strings back and forth. In fact, all the primitive C# (.NET) types can be passed in web service messages with no problem. The mechanism that translates parameters and return values from object to XML is called *serialization*. The primitive types have built-in serialization, making it effortless to use them.

The challenge comes when passing your own custom objects between client and web service. If you think about message types such as purchase orders, invoices, and so on, it is cumbersome to send the XML for them as a string. Doing so also masks their schema from the WSDL, which clients rely on to figure out how to communicate with your web service. Therefore, you need a mechanism to take your invoice or purchase order object and translate it to XML. In the example for this chapter, we need to figure out how to translate a MoneyQuote object to an XML message with schema that any client can read, as shown here:

```
[DataContract(Namespace =
"http://www.InformIT.com/SamsPublishing/CSharpUnleashed")]
    public class MoneyQuote
    {
        [DataMember]
        public int ID { get; set; }

        [DataMember]
        public string Author { get; set; }

        [DataMember]
        public string Quote { get; set; }
    }
```

The DataContract attribute specifies that this is a data object that can be included as a web service method or return type and subsequently serialized into an XML message. Notice that I also used the same namespace, with the Namespace property, as on the ServiceContract attribute for the IMoneyQuote interface.

The DataMember attributes state that a property or field can be included in the XML message.

Now, in addition to primitive types, such as int and string, this web service can communicate via a custom type, MoneyQuote. Here's the new definition of the IMoneyQuote interface, based on the latest changes:

```
[ServiceContract(Namespace=
"http://www.InformIT.com/SamsPublishing/CSharpUnleashed")]
    public interface IMoneyTalkService
    {

        [OperationContract]
        string GetQuoteString();

        [OperationContract(Name="GetQuote")]
        MoneyQuote GetQuote();
```

```
    [OperationContract(Name = "GetQuoteByID")]
    MoneyQuote GetQuote(int id);
}
```

You can see that the return types are now `MoneyQuote`, the object we just made serializable via `DataContract` and `DataMember` attributes.

After the interface (contract) and serializable data types have been defined, you can implement the interface, which is discussed next.

Implementing Web Service Logic

Implementing an interface is the easiest part of building a web service because it is what most people are familiar with: writing code. The cool thing is that with the contract in place, you have a good idea of how your code will be used by clients.

This implementation will use a super-scalable, dynamic data-driven set of algorithms for serving data in an intelligent manner. I was considering patenting it but decided to share it specifically with you. Listing 34.2 reveals this incredible implementation for the web service defined by the `IMoneyQuote` interface.

LISTING 34.2   A WCF Web Service Implementation

```
using System;
using System.Collections.Generic;

namespace Chapter_34
{
// NOTE: If you change the
// class name "Service1" here, you
// must also update the reference to
// "Service1" in Web.config and in
// the associated .svc file.
    public class MoneyService : IMoneyTalkService
    {
        Dictionary<int, MoneyQuote> m_quotes =
            new Dictionary<int, MoneyQuote>
            {
                {
                    1,
                    new MoneyQuote
                    {
                        ID = 1,
                        Author = "J. Mayo",
                        Quote =
```

LISTING 34.2   Continued

```
"A penny saved is too small, make it a buck."
                    }
                },
                {
                    2,
                    new MoneyQuote
                    {
                        ID = 2,
                        Author = "Joe M.",
                        Quote =
"Keep your wooden nickel. It'll be worth something someday."
                    }
                },
                {
                    3,
                    new MoneyQuote
                    {
                        ID = 3,
                        Author = "J. M.",
                        Quote =
"It's your dime, but you're better off dialing 10-10-XXX."
                    }
                }
            };

        public string GetQuoteString()
        {
            int rndKey = new Random().Next(3) + 1;
            return m_quotes[rndKey].Quote;
        }

        public MoneyQuote GetQuote()
        {
            int rndKey = new Random().Next(3) + 1;
            return m_quotes[rndKey];
        }

        public MoneyQuote GetQuote(int id)
        {
            return m_quotes[id];
        }
    }
}
```

Okay, perhaps Listing 34.2 wasn't as mind blowing as advertised. However, if you consider a LINQ to SQL (or another LINQ provider) solution, you might envision a practical implementation of data-driven web service logic.

The true implementation in Listing 34.2 uses a generic dictionary, populated with object initialization syntax, which I discussed in Chapter 17, "Parameterizing Type with Generics and Writing Iterators."

The skeleton code for the service includes a note explaining how you should change the reference to Service1 in both the web.config file and the *.svc file. You can find the following line in web.config under configuration\system.serviceModel\services:

```
<service name="Chapter_34.Service1"
        behaviorConfiguration="Chapter_34.Service1Behavior">
```

which you should change to

```
<service name="Chapter_34.MoneyService"
        behaviorConfiguration="Chapter_34.Service1Behavior">
```

to reflect the name of the web service implementation class in Listing 34.2.

To change the *.svc code, rename the Service1.svc file to MoneyService.svc. Then, right-click MoneyService.svc and select View Markup. Change the @ServiceHost directive from

```
<%@ ServiceHost Language="C#" Debug="true"
    Service="Chapter_34.Service1"
    CodeBehind="MoneyService.svc.cs" %>
```

to

```
<%@ ServiceHost Language="C#" Debug="true"
    Service="Chapter_34.MoneyService"
    CodeBehind="MoneyService.svc.cs" %>
```

At this point, you have working code, and changes to the configuration enable the web service to execute. The next section expands upon the configuration to give you a better understanding of what it means

Configuring a Web Service

In addition to specifying a contract for the web service through a C# interface and applicable attributes, you must also set configuration options so that clients can figure out how to communicate with your web service. You need to specify address, binding, and contract, which some refer to as the ABCs of WCF web services and define message exchange parameters to enable discovery. The following excerpt from web.config contains pertinent settings for the MoneyQuote example in this chapter:

```
<system.serviceModel>
    <services>
        <service name="Chapter_34.MoneyService"
                behaviorConfiguration="Chapter_34.Service1Behavior">
            <!-- Service Endpoints -->
            <endpoint address=""
                    binding="wsHttpBinding"
                    contract="Chapter_34.IMoneyTalkService">
                <!--
                Upon deployment, the following identity element
                should be removed or replaced to reflect the
                identity under which the deployed service runs.
                If removed, WCF will infer an appropriate identity
                automatically.
            -->
                <identity>
                    <dns value="localhost"/>
                </identity>
            </endpoint>
        <endpoint address="mex"
                binding="mexHttpBinding"
                contract="IMetadataExchange"/>
    </service>
</services>
<behaviors>
    <serviceBehaviors>
        <behavior name="Chapter_34.Service1Behavior">
            <!-- To avoid disclosing metadata information,
            set the value below to false and remove the
            metadata endpoint above before deployment  -->
            <serviceMetadata httpGetEnabled="true"/>
                <!-- To receive exception details in faults for
                debugging purposes, set the value below to true.
                Set to false before deployment to avoid disclosing
                exception information -->
                <serviceDebug includeExceptionDetailInFaults="false"/>
        </behavior>
    </serviceBehaviors>
</behaviors>
</system.serviceModel>
```

The configuration elements, in system.serviceModel, appear under the configuration element in web.config. The services section defines information about the services and the behaviors section enhances specified entries in the services section. The following sections drill down on what these elements mean.

Service Element

The service element specifies the name of the service and behaviors, which are discussed in a later section. The name attribute is required. The name attribute of the service element must be set to the Name property of the ServiceContract attribute if it is defined. Otherwise, the name attribute must be the name of the implementation class, which is MoneyService, as defined in Listing 34.2.

Endpoint Element

The endpoint tells clients how to find the web service (address), which protocol to use (binding), and available service messages (contract).

The address attribute defines the location of the service. The preceding example has a blank address, meaning that the location of the service is at the root of the application, but you could put the subdirectory name relative to the root in this location, too.

A binding is a protocol used to communicate with the web service. With ASMX web services, discussed in Chapter 33, "Writing Traditional ASMX Web Services," your only option is HTTP. That was convenient for giving developers an easy way to get started with web services because HTTP is ubiquitous. However, WCF web services can communicate via any protocol, including HTTP, TCP/IP, and named pipes. The wsHttpBinding enables communication via HTTP, which is common.

The previous section on configuring the web service interface showed you how to create a web service contract. You will use the fully qualified name of the interface type for the contract.

Behavior Element

The behavior element is used to expand on the capabilities of a service. The behavior element that is set with the WCF Wizard enables HTTP Get requests, as an additional way to call the service besides sending a SOAP request. Here's the behavior element that the WCF wizard adds to web.config:

```
<behavior name="Chapter_34.Service1Behavior">
    <!-- To avoid disclosing metadata information,
    set the value below to false and remove the
    metadata endpoint above before deployment -->
    <serviceMetadata httpGetEnabled="true"/>
        <!-- To receive exception details in faults
        for debugging purposes, set the value below
        to true.  Set to false before deployment to
        avoid disclosing exception information -->
        <serviceDebug includeExceptionDetailInFaults="false"/>
 </behavior>
```

The name attribute of the behavior element must match the behaviorConfiguration of the service element you saw earlier. This is what associates a behavior with a service.

There is also a serviceDebug element that makes it easier to debug exceptions in the service by returning exception details in the fault message that is sent back to the client if an exception occurs. Because it is set to false by default, you need to set it to true to get this behavior. Remember to set it back to false for deployment, especially if you have non-.NET clients, because they have no concept of what a .NET exception means. Besides, it would be more secure to avoid giving an arbitrary client access to exception information that might be exploited.

Now that the web service is coded and configured, clients can begin using, or consuming, it.

Consuming a Web Service

Knowing the address of a web service, what protocol to use, and how to format the XML messages to send and receive, you can build code that makes a network request to communicate. It wouldn't be too hard to do by using the .NET Framework SDK networking APIs, as explained in Chapter 30, "Using .NET Network Communications Technologies," combined with LINQ to XML, but there is a much easier way. You can use VS2008 to point at the web service and automatically generate a proxy.

WHAT IS A PROXY?

A proxy is a class that you can use like any other object by instantiating it and calling its methods. The proxy takes care of figuring out how to convert your method call into the contract format described by the web service, converting the results to XML, selecting the right binding and transmitting the results to the address specified by the web service.

All this information to create the proxy is described in the WSDL—the open standards document you learned about earlier that contains all the information you need to communicate with the web service. This is the big deal about the WSDL, because now you don't have to write all the plumbing code. Even more important, clients on other platforms can read the WSDL and communicate with your web service, too. The following sections describe how to set up a web service proxy and write code to use that proxy to communicate with a web service.

Creating a Service Reference

A client application in VS2008 can use a service reference to communicate with a WCF web service. The example in this chapter is a simple console application, but it could be any application type, including Windows Forms, WPF, ASP.NET, Silverlight, Windows service, or even another web service.

After you've added a new console application to the same solution as the WCF web service, right-click the project, select Add Service Reference, and you'll see the Add Service Reference window, as shown in Figure 34.3.

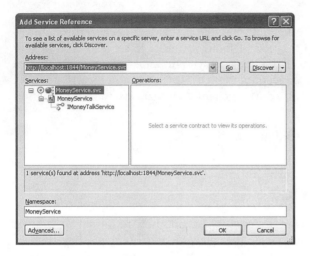

FIGURE 34.3   Adding a service reference to a client project.

To get the service to appear as in Figure 34.3, click the Discover button, which works for finding services in the same solution. Then enter a namespace. I used `MoneyService`, which means that the fully qualified namespace of the service will be `ServiceClient.MoneyService.MoneyQuote`. `ServiceClient` is the namespace of the console application project that I'm creating to consume the web service, `MoneyService` is the namespace added in the Add Service Reference window, and `MoneyQuote` is the name of the proxy and is also the name of the service itself.

Now you can write code to consume the web service.

Writing Client Code to Call a Web Service

Client code must instantiate the proxy and then call the web service method, as if it were calling a method on any other object. The difference is that the proxy takes care of all communication over the network for you. Listing 34.3 contains client code that calls the methods of `MoneyService`.

LISTING 34.3   Client Code Calling a Web Service

```
using System;
using ServiceClient.MoneyService;

namespace ServiceClient
{
    class Program
    {
        static void Main(string[] args)
        {
            var moneySvc = new MoneyTalkServiceClient();
```

LISTING 34.3   Continued

```
            string quoteString = moneySvc.GetQuoteString();
            Console.WriteLine(
                "Money Quote String: " + quoteString);

            MoneyQuote quote = moneySvc.GetQuote();
            Console.WriteLine(
                "\nMoney Quote ID: " + quote.ID +
                ", Author: " + quote.Author +
                "\nQuote: " + quote.Quote);

            MoneyQuote quoteByID = moneySvc.GetQuoteByID(2);
            Console.WriteLine(
                "\nMoney Quote ID: " + quoteByID.ID +
                ", Author: " + quoteByID.Author +
                "\nQuote: " + quoteByID.Quote);

            Console.ReadKey();
        }
    }
}
```

Remember, if you named the service reference different than the preceding code, then you should fully qualify the service name or add a using directive for its namespace.

The using declaration at the top of the listing specifies the namespace for the proxy generated when you add a service reference to the project. The moneySvc variable holds a reference to the proxy. In each case, you can see that the message being sent to the web service is invoked via a method call that matches the methods (via method name, parameters, and return types) defined in the web service contract.

Summary

You learned that to create a WCF web service you must define an interface, data, and class to implement the interface. You have attributes that expose the interface as a web service and other attributes that define the custom data used by the web service.

As for consuming web services, you learned how to create a proxy and then saw how to write code that uses the proxy to communicate with the web service.

This concludes this part of the book on .NET networking technologies. The next part begins discussing architecture and introduces tools and concepts to help you pull all the things you've learned about so far into a whole for creating applications, beginning with the VS2008 Class Designer.

PART 8

Examining .NET Application Architecture and Design

Using the Visual Studio 2008 Class Designer

W hen you go on a long trip or travel somewhere you've never been, it's often useful to have a map. Sometimes the map isn't as good as it needs to be and you still get lost, but usually the map helps out. Of course, I never get lost, but I've heard of others who do.

Most programmers never admit to being lost in code or meandering into applications only to realize their design could have been better. It's kind of like going somewhere new without a map and refusing to stop to ask for directions. A programmer's map, if they should choose to create or use one, is often an object diagram that graphically depicts the relationship between objects. This object diagram can help visualize code, if it already exists, or help to plan the development of code, if creating the object diagram.

VS2008 has a tool called the Class Designer to help you visualize or create object diagrams. It can prove useful in understanding an existing code base or even helping to create and design the relationships between objects. This chapter explains the visualization and creation features of the VS2008 Class Designer, which will, I hope, help you avoid becoming lost in code.

Visualizing Code

The VS2008 Class Designer can be used effectively to obtain a graphical representation of the objects in your code and the relationships between them. To show how this works, I walk you though creating a simple code base and then show what the generated object diagram will be for that code. This way, you'll see the relationship between the C# code and the objects that appear in the designer.

The example in this chapter uses a console application for simplicity. So, you can create the solution with a console application project and follow along if you like. In keeping with the Hospital example used in previous chapters, I refer to the project as Hospital.

Getting Started Viewing Objects

In the Hospital application, `HospitalStaff` objects hold various types of hospital workers, including doctors and nurses. To represent this, add the following class to the Hospital project:

```
namespace Chapter_35
{
    class HospitalStaff
    {
        public string Name { get; set; }
        public string Position { get; set; }
    }
}
```

`HospitalStaff` is just a regular class with properties. I'll add on and morph it later; but for right now, I just want to demonstrate what it looks like in the class designer.

The toolbar in Solution Explorer has a button for opening the Class Designer, with a tooltip that says View Class Diagram, as shown in Figure 35.1.

FIGURE 35.1   The View Class Diagram button in Solution Explorer.

Select the Hospital project and then click the View Class Diagram button, shown in Figure 35.1, to open a new Class Designer file. Figure 35.2 show all the objects in the Hospital project, including `HospitalStaff`.

You can see both the `Program` class, which contains `Main`, and the `HospitalStaff` object in the center of the Class Designer. Although you can't see it in the book, both of these objects are colored with a gradient of blue. I've expanded each of these classes by clicking their chevrons in the upper-right corner. You can also see that there is a Methods section in `Program` and a Properties section in `HospitalStaff`. Fields and events would also appear in the diagram of their containing object, if defined. This provides a view of each object and its contents, which tells you a lot in a single glance, which is the benefit of visualization.

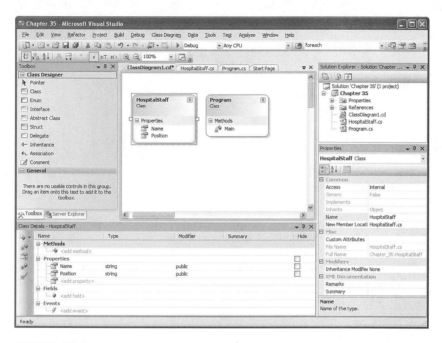

FIGURE 35.2   An object in a class diagram.

In a later section of this chapter, I show you how to create these diagrams, which is facilitated by the toolbox on the left side of Figure 35.2 and the Class Details grid at the bottom of Figure 35.2. The Solution Explorer displays the new Class Diagram file, ClassDiagram1.cd, which you can rename. You can add as many class diagrams as you need to obtain different views of your project. In case you're curious, a class diagram can show you only the objects within the same project but not across different projects in a solution.

I sincerely believe that physicians measure their effectiveness in units of pain. If you don't believe me, it's probably been a while since your last doctor's visit. Nevertheless, such practice screams for a struct as a value type representation as follows:

```
namespace Chapter_35
{
    struct UnitOfPain
    {
        private bool m_doesThisHurt;

        public long Multiply()
        {
            return m_doesThisHurt ?
```

```
            unchecked(long.MaxValue + 1) :
            long.MaxValue;
        }
    }
}
```

In addition to quality metrics, other medical tools of the trade include the dreaded instrument collection. Here's an enum to represent those:

```
namespace Chapter_35
{
    enum Instruments
    {
        Scalpel,
        Needle,
        Hacksaw,
        Drill
    }
}
```

Now that you have an assortment of C# types, let's see what it looks like. This time, we'll create a new class diagram by clicking the View Class Diagram button, which creates the ClassDiagram2.cd item, as shown in Figure 35.3.

FIGURE 35.3   Class diagram with enum and struct.

In Figure 35.3, you can see that the value types, enum and struct, have square edges. The enum is even more different with a purplish color and no sections, which makes sense because enums only have values.

I obtained the image in Figure 35.3 by right-clicking the Class Designer surface and selecting Export Diagram as Image.

So far, there aren't any relationships between images, but the next section shows you what that looks like.

Observing Associations, Inheritance, and Interfaces

A HospitalStaff object is somewhat general because it can be a doctor, nurse, intern, or one of many other professionals working in a hospital. They all have Name and Position properties in common, but each has its own specialization. I'll represent one of these specializations with inheritance, creating the Doctor class here:

```
namespace Chapter_35
{
    class Doctor : HospitalStaff
    {
        public Patient Patient { get; set; }
    }
}
```

Because Doctor derives from HospitalStaff, you'll see the representation in a new class diagram that you generate. Unfortunately, VS2008 doesn't model the association between Doctor and Patient, based on the Patient property in Doctor. Later in this chapter, you'll see how to create such an association in the class designer.

CLOSE PREVIOUS DIAGRAMS

It might help to close previous diagrams before starting new ones as you move through this chapter. This will prevent accidentally adding objects to a previous diagram.

This time, we'll do something different. When there are too many objects to view and you want to see only a subset, you can select only the files with those objects and then click the View Class Diagram button. This differs from previous examples that selected only the project, resulting in every object in the project appearing in the class diagram. Figure 35.4 shows the result of selecting only the HospitalStaff.cs and Doctor.cs files.

FIGURE 35.4   Inheritance visualization.

You can see the inheritance relationship, in Figure 35.4, where `Doctor` derives from `HospitalStaff`.

Another relationship you can view in Class Designer is interface implementation. The `IAmSick` interface here will be implemented by the `Patient` class:

```
namespace Chapter_35
{
    interface IAmSick
    {
        void Barf();
    }
}
```

This is a particularly useful interface because it can apply equally to alcoholics, toddlers, and readers who don't think I'm funny. Presently, it serves as a demonstration with the Patient class:

```
using System;

namespace Chapter_35
{
    class Patient : IAmSick
    {
        #region IAmSick Members

        public void Barf()
        {
            throw new NotImplementedException();
        }

        #endregion
    }
}
```

To view the relationship between the `Patient` class and `IAmSick` interface, select the Patient.cs and IAmSick.cs files in Solution Explorer and click the View Class Diagram button. The results appear in Figure 35.5.

Although you can't see it in the book, the `IAmSick` interface is colored with a gradient of green. Classes that implement interfaces, as does `Patient` in Figure 35.5, indicate their relationship with the interface via a symbol that looks like and is often referred to as a lollipop.

This section outlined the essentials of visualization so that you could look at a class diagram and get a feel for the relationships between objects in the same project. The next section builds upon what you've learned here and shows you the other side of the Class Designer story: how to create a class diagram.

FIGURE 35.5   Interface visualization.

Building an Object Model with the Class Designer

Instead of visualizing the objects of an existing C# application, you can use the Class Designer to create the objects from scratch. This is effective if you already have a design or even if you're doing the object model for the first time in the Class Designer. The following sections show you how to add object to the Class Designer, configure the objects, and build associations between objects.

To get started, if you're following along, create a new console application called CreateHospital. All the work in following sections will be in the CreateHospital project.

A HospitalStaff object is somewhat general because it can be a doctor, nurse, intern, or one of many other professionals working in a hospital. They all have Name and Position properties in common, but each has its own specialization. I'll represent one of these specializations with inheritance, creating the Doctor class with the following steps:

1. Right-click the CreateHospital project, select Add, New Item, select Class Diagram, and name it HospitalDiagram.cd. You can click the Class Diagram button on the Solution Explorer toolbar, as done earlier in this chapter, but I want to show you how to do it this way, too. The results are in Figure 35.6.

2. The toolbox on the left side of Figure 35.6 contains controls that represent C# objects. To use them, you drag and drop them from the toolbar to the Class Designer and then configure their members in the Class Details window at the bottom of Figure 35.6 and set properties in the Properties window, which is collapsed to the right in Figure 35.6.

3. Drag and drop an Abstract Class control from the toolbox to the Class Designer.

4. When the New Abstract Class window appears, shown in Figure 35.7, change the Class Name to HospitalStaff, and then click the OK button.

   As in Figure 35.7, any time you add a new object to the Class Designer, you'll see a new window with parameters specific to that object type to help you configure the object.

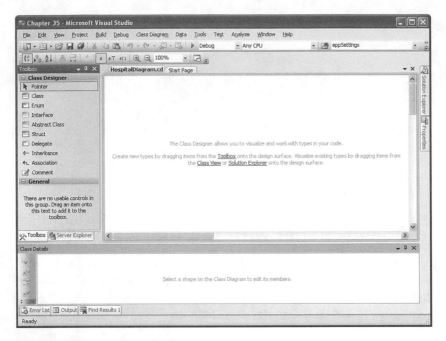

FIGURE 35.6   VS2008 with an empty class diagram.

FIGURE 35.7   Creating a new abstract class.

5. Right-click the new `HospitalStaff` object, hover over the Add menu, and observe that there are entries for Method, Property, Field, Event, Constructor, Destructor, and Constant. Select Property and notice that you get a new property entry in the `HospitalStaff` class in the Class Designer, which is highlighted so that you can rename it. Type *Name* as the property ID, as shown in Figure 35.8.

6. Now look at Class Details at the bottom of Figure 35.8. The default type for a property is int, so I changed it to string. There is a space for changing the access modifier, which I left as public. Also notice the Comment column where I added a comment. You can change the property name, type, access, and documentation in a single place. In addition, you can add fields, methods, and events through the Class Details window, which is a quick way to build the shell of an object.

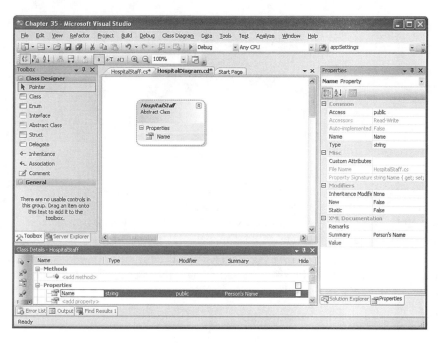

FIGURE 35.8   Configuring an object in Class Designer.

7. On the right side of Figure 35.8, in the Properties window, you can see much more detail in configurability. Whatever you click in the Class Designer will cause a context-sensitive change in the Properties window so that you can provide detailed configuration options. Now, click one time on the HospitalStaff class and change the Summary property in the Properties window to base class for hospital workers.

8. Double-click HospitalStaff and observe that it created the following code in the HospitalStaff.cs file:

```
using System;
using System.Collections.Generic;
using System.Text;

namespace CreateHospital
{
    /// <summary>
    /// base class for hospital workers
    /// </summary>
    public abstract class HospitalStaff
    {
        /// <summary>
        /// Person's Name
        /// </summary>
        public string Name
        {
```

```
            get
            {
                throw new System.NotImplementedException();
            }
            set
            {
            }
        }
    }
}
```

9. In the preceding code, you can see that everything is done for you, except for the implementation: The class has an `abstract` modifier, the `Name` property has been created, and XML documentation comments are added. Next, go back to the Class Designer and add a `Class` object, named `Doctor`, below `HospitalStaff`.

10. To show that `Doctor` derives from `HospitalStaff`, click the Inheritance control in the toolbox—the one with the line and a closed arrow on the end. Click `Doctor` and then click `HospitalStaff`. The results are in Figure 35.9.

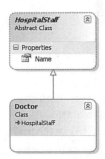

FIGURE 35.9   Creating an inheritance relationship in Class Designer.

11. As you can see, in Figure 35.9 there is an arrow from the derived class, `Doctor`, to the base class `HospitalStaff`. The following shows how this visual resolves to code:

```
using System;
using System.Collections.Generic;
using System.Text;

namespace CreateHospital
{
    public class Doctor : HospitalStaff
    {
    }
}
```

12. The preceding code is regular C# inheritance. The HospitalStaff code isn't changed by this, and it shouldn't be because base classes should never know which classes derived from them. You could have nearly predicted that result, but the next step with an association might surprise you a little bit. Add another class to the diagram and name it Patient.

13. Click the association control in the toolbox—the one with a line and an open arrow. Click Patient and then click on Doctor. You can see the results in Figure 35.10.

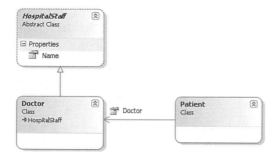

FIGURE 35.10   Creating an association relationship in Class Designer.

14. The association in Figure 35.10 says that Patient has a Doctor. In code, you can often add a field to an object and have this relationship where your object has a reference to another object. However, the Class Designer goes one more step beyond that by using a property, as shown here:

```
using System;
using System.Collections.Generic;
using System.Text;

namespace CreateHospital
{
    public class Patient
    {
        public Doctor Doctor
        {
            get
            {
                throw new System.NotImplementedException();
            }
            set
            {
            }
        }
    }
}
```

15. From the preceding code, there is a property that references the `Doctor` from `Patient`. As a practical matter, a property provides better encapsulation and maintainability than a field, and some people, including myself, like this approach. Adding the association from `Patient` to `Doctor` doesn't change the code in `Doctor`. You can add an association from `Doctor` to `Patient` if you like, which would then add a property of type `Patient` to the `Doctor` class.

As you can see, the Class Designer helps you build the shell of an application in a short amount of time. You can also use it as a basic tool for building object models. This is similar to a UML Static Structure diagram, but with limitations on relationships and more options in object types and members. I've used it effectively on projects where the object model surpasses the simplicity of data entry and reporting applications.

Summary

The VS2008 Class Designer gives you two capabilities: to view existing applications and to create new applications. The benefits of viewing existing applications are that you get a better feel for the relationships between parts of the code and how it works. You saw how to create new diagrams where you could control which objects appear and benefit from the ability to obtain different views of the application.

You also learned how to use the Class Designer to build an object model, adding objects and configuring them. As you build objects, you can see the code that VS2008 generates on each change. This could be a useful technique for building the shell of an application quickly and helping you with detailed design before jumping into code. Of course, you can still code the application first, but the future benefits derived from reduced cost and ease of maintenance make using this designer for upfront work even more compelling.

Now that you've seen object models being created in this chapter, the next chapter builds on this by introducing you to design patterns—those in the .NET Framework and a couple that you can use yourself.

CHAPTER 36

Sampling Design Patterns in C#

Some of us have our favorite word puzzles, whether crossword, word find, or cryptogram. At one time, I was fond of cryptograms, which typically resulted in a quote or saying by a famous person. At first, the task was hard, but over a series of weeks, solving the puzzles became much easier. There were tricks and techniques that helped get a start on solving it, and once key letters were discovered, the rest of the cryptogram unraveled quickly.

As our ability to solve puzzles can improve quickly, so can our ability to write object-oriented applications with C#. The concept of creating relationships between objects might be puzzling at first, but we eventually learn tricks and techniques that help us make sense of how an application should be built. These tricks and techniques exist in what is called design patterns, which the next section defines.

Overview of Design Patterns

A design pattern is a general way to organize objects in a way that solves common problems. When I first learned about design patterns, one of the things I realized was that I was already using some of them and didn't know it, which is common for people who have been writing object-oriented applications for a while. Some design patterns are simple, and others are more sophisticated. The subject of design patterns fills entire books, and so this chapter discusses just a couple of design patterns that are common in the .NET Framework and shows you how you can take advantage of them to solve real-world problems.

As a reusable set of components, the .NET Framework Class Library employs many design patterns to add in extensibility and reuse. The following sections explain a couple design patterns that you will encounter every day and explain how and why some of the .NET libraries work the way they do. More specifically, you'll learn about the iterator, proxy, and template patterns.

The Iterator Pattern

To iterate means to visit each member of an array, collection, or other object that exposes collection-like behavior. To understand how common the iterator pattern is, think about the last time you wrote a `foreach` loop. Because you already know how to write a `foreach` loop, I'll start with what the iterator pattern is and then show you how the `foreach` loop uses it. You'll also learn a special trick the `foreach` loop uses to iterate through collections.

The first thing you need to know about the iterator pattern is that a client object that wants to iterate over a collection needs to know whether it can do so. The next thing the client object does is to figure out how it wants to iterate (forward, reverse, and so on). These two tasks are managed in a consistent way through the IEnumerable and IEnumerator interfaces.

Implementing `IEnumerable`

The IEnumerable interface exposes the contract that says, "I can iterate." That means that a client object can ask a collection object if it has the capability to iterate by the fact that it exposes the IEnumerable interface. Here's a protracted example that makes this point:

```
var hospStaff = new HospitalStaff
{
    Doctor = "Marcus",
    Nurse = "Nancy",
    Intern1 = "Dmitri",
    Intern2 = "Helga"
};

if (hospStaff is IEnumerable<string>)
{
    // iterate through hospStaff
}
```

The preceding code checks to see whether HospitalStaff, hospStaff, implements the IEnumerable<string> interface. If so, it iterates through hospStaff members. I also initialized the HospitalStaff members with strings. Here's part of the HospitalStaff implementation:

```
class HospitalStaff : IEnumerable<string>
{
```

```
        public string Doctor { get; set; }
        public string Nurse { get; set; }
        public string Intern1 { get; set; }
        public string Intern2 { get; set; }

        public IEnumerator<string> GetEnumerator()
        {
            throw new NotImplementedException();
        }

        IEnumerator IEnumerable.GetEnumerator()
        {
            throw new NotImplementedException();
        }
    }
```

As you can see, my data store for `HospitalStaff` isn't sophisticated, consisting of four string properties: `Doctor`, `Nurse`, `Intern1`, and `Intern2`. The goal is to be able to return each of these values as if `HospitalStaff` were a collection. If you wrote your own collection, it would probably implement some data structure like a skip list, binary tree, or some other collection.

.NET FRAMEWORK COLLECTIONS?

If you need to write your own collection type, the `IEnumerable` and `IEnumerator` will be instrumental to helping you do this. However, as I recommended in Chapter 1, "Introducing the .NET Platform," the .NET Framework is built for reuse and is the first place you should look for classes that do what you need. In the case of collections, there are many collection classes in the `System.Collections` (nongeneric) and `System.Collections.Generic` (generic) namespaces to handle most needs. That said, if you have a better hash algorithm or need something that isn't there, such as a binary tree, use the techniques in this chapter to make them iterable.

Because `HospitalStaff` implements `IEnumerable<string>`, it must implement `GetEnumerator`. Also, if you recall from Chapter 14, "Implementing Abstract Classes and Interfaces," you must implement the members of all interfaces in the interface inheritance hierarchy. Because `IEnumberable<T>` derives from `IEnumerable`, you must implement `IEnumerable.GetEnumerator`. This is one of the cases where explicit interface implementation is required because you need to disambiguate calls between `IEnumerable<T>.GetEnumerator` and `IEnumerable.GetEnumerator`.

As you can see, both implementations of `GetEnumerator` return an object that implements the `IEnumerator` interface. The next section explains the `IEnumerator` implementation.

Implementing `IEnumerator`

A class that implements the `IEnumerator` interface says that "I perform the actual iteration." To accomplish this, the class must implement members that allow a client to reset
the collection to the beginning, establish what the current item to read is, and allow the
client to move to the next item. Thereafter, the client simply loops, performing read and
move to next operations until all items of the collection are read. To accomplish this, the
`IEnumerator` interface contains a `Reset` method, `MoveNext` method, and a `Current` property. Here's an update to the `HospitalStaff` class with only a shell for implementing the
`IEnumerator` interface:

```csharp
private class HospitalStaffEnumerator : IEnumerator<string>
{
    public void Reset()
    {
        throw new NotImplementedException();
    }

    public bool MoveNext()
    {
        throw new NotImplementedException();
    }

    public string Current
    {
        get { throw new NotImplementedException(); }
    }

    object IEnumerator.Current
    {
        get { throw new NotImplementedException(); }
    }

    public void Dispose()
    {
        throw new NotImplementedException();
    }
}
```

Here, you can see that `HospitalStaffEnumerator` implements the `IEnumerator<string>`
interface, including `Reset` method, `MoveNext` method, and `Current` property. Because
`IEnumerator<T>` derives from `IEnumerator` (nongeneric), it must implement `IEnumerator`
members, too. This requirement is satisfied through `Reset` and `MoveNext`, which have the
same signature of both interfaces. However, `IEnumerator<string>` is strongly typed,
meaning that the `Current` property of type string implements `IEnumerator<T>.Current`.

That means that you need an explicit implementation of IEnumerator.Current, which returns type object.

IEnumerator<T> implements IDisposable too, requiring it to implement the Dispose method. Chapter 15, "Managing Object Lifetime," has a detailed explanation of how to implement the dispose pattern with IDisposable, so I won't repeat that here. However, you should implement IDisposable properly, rather than pass it over as I do in this example—because the focus here is on the iterator pattern.

The following sections break down implementation of IEnumerator, including construction, Reset method implementation, MoveNext method implementation, and Current property implementation.

IEnumerator-Derived Type Construction and Instantiation

Because HospitalStaff has the information to be iterated over, the HospitalStaffEnumerator (the IEnumerator-derived type) needs access to the information. A convenient way to accomplish this is to pass a constructor parameter, referencing the current HospitalStaff instance, to the HospitalStaffEnumerator constructor. The following example shows how to implement the HospitalStaffEnumerator to handle this:

```
private HospitalStaff m_hospStaff;


public HospitalStaffEnumerator(HospitalStaff hospStaff)
{
    m_hospStaff = hospStaff;
}
```

The preceding code is a field and constructor for HospitalStaffEnumerator. The m_hospStaff field will hold a reference to the HospitalStaff instance. This reference is set in the constructor. Notice the hospStaff parameter in the constructor and how it is assigned to m_hospStaff. Now, other HospitalStaffEnumerator members have access to HospitalStaff.

If you recall, the GetEnumerator method of HospitalStaff (the IEnumerable-derived type) must return an IEnumerator. The following code shows you this implementation and how GetEnumerator will instantiate and return an instance of HospitalStaffEnumerator:

```
public IEnumerator<string> GetEnumerator()
{
    return new HospitalStaffEnumerator(this);
}
```

The preceding code instantiates HospitalStaffEnumerator, which is the proper return type—an IEnumerator<string>. See how GetEnumerator passes this when instantiating HospitalStaffEnumerator. The this is a reference to the current instance of

36

HospitalStaff, enabling the new instance of HospitalStaffEnumerator to access the HospitalStaff instance.

Next, I want to show you a case for a nested type. Recall from Chapter 8, "Designing Objects," that class members can be nested types. One of the primary reasons to create a nested type is because it exists solely for the purpose of providing services to its containing class. That is the exact situation with IEnumerator-derived types. Therefore, it makes sense to nest HospitalStaffEnumerator as a member inside of HospitalStaff, as shown here:

```
class HospitalStaff : IEnumerable<string>
{
...
    public IEnumerator<string> GetEnumerator()
    {
        return new HospitalStaffEnumerator(this);
    }

...

    private class HospitalStaffEnumerator : IEnumerator<string>
    {
        private HospitalStaff m_hospStaff;

        public HospitalStaffEnumerator(HospitalStaff hospStaff)
        {
            m_hospStaff = hospStaff;
        }
...
    }
}
```

HospitalStaffEnumerator is private because no other class needs to use it. Also, normal classes in a namespace are either internal or public, but nested classes can have any access modifier, just like other class members.

Once the IEnumerator-derived type, HospitalStaffEnumerator, has a reference to its containing class, other HospitalStaffEnumerator members can access HospitalStaff members. The next section begins discussing these other members, starting with the Reset method.

Resetting an IEnumerator

The purpose of the Reset method in the IEnumerator is to initialize the collection so that iteration can begin at a specified point. The following implementation reflects that intention:

```
    private int m_currentPos;

    public void Reset()
    {
        m_currentPos = -1;
    }
```

Reset modifies m_currentPos to -1, which is one position just prior to the first position of a zero-based collection. This is intentional because the protocol for using an iterator is to call MoveNext before reading the current value, which is the next IEnumerator method we'll look at.

Moving the IEnumerator to the Next Position

For a client class to get the next available value from an IEnumerator-derived type, such as HospitalStaffEnumerator, it must call MoveNext. Here's the implementation of MoveNext for HospitalStaffEnumerator:

```
    private const int Doctor = 0;
    private const int Nurse = 1;
    private const int Intern1 = 2;
    private const int Intern2 = 3;

    public bool MoveNext()
    {
        if (m_currentPos == Intern2)
        {
            return false;
        }

        ++m_currentPos;

        switch (m_currentPos)
        {
            case Doctor:
                m_currentVal = m_hospStaff.Doctor;
                break;
            case Nurse:
                m_currentVal = m_hospStaff.Nurse;
                break;
            case Intern1:
                m_currentVal = m_hospStaff.Intern1;
                break;
            case Intern2:
                m_currentVal = m_hospStaff.Intern2;
                break;
```

36

```
                default:
                    string message =
                        m_currentPos < 0 ?
                        "Call MoveNext before reading Current" :
                        "You've read all data - call Reset or GetEnumerator";
                    throw new IndexOutOfRangeException(message);
            }

            return true;
        }
```

This switch statement uses previously defined constants to make the code more readable. It could have been a nice opportunity to define an enum type, too. As you can see, I don't have a data structure worth talking about to maintain—the code only assigns positions to each value, keeps track of those positions via the m_currentPos field, and saves the proper value in m_currentVal. In reality, you would be keeping track of where you were in a data structure, such as a tree.

MoveNext returns a bool that indicates whether there are any more records to read. The first part of the algorithm returns false after m_currentPos is equal to Intern2, which is the last value to return. Otherwise, it returns true at the end of the algorithm to let the caller know that it can continue reading values.

You can see that I've added some error processing to the default case. This makes two points: You should include error information that gives a programmer the opportunity to figure out what a problem is, and you should use existing classes in the .NET Framework when possible. In this case, there are two reasons why the exception would be thrown: Either they called Current before calling MoveNext for the first time or they mistakenly called MoveNext after it had returned false. The IndexOutOfRangeException is an acceptable exception type to throw because it reflects what the real problem is—the user is trying to read before or after the contents of the collection, which is invalid.

The final IEnumerator member to cover is Current, which is next.

Reading a Value from an IEnumerator

The Current property returns the next available value from an IEnumerator-derived object. The following code shows how this is implemented for HospitalStaffEnumerator:

```
        public string Current
        {
            get { return m_currentVal; }
        }
```

The implementation of Current returns the private field m_currentVal. As you may recall, the MoveNext method determines what m_currentVal is set to.

Notice that Current is read-only (no set accessor). This is safe because you don't want client code trying to set it. The fact that it is read-only also precludes using an auto-implemented property in its place, in addition to the fact that MoveNext needs a way to set the value that Current returns.

This completes the implementation of the IEnumerator-derived type HospitalStaffEnumerator. Now, you can write code to use the iterator you've just constructed.

Using the Iterator in Client Code

In most cases, you can use a foreach to iterate through the members of a collection, but I want to show you the code to do it manually. In fact, this is a good technique to know because sometimes you encounter code that for some reason or another calls IEnumerator methods explicitly. The following example demonstrates the manual approach:

```
if (hospStaff is IEnumerable<string>)
{
    IEnumerator<string> hospStaffEnumerator = hospStaff.GetEnumerator();
    string name;
    hospStaffEnumerator.Reset();

    while (hospStaffEnumerator.MoveNext())
    {
        name = hospStaffEnumerator.Current;

        Console.WriteLine(name);
    }
}
```

The preceding code fleshes out the if statement you saw earlier, checking to see whether it is possible for the object to support iteration. In most cases, you'll use a foreach loop, as shown here:

```
foreach (var name in hospStaff)
{
    Console.WriteLine(name);
}
```

That's a little easier to code. When you run this example, you'll get a NotImplementedException from the Dispose method, indicating that foreach called it, which is another benefit of using the foreach loop—not the fact that you got the exception (which was an unimplemented part of the example), but because you have the opportunity to implement the Dispose pattern and clean up any resources you might have been using.

Surprising Behavior in the `foreach` Loop

One surprising feature for many new C# programmers is that the `foreach` loop doesn't need objects to implement IEnumerable or IEnumerator. Listing 36.1 demonstrates new implementation called HospitalStaffWithoutIEnumerator.

LISTING 36.1   Collection Without **IEnumerable/IEnumerator** Interfaces

```csharp
using System;
using System.Collections.Generic;
using System.Linq;
using System.Text;

namespace Chapter_36
{
    class HospitalStaffWithoutIEnumerator : IDisposable
    {
        public string Doctor { get; set; }
        public string Nurse { get; set; }
        public string Intern1 { get; set; }
        public string Intern2 { get; set; }

        private int m_currentPos = -1;
        private string m_currentVal = string.Empty;

        private enum Staff
        {
            Doctor,
            Nurse,
            Intern1,
            Intern2
        }

        public HospitalStaffWithoutIEnumerator GetEnumerator()
        {
            return this;
        }

        public bool MoveNext()
        {
            if (m_currentPos == (int)Staff.Intern2)
            {
                return false;
            }

            ++m_currentPos;
```

LISTING 36.1 Continued

```csharp
        Staff staffMbr;

        if (Enum.IsDefined(typeof(Staff), m_currentPos))
        {
            staffMbr = (Staff)Enum.ToObject(
                    typeof(Staff), m_currentPos);
        }
        else
        {
            string message =
                    m_currentPos < 0 ?
                    "Call MoveNext before reading Current" :
                    "You've read all data - call Reset or GetEnumerator";
            throw new IndexOutOfRangeException(message);
        }

        switch (staffMbr)
        {
            case Staff.Doctor:
                m_currentVal = Doctor;
                break;
            case Staff.Nurse:
                m_currentVal = Nurse;
                break;
            case Staff.Intern1:
                m_currentVal = Intern1;
                break;
            case Staff.Intern2:
                m_currentVal = Intern2;
                break;
            default:
                throw new InvalidOperationException(
                    "This code should never execute.");
        }

        return true;
    }

    public string Current
    {
        get { return m_currentVal; }
    }

    public void Dispose()
    {
```

36

LISTING 36.1   Continued

```
            throw new NotImplementedException();
        }
    }
}
```

The class in Listing 36.1 does implement `IDisposable`, resulting in the `foreach` recognizing the `IDisposable` interface and calling the `Dispose` method.

Instead of returning `IEnumerator<string>`, the `GetEnumerator` returns type `HospitalStaffWithoutIEnumerator`. The `foreach` loop recognized only that the method name is `GetEnumerator` (without parameters). Instead of instantiating an `IEnumerator`-derived type, `GetEnumerator` returns a reference to its own instance.

Again, the `foreach` loop cares only that the instance returned from `GetEnumerator` implements the `MoveNext` and `Current` methods. This time I implemented the `MoveNext` to use an enum so that you could see another example of enums. If you're a little rusty on how enums work, Chapter 6, "Using Arrays and Enums," explains them along with the `Enum` class API. The `MoveNext` method and `Current` property perform the same tasks as you saw earlier when implemented as members of the `HospitalStaffEnumerator`.

What's missing is the `Reset` method. It would never be called, even if you did implement it. Instead, the code initializes the `m_currentPos` field where it's declared, which is what the `Reset` method was doing in the `HospitalStaffEnumerator` class in earlier examples.

WHY NO RESET?

The iterator pattern was conceived in a time when most applications ran on a single thread of execution. From that perspective, it might be convenient to reuse the collection and iterate over it again, which is why `Reset` could be handy. However, as multicore and multiprocessor machines open the opportunity (or requirement) for multithreaded programming, this practice becomes more dangerous. In fact, it would be much safer to ensure that each thread gets its own copy of a collection or synchronize access to the collection to prevent corruption. In this case, you don't want any thread to call `Reset` on a collection because of the havoc it could cause. Sure, you might build a clever implementation that works just fine, but the C# designers recognized that the task is more difficult than it needs to be. Therefore, looking ahead, they implemented the `foreach` to not call `Reset`. Furthermore, the implementation of iterators in C# 2.0 generates a `Reset` method, behind the scenes, that throws a `NotImplementedException` if called.

Here's the `foreach` implementation that uses the new class:

```
            var hospStaff = new HospitalStaffWithoutIEnumerator
            {
                Doctor = "Marcus",
                Nurse = "Nancy",
```

```
        Intern1 = "Dmitri",
        Intern2 = "Helga"
    };

    foreach (var name in hospStaff)
    {
        Console.WriteLine(name);
    }
```

As you can see, there is absolutely no difference, except for the name of the new class.

The problem you face now is that you might have simplified the code for your own use, but the implementation is limited. For example, what if your code needs to work for other code that requires IEnumerable and IEnumerator types. In addition, other languages might expect collections to implement these interfaces also, which makes your code less than reusable in all environments.

Although the HospitalStaffWithoutEnumerator class was simpler than HospitalStaff, it can be even simpler. Let's revisit iterators in the next section to show you the best way to solve this problem of having IEnumerable and IEnumerator interfaces with an even simpler implementation.

Simplifying the Iterator Pattern with C# Iterators

In Chapter 17, "Parameterizing Type with Generics and Writing Iterators," I explained how to use iterators, but it might have been difficult to fully appreciate what they do for you. In this chapter, I covered the iterator pattern in depth, with one benefit being that you can now see how iterators greatly simplify the task of implementing the iterator pattern. The following code illuminates this benefit:

```
class HospitalStaffWithIterators : IEnumerable<string>
{
    public string Doctor { get; set; }
    public string Nurse { get; set; }
    public string Intern1 { get; set; }
    public string Intern2 { get; set; }

    public IEnumerator<string> GetEnumerator()
    {
        yield return Doctor;
        yield return Nurse;
        yield return Intern1;
        yield return Intern2;
    }

    IEnumerator IEnumerable.GetEnumerator()
    {
        throw new NotImplementedException();
    }
}
```

36

This example has significantly less code. You don't need to implement a separate IEnumerator, along with all the plumbing required to make sure it works. The only thing you must do is have your class implement IEnumerable<T> and then use yield return statements in GetEnumerator.

The example above shows how easy iterators are to use. Remember that with GetEnumerator you must return an IEnumerable<T>, but all other iterator types return IEnumerator<T>. The yield return statements each return an element to the calling code and only move to the next yield return when calling code performs a MoveNext operation. The code above returns four values – one for each yield return statement.

The next section moves you to a totally new pattern that is both common and useful, the Proxy pattern.

Implementing the Proxy Pattern

The proxy pattern does what its name suggests—it is a single object that you use in place of another. The proxy object acts on behalf of the real object, often encapsulating complexity and low-level plumbing code that you would rather not duplicate.

You've seen the proxy pattern used in earlier chapters on remoting, ASMX web services, and WCF web services. In each of those cases, you instantiated an object, which was the proxy, and that proxy communicated with the real object that was either in another AppDomain, process, or across a network. The proxy simplified your work because it took care of all the plumbing code associated with communications. Any time you need to hide the complexity of an operation inside of an object, you can use the proxy pattern.

Example of the Proxy Pattern

The example I use in this chapter reuses Socket client and server code from Chapter 30, "Using .NET Network Communications Technologies." The server code will stay the same, but I've wrapped the client code in a proxy, which you can see in Listing 36.2. Remember to start the MoneyServer before running the code in Listing 36.2. I've copied the code from the Chapter 30 solution to this chapter's solution so that you don't have to go looking for it.

LISTING 36.2   A Proxy for Encapsulating TCP/IP Calls to a Server

```
using System;
using System.IO;
using System.Net;
using System.Net.Sockets;
using System.Text;

namespace ProxyDemo
{
```

LISTING 36.2   Continued

```csharp
/// <summary>
/// proxy for managing communication with server
/// </summary>
class MoneyTalkProxy : IDisposable
{
    bool m_disposed;

    const int StreamSize = 256;
    const int  Port = 2010;
    const string LocalHost = "localhost";
    IPEndPoint ipEndPt = new IPEndPoint(
        new IPAddress(
            new byte[] { 127, 0, 0, 1 }),
        Port);
    ASCIIEncoding AsciiEnc = new ASCIIEncoding();
    byte[] inStreamBytes = new byte[StreamSize];
    byte[] outStreamBytes = new byte[StreamSize];
    TcpClient myClient = new TcpClient(LocalHost, Port);
    Stream myStream;

    public MoneyTalkProxy()
    {
        myStream = myClient.GetStream();
        outStreamBytes = AsciiEnc.GetBytes(
            "What is the secret of making money?");
    }

    public string GetAdvice()
    {
        myStream.Write(
            outStreamBytes, 0, outStreamBytes.Length);

        // clean garbage chars from byte array
        for (int i = 0; i < inStreamBytes.Length; i++)
        {
            inStreamBytes[i] = 0;
        }

        // retrieve response from server
        myStream.Read(
            inStreamBytes, 0, inStreamBytes.Length);
        var freeAdvice = AsciiEnc.GetString(
            inStreamBytes, 0, inStreamBytes.Length);

        return freeAdvice;
```

LISTING 36.2   Continued

```csharp
        }

        public void Close()
        {
            Dispose();
        }

        public void Dispose()
        {
            Dispose(true);
            GC.SuppressFinalize(this);
        }

        protected void Dispose(bool disposing)
        {
            if (!m_disposed)
            {
                if (disposing)
                {
                    // close session with server
                    outStreamBytes = AsciiEnc.GetBytes("bye");
                    myStream.Write(
                        outStreamBytes, 0, outStreamBytes.Length);
                }
                else
                {
                    throw new InvalidOperationException(
                        "Client code forgot to call Dispose() - " +
                        "Server connection was not properly terminated!");
                }

                m_disposed = true;
            }
        }

        ~MoneyTalkProxy()
        {
            Dispose(false);
        }
    }
}
```

Most of what the code in Listing 36.2 does was explained in Chapter 30, which you can review to understand what it does. The differences that you need to know are in initialization and destruction of the object.

Rather than a single monolithic application as was demonstrated in Chapter 30, the MoneyTalkProxy initializes its state in fields and its constructor. These are the items that will need to be set for each method call in the object. Therefore, they are initialized only one time. This strategy also reduces overhead should multiple calls on the same object need to be made.

As you can see, MoneyTalkProxy implements IDisposable and implements the .NET dispose pattern. The benefit of this is that it allows the calling code to determine how long the connection should stay open. Typically, this will be for a single use of the object, and then it will be disposed. When the object is disposed of, it sends a "bye" to the server, indicating its intent to end the conversation. This particular example simulates only the type of communications that happen between client and server. In real life, however, you replace this code with whatever disconnect sequence protocol was specified for communicating with the server.

Using the Proxy Object

To communicate with the server, client code needs only to instantiate the proxy, make a method call, and then close the proxy. Here's an example, with the client code forgetting to dispose of the proxy:

```
var moneyProxy = new MoneyTalkProxy();


string advice = moneyProxy.GetAdvice();


Console.WriteLine(advice);
```

Here, you can see how simple it is to communicate with the server; the proxy takes care of all the plumbing for you. The problem with the preceding code is that it doesn't dispose of the proxy, resulting in failing to disconnect from the server. Closer inspection of Listing 36.2 reveals that if the client doesn't call Close or Dispose, the Garbage Collector will invoke the finalizer, ~MoneyTalkProxy, which calls Dispose, setting the dispose parameter to false, and resulting in InvalidOperationException being thrown. As mentioned in Chapter 15, code invoked through the finalizer should never touch managed objects because they could have already been disposed of. Therefore, some people would regard the approach I took here of being a safer strategy because it lets the developer know immediately what the problem is—client code forgot to call Close or Dispose, which is a serious scalability issue. Here's a safer way to do this if you want to use the Close method:

```
MoneyTalkProxy moneyProxy = null;
string advice = string.Empty;

try
{
    moneyProxy = new MoneyTalkProxy();

    advice = moneyProxy.GetAdvice();
```

```
        Console.WriteLine(advice);
    }
    finally
    {
        moneyProxy.Close();
    }
```

Chapter 11, "Error and Exception Handling," provides more information about the try/finally block, which is a good way to clean up resources for objects that are not IDisposable. Alternatively, because the proxy is IDisposable, you might even prefer to implement it with a using statement, like this:

```
    using (var moneyProxy = new MoneyTalkProxy())
    {
        string advice = moneyProxy.GetAdvice();

        Console.WriteLine(advice);
    }
```

The using statement lets you write even less code and is equivalent to the preceding try/finally code. Reminder: The using statement will guarantee that Dispose is called when its block of statements completes, regardless of whether an exception occurs.

If you have complex code that you want to encapsulate, need to initiate calls to a server from multiple parts of your application and want to avoid duplication, or have different methods to the server that use the same setup and teardown code, the proxy pattern can be helpful.

Another pattern that is common in the .NET Framework is the template pattern, discussed next.

Implementing the Template Pattern

The template pattern occurs when a base class calls a sequence of virtual methods that a derived class can implement. It takes advantage of the object-oriented principle of polymorphism, where the base class defines the process and derived classes participate with specialized behavior.

Windows Forms, WPF, and ASP.NET applications make extensive use of the template pattern. Each of these technologies has an inheritance hierarchy for the form, and one object in this hierarchy drives the life cycle of the form. The form life cycle exposes events you can hook up to, such as the Load event, but it also implements virtual methods at the same times as these events.

How the Template Pattern Is Used in the .NET Framework

In Chapter 27, "Building Web Applications with ASP.NET," I described the page life cycle of a web form. The description was in the form of events, but you could also handle the stages of the page life cycle by overriding corresponding virtual methods. Here's an example of a code-behind file that does that:

```
public partial class _Default : System.Web.UI.Page
{
    protected override void OnInit(EventArgs e)
    {
        base.OnInit(e);
    }
    protected override void OnLoad(EventArgs e)
    {
        base.OnLoad(e);
    }
    protected override void OnPreRender(EventArgs e)
    {
        base.OnPreRender(e);
    }
}
```

Instead of using the event pattern Page_EventName, the overrides use the pattern OnEventName. Notice how each override calls the base class method of the same name. As you may recall from Chapter 9, "Implementing Object-Oriented Principles," polymorphism will ensure that your method (in your derived class) is called first, and you must explicitly invoke the base class virtual method to ensure it executes. This is important because the base class invokes the event for Page_EventName, which will not be done if you forget to call base.OnEventName in your OnEventName override. Here's a dramatization of how the base class is calling its virtual methods:

```
OnInit(EventArgs.Empty);
OnLoad(EventArgs.Empty);
// invoke cached events
// invoke postback event
OnPreRender(EventArgs.Empty);
```

It doesn't look exactly like that, but the point is that the base class is calling its OnEventName virtual methods, one after the other, and you have the opportunity in the derived class to implement an override to be called and specialize the behavior that occurs during the web form life cycle.

An Example of Implementing the Template Pattern

A take-off of the hospital theme I've used in this book is a program for managing appointments. I've modeled the appointment process as a patient scheduling an appointment, signing in once he has arrived, getting screened, the doctor performing a diagnosis, and treatment. This can be implemented via the template pattern because there are different ways this process can be performed, depending on who is performing it. Figure 36.1 shows the objects participating in this process: a base class named Appointments and two derived classes, HospitalAppointments and ClinicAppointments.

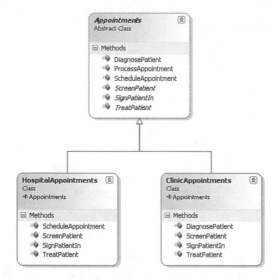

FIGURE 36.1   Object hierarchy for managing appointments using the template pattern.

The style of class diagram of the hospital theme I've used in this in Figure 36.1 might look familiar; I built it with ease using the Class Designer that I discussed in Chapter 35, "Using the Visual Studio 2008 Class Designer." I then followed up to tweak the code and add a basic implementation to make the demo work.

The Appointments base class drives the appointment scheduling process through the ProcessAppointment method. It calls each of the steps needed to complete an appointment, relying on virtual methods for derived classes HospitalAppointments and ClinicAppointments to override. Here's the Appointments implementation:

```
public abstract class Appointments
{
    public void ProcessAppointment()
    {
        ScheduleAppointment();
        SignPatientIn();
        ScreenPatient();
        DiagnosePatient();
        TreatPatient();
    }
```

```
    public virtual void ScheduleAppointment()
    {
        Console.WriteLine("No Schedule - Emergency or Walk-In");
    }

    public abstract void SignPatientIn();

    public abstract void ScreenPatient();

    public virtual void DiagnosePatient()
    {
        Console.WriteLine("Patient diagnosis is already on file.");
    }

    public abstract void TreatPatient();
}
```

As explained, ProcessAppointments calls the other methods. Notice that all the methods are either abstract or virtual. An abstract method is implicitly virtual, but has another important behavior, as covered in Chapter 14, of forcing derived classes to provide an override implementation. Because of the hospital theme I've used in this of this, the Appointments class can guarantee that derived classes will have implementations of SignPatientIn, ScreenPatient, and TreatPatient. Because Appointments has default implementations of ScheduleAppointment and DiagnosePatient, which are virtual, they are also optional for derived classes to implement. To demonstrate, here's the HospitalAppointments implementation:

```
public class HospitalAppointments : Appointments
{
    public override void ScheduleAppointment()
    {
        Console.WriteLine("Doctor refers patient and sets up appointment.");
    }

    public override void SignPatientIn()
    {
        Console.WriteLine("Sign in and wait for scheduled appointment time.");
    }

    public override void ScreenPatient()
    {
        Console.WriteLine("Get vital signs and consult on procedure.");
    }

    public override void TreatPatient()
    {
```

```
            Console.WriteLine("Operate.");
        }
    }
```

The HospitalAppointments class here implements everything but Diagnose, making the assumption that a clinic or doctor has already done this and leaving the default implementation of Appointments to execute. Similarly, here's the ClinicAppointments implementation of the hospital theme I've used in this:

```
    public class ClinicAppointments : Appointments
    {
        public override void SignPatientIn()
        {
            Console.WriteLine("Take a number and wait.");
        }

        public override void ScreenPatient()
        {
            Console.WriteLine("Get height, weight, and take blood pressure.");
        }

        public override void DiagnosePatient()
        {
            Console.WriteLine("Doctor examines patient.");
        }

        public override void TreatPatient()
        {
            Console.WriteLine("Write subscription for pills.");
        }
    }
```

Assuming that you can just walk into a clinic without an appointment, ClinicAppointments doesn't implement ScheduleAppointment, leaving the implementation to the default provided by Appointments.

Next, the code that calls this class will take advantage of polymorphism to ensure that the appropriate methods of the hospital theme I've used in this are called. Here's how this code is used:

```
        Console.WriteLine("\nProcessing Hospital Appointment:\n");


        Appointments hospAppt =
            new HospitalAppointments();


        hospAppt.ProcessAppointment();
```

```
Console.WriteLine("\nProcessing Clinic Appointment:\n");

hospAppt = new ClinicAppointments();

hospAppt.ProcessAppointment();
```

And to truly demonstrate what happened, here's the output:

```
Processing Hospital Appointment:


Doctor refers patient and sets up appointment.
Sign in and wait for scheduled appointment time.
Get vital signs and consult on procedure.
Patient diagnosis is already on file.
Operate.

Processing Clinic Appointment:

No Schedule - Emergency or Walk-In
Take a number and wait.
Get height, weight, and take blood pressure.
Doctor examines patient.
Write subscription for pills.
```

In the code, the compile-time type of hospAppt is Appointments, but the runtime type is the derived types HospitalAppointments and then ClinicAppointments. Each time ProcessAppointments is invoked, it will execute each method of Appointments, which actually calls the derived class members polymorphically, if they provide an implementation of the hospital theme I've used in this.

So, in the output for HospitalAppointment, you can see that it contains the line Diagnosis already on file, which is from Appointments. Similarly, the output for ClinicAppointment contains the line No Schedule - Emergency or Walk-In, which is also from Appointments.

This is the template pattern in action. Every method will execute, but derived classes either implement methods they must, because they are abstract in the base class, or optional methods. The .NET Framework uses the template pattern in many places, but you can use it to achieve similar goals where each method must be executed of the hospital theme I've used in this but where certain parts of the algorithm can be customized by derived classes.

Summary

The .NET Framework uses design patterns extensively. You've seen a few of them used in this chapter, including the iterator pattern, the proxy pattern, and the template pattern. There are many more design patterns than what you've seen here, but a comprehensive listing was not the goal. Instead, you had the opportunity to see many of the concepts from earlier chapters come together in a more practical setting.

With the iterator pattern, you saw how interfaces can be used to provide a generalized structure or framework that supports many different scenarios. By seeing how complex it is to create an iterator, you can also understand and have a better appreciation for the simplicity of the C# language feature called iterators.

If you build applications that communicate across a network or generally have a need to simplify the interface to another part of code, you can now accomplish this with the proxy pattern. The example in this chapter also gave you a practical implementation of the dispose pattern and reinforced the value of interfaces for giving specialized capabilities to diverse sets of objects. This example also reinforced the object-oriented principle of encapsulation and how important it is to hide the internal plumbing of an object from consuming code. You were also reminded of the role of the CLR in object creation and destruction and how the Garbage Collector affects your objects.

Finally, the template pattern should help you understand how UI frameworks manage object life-cycle processes. An extra bonus was a practical example of how the object-oriented principle of polymorphism gives you powerful capabilities to solve problems in an elegant way.

The previous chapter discussed class diagrams and object models; this chapter built upon that by showing a few ways that objects can be combined to solve problems and pull together many concepts from previous chapters. The next chapter takes you a step further and looks at different ways that you can put objects together to build entire applications.

CHAPTER 37

Building N-Tier/ Layer Systems

Anytime I'm traveling through a new town, something I do (besides getting lost or mugged) is observe the buildings and houses. Yes, I'm the klutz who trips on a crack on a busy New York sidewalk, falling flat on my face for not paying attention to where I'm going. Whenever I can keep embedded concrete off my face, I enjoy the architecture.

In many ways, the design and construction of a building can be compared to software engineering. We deal with enormous complexity at times, combining components, and building applications that pull these many pieces together into a comprehensive application that delivers value to users.

A single chapter in a book can't possibly tell you all there is to know about software architecture. However, various techniques have been effective for me over the years. Not only that, but I've also seen the same architectural practices used by other professional software engineers. In this chapter, I share some of what has worked for me and give you a few other tips.

Potential Drag-and-Drop Problems

There are many opinions about how to build applications, and I tend to respect the majority of approaches. This section might be a little controversial because there are lots of what-ifs, second-guessing, and alternative choices. Nevertheless, one of the areas that many developers have trouble with is the difference between good and bad rapid application development (RAD), aka drag-and-drop application development.

You've seen many examples of what I consider effective RAD, with LINQ to SQL/Entities, UI designers for Windows Forms, WPF, and ASP.NET, and data binding via an `ObjectDataSource` control (and its equivalents in other technologies). However, some practices cause more problems than others. The following sections walk you through a scenario that could tangle you into a web of spaghetti code.

A RAD Application in 5 Minutes

It takes less than 5 minutes to start VS2008, create a Web Application, open a database in Server Explorer, and drag and drop a table onto the design surface. If you click a few check boxes on the Action list and select Auto Format, you can get paging, editing, and a nice appearance for a page that allows you to manipulate the data in the selected table, as shown in Figure 37.1. Impressive, no?

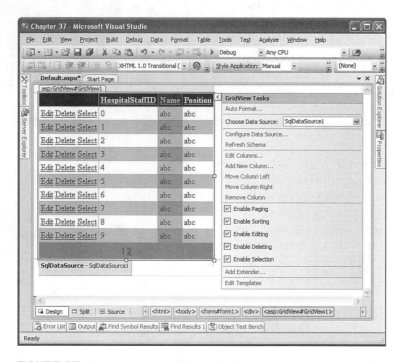

FIGURE 37.1   Drag-and-drop UI in ASP.NET.

This was easy to do, and it offers a lot of functionality with little effort. Imagine how quickly you could expose editing capabilities for your entire database. You could become popular with managers by impressing them with your development speed.

However, there's another perspective of building applications in this manner that you should consider, and the value of this approach can only be revealed with time.

What Harm Is a Little Bit of Productivity?

As in many aspects of software engineering, there are trade-offs between one approach and another. At the heart of the current subject is the value of RAD versus well-designed applications. This could stir up some more controversy, so perhaps I should qualify the discussion.

Traditionally, pure RAD development results in quick applications, often referred to as prototypes. Sometimes the desire for "quick" over "that which is more thought out" is stronger. However, there is a place for prototypes and RAD code and another for applications with more analysis and design. RAD code is more often than not of poor quality. It doesn't consider error handling, extensibility, maintenance, and other quality factors that go into an application. It's more of a veneer of a true application—kind of like the proxy pattern that I talked about in the preceding chapter, where it looks just like the object that does the work, but it actually doesn't. It's a prototype waiting for the true application to be built.

A common problem with RAD code is that users have an elevated expectation of the value of what they have been given. All they can see is the nice colors from autoformatting, and other bells and whistles, and are happy with having the application so quickly. However, the reality is that problems begin to creep into the application, growing like fungus. Because it isn't robust, the application will break when the user does something it wasn't designed to do. Users will see error messages designed for the eyes of developers. All too often, the application will break if it isn't hosted in the exact environment it was intended to run in, which is often the developer's machine and not the user's.

Another ailment of RAD code is the insidious problem of maintainability. The user will begin asking for bug fixes and new features. Think about the drag-and-drop demo of the previous section. Where do you add business logic? If an error occurs, how does the developer figure out what it is? There are events to hook up to, but patches are often copy and pasted between the event handlers in a code-behind page, resulting in spaghetti code that even the original developer can't figure out days (perhaps only hours) later. This is just the beginning of a crisis mode on a software project that was never conceived properly from day one.

Again, my apologies if this has been uncomfortable, but sometimes you have to see things for what they really are. RAD can be good when used properly but less than advantageous when applied incorrectly. So, now that I've talked about what could cause problems, it's time to talk about what has the most potential to help you avoid problems. The rest of this chapter discusses a couple strategies that improve chances of long-term benefits, resulting in greater project life-cycle savings and less frustration through code that is easier to maintain.

Introducing N-Layer/N-Tier

A couple terms are often used interchangeably when speaking about application architectures: *N-Layer* and *N-Tier*. However, both of these terms mean different things. The primary difference is that N-Layer is logical and N-Tier is physical.

Early Application Architectures

To appreciate what N-Layer and N-Tier give you, you have to look at what was being used before them (and is sometimes being used today). When an application doesn't have any architecture, it is usually just written so that events or user input are handled wherever they occur. There is much duplication, copy and pasting, and little thought is given to reusing objects or any type of practices that enhance maintainability. This is often the result of RAD gone bad.

Another widely used architecture, predating N-Layer or N-Tier, is client/server. This is where you have a client machine, perhaps a desktop or some other terminal, that communicates with a server that performs timesharing or holds a centralized database. The client/server architecture is useful to add more scalability to mainframe and server machines and push much of the processing onto a desktop.

Over time, the need for scalability increased, as did the need to manage complexity, which is where N-Layer and N-Tier come in. There was a need to divide up the work of an application into manageable pieces.

N-Layer Architecture

N-Layer is an architectural approach designed to help manage application complexity, increase maintainability, and reduce the cost of an application over its life cycle. Essentially, you divide the application into logical layers where higher-level layers communicate with lower-level layers that provide services. Figure 37.2 illustrates the relationship between layers of a basic three-layer application.

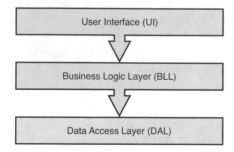

FIGURE 37.2   N-Layer application architecture.

The diagram in Figure 37.2 has three layers: User Interface (UI), Business Logic Layer (BLL), and Data Access Layer (DAL). The UI layer is responsible for interacting with a user. It displays information to and receives input from the user—nothing more. Arrows moving downward in the architecture demonstrate the direction of invocation. For example, if a user fills in a form and clicks a Submit button, the UI layer collects form information, possibly converts it to a form acceptable by a method in the BLL, and then calls a method on the BLL with the information that the user provided.

The BLL is responsible for any business logic associated with an application. For example, if a doctor or nurse uses a syringe to give someone a shot, the program will take input that one syringe was removed from stock. The implications for the business logic could be to determine whether the number of syringes dropped below a certain level and that more need to be ordered. The process of making the ordering determination, calling other objects that would be responsible for restocking, and coordinating any associated workflow belongs to the business objects in the BLL. If you think about it, there are many business rules that an application must implement that properly belong in business objects in the BLL. Part of the BLL's job is to work with data, but not to know about the persistence mechanism for performing create, read, update, or delete (CRUD) operations with a database. The BLL calls the DAL to do this, as you can see by the arrow in Figure 37.2 between BLL and DAL.

The DAL understands all there is to know about communicating with the database (or other persistence mechanism that stores the data). The BLL should have little or no knowledge about how the database works. The DAL will expose CRUD operations so that the BLL can simply make a call and send or get back an object or collection of objects that holds the data it needs to work with. The DAL is where you can put ADO.NET objects, if you're using ADO.NET. Optionally, you can use the LINQ to SQL DataContext as your DAL, which saves you a lot of work so that you don't have to use ADO.NET objects or some other API to create plumbing code. Regardless, by having the DAL in place, you can make your BLL much simpler to work with.

This was a description of a three-layer architecture, but there isn't a hard-and-fast rule for how many layers you need. If you need more layers (for instance, for additional navigation control between the UI layer and BLL), and it makes sense for your application, it is fine. Three-layer architectures are common and typically work well.

As I said, N-Layer is logical. That means you can have all your objects in the same assembly or have objects in lower layers in a separate assembly. Either way is generally no problem. If you prefer to make it easy to perform unit testing on code where your unit tests are external to the application, you might find it useful to separate BLL and DAL into a separate assembly. There are also N-Layer applications where every layer is in a separate assembly. This increases complexity, but some people prefer the explicit separation to make what goes where obvious to developers on the team. I show you examples of each of these N-Layered approaches in later parts of this chapter.

As opposed to the logical nature of N-Layer, N-Tier refers to the physical separation of application components.

N-Tier Architecture

A tier is an application component (part of the application) that physically resides on a separate computer. Given this perspective, an N-Tier architecture is one where the application is divided into *N* computer systems.

If an application and its data resides on a single desktop machine, it is single tier. That application could have many layers, perhaps three, but they reside on the same machine. If you would like to consider stored procedures, functions, or SQL-CLR code that resides in

SQL Server as a layer and if the application is on a desktop machine, while the database is on the server, you have a two-tier architecture, much like client/server.

You could also have a web application that renders in a browser, executes on the web server, and contains logic from a separate database server. This could be called a three-tier architecture.

If that same application was built with Silverlight, you have a XAML UI layer, a C# Silverlight code-behind layer, an ASP.NET web form code-behind layer, a BLL with business objects, a LINQ to SQL DataContext DAL, and then SQL Server logic. This would mean that the application has a six-layer/three-tier architecture.

Architecture Shouldn't Be Academic

Perhaps if you were to implement a service-oriented architecture (SOA) with multiple layers, you would have more layers and tiers. What you should get out of this is that any conversation about N-Layer and N-Tier should be accurate to promote effective communication and be descriptive of the application being built.

Another benefit of defining and discussing architecture is that the explicit definition of layers and tiers helps you reason about how the application should be built. Because object- and component-based APIs abstract the plumbing of the system from you, it is easy to be lulled into a sense of security that everything is being taken care of. However, understanding the tiers of your application opens your eyes to the implication of communications across a wire, which has performance and scalability issues.

To provide a more specific example, remember the proxy pattern from Chapter 36, "Sampling Design Patterns in C#," and how it provides location transparency when used to make method calls to web services and other technologies where out-of-process communication is required. If you use that proxy like a normal object, it is possible that you'll be making many calls across the wire, which could kill performance and scalability. Knowing about the communication resulting from the additional tier helps you understand that you should design your application to make fewer calls that pass more data at one time, rather than many calls that pass a small amount of data. In other words, calls should be chunky, not chatty. The focus on layers, tiers, and architecture helps you identify these issues and solve problems in design so that you don't ship code that will come back to haunt you later.

N-Layer Architecture Examples

Talking about architecture is nice, but it is often essential to see exactly how it can be implemented. The following sections concentrate on showing you how to set up applications for N-Layer architectures. You'll see examples of both web and desktop applications. The examples include layered architectures within a single assembly and divided among assemblies.

Earlier chapters in Part IV and V of this book showed you how to set up and code projects for desktop and Web Applications, so I don't need to go into that level of detail here.

What you will see is the solution setup and skeleton code that communicates between layers. Let's get started with an N-Layer architecture within a single assembly.

N-Layer/Single-Assembly Architectures

The following examples show both a WPF and website project, each of which creates a single physical assembly for their project. Perhaps, from the perspective of VS2008, this should be called an N-Layer/single-project approach, but I split hairs because, although it is a deployment issue, it doesn't affect the development experience one way or another.

N-Layer/Single-Assembly Desktop Applications

The example in this section shows an example of an N-Layer application that you can build with WPF. Because this discussion focuses on architecture, refer to Chapter 26, "Creating Windows Presentation Foundation (WPF) Applications," for the technical details of WPF if you need a refresher. There are two parts to this example: retrieving data and adding data. This should give you an idea about how you can make your application communicate effectively between layers. First of all, let's examine the solution and project, as shown in Figure 37.3.

FIGURE 37.3   Desktop N-Layer single-assembly architecture solution.

Figure 37.3 shows how I added BLL and DAL folders to explicitly state where each layer should go. I left the UI layer at the project level but could have added that to a folder, too. The naming convention is for demonstration purposes only, and you might have something that is more meaningful for your project. Either convention is fine if it works for you.

Window1.xaml, the startup window, needs to display doctors. The AddWindow will let you add a new doctor to the database. To accomplish these tasks, both Window1.xaml and AddWindow.xaml access the `HospitalManager` class that you see in the BLL folder in the HospitalManager.cs file. For `HospitalManager` to work with data, it uses `HospitalDataContext`, which is located in the DAL folder and defined by the Hospital.dbml. Figure 37.4 is a visual generalization of this process.

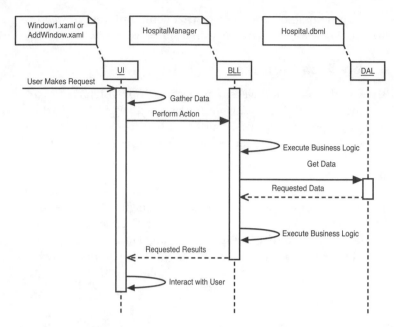

FIGURE 37.4   Sequence diagram for communication between layers.

In Figure 37.4, the boxes labeled UI, BLL, and DAL could represent any object in that particular layer. The notes show the files containing objects from this particular example. There is much greater detail here than in Figure 37.2, describing in a general nature what types of communication occurs between layers. The timeline for the process starts at the top and moves to the right and down.

As you can see, the user makes a request of the application, such as displaying data or adding a new record. The system gathers data and passes it to an object in the BLL. The BLL can optionally run business rules before or after requesting data from the DAL. Eventually, the results make their way back to the UI layer, which then displays information or interacts with the user in a way that makes sense for the particular process.

Let's drill-down a little deeper to help you make the connection between the architecture and how it is eventually implemented in code. In the first example, you'll see how to display data in the UI The following code shows the XAML for how the U gets its data:

```
<Window ...
    xmlns:local="clr-namespace:DesktopNLayerSingleAssembly.BLL"
    Title="Window1" Height="300" Width="300">
    <Window.Resources>
        <ObjectDataProvider x:Key="hospitalDataSource"
            ObjectType="{x:Type local:HospitalManager}"
            MethodName="GetDoctors">
        </ObjectDataProvider>
        <DataTemplate x:Key="doctorsTemplate">
```

```
        ...
      </DataTemplate>
   </Window.Resources>
```

This code isn't too different from what I showed you in the "Data Binding" section of Chapter 26. The `local` namespace references the `DesktopNLayerSingleAssembly.BLL` namespace, which is the same namespace for objects in the project's BLL folder. VS2008 created that namespace by default, but as you already know, you can use whatever namespace you want.

The `ObjectDataProvider` identifies the business object to use, `HospitalManager`, which is part of the BLL. It will call the `GetDoctors` for a list of items to display. This is an example of effective RAD. (I'll bet you thought I didn't like RAD.) It allows us to use data binding in the UI but still gives us the maintainability of a layered architecture because it calls into a business object for services. The next code shows the implementation of the `GetDoctors` method:

```
using System;
using System.Collections.Generic;
using System.Linq;
using DesktopNLayerSingleAssembly.DAL;

namespace DesktopNLayerSingleAssembly.BLL
{
    class HospitalManager
    {
        public List<HospitalStaff> GetDoctors()
        {
            using (var staffCtx = new HospitalDataContext())
            {
                return
                    (from staff in staffCtx.HospitalStaffs
                     where staff.Position == "Doctor"
                     select staff)
                    .ToList();
            }
        }
    }
    ...
}
```

Here you can see that `GetDoctors` performs filtering to ensure the results are what is expected. Even if a business object doesn't do much work today, I've found that it is good to code and use it anyway. Tomorrow, when you're asked to add a new feature or perform maintenance, you don't have to rework the code or try to figure out where to make the changes; you can just go to the business object and add it.

The BLL is also where most of your design patterns are implemented and where complex interactions between objects take place.

We don't have to code the DAL because it uses LINQ to SQL, which takes care of connecting, sending queries, retrieving results, and returning those results as a sequence of objects. This is a lot of work that you would have been required to do yourself in earlier versions of .NET when using ADO.NET.

Displaying data is often a simple task, as was the previous example. Next, let's look at a more complex scenario that you'll need to know how to implement. The tasks of inserting, updating, or deleting data tend to be a little more involved. The next example shows you how to add data to a system, insert (a process generally representative of how you can approach the other two operations), update, and delete. The following example is the code-behind in AddWindow.xaml.cs, with the button `Click` event that the user presses to add a new hospital staff member:

```
private void btnAddStaff_Click(
object sender, RoutedEventArgs e)
      {
          new HospitalManager()
              .AddStaff(
                  txtName.Text,
                  txtPosition.Text);
      }
```

I use the code-behind as part of the UI layer, not to hold business logic. The problem with putting business logic in the UI layer is that you quickly accumulate duplicate code in different methods that becomes difficult to maintain. Putting the business logic down into BLL objects promotes reuse of code because I push the logic into a common object that can be called by multiple events on the same UI or different UIs. Then, if I need to fix a bug or add a feature, there is a common location for it. The only code that I ever put in the UI layer is to interact with the user.

The `btnAddStaff_Click` event handles the `Click` event of the `btnAddStaff` `Button` control. It instantiates the business object (in the BLL), `HospitalManager`, and calls the `AddStaff` method, passing in values from other UI controls. The `AddStaff` method, shown here, saves the values to the database:

```
        private List<string> positions = new List<string>
        {
            "Doctor", "Nurse", "Intern1", "Intern2"
        };

        public void AddStaff(string name, string position)
        {
            if (!positions.Contains(position))
            {
                throw new ArgumentException(
                    "Invalid Position!", "position");
            }
```

```
using (var staffCtx = new HospitalDataContext())
{
    staffCtx
        .HospitalStaffs
        .InsertOnSubmit
        (
            new HospitalStaff
            {
                Name = name,
                Position = position
            }
        );

    staffCtx.SubmitChanges();
}
}
```

As you can see, `AddStaff` does more than just save the new staff member. It checks the
value of position to see whether it is valid. You could add business logic before or after the
save operation. In fact, you can do many things in a business object method to implement the business rules of your application. This is just one example. Again, using LINQ
to SQL, you don't have to write any of the database plumbing code because it is done for
you.

N-Layer/Single-Assembly Web Application Notes

Besides a different technology set, architecture for the web scenario isn't very different
from the desktop scenario. Rather than just say so, I do have an example that demonstrates a few of the nuances of how the web architecture is implemented.

Before walking through the code, let's explore the solution and project setup for a website
(see Figure 37.5).

FIGURE 37.5   Website project for N-Layer/single-assembly architecture.

With a website, custom object files must be located in the App_Code folder, as shown in Figure 37.5. Similar to the WPF application in the previous section, I've chosen to divide the layers into BLL and DAL folders, which are optional.

The first process to cover is displaying data. Here's the HTML from Default.aspx, the start page:

```
<asp:ListView
    ID="ListView1" runat="server"
    DataSourceID="DoctorsDataSource">
...
</asp:ListView>
<asp:ObjectDataSource
    ID="DoctorsDataSource" runat="server"
    OldValuesParameterFormatString="original_{0}"
    SelectMethod="GetDoctors"
    TypeName="HospitalManager">
</asp:ObjectDataSource>
```

The preceding code shows that I've used the ObjectDataSource for binding data to the ListView. The ObjectDataSource is a nice compromise between RAD UI development and N-Layer development—I get the productivity of building a UI fast, yet have the maintainability and flexibility of having a BLL.

As you can see, the business object to be called is HospitalManager and the method is GetDoctors. Here's the GetDoctors method:

```
using System;
using System.Collections.Generic;
using System.ComponentModel;
using System.Linq;
using DAL;

[DataObject]
public class HospitalManager
{
    [DataObjectMethod(DataObjectMethodType.Select)]
    public List<HospitalStaff> GetDoctors()
    {
        using (var staffCtx = new HospitalDataContext())
        {
            return
                (from staff in staffCtx.HospitalStaffs
                 where staff.Position == "Doctor"
                 select staff)
                .ToList();
        }
```

```
    }

...
}
```

The preceding code calls into the DAL, which is defined by Hospital.dbml. Notice how I used `DataObject` and `DataObjectMethod` attributes. They allow this object to appear when running the `ObjectDataSource` Wizard, which filters out all other objects in the project, except for the ones with the `DataObject` attribute. The `DataObjectMethodType` parameter can be set to `Select`, `Fill`, `Insert`, `Update`, or `Delete` and allows the `ObjectDataSource` Wizard to filter only those method types that match the operation being configured. For example, the `ObjectDataSource` page that allows you to pick a `Select` method has a check box for filtering methods. When that check box is selected, only the object methods decorated with `DataObjectMethod(DataObjectMethodType.Select)` will appear in the drop-down list, rather than every method in the object.

The scenario for adding a staff member is similar to the WPF example. Here's the event handler for the `Click` event on `btnAddStaff` in the code-behind of the AddStaff.aspx page:

```
    protected void btnAddStaff_Click(
object sender, EventArgs e)
    {
        new HospitalManager()
            .AddStaff(
                txtName.Text,
                txtPosition.Text);
    }
```

All this code does is pass control parameters to the `AddStaff` method of the `HospitalStaff` business object. This is the right way to do it because you don't want to put business logic in the code-behind file. Any business logic should be in the `HospitalManager` object, which is part of the BLL, shown here:

```
    private List<string> positions = new List<string>
        {
            "Doctor", "Nurse", "Intern1", "Intern2"
        };

    [DataObjectMethod(DataObjectMethodType.Insert)]
    public void AddStaff(string name, string position)
    {
        if (!positions.Contains(position))
        {
            throw new ArgumentException(
                "Invalid Position!", "position");
        }
```

37

```
using (var staffCtx = new HospitalDataContext())
{
    staffCtx
        .HospitalStaffs
        .InsertOnSubmit
        (
            new HospitalStaff
            {
                Name = name,
                Position = position
            }
        );

    staffCtx.SubmitChanges();
}
}
```

The preceding code is exactly the same as in the WPF example, except that the AddStaff method is decorated with the DataObjectMethod attribute, which allows this method to appear in any filters for data-binding objects in the UI. In this scenario, I chose to call into the BLL from an event handler, but it's your choice because now you have the flexibility of changing code in HospitalStaff.

This and the previous section introduced a way that you can create N-Layer architectures within the same assembly. Another options is to build layers into separate assemblies, which you'll learn about in the next section.

N-Layer/Multiple-Assembly Architectures

Some projects separate the layers of their architecture into separate assemblies. This makes the separation more explicit, reducing the opportunity for developers to bleed application responsibilities between layers. It also opens the opportunity to make code more shareable among multiple projects or even facilitate upcoming changes (perhaps, for example, making it easier to switch from one DBMS to another). There are pros and cons for doing this, and you'll have to pick whether a multiple-assembly or single-assembly separation of your architecture makes sense for you. The following sections show you how to do this with VS2008.

In this example, I show you how to separate your BLL and DAL layers into a separate class library project, which creates an assembly that is a DLL. The scenario is exactly the same as the previous section on WPF, except for the location of the code. Figure 37.6 shows the solution and project that holds this architecture.

In Figure 37.6, you can see that there is a WPF project that contains the XAML files for the UI layer and a class library project, BllDalLib, that contains the BLL and DAL layer.

When you use a class library, you must create a reference from the UI layer project to the class library project. You can see this in Figure 37.6 where there is a branch under the References folder of the DesktopNLayerMultipleAssembly (UI layer) project named

BllDllLib. To create this reference, right-click the References folder, select Add Reference, click the Projects tab, select the BllDllLib project, and click the OK button.

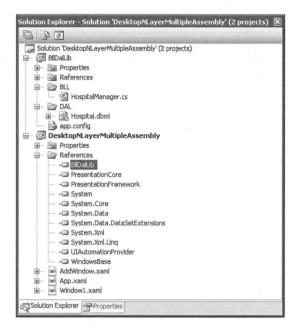

FIGURE 37.6   Desktop project for N-Layer/multiple-assembly architecture.

In addition to ensuring your references are set, gotchas to watch out for include access modifiers and namespaces. If you are trying to reference a class that is in the class library project, you will sometimes see the following message:

```
The type or namespace name 'HospitalManager' could not be found (are you missing a
using directive or an assembly reference?)
```

What is sometimes confusing is that you get the same message when you don't have a reference, as previously explained, or if you don't have a using directive for the name-space of the class you are trying to instantiate. Remember to check both situations.

Also, ensure you give public access to the object types you create in your class library. By default, the skeleton code creates a class without an access modifier, meaning that it has internal access. As you may recall, internal types are visible only within the same assembly they are defined in, which is the class library assembly in this case. Therefore, the code in your UI layer project, DesktopNLayerMultipleAssembly, will not be able to see the new class until you give it a public modifier.

The solutions to all these problems (missing references, different namespaces, and default access modifiers) were covered in earlier chapters, but you might not have understood the full implications of them. At least now you can see how some of that knowledge can assist you in practical ways at a high level.

Although the BLL is in a different assembly, none of your code changes. The only differences might be that you need to update a using directive or handle a namespace differently. You've already seen the same UI, BLL, and DAL code twice, so I won't repeat it again.

Now you have a reusable component that can be used by another application or even another UI technology. Perhaps this UI technology was ASP.NET. Next, I show you an example that demonstrates how to use the same Class library for both a WPF and an ASP.NET application.

First, I added an ASP.NET website to the same solution that I used for the WPF application that references the BllDalLib class library. Then I added a Default.aspx and AddStaff.aspx page with the same logic that I used in the website architecture with a single assembly. Figure 37.7 shows what the updated solution and project looks like.

FIGURE 37.7   Web project for N-Layer/multiple-assembly architecture.

Figure 37.7 shows how the website project has a reference to BllDalLib, which appears as a *.dll in the Bin folder. You can add this reference the same way as in the WPF project discussed previously. Also, just as with the previous WPF project, watch out for gotchas with namespaces and access modifiers. The code in this website project, besides namespace adjustments, is exactly the same as the website project for a single-assembly N-Layer architecture.

The big takeaway from this scenario is the code reuse. You can use that same BllDalLib class library with any type of .NET project, including Windows Forms, Windows service, ASMX web service, WCF web service, WPF, ASP.NET, Silverlight, and whatever other project type that occurs in the future.

The one thing you have to watch out for on ASP.NET projects if you want to create a reusable DLL is to not allow ASP.NET-specific technologies to bleed into the BLL. For example, it's possible to reference the System.Web namespace and get a reference to the current Context via the static HttpContext class so that you can use Request, Response, Session, and other ASP.NET intrinsics in BLL classes. However, these objects are not available in non-ASP.NET-based technologies, such as WPF, and make the code less reusable than you might desire. There are two techniques for avoiding ASP.NET intrinsic bleed-through: encapsulation and data transformation.

With encapsulation, you can create a class that accesses intrinsic objects, such as Session state through public method calls. If you give that class an interface, then if you want to reuse the code, all you have to do is create a new class with the same interface as the one that encapsulates the intrinsics but change the implementation so that it uses other data stores. This is sometimes easier said than done, especially when you consider access to HTTP-specific intrinsics, such as Request and Response, but it depends on what you're using them for; you'll have to evaluate your own situation to see whether this will work for you.

Another technique is to transform the data from intrinsics into something that the BLL can accept. For example, instead of accessing Session in the BLL, add a parameter to the BLL method that needs the information. Then have the UI layer pull that data out of Session state and pass it to the BLL in a form, such as a string, or custom object, that makes the BLL class more reusable across different technologies. Again, just another idea that may or may not work for you. However, I've used both techniques successfully and achieved reuse goals in a way that is understandable and maintainable.

Summary

Trying to figure out the right way to build an application isn't always easy when starting with a new technology. Fact is, there are more opinions on the subject than you can count. However, one of the goals of this chapter wasn't to specify a dogmatic approach to architecture, but rather show you a few techniques that have worked for me and for others.

First in this chapter, I wanted to steer you away from a full-blown RAD approach, which often gets people and projects into trouble. I explained some of the things that can go wrong, but then turned my attention to architectural approaches that can increase the chances of project success and reduce cost over the application life cycle.

After learning about N-Layer/N-Tier architectures, you saw how to implement N-Layer applications in different ways. This included both a desktop and Web Application implementing an N-Layer architecture in a single assembly and then the same thing with multiple assemblies. The multiple-assembly scenario opened some new gotchas that you should be aware of, and I showed you how to work around them.

The last architectural-related subject I cover in this book is a new technology, Windows Workflow, which enables you to graphically create applications that follow a process. You can learn about Windows Workflow in the next chapter.

37

CHAPTER **38**

Automating Logic with Windows Workflow

Sometimes it seems like you have to go through a long and drawn-out process to get anything done in life. Last year, I helped my son register for his first year in college. You start by applying to the college and then wait for acceptance, attend orientation, and schedule classes. At any step along the way, if something is out of order, you end up going in circles between offices until it's fixed. When that's all done, you have to pay for it—the tuition that is, not the hassle of the process.

I wonder if they implemented their student enrollment system with Windows Workflow (WF). Although computers won't completely eliminate the frailties of the human condition, you can use tools like WF to make processes better. Regardless, WF is a way to easily develop .NET applications that follow a process—aka workflow.

In this chapter, you learn how to create two types of workflow: sequence and state. The first section shows you how to create a Workflow application and work with other windows and designers in the project.

Starting a Workflow Project

VS2008 has a project known as a Workflow application. To get started, select File, New, Project. When the New Project window appears, select Workflow (under the Visual C# branch), select Sequential Workflow Console Application, fill out the fields as you like, and then click the OK button. The results will look similar to Figure 38.1.

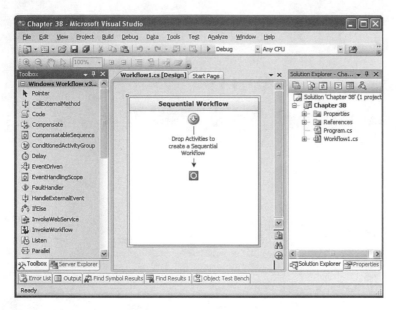

FIGURE 38.1   Parts of a Workflow project.

In the middle of the Workflow project shown in Figure 38.1 resides the design surface. This is where you do most of your work to construct the workflow. As you can see, it is graphical in nature, and you will build the workflow by connecting activities.

The toolbox holds activities you can use to build the workflow. These include IfElse, Code, and Sequence (so you can have a sequential workflow inside of a sequential work-flow—nested).

In the designer, the round arrow is green and represents the start condition. The square with a circle is red and represents the ending condition. You'll begin working in between these two icons, where it says Drop Activities, to create a sequential workflow, which you learn how to do next.

Building a Sequential Workflow

This section shows you how to create and call a workflow.

Creating the Workflow

To give you a feel for how workflows operate, this section creates a simple workflow that handles hospital appointments. Consider what a person must do from start to finish of a hospital appointment: schedule an appointment, travel to the doctor's office, check-in, wait, receive an examination, and then perform whatever actions are appropriate based on the doctor's recommendations. Scenarios like this surround us every day, where we need to perform a sequence of activities. The following steps describe how to create a workflow similar to the hospital appointment scenario just described:

1. Drop a Code activity onto the design surface.

2. In the Properties window, set Name to **CheckIn** and ExecuteCode to **DoPaperwork**. Figure 38.2 shows what this looks like.

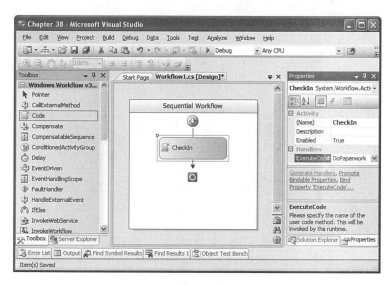

FIGURE 38.2   The **CheckIn Code** activity.

You have now created a workflow with a single activity. A Code activity allows you to add code into your workflow, which is described in the next step.

3. Right-click the designer, select View Code, and modify the DoPaperwork method as follows. (Remember to add the m_waitList and PatientName properties to the WorkFlow1 class.)

```
private List<string> m_waitList = new List<string>();


public string PatientName { get; set; }

private void DoPaperwork(object sender, EventArgs e)
{
    m_waitList.Add(PatientName);
}
```

To continue with the workflow, we need to verify that the patient filled in the paperwork properly. If so, we'll be happy and move the patient to the front of the line as a reward. If not, we need to make the patient correct the paperwork. To get started, drop an IfElse activity onto the designer below CheckIn and change its Name property to **VerifyPaperwork**. Change the names of ifElseBranchActivity1 to **IsGood** and ifElseBranchActivity2 to **ResolveProblem**. Figure 38.3 shows the results.

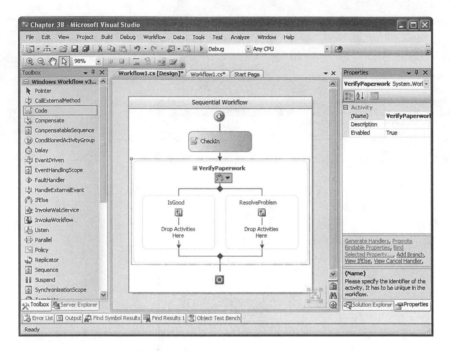

FIGURE 38.3   The **IfElse** activity.

The IfElse activity allows you to take different branches based on a condition. This example demonstrates how to have a good condition and a default condition.

There is a round icon with an exclamation point (it's red) at the top of the IsGood branch. Hovering over this icon and selection in the Action list, you'll see the message Property 'Condition' is not set. We need to specify a condition that defines whether this branch should execute. If you click this item or click IsGood, you'll see a Condition property in the Properties window. Working in the Properties window, select Code Condition from the Condition drop-down list, expand the Condition branch, and type **CheckPaperwork** into the Condition value. Implement the CheckPaperwork method as follows:

```
private void CheckPaperwork(object sender, ConditionalEventArgs e)
{
    e.Result = m_waitList.Contains(PatientName);
}
```

Next, add Code activities to both IsGood and ResolveProblem.

For the Code activity in IsGood, set its properties: Name to **Reward** and ExecuteCode to **MoveToFrontOfLine**.

For the Code activity in ResolveProblem, set its properties: Name to **Scold** and ExecuteCode to **FixPaperwork**.

Implement MoveToFrontOfLine and FixPaperwork as follows:

```
private void MoveToFrontOfLine(object sender, EventArgs e)
{
    Console.WriteLine("Hooray, paperwork is correct!");
}

private void FixPaperwork(object sender, EventArgs e)
{
    if (!m_waitList.Contains(PatientName))
    {
        m_waitList.Add(PatientName);
    }
}
```

Next, add a Code activity below the IfElse. Set its Name to **SeeDoctor** and ExecuteCode to **ExaminePatient**. Implement ExaminePatient as follows:

```
private void ExaminePatient(object sender, EventArgs e)
{
    Console.WriteLine("You're healthy.");
}
```

Figure 38.4 shows the final workflow.

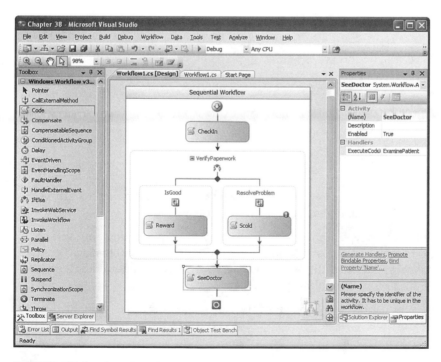

FIGURE 38.4   Complete sequential workflow.

Executing the Workflow

To understand how the workflow executes, let's examine the code that the Workflow Project Wizard creates, located in the Program.cs file:

```
static void Main(string[] args)
{
    using(WorkflowRuntime workflowRuntime = new WorkflowRuntime())
    {
        AutoResetEvent waitHandle =
            new AutoResetEvent(false);

        workflowRuntime.WorkflowCompleted +=
            delegate(object sender, WorkflowCompletedEventArgs e)
            {
                waitHandle.Set();
            };

        workflowRuntime.WorkflowTerminated +=
            delegate(object sender, WorkflowTerminatedEventArgs e)
            {
                Console.WriteLine(e.Exception.Message);
                waitHandle.Set();
            };

        WorkflowInstance instance =
            workflowRuntime.CreateWorkflow(
                typeof(Chapter_38.Workflow1));

        instance.Start();

        waitHandle.WaitOne();
    }
}
```

The WorkflowRuntime is a runtime engine that manages workflows. It handles starting, stopping, and a set of events that you can hook up to in your code.

The waitHandle variable, of type AutoResetEvent, is used to keep the program running until the workflow completes. We have handlers hooked up to the WorkflowCompleted and WorkflowTerminated events of the WorkflowRuntime that will call set on waitHandle, allowing the program to continue running to the end of Main.

After hooking up event handlers, the code uses the runtime, workflowRuntime, to create an instance of the workflow. Chapter_38.Workflow1 is the class (workflow code-behind) containing the code you implemented in the previous section.

The workflow begins execution when we call Start on the new workflow instance, instance. This starts the workflow on a new thread, making the call to waitHandle.WaitOne necessary to ensure the program doesn't close before the workflow is done.

Building a State Workflow

The process in the preceding section was created as a sequential workflow. However, there might be a scenario in which it would make sense to create that workflow as a state workflow. The next couple of sections explain how the hospital appointment system can be implemented as a state workflow and the steps for creating the state workflow.

Overview of the Hospital Appointment State Workflow

State workflows are like state machines in that the process executes by being in one state or another. Particular actions cause a transition from one state to another. Figure 38.5 shows a state diagram for a hospital appointment system.

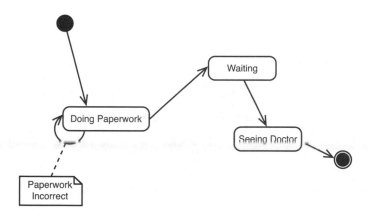

FIGURE 38.5   State diagram for hospital appointments.

In the state diagram in Figure 38.5, the initial stage moves from the upper-left black dot to the Doing Paperwork state when the patient walks into the office. The patient will stay in the Doing Paperwork state as long as he or she keeps making mistakes. However, when the paperwork is good, the patient moves to the Waiting state. When the doctor is ready, the patient moves to the Seeing Doctor state. Finally, after the patient's examination is complete, the patient moves to the final state, which is the black dot with a circle toward the bottom right.

Creating Workflow States

With a state workflow, you don't have to write a lot of code to manage the process; you just add the states, logic for each state, and then invoke the transition to the next state.

To get started, create a new project, but this time select the State Machine Workflow console application. You'll see an initial screen that looks similar to Figure 38.6.

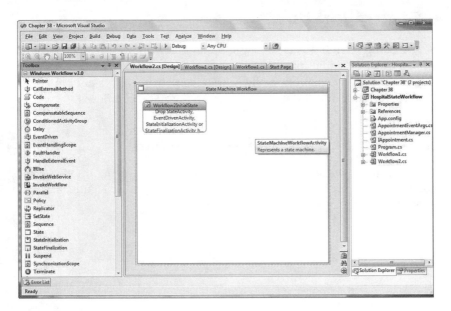

FIGURE 38.6   State machine project for hospital appointments.

State workflows have optional initial and final states and one or more states in between. The WorkflowInitialState1 that you see in Figure 38.6 is the initial state. The following steps explain how to implement the state machine shown in Figure 38.6 via a state workflow:

1. Drop three state activities onto the design surface and set their Name properties as follows:

    a.   DoingPaperwork

    b.   Waiting

    c.   SeeingDoctor

2. Add a state activity to the diagram and set its Name property to Workflow1FinalState.

3. Select the design surface, not any of the states, and observe the Property window. The InitialStateName property is already set to Workflow1InitialState. Now set the CompletedStateName property to Workflow1FinalState. Both Workflow1InitialState and Workflow1FinalState have icons that indicate their purpose. You can see the states and their icons in Figure 38.7.

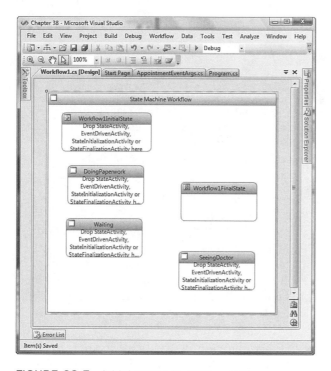

FIGURE 38.7   Initial states in state workflow.

As you might guess, states alone are not enough to create a useful workflow. You'll need code that drives the machine and communicates with the workflow runtime to pass information. We'll accomplish this by creating what is called an ExternalDataExchangeService.

Communicating from Host to Workflow: Implementing ExternalDataExchangeService

You might be wondering why we can't just take an instance of the workflow and call it to pass information in, but it isn't that easy. You see, the workflow is running on a separate thread, meaning that you have to marshal information from the thread of the host application, which is a console application in this case, to the thread that the workflow executes on. The following steps describe the details and process of implementing ExternalDataExchangeService:

1. Before hooking up the ExternalDataExchangeService, you need to create an interface that defines communication from the host to the workflow, build a class that implements that interface, and then add the ExternalDataService to the workflow runtime, setting its reference to the class that implements the interface. When that is done, you can hook up states in the state workflow to handle events that were

defined by the interface that the host is calling through. Here's the interface we'll use for this application:

```
[ExternalDataExchange]
    public interface IAppointment
    {
    event EventHandler<AppointmentEventArgs> PatientArrived;
    event EventHandler<AppointmentEventArgs> PaperworkDone;
    event EventHandler<AppointmentEventArgs> DoctorReady;
    event EventHandler<AppointmentEventArgs> AppointmentComplete;

    }
```

This is an interface, just like you've learned about in Chapter 14, "Implementing Abstract Classes and Interfaces." You've seen interfaces implemented repeatedly throughout multiple chapters of this book, primarily to facilitate communication between objects. (For example, the calling code uses the interface for a common contract of type members it can use, and the called code implements the interface with code that is specific to that application.) In the case of this program, the interface is used by the state machine to know which events each state can react to, which you'll see after building the code to implement the ExternalDataExchangeService.

The ExternalDataExchange attribute is necessary for indicating to workflow runtime that this interface supports the ExternalDataExchangeService. As explained in Chapter 16, "Declaring Attributes and Examining Code with Reflection," attributes are specific to supporting some tool or application, which in this case is the workflow runtime. The ExternalDataExchange attribute is required.

2. AppointmentEventArgs, the generic EventHandler type, is instrumental in being able to pass information to the workflow. You learned about events in Chapter 11, "Error and Exception Handling," and generic types in Chapter 17, "Parameterizing Type with Generics and Writing Iterators," and can now see how convenient it is to declare events with a custom EventArgs-derived type. In this case, however, AppointmentEventArgs derives from ExternalDataEventArgs, which derives from EventArgs, as shown here:

```
[Serializable]
    public class AppointmentEventArgs : ExternalDataEventArgs
    {
    public string PatientName { get; set; }

    public AppointmentEventArgs(Guid instanceID)
        : base(instanceID)
    {
        PatientName = string.Empty;
        WaitForIdle = true;
    }

    }
```

Besides deriving from `ExternalDataEventArgs`, there are important elements of `AppointmentEventArgs` that are critical to making this work as a means of sharing host information with your workflow: marking the type as `Serializable`, implementing the proper constructor, and setting `WaitForIdle`.

As you may recall, the workflow is running on its own thread, and there could be many instances of the workflow. Because of this complexity, you can't just call the workflow and send the information. It must be marshaled from the host to the workflow. To mashal the type, it must be serializable, which is why the `Serializable` attribute decorates the `AppointmentEventArgs` class.

The constructor parameter `instanceID` identifies the specific workflow instance to communicate with. The `ExternalDataEventArgs` holds this value as a standard data item for correlating communication between the host and the workflow.

3. Another `ExternalDataEventArgs` member is `WaitForIdle`. This particular property is important to workflow management. Later, you'll see how the host drives the workflow by invoking methods that fire the events to enable state changes. When one of these events occur before a state is ready, you'll receive the following exception:

    ```
    Event "PatientArrived" on interface type "HospitalStateWorkflow.IAppointment"
    for instance id "0882dbfc-a923-46bb-9ab6-52e78318af24" cannot be delivered.
    ```

4. In addition to that error message, if you drill down on the exception, inspecting the `InnerException`, you'll see the following message:

    ```
    Event Queue operation failed with MessageQueueErrorCode QueueNotFound for
    queue 'Message Properties
    Interface Type:HospitalStateWorkflow.IAppointment
    Method Name:PatientArrived
    CorrelationValues:

        '.
    ```

    There's a lot of plumbing behind the scenes of the `ExternalDataExchangeService`, including correlating the caller with the receiver and message queues to facilitate communication, and all of this can get out of whack because the thread for the host and the thread for the caller are executing at their own pace, which is the nature of multithreading. For all the complex explanation, which you would normally never care about, it all comes down to the fact that the host was making a call to the service, and the service wasn't ready for it. One solution is to ensure that `WaitForIdle` is set to `true` so that a call from the host has to wait for the workflow to be in the proper state to receive the value. Another solution is to ensure there is a state that handles that event and the workflow is currently in state before firing the event, which you'll learn how to do later in this chapter. In other words, `WaitForIdle` keeps the application from getting the cart before the horse.

5. Next, let's look at the class that implements the `Iappointment` interface. This is the same class that the host uses to define the `ExternalDataExchangeService` and the

same class that is used to drive the workflow. The `AppointmentManager` class here implements the `Iappointment` interface:

```
[Serializable]
    class AppointmentManager : IAppointment
    {
    public event EventHandler<AppointmentEventArgs> PatientArrived;
    public event EventHandler<AppointmentEventArgs> PaperworkDone;
    public event EventHandler<AppointmentEventArgs> DoctorReady;
    public event EventHandler<AppointmentEventArgs> AppointmentComplete;

    public void DoPaperwork(Guid instanceID, string name)
    {
        PatientArrived(
            this,
            new AppointmentEventArgs(instanceID)
            {
                PatientName = "Joe"
            });
    }

    public void Wait(Guid instanceID, string name)
    {
        PaperworkDone(
            this,
            new AppointmentEventArgs(instanceID)
                {
                    PatientName = name
                });
    }

    public void SeeDoctor(Guid instanceID, string name)
    {
        DoctorReady(
            this,
            new AppointmentEventArgs(instanceID)
            {
                PatientName = name
            });
    }

    public void GoHome(Guid instanceID, string name)
    {
        AppointmentComplete(
            this,
            new AppointmentEventArgs(instanceID)
```

```
            {
                PatientName = name
            });
        }
    }
```

AppointmentManager is decorated with the Serializable attribute to facilitate communication with the workflow. Its events implement the Iappointment inter-face, and it contains convenient methods that fire those events.

Taking the DoPaperwork method as an example, you can see how it raises the PatientArrived event, passing itself and AppointmentEventArgs as arguments. The parameters passed to DoPaperwork, and other methods, hold values necessary for instantiating AppointmentEventArgs, including the instanceID that identifies the workflow instance to communicate with.

6. Just like DoPaperwork, all other methods of AppointmentManager receive parameter values that are passed as arguments from the host. Here's the implementation of the host that does this:

```
static void Main(string[] args)
{
    using(WorkflowRuntime workflowRuntime
            = new WorkflowRuntime())
    {
        AutoResetEvent waitHandle
            = new AutoResetEvent(false);
        workflowRuntime.WorkflowCompleted +=
            delegate(
                object sender,
                WorkflowCompletedEventArgs e)
            {
                waitHandle.Set();
            };
        workflowRuntime.WorkflowTerminated +=
            delegate(
                object sender,
                WorkflowTerminatedEventArgs e)
            {
                Console.WriteLine(e.Exception.Message);
                waitHandle.Set();
            };

        var extDatEx = new ExternalDataExchangeService();
        workflowRuntime.AddService(extDatEx);
```

```
        var apptMgr = new AppointmentManager();
        extDatEx.AddService(apptMgr);

        WorkflowInstance instance =
         workflowRuntime.CreateWorkflow(
                typeof(HospitalStateWorkflow.Workflow1));
        instance.Start();

        var name = "Joe";

        apptMgr.DoPaperwork(instance.InstanceId, name);
        apptMgr.Wait(instance.InstanceId, name);
        apptMgr.SeeDoctor(instance.InstanceId, name);
        apptMgr.GoHome(instance.InstanceId, name);

        waitHandle.WaitOne();
        Console.ReadKey();
    }
  }
```

7. To set up the ExchangeDataExchangeService, you must first add an instance of
    ExternalDataExchangeService to the workflow runtime services, shown here:

    ```
        var extDatEx = new ExternalDataExchangeService();

        workflowRuntime.AddService(extDatEx);
    ```

8. The order of operations here counts because you'll receive a runtime exception if
    you try to configure ExternalDataExchangeService first. Next, you can configure
    the ExternalDataExchangeService, as follows:

    ```
        var apptMgr = new AppointmentManager();

        extDatEx.AddService(apptMgr);
    ```

    This is the AppointmentManager that was shown previously that implements the
    IAppointment interface. Now that AppointmentManager is added to the services of the
    ExternalDataExchangeService, it can participate in communication between host
    and workflow.

9. After the ExternalDataExchangeService has been set up, you can use
    AppointmentManager to drive the workflow, as follows:

    ```
        apptMgr.DoPaperwork(instance.InstanceId, name);
        apptMgr.Wait(instance.InstanceId, name);
        apptMgr.SeeDoctor(instance.InstanceId, name);
        apptMgr.GoHome(instance.InstanceId, name);
    ```

You've seen the implementation of each of these methods in AppointmentManager. They
fire events that implement the IAppointment interface. Now that all the code to facilitate
communication is in place, we can return to the workflow and implement state activities
to ensure the workflow reacts properly to the events fired by the host.

Handling Events in the State Workflow

The preceding section showed how to implement the ExternalDataExchangeService, which involved a lot of coding. That was so that the host could raise events that drive the state machine defined by the state workflow. Next you'll see how to finish building the workflow that we started earlier so that it can respond to those events and implement the logic associated with the hospital appointment system. The following steps show you how to do so:

1. Drop EventDriven activities on Workflow1InitialState, DoingPaperwork, Waiting, and SeeingDoctor states.

2. Double-click the EventDriven activity in Workflow1InitialState. You'll see a Sequence workflow that you can add items to.

3. Add a HandleExternalEvent activity, click InterfaceType in the Properties window, and select IAppointment. Then set the EventName property to PatientArrived. This is the IAppointment interface created earlier in this chapter when configuring the ExchangeDataEventService.

4. Add a Code activity and set its ExecuteCode property to StartAppointment.

5. Add a SetState activity and set its StartState property to DoingPaperwork. The SetState activity is necessary for setting what the next state in the workflow should be. You can put whatever activities are necessary in the workflow to make this decision. Figure 38.8 shows the final configuration of the EventDriven activity. Each of the states in this particular state workflow will be similar.

   Figure 38.8 shows a breadcrumb trail at the top-left side of the designer. You can click the Workflow1 link to go back to the main state workflow.

6. Double-click the EventDriven activity in the DoingPaperwork state.

7. Add a HandleExternalEvent activity, click InterfaceType in the Properties window, and select IAppointment. Then set the EventName property to PaperworkDone.

8. Add a Code activity and set its ExecuteCode property to DoPaperwork.

9. Add a SetState activity and set its StartState property to Waiting.

10. Click the Workflow1 link to go back to the main state workflow.

11. Double-click the EventDriven activity in the Waiting state.

12. Add a HandleExternalEvent activity, click InterfaceType in the Properties window, and select IAppointment. Then set the EventName property to DoctorReady.

13. Add a Code activity and set its ExecuteCode property to WaitingForDoctor.

14. Add a SetState activity and set its StartState property to SeeingDoctor.

15. Click the Workflow1 link to go back to the main state workflow.

16. Double-click the EventDriven activity in the SeeingDoctor state.

17. Add a HandleExternalEvent activity, click InterfaceType in the Properties window, and select IAppointment. Then set the EventName property to AppointmentComplete.

18. Add a Code activity and set its ExecuteCode property to InWithDoctor.

19. Add a SetState activity and set its StartState property to Workflow1FinalState.

38

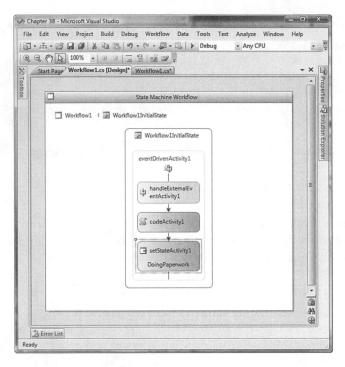

FIGURE 38.8   **EventDriven** activity implementation.

20. Implement the code for the Code activities as follows:

```
private void StartAppointment(object sender, EventArgs e)
{
    Console.WriteLine("Patient Arrived.");
}

private void DoPaperwork(object sender, EventArgs e)
{
    Console.WriteLine("Doing Paperwork.");
}

private void WaitingForDoctor(object sender, EventArgs e)
{
    Console.WriteLine("Waiting For Doctor");
}

private void InWithDoctor(object sender, EventArgs e)
{
    Console.WriteLine("Seeing Doctor");
}
```

The workflow is now complete. If you click Workflow1 in the breadcrumb trail, you'll see all the states connected, as shown in Figure 38.9.

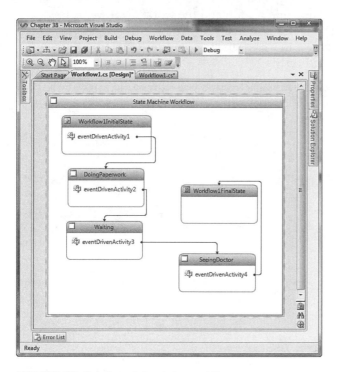

FIGURE 38.9   Complete state workflow.

As you can see in Figure 38.9, all the states have linkages between them so that you can see the flow. When you run the application, it will produce the following output:

```
Patient Arrived.
Doing Paperwork.
Waiting For Doctor
Seeing Doctor
```

Each element of the output was produced by methods identified in the ExecuteCode properties of Code activities in EventDriven activities of states in the state workflow that were invoked by events fired by the host.

Summary

In this chapter, you learned how to use Windows Workflow to implement both sequential and state workflows. Sequential workflows allow a flow of logic that begins at one point and ends at another. State workflows focus primarily on the states that the application is in at a specific point in time, with events that drive the transitions from one state to another.

Another thing you learned was how to set up an `ExternalDataExchangeService`, which facilitates communication between a host application and the workflow it wants to communicate with. Setting up an ExternaDataExchangeService is a detailed process, so be sure to double-check each step, as shown in this chapter, to ensure communication between client and workflow occurs properly.

This completes this part of the book. The next part shows you how to work with more advanced concepts supported by the .NET Framework Class Library.

PART 9

Surveying More of the .NET Framework Class Library

Managing Processes and Threads

Between work, family, friends, and other activities, most of us have pretty busy lives. My wife continually says that she needs two of me. That would be great—the doppelganger can do all the work.

Unfortunately, cloning technology isn't ready for prime time. Instead, we find other ways to deal with our schedule, often multitasking to help accomplish what we need or want. Still, there is only one of us, and for all the juggling of time we attempt, a limit of 24 hours—sleep constrains us.

Just like there is only so much one person can do, it wasn't too long ago when computers could do only one thing at a time. However, that has been changing. Multiprocessing, where the OS quickly switches between processes, giving each process a time slice (or quantum), has become common. This simulates doing multiple things at the same time, but there is only one operation being executed on the machine at a time, regardless of which process is running.

More recently, hardware (and CPUs especially) has advanced to the point that multiprocessing does mean that your computer is performing multiple operations at the same time. Multicore processors can run multiple logical CPUs in a single physical CPU. Furthermore, desktop and server computers are shipping with multiple physical processors. The Microsoft Windows operating systems have been able to take advantage of multicore/multiprocessing systems for many years now.

With the advent of hardware and operating systems that support multiprocessing, demand has increased in financial, scientific, and other market sectors for taking advantage of these capabilities. The trend is that this demand will spread into other market sectors, hungry for processing power and desiring to exploit the new and improving capabilities that hardware and OS vendors are delivering.

To meet this demand, you as a developer can learn about how to manage multiple processes and threads and become skilled in the issues involved. This chapter is designed to help you move in that direction by using the C# and .NET APIs and services for managing processes and threads. In addition, you learn about synchronization methods to help you build multithreaded programs that can be more reliable. Before we move into multithreading, the first section of this chapter introduces the process APIs supported through the .NET Framework Class Library.

.NET Process Support

The System.Diagnostics namespace has a class named Process and, as its name suggests, it helps manage processes. You can use it to launch a new process or work with existing processes.

Launching a New Process

This section covers a subject that most people are interested in: how to make code launch and execute another program. We'll use a couple examples to demonstrate how to start processes and further see how to manipulate properties of the process to make it behave the way you want.

Process Quick Start

At its essence, creating a new process involves calling the static Start method of the Process class. The following statement runs the Windows calc.exe utility:

```
Process.Start("calc");
```

As you can see, the extension is optional. An example like this might be useful for a menu that invokes other programs while you're working with an application. Typically, you need to specify arguments, which the next example demonstrates:

```
Process.Start("devenv", "..\\..\\Program.cs");
```

Because VS2008 Express is free, why edit code with Notepad? The preceding statement launches VS2008, devenv.exe, and passes a parameter that is the file to be opened. You can include a list of options in the parameter list, as if typing the options on the command line.

Opening Processes with Credentials

Sometimes you need to load an application with credentials, which the next code example demonstrates. The password to pass to the process is a .NET SecureString, which encrypts a string in memory and ensures that it is cleaned up when the process exits. Here's an example:

```
var secPwd = new SecureString();


"password"
    .ToCharArray()
    .Cast<char>()
    .ToList()
    .ForEach
    (
        ch => secPwd.AppendChar(ch)
    );
```

Populating a SecureString isn't as simple as assignment, so you need to set each individual character. The preceding code uses LINQ to Objects (Chapter 19, "Accessing Data with LINQ") and a lambda expression (Chapter 18, "Using Lambdas and Expression Trees") to append characters from the literal password string (Chapter 5, "Manipulating Strings"), to the SecureString, secPwd.

As in the SecureString example, I've used credentials that don't mean anything. You don't think I'm going to give you the password to my system, do you? You'll want to replace password, user ID, and machine or domain names with your own credentials. Here's how to pass credentials to Process.Start to launch an application with a specified identity:

```
Process.Start(
    @"C:\Program Files\Microsoft Visual Studio 9.0\Common7\IDE\devenv.exe",
    "UserName",
    secPwd,
    "MachineOrDomain");
```

The first thing you'll notice is that I used a fully qualified path to devenv in this example, which is required. If you don't fully qualify the path like this, you'll receive a Win32Exception with the message "The parameter is incorrect". I know this is incredibly meaningful—not! So, you might want to remember this for when it happens to you.

If the userName, password, or domain parameters are incorrect, you'll receive a Win32Exception message that says "Logon failure: unknown user name or bad password", which is a little better.

Another tip is that the domain parameter can be either a domain or machine name. This is handy because now you can test this code on an account for your computer and specify the machine name.

If you want more control over a process, such as whether it should display the console window or capturing output, you can instantiate the Process class and set its properties. The following sections show you how to do this and share a few tips to help you work around common problems.

39

Setting `ProcessStartInfo`

One process property that you must set when working with a `Process` instance is `StartInfo`, which holds all the information for the file to run, arguments, and more for customizing the process. Here's an example that builds upon previous examples and shows a few `StartInfo` properties that you might want to use:

```
var startInfo = new ProcessStartInfo();
startInfo.FileName = "devenv";
startInfo.Arguments = "Program.cs";
startInfo.WorkingDirectory = @"..\..";
startInfo.WindowStyle = ProcessWindowStyle.Maximized;
startInfo.ErrorDialog = true;

var proc = new Process();
proc.StartInfo = startInfo;
proc.Start();
```

The `FileName` and `Arguments` properties of `StartInfo` are the same as their corresponding parameter names in the static `Start` method that you saw earlier. The `WorkingDirectory` property sets the place where the program will execute. This allowed me to just specify the filename, Program.cs, as the argument, rather than fully qualifying the name. You can set the window that opens to any value of the `ProcessWindowStyle` enum, which can be `Hidden`, `Maximized`, `Minimized`, or `Normal`. The `ErrorDialog` option, when set to `true` as in the preceding example, will display a message box with an error if the process doesn't start properly. You can test it by changing `devenv` to a misspelled version (for example, `deven` without the v).

Managing Process Streams

The `Process` class also exposes input, output, and error streams, allowing you to send input and capture output to/from the process. Here's an example that demonstrates how to capture the output stream of a call to `osql`, the SQL Server command-line tool, to execute a query:

```
var startInfo = new ProcessStartInfo();
startInfo.FileName = "osql";
startInfo.Arguments = "-E -dNorthwind -Q\"select top 10 * from
    customers\"";
startInfo.RedirectStandardOutput = true;
startInfo.UseShellExecute = false;
var proc = new Process();
proc.StartInfo = startInfo;

proc.Start();

using (StreamReader rdr = proc.StandardOutput)
{
```

```
        Console.WriteLine("--- begin output ---");
        Console.WriteLine(rdr.ReadToEnd());
        Console.WriteLine("--- end output ---");
    }
```

To make this work, you have to set properties on both the `ProcessStartInfo` and call methods on the `Process` class. The sequence of operations makes a difference when reading the output stream. If you leave any of the steps out, this won't work.

The two properties you must set on the `ProcessStartInfo` are `RedirectStandardOutput` and `UseShellExecute`. Set `RedirectStandardOutput` to `true` to use it. Remember, you can't just attach to the process output stream; you must perform this step.

The `UseShellExecute` defaults to `true`, meaning that the process will use the OS shell to run. This enables features like specifying a filename such as MyFile.doc and the OS opening the document in Microsoft Word because the *.doc extension has an OS shell association with Microsoft Word. Setting `UseShellExecute` to `false` enables access to streams, but it also turns off the features given to you by the OS shell, and you can't use `ErrorDialog`, as shown in the previous section.

Notice that the output stream assignment, `proc.StandardOutput` to the `StreamReader`, `rdr`, occurs after `proc.Start`, which is the required sequence. I used `ReadToEnd` on `rdr` to read output from the stream, but `rdr` is just a `StreamReader`, and you can use any of the `ReadX` methods and their overloads as you need.

A couple more observations to make is that this version of `Arguments` on `startInfo` contains multiple parameters—something you haven't seen yet because previous examples used only a single argument. Also, the `osql` command used assumes you have the Northwind database installed on the default instance. You can type `osql /?` on the command-line to get a list of available options or check SQL Server Books Online (a free download from Microsoft or ships with a version of SQL Server) to get a set of arguments that will work on your system.

This example works for `StandardOutput`, but you would use similar techniques for `StandardInput` and `StandardError`. One notable exception, which you already know or will quickly realize, is that you'll need to use a `StreamWriter` (rather than `StreamReader`) with `StandardInput`.

Now that you know how to start applications in their own process, you might also be interested in knowing how to work with existing processes, which is covered in the next section.

Working with Existing Processes

The `Process` class helps you work with existing processes, in addition to creating new ones. The following sections show you how to get a list of processes, extract information about those processes, find a specific process, and manipulate a process.

Getting a List of Processes

The `Process` class has a method named `GetProcesses` that helps you get a list of all processes running on your system. Here's an example:

```
Process.GetProcesses()
    .ToList()
    .ForEach(
        proc => Console.WriteLine(proc.ProcessName));
```

The preceding example prints out a list of all the processes on your machine.

Reading Process Details

The Process class also has a suite of properties that you can use to get information on the process. Here's an example:

```
Process.GetProcesses()
    .ToList()
    .ForEach(
        proc =>
            {
                Console.WriteLine(
                    "Name: {0}, ID: {1}, Memory: {2}",
                    proc.ProcessName,
                    proc.Id,
                    proc.WorkingSet64);
            });
```

This example displays the name of the process, process ID, and the amount of memory being used by the process. There are several more properties to use that can be found in the .NET Framework Class Library documentation for the Process class.

Finding a Specific Process

A lot of times, you'll be looking for a specific process to get information on. The following example shows you how:

```
var fireFoxProc =
    from proc in Process.GetProcesses()
    where proc.ProcessName == "firefox"
    select proc;
```

Notice that I filtered the query on the process name, which is the filename without the extension. Important: If you try to append the filename extension, you'll never find the process.

Killing Processes

It's a known fact that sometimes processes misbehave. They hang or get stuck, and you need to stop them somehow. However rude it might be, your only choice might be to kill the process. Firefox has been hanging on me lately and has been on my mind as a process that needs to be killed on occasion, so it gets honorable mention for this particular example:

```
(from proc in Process.GetProcesses()
 where proc.ProcessName == "firefox"
 select proc)
 .ToList()
 .ForEach(ff => ff.Kill());
```

Yes, I know modern browsers have tabbed interfaces, and I don't need to have multiple copies open, but it's an old habit. Regardless, you might find a situation where there are multiple copies of an application open and you need to close them all. The preceding example calls Kill on each process it finds that matches the criteria in the where clause.

You should now have a good set of tools to work with processes. The next section explains how to work with threads that belong to processes.

Multithreading Overview

A thread is a unit of execution, and multithreading is the capability to run multiple units of execution simultaneously. Multithreading offers opportunities to improve the performance of your application and make a program more responsive to the user.

For example, if you have work that takes time to perform and that work can be logically divided into pieces, you can divide the work into multiple threads. Sometimes launching a bit of work onto a thread can make a user interface more responsive, too.

Just because multithreading is available doesn't mean it should be used in every situation. There is overhead associated with threading as well as complexity, so you'll want to think about whether the benefits outweigh the overhead or complexity. As in most decisions you have to make, you'll must evaluate these trade-offs.

Creating New Threads

The act of creating and invoking a new thread in C# is relatively straightforward. The process involves creating a Thread object, instantiating a ThreadStart delegate with a delegate method handler, and passing the ThreadStart delegate to the new Thread object. All that's remaining is to start the thread and off it runs. The following example shows how to create and execute a new thread:

```
private static void StartThread()
{
    var th = new Thread(new ThreadStart(SayHello));

    th.Start();
}

public static void SayHello()
{
    Console.WriteLine("Hello from a single thread.");
}
```

39

And here's the output:

```
Hello from a single thread.
```

The preceding example has a SayHello method, which is executed as part of the thread in this program. All the thread creation and initialization occurs in the following line:

```
var th = new Thread(new ThreadStart(SayHello));
```

The Thread object, th, is an instance of a Thread object with a new ThreadStart delegate as its parameter. The delegate method handler for the ThreadStart delegate is the SayHello method of the same class. SayHello could have been an instance method also, which means that you would have needed to instantiate the containing class and use the class instance reference to specify SayHello. I made it static to reduce code and simplify the example.

Now the thread exists, but it's idle, waiting for directions. It's said to be in the unstarted state. To get this thread running, the program invokes the Start method of the Thread object, th.

Running Code in a Thread with Less Code

The previous example took several steps to run, instantiating the thread, instantiating the ThreadStartDelegate, and executing start. Here's an example that takes a lambda to show a more terse syntax.

Passing Parameters to Threads

The previous example just executed a method on a thread, but sometimes you need to pass information to the thread. Here's an example that uses a ParameterizedThreadStart delegate, rather than a ThreadStart delegate, to pass information to a method running on the thread:

```
private static void StartParameterizedThread()
{
    var th = new Thread(new ParameterizedThreadStart(SayHello));

    th.Start("Joe");
}

public static void SayHello(object name)
{
    Console.WriteLine(
        "Hello {0} from a parameterized thread.",
        name as string);
}
```

Notice that the argument to the Thread constructor in StartParameterizedThread is now a ParameterizedThreadStart delegate. Also, the call to Start contains the parameter that is passed. Because the method signature defined by `ParameterizedThreadStart` takes a parameter of type object, the `SayHello` overload has an object parameter, `name`. I converted it to a string in the `WriteLine` method for illustrative purposes, even though I didn't need to because `WriteLine` will call `ToString` on the object anyway.

Using the `ThreadPool`

When you execute code with the `Thread` class, each individual invocation of `Start` instantiates a new thread. If you have only a single thread to launch, this is usually not a problem. If you have many threads executing in the same application or are starting many threads to work on pieces of the same job, however, you must beware of the overhead associated with too many threads.

The isn't an exact definition of what "too many threads" means because computers vary in configuration, power, processors, and operating systems, to name a few variables. Therefore, you will have to do research on your own system to see where the tradeoffs are between managing how many threads can run for the best performance.

There is also complexity associated with throttling threads yourself to ensure that too many aren't running at the same time. To relieve you from needing to manage this complexity yourself, you could use the `ThreadPool` instead. The `ThreadPool` is an object that ensures that only a specified number of threads in a process can run at the same time and that a minimum number of threads will be instantiated and ready for use. You can read the values for the maximum and minimum number of threads by calling `GetMaxThreads` and `GetMinThreads`, respectively, on the `ThreadPool` type. Similarly, you can adjust these numbers by calling the `SetMaxThreads` and `SetMinThreads` on the `ThreadPool` type. This way, you can tweak the `ThreadPool` to maximize performance on your system. Here's an example that runs a thread on the `ThreadPool`:

```
ThreadPool.QueueUserWorkItem(new WaitCallback(SayHello), "Joe");
```

```
ThreadPool.QueueUserWorkItem(
    stateInfo =>
        {
            int minWorker;
            int maxWorker;
            int minIOCompletionPort;
            int maxIOCompletionPort;

            ThreadPool.GetMinThreads(out minWorker, out minIOComple-
tionPort);
            ThreadPool.GetMaxThreads(out maxWorker, out maxIOComple-
tionPort);

            Console.WriteLine(
                "Worker Threads - Min: {0} Max: {1}\n" +
                "IO Completion Threads - Min: {2} Max: {3}",
```

39

```
                    minWorker,
                    maxWorker,
                    minIOCompletionPort,
                    maxIOCompletionPort);
            });
```

The first example invokes the `SayHello` method on a thread in the `ThreadPool`, just by calling `ThreadPool.QueueUserWorkItem`. The second parameter is an object you can use to pass any state. Because the signature of the `SayHello` method that takes type object and prints it out as a name conforms to both the `ParameterizedThreadStart` and `WaitCallback` delegates, it will work for this example, too, regardless of what the method does.

The second call to `QueueUserWorkItem` uses a lambda expression rather than the `WaitCallback` delegate. The lambda has a single parameter, which is interpreted as type object so that it will conform to the signature of `WaitCallback`. The contents of the lambda show how to use the `GetMinThreads` and `GetMaxThreads` methods. They show that the minimum is 1 worker thread and 1 IO completion thread and the maximum is 25 worker threads and 1,000 IO completion threads, which are the defaults.

Thread Synchronization

Using the techniques from previous sections, it's easy to create multiple threads of execution. As long as each thread minds its own business, the program runs fine. In many situations, however, this is not practical. It's often necessary for multiple threads to share a resource. Without control, the behavior of multithreaded programs sharing a resource yields nondeterministic results.

To provide that control, C# allocates methods to coordinate activities between threads. This coordination is properly termed *synchronization*. Correct implementation of synchronization enables programs to take advantage of performance benefits of multithreading and helps maintain the integrity of object state and data. The following sections discuss different ways to synchronize threads.

The C# lock Statement

C# has a `lock` statement that allows only one thread at a time to execute a block of code. The following example ensures that only a single thread can access a list of emergency room patients:

```
private static object m_erPatientsLock = new object();
private static List<string> m_erPatients = new List<string>();

private static void LockThreads()
{
    lock (m_erPatientsLock)
    {
        m_erPatients.Add("John Smith");
```

```
        }
    }
```

The preceding code has a List<string> that holds patient names of those who have signed into the emergency room. This is an important list, and if someone's name is added twice or not added at all, bad things will happen. Because this is a multithreaded application, the preceding code uses the lock statement to ensure that only one thread at a time can access this list.

Notice that the parameter to the lock statement, m_erPatientsLock, is a static field of type object. Any thread that reaches the lock will check to ensure that the Common Language Runtime (CLR) doesn't have m_erPatientsLock marked as locked. If m_erPatientsLock is marked as locked, the thread will wait. Otherwise, the thread will enter the lock block, and the CLR will mark m_erPatientsLock as locked to keep the next thread out. When a thread that is executing the code in the lock statement is done, it leaves the lock block, and the CLR marks m_erPatientsLock as not being locked so that the next waiting thread can enter the lock block.

Inside lock: the Monitor Class

The C# lock statement makes it easy to synchronize access to a block of code, but it is a C# language construct that is translated into code that implements the .NET Monitor class. As you may recall, C# does something similar with the using statement to simplify code that would have otherwise implemented a try/finally block. Here's a block of code using the Monitor class, which is equivalent to the lock statement in the previous example:

```
try
{
    Monitor.Enter(m_erPatientsLock);

    m_erPatients.Add("John Smith");
}
finally
{
    Monitor.Exit(m_erPatientsLock);
}
```

Here we use a try/finally block where Monitor.Enter executes in the try block. Monitor.Exit needs to execute in the finally block to ensure that the lock on m_erPatientLock is released. Otherwise, only one thread will execute the code and, if there is an exception in the try block, it is possible that no other thread will be able to execute that code, causing a deadlock.

At this point, you might be wondering why you would want to use Monitor if the lock statement is easier syntax. The Monitor class has additional features, such as timeouts. So, if you need these features, you can use a Monitor instead. Here's an example of setting a timeout:

39

```
        try
        {
            if (!Monitor.TryEnter(m_erPatientsLock, 300))
            {
                return;
            }

            m_erPatients.Add("John Smith");
        }
        finally
        {
            Monitor.Exit(m_erPatientsLock);
        }
```

The TryEnter method has a second parameter that lets you set a number of milliseconds to wait before timing out. This can help avoid deadlock. The TryEnter returns true if it can acquire the lock within the specified amount of time (and false otherwise).

Balancing Access Between Reader and Writer Threads

Sometimes writing to a resource can be rare, but reading from the resource can be frequent. If you have a situation like this, it could be better to use a ReaderWriterLockSlim class to make your program more responsive, rather than causing a bottleneck with a lock statement.

If you use ReaderWriterLockSlim, all reader threads that want to access shared state can do so at the same time. However, only one writer thread can access shared state at a time. This is safe because it ensures that readers access consistent information only, instead of accidentally reading the wrong information in the middle of a write:

```
        private static ReaderWriterLockSlim m_erPatientsRWLock = new ReaderWriter-
LockSlim();


        private static void ReaderThread()
        {
            try
            {
                m_erPatientsRWLock.EnterReadLock();

                int count = m_erPatients.Count;
            }
            finally
            {
                m_erPatientsRWLock.ExitReadLock();
            }
        }
```

```
    private static void WriterThread()
    {
        try
        {
            m_erPatientsRWLock.EnterWriteLock();

            m_erPatients.Add("John Smith");
        }
        finally
        {
            m_erPatientsRWLock.ExitWriteLock();
        }
    }
```

Instead of using an object to lock on, the `ReaderWriterLockSlim`, `m_erPatientsRWLock`, is a private field, which will define the single object to synchronize on. The `ReaderThread` method will be called by threads wanting to read from shared state, and the `WriterThread` method will be called from threads wanting to modify shared state.

While there is no writer thread waiting at `m_erPatientsRWLock.EnterWriteLock` inside of the `WriterThread` method, all the reader threads that enter `ReaderThread` will be granted access at `m_erPatientsRWLock.EnterReadLock`. As soon as a writer thread begins waiting, no more reader threads will be allowed in, and the rest of the reader threads will continue to execute until finished. When all the reader threads have executed `m_erPatientsRWLock.ExitReadLock`, one writer thread will be able to execute past `m_erPatientsRWLock.EnterWriteLock`. Then, after the writer thread executes `m_erPatientsRWLock.ExitWriteLock`, all new reader threads will be able to run again.

One more scenario is that if the writer thread completes and there are other writer threads waiting, the writer threads execute before any reader threads. If this could potentially cause thread-starvation scenarios for your reader threads, consider one of the other synchronization mechanisms discussed earlier. `ReaderWriterLockSlim` is for scenarios where you expect there to be more readers than writers.

Summary

You now have several bits of knowledge that can help you work with processes and threads in C#. You can start new processes, pass parameters, set pertinent properties, and capture process IO. In this chapter, you also learned how to work with existing processes, reading info about them, finding specific processes, and even killing processes that you don't want to run.

This chapter also presented multithreaded applications in C#. You learned how to create and start a thread, including declaring a thread argument and passing it a delegate with the method to be invoked, and how to execute the thread.

To keep threads from wreaking havoc with shared data, it's often necessary to use synchronization objects. Proper thread synchronization helps manage access to program data. The sample program in this chapter used `lock` statements, `Monitor` classes, and `ReaderWriterLockSlim` classes to synchronize access to shared state.

The next chapter takes a slightly different direction in your journey of applying C# to build .NET applications. You'll learn how to use globalization and localization features to make programs more world–friendly.

CHAPTER 40

Localizing and Globalization

If everyone were the same, this world would be a pretty boring place. With the plethora of cultures, ideas, and means of communication, there needs to be a way to make applications and information accessible on the desktop and over the Internet. This is the role of localization.

Localization is the process of making computer programs accessible to a diverse cultures. A localized program identifies selected cultures and presents information, such as language, fonts, and graphics, in a specific manner for each culture. This way, a person in Italy, Thailand, or anywhere else can have the same user experience as a person in the United States.

Resource Files

Setting up and using resource files is the primary means of localizing programs. *Resource files are specialized binary files* that can be bound to a standalone DLL or added into a program assembly. They contain strings, graphics, and other binary resources that assist in localizing a program.

Creating a Resource File

The resource generator utility ResGen is a string resource creation utility that comes with the Microsoft .NET Framework SDK. Given a properly formatted .txt (text) file, ResGen converts it into a .resources (binary resources) file that can subsequently be added to an assembly.

> **NOTE**
>
> In simplistic terms, an assembly is a unit of deployment. Assemblies are covered in more detail in later chapters, but for now, it will be helpful to think of them as executable files or dynamic link libraries (DLLs).

Without a special resource creation tool, string resources begin life as a specially formatted .txt file. They have headers, comments, and name/value pairs, as shown in Table 40.1.

TABLE 40.1   .txt Resource File Elements

Element	Description
[header]	Optional file header
;	Optional comment marker
Name = value	Resource string declaration

Header elements must match the filename without the extension. For example, if the resource file's name is myResources.txt, the header contents must be [myResources]. Comments are useful for delimiting groups of resource strings or adding more information to the use of a string. All comments are removed from compiled resources.

Name/value pairs are the reason for the resources file. The name portion is used as a key in programs to identify a particular string resource. A value is the string itself. An example .txt resource file is shown in Listing 40.1.

LISTING 40.1   .txt Resource File: strings.txt

```
[strings]


;———————————————————;
;                   ;
;   This file holds default resource  ;
;   strings for the sample StringRes  ;
;   program in C# Unleashed.          ;
;                   ;
;———————————————————;


;
; A standard greeting
;
greeting = Hello
```

Because the filename of the code in Listing 40.1 is strings.txt, the header text is [strings], according to the rules for the header element. There are comments describing the purpose of the resource file and a shorter comment describing the greeting string resource. The following example shows how to prepare the resources file for use:

```
resgen strings.txt
al /out:strings.resources.dll /embed:strings.resources
```

The first line uses the ResGen utility (discussed previously) to convert the strings.txt file into a strings.resources file. The second line uses the assembly generation tool, included in the .NET Framework SDK, to create a DLL. The first parameter is the /out option, which works the same as the /out option when invoking the C# compiler. The /embed option identifies the binary resource file. The example creates the file strings.resources.dll, which can be used by any application to obtain predefined resources.

There are a couple things to do when using resources. First, declare an instance of the ResourceManager class, which assists in using resources; then use ResourceManager class members to access resources. This is demonstrated in Listing 40.2.

LISTING 40.2   Using Resources: StringRes.cs

```
using System;
using System.Resources;

namespace StringRes
{
    /// <summary>
    /// Example of Using String Resources.
    /// </summary>
    class StringRes
    {
        static void Main(string[] args)
        {
            ResourceManager rm =
                ResourceManager.CreateFileBasedResourceManager(
                "strings", ".", null);

            Console.WriteLine("Greeting: {0}",
                            rm.GetString("greeting"));
        }
    }
}
```

And the output is

```
Greeting: Hello
```

Listing 40.2 includes the System.Resources namespace, which contains the ResourceManager class. Within the Main method, an instance of the ResourceManager class is instantiated with the `CreateFileBasedResourceManager` method, which takes three parameters.

The first parameter is the name of the resource file. The .resources extension is assumed. The second parameter specifies the directory where the .resources file is located. The example specifies the current directory. The third parameter is `null`, specifying that the type of `ResourceSet` is the default `ResourceSet`. A `ResourceSet` is a class that stores properties as a hash table and can be derived from, enabling the third parameter of the `CreateFileBasedResourceManager()` method to indicate the type of a customized `ResourceSet`.

Within the `Console.WriteLine` method, a single parameter obtains the greeting resource to display on the screen. This resource is obtained by using the `GetString` method of the `ResourceManager` object. The parameter is a string with the name of the key to the resource being used. As evident in the results, the parameter is the value part of the greeting resource from Listing 40.1. The code in Listing 40.2 is compiled with the following command line:

```
csc StringRes.cs
```

Writing a Resource File

Resource files may be created programmatically. This is useful for automated .resources file generation utilities or resource tools in IDEs. The steps involved in creating a .resources file are to open a `ResourceWriter` stream, add whatever resources are needed, and then close the stream. Listing 40.3 demonstrates this procedure.

LISTING 40.3 Writing a Resource File: ResWrite.cs

```
using System;
using System.Resources;

namespace ResWrite
{
    /// <summary>
    /// Resource Writing Example
    /// </summary>
    class ResWrite
    {
        static void Main(string[] args)
        {
            IResourceWriter resWriter =
                new ResourceWriter("strings.resources");

            resWriter.AddResource("thanks",  "Thank you.");
            resWriter.AddResource("welcome", "You're welcome.");
```

LISTING 40.3   Continued

```
            resWriter.Close();
        }
    }
}
```

The default `ResourceWriter` class in the `System.Resources` namespace implements `IResourceWriter`. This is why it's possible to create an `IResourceWriter` object within the `Main` method of Listing 40.3. The `ResourceWriter` constructor accepts a string parameter specifying the resource file to create. If a file by that name exists, it will be overwritten.

String resources are added with the `AddResource` method of the `resWriter` object. Its parameters conform to the name/value pair format of resources with the first parameter as the name and the second parameter as the `value`. The `resWriter` stream is then closed with the `Close()` method. This program is compiled with the following command line:

```
csc ResWrite.cs
```

Reading a Resource File

The `ResourceReader` class is also useful in creating resource manipulation utilities and IDE tools to manage resources. A utility uses the `ResourceReader` functionality to read in an existing resource file, the program performs any necessary manipulations, and then the `ResourceWriter` helps write the new resources back to the persistent .resources file. Listing 40.4 shows how to read resources.

LISTING 40.4   Reading a Resource File: ResRead.cs

```
using System;
using System.Resources;
using System.Collections;

namespace ResRead
{
    /// <summary>
    /// Resource Reading Example
    /// </summary>
    class ResRead
    {
        static void Main(string[] args)
        {
            IResourceReader resReader =
                new ResourceReader("strings.resources");

            IDictionaryEnumerator resEnumerator =
```

40

LISTING 40.4   Continued

```
            resReader.GetEnumerator();

        while (resEnumerator.MoveNext())
        {
            Console.WriteLine("{0} = {1}",
                resEnumerator.Key, resEnumerator.Value);
        }
        resReader.Close();
    }
  }
}
```

And here's the output:

```
greeting = Hello.
thanks = Thank you.
welcome = You're welcome.
```

The IResourceReader object is created, similar to the IresourceWriter, by instantiating a new ResourceWriter with the .resources file specified as its constructor parameter. The IResourceReader may be used as a collection of resources by obtaining an enumerator and iterating through the list of resources. This program prints each resource to screen and then closes the ResourceReader stream with the Close method. Listing 40.4 is compiled with the following command line:

```
csc resread.cs
```

Converting a Resource File

Another use of ResGen is to convert between .txt, .resources, and .resx files. Resx files are XML format files used for binary resources such as graphics, fonts, icons, and cursors. For example, the following command line converts the .resources file to a .resx file:

```
resgen strings.resources strings.resx
```

This produces an XML format file, as shown in Listing 40.5. The same exact file would have been generated if you had performed the following command line:

```
resgen strings.txt strings.resx
```

Alternatively, it's possible to generate .txt files from either .resx or .resources files. As explained earlier, it's possible to convert .txt and .resx files to .resources files. This is the most common scenario as .resources files are added to assemblies. Because of its binary format, the .resources file is barely readable, which can be verified by opening up a .resources file in Notepad.

> **WARNING**
>
> If a .resx or .resources file already contains graphics, it can't be converted to a .txt file, which only holds strings.

LISTING 40.5   Generated .resx File: strings.resx

```
<root>
  <xsd:schema id="root" targetNamespace="" xmlns=""
xmlns:xsd="http://www.w3.org/2001/XMLSchema" xmlns:msdata="urn:schemas-microsoft-
com:xml-msdata">
    <xsd:element name="root" msdata:IsDataSet="true">
      <xsd:complexType>
        <xsd:choice maxOccurs="unbounded">   .
          <xsd:element name="data">
            <xsd:complexType>
              <xsd:sequence>
                <xsd:element name="value" type="xsd:string"
                ➥minOccurs="0" msdata:Ordinal="1" />
                <xsd:element name="comment"
                ➥type="xsd:string" minOccurs="0" msdata:Ordinal="2" />
              </xsd:sequence>
              <xsd:attribute name="name" type="xsd:string" />
              <xsd:attribute name="type" type="xsd:string" />
              <xsd:attribute name="mimetype"
              ➥type="xsd:string" /> </xsd:complexType>
          </xsd:element>
          <xsd:element name="resheader">
            <xsd:complexType>
              <xsd:sequence>
                <xsd:element name="value" type="xsd:string"
                ➥minOccurs="0" msdata:Ordinal="1" />
              </xsd:sequence>
              <xsd:attribute name="name" type="xsd:string"
              ➥use="required" />
            </xsd:complexType>
          </xsd:element>
        </xsd:choice>
      </xsd:complexType>
    </xsd:element>
  </xsd:schema>
  <data name="thanks">
    <value>Thank you.</value>
  </data>
  <data name="welcome">
```

LISTING 40.5   Continued

```
    <value>You're welcome.</value>
  </data>
  <resheader name="ResMimeType">
    <value>text/microsoft-resx</value>
  </resheader>
  <resheader name="Version">
    <value>1.0.0.0</value>
  </resheader>
  <resheader name="Reader">
    <value>System.Resources.ResXResourceReader</value>
  </resheader>
  <resheader name="Writer">
    <value>System.Resources.ResXResourceWriter</value>
  </resheader>
</root>
```

The header at the top of Listing 40.5 indicates that this is an XML file. There's a <root> element enclosing several subelements. The first of these is the XML schema definition, which defines the format, types, and constraints on the resources. The second portion of this file is the set of <data> elements, holding the name/value pairs used in programs. The name part is an attribute of the <data> element, and the value part is a <value> subelement of the <data> element. The final elements of the file are MIME type information, versioning information, and reader and writer class definitions.

Creating Graphical Resources

The .NET Framework SDK includes a couple of sample programs that help manage graphical resources. One is the ResXGen program, which adds a graphic to a .resx file. The other is the ResEditor program, which manages all types of resources for .resources files. An added bonus is that these two utilities come with source code, enabling you to examine graphical resource manipulation code in detail.

The source code is located in subdirectories at C:\Program Files\Microsoft.Net\FrameworkSDK\Samples\tutorials\resourcesandlocalization on my computer. If you've customized your directory structure, search for the relative location of the Samples directory on your own system. Each executable can be compiled by running the build.bat batch file in its respective directory.

TIP

For convenience, I copied the ResEditor and ResXGen executables into my C:\Program Files\Microsoft.Net\FrameworkSDK\bin directory, which is in my PATH environment variable and makes each utility accessible from my command line without having to specify the long path.

The ResXGen Utility

The ResXGen utility generates a .resx XML formatted file for graphical resources. The actual formatting within the .resx file is done via the base class library's System.Serialization.Formatters.Binary.BinaryFormatter and then encoded to a base-64 format. To demonstrate the ResXGen utility, copy un.jpg, a JPEG picture of the United Nations flag, from the C:\Program Files\Microsoft.Net\FrameworkSDK\Samples\ tutorials\resourcesandlocalization\graphics\cs\images directory into a local working directory and run the following command line:

```
ResXGen /i:un.jpg /o:graphics.resx /n:flag
```

The /i option is the input graphic file, the /o option is the output .resx file, and the /n option is the resource key name used in programs to identify this resource. The help option, /?, explains all the other options available. Another option, /s, generates the XML schema definition of a .resx file. The result is relatively the same as the <xsd:schema> element from Listing 40.5 and a little more explanatory information. Here's how to generate the XML schema definition:

```
ResXGen /s
```

Between the ResGen and ResXGen utilities, the job of creating a .resources file gets done, but there are limitations. For instance, each of these utilities generates a new .resources file each time it runs. There are no options to add a .txt or .resx file to a .resources file without wiping out the existing .resource file's current content. Therefore, by using only these two utilities, ResGen and ResXGen, the only way to generate an assembly is to create separate .resources files and add them separately to an assembly, as the following example demonstrates:

```
ResXGen /i:un.jpg /o:unflag.resx /n:flag
ResGen unflag.resx unflag.resources
ResGen strings.txt strings.resources
al /out:graphics.resources.dll /embed:strings.resources
al /out:graphics.resources.dll /embed:unflag.resources
```

In this example, ResXGen creates the unflag.resx file from the un.jpg graphics file. Then the unflag.resx is converted to unflag.resources, and strings.txt is converted to strings.resources with ResGen. Finally, both .resources files just generated are added to the graphics.resources.dll library with the al utility. You could reduce the pain of all this work by modifying the source code of the ResXGen utility or use a batch or make a file for automation. Another alternative is the ResEditor utility.

The ResEditor Utility

The ResEditor utility is a graphical program that enables manipulation of .resources files. The ResEditor screen is shown in Figure 40.1.

40

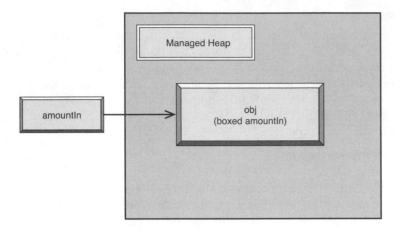

FIGURE 40.1   The **ResEditor** utility.

For Figure 40.1, I clicked the Open button to select a file and chose the unflag.resources file. I create a new string resource by making a new entry in the Add section, typing the name **greeting** in the first text box, selecting the System.String item in the drop-down list, and clicking the Add button. This created the greeting entry in the first column of the main list box under the Strings heading. Then I typed the value **Hello** into the second column of the same row where the greeting name is entered. Figure 40.1 shows another string entry, thanks, being entered into the Add section. Finally, any changes can be made by clicking the Save button and entering a new .resources filename.

Using Graphical Resources

Using graphical resources is similar to using string resources. Just create a ResourceManager and then get the resource. In Listing 40.6, the GetObject method of the ResourceManager obtains the binary Graphics object. With the Graphics object in hand, it can be manipulated according to how that type of resource would normally be manipulated in a program. Listing 40.6 shows how a JPEG image file resource is obtained and used in an application.

LISTING 40.6   Using Graphical Resources: GraphRes.cs

```
using System;
using System.Drawing;
using System.Collections;
using System.ComponentModel;
using System.Windows.Forms;
using System.Data;
using System.Resources;
```

LISTING 40.6   Continued

```
namespace GraphicRes
{
    /// <summary>
    /// Graphics Resources Demonstration.
    /// </summary>
    public class GraphicResFrm : System.Windows.Forms.Form
    {
        private PictureBox flagPic;
        private Label       HelloLbl;
        private System.ComponentModel.Container components = null;

        public GraphicResFrm()
        {
            InitializeComponent();
        }

        private void InitializeComponent()
        {
            this.HelloLbl = new Label();
            this.flagPic  = new PictureBox();
            this.SuspendLayout();
            //
            // HelloLbl
            //
            this.HelloLbl.Font       = new Font(
                "Microsoft Sans Serif",
                14.25F,
                FontStyle.Regular,
                GraphicsUnit.Point,
                ((byte)(0)));
            this.HelloLbl.Location  = new Point(24, 136);
            this.HelloLbl.Name      = "HelloLbl";
            this.HelloLbl.Size      = new Size(240, 32);
            this.HelloLbl.TabIndex  = 1;
            this.HelloLbl.Text      = "label1";
            this.HelloLbl.TextAlign =
                ContentAlignment.MiddleCenter;
            //
            // flagPic
            //
            this.flagPic.Location = new Point(64, 24);
            this.flagPic.Name     = "flagPic";
            this.flagPic.Size     = new Size(160, 96);
            this.flagPic.SizeMode =
                PictureBoxSizeMode.StretchImage;
```

LISTING 40.6   Continued

```
        this.flagPic.TabIndex = 0;
        this.flagPic.TabStop  = false;
        //
        // GraphicResFrm
        //
        this.AutoScaleBaseSize = new Size(5, 13);
        this.ClientSize        = new Size(292, 197);
        this.Controls.AddRange(new Control[] {
        this.HelloLbl,
        this.flagPic});
        this.Name = "GraphicResFrm";
        this.Text = "Graphical Resources Demo";
        this.Load += new
            System.EventHandler(this.GraphicResFrm_Load);
        this.ResumeLayout(false);
    }

    /// <summary>
    /// The main entry point for the application.
    /// </summary>
    static void Main()
    {
        Application.Run(new GraphicResFrm());
    }

    private void GraphicResFrm_Load(object sender,
                                   System.EventArgs e)
    {
        ResourceManager graphRes  = ResourceManager.
        CreateFileBasedResourceManager(
            "unflag", ".", null);
        ResourceManager stringRes = ResourceManager.
        CreateFileBasedResourceManager(
            "strings", ".", null);

        flagPic.Image = (System.Drawing.Image)
            graphRes.GetObject("flag");

        HelloLbl.Text = stringRes.GetString("greeting");
    }
  }
}
```

The majority of Listing 40.6 is just Windows Forms code supporting the main form and its PictureBox and Label controls. The pertinent part of the listing is the

GraphicResFrm_Load method that is called when the form is loaded to screen. It creates two ResourceManager objects: graphRes and stringRes.

The graphRes object is created with the unflag.resources file. This is where the un.jpg resource is stored. The un.jpg resource was the value with a name of flag. To obtain this resource, the program uses the GetObject() method of the graphRes object and stores it in the Image property of the flagPic object, which is a Windows Forms PictureBox control. This action displays the United Nations flag on the form.

The string resource is obtained the same way as shown earlier in this chapter. The value obtained from the GetString method of the stringRes object is stored in the Text property of the HelloLbl object, which is a Windows Forms Label control. The form produced from Listing 40.6 is shown in Figure 40.2. Listing 40.6 was compiled with the following command line:

```
csc /t:winexe GraphRes.cs
```

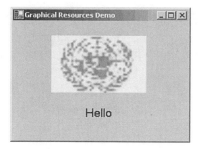

FIGURE 40.2   Displaying a graphical resource.

Multiple Locales

The purpose of resource files is to support multiple locales. The official way of specifying locales is via cultures, as specified in RFC 1766, ISO 639, and ISO 6133. Cultures are denoted with four-character designations. The first two characters specify the language in lowercase, and the second two specify the country or region in uppercase. Table 40.2 contains some examples of culture designations. The total list is much too large to be included here. You can check out the RFC and ISOs listed previously for further information.

TABLE 40.2   Sample List of Cultures

Tag	Description
de_CH	Swiss German
En	English

TABLE 40.2   Sample List of Cultures

Tag	Description
en_US	U.S. English
en_GB	British English
It	Italian
Ja	Japanese

A separate resource file must be created for each locale. There are multiple ways to deploy these resources: compiled into a program, via satellite assembly, or via a global assembly. Your choice depends on what the program is trying to accomplish. There is also a sequence of steps a program goes through to figure out which resources it should use.

Implementing Multiple Locales

Through a combination of resource files and a directory structure geared toward targeted cultures, any program can be localized. The directory structure corresponds to each culture implemented in a program. The following directory structure supports localization for a program named MultiCulture:

```
MultiCulture
   en
   en-US
   en-GB
   ja
```

The MultiCulture directory holds the executable program, and each of the subdirectories holds libraries with localized resources corresponding to the culture specified in the directory name. Each resource file contains the resources as specified in Table 40.3.

TABLE 40.3   Resource File Contents

Culture	Flag/Greeting
En	en-US.jpg/Hi
en-US	en-US.jpg/Hi
en-GB	en-GB.jpg/Hello
It	it.jpg/ciao
Ja	ja.jpg/Konnichiwa
Unspecified	un.jpg/Hello

Create each resource file in its corresponding directory with the name pattern MultiCulture.<culture>.resources. For example, the Japanese resource file would be built in the ja subdirectory with the name multiculture.ja.resources. Then create an assembly named MultiCulture.Resources.Dll in each directory with a localized resource file. The following example shows how to create the Japanese assembly:

```
al /out:MultiCulture.Resources.Dll /c:ja /embed:MultiCulture.ja.resources,MultiCul-
ture.ja.resources,Private
```

This follows the same method of creating resource files from assemblies that was explained earlier in this chapter. The only difference is the /c option, which specifies the culture. Remember to perform this task in each culture subdirectory, substituting culture abbreviations as appropriate.

If the appropriate culture subdirectory is present, a localized program can automatically pick up the resources corresponding to its default locale. For example, the default culture on my computer is en-US, resulting in the resources from the en-US culture subdirectory being used in the MultiCulture localized program. Listing 40.7 shows this program.

LISTING 40.7   A Localized Program: MultiCulture.cs

```csharp
using System;
using System.Drawing;
using System.Collections;
using System.ComponentModel;
using System.Windows.Forms;
using System.Data;
using System.Resources;
using System.Threading;
using System.Globalization;

namespace MultiCulture
{
    /// <summary>
    /// Summary description for MultiCulture.
    /// </summary>
    public class MultiCulture : System.Windows.Forms.Form
    {
        ResourceManager multiRes;

        private System.Windows.Forms.PictureBox flagPic;
        private System.Windows.Forms.Label greetingLbl;
        private System.Windows.Forms.ComboBox cultureCbx;

        private System.ComponentModel.Container components
            = null;

        public MultiCulture()
        {
            InitializeComponent();
            multiRes = new ResourceManager("multiculture",
                this.GetType().Assembly);
```

40

LISTING 40.7   Continued

```
        }

        private void InitializeComponent()
        {
            this.flagPic
                = new System.Windows.Forms.PictureBox();
            this.cultureCbx
                = new System.Windows.Forms.ComboBox();
            this.greetingLbl
                = new System.Windows.Forms.Label();
            this.SuspendLayout();
            //
            // flagPic
            //
            this.flagPic.Location
                = new System.Drawing.Point(64, 24);
            this.flagPic.Name = "flagPic";
            this.flagPic.Size
                = new System.Drawing.Size(168, 104);
            this.flagPic.SizeMode
    = System.Windows.Forms.PictureBoxSizeMode.StretchImage;
            this.flagPic.TabIndex = 0;
            this.flagPic.TabStop = false;
            //
            // cultureCbx
            //
            this.cultureCbx.DisplayMember = "en-US";
            this.cultureCbx.DropDownWidth = 121;
            this.cultureCbx.Items.AddRange(new object[] {
                                            "en-US",
                                            "en-GB",
                                            "ja-JP",
                                            "de-CH",
                                            "it",
                                            "mars"});
            this.cultureCbx.Location
                = new System.Drawing.Point(88, 216);
            this.cultureCbx.Name = "cultureCbx";
            this.cultureCbx.Size
                = new System.Drawing.Size(121, 21);
            this.cultureCbx.TabIndex = 2;
            this.cultureCbx.Text = "en-US";
            this.cultureCbx.SelectedIndexChanged += new
                System.EventHandler(
                this.cultureCbx_SelectedIndexChanged);
            //
```

LISTING 40.7   Continued

```
        // greetingLbl
        //
        this.greetingLbl.Font = new System.Drawing.Font(
                "Microsoft Sans Serif",
                14.25F,
                System.Drawing.FontStyle.Regular,
                System.Drawing.GraphicsUnit.Point,
                ((System.Byte)(0)));
        this.greetingLbl.Location
            = new System.Drawing.Point(64, 160);
        this.greetingLbl.Name = "greetingLbl";
        this.greetingLbl.Size
            = new System.Drawing.Size(168, 23);
        this.greetingLbl.TabIndex = 1;
        this.greetingLbl.Text = "greeting";
        this.greetingLbl.TextAlign
          = System.Drawing.ContentAlignment.MiddleCenter;
        //
        // MultiCulture
        //
        this.AutoScaleBaseSize
            = new System.Drawing.Size(5, 13);
        this.ClientSize
            = new System.Drawing.Size(292, 273);
        this.Controls.AddRange(
            new System.Windows.Forms.Control[] {
                this.cultureCbx,
                this.greetingLbl,
                this.flagPic});
        this.Name = "MultiCulture";
        this.Text = "Localization Demo";
        this.Load += new
            System.EventHandler(this.MultiCulture_Load);
        this.ResumeLayout(false);
    }

    /// <summary>
    /// The main entry point for the application.
    /// </summary>
    static void Main()
    {
        Application.Run(new MultiCulture());
    }

    private void SetLocalizedResources()
    {
```

LISTING 40.7   Continued

```
            flagPic.Image
                = (System.Drawing.Image)
                multiRes.GetObject("flag");

            greetingLbl.Text
                = multiRes.GetString("greeting");
        }

        private void MultiCulture_Load(object sender,
                                            System.EventArgs e)
        {
            SetLocalizedResources();
        }

        private void cultureCbx_SelectedIndexChanged(
            object sender, System.EventArgs e)
        {
            Thread.CurrentThread.CurrentUICulture = new
        CultureInfo(this.cultureCbx.SelectedItem.ToString());

            SetLocalizedResources();
        }
    }
}
```

The first difference between this program and demos in earlier sections is the way the resources are used. Earlier programs declared `ResourceManager` classes that used .resources files directly. The MultiCulture program in Listing 40.7 uses the satellite assemblies located in each culture subdirectory. The manner in which it finds the appropriate assembly is hidden within the `ResourceManager` class. This program enables this functionality in the way it initializes the `ResourceManager` instance.

The `ResourceManager` object is declared as a class field and initialized in the `MultiCulture` form constructor. The `ResourceManager` constructor accepts two parameters. The first is the root name of the resources to read. Because each file is named multiculture.resources.dll, the root name is `multiculture`. The second parameter identifies the main assembly for the resources, which is the `MultiCulture` assembly. The MultiCulture program is compiled with default resources, in case a requested culture doesn't have a specific culture subdirectory. The following command line compiles Listing 40.7:

```
csc /t:winexe /res:multiculture.resources MultiCulture.cs
```

In this command line, the `/t:winexe` option keeps the pesky console window from popping up every time the program is run. The default .resources file, identified in the `/res` option, contains resources from the unspecified column of Table 40.3 and doesn't have a culture abbreviation in the name.

The `SetLocalizedResources` method sets the `PictureBox` and `Label` controls, similar to earlier examples. This method is called by the `MultiCulture_Load` method, which is invoked when the form loads. It's also called by the `cultureCbx_SelectedIndexChanged` method.

The `cultureCbx_SelectedIndexChanged` method is instrumental in enabling dynamic localization in this program. It's called when a new item in the drop-down list is selected. The following busy line of code changes the program's culture:

```
Thread.CurrentThread.CurrentUICulture =
    new CultureInfo(this.cultureCbx.SelectedItem.ToString());
```

This command resets the `CurrentUICulture` property of the `CurrentThread` object, which is the current thread this program is running in. The value placed into the `CurrentUICulture` property is a `CultureInfo` object. It's initialized with the culture identifier that the user selected from the drop-down list.

> **WARNING**
>
> `Thread.CurrentThread` contains both `CurrentCulture` and `CurrentUICulture` properties. Be sure to use the `CurrentUICulture` property (with the UI in the middle) when changing locales. It might save a few hours' worth of headaches when you try to change a program's culture and nothing happens.

`CultureInfo` is the standard base class library class for localization. It holds pertinent information for calendars, numbers, and string formatting. In its current role, it's the primary means of providing dynamic manipulation of cultures. Figure 40.3 shows the `MultiCulture` program.

FIGURE 40.3   The **MultiCulture** program.

Finding Resources

A localized application follows a specific path when resolving where it obtains resources. As would be expected, this resolution strategy is based on moving from the most-specific to a general source of resources. The resource resolution process follows these steps and ends whenever a resource is found or an exception is thrown:

1. Search the global assembly cache for the specific resource. The global assembly cache is discussed in detail in a later chapter, but for now think of it as a central repository for all programs on a machine to access.

2. Search culture subdirectories of the localized program.

3. Search the global assembly cache for parent resources. For instance, if the original resource selected, but not found, was en-US, search the global assembly cache for en only.

4. Search culture subdirectories of the localized program for the parent resources.

5. Search culture subdirectories of the localized program for parent resources of the last parent resource searched. A resource has only a single parent, but the chain of parents can extend multiple levels.

6. Use the default resource. This is the unspecified resource that was compiled with the main assembly.

7. If the resource is not found, throw a `System.Argument.Exception`.

> **TIP**
>
> To reduce complexity, it's useful to begin localizing a program with only two cultures. Imagine what would happen if a more meaningful resource name was desired after all locales had been created. If this happens often enough during development, it would get annoying to change every resource file.
>
> Also seriously consider having default parent culture resources for every subculture you support. This way you could do a quick modification for a new subculture, allowing the majority of resources to default to the parent, while concentrating on those resources specific to the subculture.

Experimenting with this resolution process can be done with the `MultiCulture` program. For example, selecting en-GB, it, or ja will use the resources from the corresponding culture subdirectories. Because en-US doesn't have a culture subdirectory, it defaults to its parent, en, which happens to have a U.S. flag and greeting. The de-CH culture doesn't have any resources of its own, and must use the default assembly, which was compiled into the main `MultiCulture` assembly. Finally, although there has been much speculation as to whether there is life on the planet Mars, the mars locale is not installed on this operating system, generating an exception when selected.

Summary

Program localization is supported through resources. There are several ways to generate resources, depending on the resource type. The available formats are text files with name/value pairs of strings or XML files, which are specifically suited to binary resources. These two file types are then converted to binary resource files, which may be included in assemblies.

The ResGen tool, included in the .NET Framework SDK, enables conversion between different resource types. The ResXGen and ResEditor are sample programs included with the .NET Framework SDK that help manage resources.

Resource files are placed in specified directories so that localized programs can find the right resources. ResourceManager is the primary class, providing management of resources for program use. Assigning CultureInfo objects to the CurrentUICulture property of the current thread may dynamically change cultures. Localized programs use a resolution process to find the most-specific resources available. A combination of specialized culture subdirectories and resource files makes program localization a straightforward process.

CHAPTER 41

Performing Interop (P/Invoke and COM) and Writing Unsafe Code

An important consideration in any project is reuse of existing code. The ability to access legacy code containing business logic or low-level system functionality could lead to significant benefits in time and cost. To meet this demand, C# provides a mechanism to access legacy systems, with a feature known as PInvoke, short for Platform Invoke.

Unsafe code permits a block of code to use pointers, low-level types that allow indirect access to memory and other types. This opens new opportunities for optimization and interfaces to operating system or legacy code that requires pointers. The primary reason for unsafe code blocks is to separate safe C# code from pointer-related code, which could cause problems if mixed together.

COM has been the most successful binary reuse component framework ever. Every machine running any flavor of Windows is probably running at least one COM application, and that's in addition to the OS itself. .NET technology builds upon the successful aspects of COM through its promotion of component concepts and cross-language interoperability. Because of the tremendous base of COM applications in use today, .NET programs must have the capability to reuse existing COM components.

The .NET platform supports a method of communication between .NET and COM known as COM Interop, which supports making COM objects appear as managed objects to .NET components and making .NET components appear as COM objects to unmanaged code. Another related technology is COM+ services, which is supported extensively by .NET.

Unsafe Code

Unsafe code, as defined in the next section, permits the use of pointers, which supports certain performance optimizations and interface to legacy code and operating systems. Unsafe code is identified with a special keyword, unsafe, which marks either a block of code or a field. This establishes an unsafe context where pointer operations can be implemented.

There are special keywords associated with unsafe contexts, making it easier to work with pointers. The fixed keyword helps pin down objects in memory so that the Garbage Collector doesn't move them in the middle of an operation. Obtaining the size of a pointer or field can be accomplished by using the sizeof operator. The stackalloc operator enables memory to be allocated on the stack. In addition to keywords, a few other operators facilitate pointer operations, such as the dereferencing operator (*), the address of operator (&), and the indirection operator (->).

What Do You Mean My Code Is Unsafe?

A subject of much confusion and discussion, C# brings a whole new vocabulary relating to whether code is safe, unsafe, managed, or unmanaged. For full understanding of the issues in this chapter, it's important to define what these terms are and why they're important:

▶ **Safe**—The normal mode of operation in a C# program is safe. When code is safe, its type is safe and secure. Although there may not be a formal type of code called safe, it's illustrative to differentiate it from unsafe code.

▶ **Unsafe**—Unsafe code is identified by the unsafe keyword. This is code that is allowed to use pointers. It's also the only place that certain statements and operators such as fixed, sizeof, and stackalloc may be used. Unsafe code is more complex and prone to error than normal safe code, so it requires the unsafe keyword to separate it from normal safe C# code.

Although unsafe code permits operations that are not part of normal C# practices, unsafe code is still managed. It's managed because the Common Language Runtime (CLR) or Virtual Execution System (VES) still has control over the code and still manages memory.

▶ **Managed**—All C# code is managed. Managed code is under control of the CLR, which has full control of all memory and security operations. Unsafe code is still managed code.

Managed types are all reference types and value types with a nested reference type. Managed types reside on the heap and are managed by the CLR.

▶ **Unmanaged**—Native code, such as that accessed through Platform Invoke or COM Interop, is unmanaged. Code that is unmanaged is not controlled by the CLR.

Unmanaged types include all value types (without nested reference types), enums, and pointers.

The Power of Pointers

A pointer is an indirect address to another object. At its most basic level, it's similar to an object reference but much more powerful. References provide a mechanism to refer to an object, but pointers can be arithmetically manipulated to move forward and backward through a group of objects. Pointers can be set to any addressable location and even view memory locations where no object exists.

Classification-wise, a pointer type is considered a peer of value and reference types. Pointers are declared as a specific value or reference type. This means that they hold the address of the type it is declared as. For instance, a pointer to an int is declared like one of the following:

```
int *intPtr;
```

or

```
int* intPtr;
```

or

```
int * intPtr;
```

This creates an uninitialized integer pointer. The asterisk (*) means that intPtr is a pointer. The keyword, int, indicates the type this pointer can hold an address of. This is the same as any other field declaration except it has the * to indicate that it is a pointer.

Pointers hold addresses of objects. Therefore, in most cases it would be illogical to assign a field value to a pointer. The address-of operator (&), shown in the following example, is used to load a value into a pointer:

```
int myInt = 7;
intPtr = &myInt;
```

The address-of operator, &, returns the memory address of a field. In this example, the address of the myInt variable is assigned to the intPtr pointer. Now intPtr refers to the value held by myInt.

Right now, the value of myInt is 7, and the value of intPtr is the address of myInt. This is nice, but the real benefit of intPtr comes when it can be used to indirectly read the value from myInt. The following example shows how to use the indirection operator to enable a pointer to read the value from a normal field:

```
int retrievedInt = *intPtr;
```

Now the value of myInt, 7, has been assigned to retrievedInt through the int pointer, intPtr. This was made possible by the dereferencing operator (*), which returns the value of the field it is pointing to.

At this point, the * has been used twice in the context of pointers. The first time it was used in the declaration of a pointer to specify that this is a pointer type declaration, as opposed to a reference type or value type declaration. The second time it was used as an indirection operator, returning the value of the object it pointed to. This one operator, *, is used for both pointer declaration and pointer indirection.

Pointers may have multiple levels of indirection, which is essentially a pointer to a pointer. Here's an example of how to declare a pointer to a pointer.

```
int **intPtrPtr = &intPtr;
```

The address of `intPtr`, which is a pointer itself, is assigned to another pointer, `intPtrPtr`. This time, two *'s are needed to declare `intPtrPtr` because it is a pointer to a pointer of type `int`. Although further levels of indirection are possible, it may be quite rare that they would be necessary.

An interesting relationship exists between arrays and pointers, where pointers may be represented as arrays. The following example shows how to use a pointer as an array:

```
int myInt = intPtr[0]; // myInt = 7
```

This time, `intPtr` was used just like an array. Because it has only one element, the example accessed the first (zero-based) element in the array, which returned the value 7. Pointing to just the first element of an array won't accomplish much, and hints at the need for some mechanism to get to the other elements of the array. One obvious solution is to use an index into the array to get to the elements necessary. However, there's another way to do this—with pointer arithmetic, as shown in Listing 41.1.

LISTING 41.1   Pointer Arithmetic: PointerArithmetic.cs

```
using System;

/// <summary>
///     Pointer Arithmetic Demonstration.
/// </summary>
class PointerArithmetic
{
    struct IntStruct
    {
        public int one;
        public int two;
        public int three;

        public IntStruct(int first, int second, int third)
        {
            one   = first;
            two   = second;
```

LISTING 41.1   Continued

```
                three = third;
        }
    }

    unsafe static void Main(string[] args)
    {
        IntStruct myIntStruct = new IntStruct(3, 5, 7);

        int *intPtr = (int *)&myIntStruct;

        Console.WriteLine(
            "\nPointer with array indexing - \n");

        for (int i=0; i < 3; i++)
        {
            Console.WriteLine("intPtr[]: {0}", intPtr[i]);
        }

        Console.WriteLine("\nPointer arithmetic - \n");

        for (int i=0; i < 3; i++)
        {
            Console.WriteLine("*intPtr: {0}", (*intPtr)++);
        }

    Console.WriteLine("\nPointer to member access with dereferencing (*) operator)
- \n");
    IntStruct *isPtr = &myIntStruct;
    Console.WriteLine("(*isPtr).one:   {0}", (*isPtr).one);
    Console.WriteLine("(*isPtr).two:   {0}", (*isPtr).two);
    Console.WriteLine("(*isPtr).three: {0}", (*isPtr).three);
        }
}
```

And here's the output:

```
Pointer with array indexing -

intPtr[]: 3
intPtr[]: 5
intPtr[]: 7

Pointer arithmetic -

*intPtr: 3
```

LISTING 41.1   Continued

```
*intPtr: 5
*intPtr: 7

Pointer member access -

isPtr->one:    3
isPtr->two:    5
isPtr->three: 7
```

The first `for` loop in Listing 41.1 uses array indexing to access each member of the `IntStruct`. Although `myIntStruct` is a `struct`, its members are sitting in a contiguous block of memory, which is accessible by a pointer. The indexer serves as an offset from the address the pointer actually points to.

The second `for` loop uses pointer arithmetic to move the pointer to the next location in memory. The actual location moved to in memory is relative to the size of the pointer type. As with any other C# expression, addition, subtraction, increment, or decrement operators may be used to arithmetically manipulate the value of a pointer.

Listing 41.2 shows how to compile this program. The `/unsafe` command-line option is required.

LISTING 41.2   Compilation Instructions for Listing 41.1

```
csc /unsafe PointerArithmetic.cs
```

The last part of Listing 41.1 shows how to use the indirection operator, `->`, to reference the members of the `myIntStruct` struct. This is how pointers reference struct members, rather than using the dot operator.

Going back to the second `for` loop of Listing 41.1, the post-increment operator modifies the value of the pointer so that its value is now at the next address. The type of pointer determines what that next address will be. Because an `int` is 4 bytes long, the post-increment operator would yield an address that is 4 bytes beyond its current location.

The `sizeof()` Operator

Knowing the size of a type can help in several areas. For instance, if the program had only a certain amount of memory to work with, it would need to keep track of where the pointer was in a loop to make sure it didn't go too far. To help with these types of scenarios, the `sizeof()` operator is available. The `sizeof()` operator may be used only on unmanaged types. Listing 41.3 demonstrates how to use the `sizeof()` operator.

LISTING 41.3   Using the **sizeof()** Operator

```
using System;

/// <summary>
```

LISTING 41.3   Continued

```
///     sizeof operator demo
/// </summary>
class SizeOfDemo
{
    unsafe static void Main(string[] args)
    {
        Console.WriteLine("\nsizeof Operator Demo\n");

        Console.WriteLine("sizeof(bool):    {0}", sizeof(bool));
        Console.WriteLine("sizeof(char):    {0}", sizeof(char));
        Console.WriteLine("sizeof(byte):    {0}", sizeof(byte));
        Console.WriteLine("sizeof(short):   {0}", sizeof(short));
        Console.WriteLine("sizeof(int):     {0}", sizeof(int));
        Console.WriteLine("sizeof(long):    {0}", sizeof(long));
        Console.WriteLine("sizeof(float):   {0}", sizeof(float));
        Console.WriteLine("sizeof(double):  {0}", sizeof(double));
        Console.WriteLine("sizeof(decimal): {0}", sizeof(decimal));
    }
}
```

And here's the output:

```
sizeof Operator Demo

sizeof(bool):    1
sizeof(char):    2
sizeof(byte):    1
sizeof(short):   2
sizeof(int):     4
sizeof(long):    8
sizeof(float):   4
sizeof(double):  8
sizeof(decimal): 16
```

The code in Listing 41.3 shows the sizeof() operator used with the C# primitive types. The sizeof() operator tells the number of bytes a pointer will move when it is incremented or decremented by one. Listing 41.4 shows how to compile Listing 41.3.

LISTING 41.4   Compilation Instructions for Listing 41.3

```
csc /unsafe SizeOfDemo.cs
```

The `stackalloc` Operator

A common requirement when working with pointers is to have a pool of memory to work with to accomplish a task. The `stackalloc` operator allocates memory on the stack and may be used only on unmanaged types. There's no need to explicitly free memory obtained through `stackalloc` because it's returned to the system when the routine ends. Listing 41.5 shows how to use the `stackalloc` operator.

LISTING 41.5   **`stackalloc`** Demonstration: StackAllocDemo.cs

```csharp
using System;


/// <summary>
///     stackalloc demo.
/// </summary>
class StackAllocDemo
{
    unsafe static void Main(string[] args)
    {
        string myString = "Unsafe is still Managed!";

        char *charArr = stackalloc char[myString.Length];
        char *charPtr = charArr;

        Console.WriteLine("\nCreating String...\n");

        int count = 0;
        foreach(char character in myString)
        {
            *charPtr++ = character;
            Console.Write("{0} ", charArr[count++]);
        }
        Console.WriteLine();
    }
}
```

And the output is

```
Creating String...


U n s a f e   i s   s t i l l   M a n a g e d !
```

The example in Listing 41.5 loads a string into a block of `stackalloc`-allocated memory. The memory is allocated by using array-like syntax. Instead of the new statement, it uses `stackalloc`. The block of memory allocated by `stackalloc` must be assigned to a pointer of the type that was allocated, which is a char * named charArr. The reason it's named charArr is because it will be used with array syntax later in the program. Here's the line using the stackalloc operator:

```
char *charArr = stackalloc char[myString.Length];
```

The charArr pointer needs to remain stationary, so its address is assigned to the charPtr character pointer. Note that the address of a pointer is assigned with the pointer type itself as opposed to a field that requires the address-of operator, &,. The address assignment is shown here:

```
char *charPtr = charArr;
```

Within the foreach loop, each character of the string is copied to the memory that was allocated with stackalloc. The indirection operator is used to assign the character value to the proper memory position. After dereferencing and assignment, the location of the charPtr is incremented to the next character position, as shown in the following statement:

```
*charPtr++ = character;
```

After each character is assigned to its corresponding position in the allocated memory block, the value of that location in memory is printed to the console. The reason we left the charArr character pointer alone was so that it can be used with array-like syntax to reference each character. The count field is used to index into the allocated memory and is then incremented. The line showing element access with the charArr pointer is shown here:

```
Console.Write("{0} ", charArr[count++]);
```

The stackalloc program from Listing 41.5 can be compiled with the command-line from Listing 41.6.

LISTING 41.6   Compilation Instructions for Listing 41.5

```
csc /unsafe StackAllocDemo.cs
```

TIP

The stackalloc operator allocates memory on the stack. If there's a need to allocate heap memory, you should create a class that uses PInvoke to call operating system memory allocation routines. For example, the Windows HeapAlloc() and HeapFree() functions allocate and free heap memory.

The fixed Statement

The fixed statement keeps moveable objects pinned while accessing them with a pointer. When using the fixed statement, you pin a variable, which is then considered pinned. Because of garbage collection and other memory-optimization processes, there would be no guarantee that the object being pointed to in one operation would be the same the next time the pointer was referenced. The `fixed` statement guarantees that moveable objects stay put.

There are two categories of variables to consider when using the `fixed` statement: fixed and movable. Fixed variables include local variables and value types, values resulting from a struct member access where the struct is fixed, and pointer indirection or pointer member access.

Moveable variables include reference types, `ref` and `out` parameters, a boxed variable, and static variables. Listing 41.7 shows how to use the `fixed` statement.

LISTING 41.7   **fixed** Statement Demo: FixedStatementDemo.cs

```
using System;


/// <summary>
///     fixed Statement Demo.
/// </summary>
class FixedStatementDemo
{
    unsafe static int strstr(string subString,
                             string searchString)
    {
        int  pos  = 0;
        bool found = false;
        char *tmpPtr;

        fixed (char *stringPtr = searchString)
        {
            char *charPtr = stringPtr;

            for(int i=0; i < searchString.Length; i++)
            {
                if (subString[0] != *charPtr++)
                    continue;

                pos     = i;
                tmpPtr = charPtr;

                for(int j=1; j < subString.Length; j++)
                {
                    found = true;

                    if (subString[j] != *tmpPtr++)
                    {
```

LISTING 41.7   Continued

```
                    found = false;
                    pos = 0;
                    break;
                }
            }

            if (found)
                return pos;
        }
    }
    return -1;
}

static void Main(string[] args)
{
    string subString    = "an";
    string searchString = "banana";

    int pos = strstr(subString, searchString);

    if (pos == -1)
        Console.WriteLine(
            "'{0}' not found in '{1}'",
            subString, searchString);
    else
        Console.WriteLine(
            "Found '{0}' in '{1}' at position {2}",
            subString, searchString, pos+1);
}
}
```

And here's the output:

```
Found 'an' in 'banana' at position 2
```

The first thing to notice about the example in Listing 41.7 is that the fixed statement is inside the strstr() method. It would have been easy to pin the strings before calling strstr() and then send in pointers, but that would have violated an important rule when using the fixed statement: Objects should only be pinned for the minimum amount of time necessary.

The rationale for this rule is simple when you consider the reason for pinning a variable. A pinned variable can't be garbage collected. To prevent the pinned variable from being garbage collected, some mechanism must be in place to recognize that this variable is pinned. This involves overhead that won't exist if the object is not pinned.

Therefore, the `fixed` statement is placed inside the `strstr()` method, and the routine is optimized to spend the minimal amount of time finding a substring within a string. The `fixed` statement assigns the moveable object to a pointer of a compatible type, as shown here:

```
fixed (char *stringPtr = searchString)
```

This creates a read-only pointer. Another pointer must be created and assigned the value of `stringPtr` to read the rest of the string:

```
char *charPtr = stringPtr;
```

We want to rip through the search string in a linear fashion, so the first thing done is to keep reading until the first characters match. When the characters don't match, skip all other loop processing:

```
if (subString[0] != *charPtr++)
    continue;
```

There's similar logic throughout this routine, but the point is to do what's necessary and leave as soon as possible. Listing 41.8 shows how to compile the code in listing 41.7, again using the /unsafe command-line option.

LISTING 41.8   Compilation Instructions for Listing 41.7

```
csc /unsafe FixedStatementDemo.cs
```

Platform Invoke

Platform Invoke—PInvoke —provides a means for C# programs to execute native code. This is of great help when there's a need to reuse legacy code or communicate with systems that don't have other readily available interfaces. When legacy code is wrapped in a DLL, it can be called with C# through PInvoke.

Another use of PInvoke is to access existing operating system and third-party DLLs. Using PInvoke is as simple as declaring the method prototype as static extern and decorating it with the DllImport attribute. Listing 41.9 has a couple examples of how to use the DllImport attribute to implement PInvoke.

LISTING 41.9   Platform Invoke Demo: PinvokeDemo.cs

```
using System;
using System.Runtime.InteropServices;

/// <summary>
///     Platform Invocation Demo.
/// </summary>
```

LISTING 41.9   Continued

```
class PInvokeDemo
{
    const int ABORT_RETRY_IGNORE = 2;

    [DllImport("user32.dll")]
    static extern int MessageBox(
        int hWnd, string message, string title, int options);

    [DllImport("user32.dll",
        EntryPoint="MessageBox", CharSet = CharSet.Unicode)]
    static extern int SpecialMessageBox(
        int hWnd, string message, string title, int options);

    static void Main(string[] args)
    {
        MessageBox(
            0, "Plain Message Box", "PInvoke Example #1", 0);

        SpecialMessageBox(
            0, "Special Message Box", "PInvoke Example #2",
            ABORT_RETRY_IGNORE);
    }
}
```

Listing 41.9 has two examples of how to use the DllImport attribute. The first example contains a positional parameter to specify which DLL has the function we want to call. It uses the MessageBox call to display the Windows message box on the screen, as shown in Figure 41.1.

FIGURE 41.1   Plain message box.

The DllImport attribute in the second example is more detailed, with the EntryPoint and CharSet named parameters. The EntryPoint named parameter specifies the name of the method being called. This permits the method declaration being decorated to have any other name. In this example, the method is called SpecialMessageBox().

The CharSet named parameter specifies two things: what character set to translate when marshalling strings to native code, and method name mangling. Windows commonly uses a name-mangling convention for multiple versions of a method. Methods ending in A accept ANSI strings, and methods ending in W accept Unicode strings. When neither of these name-mangling conventions is used in either the EntryPoint named parameter or the method name of the declaration, PInvoke uses the CharSet named parameter to select the appropriate function.

Options for the CharSet named parameter include members of the CharSet enum: Ansi, Auto, None, and Unicode. Ansi and Unicode specify which character set to use when marshalling strings. None means that no CharSet is specified. Auto, the default, is platform-dependent. For example, Windows NT is Unicode and Windows 9x is Ansi. Figure 41.2 shows what the second message box looks like. Listing 41.10 contains the command line for compiling the example in Listing 41.9.

FIGURE 41.2   Special message box.

LISTING 41.10   Compilation Instructions for Listing 41.9

```
csc FixedStatementDemo.cs
```

Communicating with COM from .NET

One of the most likely interop scenarios is communicating from .NET to existing COM components. This can allow preservation of existing infrastructure and reduction in overall development cost.

COM components may be called via either early or late binding. Via early binding, legacy COM components can be made to appear as managed objects in the .NET environment. This is accomplished by a utility that reads an existing type library and creates a proxy for the .NET component to interact with.

Early bound components are those that are bound at compile time. This promotes type safety and improves a program's overall performance.

However, sometimes a type library may not be available. In these cases, it's necessary to use late-bound techniques. Late binding occurs at runtime. This has its drawbacks, however, because of additional overhead with the late-binding process and the possibility of exceptions raised if a method doesn't exist or is specified incorrectly.

Early-Bound COM Component Calls

Early-bound calls require the use of a .NET Framework to create a proxy for the COM component. The proxy is then compiled into the C# program where the COM component can be instantiated and called just like any other managed component. Listing 41.10 shows a method from a COM component written in C++.

LISTING 41.10   A C++ COM Component: ComObj.dll

```
STDMETHODIMP CCom4DotNet::GetResponseFromCom(void)
{
    printf("Hello from COM!");
    return S_OK;
}
```

This code simply prints a sentence to the console when called. The following instructions should help in creating this component in Visual Studio.NET:

1. Select File, New, and then the Project. When the Project window pops up, select ATL Project and name it **ComObj.dll**. The IDE will build a skeleton with many files.

2. From the Solution Explorer window, right-click, select Add, Add Class. When the wizard pops up, select ATL Control and name the component **Com4DotNet**. This creates a class named CCom4DotNet and an interface named ICom4DotNet.

3. After the CCom4DotNet class has been created, go to the Class View window and right-click the ICom4DotNet interface. Select Add, Add Method. When the wizard pops up, name the method **GetResponseFromCom** (with no parameters).

4. Go to the CCom4DotNet class where the GetResponseFromCom() method shell is defined and add the contents shown in Listing 41.10. This completes creation of the COM component necessary for this example.

The COM component from Listing 41.10 should have an associated type library. Type libraries are input into the TlbImp command to create a proxy object called a runtime callable wrapper (RCW). A C# program doesn't need to worry about underlying plumbing, such as reference counting, HRESULTS, and so on because the RCW takes care of all these tasks. The following command line creates an RCW named ComObj.dll:

```
tlbimp _ComObj.tlb
```

The ComObj.dll must be referenced by a C# program, just as any other .NET library. Listing 41.11 shows a C# program calling a COM component.

LISTING 41.11   A C# Program Calling a COM Component: TalkToCom.cs

```
using System;
using ComObj;

namespace TalkToCom
{
    /// <summary>
    /// Calls a COM Component.
    /// </summary>
    class CallCom
    {
```

LISTING 41.11   Continued

```
        static void Main(string[] args)
        {
            CCom4DotNet c4dn = new CCom4DotNet();
            c4dn.GetResponseFromCom();
        }
    }
}
```

And here's the output:

```
Hello from COM!
```

The namespace for referencing the COM component corresponds to the name of the file containing it because that's the method TlbImp used during creation of the RCW. Within the Main method, the COM component is instantiated the same as a normal C# object. The GetResponseFromCom method prints to the console from the COM component method, as shown in the output.

Late-Bound COM Component Calls

For times when a type library isn't available, or there's a dynamic invocation requirement, a C# program can perform a late-bound call to a COM component. Listing 41.12 demonstrates how to do this.

LISTING 41.12   Late-Bound COM Component Invocation: TalkToComLater.cs

```
using System;
using System.Runtime.InteropServices;
using System.Reflection;

namespace TalkToComLater
{
    /// <summary>
    /// Makes a late bound call to a COM Component.
    /// </summary>
    class CallComLater
    {
        static void Main(string[] args)
        {
            Type lateBoundType
                = Type.GetTypeFromProgID("ComObj.Com4DotNet");

            object lateBoundObject
                = Activator.CreateInstance(lateBoundType);

            lateBoundType.InvokeMember(
```

LISTING 41.12   Continued

```
                      "GetResponseFromCom",
                      BindingFlags.Default¦
                      BindingFlags.InvokeMethod,
                      null,
                      lateBoundObject,
                      null);
        }
    }
}
```

And here's the output:

```
Hello from COM!
```

Late-bound COM component invocations are performed using C# reflection. The program in Listing 41.12 invokes the COM component containing the code from Listing 41.10. It first obtains a ProgID from the COM object, as listed in the Windows registry. When a type object is obtained, an object is created using the static CreateInstance method of the Activator class. The GetResponseFromCom method of the COM component is then invoked with the InvokeMember method of the Type object, lateBoundType.

Exposing a .NET Component as a COM Component

C# components are accessible as COM components with the use of a couple of .NET Framework tools to create an unmanaged proxy and enter the proper settings in the registry. This enables unmanaged code to use .NET components as if they were COM components. Listing 41.13 shows a C# component to be exposed as a COM component.

LISTING 41.13   A C# Component Exposed as a COM Component: CallFromCom.dll

```
using System;


public interface ICSharp
{
    string GetResponseFromCSharp();
}


namespace CallFromCom
{
    /// <summary>
    /// C# DLL to be called as a COM object.
    /// </summary>
    public class CallCSharp: ICSharp
    {
        public string GetResponseFromCSharp()
```

LISTING 41.13   Continued

```
        {
            return "Hello from C#!";
        }
    }
}
```

The code in Listing 41.13 appears as any other C# library. To expose this library as a COM object, use the RegAsm utility as shown on the following command line:

```
RegAsm CallFromCom.dll /tlb:CallFromCom.tlb
```

This command line registers the C# library as a COM component. In addition, the /tlb option creates a type library to facilitate early binding. To generate a type library without registering the library, use the TlbExp program as shown in the following command line:

```
TlbExp CallFromCom.dll
```

This creates a type library named CallFromCom.tlb. If you needed another name, you could use the /out command-line option. For a list of all command-line options for RegAsm, TlbExp, or TlbImp, just type the command name with the –h option.

After a C# program has been registered with RegAsm, it can be called as a COM component by any other program. The Visual Basic program shown in Figure 41.3 calls the C# COM component when its button is clicked. The code that calls the C# COM component is shown in Listing 41.14.

LISTING 41.14   Calling a C# Component Exposed as a COM Component

```
Private Sub Command1_Click()
    Dim myCSharp As New CallCSharp.CallCSharp
    myString = myCSharp.GetResponseFromCSharp()
    response = MsgBox(myString, vbOKOnly, "Response From C#")
End Sub
```

The RegAsm program automatically registered the CallCSharp object under the CallCSharp namespace. This is why the object is instantiated as CallCSharp.CallCSharp. After the C# COM object has been instantiated, its members can be called just like any other COM object. Figure 41.4 shows the message box that pops up when the button shown in Figure 41.3 is clicked.

> **NOTE**
>
> The C# COM object should be copied into the same directory as the VB program or added to the Global Assembly Cache with the gacutil /i command.

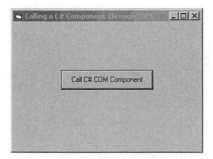

FIGURE 41.3   AVB program calling a C# COM component.

FIGURE 41.4   A message box showing the response from a C# COM component.

Introduction to .NET Support for COM+ Services

The .NET Framework provides extensive support for COM+ services such as transactions, JIT activation, object pooling, and others. COM+ services are activated through the use of attributes, which decorate a specific C# element as appropriate. These attributes are analogous to the COM+ concepts you may already be familiar with. To get started, let's take a look at Listing 41.15, a minimal C# program that will be registered as a COM+ component.

LISTING 41.15   A Minimal C# COM+ Component

```
using System;
using System.Reflection;
using System.EnterpriseServices;

[assembly: ApplicationName("CPSkel")]
[assembly: AssemblyKeyFileAttribute(@"..\..\CPSkel.snk")]

namespace ComPlusServices
{
    /// <summary>
    /// COM+ Service Skeleton.
    /// </summary>
    public class CPSkel : ServicedComponent
    {
        public CPSkel()
        {
        }
    }
}
```

The primary part of the code in Listing 41.15 that makes it a COM+ service is the fact that the CPSkel class is derived from System.EnterpriseServices.ServicedComponent. The other step necessary to make this C# program work as a COM+ service is to register it. The ApplicationName attribute identifies the COM+ name, and the AssemblyKeyFile attribute specifies the strong name key to register the assembly with. The following command line shows how to create a strong name key:

```
sn -k CPSkel.snk
```

The sn program creates a public key pair to be used when the assembly is registered. It uniquely identifies the assembly it is used with. The RegSvcs program registers the C# library as a COM+ service, as shown here:

```
D:\My Documents\Visual Studio Projects\Chapter 41
➥\ComPlusServices\bin\Debug>RegSvcs ComPlusServices.dll
RegSvcs - .NET Services Installation Utility
➥Version 1.0.2914.16
Copyright (C) Microsoft Corp. 2000-2001.  All rights reserved.

Installed Assembly:
        Assembly: D:\My Documents\Visual Studio Projects
        ➥\Chapter 41\ComPlusServices\bin\Debug\ComPlusServices.dll
        Application: CPSkel
        TypeLib: d:\my documents\visual studio projects
        ➥\chapter 41\complusservices\bin\debug\ComPlusServices.tlb
```

This registers a COM+ service named CPSkel and generates a type library named ComPlusServices.tlb. Figure 41.5 shows what this new service looks like in the Component Services Explorer. The program in Listing 41.15 didn't have any class members other than a constructor. However, Figure 41.5 shows that the CPSkel COM+ service contains interfaces for object, IDisposable, and others, showing that it hasn't lost any of its managed behavior.

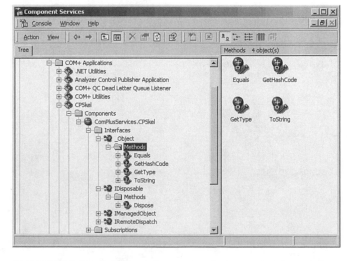

FIGURE 41.5   A C# program registered as a COM+ service.

Transactions

A transaction is a way to combine multiple actions into a single body of work to guarantee that all actions either succeed or fail together. C# programs can participate in COM+ services transactions by inheriting from the ComPlusServices class and marking their classes with a Transaction attribute. Listing 41.16 shows how to create a COM+ services transactional component in C#.

LISTING 41.16   A COM+ Transactional Component in C#: **CPTrans.cs**

```csharp
using System;
using System.Reflection;
using System.EnterpriseServices;

[assembly: ApplicationName("CPTrans")]
[assembly: AssemblyKeyFileAttribute(@"..\..\CPTrans.snk")]

namespace ComPlusServices
{
    /// <summary>
    /// COM+ Transaction Service.
    /// </summary>
    [Transaction(TransactionOption.Required)]
    public class CPTrans : ServicedComponent
    {
        public CPTrans()
        {
        }

        [AutoComplete]
        public bool PayBill()
        {
            // debit from account
            // send amount to creditor
            // record transaction
            return true;
        }
    }
}
```

To indicate that a component supports COM+ services transactions, apply the `Transaction` attribute to the class. The parameter to the `Transaction` attribute is a member of the `TransactionOption` enum, which specifies the type of automatic transaction to execute.

Another transaction-related attribute is `AutoComplete`, which enables a transaction to commit automatically if all items succeed. However, if an exception is raised, `AutoComplete` causes the transaction to abort.

JIT Activation

Just-In-Time (JIT) activation is the capability to instantiate a new component when it's needed and have that component go away automatically when it's no longer needed. By using COM+ services and associated attributes, a C# component can participate in JIT activation. Listing 41.17 shows a C# component implemented to use COM+ services JIT activation.

LISTING 41.17   A C# Component Configured for JIT Activation: CPJit.cs

```
using System;
using System.Reflection;
using System.EnterpriseServices;

[assembly: ApplicationName("CPJit")]
[assembly: AssemblyKeyFileAttribute(@"..\..\CPJit.snk")]

namespace ComPlusServices
{
    /// <summary>
    /// COM+ Transaction Service.
    /// </summary>
    [JustInTimeActivation]
    public class CPJit : ServicedComponent
    {
        public CPJit()
        {
        }
    }
}
```

Implementing JIT activation requires specifying the `JustInTimeActivation` attribute. JIT activation is `true` by default, but if you want to turn it off, specify `false` as the first attribute parameter.

Object Pooling

Another COM+ service enabling efficient use of resources is object pooling. An object pool is a group of components that stay activated and ready for connections at all times. This reduces the overhead associated with activation and deactivation of components. Listing 41.18 shows how to implement COM+ services object pooling.

LISTING 41.18   COM+ Services Object Pooling Implemented in C#: CPPool.cs

```csharp
using System;
using System.Reflection;
using System.EnterpriseServices;

[assembly: ApplicationName("CPPool")]
[assembly: AssemblyKeyFileAttribute(@"..\..\CPPool.snk")]

namespace ComPlusServices
{
    /// <summary>
    /// COM+ Transaction Service.
    /// </summary>
    [ObjectPooling(Enabled=true,
    MinPoolSize=5, MaxPoolSize=11)]
    public class CPPool : ServicedComponent
    {
        public CPPool()
        {
        }

        public override void Activate()
        {
        }

        public override void Deactivate()
        {
        }

        public override bool CanBePooled()
        {
            return true;
        }
    }
}
```

The `ObjectPooling` attribute has three parameters: `Enabled`, `MinPoolSize`, and `MaxPoolSize`. The `Enabled` parameter turns object pooling on. The `MinPoolSize` parameter specifies the minimum number of objects held in the pool, and the `MaxPoolSize` parameter specifies the maximum number of objects to be held in the pool.

Three methods are associated with object pooling: `Activate()`, `Deactivate()`, and `CanBePooled()`. The `Activate()` method is invoked when an object is pulled from the pool for use. When the object is returned to the pool, its `Deactivate()` method is invoked. The `CanBePooled()` method informs a requester about whether the object can be pooled.

Other Services

COM+ services include several other technologies not listed in this chapter, such as roles, security, and message queuing. Using the techniques described in other sections and examining the applicable attributes in the `System.EnterpriseServices` namespace, you can implement these other COM+ services in C#.

> **NOTE**
>
> C# and COM+ services security are mutually exclusive. That is, you can use either one or the other but not both in the same program. Because this book focuses on how to use C# with .NET, I've included Chapter 44, "Securing Code," which covers security in the managed environment.

Summary

Unsafe code allows you to use pointers, a low-level mechanism designed to help optimize some routines. Pointers operate by holding the address of objects and providing indirect access to an object's value and member-wise access to structs. Pointers also may be manipulated arithmetically.

A few keywords assist working with unsafe code. The `sizeof()` operator returns the number of bytes in a variable. Memory allocation is performed with the `stackalloc` operator. Because there's no guarantee that a moveable object in memory will stay in place, the `fixed` statement is used to pin a movable object in memory.

Platform Invoke—`PInvoke`—is a capability that allows C# programs to call native code libraries. To use `PInvoke`, methods are decorated with the `DllImport` attribute.

The ability to communicate with legacy COM applications is absolutely essential for some C# development projects. Through COM Interop, a C# program can call methods of any COM component. The process of making this happen involves both early- and late-binding techniques.

A .NET component may also be exposed as a COM component. The C# component doesn't need anything special within the code. However, there are utilities that register the C# component and generate a type library.

C# provides full support for COM+ services. By inheriting from the `System.EnterpriseServices.ComPlusServices` class, a C# program inherits all functionality necessary to operate as a COM+ service. Specific COM+ services are implemented by adding appropriate attributes to C# program elements. Special utilities are available to register a C# program as a COM+ service.

41

CHAPTER 42

Instrumenting Applications with System.Diagnostics Types

In several situations, runtime debugging and tracing are desirable. Often it's easy to turn on debugging in a program, let it run, and watch a console screen for specific printouts representing the state of the program during execution. This is a quick way of isolating system failures during development.

For critical code, it may be useful to install a runtime trace facility. This provides a means to capture real-time information on production code and interact with administrators or analysts on what could be causing a problem.

The system libraries have facilities for supporting runtime debugging and tracing. This includes attributes and switches for conditional debugging and multilevel conditions for controlling trace output. It's also possible to monitor the logical implementation of code with assertions.

The System.Diagnostics namespace has two primary classes for runtime debugging: Debug and Trace. For the most part, their functionality is similar; the primary difference between the two comes from how they are used. The Debug class is strictly for development environments and requires a DEBUG directive or command-line option to be specified to activate its functionality. The Trace class is automatically activated and doesn't require any directive or command-line options. This is because the Trace class is for programs to be deployed with debugging capability. Debugging code introduces overhead in a program. If programs should not be deployed with debugging information, which reduces overhead, use the Debug class. However, if there's a need to have debugging information available in deployment and the overhead is acceptable, the Trace class does the trick.

It's agreed that a program must run correctly and produce accurate results, but in many systems this isn't enough. Enterprise-class applications are of such mass that they must also be scalable. Verifying the scalability of an application traditionally requires specialized tools and bolted-on functionality to support monitoring. Now there's help, using the performance counter capability of the System.Diagnostics namespace.

Performance counters present an object framework for supporting application monitoring. The framework hooks into the operating system performance counter system to access available counters. In addition, the performance counter framework can be extended for customized counters and data sampling. Such samples may be collected efficiently with timers, which, as their name suggests, enable periodic execution of logic via specified time intervals. By using either built-in or customized performance counters, a program can be monitored under various conditions to verify its performance and scalability.

Simple Debugging

In its simplest form, runtime debugging is just a matter of printing out statements to the console. The Debug class, a member of the System.Diagnostics namespace, has two methods for supporting explicit debugging: Write and WriteLine. These methods work similarly to their Console class counterparts. Listing 42.1 shows an example that uses the WriteLine method of the Debug class.

LISTING 42.1   A Simple Debugging Example: PlainDebugDemo.cs

```
#define DEBUG

using System;
using System.Diagnostics;

/// <summary>
///     Plain Debug Demo.
/// </summary>
class PlainDebugDemo
{
    static void DebuggedMethod()
    {
        Debug.WriteLine("Debug: Entered MyMethod()");
    }

    static void Main(string[] args)
    {
        TextWriterTraceListener myListener =
            new TextWriterTraceListener(Console.Out);

        Debug.Listeners.Add(myListener);
```

LISTING 42.1   Continued

```
        DebuggedMethod();
    }
}
```

And here's the output:

```
Debug: Entered MyMethod()
```

Setting up a program for debugging requires statements to specify where debug output should be sent. The `Main` method in Listing 42.1 creates a `TextWriterTraceListener` class that directs debugging output to the console window. It then adds the listener to the collection of `Debug` listeners.

Listing 42.1 used a `TextWriter` object, `Console.out`, as its output destination. However, debug output could have been just as well sent to a file by instantiating a `Stream` object and providing it as the parameter to the `TextWriterTraceListener` instantiation. The `TextWriterTraceListener` class also has methods to flush and close debug output with the `Flush` and `Close` methods, respectively.

The `Listeners` collection of the `Debug` class accepts any derived `TraceListener` class. Therefore, it's possible to create customized trace listeners by deriving them from either the `TraceListener` or `TextWriterTraceListener` classes.

After an output destination has been set up, the program invokes the `DebuggedMethod` method, which calls the `WriteLine` method of the `Debug` class. This produces the output shown following the listing.

There are a couple ways to enable debugging. At the top of Listing 42.1 is a `#define DEBUG` directive, enabling the operation of the `Debug` class. In addition, Listing 42.2 shows how to enable debugging with the command-line option, `/d:DEBUG`. One or the other of these methods, directive or compilation option, enables debugging, but they both are not required together. If neither of these, directive or compilation option, is present, the `Debug` class does not operate, and there would be no output.

LISTING 42.2   Compilation Instructions for Listing 42.1

```
csc /d:DEBUG PlainDebugDemo.cs
```

Conditional Debugging

A program's capability to turn debugging on and off as needed is called conditional debugging. During development, output from debugging can clutter up normal output or force paths of execution that aren't necessary on every run. The `System.Diagnostics` namespace has both attributes and switches to turn debugging on and off as necessary. Listing 42.3 shows how to use attributes to control conditional debugging.

LISTING 42.3   Debugging with Conditional Attributes: ConditionalDebugDemo.cs

```csharp
#define DEBUG

using System;
using System.Diagnostics;

/// <summary>
///     Conditional Debug Demo.
/// </summary>
class ConditionalDebugDemo
{
    static bool Debugging = true;

    [Conditional("DEBUG")]
    static void SetupDebugListener()
    {
        TextWriterTraceListener myListener =
            new TextWriterTraceListener(Console.Out);

        Debug.Listeners.Add(myListener);
    }

    [Conditional("DEBUG")]
    static void CheckState()
    {
        Debug.WriteLineIf(Debugging, "Debug: Entered CheckState()");
    }

    static void Main(string[] args)
    {
        SetupDebugListener();

        CheckState();
    }
}
```

And here's the output:

```
Debug: Entered CheckState()
```

Two features of Listing 42.3 are of primary interest: the Conditional attribute and a
Boolean condition on output. The Conditional attribute is placed at the beginning of a
method that can be turned on and off at will. The condition causing the method to be
invoked is either the #define DEBUG directive at the top of the listing or the command

line /d:DEBUG option, shown in Listing 42.4. If neither of these, directive or command-line option, is present, the methods with the Conditional attribute are invoked when called by the Main method.

LISTING 42.4   Compilation Instructions for Listing 42.3

```
csc /d:DEBUG ConditionalDebugDemo.cs
```

The second item of interest in Listing 42.3 is the Boolean condition parameter of the WriteLineIf method in the CheckState method. The WriteLineIf method of the Debug class has a first parameter that takes a bool. In the example, the static class field Debugging is used as an argument. It's set to true, but had it been set to false, there would have been no output.

The examples presented so far expect that the code will be recompiled to turn debugging on and off. In a development environment, this is fine. In production, however, such luxury is not likely to be available. That's why the example in Listing 42.5 uses the BooleanSwitch and Trace classes.

LISTING 42.5   Implementing Debugging with a Boolean Switch: BooleanSwitchDemo.cs

```
using System;
using System.Diagnostics;

/// <summary>
///     BooleanSwitch Demo.
/// </summary>
class BooleanSwitchDemo
{
    BooleanSwitch traceOutput = new
        BooleanSwitch("TraceOutput", "Boolean Switch Demo");

    void SetupDebugListener()
    {
        TextWriterTraceListener myListener =
            new TextWriterTraceListener(Console.Out);

        Trace.Listeners.Add(myListener);
    }

    void CheckState()
    {
        Trace.WriteLineIf(traceOutput.Enabled,
            "Debug: Entered CheckState()");
    }

    static void Main(string[] args)
```

LISTING 42.5   Continued

```
    {
        BooleanSwitchDemo bsd = new BooleanSwitchDemo();

        bsd.SetupDebugListener();
        bsd.CheckState();
    }
}
```

And here's the output:

```
Debug: Entered CheckState()
```

The CheckState method of Listing 42.5 is similar to the same method in Listing 42.3, except that the WriteLineIf method uses the Enabled property of a BooleanSwitch object as its first parameter. The BooleanSwitch class is instantiated with a first parameter as the display name and a second parameter as a description.

An entry must be added to the program's configuration file to turn on tracing. Listing 42.6 shows how to add the BooleanSwitch display name entry into the configuration file. The configuration file must have the same name as the executable with a .config extension.

LISTING 42.6   **BooleanSwitch** entry in Configuration File: BooleanSwitchDemo.config

```
<configuration>
    <system.diagnostics>
        <switches>
            <add name="TraceOutput" value="1" />
        </switches>
    </system.diagnostics>
</configuration>
```

LISTING 42.7   Compilation Instructions for Listing 42.5

```
csc /d:TRACE BooleanSwitchDemo.cs
```

Runtime Tracing

Runtime tracing is the ability to perform debug tracing while a program is running. Sometimes it's necessary to have more control over what debugging information is displayed. Specific types of problems often indicate what information should be displayed in trace output. The TraceSwitch class is similar to the BooleanSwitch class in that it allows you to create a configuration file or set an environment variable. However, its real value comes in being able to specify a finer degree of granularity in determining what information is displayed. Listing 42.8 demonstrates how to use the TraceSwitch class.

LISTING 42.8   **TraceSwitch** Class Demo: TraceSwitchDemo.cs

```csharp
using System;
using System.Diagnostics;

/// <summary>
///     TraceSwitch Demo.
/// </summary>
class TraceSwitchDemo
{
    public static TraceSwitch traceOutput = new
        TraceSwitch("TraceOutput", "TraceSwitch Demo");

    void SetupDebugListener()
    {
        TextWriterTraceListener myListener =
            new TextWriterTraceListener(Console.Out);

        Trace.Listeners.Add(myListener);
    }

    void CheckState()
    {
        Trace.WriteLineIf(traceOutput.TraceInfo,
            "Trace: Entered CheckState()");
    }

    static void Main(string[] args)
    {
        TraceSwitchDemo tsd = new TraceSwitchDemo();

        tsd.SetupDebugListener();
        tsd.CheckState();
    }
}
```

And here's the output:

```
Trace: Entered CheckState()
```

The implementation of the TraceSwitch is similar to the BooleanSwitch, except that the first parameter to the WriteLineIf method in the CheckState method is the TraceInfo property of the TraceSwitch class. This parameter can be any of the possible values corresponding to a member of the TraceLevel enum, shown in Table 42.1.

TABLE 42.1   **TraceLevel** Enum

TraceLevel **Enum**	**Description**
Verbose	Output everything
Info	Output info, error, and warning
Warning	Output error and warning
Error	Output error
Off	Output nothing

TraceSwitch must be set in a configuration file. Values may be from 0 to 4, with Verbose equal to 4 and descending to Off, which is equal to 0. It's possible to create a custom switch by inheriting the Switch class and defining Boolean properties with your own unique names that map to the available members of the TraceLevel enum. The configuration file in Listing 42.9 has TraceOutput set to 3, which causes evaluation of TraceInfo to return true.

LISTING 42.9   **TraceSwitch** entry in Config File: TraceSwitchDemo.config

```
<configuration>
    <system.diagnostics>
        <switches>
            <add name="TraceOutput" value="3" />
        </switches>
    </system.diagnostics>
</configuration>
```

LISTING 42.10   Compilation Instructions for Listing 42.8

```
csc /d:TRACE TraceSwitchDemo.cs
```

Making Assertions

Another common debugging task is to check the state of a program at various intervals for logical consistency. This is performed with the Debug.Assert method. By sprinkling Assert methods at strategic points in a routine, such as preconditions, intermediate state, and postconditions, you can verify that routine's logical consistency. Whenever the assertion proves false, a given message is displayed in the form of a message box. Listing 42.11 has a simple program demonstrating the mechanics of the Assert method.

LISTING 42.11   Assertion Demonstration: AssertDemo.cs

```
using System;
using System.Diagnostics;

/// <summary>
///     Assertion Demonstration.
/// </summary>
class AssertDemo
{
    static void Main(string[] args)
    {
        decimal profit = -0.01m;

        // do some calculations

        Debug.Assert(profit >= 0.0m,
            "Illogical Negative Profit Calculation");
    }
}
```

The example in Listing 42.11 simulates some fictitious profit calculation that should never return a negative result. The Debug.Assert method takes two parameters. The first is the logical condition to check, which should evaluate to a Boolean true or false. In this case, it's making sure the profit is always zero or greater. The second parameter is the message to be displayed. The example forces the assertion to evaluate to false, displaying the message shown in Figure 42.1.

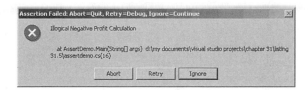

FIGURE 42.1   Assertion message box.

Assertions are designed to work only in debugging mode. Therefore, you will want to add a /define switch to the command-line when debugging. This program can be compiled with the command line in Listing 42.12.

LISTING 42.12   Compilation Instructions for Listing 42.11

```
csc /d:DEBUG AssertDemo.cs
```

Accessing Built-In Performance Counters

The performance counter framework provides access to existing operating system counters. The help files associated with the operating system performance monitor application have more information on what counters are available.

Using a performance counter involves declaring a PerformanceCounter object, initializing its properties as desired, and requesting the counter value at various intervals to watch performance. The program in Listings 42.13 and 42.14 comprises a fictitious ordering system that demonstrates the use of system performance counters. The program is sufficiently equipped to degrade system performance, where the effects can be observed by watching the performance counter. The project in Listing 42.13 is a Windows Forms project, which is different from the typical Console application most of this book has used. Hopefully, you'll find it to be a welcome change and helpful for working with GUI technology.

LISTING 42.13   System Performance Counter Demo: OrderClient.cs

```
using System;
using System.Drawing;
using System.Collections;
using System.ComponentModel;
using System.Windows.Forms;
using System.Data;
using System.Threading;
using System.Diagnostics;

namespace OrderingClient
{
    /// <summary>
    /// Performance Counter Demo.
    /// </summary>
    public class OrderClient : System.Windows.Forms.Form
    {
        private System.Windows.Forms.Label maxOrdLbl;
        private System.Windows.Forms.Label curOrdLbl;
        private System.Windows.Forms.TextBox maxOrdTxt;
        private System.Windows.Forms.Label curOrdResultLbl;
        private System.Windows.Forms.Button updateBtn;
        private int maxOrders;
        private int curOrders;
        private OrderProcessor orderProc;
        private System.Windows.Forms.Timer orderTimer;
        private System.Windows.Forms.Timer countTimer;
        private System.Windows.Forms.Label threadLbl;
        private System.Windows.Forms.Label threadResultLbl;
```

LISTING 42.13   Continued

```
    private System.Diagnostics.PerformanceCounter
        threadCounter;

    private System.ComponentModel.IContainer components;

    public OrderClient()
    {
        InitializeComponent();
        maxOrders = 10;
        maxOrdTxt.Text = maxOrders.ToString();
        orderProc = new OrderProcessor();
        curOrders = orderProc.CurNoOrders;
        curOrdResultLbl.Text = curOrders.ToString();
    }

    /// <summary>
    /// Clean up any resources being used.
    /// </summary>
    protected override void Dispose( bool disposing )
    {
        if( disposing )
        {
            if (components != null)
            {
                components.Dispose();
            }
        }
        base.Dispose( disposing );
    }

    private void InitializeComponent()
    {
        this.components =
            new System.ComponentModel.Container();
        this.maxOrdTxt =
            new System.Windows.Forms.TextBox();
        this.updateBtn =
            new System.Windows.Forms.Button();
        this.maxOrdLbl =
            new System.Windows.Forms.Label();
        this.curOrdLbl =
            new System.Windows.Forms.Label();
        this.orderTimer =
            new System.Windows.Forms.Timer(
                this.components);
```

42

LISTING 42.13   Continued

```
            this.curOrdResultLbl =
                new System.Windows.Forms.Label();
            this.countTimer =
                new System.Windows.Forms.Timer(
                    this.components);
            this.threadLbl =
                new System.Windows.Forms.Label();
            this.threadResultLbl =
                new System.Windows.Forms.Label();
            this.threadCounter =
                new System.Diagnostics.PerformanceCounter();
              ((System.ComponentModel.ISupportInitialize)
                    (this.threadCounter)).BeginInit();
            this.SuspendLayout();

            this.maxOrdTxt.Location =
                new System.Drawing.Point(152, 24);
            this.maxOrdTxt.Name = "maxOrdTxt";
            this.maxOrdTxt.TabIndex = 2;
            this.maxOrdTxt.Text = "";
            this.maxOrdTxt.TextAlign =
              System.Windows.Forms.HorizontalAlignment.Right;

            this.updateBtn.Location =
                new System.Drawing.Point(104, 152);
            this.updateBtn.Name = "updateBtn";
            this.updateBtn.TabIndex = 4;
            this.updateBtn.Text = "Update";
            this.updateBtn.Click +=
                new System.EventHandler(this.updateBtn_Click);

            this.maxOrdLbl.Location =
                new System.Drawing.Point(40, 24);
            this.maxOrdLbl.Name = "maxOrdLbl";
            this.maxOrdLbl.TabIndex = 0;
            this.maxOrdLbl.Text = "Max Orders:";
            this.maxOrdLbl.TextAlign =
                System.Drawing.ContentAlignment.MiddleRight;

            this.curOrdLbl.Location =
                new System.Drawing.Point(40, 64);
            this.curOrdLbl.Name = "curOrdLbl";
            this.curOrdLbl.TabIndex = 1;
            this.curOrdLbl.Text = "Current Orders:";
            this.curOrdLbl.TextAlign =
                System.Drawing.ContentAlignment.MiddleRight;
```

LISTING 42.13   Continued

```
            this.orderTimer.Enabled = true;
            this.orderTimer.Interval = 2000;
            this.orderTimer.Tick +=
                new System.EventHandler(this.orderTimer_Tick);

            this.curOrdResultLbl.BorderStyle =
                System.Windows.Forms.BorderStyle.Fixed3D;
            this.curOrdResultLbl.Location =
                new System.Drawing.Point(152, 64);
            this.curOrdResultLbl.Name = "curOrdResultLbl";
            this.curOrdResultLbl.Size =
                new System.Drawing.Size(100, 20);
            this.curOrdResultLbl.TabIndex = 3;
            this.curOrdResultLbl.TextAlign =
                System.Drawing.ContentAlignment.MiddleRight;

            this.countTimer.Enabled = true;
            this.countTimer.Interval = 1000;
            this.countTimer.Tick +=
                new System.EventHandler(this.countTimer_Tick);

            this.threadLbl.Location =
                new System.Drawing.Point(40, 104);
            this.threadLbl.Name = "threadLbl";
            this.threadLbl.TabIndex = 1;
            this.threadLbl.Text = "Thread Count:";
            this.threadLbl.TextAlign =
                System.Drawing.ContentAlignment.MiddleRight;

            this.threadResultLbl.BorderStyle =
                System.Windows.Forms.BorderStyle.Fixed3D;
            this.threadResultLbl.Location =
                new System.Drawing.Point(152, 104);
            this.threadResultLbl.Name = "threadResultLbl";
            this.threadResultLbl.Size =
                new System.Drawing.Size(100, 20);
            this.threadResultLbl.TabIndex = 3;
            this.threadResultLbl.TextAlign =
                System.Drawing.ContentAlignment.MiddleRight;

            this.threadCounter.CategoryName =
                ".NET CLR LocksAndThreads";
            this.threadCounter.CounterName =
                "# of current physical Threads";
            this.threadCounter.InstanceName =
                "OrderingClient";
```

LISTING 42.13 Continued

```
        this.AutoScaleBaseSize =
            new System.Drawing.Size(5, 13);
        this.ClientSize =
            new System.Drawing.Size(288, 197);
        this.Controls.AddRange(
            new System.Windows.Forms.Control[] {
                this.threadLbl,
                this.threadResultLbl,
                this.updateBtn,
                this.curOrdResultLbl,
                this.maxOrdTxt,
                this.curOrdLbl,
                this.maxOrdLbl});
        this.Name = "OrderClient";
        this.Text = "Order Client";
        ((System.ComponentModel.ISupportInitialize)
            (this.threadCounter)).EndInit();
        this.ResumeLayout(false);
    }

    static void Main()
    {
        Application.Run(new OrderClient());
    }

    private void updateBtn_Click(object sender, System.EventArgs e)
    {
        maxOrders = Convert.ToInt32(maxOrdTxt.Text);
    }

    private void orderTimer_Tick(object sender, System.EventArgs e)
    {
        orderTimer.Enabled = false;
        Thread th = new Thread(new ThreadStart(ProcessOrders));
        th.Start();

        orderTimer.Enabled = true;
    }

    private void countTimer_Tick(object sender, System.EventArgs e)
    {
        countTimer.Enabled = false;
        curOrdResultLbl.Text = orderProc.CurNoOrders.ToString();
        threadResultLbl.Text = threadCounter.NextValue().ToString();
```

LISTING 42.13   Continued

```csharp
                countTimer.Enabled = true;
        }

        private void ProcessOrders()
        {
            for (curOrders = orderProc.CurNoOrders;
                  curOrders <= maxOrders;
                  curOrders++)
            {
                curOrdResultLbl.Text = curOrders.ToString();
                orderProc.ProcessOrder();
            }
        }
    }
}
```

LISTING 42.14   Server Component of System Performance Counter Demo: OrderProcessor.cs

```csharp
using System;
using System.Threading;

namespace OrderingClient
{
    /// <summary>
    /// Summary description for OrderProcessor.
    /// </summary>
    public class OrderProcessor
    {
        private static int curNoOrders = 0;
        private Random rand;

        public OrderProcessor()
        {
            rand = new Random();
        }

        public int ProcessOrder()
        {
            Thread th = new Thread(new ThreadStart(doOrder));
            th.Start();

            curNoOrders++;
            return 0;
        }
```

LISTING 42.14   Continued

```
    public int CurNoOrders
    {
        get
        {
            return curNoOrders;
        }
        set
        {
            curNoOrders = value;
        }
    }

    private void doOrder()
    {
        for (int delay = rand.Next(10000000);
            delay >= 0;
            delay—)
            ;

        curNoOrders—;
    }
  }
}
```

The performance counter framework belongs to the System.Diagnostics namespace. Performance counters are declared like any other class, as follows:

```
    private System.Diagnostics.PerformanceCounter
        threadCounter;
```

This particular performance counter keeps track of the number of .NET Common Language Runtime (CLR) threads. Three pertinent properties of a performance counter are required (CategoryName, CounterName, and InstanceName), as shown next:

```
        this.threadCounter.CategoryName =
            ".NET CLR LocksAndThreads";
        this.threadCounter.CounterName =
            "# of current physical Threads";
        this.threadCounter.InstanceName =
            "OrderingClient";
```

Performance counters are broken into categories that help organize each counter into a logical related group. The preceding example sets the category for the threadCounter object to ".NET CLR LocksAndThreads". An examination of this category in the .NET Framework documentation shows that this category has counters for different types of threads and other counters associated with thread synchronization. This example assigns the "# of current physical Threads" counter to the CounterName property of the threadCounter object. The InstanceName property holds the name of the executable file whose count property will be monitored.

To get the value of the counter, call the NextValue method of the PerformanceCounter object. The following example shows how to do this:

```
threadResultLbl.Text = threadCounter.NextValue().ToString();
```

The example converts the integer value returned from the NextValue method into a string and places it into a Windows Forms label control for presentation onscreen. Figure 42.2 shows what the code from Listings 42.13 and 41.14 looks like when compiled and executed. Increasing the number in the Max Orders text box stresses the system. This can be observed by watching the numbers change more sluggishly, indicating performance degradation.

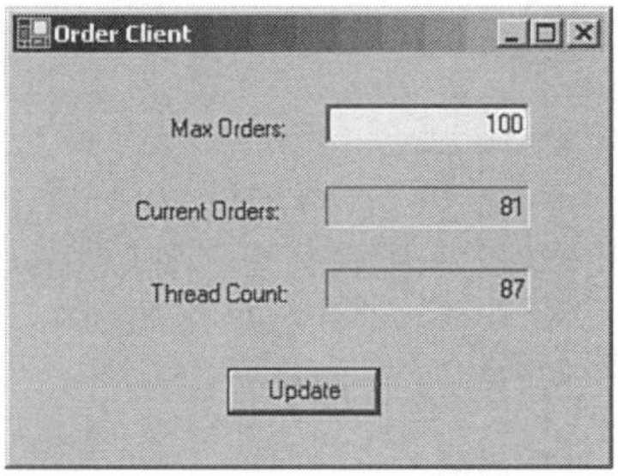

FIGURE 42.2   A system performance counter.

The program from Listings 32.1 and 32.2 uses threads extensively. OrderClient uses threads to execute its loop efficiently. It finishes quickly so that it doesn't hold up any other program activities, such as the ability to update Max Orders, update the count fields, and execute timers.

The OrderProcessor class uses threads so that it can accept orders efficiently without making the client block for each order. Otherwise, there would be no telling how long it could take to process an order, because the program is set to take a random amount of time for each order. This simulates the nature of many ordering systems, which typically have multiple types of orders and several options or variables that make the amount of time for each order practically unpredictable.

TIP

As the world turns, Moore's law has my faithful but inadequate computer dragging behind in performance. If you don't experience significant performance hits when incrementing Max Orders in this program, bump up the number of zeros in the rand.Next method in the for loop initializer of the doOrder method in Listing 32.2.

Implementing Timers

It would be easy to use existing C# constructs, such as sleeping threads or for and while loops, to control the periodic collection of performance counter data. The primary problems with these methods are their synchronous nature. Furthermore, loops such as for and while deliver a significant performance hit. A better solution for performing logic via specified intervals is the timer.

A timer can be set for a specified time interval, executing a callback routine whenever that interval elapses. The primary benefit of this approach is the asynchronous behavior of the timer, which delivers much better performance than synchronous methods discussed earlier. Just set the timer interval, assign a callback routine to execute, and then move on and process the rest of the program logic. The following example shows how timers are declared:

```
private System.Windows.Forms.Timer orderTimer;
private System.Windows.Forms.Timer countTimer;
```

These timers are members of the System.Windows.Forms namespace. The orderTimer will fire periodically to make sure the number of orders being processed go up to, but not over, the maximum number of orders. The countTimer fires periodically to update the number of orders being processed and to get and display the current value of the threadCounter performance counter. Here's an example of how the timers are set up:

```
this.orderTimer.Enabled = true;
this.orderTimer.Interval = 2000;
this.orderTimer.Tick +=
    new System.EventHandler(this.orderTimer_Tick);

this.countTimer.Enabled = true;
this.countTimer.Interval = 1000;
this.countTimer.Tick +=
    new System.EventHandler(this.countTimer_Tick);
```

Both of these timers have their Enabled properties set to true, meaning that the timers are turned on. A timer can be turned off by setting the Enabled property to false; this is necessary when a program is in the middle of a callback and doesn't want the timer firing while a previous callback based on that timer is still executing.

Setting the Interval property to 1000 makes the timer tick approximately every second. Thus, the orderTimer will tick about every 2 seconds, and the count timer will tick about once per second.

WARNING

Because they are based on the underlying operating system timer, don't bet on timers having a great degree of accuracy. This is because various operating system events may preclude the tick event from firing on time. Therefore, the safest assumption to make with timers is that they provide an approximate timing mechanism.

Callback routines are attached to the Tick event of a timer with the EventHandler dele-gate. The orderTimer timer calls the ordertimer_Tick method, and the countTimer timer calls the countTimer_Tick method when their respective Tick events fire. Listing 32.1 has the full code that shows what these routines do when their Tick event fires.

Building a Customized Performance Counter

Often, the system performance counters are enough for monitoring a system's perfor-mance. However, sometimes you need a specialized counter that gives a unique picture of what's happening in a specific program. Making customized performance counters is possible because of the extensible nature of the performance counter framework.

Implementing a customized performance counter requires creating a new counter type and a new category to hold the new counter. The performance counter will be instantiated with the new counter and category definitions. Additional logic is necessary to load the custom performance counter with program specific data. Listings 42.15 and 42.16 show how to implement custom performance counters.

LISTING 42.15   Client Using Data from Custom Performance Counter: CustomOrderClient.cs

```
using System;
using System.Drawing;
using System.Collections;
using System.ComponentModel;
using System.Windows.Forms;
using System.Data;
using System.Threading;
using System.Diagnostics;


namespace OrderingClient
{
    /// <summary>
    /// Summary description for Form1.
    /// </summary>
    public class CustomClient : System.Windows.Forms.Form
    {
        private System.Windows.Forms.Label maxOrdLbl;
        private System.Windows.Forms.Label curOrdLbl;
        private System.Windows.Forms.TextBox maxOrdTxt;
        private System.Windows.Forms.Label curOrdResultLbl;
        private System.Windows.Forms.Button updateBtn;
        private int maxOrders;
        private int curOrders;
        private CustomOrderProcessor orderProc;
        private System.Windows.Forms.Timer orderTimer;
        private System.Windows.Forms.Timer countTimer;
```

LISTING 42.15   Continued

```csharp
    private System.Windows.Forms.Label threadLbl;
    private System.Windows.Forms.Label threadResultLbl;
    private System.Diagnostics.PerformanceCounter
        threadCounter;
    private System.ComponentModel.IContainer components;

    public CustomClient()
    {
        InitializeComponent();
        maxOrders = 10;
        maxOrdTxt.Text = maxOrders.ToString();
        orderProc = new CustomOrderProcessor();
        curOrders = orderProc.CurNoOrders;
        curOrdResultLbl.Text = curOrders.ToString();
    }

    /// <summary>
    /// Clean up any resources being used.
    /// </summary>
    protected override void Dispose( bool disposing )
    {
        if( disposing )
        {
            if (components != null)
            {
                components.Dispose();
            }
        }
        base.Dispose( disposing );
    }

    private void InitializeComponent()
    {
        this.components =
            new System.ComponentModel.Container();
        this.maxOrdTxt =
            new System.Windows.Forms.TextBox();
        this.threadLbl =
            new System.Windows.Forms.Label();
        this.orderTimer =
            new System.Windows.Forms.Timer(this.components);
        this.updateBtn =
            new System.Windows.Forms.Button();
        this.threadResultLbl =
            new System.Windows.Forms.Label();
        this.curOrdResultLbl =
```

LISTING 42.15   Continued

```
            new System.Windows.Forms.Label();
        this.threadCounter =
            new System.Diagnostics.PerformanceCounter();
        this.curOrdLbl =
            new System.Windows.Forms.Label();
        this.countTimer =
            new System.Windows.Forms.Timer(this.components);
        this.maxOrdLbl =
            new System.Windows.Forms.Label();
        ((System.ComponentModel.ISupportInitialize)
            (this.threadCounter)).BeginInit();
        this.SuspendLayout();

        this.maxOrdTxt.Location =
            new System.Drawing.Point(152, 24);
        this.maxOrdTxt.Name = "maxOrdTxt";
        this.maxOrdTxt.TabIndex = 2;
        this.maxOrdTxt.Text = "";
        this.maxOrdTxt.TextAlign =
          System.Windows.Forms.HorizontalAlignment.Right;

        this.threadLbl.Location =
            new System.Drawing.Point(40, 104);
        this.threadLbl.Name = "threadLbl";
        this.threadLbl.TabIndex = 1;
        this.threadLbl.Text = "Thread Count:";
        this.threadLbl.TextAlign =
            System.Drawing.ContentAlignment.MiddleRight;

        this.orderTimer.Enabled = true;
        this.orderTimer.Interval = 2000;
        this.orderTimer.Tick +=
            new System.EventHandler(this.orderTimer_Tick);

        this.updateBtn.Location =
            new System.Drawing.Point(104, 152);
        this.updateBtn.Name = "updateBtn";
        this.updateBtn.TabIndex = 4;
        this.updateBtn.Text = "Update";
        this.updateBtn.Click +=
            new System.EventHandler(this.updateBtn_Click);

        this.threadResultLbl.BorderStyle =
            System.Windows.Forms.BorderStyle.Fixed3D;
        this.threadResultLbl.Location =
            new System.Drawing.Point(152, 104);
```

LISTING 42.15   Continued

```
            this.threadResultLbl.Name = "threadResultLbl";
            this.threadResultLbl.Size =
                new System.Drawing.Size(100, 20);
            this.threadResultLbl.TabIndex = 3;
            this.threadResultLbl.TextAlign =
                System.Drawing.ContentAlignment.MiddleRight;

            this.curOrdResultLbl.BorderStyle =
                System.Windows.Forms.BorderStyle.Fixed3D;
            this.curOrdResultLbl.Location =
                new System.Drawing.Point(152, 64);
            this.curOrdResultLbl.Name = "curOrdResultLbl";
            this.curOrdResultLbl.Size =
                new System.Drawing.Size(100, 20);
            this.curOrdResultLbl.TabIndex = 3;
            this.curOrdResultLbl.TextAlign =
                System.Drawing.ContentAlignment.MiddleRight;

            this.threadCounter.CategoryName =
                ".NET CLR LocksAndThreads";
            this.threadCounter.CounterName =
                "# of current physical Threads";
            this.threadCounter.InstanceName =
                "CustomClient";

            this.curOrdLbl.Location =
                new System.Drawing.Point(40, 64);
            this.curOrdLbl.Name = "curOrdLbl";
            this.curOrdLbl.TabIndex = 1;
            this.curOrdLbl.Text = "Current Orders:";
            this.curOrdLbl.TextAlign =
                System.Drawing.ContentAlignment.MiddleRight;

            this.countTimer.Enabled = true;
            this.countTimer.Interval = 1000;
            this.countTimer.Tick +=
                new System.EventHandler(this.countTimer_Tick);

            this.maxOrdLbl.Location =
                new System.Drawing.Point(40, 24);
            this.maxOrdLbl.Name = "maxOrdLbl";
            this.maxOrdLbl.TabIndex = 0;
            this.maxOrdLbl.Text = "Max Orders:";
            this.maxOrdLbl.TextAlign =
                System.Drawing.ContentAlignment.MiddleRight;
```

LISTING 42.15   Continued

```csharp
            this.AutoScaleBaseSize =
                new System.Drawing.Size(5, 13);
            this.ClientSize =
                new System.Drawing.Size(288, 197);
            this.Controls.AddRange(
                new System.Windows.Forms.Control[] {
                    this.threadLbl,
                    this.threadResultLbl,
                    this.updateBtn,
                    this.curOrdResultLbl,
                    this.maxOrdTxt,
                    this.curOrdLbl,
                    this.maxOrdLbl});
            this.Name = "CustomClient";
            this.Text = "Custom Client";
            this.Closing +=
                new System.ComponentModel.CancelEventHandler(
                    this.CustomClient_Closing);
            ((System.ComponentModel.ISupportInitialize)
                (this.threadCounter)).EndInit();
            this.ResumeLayout(false);
        }

        static void Main()
        {
            Application.Run(new CustomClient());
        }

        private void updateBtn_Click(
            object sender, System.EventArgs e)
        {
            maxOrders = Convert.ToInt32(maxOrdTxt.Text);
        }

        private void orderTimer_Tick(
            object sender, System.EventArgs e)
        {
            orderTimer.Enabled = false;

            Thread th = new Thread(
                new ThreadStart(ProcessOrders));
            th.Start();

            orderTimer.Enabled = true;
        }
```

LISTING 42.15   Continued

```csharp
        private void countTimer_Tick(
            object sender, System.EventArgs e)
        {
            countTimer.Enabled = false;

            curOrdResultLbl.Text =
                orderProc.CurNoOrders.ToString();
            threadResultLbl.Text =
                threadCounter.NextValue().ToString();

            countTimer.Enabled = true;
        }

        private void ProcessOrders()
        {
            for (curOrders = orderProc.CurNoOrders;
                 curOrders <= maxOrders;
                 curOrders++)
            {
                curOrdResultLbl.Text = curOrders.ToString();
                orderProc.ProcessOrder();
            }
        }

        private void CustomClient_Closing(object sender,
            System.ComponentModel.CancelEventArgs e)
        {
            orderProc.Dispose();
        }
    }
}
```

LISTING 42.16   Server Implementing a Custom Performance Counter:
CustomOrderProcessor.cs

```csharp
using System;
using System.Threading;
using System.Diagnostics;

namespace OrderingClient
{
    /// <summary>
    /// Summary description for CustomOrderProcessor.
    /// </summary>
    public class CustomOrderProcessor : IDisposable
```

LISTING 42.16   Continued

```
{
    private PerformanceCounter orderCounter;
    private Random rand;

    public CustomOrderProcessor()
    {
        rand = new Random();

        CounterCreationDataCollection myCounters =
            new CounterCreationDataCollection();

        CounterCreationData myCounterCreationData =
            new CounterCreationData();

        myCounterCreationData.CounterName =
            "Order Count";
        myCounterCreationData.CounterHelp =
            "Displays number of orders being processed.";
        myCounterCreationData.CounterType =
            PerformanceCounterType.NumberOfItems32;

        myCounters.Add(myCounterCreationData);

        if (PerformanceCounterCategory.Exists(
            "Order Processor"))
        {
            PerformanceCounterCategory.Delete(
                "Order Processor");
        }

        PerformanceCounterCategory.Create(
            "Order Processor",
            "OrderProcessor class counters",
            PerformanceCounterCategoryType.MultiInstance,
            myCounters);

        orderCounter = new PerformanceCounter(
            "Order Processor",
            "Order Count",
            false);

        orderCounter.RawValue = 0;
    }

    public int ProcessOrder()
    {
```

42

LISTING 42.16   Continued

```
        Thread th = new Thread(new ThreadStart(doOrder));
        th.Start();

        CurNoOrders++;
        return 0;
    }

    public int CurNoOrders
    {
        get
        {
            return (int)orderCounter.NextValue();
        }
        set
        {
            orderCounter.RawValue = value;
        }
    }

    private void doOrder()
    {
        for (int delay = rand.Next(1000000);
            delay >= 0;
            delay—)
            ;
        CurNoOrders—;
    }

    public void Dispose()
    {
        PerformanceCounterCategory.Delete(
            "Order Processor");
    }
    }
}
```

The interesting bits of this program are in Listing 42.15. The custom counter is initialized in the constructor, and the updates are managed with the CurNoOrders property. The two primary classes supporting custom counters are CounterCreationDataCollection and CounterCreationData, which are each instantiated with default constructors, as shown here:

```
    CounterCreationDataCollection myCounters =
        new CounterCreationDataCollection();
```

```
CounterCreationData myCounterCreationData =
    new CounterCreationData();
```

The `CounterCreationData` class holds counter definition properties that must be set to create a new counter. The `CounterName` property is a user-defined name of a counter. The `CounterType` property may be any member of the `PerformanceCounterType` enum, which are listed in Table 42.2. The following code sets the `CounterCreationData` properties, including the `CounterHelp` property, which is a description of the custom counter:

```
myCounterCreationData.CounterName =
    "Order Count";
myCounterCreationData.CounterHelp =
    "Displays number of orders being processed.";
myCounterCreationData.CounterType =
    PerformanceCounterType.NumberOfItems32;
```

TABLE 42.2   Members of the **PerformanceCounterType** Enum

Counter Name	Description
AverageBase	Denominator for AverageCount32 and AverageCount64
AverageCount64	64-bit average count
AverageCount32	32-bit average count
AverageTimer32	32-bit average elapsed time
CounterDelta32	32-bit difference between counts
CounterDelta64	64-bit difference between counts
CounterMultiBase	Denominator for CounterMultiTimer, CounterMultiTimerInverse, CounterMultiTimer100Ns, and CounterMultiTimer100NsInverse
CounterMultiTimer	Multiple time samplings—in use
CounterMultiTimer100Ns	Multiple time samplings in 100-nanosecond units
CounterMultiTimerInverse	Multiple time samplings—not in use
CounterTimer	Time sampling—in use
CounterTimerInverse	Time sampling—not in use
CountPerTimeInterval32	32-bit count per time interval
CountPerTimeInterval64	64-bit count per time interval
ElapsedTime	Difference between timer start and sample
NumberOfItems32	32-bit count
NumberOfItems64	64-bit count
NumberOfItemsHEX32	32-bit hexadecimal count
NumberOfItemsHEX64	64-bit hexadecimal count
RateOfCountsPerSecond32	32-bit number of counts per second
RateOfCountsPerSecond64	64-bit number of counts per second
RawBase	Denominator for RawFraction

TABLE 42.2   Continued

Counter Name	Description
RawFraction	Numerator of a fractional count
SampleBase	Denominator representing number of samplings
SampleCounter	Number of ones returned from 0 or 1 count
SampleFraction	Percentage of ones returned from 0 or 1 count
Timer100Ns	Time in 100-nanosecond units—in use
Timer100NsInverse	Time in 100-nanosecond units—not in use

After the new counter has been defined, add the `CounterCreationData` object to the `CounterCreationDataCollection` object. This completes definition of the counter, and now the counter must be added to a category. To create the `CounterCategory`, call the static `Create` method of the `PerformanceCounterCategory` class with four parameters: category name, category description, PerformanceCounterCategoryType, and the `CounterCreationDataCollection` object just described. Multiple counters may be added to a category by just adding more `CounterCreationData` counters to the `CounterCreationDataCollection` object used as the fourth parameter to the `Create` method of the `PerformanceCounterCategory` class. Here's the definition of the customized counter with a custom category:

```
myCounters.Add(myCounterCreationData);


if (PerformanceCounterCategory.Exists(
    "Order Processor"))
{
    PerformanceCounterCategory.Delete(
        "Order Processor");
}

PerformanceCounterCategory.Create(
    "Order Processor",
    "OrderProcessor class counters",
    PerformanceCounterCategoryType.MultiInstance,
    myCounters);
```

This example also contains a check for whether the new category exists. If this is true, the category is deleted before it is re-created. If a performance counter category already exists, it can't be re-created, and therefore a runtime exception is thrown. This program could just as well have used an exception handler around this code, which might be better form. However, to be instructive, this example shows how to use the `Exists` and `Delete` methods of the `PerformanceCounterCategory` class. There's also a `Delete` method call in the `Dispose` method so that the program doesn't leave counters laying around unnecessarily.

The performance counter object for this new custom performance counter is declared the same as any other performance counter. One important item to address is that a program must manage the custom counter itself, updating its value as appropriate. This performance counter value is initialized by setting its RawValue property to 0, as the following code shows:

```
orderCounter = new PerformanceCounter(
    "Order Processor",
    "Order Count",
    false);

orderCounter.RawValue = 0;
```

Subsequent management of the custom performance counter resides in the CurNoOrders property. The get accessor obtains the NextValue, a float result, and casts it to an int before returning the value. The set accessor directly sets the counter's RawValue property. Here's the CurNoOrders property:

```
public int CurNoOrders
{
    get
    {
        return (int)orderCounter.NextValue();
    }
    set
    {
        orderCounter.RawValue = value;
    }
}
```

Custom performance counters present a unique view of special conditions within a program. They provide insight not available with the generalized view of system performance counters. Figure 42.3 shows the executed program from Listings 42.15 and 42.16. Here are the compilation instructions:

```
csc /t:winexe /out:CustomClient.exe CustomClient.cs CustomOrderProcessor.cs
```

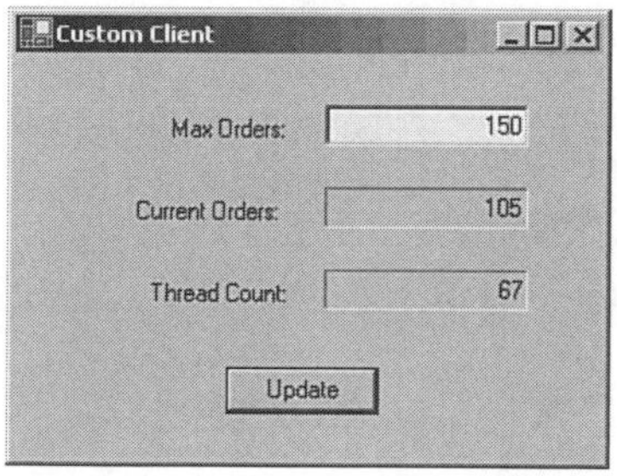

FIGURE 42.3   A custom performance counter.

Analyzing Performance with Sampling

Previous programs in this chapter provided interesting statistics to look at and even provided a general idea of what was happening with system performance. This is nice, but sometimes you need to zero in on what's going on with a program and get a better picture of a more sophisticated scenario. Performance counter sampling does just that.

Sampling is the capability to perform specialized calculations between successive performance counter results. This is especially relevant in tracking averages and discovering trends. Listings 42.17 and 42.18 show how to create a custom performance counter that performs sampling.

LISTING 42.17   Sampling Client: SampleClient.cs

```
using System;
using System.Drawing;
using System.Collections;
using System.ComponentModel;
using System.Windows.Forms;
using System.Data;
using System.Threading;
using System.Diagnostics;

namespace OrderingClient
{
    /// <summary>
    /// Summary description for Form1.
    /// </summary>
    public class SampleClient : System.Windows.Forms.Form
    {
        private System.Windows.Forms.Label maxOrdLbl;
        private System.Windows.Forms.TextBox maxOrdTxt;
        private System.Windows.Forms.Button updateBtn;
        private int maxOrders;
        private int curOrders;
        private CustomSamplingProcessor orderProc;
        private System.Windows.Forms.Timer orderTimer;
        private System.Windows.Forms.Timer countTimer;
        private System.Windows.Forms.Label threadLbl;
        private System.Windows.Forms.Label threadResultLbl;
        private System.Diagnostics.PerformanceCounter
            threadCounter;
        private System.Windows.Forms.Label ordRateResultLbl;
        private System.Windows.Forms.Label ordRateLbl;
        private System.ComponentModel.IContainer components;
```

LISTING 42.17   Continued

```csharp
public SampleClient()
{
    InitializeComponent();
    maxOrders = 10;
    maxOrdTxt.Text = maxOrders.ToString();
    orderProc = new CustomSamplingProcessor();
    curOrders = orderProc.CurNoOrders;
    ordRateResultLbl.Text = curOrders.ToString();
}

/// <summary>
/// Clean up any resources being used.
/// </summary>
protected override void Dispose( bool disposing )
{
    if( disposing )
    {
        if (components != null)
        {
            components.Dispose();
        }
    }
    base.Dispose( disposing );
}

private void InitializeComponent()
{
    this.components =
        new System.ComponentModel.Container();
    this.maxOrdTxt =
        new System.Windows.Forms.TextBox();
    this.ordRateResultLbl =
        new System.Windows.Forms.Label();
    this.threadLbl =
        new System.Windows.Forms.Label();
    this.ordRateLbl =
        new System.Windows.Forms.Label();
    this.orderTimer =
        new System.Windows.Forms.Timer(
            this.components);
    this.updateBtn =
        new System.Windows.Forms.Button();
    this.threadResultLbl =
        new System.Windows.Forms.Label();
    this.threadCounter =
        new System.Diagnostics.PerformanceCounter();
```

42

LISTING 42.17   Continued

```
            this.countTimer =
                new System.Windows.Forms.Timer(
                    this.components);
            this.maxOrdLbl =
                new System.Windows.Forms.Label();
            ((System.ComponentModel.ISupportInitialize)
                (this.threadCounter)).BeginInit();
            this.SuspendLayout();

            this.maxOrdTxt.Location =
                new System.Drawing.Point(152, 24);
            this.maxOrdTxt.Name = "maxOrdTxt";
            this.maxOrdTxt.TabIndex = 2;
            this.maxOrdTxt.Text = "";
            this.maxOrdTxt.TextAlign =
              System.Windows.Forms.HorizontalAlignment.Right;

            this.ordRateResultLbl.BorderStyle =
                System.Windows.Forms.BorderStyle.Fixed3D;
            this.ordRateResultLbl.Location =
                new System.Drawing.Point(152, 64);
            this.ordRateResultLbl.Name = "ordRateResultLbl";
            this.ordRateResultLbl.Size =
                new System.Drawing.Size(100, 20);
            this.ordRateResultLbl.TabIndex = 3;
            this.ordRateResultLbl.TextAlign =
                System.Drawing.ContentAlignment.MiddleRight;

            this.threadLbl.Location =
                new System.Drawing.Point(40, 104);
            this.threadLbl.Name = "threadLbl";
            this.threadLbl.TabIndex = 1;
            this.threadLbl.Text = "Thread Count:";
            this.threadLbl.TextAlign =
                System.Drawing.ContentAlignment.MiddleRight;

            this.ordRateLbl.Location =
                new System.Drawing.Point(40, 64);
            this.ordRateLbl.Name = "ordRateLbl";
            this.ordRateLbl.TabIndex = 1;
            this.ordRateLbl.Text = "Orders/Sec:";
            this.ordRateLbl.TextAlign =
                System.Drawing.ContentAlignment.MiddleRight;

            this.orderTimer.Enabled = true;
            this.orderTimer.Interval = 2000;
```

LISTING 42.17   Continued

```
            this.orderTimer.Tick +=
                new System.EventHandler(
                    this.orderTimer_Tick);

            this.updateBtn.Location =
                new System.Drawing.Point(104, 152);
            this.updateBtn.Name = "updateBtn";
            this.updateBtn.TabIndex = 4;
            this.updateBtn.Text = "Update";
            this.updateBtn.Click +=
                new System.EventHandler(
                    this.updateBtn_Click);

            this.threadResultLbl.BorderStyle =
                System.Windows.Forms.BorderStyle.Fixed3D;
            this.threadResultLbl.Location =
                new System.Drawing.Point(152, 104);
            this.threadResultLbl.Name =
                "threadResultLbl";
            this.threadResultLbl.Size =
                new System.Drawing.Size(100, 20);
            this.threadResultLbl.TabIndex = 3;
            this.threadResultLbl.TextAlign =
                System.Drawing.ContentAlignment.MiddleRight;

            this.threadCounter.CategoryName =
                ".NET CLR LocksAndThreads";
            this.threadCounter.CounterName =
                "# of current physical threads";
            this.threadCounter.InstanceName =
                "SampleClient";

            this.countTimer.Enabled = true;
            this.countTimer.Interval = 1000;
            this.countTimer.Tick +=
                new System.EventHandler(
                    this.countTimer_Tick);

            this.maxOrdLbl.Location =
                new System.Drawing.Point(40, 24);
            this.maxOrdLbl.Name = "maxOrdLbl";
            this.maxOrdLbl.TabIndex = 0;
            this.maxOrdLbl.Text = "Max Orders:";
            this.maxOrdLbl.TextAlign =
                System.Drawing.ContentAlignment.MiddleRight;
```

LISTING 42.17   Continued

```
            this.AutoScaleBaseSize =
                new System.Drawing.Size(5, 13);
            this.ClientSize =
                new System.Drawing.Size(288, 197);
            this.Controls.AddRange(
                new System.Windows.Forms.Control[] {
                    this.threadLbl,
                    this.threadResultLbl,
                    this.updateBtn,
                    this.ordRateResultLbl,
                    this.maxOrdTxt,
                    this.ordRateLbl,
                    this.maxOrdLbl});
            this.Name = "SampleClient";
            this.Text = "Sample Client";
            this.Closing +=
                new System.ComponentModel.CancelEventHandler(
                    this.SampleClient_Closing);
            ((System.ComponentModel.ISupportInitialize)
                (this.threadCounter)).EndInit();
            this.ResumeLayout(false);
        }

        static void Main()
        {
            Application.Run(new SampleClient());
        }

        private void updateBtn_Click(object sender,
            System.EventArgs e)
        {
            maxOrders = Convert.ToInt32(maxOrdTxt.Text);
        }

        private void orderTimer_Tick(object sender,
            System.EventArgs e)
        {
            orderTimer.Enabled = false;

            Thread th = new Thread(
                new ThreadStart(ProcessOrders));
            th.Start();

            orderTimer.Enabled = true;
        }
```

LISTING 42.17   Continued

```csharp
        private void countTimer_Tick(object sender,
            System.EventArgs e)
        {
            countTimer.Enabled = false;

            ordRateResultLbl.Text =
                ((int)orderProc.OrderRate).ToString();
            threadResultLbl.Text =
                threadCounter.NextValue().ToString();

            countTimer.Enabled = true;
        }

        private void ProcessOrders()
        {
            for (curOrders = orderProc.CurNoOrders;
                curOrders <= maxOrders;
                curOrders++)
            {
                orderProc.ProcessOrder();
            }
        }

        private void SampleClient_Closing(object sender,
            System.ComponentModel.CancelEventArgs e)
        {
            orderProc.Dispose();
        }
    }
}
```

LISTING 42.18   Custom Performance Counter Sampling: CustomSamplingProcessor.cs

```csharp
using System;
using System.Threading;
using System.Diagnostics;

namespace OrderingClient
{
    /// <summary>
    /// Summary description for CustomSamplingProcessor.
    /// </summary>
    public class CustomSamplingProcessor : IDisposable
    {
        private PerformanceCounter orderCounter;
```

LISTING 42.18   Continued

```
    private CounterSample      orderSample;
    private static int curNoOrders = 0;
    private Random rand;

    public CustomSamplingProcessor()
    {
        rand = new Random();
        CounterCreationDataCollection myCounters =
            new CounterCreationDataCollection();
        CounterCreationData myCounterCreationData =
            new CounterCreationData();
        myCounterCreationData.CounterName =
            "Order Count";
        myCounterCreationData.CounterHelp =
            "Displays the of orders being processed.";
        myCounterCreationData.CounterType =
          PerformanceCounterType.RateOfCountsPerSecond32;
        myCounters.Add(myCounterCreationData);

        if (PerformanceCounterCategory.Exists(
            "Order Processor"))
        {
            PerformanceCounterCategory.Delete(
                "Order Processor");
        }

        PerformanceCounterCategory.Create(
            "Order Processor",
            "OrderProcessor class counters",
            myCounters);

        orderCounter = new PerformanceCounter(
            "Order Processor",
            "Order Count",
            false);

        orderCounter.RawValue = 0;
        orderSample = new CounterSample();
        orderSample = orderCounter.NextSample();
    }

    public int ProcessOrder()
    {
        Thread th = new Thread(new ThreadStart(doOrder));
        th.Start();
```

LISTING 42.18   Continued

```
        CurNoOrders++;
        return 0;
    }

    public int CurNoOrders
    {
        get
        {
            return curNoOrders;
        }
        set
        {
            curNoOrders = value;
        }
    }

    public float OrderRate
    {
        get
        {
            CounterSample tempSample
                = new CounterSample();
            tempSample = orderCounter.NextSample();

            float sample = CounterSample.Calculate(
                orderSample, tempSample);

            orderSample = tempSample;
            return sample;
        }
    }

    private void doOrder()
    {
        for (int delay = rand.Next(1000000);
            delay >= 0;
            delay--)
        ;

        CurNoOrders--;
        orderCounter.Increment();
    }

    public void Dispose()
    {
        PerformanceCounterCategory.Delete(
```

LISTING 42.18   Continued

```
            "Order Processor");
        }
    }
}
```

The example program in Listings 42.17 and 42.18 is similar to the one in Listings 42.15 and 42.16, except in the way the data is collected. During creation of the CounterCreationData instance, the CounterType property is set to RateOfCountsPerSecond32. This enables the counter to support a count of the number of orders per second processed by the CustomSamplingProcessor object. Here is the property setting:

```
        myCounterCreationData.CounterType =
            PerformanceCounterType.RateOfCountsPerSecond32;
```

Another difference in sampling is that the NextSample method of the counter object is called rather than NextValue. The NextSample method returns a CounterSample object. Here's how to declare and collect a single counter sampling:

```
        orderSample = new CounterSample();
        orderSample = orderCounter.NextSample();
```

Proper sampling of a RateOfCountsPerSecond32 type counter requires two samples. These samples are presented to the static Calculate method of the CounterSample class. The result of the Calculate method is a float type value representing the number of orders per second processed. The following example shows how the details of the Calculate method are encapsulated in the read-only OrderRate property:

```
        public float OrderRate
        {
            get
            {
                CounterSample tempSample
                    = new CounterSample();
                tempSample = orderCounter.NextSample();

                float sample = CounterSample.Calculate(
                    orderSample, tempSample);

                orderSample = tempSample;
                return sample;
            }
        }
```

This counter clearly provides valuable information about the performance of the program. An average on the way up shows potential for more capacity. When the average peaks, you have a good idea of what the system limits are. And a descending average indicates overload. The output from Listings 42.17 and 42.18 are shown in Figure 42.4. Here are the compilation instructions:

```
csc /t:winexe /out:SampleClient.exe SampleClient.cs CustomSamplingProcessor.cs
```

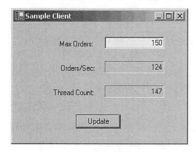

FIGURE 42.4   A custom sampling performance counter.

> **TIP**
>
> Any of the performance counters used or created in this chapter may be monitored with the Windows Performance tool. On Windows 2000, you can find the System Monitor by selecting Settings, Control Panel from the Start menu. Then open the Administrative Tools folder and run Performance.

Summary

When appropriate statements and methods are in place, runtime debugging can make program verification more efficient by allowing you to analyze console printouts or view log files for pertinent results. Runtime debugging can be turned on and off with conditional attributes, specialized output methods that accept Boolean parameters, command-line options, and preprocessing directives.

The Debug class is effective in development environments where the debugging code will be removed for deployment. Alternatively, the Trace class is the best decision for situations where code should be deployed with a debugging capability.

Runtime debugging in trace-enabled code can be controlled with Boolean switches or multilevel trace switches. Each option provides a means of controlling the level of debugging with less disruption to a customer.

The Debug.Assert method assists in verifying the logical consistency of an application during debugging. When a specified constraint fails, the Assert method notifies the user with a message box displaying information about the reason for the failure.

Runtime detection of program errors is an important capability. Similarly, it's important to monitor the performance of a program. The next chapter shows how to capture runtime performance of an application.

The System.Diagnostics namespace includes a framework for supporting performance counters. Performance counters enable a program to be monitored for performance and scalability. At a basic level, predefined system performance counters can be used to examine a program's behavior.

The performance counter framework supports customized performance counters for situations where it's necessary to monitor specialized behavior. Custom performance counters identify conditions specific to an application and must be explicitly managed by the application.

Sampling provides more sophisticated monitoring of program performance. This technique takes a number of samples and performs calculations on a regular basis. More so than other methods, the results of sampling can provide much more insight into a program's capability.

PART 10

Deploying Code

Assemblies and Versioning

Assemblies are the Common Language Infrastructure (CLI) logical units of functionality, providing identity, scope, security, and version management. Composed of one or more files, assemblies solve several problems that plague executable and library files on other platforms.

Some of the more prominent aspects of assemblies are side-by-side deployment, full containment and self-description, and security. Some of these aspects are reminiscent of earlier programming methodologies but are much improved with unique approaches to avoiding known problems.

Inside Assemblies

Assemblies can be made up of one or more files. Each file can be either a module or another assembly. The contents of an assembly could include a manifest, type metadata, Intermediate Language (IL) code, and resources. One of the files in the assembly must contain a manifest. Figure 43.1 shows a possible assembly configuration.

The example in Figure 43.1 shows three different files that make up an assembly. The main file, SomeAssembly.exe, contains all four elements of an assembly, including the assembly manifest. The other files, SomePictures.resources and SomeLibrary.netmodule, contain additions to the assembly.

Resources are files that hold various types of reusable data. Possible contents include strings, icons, pictures, or sound files. An earlier chapter discussed creation of resource files to support localization.

Modules are always deployed as part of an assembly because they are not meant to be separate executable entities. A couple benefits include modularization and multilanguage integration. Modularization benefits come from the capability to separate code into logical entities, providing another way to group and manage code. Another benefit comes with the ability to pull code written in multiple languages into a single assembly. For example, if ModuleA contains code written in Managed C++ and ModuleB contains code written in VB, both of these modules can be compiled into an assembly with a C# source file that uses code in both modules. The following command line creates a module:

```
csc /target:module SomeLibrary.cs
```

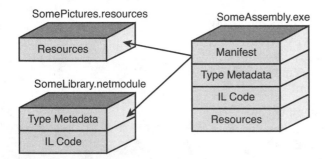

FIGURE 43.1   Assembly example.

This example creates the file `SomeLibrary.netmodule`. When you have a module, as created here, the following command line can add the module to an assembly:

```
csc SomeAssembly.cs /addmodule:SomeLibrary.netmodule
```

That command line creates a new assembly, `SomeAssembly.exe`, which includes a reference to the module `SomeLibrary.netmodule`. The `/addmodule` command-line option makes the resulting `SomeAssembly.exe` assembly reference the `SomeLibrary.netmodule` file. Therefore, the `SomeLibrary.netmodule` file must be in the same directory as the `SomeAssembly.exe`; otherwise, a `FileNotFoundException` exception is generated.

Manifests

As mentioned earlier, every assembly must have a manifest. The manifest may reside in its own file or within another file with other assembly elements. Manifests contain metadata about the assembly. Table 43.1 lists manifest contents.

TABLE 43.1   Manifest Contents

Content Type	Description
Culture	Localization info
Files	List of files inside assembly
Name	Name of assembly

TABLE 43.1   Continued

Content Type	Description
References	Referenced assemblies
Strong name	Public key info
Types	List of types inside assembly
Version	Version number of assembly

Attributes

Several attributes decorate assemblies for various purposes. These attributes can be categorized as identity, informational, manifest, and strong name.

Identity

Identity attributes provide uniqueness to distinguish one assembly from another. The benefits of this are that different versions of an assembly may be running at the same time and there must be a way to tell each version apart. Programs also have the option to call the assembly they want to use by specifying culture or version requirements in their configuration files. Configuration files are explained later in this chapter. Table 43.2 outlines assembly identity attributes.

TABLE 43.2   Identity Attributes

Attribute Name	Description
AssemblyCulture	Localization Info
AssemblyVersion	Version number of assembly
AssemblyFlags	Controls side-by-side execution

Here are a couple examples of identity attributes:

```
[assembly: AssemblyCulture("en_US")]
[assembly: AssemblyVersion("1.0.*")]
```

Informational

The informational attributes impart knowledge about the origin of an assembly. These attributes tell which company created the assembly, copyright, trademark, and other proprietary information about the assembly. Table 43.3 outlines informational attributes of assemblies.

TABLE 43.3   Informational Attributes

Attribute Name	Description
AssemblyCompany	Company name
AssemblyCopyright	Copyright info
AssemblyFileVersion	Win32 file version; defaults to assembly version

43

TABLE 43.3   Continued

Attribute Name	Description
AssemblyInformationalVersion	Product version number; not used by runtime
AssemblyProduct	Product information
AssemblyTrademark	Trademark information

Here are some examples of identity attributes:

```
[assembly: AssemblyCompany("MyCompany")]
[assembly: AssemblyProduct("My Product Name")]
[assembly: AssemblyCopyright("Copyright 2001")]
[assembly: AssemblyTrademark("TM Product Name")]
```

Manifest

The manifest attributes explain what an assembly is and how it should be used. With a short name, full name, and description, a user can get a good idea of how to use the assembly. The configuration can provide insights into what environment and assembly can be used. Table 43.4 outlines assembly manifest attributes.

TABLE 43.4   Manifest Attributes

Attribute Name	Description
AssemblyConfiguration	Config info such as Release or Debug
AssemblyDefaultAlias	Short friendly name of assembly
AssemblyDescription	Summary of what assembly is
AssemblyTitle	Full friendly name of assembly

Here are a few examples of identity attributes:

```
[assembly: AssemblyTitle("My Assembly")]
[assembly: AssemblyDescription("Provides extensive widget support.")]
[assembly: AssemblyConfiguration("Release")]
```

Strong Name

The strong name attributes primarily support security. They identify the key, key file, and timing associated with various security issues. An assembly can have what is called a strong name, which consists of a combination of identity, manifest, and strong name attributes. Another section later in this chapter shows how to create a strong name for an assembly. Table 43.5 outlines strong name attributes for assemblies.

Here are three examples of identity attributes:

```
[assembly: AssemblyDelaySign(false)]
[assembly: AssemblyKeyFile("MyKey.snk")]
[assembly: AssemblyKeyName("MyKeyContainer")]
```

TABLE 43.5   Strong Name Attributes

Attribute Name	Description
AssemblyDelaySign	Indicates whether delayed signing is used
AssemblyKeyFile	Name of key file
AssemblyKeyName	Name of key container

Assembly Features

Besides being just another executable program or library, an assembly offers several features that enhance program management and execution. The features of identity, scope, versioning, and security form a basis for assigning a strong name to an assembly.

Identity

An assembly is a unit of identity. For instance, a class named MyClass in an assembly named AssemblyOne is different from a class named MyClass in an assembly named AssemblyTwo.

Scope

Through proper use of the internal modifier, assembly types are visible only within that assembly. External assemblies won't be able to see or access any types marked as internal.

Versioning

The ability to version assemblies allows a few key capabilities, such as automatic upgrades, enhanced deployment, and side-by-side execution. An assembly version is a 4-tuple separated by dots with the following format:

<major>.<minor>.<build>.<revision>

Table 43.6 shows the meaning of each position and a suggested method of implementation.

TABLE 43.6   Assembly Version Numbers

Position	Description
Major	Major release number
Minor	Minor release number
Build	Intermediate build
Revision	Hot fix number

43

The version may be specifically stated in the `AssemblyVersion` attribute or defaults may be accepted. In the following `AssemblyVersion` attribute, the major version is 1, the minor version is 0, and the build and revision version numbers will be assigned during compilation:

```
[assembly: AssemblyVersion("1.0.*")]
```

Security

Public keys and certificates make assemblies inherently more reliable and secure than the libraries and executables developed in traditional machine-compiled languages. There are two ways to secure your assemblies: strong names and digital signatures.

Strong Names

Strong names consist of assembly name, version, culture, and public key. The following command line generates a key file to be used in applying a strong name to an assembly:

```
sn -k Mykey.snk
```

After a key file has been generated, it may be referenced in an assembly by specifying the generated key filename in an `AssemblyKeyFile` attribute as follows:

```
[assembly: AssemblyKeyFile("MyKey.snk")]
```

Certificates

Certificates provide proof of code identity and are the secure complement to strong names. More specifically, a strong name alone does not guarantee authenticity of code. You need a certificate to prove identity.

Normally, certificates are obtained through certification authorities such as Verisign and Thawte. However, for testing purposes there are a couple tools in the .NET Framework SDK that make it easy to create a test certificate. The `makecert` utility creates an X.509 certificate, as the following example shows:

```
makecert mycert.cer -sk mykey
```

This command line creates an X.509 certificate named `mycert.cer` and a registry key named `mykey`. The certificate must be translated into a Software Publisher Certificate (SPC):

```
cert2spc mycert.cer mycert.spc
```

The `cert2spc` utility created a new SPC named `mycert.spc`, which contains the X.509 certificate specified in `mycert.cer`. Now that we finally have a certificate, the assembly may be signed as follows:

```
signcode /spc mycert.spc /v mykey SomeAssembly.exe
```

The `signcode` utility added the `mycert.spc` SPC, identified with the `/spc` switch, to the `SomeAssembly.exe` assembly. The key was the `mykey` registry key, which was created with the `makecert`.

Now the `SomeAssembly.exe` assembly is signed and secure.

The utilities in this section have many options to customize their functionality. Just use the –h option for help. In addition, executing the `signcode` utility without command-line options opens a wizard application that steps you through the certification process.

Configuration

Another benefit of assemblies is that they can be configured dynamically through configuration files. These files are written in XML, providing human-readable access to program configuration.

There are basically two types of configuration files: machine and application. Machine configuration files hold configuration information for all applications running on a machine. In this light, they are intended to be more generic and applicable to multiple applications. Machine configuration files are located at %runtime install path%\Config\Machine.config. When running applications, the machine configuration file is consulted first, and then the application configuration file settings are applied.

Executable application configuration files have the same name as the executable filename with the extension .config appended. For example if a program were named MyApp.exe, its configuration file would be named MyApp.exe.config. ASP.NET and web service configuration files are named web.config.

All configuration files have a `<configuration>` root element. Subsections are divided into startup, runtime, remoting, crypto, class API, and security settings. This chapter focuses specifically on assemblies, so I discuss startup and runtime settings in the next couple sections.

Startup Configuration

Startup configuration options are specified within the `<startup>` section of a configuration file. You would use this section to specify which version of the CLR to use. In version 1.0, the only optins was to use the requiredRuntime element, which could be configured as follows:

```
<configuration>
   <startup>
      <requiredRuntime version="1.0.2914.0" safeMode="true"/>
   </startup>
</configuration>
```

According to this configuration file, a program must run with CLR version 1.0.2914.0. Setting the `safeMode` attribute to `true` enables a registry search to see whether this assembly was redirected to run against another version of the CLR.

In .NET v1.1 and higher, you should use the supportedRuntime element instead, which allows you to specify all of the runtimes your application supports. Here's an example:

```
<configuration>
   <startup>
      <supportedRuntime version="v2.0.50727" />
      <supportedRuntime version="v1.1.4322" />
   </startup>
</configuration>
```

This example states that the application supports both the v1.1 and v2.0 versions of the .NET CLR. You would order them with the most preferred CLR at the top of the list. In this example, the application would load with v2.0 of the CLR but would then run with v1.1 of the CLR if v2.0 wasn't available.

Runtime Configuration

There are three possible options for runtime configuration: concurrent garbage collection, assembly version redirection, and assembly location. All are subelements of the <runtime> section.

Concurrent Garbage Collection

Concurrent garbage collection occurs when the garbage collector runs in a separate thread from the application. This is good for performance when an application has a lot of user interaction. However, you would want to disable it to optimize performance for server-bound operations. The following example shows how to disable concurrent garbage collection:

```
<configuration>
   <runtime>
      <gcConcurrent enabled="false"/>
   </runtime>
</configuration>
```

Concurrent garbage collection is disabled by setting the enabled attribute of the <gcConcurrent> element to false. The default for concurrent garbage collection is true.

Assembly Version Redirection

Normally, assemblies run against other specified assemblies as specified at compile time. However, configuration files enable redirection from one assembly to another at runtime. This is useful when a third-party library is upgraded and is also backward-compatible with the older version. The following example shows how to redirect an assembly:

```
<configuration>
    <runtime>
        <assemblyBinding xmlns="urn:schemas-microsoft-com:asm.v1">
            <dependentAssembly>
                <assemblyIdentity name="SomeAssembly"
```

```
                               publickeytoken="fa3a9d02dc01aa10"
                               culture="en-us" />
                 <bindingRedirect oldVersion="1.0.0.0"
                               newVersion="2.0.0.0"/>
            </dependentAssembly>
         </assemblyBinding>
      </runtime>
  </configuration>
```

The `<assemblyBinding>` section contains the details for redirecting an assembly's binding. It contains an xmlns attribute set to `"urn:schemas-microsoft-com:asm.v1"`, which is a mandatory entry. The two elements within the `<assemblyBinding>` section are `<assemblyIdentity>` and `<bindingRedirect>`.

The `<assemblyIdentity>` element identifies the assembly to redirect. Its first parameter, name, is the name of the assembly. The publickeytoken and culture attributes are optional. However, if you wanted to add the publickeytoken, an easy way to obtain it is by using the strong name utility with the -T option, as follows:

```
sn -T SomeAssembly.dll
```

The `<bindingRedirect>` element has an oldVersion attribute, which specifies the preexisting version of the assembly, and a newVersion attribute, which specifies the new assembly to redirect to.

Assembly Location

There are two assembly location elements to find where a given assembly resides: `<codeBase>` and `<probing>`. The `<codeBase>` element specifies where the runtime can find a shared assembly. The following example demonstrates the `<codeBase>` element:

```
<configuration>
  <runtime>
    <assemblyBinding xmlns="urn:schemas-microsoft-com:asm.v1">
      <dependentAssembly>
        <assemblyIdentity name="SomeAssembly" publicKeyToken="b77a5c561934e089" />
        <codeBase version="1.0.0.0" href="file:///C:\Program Files\Some Applica-
tion" />
      </dependentAssembly>
    </assemblyBinding>
  </runtime>
</configuration>
```

The version attribute of the `<codeBase>` element is optional, and version ranges are not allowed. The href attribute is mandatory and must include the protocol in the URI.

The other method of locating an assembly is via probing, which specifies which subdirectories of an application may be searched. The following example shows how to configure probing:

```
<configuration>
   <runtime>
      <assemblyBinding xmlns="urn:schemas-microsoft-com:asm.v1">
         <probing privatePath="subdir1;subdir2\subsubdir;subdir2"/>
      </assemblyBinding>
   </runtime>
</configuration>
```

The private attribute of the `<probing>` element specifies the subdirectories to search. A semicolon separates each subdirectory.

MMC Configuration Tool

This section shows how to create the text-based XML configuration files. For those who prefer a graphical tool with wizards, there is an easier way to produce configuration files: the MMC snap-in called the .NET Admin Tool at %windir%\Microsoft.NET\Framework\ v1.0.xxxx (where %windir% is the environment variable for your Windows directory and xxxx is the most current build). With the knowledge gained from this section, using the .NET Admin Tool should be quite easy.

Deployment

Assemblies can be deployed as either private or shared. A private assembly resides in the same directory, or a subdirectory, as its main program. Private directories don't need any special configuration or handling to work with a program. Just copy them where they go and they work.

Shared assemblies are another matter. As the name suggests, multiple programs may execute a shared assembly. Special preparation is required to give the assembly a strong name and deploy it to a central repository called the global assembly cache (GAC) . The following command line demonstrates how to add an assembly to the GAC:

```
gacutil -i SomeAssembly.dll
```

The `gacutil` utility has several other options that can be viewed with the `-h` option. All assemblies added to the GAC must have a strong name. See the "Assembly Features/Strong Names" section earlier in this chapter for information about adding strong names to an assembly.

Summary

Assemblies can be composed of several elements, including manifests, type catalogs, IL code, and resources. These elements may be in separate files. A manifest is required.

Features of assemblies include identity, scope, versioning, and security. These features are combined to form the strong name of an assembly.

The runtime behavior of an assembly can be altered with configuration files. These behaviors include concurrent garbage collection, binding, and location.

Simply copying assemblies to where they need to be and executing them is all that is required for private assemblies. Shared assemblies require an extra step of assigning a strong name and adding them to the global assembly cache. They're self-contained entities that don't require external catalogs or registries to enable their execution.

43

Securing Code

The .NET security model introduces a significant security enhancement, referred to as *code-based security*. The need for code-based security has grown out of recent years' experience in which foreign code is accessible and downloadable to computers from diverse sources throughout the Internet. Code-based security makes a system more secure by limiting the capability of code to perform specified actions.

Traditional role-based security is also a major component of the .NET security model. *Role-based security* controls the ability of agents or individuals to perform actions on a computing system. The security types are managed by specific policies, which guide their implementation. Tools, such as public key signatures, encryption, and security certificates, assist in implementation of the security policy, for both code- and role-based security.

Code-Based Security

Code-based security is implemented via a multifaceted approach that pulls together cooperative security mechanisms to determine what an assembly is allowed to do in a system. Through the security mechanisms of evidence, code groups, security levels, and security policy, an assembly is assigned permissions in a computer system.

A code-based security policy is constructed by use of evidence, permissions, code groups, and security policy levels. Each assembly contains evidence, which is used to categorize it into a code group. Each code group has permissions that are assigned to an assembly belonging to that code group. The union of all the permissions from the code group to which the assembly belongs is then given to the assembly. Finally, there are security policy levels, each with its own set of code groups, which the assembly is evaluated against. The final set of permissions for an assembly is based on the intersection of the permissions from each security policy level. The following sections go into more detail about how these pieces fit together.

Evidence

The information examined to determine an assembly's permissions is called *evidence*. There are seven primary types of evidence, as shown in Table 44.1.

TABLE 44.1   Types of Evidence

Type	Description
Application directory	Where the application is installed
Hash	MD5 or SHA1 cryptographic hash
Publisher	Software publisher's signature
Site	Web or Internet site where software came from
Strong name	Assembly's cryptographic strong name
URL	URL where software came from
Zone	Zone where software originated

In a couple more sections, you'll see how evidence is used to classify assemblies into code groups. Each code group has criteria upon which to compare evidence to see if an assembly belongs to that group.

Permissions

The .NET Framework includes named permission sets that define sets of permissions that can be granted to assemblies. Table 44.2 lists the available named permission sets. Only three of the permission sets may be modified: `Internet`, `LocalIntranet`, and `Everything`.

TABLE 44.2   Named Permission Sets

Permission	Description
Nothing	No permissions.
Execution	Can run, but has no access to system resources.
Internet	Has permissions for when origin is unknown.
LocalIntranet	Code has enterprise permissions.
Everything	All permissions except security verification.
FullTrust	No limits.

The code groups to which an assembly belongs determine the set of permissions that can be granted. The next section goes into greater detail on the relationship between code groups and assemblies.

Code Groups

Assemblies are classified into code groups based on the evidence presented by the assembly. A code group is a member of a hierarchical structure that is used to logically classify types of assemblies. As an intermediate step to full determination of permissions, assemblies are granted permissions based on the code groups to which they belong. Later sections on security policy level and security requests explain how the final permissions are granted to an assembly. Figure 44.1 shows a code group hierarchy that could be implemented on a system.

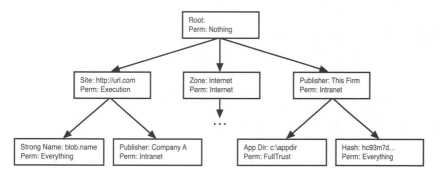

FIGURE 44.1   A code group hierarchy.

Every hierarchy has a Root group, which represents all code. Child groups represent specializations that help categorize code. In Figure 44.1, each group is represented by a rectangle with a group name, membership condition, and permission. The first line shows the group name and membership condition, separated by a colon. Except for the Root group, each group name is one of the types of evidence from Table 44.1. The second line shows the permission associated with that group, after the word Perm and a colon. Permissions correspond to entries in Table 44.2. The code group hierarchy may be shaped and extended as far as necessary. Also, evidence may be repeated throughout the hierarchy.

It is expected that an assembly will be a member of multiple code groups. Membership determination begins at the Root group and continues to child groups. If an assembly matches the membership criteria for a group, it may be evaluated for membership in that group's children (if any). An assembly must have membership in all parents of a group before it may be evaluated with that group.

To trace how permissions are assigned with code groups, consider an assembly with a publisher certificate for This Firm and located at c:\appdir. As shown in Figure 44.2, this assembly automatically belongs to the Root group, which has a membership condition of all code. The assembly doesn't come from the Internet and its Url is not http://url.com, so it doesn't belong to the Site or Zone groups on the second level. However, it does have a publisher certificate from This Firm and, therefore, belongs to the Publisher group. Because this assembly does not belong to the Site group on the second level, it won't be evaluated against the Strong Name and Publisher child groups on the third level. Similarly, this assembly will not be evaluated for membership in any child groups of the Zone group on the second level. However, the assembly will be evaluated for membership in the children, on the third level, of the Publisher group, on the second level. As it turns out, the assembly is located in c:\appdir and is a member of the Application Directory group. In this example, I make the assumption that the hash code for this assembly doesn't match the one in the Hash group.

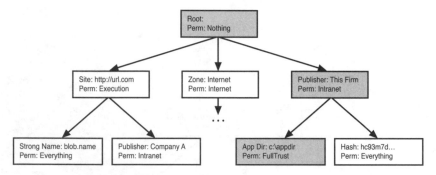

FIGURE 44.2   Code group membership.

Permissions for this assembly are determined by taking the union of all code groups to which it belongs. Therefore, this assembly has the permissions contained in the Root + Publisher + Application Directory, which are Nothing + Intranet + FullTrust.

This is not the final word in the allowable permissions for this assembly. You see, code groups belong to security policy levels, and the assembly must be evaluated with the code group of each security policy level, which is the subject of the next section.

Security Policy Levels

After classification into code groups and accumulating allowable permissions, an assembly is then evaluated according to the four security policy levels: Enterprise, Machine, User, and Application Domain. The security policy level evaluation grants the intersection of the results of the code level permissions with each security level. This is different from the code group permission determination, which grants the union of all permissions to an assembly. Table 44.3 lists the security policy levels.

A host, such as a browser or other application that can host the CLR, sets the application domain policy level. The system administrator sets Enterprise, Machine, and User policy levels. In addition, a user may set the User policy level.

TABLE 44.3   Security Policy Levels

Level	Description
Enterprise	Managed code belonging to the enterprise
Machine	Managed code on the computer
User	Managed code belonging to the operating system user when the CLR starts
Application Domain	Managed code in the application domain

When determining permissions, the code group membership of each security policy level is evaluated and permissions are assigned for each security policy level. Then the intersection of the permissions from each policy level is taken to get the next set of permissions. For example, review the following set of permissions for a given assembly:

▶ Enterprise: Execution + Intranet

▶ Machine: Intranet + Internet

▶ User: FullTrust + Intranet

The intersection, or common element, of these security policy levels is the Intranet named permission set. Therefore, the security policy has granted the Intranet permission to this assembly.

Although the security policy has granted permission to this assembly, it is not the final word in what permissions the assembly will have. That's because the assembly itself must specify what permissions it wants.

Permission Requests

The final permissions an assembly receives are always a subset of the permissions granted by security policy. In other words, an assembly may have permissions that are equal to or less than the permissions specified in the security policy. This final set of permissions depends on what the assembly requests.

There are two ways for assemblies to request permissions: declarative and imperative. Declarative requests are performed using C# attributes and are evaluated at assembly load time. Imperative requests are made by instantiating a permission object and invoking the appropriate request method. Imperative requests are evaluated at runtime. Listing 44.1 shows how to make a declarative security request.

LISTING 44.1   A Declarative Security Request

```
using System;
using System.Security.Permissions;

[assembly:ReflectionPermissionAttribute(
SecurityAction.RequestMinimum, ReflectionEmit=false)]
```

LISTING 44.1   Continued

```
class CodeGroups
{
    static void Main(string[] args)
    {
    }
}
```

Declarative security requests may be applied at the assembly, class, or member level. The declarative security request in Listing 44.1 applies to the entire assembly. The particular request is for the ReflectionPermission. This requests asks for reflection to be given as a minimum requirement and the request does not include reflection emit capabilities.

Three types of permission requests can be made with a declarative request: RequestMinimum, RequestOptional, and RequestRefused. Minimal permissions are ones that an assembly must have to operate. Optional permissions are nice to have, but the assembly can find a way to deal with the situation if they're not available. Refused permissions are those that the assembly doesn't want. These permission requests are members of the SecurityAction enum. When determining permissions for declarative requests, the following steps are taken by the CLR:

1. Take the union of minimal and optional permissions.
2. Remove the refused permissions from the results of step 1.
3. Take the intersection of the security policy permissions and the results of step 2.

The System.Security.Permissions namespace contains specifications for the reflection permission and others. Table 44.4 provides a quick list of what permissions are available.

TABLE 44.4   Individual Permissions

	Read and write environment variables
	Read access to a file
	Append, read, or write to a file
	Controls access and amount of virtual file system
	Control access and amount of generic isolated storage
	Role-based security checks
	Access for a software publisher
	Can use C# reflection
	Access operating system registry
	Security permissions that can be invoked
	Access to software from a specific website
	Access to assembly with a specific strong name
UI	User interface and clipboard
	Access to software from a location on the Internet
Zone	Access to specified zones

Imperative security requests are a part of the code. They're performed by instantiating an object of the appropriate permission type and calling the `Demand()` method. Listing 44.2 shows how to use imperative security requests.

LISTING 44.2   An Imperative Security Request

```
using System;
using System.Security;
using System.Security.Permissions;

class CodeGroups
{
    static void Main(string[] args)
    {
        CodeGroups cg = new CodeGroups();
        cg.MakeDemand();
    }

    public void MakeDemand()
    {
        try
        {
            UIPermission uip = new UIPermission(
                UIPermissionWindow.AllWindows,
                UIPermissionClipboard.AllClipboard);

            uip.Demand();
        }
        catch(SecurityException se)
        {
            Console.WriteLine("UI Permission Refused");
        }
    }
}
```

Within the `MakeDemand()` method, a `UIPermission` object is instantiated. A `UIPermission` allows code to create windows and access the clipboard. The `UIPermission` object in Listing 44.2 is instantiated with parameters that request permissions for performing all types of window operations and performing all actions with the clipboard. The request is made by invoking the permission object's `Demand()` method. If the request succeeds, all is well and the program continues. However, a `SecurityException` exception is raised if the assembly is not allowed the `UIPermission` permission.

Implementing Security Policy

The creation of permissions associated with code groups and security policy levels forms the security policy of a computer system. Fortunately, the CLR comes configured with a default security policy that provides some protection against the wilds of the Web. With knowledge of how permissions are granted, you're ready to create security policies to meet the needs of your code and computer system.

Security policy can be viewed and changed with the `caspol.exe` utility. For example, the following command line prints the current security policy:

```
caspol -l
```

The output of this command would fill a few pages with the default security policy that comes with the .NET Framework installation. For a more focused view, involving code groups, use the `-lg` option as follows:

```
caspol -lg
```

And here's the output:

```
Security is ON
Execution checking is ON
Policy change prompt is ON

Level = Machine

Code Groups:

1.  All code: Nothing
    1.1.  Zone - MyComputer: FullTrust
    1.2.  Zone - Intranet: LocalIntranet
        1.2.1.  All code: Same site Web.
        1.2.2.  All code: Same directory FileIO - Read, PathDiscovery
    1.3.  Zone - Internet: Internet
        1.3.1.  All code: Same site Web.
    1.4.  Zone - Untrusted: Nothing
    1.5.  Zone - Trusted: Internet
        1.5.1.  All code: Same site Web.
    1.6.  StrongName -
00240000048000009400000006020000002400005253413100040000010000
10007D1FA57C4AED9F0A32E84AA0FAEFD0DE9E8FD6AEC8F87FB03766C834C
99921EB23BE79AD9D5DCC1DD9AD236132102900B723CF980957FC4E177108
FC607774F29E8320E92EA05ECE4E821C0A5EFE8F1645C4C0C93C1AB99285D
622CAA652C1DFAD63D745D6F2DE5F17E5EAF0FC4963D261C8A12436518206
```

```
DC093344D5AD293: FullTrust
    1.7.   StrongName -
000000000000000004000000000000000: FullTrust
Success
```

As you can see, the default security policy is composed of Zone, All Code, and Strong Name evidence. The most often used option for developers may be the -u option, to configure the User security policy level. To target a specific policy level, such as User, specify its option on the command line as follows:

```
caspol -u -lg
```

And here's the output:

```
Security is ON
Execution checking is ON
Policy change prompt is ON

Level = User

Code Groups:

1.  All code: FullTrust
Success
```

This example performs a group listing on the User security policy level. The default policy level without an option is the Machine policy level. The following commands show how to add a code group to the security policy:

```
caspol -ag 1.1 -appdir FullTrust
caspol -lg
```

And here's the output:

```
Security is ON
Execution checking is ON
Policy change prompt is ON

Level = Machine

Code Groups:

1.  All code: Nothing
    1.1.   Zone - MyComputer: FullTrust
        1.1.1.   ApplicationDirectory: FullTrust
    1.2.   Zone - Intranet: LocalIntranet
        1.2.1.   All code: Same site Web.
        1.2.2.   All code: Same directory FileIO - Read, PathDiscovery
```

44

```
    1.3.  Zone - Internet: Internet
       1.3.1.  All code: Same site Web.
    1.4.  Zone - Untrusted: Nothing
    1.5.  Zone - Trusted: Internet
       1.5.1.  All code: Same site Web.
    1.6.  StrongName -
0024000004800000940000000602000000240000525341310004000001000
10007D1FA57C4AED9F0A32E84AA0FAEFD0DE9E8FD6AEC8F87FB03766C834C
99921EB23BE79AD9D5DCC1DD9AD236132102900B723CF980957FC4E177108
FC607774F29E8320E92EA05ECE4E821C0A5EFE8F1645C4C0C93C1AB99285D
622CAA652C1DFAD63D745D6F2DE5F17E5EAF0FC4963D261C8A12436518206
DC093344D5AD293: FullTrust
    1.7.  StrongName -
00000000000000000400000000000000: FullTrust
Success
```

The –ag option performs an add group operation. In the example, a new code group was
added below the parent, specified by the number 1.1. The new group, added at location
1.1.1, was for ApplicationDirectory membership and was given FullTrust permissions.
The new ApplicationDirectory group was shown in the output. To remove this group,
type the following command line:

```
caspol -rg 1.1.1
```

This removes the group we just added, which was at location 1.1.1 in the policy. For
more help on how to configure security policy, use the –h option.

Role-Based Security

The .NET Framework includes a suite of classes specialized for traditional role-based security. These classes permit code to grant and restrict access to specified agents and users to
support a security policy. The primary object in role-based security is the Principal
object. It contains both a user identity and a role.

The .NET Framework contains two methods of managing role-based security: Windows and
Generic. The first is through the native Windows security system, and the other is a more
general and independent mechanism. Listing 44.3 shows how to find a given role using
the native Windows security system.

LISTING 44.3   Role-Based Security with **WindowsPrincipal**

```
using System;
using System.Threading;
using System.Security.Principal;

class WinPerm
{
```

LISTING 44.3   Continued

```
    static void Main(string[] args)
    {
        AppDomain.CurrentDomain.SetPrincipalPolicy(
                PrincipalPolicy.WindowsPrincipal);

        WindowsPrincipal wp
                = (WindowsPrincipal) Thread.CurrentPrincipal;

        if (wp.IsInRole(WindowsBuiltInRole.PowerUser))
        {
            Console.WriteLine("Access Granted!");
        }
        else
        {
            Console.WriteLine("Access Denied!");
        }
    }
}
```

The call to AppDomain.CurrentDomain.SetPrincipalPolicy() method initializes the current thread with WindowsPrincipal representing the current user. The WindowsPrincipal object is extracted from the CurrentPrincipal property of the current thread. Listing 44.3 uses the IsInRole() method of the WindowsPrincipal object to determine whether the current user is in the PowerUser role. The parameter to the IsInRole() method is a member of the WindowBuiltInRole enum.

The more general method of implementing role-based security is through the GenericPrincipal and GenericIdentity objects. Listing 44.4 shows how to use general role-based security.

LISTING 44.4   Role-Based Security with **GenericPrincipal**

```
using System;
using System.Threading;
using System.Security.Principal;

class GenPerm
{
    static void Main(string[] args)
    {
        GenericIdentity gid
                = new GenericIdentity("Administrator");

        String[] Roles = {"Administrator", "Developer"};

        GenericPrincipal gp
```

LISTING 44.4   Continued

```
            = new GenericPrincipal(gid, Roles);

    Thread.CurrentPrincipal = gp;

    if (gp.Identity.Name == "Administrator")
    {
        Console.WriteLine("Good to go!");
    }
    else
    {
        Console.WriteLine("Not in this lifetime!");
    }
    }
}
}
```

Listing 44.4 creates a GenericIdentity object with a username. It then passes the GenericIdentity and an array of roles as parameters to create a new GenericPrincipal object. The flexibility of the GenericIdentity and GenericPrincipal objects makes it easy to create permissions infrastructures independent of the underlying operating system.

Security Utilities

The .NET Framework comes with several security-related utilities. Some will be familiar from this and previous chapters. Although I do not go into detail about all of them, they're listed in Table 44.5 to give you an idea about what is available. Remember to use the –h option on the command line for help on how to use each utility.

TABLE 44.5   .NET Security Utilities

Name	Description
Makecert.exe	Creates test X.509 certificates
Certmgr.exe	Manages certificate trust and revocation lists
Chktrust.exe	Checks validity of a file signed with a certificate
Caspol.exe	Manages security policy
Signcode.exe	Signs an assembly
Storeadm.exe	Isolated storage management
Permview.exe	View an assembly's permissions
Peverify.exe	Checks whether an assembly can be verified during JIT compilation
Secutil.exe	Extracts keys and certificates from an assembly
Setreg.exe	Sets signatures and certificates in the registry
Cert2spc.exe	Creates test software publisher certificates
Sn.exe	Strong name tool that generates keys for assemblies

Summary

Creating a security policy for code-based security includes combining evidence, code groups, permissions, and security policy levels. The evidence is the information revealed about an assembly. Code groups use evidence to categorize assemblies and grant permissions. Through a process of unions of the code groups and intersections of security policy levels, a security policy is applied to an assembly.

Assemblies can request permissions at load time and runtime. Imperative requests are made in code, and declarative requests are made with C# attributes.

Role-based security includes native Windows and generic request mechanisms. The native Windows `Principal` and `Identity` objects interoperate with the operating system to provide role and identity security. The generic `Principal` and `Identity` objects are more flexible for working with other security systems.

Several security utilities are available for working with certificates, keys, signatures, and other security issues.

44

Creating Visual Studio 2008 Setup Projects

Stores and companies often sell their merchandise in packages that contain the main item, accessories, and instructions. Recently, I bought a new laptop computer that was packaged like this. The computer was covered with Styrofoam, and another box contained the power cord, software, and instructions. Everything was packaged nicely so that I could find the bits and set it up quickly.

Manufactured goods, such as my laptop, are a lot like software. Many applications have setup programs that put everything where it goes and give you instructions on how to get started. A professional setup can also indicate a certain amount of professionalism in the application you've built, and it provides an opportunity to make a positive first impression on your customer.

Running the VS2008 Setup Project Wizard

To get started, create a console, Windows Forms, or WPF application that performs some simple function, such as displaying "Hello C#!" Previous chapters discussed how to do this, and we just want to use the program so that we can build a setup application for it. For our current purposes, it doesn't matter what the program does.

1. To create the setup project, right-click the solution, select New Project, open the Other Project Types branch, select Setup and Deployment, select Setup Wizard, name it **MyAppSetup**, and click OK. You'll see the Welcome screen in Figure 45.1. Click Next to move to the Project Type screen, as in Figure 45.2.

FIGURE 45.1   Setup Wizard Welcome screen.

2. The Choose a Project Type screen in Figure 45.2 has four choices: Windows, Web, Merge Module, or CAB. You could use this to deploy a Web Application, assuming that the destination machine has IIS installed. The majority of settings for web apps are identical to Windows apps. You could also create a merge module, which might be ideal for a class library project for a reusable DLL that you would want to include in other setup projects. The CAB file option allows you to compress setup content and enables you to divide the setup project into pieces that facilitate distribution via multiple physical media artifacts, such as a multi-CD installation. The Windows option illustrates the majority of features you'll need, so accept the default selection of Windows Application and click Next, which brings you to the Project Outputs window, shown in Figure 45.3.

3. The most important item in Figure 45.3 is Primary Output from Chapter 45, which contains the executable file from the specified project. If you have localized resources to deploy, you would check the Localized Resources check box, too. For production deployments, you won't ever need to check the other boxes. If you have a reason to deploy a solution so that other developers can access everything, you can select the other options to deploy code and all the other resources with your project. Click Next to show the Include Files window, as shown in Figure 45.4.

4. The Include Files window, as shown in Figure 45.4, allows you to add files to the setup that aren't part of the project being added. Click the Next button to show the Create Project window.

5. The Create Project window summarizes the choices you've made. Click the Finish button to produce the new setup project, which appears as a project under your solution.

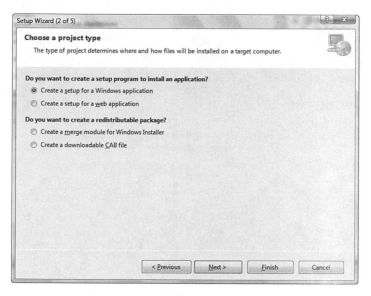

FIGURE 45.2   Setup Wizard Project Type window.

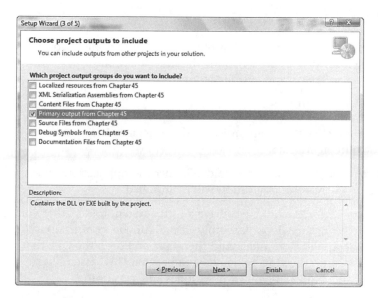

FIGURE 45.3   Setup Wizard Project Outputs window.

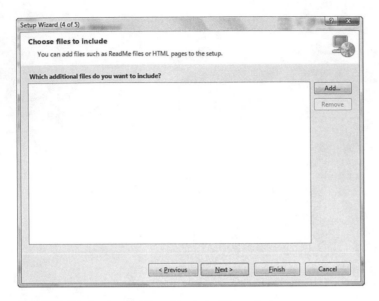

FIGURE 45.4   Setup Wizard Include Files window.

Additional Setup Configuration

When the Setup Wizard runs, you have several screens of information that allow you to configure the setup project even further. Options include the file system, file types, registry, launch conditions, user interface, and custom actions.

File System Setup

To configure the file system, right-click the setup project and select View, File System. You'll see the screen, as shown in Figure 45.5.

A typical task to perform in the file system is to add folders under the Application folder, which is the destination folder where your application will be installed.

By right-clicking File System on Target Machine, you have a list of system folders that you can define to add files to—one being the Global Assembly Cache. All you need to do is define the GAC folder, open the Application folder, and then drag and drop the DLL that you want to install into the GAC into the GAC folder. Remember that GAC assemblies must be strong named, as explained in Chapter 43, "Assemblies and Versioning."

Another useful technique is to add a shortcut to the Start menu. Just right-click in the Application folder, create a shortcut, rename the shortcut appropriately, add a folder to User Programs menu for your company or application, and drag and drop the shortcut into that new folder.

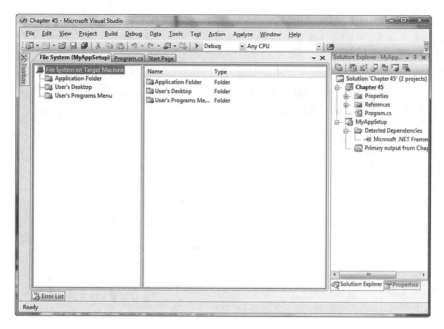

FIGURE 45.5   Setup project file system.

Creating Registry Settings

Because of the potential for making mistakes in the registry that could mess up your computer, it's often safer to use the XML application configuration file, as explained in Chapter 25, "Writing Windows Forms Applications," for Windows Forms apps (works the same for WPF) or the web.config file for web apps, as explained in Chapter 27, "Building Web Applications with ASP.NET," for application-specific settings. However, sometimes you still need to make registry settings for cross-application settings or to integrate with other tools, such as VS2008 add-ins.

Therefore, you can create registry settings by right-clicking the setup project and selecting View, Registry. You'll see a folder tree that emulates the registry keys. You can right-click and add your own keys and values as necessary.

File Types

Some programs produce and consume specific file types. You can specify the file types that your program works with; doing so creates a Windows file association for your file extension with your program.

You can right-click, select View, File Types to see the File Types Editor. Then, right-click on File Types and select Add File Type. At this point, you can give the file type a name and then open the Properties window and specify the file extension.

After you've done this, ensure your application handles the args parameter in Main to open and work with any file that is selected in Windows.

User Interface

To configure the user interface, right-click the setup project, select View, User Interface. Doing so displays the screen shown in Figure 45.6.

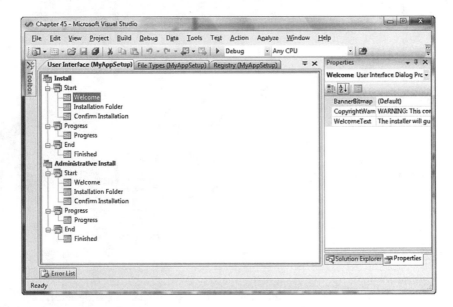

FIGURE 45.6   Setup project user interface.

Each of the User Interface windows has a BannerBitmap property in the Properties window where you can set the image that appears at the top of the Setup Wizard for your application.

You have some options for the user interface, but they're limited in that you can add only window types that are available via the setup project. You can right-click the User Interface tree and select Add Dialog to bring up the window shown in Figure 45.7.

You have several options to add new windows. For example, the License Agreement and Read Me dialog windows are common additions.

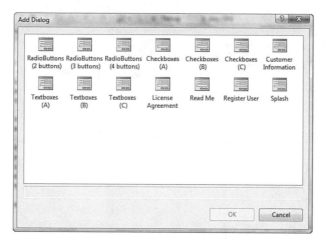

FIGURE 45.7   Setup project Add Dialog.

Launch Conditions

A launch condition allows you to ensure that a specific file, registry entry, or application is installed on the target machine prior to installation. For example, if you have an application that communicates with Microsoft Excel, you could add a launch condition that ensures the version of Excel you need is already installed. You can also configure the condition to display the error message you want if Excel isn't there. The program won't install if your launch conditions aren't met.

To configure a launch condition, right-click the setup project and select View, Launch Condition.

Custom Actions

If there are one or more actions your application needs to take to set up, you can add a custom action that you write code for. To configure a custom action, right-click the setup project; select View, Custom Action. You'll see the screen shown in Figure 45.8

The custom action is part of an external project, typically a class library project, which is a DLL. In the custom action project, you right-click, select Add, New Item, and then select Installer File.

Notice that there are branches for Install, Uninstall, Commit, and Rollback. The installer file in your custom installer derives from the Installer class, which contains virtual methods for `Install`, `Uninstall`, `Commit`, and `Rollback`. You can override these methods, and they will be called by the setup program. The custom installer is the last thing to run during setup; it assures you that all files are in place.

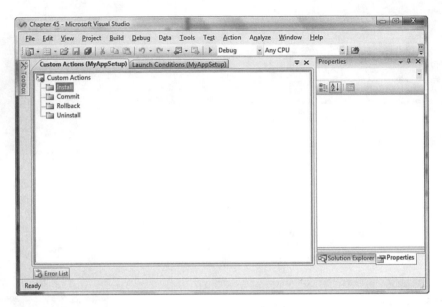

FIGURE 45.8   Setup project Custom Action window.

After you have a custom installer, add it to your setup project by right-clicking, selecting Add, Project Output, and then selecting the primary output for your custom action project. Then right-click Custom Actions in the Custom Actions window, as shown in Figure 45.8, and select Add Custom Action.

Summary

This chapter showed you how to create a setup project for your application. You can run the wizard and select items that you need for setup.

After setup, you can continue to configure setup by adding files to the file system, adding file types, configuring the user interface, adding registry settings, creating launch conditions, and even creating custom actions for items that the setup doesn't take care of natively.

CHAPTER 46

Deploying Desktop Applications

A continuing trend in retail service is to get what you want, the way you want, when you want it. From fast-food restaurants to services you can order by phone or quick Internet search, people are enjoying the benefits of greater service and technology all the time. I can hear some of you now saying I didn't receive some of the service that you did recently. Yes, I've seen that, too, but would prefer to keep things positive.

The same situation holds for desktop application deployment. There was a time when all deployments were performed manually by an administrator who was responsible for obtaining a CD and running an install on every computer in the company. The expense of this process is one of the reasons why web applications have become so popular. However, now you have a middle-ground position where you can have the richness of the desktop application with the ease of deployment of the Internet via a technology called ClickOnce. Just like retail services, deployment is getting better and more convenient.

Deploying via ClickOnce

In .NET you have XCopy deployment because assemblies can be standalone entities. However, sometimes you want more flexibility in deployment, instead of investing in all the work it takes to deploy applications yourself.

ClickOnce deployment is designed to ease the cost of deployment of desktop applications by making it easy for customers to download and run your applications. ClickOnce enables you to deploy your application to a single network share or Internet location and allow users to download and install that software with minimal effort. Whenever new versions of an application are available, users can update their existing software over a network connection.

To get started, create a simple Windows Presentation Foundation (WPF) application to deploy.

To implement Click-Once, right-click the project in Solution Explorer and select Publish. Doing so displays a wizard for you to specify publishing options, such as the IIS virtual directory where you want to deploy to, as shown in Figure 46.1.

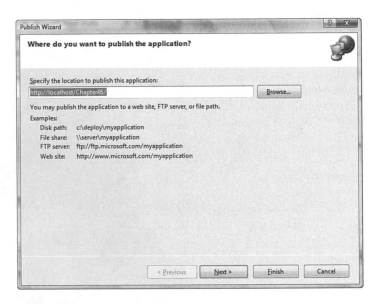

FIGURE 46.1   Publish Wizard location.

As shown in Figure 46.1, you can deploy to a website, FTP, or file location. We'll use the HTTP option so that we can deploy from a website.

After you click Next, the wizard gives you the option to allow your program to be used either online only or online and offline.

The difference between the online and offline options is that online forces you to launch the application from the website each time. The implications of this are that you must be connected to the Internet, which requires that you understand how the application would be used and what restrictions, if any, the user will incur regarding where they use the application.

The offline option allows the user to run the program at any time. This means that the application can have a shortcut menu item in your Start menu and doesn't require Internet access. The application itself is stored on your machine in a place called isolated storage, which is a sandbox environment that keeps the application from accessing any other resources on your system without your permission. Chapter 44, "Securing Code," explained how code-access security works and how you can control which permissions this application has.

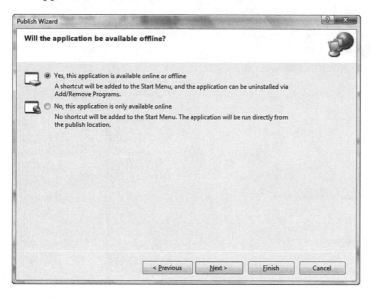

FIGURE 46.2   Publish Wizard, online or offline.

Click Next to get a confirmation of what you want to do and then click Finish. ClickOnce publishing will begin.

If you use Windows Vista, you must run VS2008 as Administrator to have permissions to deploy to IIS. For Vista, also ensure that IIS 6 Metabase and IIS 6 Configuration Compatibility are installed. Independent of OS, you need to have IIS and ASP.NET installed, which aren't installed by default. If you leave out any of the configuration items in this paragraph, the deployment will not work.

This launches a helper screen that allows customers to download the application, as shown in Figure 46.3.

Clicking Install will cause the Windows Forms application to load over the network or Internet to your machine. After working through security warnings or any dialog boxes that pop up from firewalls and other security software, you will see a dialog box that enables you to install your application.

After installation, your application will run. If you selected the online and offline deployment mode, you'll see a folder on the Start menu for launching your application.

Configuring ClickOnce

The Publish window allows you to modify the publication information associated with your application. You can find the publish configuration options by double-clicking the Properties folder in the solution and then clicking the Publish tab. Figure 46.4 shows the available options.

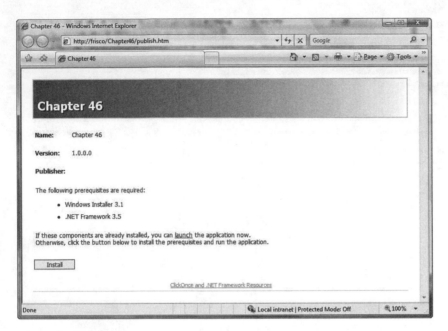

FIGURE 46.3   Application launch screen.

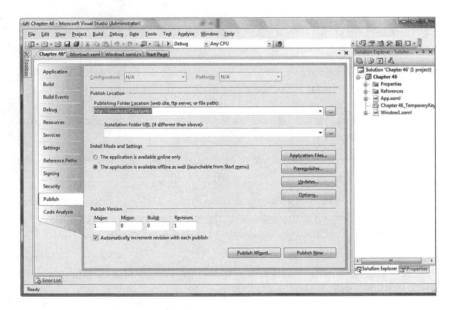

FIGURE 46.4   ClickOnce publishing options.

One of the things you'll want to do is to deploy new versions of your application. You can do this by updating the version number and then clicking the Publish button. When you do this, users will receive a prompt asking them if they would like to download and use the next version.

Summary

ClickOnce is a useful technology for helping you deploy desktop applications over the Internet, FTP, or file system. It reduces the cost of deployment, making desktop application deployment more affordable.

You can use ClickOnce by running a Publish Wizard, which will deploy the application to a website of your choice. After you've published, you can update settings and republish so that users can have the latest features with one click.

46

Publishing Web Applications

A lot of work goes into designing and building a new airplane. When it is ready, some brave pilot will test it. They've got to pay these people a lot of money to get into an untested vehicle that could stop flying from a mile in the air. Anyway, after the airplane has been certified, it can be put into production. However, a lot of work is required to put the airplane in service. Pilots must be trained, maintenance equipment must be in place, and schedules must be established.

Just like a new type of airplane that is ready to fly, you've built a Web Application with ASP.NET, ASP.NET AJAX, and Silverlight that you need to deploy so that people can use it. In VS2008, you have a nice sandbox environment that just works. However, you need to set up a web server so that you can put your website into production. Until you've tested your website in the environment that it will be used, it won't be ready to fly.

The Anatomy of a Web Application

ASP.NET has specific places for certain files to be placed. You learned about this in Chapter 27, "Building Web Applications with ASP.NET." This section reinforces a couple of those items so that you can understand the essential organization of an ASP.NET website in production.

First you will have an application root, which is the top-level folder where your application resides. In the root, you need a start page, typically Default.aspx, and web.config. In addition, you must have a bin folder under the root, which holds assemblies that your Web Application uses. Figure 47.1 shows what this folder looks like.

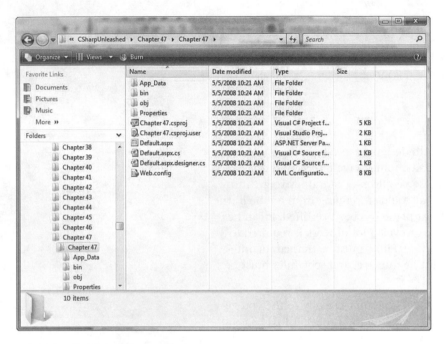

FIGURE 47.1   ASP.NET Web Application root folder.

From Figure 47.1, you can see that there is a Chapter 47 folder that contains a bin folder, a Default.aspx, and web.config. Other folders may or may not exist, depending on which features your Web Application implements.

Web Server Setup

As indicated earlier, VS2008 (and VS2005) has an integrated web server. However, the integrated web server can operate only on your computer and isn't built to support normal web server operations. The benefits are that you don't need to set up a separate web server, and it's more secure.

However, you will eventually need to deploy to a web server for your intended audience to use the application. Therefore, you must ensure that Internet Information Services (IIS), which is your OS web server, is set up.

Normally, IIS doesn't install by default, and you'll need to manually install it. You can do that via the Control Panel. Select Programs and Features for Vista or Add or Remove Programs for Windows XP, and then choose to Add or Remove Windows Components. Each OS interface is just a little bit different, but the general procedures are similar. When you do this, make sure you choose to install ASP.NET, too.

You can run the following command line to reinstall ASP.NET after installing IIS:

```
aspnet_regiis -i
```

The preceding command line is also necessary if you ever uninstall and then reinstall IIS because the reinstall will not automatically install ASP.NET for you.

The process for setting up the web server is different for Windows Server 2000, Windows Server 2003, and Windows Server 2008. Refer to the documentation on the servers for instructions. As of Windows Server 2003, you also have a web server–only SKU.

Virtual Directory Setup

Deploying to the developer machine might be an option to test deployment before deploying to a normal web server. A lot of companies have a test server, often referred to as a staging server, for testing before launching an application to production. So, the process might be to get the application running on the local developer machine, push it to staging, and then push it to production, as each quality gate is satisfied.

If you're deploying to a desktop OS, such as Windows XP or Vista, you have only a single web application in IIS. Therefore, it is often more convenient to deploy to a virtual directory, under the web application, where you can deploy as many applications as you like. Assuming that you've set up IIS as discussed in the previous section, here are the steps for creating a virtual directory in IIS:

1. Open IIS and locate the website, named Default Web Site by default.
2. Right-click the Web Application, type the Alias as Chapter47, and select Add Virtual Directory. You'll see the window in Figure 47.2.

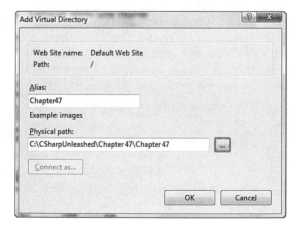

FIGURE 47.2   Virtual directory setup.

1. Click the ellipsis by the Physical Path field to select the location where the actual ASP.NET files will reside. Observe in Figure 47.3 that I've selected the root application folder, which contains Default.aspx, web.config, and the bin folder.

FIGURE 47.3   Selecting a web app physical path.

In addition, you could select another folder in your file system, but you must ensure that you give access to the Network Service user for Vista and the ASPNET user for XP at least Modify permissions on the folder.

2. When you click the OK button on the Virtual Directory window from Figure 47.2, you'll see the new virtual directory in IIS, under Default Web Site.

3. Next, you need to set the default document. Without this step, you'll likely get an error that says IIS can't find the page. This is important because the default document usually isn't set to Default.aspx, which you expect in your ASP.NET application. For XP, right-click the new virtual directory, select Properties, go to the Documents tab, add Default.aspx, and move Default.aspx to the top of the list. If Default.aspx isn't at the top of the list and you happen to have one of the other document names in your root folder, that document will be selected first when someone navigates to your site without a filename. For Vista, select the virtual directory and double-click the default document. Vista already has default.aspx in the list, but for the reason just stated, you'll want to move it to the first place in the list.

4. If you are using Vista, you must right-click the virtual directory and select Convert to Application, accept the defaults, and click OK.

5. Now you can open your website by typing the following address into your browser:

   http://localhost/Chapter47

   If you name your alias something other than the instructions in step 2, you'll need to replace Chapter47 with the alias you used.

Web Server Deployment

Setting up a Web Application on a server OS is similar to doing so on the desktop OS except that you can select Web Application rather than the virtual directory. Here are a few important points, made in the previous section, that you should keep in mind:

1. Ensure the folder you use gives at least Modify permissions to the Network Service user.

2. Ensure that Default.aspx is added to the top of your documents list.

Publishing a Web App from VS2008

In the virtual directory example, I used the existing VS2008 folder as the physical path. However, you will want to create a physical directory on your web server and then deploy the application there. VS2008 includes a publishing feature that makes deployment easy.

To publish from VS2008, right-click your web project and select Publish. You'll see a screen similar to Figure 47.4.

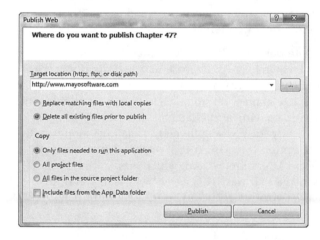

FIGURE 47.4   Publishing a web app from VS2008.

There are a few important issues with the Publishing window in Figure 47.4 that you need to know regarding deployment address, handling existing files, and copy behavior.

You can deploy to a file share, FTP site, or website. If you use the Web Site option, you must configure IIS on the server to handle Front Page Extensions, which has a protocol for helping deploy files over HTTP. When deploying to a shared hosting site, ensure that you've set the destination folder for where your application will be placed, which can default to your main folder. You can also use FTP if you prefer. The File Share option is convenient if you're deploying across your LAN, which could be much faster than the other two options.

Copying is important because, as the window says, you have the option to delete all existing files. I prefer to delete all existing files because of strangeness that could be caused by residue of other files that are obsolete. A couple of these scenarios are that your communications line bugs out during deployment, leaving you with an incomplete set of files. Sure, you would like to think that you would catch something like this, but turn your head one time, making the assumption that it will work this time because it has worked so many times before is a recipe for problems. On a busy site, you'll notice these types of problems more. Another problem with old residue is old web.config files that you might now want laying in a folder, but you've removed them from your development environment, which would be hard to figure out because you don't see the web.config in your project. On the other hand, the Replace option could be faster, but I personally prefer the clean deployment that the Delete option provides.

When deploying, the Copy option for Only Files Needed to Run This Application is generally the more secure choice. If you pick one of the other options, you put a whole lot more information on the server than what needs to be. Of course, you might have an arrangement where multiple developers are using a single location to work on files, which means that you would want to deploy everything to the server. However, source control applications such as Team System, Visual Source Safe, or even open source options such as SVN are better options than a shared folder on a web server.

Finally, I normally uncheck the App_Data options folder. As you may recall from Chapter 27, ASP.NET puts an instance of a SQL Express database in App_Data if you set up any of the web configuration options, such as security, roles, or profiles. If you're using this SQL Express database and you have SQL Express set up on the server, you might want to deploy your database this way. However, copying a full database across the wire is extremely slow and increases the opportunity for your deployment to fail, let alone waste your time and computer cycles. A better option is to visit http://www.codeplex.com and download a free utility called the Database Migration Wizard, which was written by Microsoft, and deploy your data and schema that way. This wizard will save you from babysitting a deployment for hours and let you move on with your work in minutes.

Summary

Although a normal ASP.NET web application deployment isn't rocket science after you get used to it, the process can be frustrating the first time or two you attempt it. At least now you know the process of how to deploy an ASP.NET website to a desktop or server machine. More important, you've picked up tips that will smooth out the deployment process and save you hours of time trying to figure it out.

Finally, here we are at the last chapter of *C# 3.0 Unleashed*. However, this is not actually an end, but an exciting beginning to a bright new future in computing. You now have a brand new set of tools in your software engineering backpack. I hope they help you create many wonderful technologies, and I wish you well and the best of luck in all your endeavors.

Sincerely,

Joe Mayo

PART 11

Appendixes

Compiling Programs

Throughout *C# 3.0 Unleashed: With the .NET Framework 3.5* are numerous examples of how to compile libraries and programs. Many of the common compiler options are covered in one form or another. However, several other options are also useful. The following sections group and present each option of the C# compiler in alphabetically ordered categories.

Advanced

▶ **/baseaddress:<address>**   Specifies the base address of a library.

```
csc /target:library /baseaddress:0x11110000
aLib.cs
```

▶ **/bugreport:<filename>**   Produces a file with information that can be submitted as a bug report. Information includes source code, command-line options, system information, and compiler output. The system will also prompt you for information such as a bug description and advise on how to fix the bug.

```
csc /bugreport:myreport.txt aprog.cs
```

▶ **/codepage:<id>**   Indicates the code page to compile programs with. (For instance, the id 1252 specifies the ANSI character set.)

```
csc /codepage:1252 aProg.cs
```

▶ **/errorreport:[none|prompt|queue|send]**   Identifies how to send error reports to Microsoft for errors that occur in the C# compiler.

```
csc /errorreport:send aProg.cs
```

▶ **/filealign:<size>**   Specifies the size of sections written to an output file. Can make efficient use of space on smaller devices.

```
csc /filealign:512 aProg.cs
```

▶ **/fullpaths**   Shows the full path of files where errors and warnings occur.

```
csc /fullpaths aprog.cs
```

▶ **/incremental[+|-]**   Performs a partial build on a program. Only those files that have changed will be recompiled.

```
csc /incremental aProg1.cs aProg2.cs
```

▶ **/lib:<filename>[,<filename>[. . .]]**   Specifies a directory to search for library references. Commas separate multiple directories.

```
csc /lib:dir1,dir2 /reference:alib.dll aprog.cs
```

▶ **/main:<classname>**   Specifies type containing the desired entry point when multiple Main() methods are defined in an assembly.

```
csc /main:aClass aProg1.cs aProg2.cs
```

▶ **/moduleassemblyname:<assemblyname>**   Identifies assembly to add this module to.

```
csc /moduleassemblyname:aProg aModule.netmodule
```

▶ **/nostdlib[+|-]**   Prevents mscorlib.dll, the library for the System namespace, from being imported automatically. Allows implementation of a custom System namespace.

```
csc /nostdlib /reference:customstdlib.dll aprog.cs
```

▶ **/pdb:<filename>**   Identifies name of the *.pdb file to create. Defaults to the name of the output file.

```
csc /pdb:debugFile.pdb aprog.cs
```

▶ **/recurse:[<dir>\]file**   Searches subdirectories for files. No directory defaults to the current directory.

```
csc /recurse:*.cs aProg1.cs aProg2.cs
```

▶ **/utf8output**   Converts compiler output to UTF-8 encoding. Some locales aren't able to support default encoding and so use this option with redirection to an output file.

```
csc /utf8output aProg.cs > compilerOutput.txt
```

Assemblies

▶ **/addmodule:<filename>[;<filename>[. . .]]**   Adds a module to an assembly. Semicolons separate multiple modules. A module must not contain a manifest.

```
csc /addmodule:mod1.netmodule;mod2.netmodule aprog.cs
```

▶ **/reference:[alias=]<filename>[;<filename>[. . .]]**   Imports assembly metadata so that types of the referenced assembly may be used in a program. Semicolons separate multiple directories. The referenced assembly must have a manifest. Can also use alias to support extern namespace aliases.

```
csc /reference:alib.dll aprog.cs

@BL_listitem_
```

Getting Help with the .NET Framework

The .NET Framework Class Library has grown steadily since .NET 1.0 release to manufacturing (RTM) in 2002. Currently, the .NET Framework 3.5 Class Library contains more than 11,400 object types. This is huge and more than most people can memorize in a practical way.

The reason I'm telling you this is because I've seen countless people who feel inadequate for not knowing everything there is to know about .NET. There used to be a time when a developer could pick up a language or platform and know everything about it in detail. With the pace of technology and the volume of what is available, that isn't possible, for the normal human being, anymore.

Rather than complain about what is impractical, however, I prefer to think about the problem in terms of what I can do about it and how I can be more productive in this new environment. The following tips might not be new for you, but I've found them to be helpful for myself and many others who are trying to get their head around the 500-pound gorilla in their backyards (aka the .NET Framework Class Library).

When getting help, I use a sequence of steps designed to bring me to the problem as quickly as possible, using this book as a reference, the VS2008 Help index, VS2008 Framework Class Library documentation, online searches, and favorite websites.

Read This Book

I've written this book as both a tutorial and a reference to help you find what you need quickly. When you are looking for an answer, grab it and let it help you solve your problem.

That said, 1,000 pages in a single book cannot fully cover 11,400 types, each of which has numerous pages of technical documentation. Reading this book first will give you the solid foundation you need to tackle this behemoth.

Index

Normally, I have a good idea of what I'm looking for before doing a search. So, I open the VS2008 Help index. In the index, I can quickly type in the name of what I want to search for and drill straight into the solution to a problem.

When you find a class you want to work with, such as FileInfo, click the About FileInfo Class link in the index. This one page has a wealth of information that will often solve your problem right away. For example, you'll see the formal definition of the type, inheritance hierarchy, namespace, and assembly. Many times, this page will have a code example that shows you how to solve your problem or will provide a link to a sample relevant to what you're looking for.

When the About page doesn't give you exactly what you need, look at the type members, searching for a method that takes care of what you need. Often, the code example with that type member will prove helpful. In the case of methods, you can also view the Exception list, which can be helpful in trying to figure out why an exception was raised by that method.

When the index isn't applicable or doesn't quickly yield results, I look at the .NET Framework Class Library documentation.

.NET Framework Class Library Documentation

Sometimes you know what you want to do but don't know the right class to use. In that case, it's useful to familiarize yourself with the overall structure of the .NET Framework Class Library. It's organized into namespaces, and it is not that hard to understand from a high level what the namespaces are for.

You can open the .NET Framework contents from the VS2008 Help menu. Then drill down to

.NET Development

.NET Framework SDK

.NET Framework

.NET Framework Class Library

This is the entire .NET Framework Class Library, organized into a manageable hierarchy of classes. I often poke around the hierarchy looking for classes that might do what I want them to do. It sure beats writing the code on my own when it's already done for me.

Search Engines

Most modern browsers let you add popular search engines to their interface. So, if you aren't finding the answer you need, I suggest that you look at the online search engines next.

You might be wondering why I didn't recommend the search that is part of the VS2008 Help system before this option. Actually, I recommend a VS2008 Help search after you've used the online option, simply because that is what I've found to be most productive and useful. I love Microsoft and its products, but I'm like you: When I need an answer, I need what works the fastest.

That said, occasionally online searches have yielded nothing, and so I resorted to a VS2008 Help search and found a golden nugget buried deep in a search link to somewhere in the Help files. When I have found answers in the VS2008 Help files, they've generally been of useful quality. However, the documentation is extensive, and so I normally use VS2008 Help search as a last option, behind index, contents, and online searches.

Favorite Websites

I really like MSDN at http://msdn.microsoft.com as a reliable source of information. They have multiple developer centers that focus on a specific topic. For example, one of my regular stops is the C# Developer Center, run by Charlie Calvert of Microsoft at the time of this writing. Some Developer Centers focus on other .NET Technologies such as ASP.NET, Silverlight, SQL Server, and the .NET Framework. There are even architecture and patterns and practices developer centers with tons of example code.

Microsoft also has a set of community sites, such as www.silverlight.net, www.asp.net, www.codeplex.net, and more. There are also many other good community sites run by non-Microsoft developers.

In addition to community sites, some good blogs by Microsoft and community developers specialize in .NET software development.

More sources of information include blogs, forums, and newsgroups, which can prove helpful for solving problems, but the results might or might not work for you.

Summary

Many sources of information are available to help you navigate the size and complexity of the .NET Framework Class Library. Certainly, knowledge gained from this book will help to move you forward more quickly, but you'll still need skills to find the answers that solve your problems. I hope that with *C# 3.0 Unleashed: With the .NET Framework*, you'll have solid footing to tackle tough programming challenges and be able to build upon a solid foundation, leading you to greater productivity.

Index

How can we make this index more useful? Email us at indexes@samspublishing.com

formatting strings, 106-109

forms
ASP.NET, 588-593
web forms, 588

FormView server control (ASP.NET), 594

Frame control (WPF), 563

framework class library types, 16

framework types (NET), 94-101

FrontPage Server Extensions, 643

FTP file transfers, performing, 671-675

FTP servers, files
downloading from, 673-675
uploading to, 671-673

FullAddress method, 181-182

function pointers, delegates, compared, 251

functions, 14. *See also* methods
SQL functions, using, 421

fundamentals, Windows Forms application, 516-519

G

GAC (global assembly cache), 930

garbage collection, CLR (Common Language Runtime), 12

Garbage Collector (GC), 327

GC (Garbage Collector), 327-330
class members, 335
collection process, 330
interacting with, 335-337
optimization, 330-331
running, 329

GDI+, Windows Forms applications, 536-539
Brush object, 536-537
drawing text, 537-539
fonts, 537-539
Graphics object, 536-537
Pen object, 536-537

Generated .resx File: strings.resx listing (40.5), 837-838

GenerateException method, 239

GenerateReport method, 185

generation operators, 435-436

generic collections, 396
arrays, compared, 371-372
nongeneric collections, compared, 371-372

generic delegates, 382-384

generic interfaces, 381-382

generic nodes, implementing, 373-374

generic type objects, 365

generic types
benefits of, 366-372
building, 372-387
singly linked lists, implementing, 373-381
types, defining, 384

GenericPrincipal, role-based security, 943-944

GenericSingleLinkedList collection, 373-376

GenericSingleLinkedListT, 375-376

GetAttribute method, 356-357

GetEnumerator method, 388-390

GetGeneration class member (GC), 335

GetHashCode method, 173, 200
System.Object class members, overriding, 199

GetLowerBound method, 137-138

GetModule method, 356

GetReflectionInfo method, 356

Getting Attributes from a Class listing (16.9), 356-357

Getting Files from an FTP Server listing (30.5), 673-675

GetTotalMember class member (GC), 335

GetUpperBound method, 137-138

global assembly cache (GAC), 930

globally unique identifier (GUIDs), 95-96

goto statements, 63, 74-75

graphical resource files, creating, 838-840, 843

Graphics object, 2D graphics, creating, 536-539

Graphics object (GDI+), Windows Forms applications, 536-537

grep (Global Regular Expression Print) expressions, 127-128

Grid control (WPF), 564

Grid layout, WPF (Windows Presentation Foundation), 555-559

GridSplitter control (WPF), 564

GridView server control (ASP.NET), 594

H

I

J–K

How can we make this index more useful? Email us at indexes@samspublishing.com

N

How can we make this index more useful? Email us at indexes@samspublishing.com

How can we make this index more useful? Email us at indexes@samspublishing.com

T

X–Z